THE NEW OXFORD SCHOOL ATLAS

Editorial Adviser
Patrick Wiegand

© Oxford University Press 1990
© Maps copyright Oxford University Press

Oxford University Press, Walton Street, Oxford OX2 6DP

Oxford New York
Athens Auckland Bangkok Bombay
Calcutta Cape Town Dar es Salaam Delhi
Florence Hong Kong Istanbul Karachi
Kuala Lumpur Madras Madrid Melbourne
Mexico City Nairobi Paris Singapore
Taipei Tokyo Toronto

and associated companies in
Berlin Ibadan

Oxford is a trade mark of Oxford University Press

ISBN 0 19 831667 4 (non net) ISBN 0 19 831682 8 (hardback)

First published 1990
Second edition 1993
Reprinted with corrections, 1993, 1994, Feb. 1995

Printed in Italy by G. Canale & C. S.p.A., Turin

Oxford University Press

Contents

Latitude and Longitude

The earth is a small, blue planet.
Seen from space it has no right way up.

An imaginary grid is used to pinpoint the position of any place on earth. This grid consists of lines called parallels of latitude and meridians of longitude. Both are measured in degrees.

Latitude
Parallels of latitude measure distance north or south of the equator. The equator is at latitude 0°. The poles are at latitudes 90°N and 90°S.

Longitude
Meridians of longitude measure distance east or west of the Prime (or Greenwich) Meridian. The Prime (or Greenwich) Meridian is at longitude 0°. The 180° line of longitude, on the opposite side of the earth, is the International Date Line.

The equator divides the earth into halves: the Northern Hemisphere and the Southern Hemisphere. The Prime Meridian and the 180° meridian together also divide the earth into halves: the Western Hemisphere and the Eastern Hemisphere.

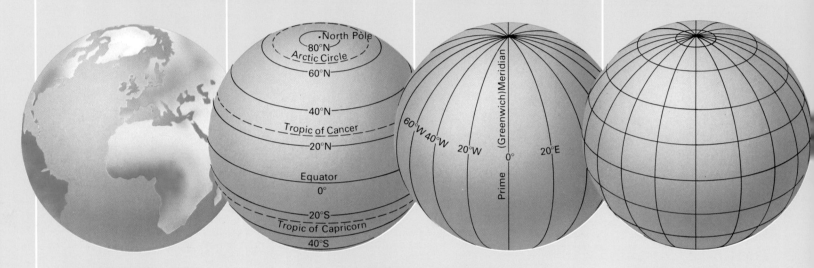

When used together, lines of latitude and longitude form a grid. The position of places on the surface of the earth can be located accurately using this grid.

To locate places really accurately, each degree of latitude and longitude can be divided into 60 minutes. Minutes can be divided into even smaller units called seconds.

Extract from a Meteosat view of Europe, 35,790 km above the equator. (This is an enlargement of the photograph of the earth shown at the top of the page.)

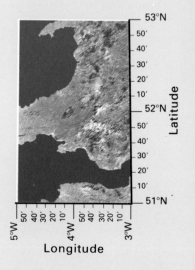

Extract from the Landsat image of the British Isles shown on page 28. This extract shows part of Wales at a scale of 1 : 4 500 000.

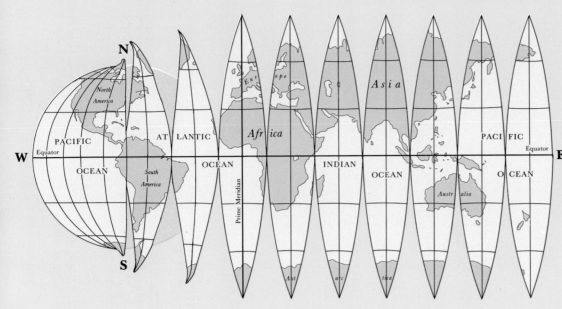

The most accurate way of looking at the earth's land and sea areas is to use a globe. Maps, however, are more convenient to use than globes. This map has been made by unpeeling strips, or gores, from the globe's surface. The map is difficult to use because gaps are left in the land and sea.
Grids of parallels and meridians that are used to turn a globe into a flat map are called map projections. It is impossible to flatten the curved surface of the earth without stretching or cutting part of it. It is important that the projection used for a world map is suitable for the purpose.

The **Oblique Aitoff projection** is also equal area. The arrangement of the land masses allows a good view of routes in the northern hemisphere. The position of North America and Asia on either side of the Arctic is shown clearly.

Mercator's projection was designed for navigators. Any straight line on the map is a line of constant compass bearing. Straight lines are not the shortest routes, however. Shape is accurate on a Mercator projection but the size of the land masses is distorted. Land is shown larger the further away is it from the equator.

——— Line of constant compass bearing

- - - - Shortest route

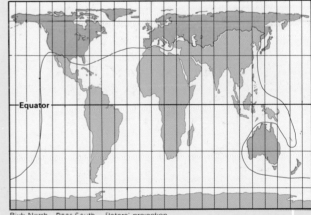

Navigation Chart.   Mercator's projection.

Peters' projection is an equal area projection. The land masses are the correct size in relation to each other, but there is some distortion in shape. This projection has been used to emphasize the size of the poor countries of the South compared with the rich countries of the North.

——— Brandt Line

▩ Rich North

▩ Poor South

Rich North—Poor South.   Peters' projection.

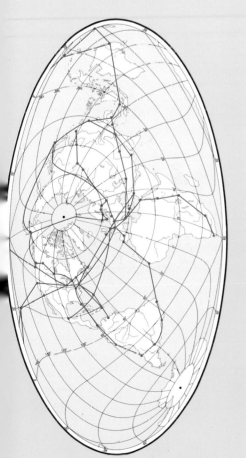

Major air routes. Oblique Aitoff projection.

Gall's projection gives a reasonable compromise between accuracy of shape and area. A modified version is used in this atlas as a general purpose world map. This map shows states which have gained their independence since 1945.

▩ States independent since 1945.

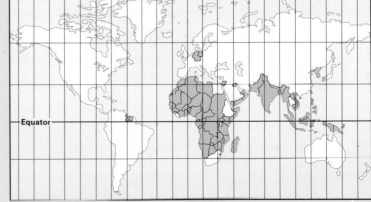

States independent since 1945.   Gall's projection.

Topographic maps show the main features of the physical and human landscape. There are small differences in the symbols and colours used for the maps of the British Isles and those for the rest of the world.

Place names

Local spellings are used. Anglicised and other common spellings are shown in brackets. This atlas has been designed for English speaking readers and so all places have been named using the Roman alphabet. Compare this extract of the map of Southern Asia with the same map printed in Bengali.

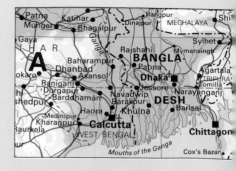

British Isles Maps

Boundaries

international

national

county

region (Scotland)

district (N. Ireland)

Communications

motorway   M6

primary road

A road

- ⊙ motorway junction
- ⬤ motorway service area

railway

canal

- ⊕ international airport
- ✦ other airport

Cities and towns

⬭ built-up areas

■ over 1 million inhabitants

● more than 100 000 inhabitants

• smaller towns

Non British Isles Maps

Boundaries

international

disputed ⋁⋁⋁⋁⋁⋁

internal

national park

Communications

motorway

other major road

track

railway

canal

✈ major airport

Cities and towns

⬭ built-up areas

■ over 1 million inhabitants

● more than 100 000 inhabitants

• smaller towns

+ historic sites

Physical features

- seasonal river/lake
- marsh
- salt pan
- ice cap
- sand dunes
- coral reef

Scale 1:1 000 000

0 ————————— 25km

Scale is shown by a representative fraction and a scale line.

Type style

Contrasting type styles are used to show the difference between physical features, settlements and administrative areas. Physical features (except for peaks) are shown in italics.

e.g. *Hautes Fagnes*   *Maas*

Peaks are shown in condensed type.

e.g. Hohe Acht 746

Settlement names are shown in upper and lower case.

e.g. Valkenswaard

Administrative areas are shown in capital letters.

e.g. LIÈGE

The importance of places is shown by the size of the type and whether the type face is bold, medium or light.

e.g. Malmédy   Bergheim   Duisburg

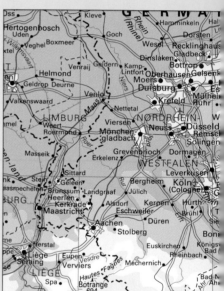

Land height

Colours on topographic maps refer only to the height of the land. They do not give information about use or other aspects of the environment.

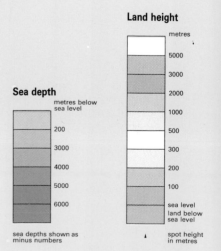

Sea depth

metres below sea level

200
3000
4000
5000
6000

sea depths shown as minus numbers

Land height

metres

5000
3000
2000
1000
500
300
200
100

sea level
land below sea level

▲ spot height in metres

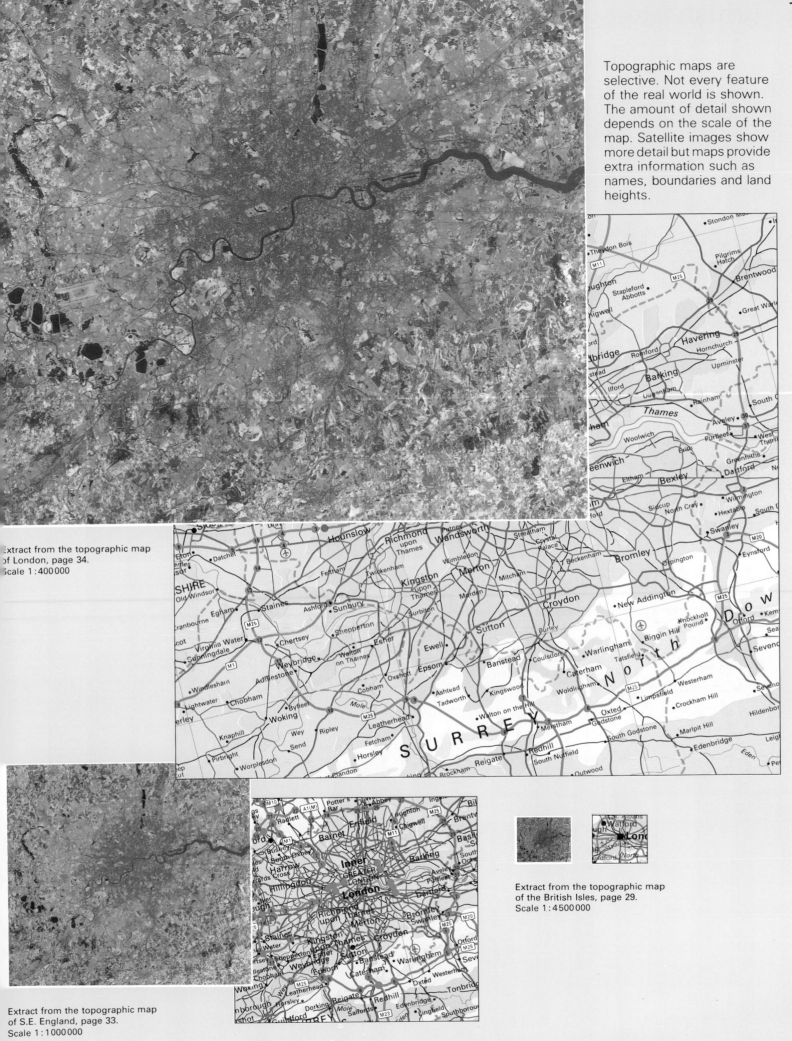

Topographic maps are selective. Not every feature of the real world is shown. The amount of detail shown depends on the scale of the map. Satellite images show more detail but maps provide extra information such as names, boundaries and land heights.

Extract from the topographic map of London, page 34.
Scale 1:400 000

Extract from the topographic map of S.E. England, page 33.
Scale 1:1 000 000

Extract from the topographic map of the British Isles, page 29.
Scale 1:4 500 000

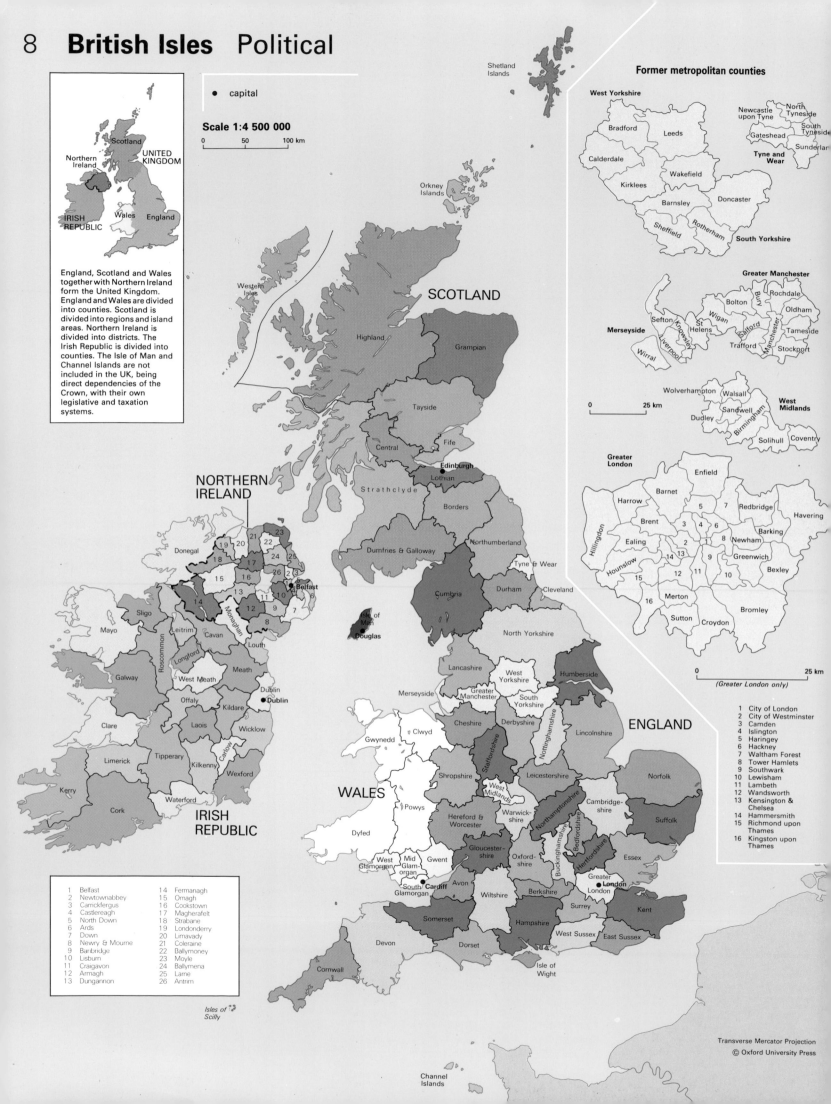

British Isles Political

● capital

Scale 1:4 500 000

0   50   100 km

England, Scotland and Wales
together with Northern Ireland
form the United Kingdom.
England and Wales are divided
into counties. Scotland is
divided into regions and island
areas. Northern Ireland is
divided into districts. The
Irish Republic is divided into
counties. The Isle of Man and
Channel Islands are not
included in the UK, being
direct dependencies of the
Crown, with their own
legislative and taxation
systems.

Former metropolitan counties

West Yorkshire

Bradford   Leeds

Calderdale   Wakefield

Kirklees   Barnsley   Doncaster

Sheffield   Rotherham

South Yorkshire

Newcastle upon Tyne   North Tyneside

Gateshead   South Tyneside   Sunderland

Tyne and Wear

Greater Manchester

Sefton   Knowsley   St Helens   Wigan   Bolton   Bury   Rochdale   Oldham

Merseyside

Liverpool   Salford   Manchester   Tameside   Trafford   Stockport   Wirral

Wolverhampton   Walsall

Dudley   Sandwell   Birmingham   **West Midlands**

Solihull   Coventry

0   25 km

Greater London

Enfield   Barnet   Harrow   Brent   Redbridge   Havering   Hillingdon   Ealing   Newham   Barking   Hounslow   Greenwich   Bexley   Merton   Bromley   Sutton   Croydon

1   2   3   4   5   6   7   8   9   10   11   12   13   14   15   16

0   25 km

(Greater London only)

1 City of London
2 City of Westminster
3 Camden
4 Islington
5 Haringey
6 Hackney
7 Waltham Forest
8 Tower Hamlets
9 Southwark
10 Lewisham
11 Lambeth
12 Wandsworth
13 Kensington &
   Chelsea
14 Hammersmith
15 Richmond upon
   Thames
16 Kingston upon
   Thames

Shetland Islands

Orkney Islands

SCOTLAND

Western Isles

Highland

Grampian

Tayside

Central   Fife

● Edinburgh
Lothian

Strathclyde

Borders

NORTHERN IRELAND

Donegal

19 20 21 23
     22
18   24 25
   17 26 2 3
15 16 13 1 4   ● Belfast
    14   11 5 10   6
       12 9   7
              8

Monaghan

Dumfries & Galloway

Northumberland

Tyne & Wear

Cumbria   Durham   Cleveland

Isle of Man
● Douglas

North Yorkshire

Lancashire

West Yorkshire

Merseyside

Greater Manchester   South Yorkshire

Humberside

Cheshire   Derbyshire   Nottinghamshire   Lincolnshire

ENGLAND

Sligo   Mayo   Leitrim   Cavan

Roscommon   Longford   Meath

Galway   West Meath

Dublin
● Dublin

Offaly   Kildare

Clare   Laois   Wicklow

Tipperary   Kilkenny   Carlow

Limerick   Wexford

Kerry   Waterford

IRISH REPUBLIC

Cork

Louth

WALES

Gwynedd   Clwyd

Powys

Dyfed

Shropshire   Staffordshire   West Midlands   Leicestershire

Warwickshire   Northamptonshire

Hereford & Worcester   Oxfordshire   Buckinghamshire   Bedfordshire   Hertfordshire   Cambridgeshire

Norfolk

Suffolk

Essex

West Glamorgan   Mid Glamorgan   Gwent

Gloucestershire

South Glamorgan   ● Cardiff

Avon   Wiltshire   Berkshire

Greater London   ● London

Somerset   Hampshire   Surrey   Kent

Devon   Dorset   West Sussex   East Sussex

Isle of Wight

Cornwall

Isles of Scilly

Channel Islands

Transverse Mercator Projection

© Oxford University Press

1   Belfast
2   Newtownabbey
3   Carrickfergus
4   Castlereagh
5   North Down
6   Ards
7   Down
8   Newry & Mourne
9   Banbridge
10 Lisburn
11 Craigavon
12 Armagh
13 Dungannon
14 Fermanagh
15 Omagh
16 Cookstown
17 Magherafelt
18 Strabane
19 Londonderry
20 Limavady
21 Coleraine
22 Ballymoney
23 Moyle
24 Ballymena
25 Larne
26 Antrim

Scotland   UNITED KINGDOM   Northern Ireland   IRISH REPUBLIC   Wales   England

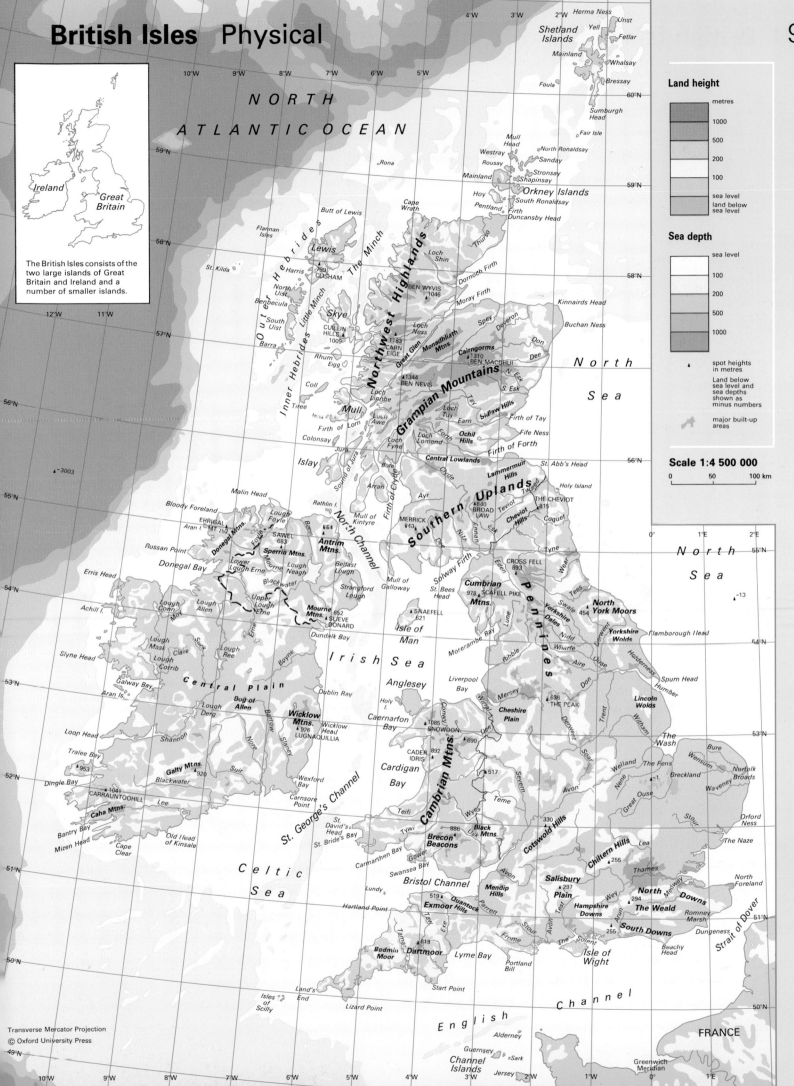

The British Isles consists of the two large islands of Great Britain and Ireland and a number of smaller islands.

Land height

	metres
	1000
	500
	200
	100
	sea level
	land below sea level

Sea depth

	sea level
	100
	200
	500
	1000

▲ spot heights in metres

Land below sea level and sea depths shown as minus numbers

major built-up areas

Scale 1:4 500 000

0   50   100 km

Transverse Mercator Projection
© Oxford University Press

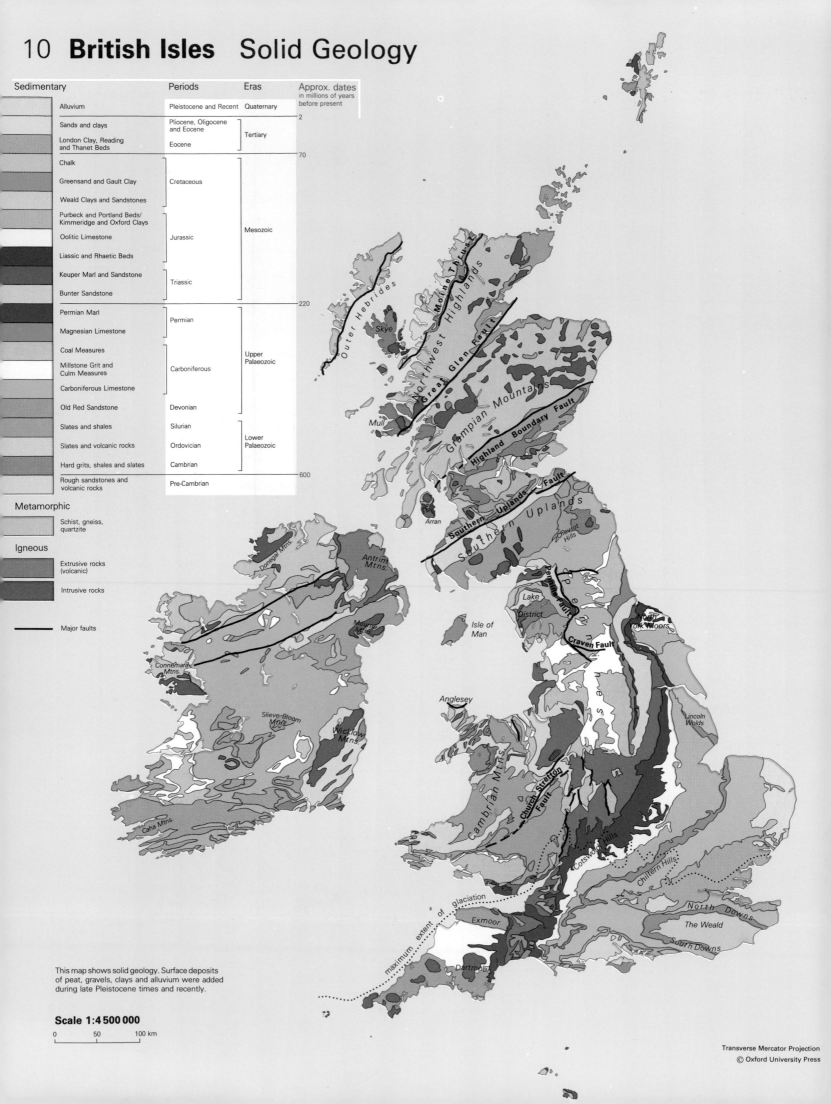

Sedimentary		Periods	Eras	Approx. dates in millions of years before present
	Alluvium	Pleistocene and Recent	Quaternary	2
	Sands and clays	Pliocene, Oligocene and Eocene	Tertiary	
	London Clay, Reading and Thanet Beds	Eocene		70
	Chalk	Cretaceous		
	Greensand and Gault Clay			
	Weald Clays and Sandstones		Mesozoic	
	Purbeck and Portland Beds/ Kimmeridge and Oxford Clays	Jurassic		
	Oolitic Limestone			
	Liassic and Rhaetic Beds			
	Keuper Marl and Sandstone	Triassic		
	Bunter Sandstone			220
	Permian Marl	Permian		
	Magnesian Limestone			
	Coal Measures	Carboniferous	Upper Palaeozoic	
	Millstone Grit and Culm Measures			
	Carboniferous Limestone			
	Old Red Sandstone	Devonian		
	Slates and shales	Silurian	Lower Palaeozoic	
	Slates and volcanic rocks	Ordovician		
	Hard grits, shales and slates	Cambrian		
	Rough sandstones and volcanic rocks	Pre-Cambrian		600

Metamorphic

Schist, gneiss, quartzite

Igneous

Extrusive rocks (volcanic)

Intrusive rocks

—— Major faults

This map shows solid geology. Surface deposits of peat, gravels, clays and alluvium were added during late Pleistocene times and recently.

Scale 1:4 500 000

0   50   100 km

Transverse Mercator Projection

© Oxford University Press

British Isles Soils

Upland peat

Lowland fen peat

Alluvial gley

Gley

Poorly drained soils

Upland peat and peat bog. Well-leached acid peat formed by high rainfall.

Lowland fen peat. Alkaline peat formed by water-logging in low areas.

Alluvial gleys. Gleying from low lying location such as flooding by sea or river.

Gleys. Gleying from underlying impermeable parent material, usually clay.

Well drained soils

Brown earths. Subsoil formed from weathering of parent material.

Argillic brown earths. Subsoil formed by the accumulation of clay leached from above.

Podzols. Subsoil has an accumulation of iron and/or aluminium.

Rendzinas and brown calcareous soils. Shallow and moderately deep soils over limestones and chalk.

major urban areas.

Brown earth

Argillic brown earth

Podzol

Rendzina

Scottish Highlands

Scottish Lowlands

Southern Uplands

The Pennines

Lake District

Donegal Mtns.

Antrim Plateau

Mountains of Mourne

Mayo Mtns.

Central Plain

Wicklow Mtns.

Munster Mtns.

Welsh Uplands

English Lowlands

Fenlands

East Anglia

London Basin

The Weald

Southwest Peninsula

Scale 1:4 500 000

0   50   100 km

Transverse Mercator Projection

© Oxford University Press

Actual surface temperature

°C
17
16
15
14
13
12
11
10
9
8
7
6
5
4
3
2
1
0
-1
-2

— isotherms reduced to sea level

→ warm currents

→ cold currents

January

Stornoway
Edinburgh
Belfast
Valentia
London
Penzance

Climate graphs for selected British Isles stations
(1951–80 averages)

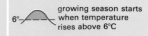

growing season starts when temperature rises above 6°C

Stornoway

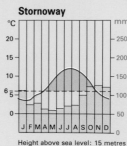

Height above sea level: 15 metres
Mean annual rainfall: 1096 mm
Mean January temperature: 4.0°C
Mean July temperature: 12.6°C

Edinburgh

Height above sea level: 61 metres
Mean annual rainfall: 642 mm
Mean January temperature: 3.0°C
Mean July temperature: 14.3°C

July

Stornoway
Edinburgh
Belfast
Valentia
London
Penzance

Belfast

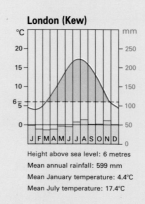

Height above sea level: 35 metres
Mean annual rainfall: 837 mm
Mean January temperature: 4.0°C
Mean July temperature: 14.6°C

London (Kew)

Height above sea level: 6 metres
Mean annual rainfall: 599 mm
Mean January temperature: 4.4°C
Mean July temperature: 17.4°C

Valentia

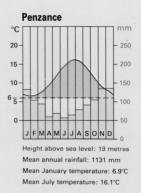

Height above sea level: 9 metres
Mean annual rainfall: 1400 mm
Mean January temperature: 6.6°C
Mean July temperature: 14.8°C

Penzance

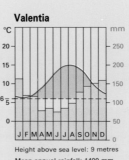

Height above sea level: 19 metres
Mean annual rainfall: 1131 mm
Mean January temperature: 6.9°C
Mean July temperature: 16.1°C

Scale 1 : 10 000 000

0   100   200 km

Transverse Mercator Projection

© Oxford University Press

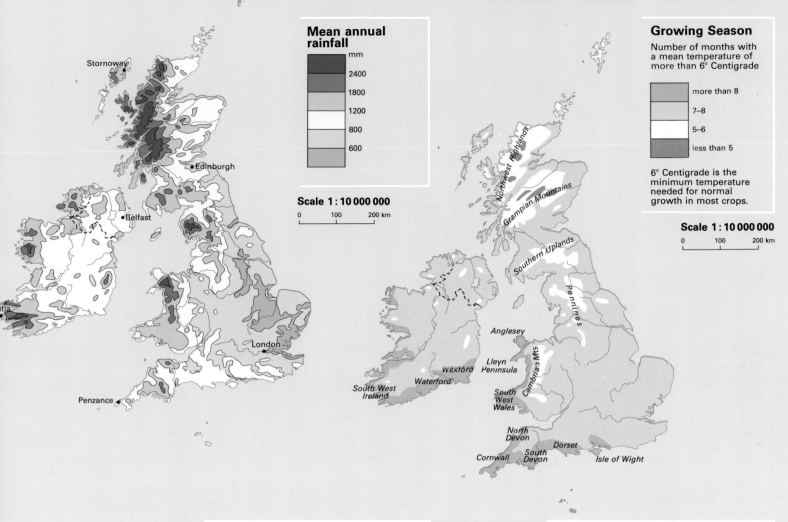

Mean annual rainfall

mm
- 2400
- 1800
- 1200
- 800
- 600

Scale 1 : 10 000 000

0   100   200 km

Stornoway
Edinburgh
Belfast
London
Penzance

Growing Season

Number of months with a mean temperature of more than 6° Centigrade

- more than 8
- 7–8
- 5–6
- less than 5

6° Centigrade is the minimum temperature needed for normal growth in most crops.

Scale 1 : 10 000 000

0   100   200 km

Northwest Highlands
Grampian Mountains
Southern Uplands
Pennines
Anglesey
Lleyn Peninsula
Cambrian Mts
Wexford
Waterford
South West Ireland
South West Wales
North Devon
Cornwall
South Devon
Dorset
Isle of Wight

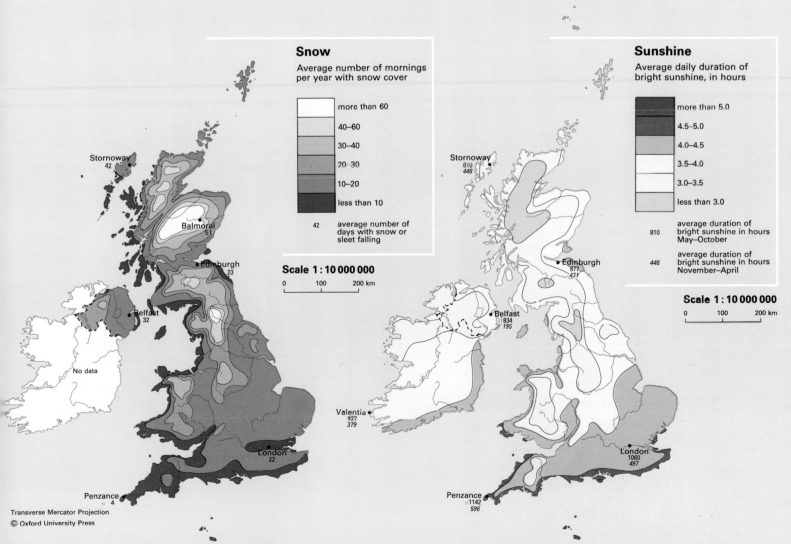

Snow

Average number of mornings per year with snow cover

- more than 60
- 40–60
- 30–40
- 20–30
- 10–20
- less than 10

42   average number of days with snow or sleet falling

Scale 1 : 10 000 000

0   100   200 km

Stornoway
42
Balmoral
51
Edinburgh
23
Belfast
32
No data
Valentia
927
379
London
22
Penzance
4

Sunshine

Average daily duration of bright sunshine, in hours

- more than 5.0
- 4.5–5.0
- 4.0–4.5
- 3.5–4.0
- 3.0–3.5
- less than 3.0

810   average duration of bright sunshine in hours May–October

446   average duration of bright sunshine in hours November–April

Scale 1 : 10 000 000

0   100   200 km

Stornoway
810
446
Edinburgh
877
471
Belfast
834
195
London
1060
497
Penzance
1142
596

Transverse Mercator Projection
© Oxford University Press

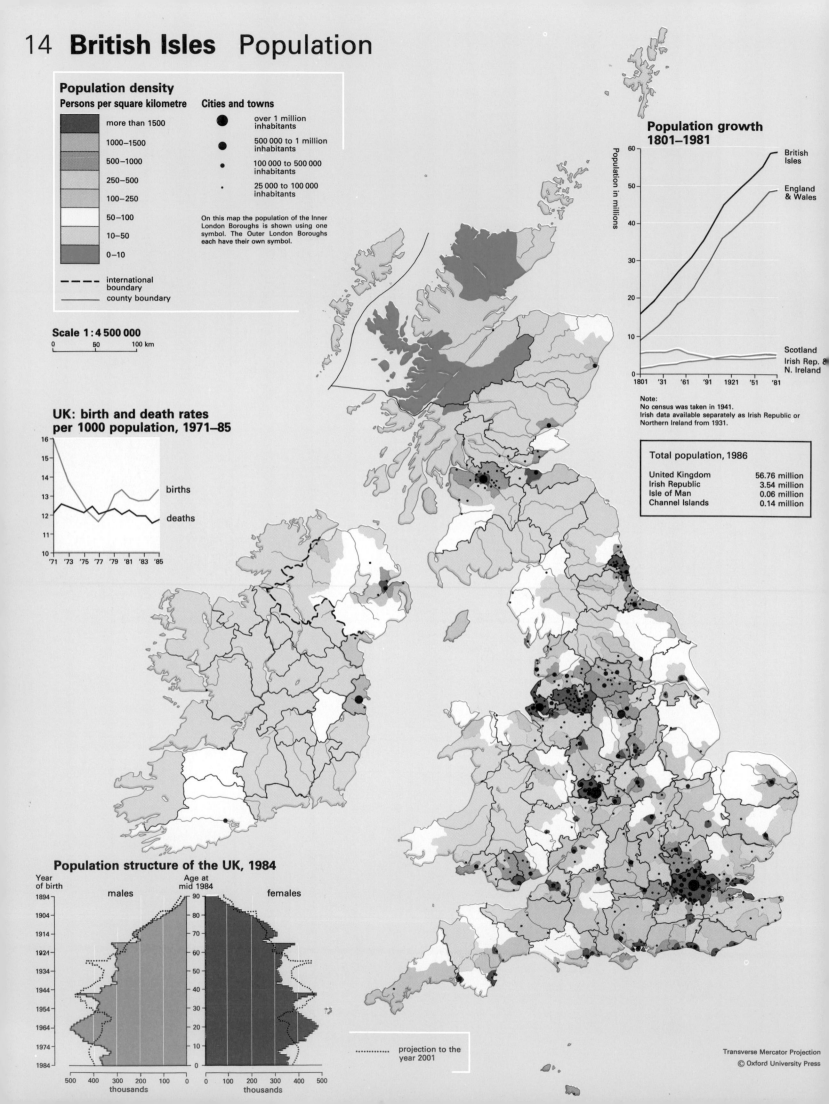

Population density

Persons per square kilometre

	more than 1500
	1000–1500
	500–1000
	250–500
	100–250
	50–100
	10–50
	0–10

Cities and towns

- over 1 million inhabitants
- 500 000 to 1 million inhabitants
- 100 000 to 500 000 inhabitants
- 25 000 to 100 000 inhabitants

On this map the population of the Inner London Boroughs is shown using one symbol. The Outer London Boroughs each have their own symbol.

- - - - international boundary
───── county boundary

Scale 1 : 4 500 000

0   50   100 km

UK: birth and death rates per 1000 population, 1971–85

births
deaths

Population growth 1801–1981

Population in millions

British Isles
England & Wales
Scotland
Irish Rep. & N. Ireland

1801 '31 '61 '91 1921 '51 '81

Note:
No census was taken in 1941.
Irish data available separately as Irish Republic or Northern Ireland from 1931.

Total population, 1986

United Kingdom	56.76 million
Irish Republic	3.54 million
Isle of Man	0.06 million
Channel Islands	0.14 million

Population structure of the UK, 1984

Year of birth

	Age at mid 1984	
males		females

1894
1904
1914
1924
1934
1944
1954
1964
1974
1984

90
80
70
60
50
40
30
20
10
0

500 400 300 200 100
thousands

0 100 200 300 400 500
thousands

· · · · · · projection to the year 2001

Transverse Mercator Projection

© Oxford University Press

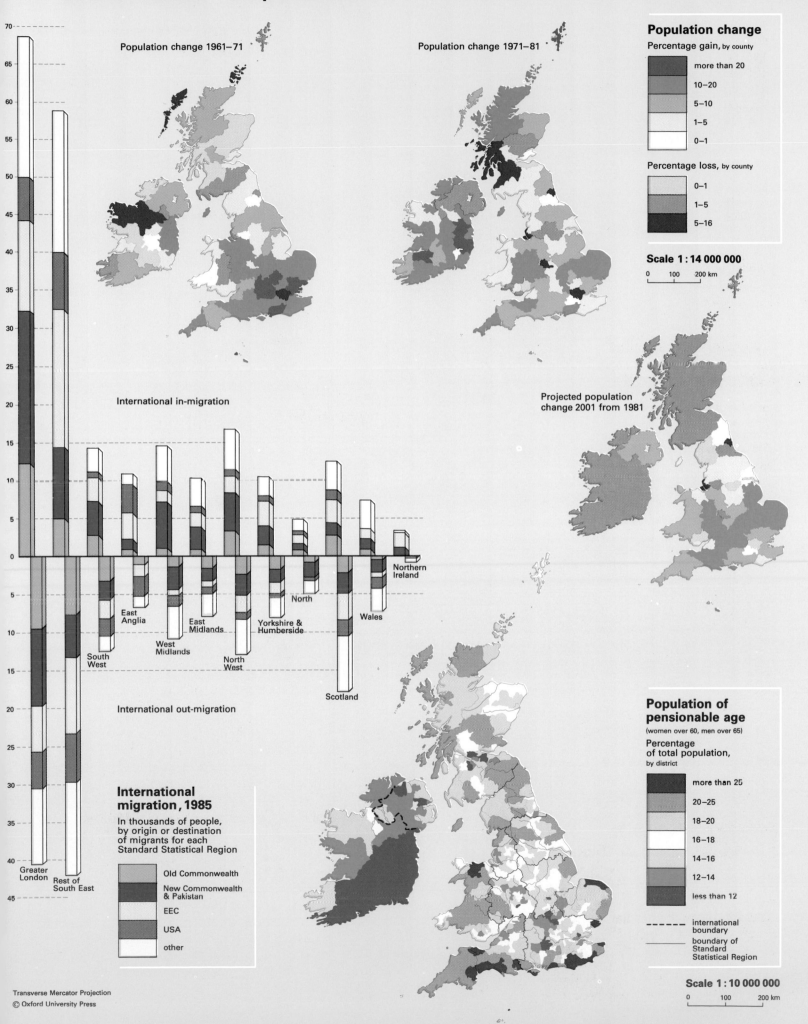

Population change 1961–71

Population change 1971–81

International in-migration

International out-migration

East
Anglia

South
West

West
Midlands

East
Midlands

North
West

Yorkshire &
Humberside

North

Scotland

Wales

Northern
Ireland

Greater
London

Rest of
South East

Population change

Percentage gain, by county

- more than 20
- 10–20
- 5–10
- 1–5
- 0–1

Percentage loss, by county

- 0–1
- 1–5
- 5–16

Scale 1 : 14 000 000

0   100   200 km

Projected population
change 2001 from 1981

**International
migration, 1985**

In thousands of people,
by origin or destination
of migrants for each
Standard Statistical Region

- Old Commonwealth
- New Commonwealth
  & Pakistan
- EEC
- USA
- other

**Population of
pensionable age**

(women over 60, men over 65)

Percentage
of total population,
by district

- more than 25
- 20–25
- 18–20
- 16–18
- 14–16
- 12–14
- less than 12

- - - international
boundary

boundary of
Standard
Statistical Region

Scale 1 : 10 000 000

0   100   200 km

Transverse Mercator Projection

© Oxford University Press

Legend

- crofting
- hill-farming—mainly sheep
- barley and wheat ⎫ arable farming predominant
- barley and oats ⎭
- oats
- improved grazing
- dairying and mixed farming
- • market gardening
- forest and woodland
- settlement and industry

Scale 1 : 4 500 000

0   50   100 km

Total farm workforce (thousands) U.K.

1956	754
1986	684

Agricultural machinery (thousands) U.K.

Tractors
1956	418
1986	510

Combine harvesters
1956	33
1986	74

Area of agricultural land by type of use 1986 (U.K.)

horticulture
stockfeeding
cereals
sole rights
other
grasses under
5 years old
common

Total area of agricultural land: 18.7 m. hectares

37.5	27.2	32.4	1.7	1.2	percentage
arable land	grasses 5 years old & over	rough grazing	woodland	other land	

Major crops as a percentage of total arable land (U.K.)

1956 / 1986

wheat, barley, oats, sugar beet, potatoes, oilseed rape, vegetables (except potatoes), rotational grass

Livestock (millions) U.K.

1956 / 1986

cattle, pigs

sheep, poultry

Selected crop yields (tons per ha.) U.K.

1956 / 1986

wheat, barley, oats, potatoes (main crop), sugar beet

North Sea

Irish Sea

Celtic Sea

English Channel

Transverse Mercator Projection

© Oxford University Press

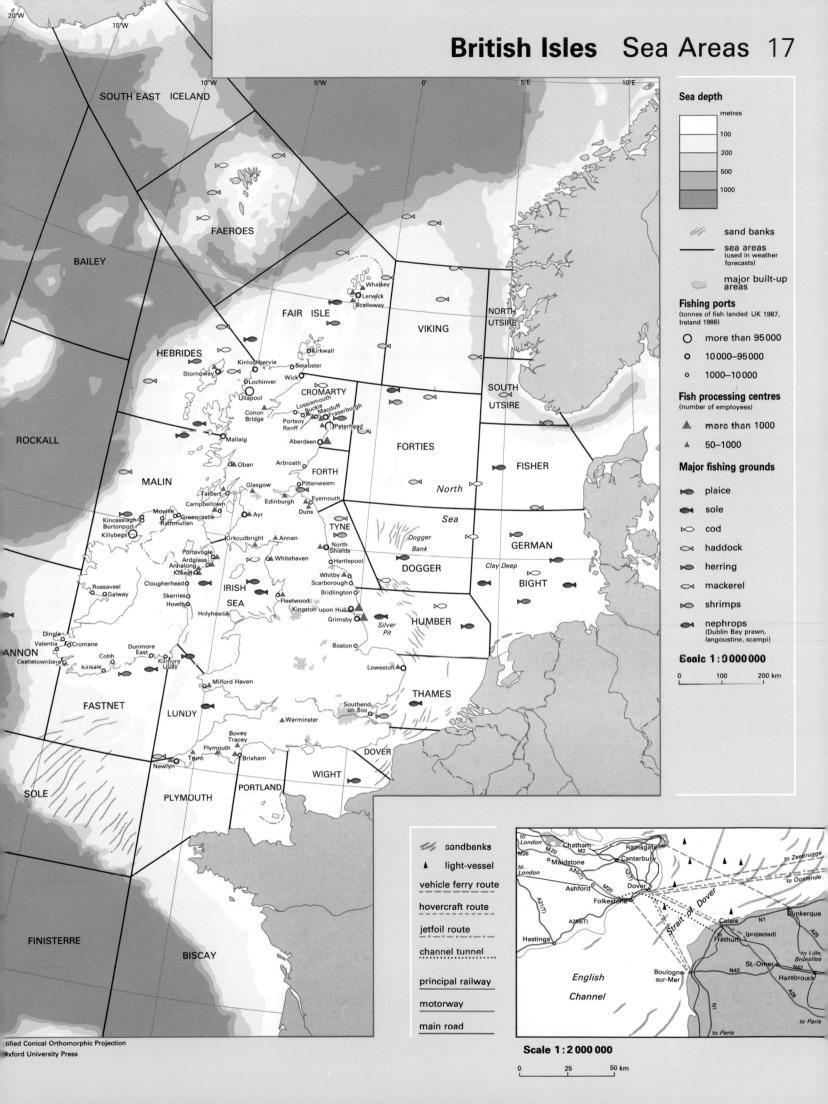

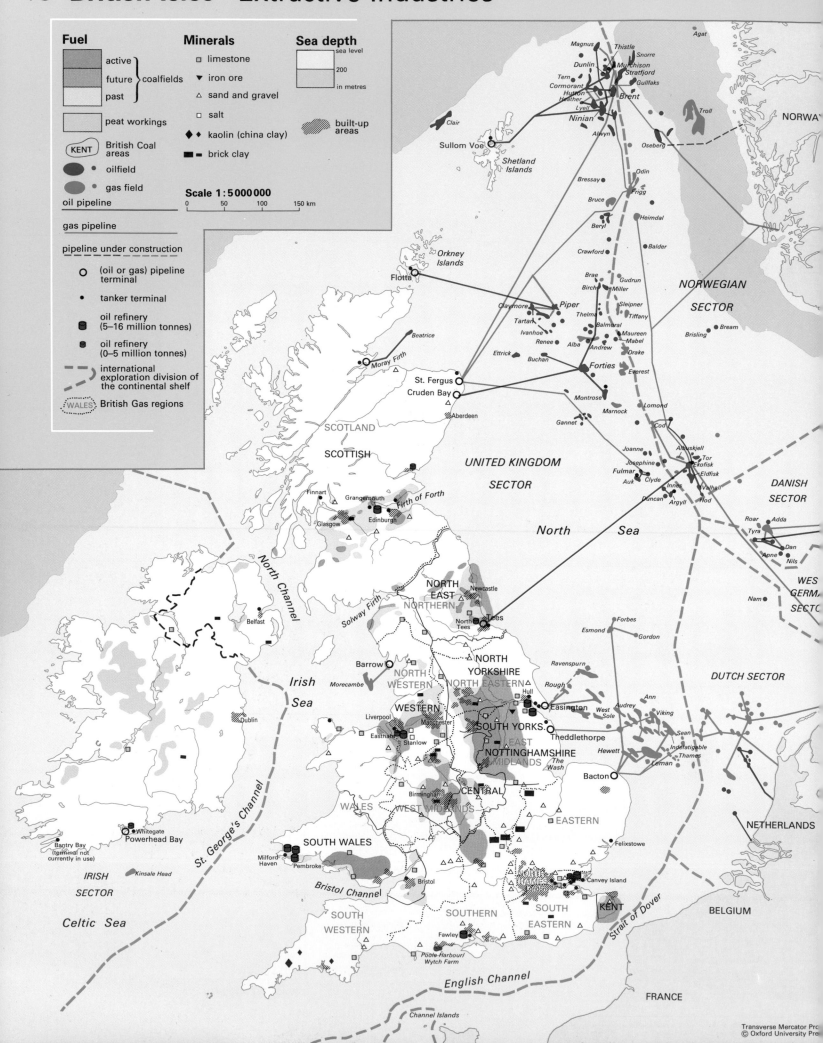

Fuel
- active ⎫
- future ⎬ coalfields
- past ⎭
- peat workings

KENT British Coal areas

- ● oilfield
- ● gas field

oil pipeline

gas pipeline

pipeline under construction

- ○ (oil or gas) pipeline terminal
- ● tanker terminal
- oil refinery (5–16 million tonnes)
- oil refinery (0–5 million tonnes)
- international exploration division of the continental shelf
- WALES British Gas regions

Minerals
- ☐ limestone
- ▼ iron ore
- △ sand and gravel
- ☐ salt
- ◆ ◆ kaolin (china clay)
- ■ ▬ brick clay
- built-up areas

Sea depth
- sea level
- 200
- in metres

Scale 1:5 000 000
0   50   100   150 km

NORWAY

Agat

Magnus · Thistle · Snorre
Dunlin · Murchison Stratfjord
Tern · Cormorant · Gullfaks
Hutton Heather · Brent
Lyell · Ninian · Troll
Clair · Alwyn
Sullom Voe · Oseberg
Shetland Islands

Odin
Bressay · Frigg
Bruce · Heimdal
Beryl
Crawford · Balder

Orkney Islands

NORWEGIAN SECTOR

Brae · Gudrun
Birch · Miller
Flotta · Claymore · Piper
Tartan · Thelma · Sleipner
Ivanhoe · Tiffany
Renee · Balmoral · Maureen · Brisling
Alba · Andrew · Mabel · Bream
Beatrice · Ettrick · Drake
Buchan · Forties
Moray Firth · Everest
St. Fergus
Cruden Bay
Aberdeen · Montrose · Lomond
Gannet · Marnock
Cod

SCOTLAND

SCOTTISH

Joanne · Alwyn
Josephine · Tor
Fulmar · Ekofisk
Auk · Clyde · Eldfisk
Duncan · Innes · Valhall
Argyll · Hod

DANISH SECTOR

Roar · Adda
Tyra
Dan
Anne · Nils

UNITED KINGDOM SECTOR

North   Sea

Finnart
Grangemouth · Firth of Forth
Glasgow · Edinburgh

Belfast

North Channel

Solway Firth

NORTH EAST · Newcastle
NORTHERN
North Tees · Tees

Forbes
Esmond · Gordon

WEST GERMAN SECTOR

Nam

Barrow
Morecambe
NORTH WESTERN
NORTH YORKSHIRE
NORTH EASTERN
Hull
Ravenspurn
Rough

Irish Sea

Dublin

Liverpool · Manchester
WESTERN
Eastham · Stanlow
SOUTH YORKS
EAST
NOTTINGHAMSHIRE
MIDLANDS
The Wash
Easington
West Sole · Audrey · Ann
Theddlethorpe · Viking
Hewett · Sean
Indefatigable
Leman · Thames
Bacton

DUTCH SECTOR

Birmingham · CENTRAL
WEST MIDLANDS
EASTERN
Felixstowe

NETHERLANDS

St. George's Channel

Whitegate
Powerhead Bay
Bantry Bay (terminal not currently in use)

IRISH SECTOR

Kinsale Head

SOUTH WALES
Milford Haven
Pembroke
Bristol Channel
SOUTH WESTERN

Fawley
Poole Harbour/Wytch Farm

Bristol
SOUTHERN
NORTH THAMES
SOUTH EASTERN
Canvey Island
KENT
Strait of Dover

BELGIUM

FRANCE

Celtic Sea

English Channel

Channel Islands

Transverse Mercator Pro
© Oxford University Pre

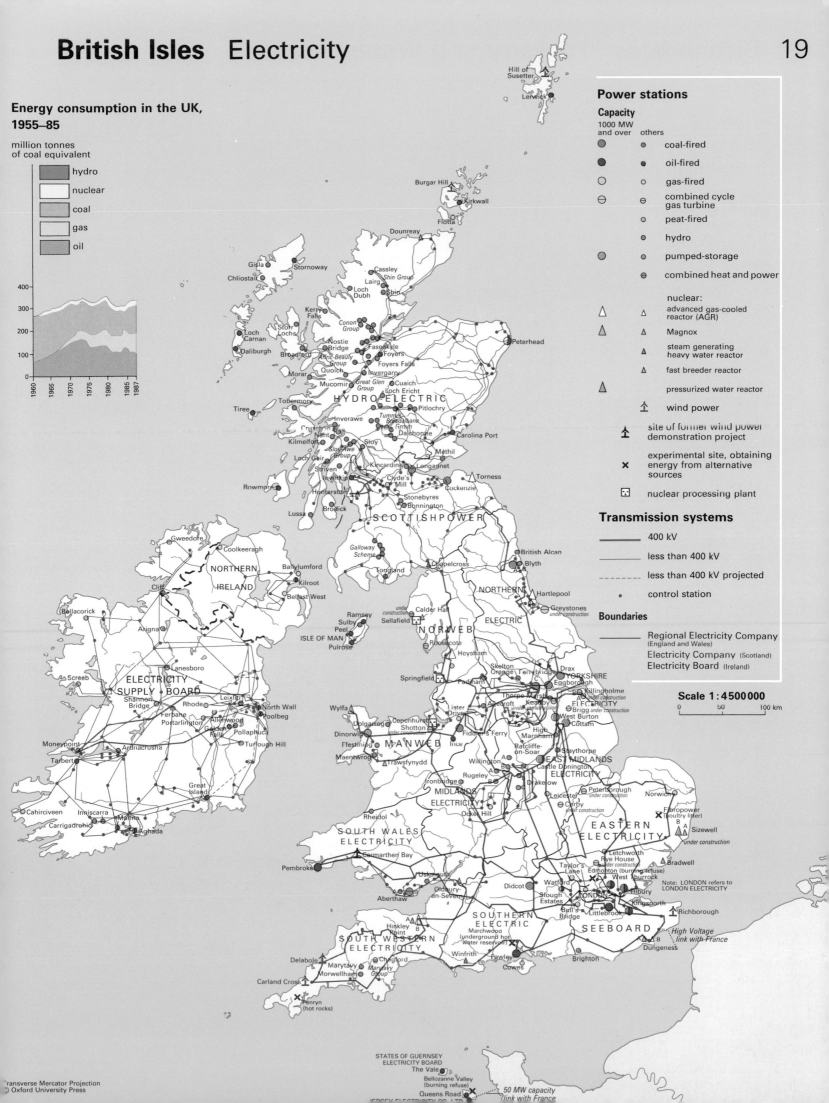

major built-up areas

Forestry

forest and woodland

forest parks

Paper mills
Annual production (tonnes)

● more than 100 000

· 25 000–100 000

Water

Water Authority boundary
(England and Wales)
Regional Council boundary
(Scotland)
Water Service Divisions
(Northern Ireland)

Surface water

rivers

21 ● major reservoirs (with capacity in millions of cubic metres of water)

Groundwater

highly productive aquifers
(porous rock)

highly productive aquifers
(jointed rock)

NB Although chalk is slightly porous, the main groundwater flow is through fissures

▾ major public supply groundwater pumping station (more than 20 000 cubic metres/day)

Scale 1 : 4 500 000

0   50   100 km

High forest tree species in Great Britain

- Sitka spruce
- Scots pine
- Lodgepole pine
- Norway spruce
- Japanese/Hybrid larch
- other conifers
- Oak
- Beech
- Ash
- Birch
- other broadleaved species

percentage of all species

Domestic water use in England and Wales, 1986

average litres per person per day

- flushing WC
- baths and showers
- washing machines
- hand washing, drinking, cooking, cleaning, outside use, etc.

Water use in England and Wales

thousand megalitres per day

water supply

Central Electricity Generating Board

industry

agriculture

1976   1980   1986

SHETLAND ISLANDS
ORKNEY ISLANDS
WESTERN ISLES

12 Loch Calder

Loch Glass 20
HIGHLAND
26 Loch Ness
GRAMPIAN
Inverurie
Glen More
Aberdeen
Fort William

25 Blackwater Res.
10 Loch of Lintrathen
18 Loch Turret
TAYSIDE
19 Glen Finglas Res.
64 Loch Ard 12
Loch Katrine
Loch Lomond 7 9
21 CENTRAL
Argyll
11 Carron Valley Res.
Loch Thom
Queen Elizabeth
FIFE
Glenrothes
LOTHIAN
11 Portmore Loch
STRATHCLYDE
BORDERS
Fruid Res. 11
12 Talla Res.
64 Megget Res.
19
23 The Border
Loch Bradan
200 Kielder Res.
DUMFRIES & GALLOWAY
NORTHUMBRIAN
Galloway
Paudhee
22 Derwent Res.
Workington
41 Cow Green Res.
41 Thirlmere 15 Selset Res.
85 Haweswater
20 Balderhead Res.
Grizedale
North Riding
Barrow-in-Furness
NORTH WEST
22 Grimwith Res.
12 Stocks Res.
YORKSHIRE
Tadcaster
ISLE OF MAN
Blackburn
Darwen
Burnley
Halifax
Rivington linked reservoirs 17
Radcliffe
Longendale linked reservoirs 19
28
11 Covenham Res.
Ellesmere Port
Ladybower Res.
Shotton
60 Delamere
Alwen Res.
11 Llyn Brenig
Snowdonia
Llyn Celyn 74
Lake Vyrnwy 59
Blithfield Res.
Foremark Res.
WELSH
18
13 SEVERN-TRENT
Rutland Water
50 Llyn Clywedog
124
Birmingham
ANGLIAN
Claerwen Res.
35 Caban Coch Res.
23 Pitsford Res.
48
Draycote Water
18
59 Grafham Water
Llyn Brianne 61
Usk Res. 12
Talybont Res.
15 Llandegfedd Res.
25 Abberton Res.
Taf Fechan 22
Dean & Wye Valley
27 Hanningfield Res.
Newport
High Wycombe
THAMES
Llangynwyd
Thatcham
Dartford
Purfleet
Northfleet
Chew Valley Lake 20
Snodland
Sittingbourne
Watchet
WESSEX
Aylesford
Maidstone
Wimbleball Lake 21
21 Bewl Water
SOUTHERN
SOUTH WEST
34
28 Roadford Res.
Colliford Lake Res.

Ards
Gortin Glen
NORTHERN
Glenariff
170 Ballyshannon Res.
WESTERN
Drum Manor
Florence Court
Parkanaur
EASTERN
Gosford
Rossmore
Castlewellan
Killykeen
Tollymore
13 Silent Valley Res.
Lough Key
Dún Á Rí
Slieve Gullion
Portumna
Donadea
Dublin
Parteen Weir Res. 465
168 Pollaphuca Res.
Avondale
Currahchase
J. F. Kennedy
Carrigadrohid Res.
Inishcarra Res.
Guagan Barra
33 57 Farran

Transverse Mercator Projection
© Oxford University Press

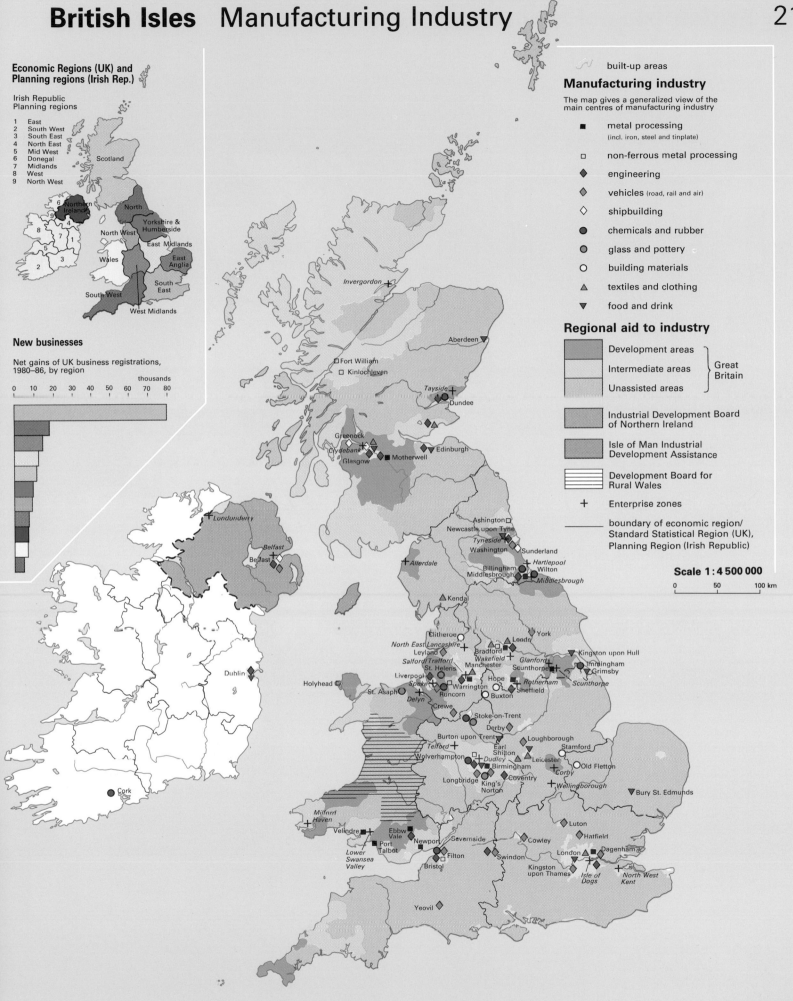

Economic Regions (UK) and Planning regions (Irish Rep.)

Irish Republic
Planning regions

1 East
2 South West
3 South East
4 North East
5 Mid West
6 Donegal
7 Midlands
8 West
9 North West

New businesses

Net gains of UK business registrations,
1980–86, by region

thousands

0 10 20 30 40 50 60 70 80

built-up areas

Manufacturing industry

The map gives a generalized view of the
main centres of manufacturing industry

■ metal processing
(incl. iron, steel and tinplate)

□ non-ferrous metal processing

◆ engineering

◆ vehicles (road, rail and air)

◇ shipbuilding

● chemicals and rubber

● glass and pottery

○ building materials

▲ textiles and clothing

▼ food and drink

Regional aid to industry

Development areas
Intermediate areas   } Great Britain
Unassisted areas

Industrial Development Board
of Northern Ireland

Isle of Man Industrial
Development Assistance

Development Board for
Rural Wales

+ Enterprise zones

boundary of economic region/
Standard Statistical Region (UK),
Planning Region (Irish Republic)

Scale 1 : 4 500 000

0   50   100 km

Transverse Mercator Projection

© Oxford University Press

Employment by region, 1987
Percentage of total employed

- Distribution, hotels, catering, repairs
- Banking, finance, insurance, business services and leasing
- Public administration and other services
- Transport and communication
- Metal goods, engineering and vehicles industries
- Other manufacturing industries
- Construction
- Energy and water supply
- Metals, minerals and chemicals
- Agriculture, forestry, fishing

----- international boundary

——— boundary of Standard Statistical Region

Scale 1 : 7 000 000

0   100   200 km

50%
40
30
20
10
0

UK data based on Standard Industrial Classification, 1980.
Irish Republic data based on Industrial Classification, 1981 Census of Ireland.

Job gains in Great Britain, 1966–84

Total 3.3 million
private services
finance
health
teaching
distribution
public administration

Job losses in Great Britain, 1966–84

Total 5.4 million
building
public utilities
general industry
textiles and clothing
heavy industry
primary industry (mining and agriculture)
'growth' industries (electronics and chemicals)

Scotland

Northern Ireland

North

Yorkshire & Humberside

North West

East Midlands

Irish Republic

Wales

East Anglia

South West

South East

West Midlands

Employment structure analysis, Great Britain 1986

Total employed population	21 105 000
Production and construction industries	6 635 000
of which manufacturing industries	5 137 000
Service industries	14 161 000

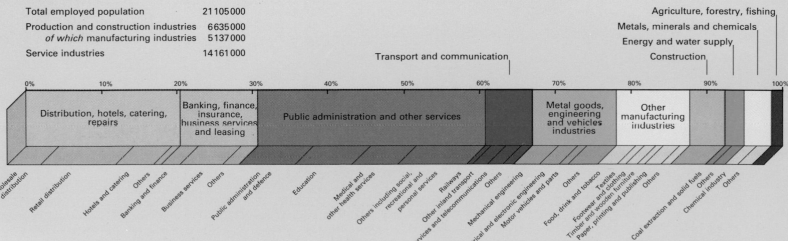

Agriculture, forestry, fishing
Metals, minerals and chemicals
Energy and water supply
Construction
Transport and communication

0%   10%   20%   30%   40%   50%   60%   70%   80%   90%   100%

Distribution, hotels, catering, repairs
Banking, finance, insurance, business services and leasing
Public administration and other services
Metal goods, engineering and vehicles industries
Other manufacturing industries

Wholesale distribution
Retail distribution
Hotels and catering
Others
Banking and finance
Business services
Others
Public administration and defence
Education
Medical and other health services
Others including social, recreational and personal services
Railways
Other inland transport
Postal services and telecommunications
Others
Mechanical engineering
Electrical and electronic engineering
Motor vehicles and parts
Others
Food, drink and tobacco
Footwear and clothing
Textiles
Timber and wooden furniture
Paper, printing and publishing
Others
Coal extraction and solid fuels
Chemical industry
Others

Employees by industry based on the Standard Industrial Classification 1980

© Oxford University Press

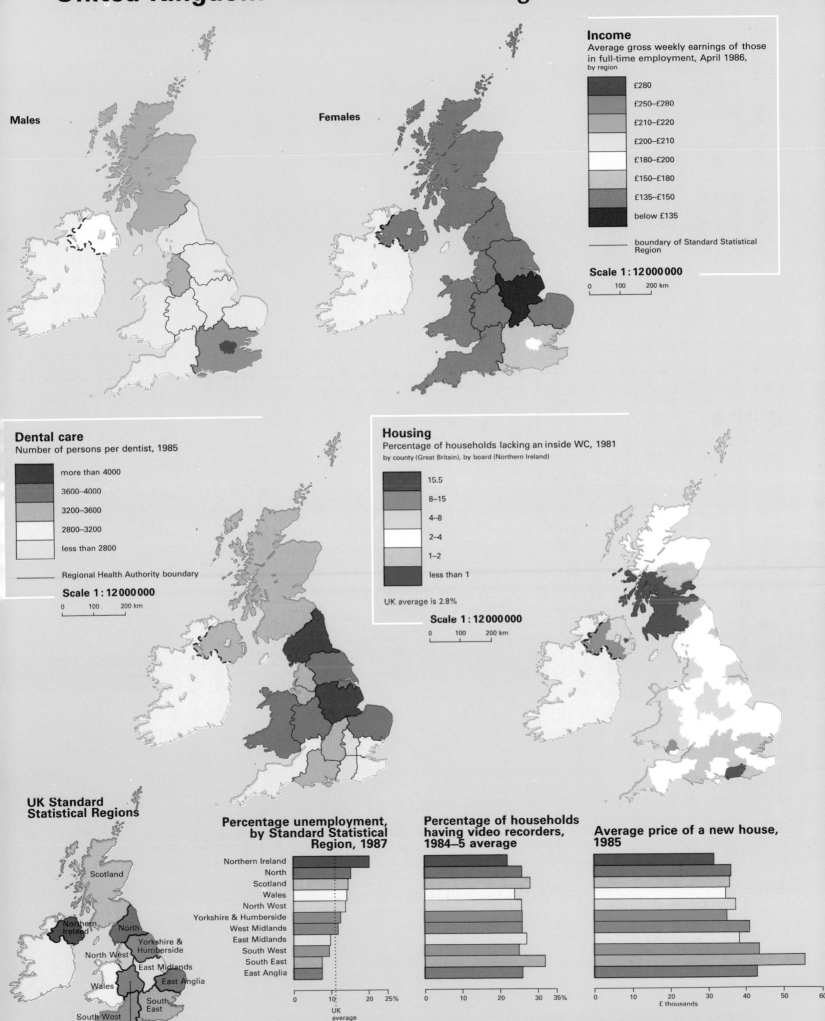

Males

Females

Income

Average gross weekly earnings of those in full-time employment, April 1986, by region

- £280
- £250–£280
- £210–£220
- £200–£210
- £180–£200
- £150–£180
- £135–£150
- below £135

—— boundary of Standard Statistical Region

Scale 1 : 12 000 000

0   100   200 km

Dental care

Number of persons per dentist, 1985

- more than 4000
- 3600–4000
- 3200–3600
- 2800–3200
- less than 2800

—— Regional Health Authority boundary

Scale 1 : 12 000 000

0   100   200 km

Housing

Percentage of households lacking an inside WC, 1981

by county (Great Britain), by board (Northern Ireland)

- 15.5
- 8–15
- 4–8
- 2–4
- 1–2
- less than 1

UK average is 2.8%

Scale 1 : 12 000 000

0   100   200 km

UK Standard Statistical Regions

Scotland

Northern Ireland

North

North West

Yorkshire & Humberside

East Midlands

Wales

East Anglia

South East

South West

West Midlands

Percentage unemployment, by Standard Statistical Region, 1987

Northern Ireland
North
Scotland
Wales
North West
Yorkshire & Humberside
West Midlands
East Midlands
South West
South East
East Anglia

0   10   20   25%

UK average

Percentage of households having video recorders, 1984–5 average

0   10   20   30   35%

Average price of a new house, 1985

0   10   20   30   40   50   60

£ thousands

Transverse Mercator Projection   © Oxford University Press

24 British Isles Communications

| motorways |
| main roads |
| principal railways |
| Channel tunnel (under construction) |
| vehicle ferry routes |
| ● major container terminals |

Scale 1:4 500 000

0   50   100 km

Transverse Mercator Projection
© Oxford University Press

British Isles Communications

Airports
Passengers in 1987

✈ more than 15 million

✈ 1–15 million

✈ less than 1 million

Airways

UK controlled airspace

other airways (beyond UK controlled airspace)

limit of Flight Information Region (FIR)

Ports
Cargo handled in 1987 (tonnes)

● more than 20 million

● 5–20 million

• 95 000–5 million

Waterways

navigable rivers

canals

major freight waterways

Scale 1 : 4 500 000

0   50   100 km

Transverse Mercator Projection
© Oxford University Press

National Parks

Areas of Outstanding Natural Beauty (England, Wales and Northern Ireland);
National Scenic Areas (Scotland)

Green Belt and proposed Green Belt (United Kingdom)

Heritage Coast (defined and proposed in England and Wales);
Coastal Conservation Zones (Scotland)

• major reserves

● internationally recognized sites
(including Special Protection Areas,
'Ramsar' Sites and Biosphere Reserves)

★ World Heritage Sites
(natural and cultural)

major built-up areas

Scale 1 : 4 500 000

0   50   100 km

The term Green Belt is now being
adopted in new development
plans in Northern Ireland.
It is gradually replacing the
Areas of Special Control, drawn
around the towns and larger
villages to control urban sprawl.

The National Parks were
joined in 1988 by the
similarly constituted
Broads Authority.

Transverse Mercator Projection
© Oxford University Press

British Isles Sport and Recreation

Greater London

Wembley Arena & Stadium
Lords
Royal Albert Hall
Ealing
Olympia
Tower of London
Boat Race
Cutty Sark
Kew Gardens
Twickenham
The Queen's Club
Wimbledon
The Oval
Kempton Park
Crystal Palace
Hampton Court Palace

Scale 1 : 2 000 000

0   25 km

Recreation

+ popular tourist attraction

river } navigable and used mainly for leisure activities

canal } navigable and used mainly for leisure activities

trail (footpath)

land over 200 metres

Major sports venues

- Association football (major club or international ground)
- Rugby Union (major club or international ground)
- Rugby League (major club)
- cricket (first class county club; test ground)
- tennis
- golf
- swimming
- athletics
- stadium for various sports
- horse racing
- horse riding
- sailing
- other water sports
- highland games
- winter sports
- rock climbing
- motor racing circuit
- - - - motor cycle race route (T.T.)
- ——— motor rally route, 1988
- ······· cycling race route, 1988

Scale 1 : 4 500 000

0   50   100 km

Transverse Mercator Projection
© Oxford University Press

Pseudo natural colour satellite image

This composite image of the British Isles has been created from 52 smaller, separate images obtained by Landsat satellite. Scanners from the satellite sense the reflection of the earth in small picture elements or pixels. For each pixel reflected radiation is recorded from several parts of the electromagnetic spectrum. This information has been reprocessed by computer to simulate a natural colour to the land areas. Adjustments have been made for the curvature of the earth when the pixels were pieced together.

British Isles

Boundaries
international
internal

Communications
motorway
other major road
railway
✈ major airport

Cities and towns
major built-up areas
■ over 1 million inhabitants
● more than 100,000 inhabitants
• smaller towns

Land height

	metres
	1000
	500
	200
	100
	sea level
	land below sea level
▲	spot height in metres

Scale 1 : 4 500 000

0   50   100 km

Transverse Mercator Projection
© Oxford University Press

Legend

Power stations
- ⚡ hydro
- ☢ nuclear

Extractive industries
- △ sand and gravel
- ▢ limestone

Land use
- arable
- dairying and mixed farming
- improved grazing
- hillfarming— mainly sheep
- woodland and forestry
- 🍎 market gardening
- major built-up area
- ✳ tourism
- major reservoir

Communications
- motorway
- major road
- principal railway
- ferry route

Industry
- metal
- zinc and aluminium
- mechanical engineering
- motor vehicles
- aerospace
- shipbuilding
- electrical engineering
- electronics/ computers
- precision instruments
- chemicals
- rubber
- glass
- cement
- nuclear processing
- textiles and carpets
- clothing and footwear
- fur and leather
- dairy
- fish processing
- brewing and distilling
- other food and drink
- furniture
- pulp and paper
- printing and publishing

Scale 1 : 1 750 000

0   25   50 km

Boundaries
- international
- national
- county

Cities and towns
- built-up areas
- ● more than 100 000 inhabitants
- • smaller towns

Communications
- motorway M5
- primary road
- A road
- ⓘ motorway junction
- ● motorway service area
- railway
- canal
- ✈ international airport
- ✈ airport

Land height

metres
500
300
200
100
sea level
▲ spot height in metres

Scale 1 : 1 000 000

0   25   50 km

Place names

Cheltenham
Gloucester
Bristol
Swindon
Trowbridge
Street
Yeovil
Poole
Weymouth
Great Torrington
Plymouth
Penzance

to Cherbourg
to Channel Is. Cherbourg
to Channel Is.
to Santander
to Roscoff
to Weymouth Portsmouth
to Cherbourg
to St-Malo
to St-Malo

Lundy
Barnsta... Bidefor...
Hartland Point
Hartland
Clove...
Bradw...
Kilkham
Bude
Bude Bay
Stratton
Holsworth...
Tintagel Head
Boscastle
Tintagel
Ottery
Launceston
Port Isaac
Camelford
Brown Willy 420
Bodmin Moor
Trevose Head
Padstow
Camel
Fowey
Lynher
Pensilva
Wadebridge
Bodmin
CORNWALL
Newquay
St. Columb Major
Liskeard
Perranporth
312 ▲
Lostwithiel
St. Agnes
St. Blazey
Looe
Whites...
St. Austell
Fowey
Polperro
Bay
Portreath
Truro
Fal
Tregony
Mevagissey
St. Ives
Redruth
Dodman Point
252 ▲
Hayle
Camborne
252 ▲
St. Mawes
St. Just
Hayle
Penryn
Newlyn
Marazion
Falmouth
Land's End
Penzance
Helston
Sennen
Mounts Bay
Mousehole
Porthleven
St. Keverne
Mullion
Coverack
Bryher
St. Martin's
Tresco
Lizard Point
Lizard
Bishop Rock
St. Mary's
St. Agnes
Hugh Town

51°N
50°N
6°W
5°W
5°W

A   B   C
1   2   3

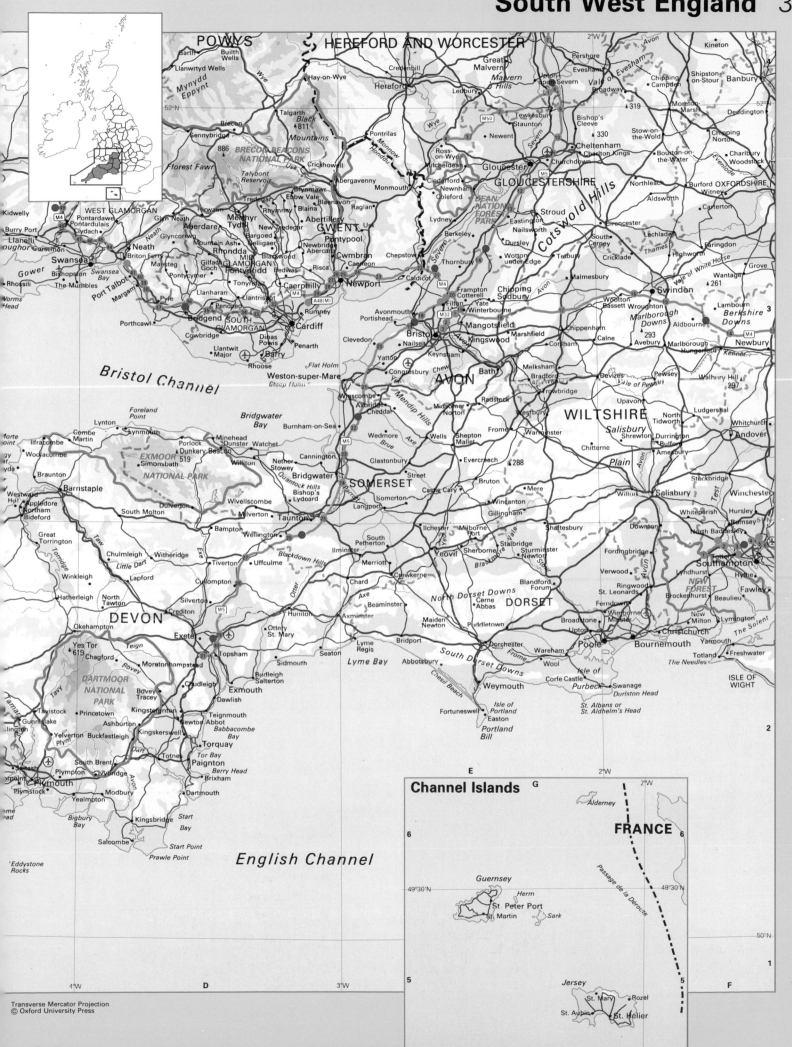

POWYS

HEREFORD AND WORCESTER

Kineton

Barth
Builth Wells
Llanwrtyd Wells

Mynydd Eppynt

Credenhill
Great Malvern
Malvern Hills
Pershore
Shipston-on-Stour
Banbury

Hay-on-Wye
Hereford
Ledbury
Evesham
Vale of Evesham
Chipping Campden
Moreton-in-Marsh
Deddington

Brecon
Sennybridge
Talgarth
Black
Mountains
811

Fforest Fawr
886
Crickhowell
Talybont Reservoir

BRECON BEACONS NATIONAL PARK

Pontrilas
Monnow
Honddu

Ross-on-Wye
Mitcheldean
Newent
Upton upon Severn
Tewkesbury
Bishop's Cleeve
Stow-on-the-Wold
Bourton-on-the-Water
Chipping Norton
Charlbury
Woodstock
Evenlode
319

Kidwelly
WEST GLAMORGAN
Pontardawe
Pontardulais
Clydach
M4
Cinderford
Newnham
Coleford
Cheltenham
Charlton Kings
Churchdown
330

Burry Port
Llanelli
Loughor
Gorseinon
Glyn Neath
Aberdare
Mountain Ash
Hirwaun
Merthyr Tydfil
New Tredegar
Rhymney
Ebbw Vale
Blaina
Abertillery
Lydney
Berkeley
GLOUCESTERSHIRE
Gloucester
M5
Stroud
Eastington
Nailsworth
Northleach
Aldsworth
Burford OXFORDSHIRE
Witney
Carterton

Neath
Rhondda
Glamorgan
Pontypridd
Bedwas
Newbridge
Abercarn
Cwmbran
Caerleon
DEAN FOREST NATIONAL PARK
Dursley
Wotton under Edge
Tetbury
Cotswold Hills
South Cerney
Cirencester
Lechlade
Faringdon
Highworth
Grove
Wantage

Swansea
Gower
Bishopston
Rhossili
The Mumbles
Swansea Bay
Port Talbot
Margam
Pyle
Porthcawl
Bridgend
Pencoed
Llanharan
Llantrisant
Caerphilly
Newport
Chepstow
Caldicot
M4
Thornbury
Frampton Cotterell
Chipping Sodbury
Yate
Winterbourne
Malmesbury
Avon
Cricklade
Vale of White Horse
Swindon
Wootton Bassett
Wroughton
Marlborough Downs
Aldbourne
Lambourn
Berkshire Downs
261
M4

Worms Head
Porthcawl
SOUTH GLAMORGAN
Cowbridge
Cardiff
Rumney
Avonmouth
Portishead
Portbury
Filton
M32
Mangotsfield
Marshfield
Chippenham
Calne
293
Avebury
Marlborough
Hungerford
Kennet
Newbury

Llantwit Major
Dinas Powis
Penarth
Barry
Rhoose
Clevedon
Nailsea
Bristol
Kingswood
Keynsham
Corsham
Devizes
Vale of Pewsey
Pewsey
13

Flat Holm
Weston-super-Mare
Steep Holm
Yatton
Congresbury
Chew
Bath
Melksham
Bradford-on-Avon
Trowbridge
Walbury Hill
297

Bristol Channel

AVON
Midsomer Norton
Radstock
Westbury
Frome
Warminster
WILTSHIRE
Salisbury
Plain
Upavon
North Tidworth
Ludgershall
Whitchurch
Andover

Foreland Point
Lynton
Lynmouth
Combe Martin
Ilfracombe
Woolacombe
Bridgwater Bay
Minehead
Dunster
Watchet
Porlock
EXMOOR
519
Dunkery Beacon
Simonsbath
NATIONAL PARK
Williton
Nether Stowey
Cannington
Bridgwater
Burnham-on-Sea
M5
Axbridge
Cheddar
Wedmore
Axe
Brue
Wells
Shepton Mallet
Evercreech
288
Chitterne
Shrewton
Durrington
Bulford
Amesbury

Morte Point
Braunton
Westward Ho!
Appledore
Northam
Bideford
Barnstaple
Dulverton
Wivelscombe
South Molton
Bampton
Wellington
Taunton
Quantock Hills
Bishop's Lydeard
SOMERSET
Langport
Somerton
Glastonbury
Street
Castle Cary
Bruton
Wincanton
Gillingham
Mere
Wilton
Salisbury
Stockbridge
Winchester

Great Torrington
Witheridge
Tiverton
Uffculme
Cullompton
Blackdown Hills
Ilminster
Chard
South Petherton
Merriott
Crewkerne
Ilchester
Yeovil
Milborne Port
Sherborne
Shaftesbury
Stalbridge
Sturminster Newton
Fordingbridge
Downton
Whiteparish
Hursley
Romsey
North Baddesley
Southampton

Chulmleigh
Winkleigh
Lapford
Little Dart
Silverton
Crediton
M5
Honiton
Ottery St. Mary
Axminster
Axe
Beaminster
Maiden Newton
North Dorset Downs
Cerne Abbas
Blandford Forum
DORSET
Verwood
Ringwood
St. Leonards
Ferndown
NEW FOREST
Lyndhurst
Brockenhurst
Beaulieu
Fawley
Hythe

DEVON
Hatherleigh
North Tawton
Okehampton
Yes Tor
619
Chagford
Exeter
Topsham
Seaton
Lyme Regis
Bridport
Puddletown
Dorchester
Wareham
Wimborne Minster
Upton
Poole
Christchurch
Bournemouth
Yarmouth
New Milton
Lymington
The Solent
Totland
Freshwater

Teign
Moretonhampstead
Bovey Tracey
Chudleigh
Dawlish
Exmouth
Sidmouth
Budleigh Salterton
Lyme Bay
Abbotsbury
Chesil Beach
Weymouth
Frome
Wool
Corfe Castle
Isle of Purbeck
Swanage
Durlston Head
The Needles
ISLE OF WIGHT

Tavy
Gunnislake
Tavistock
Princetown
DARTMOOR NATIONAL PARK
Yelverton
Buckfastleigh
Ashburton
Newton Abbot
Kingsteignton
Kingskerswell
Babbacombe Bay
Torquay
Tor Bay
Paignton
Berry Head
Brixham
Fortuneswell
Isle of Portland
Easton
Portland Bill
St. Albans or St. Aldhelm's Head

Saltash
Plymouth
Plymstock
Plympton
South Brent
Ivybridge
Modbury
Yealmpton
Totnes
Dart
Dartmouth
Bigbury Bay
Kingsbridge
Start Bay
Salcombe
Start Point
Prawle Point

Eddystone Rocks

English Channel

Channel Islands

Alderney

FRANCE

Passage de la Déroute

49°30'N

Guernsey
Herm
St. Peter Port
St. Martin
Sark

Jersey
St. Mary
Rozel
St. Aubin
St. Helier

50°N

Land use

- arable
- dairying and mixed farming
- improved grazing
- hillfarming—mainly sheep
- woodland and forestry

- market gardening
- major built-up area

Communications

- motorway
- major road
- principal railway
- ferry route

- ✳ tourism
- major reservoir

Scale 1 : 1 750 000

0   25   50 km

Power stations

- coal
- coal/oil
- oil
- gas
- ☉ nuclear

Extractive industries

- ■ coal
- △ sand and gravel
- □ limestone

Industry

- iron and steel
- metal
- aluminium
- mechanical engineering
- motor vehicles
- rail vehicles
- aerospace
- electrical engineering
- electronics/computers
- precision instruments, optics
- jewellery
- oil refining
- glass
- cement

- bricks and tiles
- nuclear processing
- textiles and carpets
- clothing and footwear
- fur and leather
- dairy
- fish processing
- sugar refining
- brewing and distilling
- other food and drink
- furniture
- pulp and paper
- printing and publishing

Boundaries

county

Communications

- motorway — M1
- primary road
- A road
- ⬤ motorway junction
- ⬤ motorway service area
- railway
- canal
- ⊕ international airport
- ✈ other airport

Cities and towns

- built-up areas
- ■ over 1 million inhabitants
- ● more than 100 000 inhabitants
- • smaller towns

Land height

metres
300
200
100
sea level
land below sea level

▲ spot height in metres

Scale 1 : 1 000 000

0   25   50 km

King's Lynn
Norwich
Peterborough
Cambridge
Bedford
Banbury
Oxford
Ipswich
Felixstowe
Harwich
Reading
London
Fawley
Portsmouth
Newhaven
Dover
Folkestone

to Oslo
Kristiansand
Esbjerg
Hamburg
Hoek van Holland
Göteborg
to Zeebrugge
to Vlissingen
to Dunkerque
to Zeebrugge
Oostende
Calais
Boulogne
to Channel Is.
Cherbourg
St-Malo
le Havre
Caen
to Dieppe

Inset map (Scale 1 : 1 000 000)

WARWICKSHIRE
Avon
M6
Rugby
Duncharch
M45
Southam
Stratford-upon-Avon
Gaydon
Byfield
Woodfo
Weedon
Halse
Kineton
Chipping Campden
Shipston-on-Stour
Banbury
Brackley
Gre
Broadway
52°N
2°W
319
Moreton-in-Marsh
Bishop's Cleeve
330
Stow-on-the-Wold
Chipping Norton
Deddington
Cheltenham
Charlton Kings
Bourton-on-the-Water
Charlbury
Bicester
GLOUCESTERSHIRE
OXFORDSHIRE
Northleach
Burford
Woodstock
Cotswold Hills
Aldsworth
Witney
Kidlington
Cirencester
Evenlode
Carterton
Oxford
Wheatley
South Cerney
Lechlade
Thames
Faringdon
Abingdon
Cricklade
Highworth
Dorc
Vale of White Horse
Didcot
Grove
Harwell
Walli
Wantage
Wootton Bassett
Swindon
261
East Ilsley
Goring
Wroughton
Lambourn
Berkshire Downs
Pangbourne
Calne
293
Avebury
Marlborough Downs
Aldbourne
M4
BERKSHIRE
Marlborough
Newbury
Thatcham
Devizes
Pewsey
Hungerford
Kennet
Vale of Pewsey
Walbury Hill
297
Kingsclere
Tadley
Upavon
Basingst
WILTSHIRE
North Tidworth
Ludgershall
Hampshire
Oakley
Overton
Salisbury
Shrewton
Durrington
Bulford
Andover
Whitchurch
Down
Plain
Avon
Chitterne
Amesbury
HAMPSHIRE
Stockbridge
M3
New Alresford
Wilton
Salisbury
Wilton
Winchester
Itchen
51°N
Whiteparish
Hursley
Twyford
Downton
Romsey
Test
Fordingbridge
North Baddesley
Eastleigh
Bishop's Waltham
Verwood
Avon
Southampton
Hythe
Hedge End
Wickham
Waterlooville
Ringwood
Lyndhurst
Locks Heath
Fareham
St. Leonards
NEW FOREST
Beaulieu
Fawley
Stubbington
Ferndowns
Brockenhurst
Southampton Water
Gosport
Por
Wimborne Minster
New Milton
Lymington
Cowes
Spithead
Fishbourne
Poole
Bournemouth
Yarmouth
ISLE OF WIGHT
Ryde
Bembri
Christchurch
Totland
Freshwater
NEWPORT
Sandow
Shanklin
The Needles
Swanage
Durlston Head
St. Catherine's Point
Ventnor

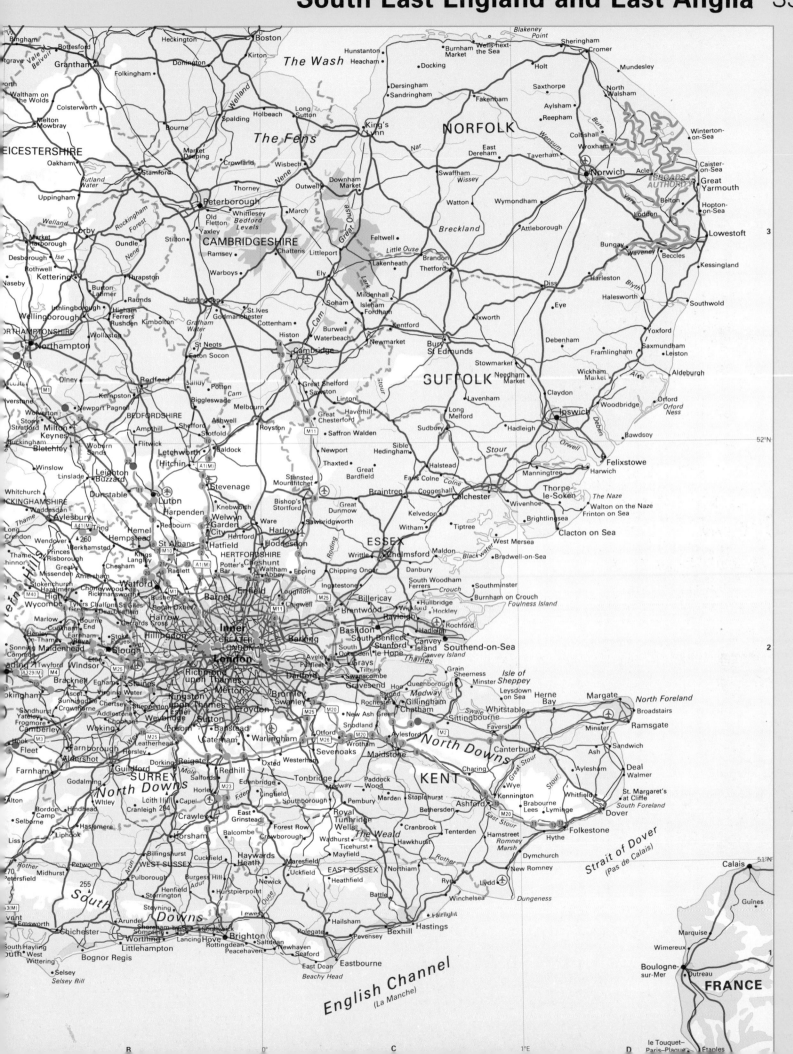

For legend see page 32.

Scale 1 : 400 000

0   10 km

BEDFORDSHIRE

HERTFORDSHIRE

ESSEX

BUCKINGHAMSHIRE

BERKSHIRE

GREATER LONDON

SURREY

KENT

Chilterns

North Downs

North Downs

Epping Forest

Thames

Grand Union Canal

Mole

Wey

Roding

Lea

Eden

Medway

Milton Keynes, Woburn Sands, Bletchley, Newton Longville, Great Brickhill, Stewkley, Linslade, Wing, Leighton Buzzard, Stanbridge, Billington, Hockliffe, Streatley, Toddington, Cranfield, Marston Moretaine, Lidlington, Ampthill, Maulden, Flitwick, Clophill, Chicksands, Langford, Shefford, Henlow, Stotfold, Letchworth, Baldock, Hitchin, Shillington, Barton-le-Clay, Kings Walden, Whitwell, Welwyn, Stevenage, Knebworth, Watton at Stone, Walkern, Braughing, Puckerage, Standon, Hadham Ford, Much Hadham, Widford, Sawbridgeworth, Hunsdon, Spellbrook, Bishop's Stortford, Stansted Mountfitchet, Clavering, Brent Pelham, Quendon, Newport, Thaxted, Great Bardfield, Henham, Elsenham, Stebbing, Takeley, Great Dunmow, Felsted, High Roding, Hatfield Heath, Sheering, Great Waltham, Little Waltham, Harlow, Matching Green, Chelmsford, Writtle, Great Baddow, Chipping Ongar, Galleywood, Stondon Massey, Ingatestone, Stock, Brentwood, Billericay, Grays Hill, Great Warley, Basildon

Woburn, Aspley Guise, Dunstable, Eaton Bray, Whipsnade, Luton, Caddington, Markyate, Harpenden, Wheathampstead, Redbourn, Welwyn Garden City, Hatfield, Essendon, Tewin, Hertford, Ware, Lower Nazeing, Roydon, Hoddesdon, Hastingwood, Fyfield, North Weald Bassett, Thornwood Common, Epping, Cuffley, Cheshunt, Waltham Abbey, Theydon Bois, Menmore, Edlesborough, Cheddington, Ivinghoe, Marsworth, Great Gaddesden, Daghall, Aston Clinton, Tring, Potten End, Berkhamsted, Hemel Hempstead, St. Albans, Colney Heath, Welham Green, Brookmans Park, Potter's Bar, Botley, Bovingdon, Chiswell Green, London Colney, Radlett, Shenley, Borehamwood, Enfield, Southgate, Edmonton, Chingford, Loughton, Stapleford Abbotts, Chigwell, Pilgrims Hatch

Wendover, Great Missenden, Prestwood, Chesham, Kings Langley, Abbots Langley, Bricket Wood, Amersham, Holmer Green, Hazelmere, Little Chalfont, Chorleywood, Watford, Bushey, Barnet, Edgware, Stanmore, Finchley, Wood Green, Haringey, Tottenham, Hornsey, Waltham Forest, Woodford, Redbridge, Wanstead, Romford, Havering, Hornchurch, Upminster, High Wycombe, Tylers Green, Loudwater, Flackwell Heath, Beaconsfield, Chalfont St. Giles, Rickmansworth, South Oxhey, Harrow, Hendon, Golders Green, Camden, Islington, Hackney, Leyton, Ilford, Barking, Dagenham

Bourne End, Cookham, Burnham Beeches, Stoke Poges, Farnham Royal, Taplow, Gerrards Cross, Chalfont St Peter, Harefield, Ruislip, Hillingdon, Uxbridge, Greenford, Brent, Wembley, Willesden, Paddington, Tower Hamlets, West Ham, Newham, Maidenhead, Bray, Slough, Iver, West Drayton, Ealing, Spouthall, Brentford, Hammersmith, Kensington & Chelsea, City of London, Westminster, Southwark, Woolwich, Rainham, Stanford le Hope, South Ockenden, Linford, Chadwell St. Mary, Aveley, Purfleet, Erith, Grays, Tilbury, West Thurrock

Eton, Windsor, Datchet, Hounslow, Richmond upon Thames, Putney, Fulham, Battersea, Lambeth, Brixton, Greenwich, Eltham, Bexley, Dartford, Greenhithe, Swanscombe, Northfleet, Gravesend, Old Windsor, Feltham, Twickenham, Wandsworth, Wimbledon, Streatham, Catford, Lewisham, Sidcup, North Cray, Wilmington, Hextable, Higham, Instead Rise

Bracknell, Ascot, Cranbourne, Egham, Staines, Ashford, Kingston upon Thames, Merton, Mitcham, Beckenham, Bromley, Swanley, South Darenth, Hartley, Virginia Water, Sunningdale, Chertsey, Shepperton, Sunbury, Walton on Thames, Weybridge, Esher, Surbiton, Morden, Croydon, Orpington, Eynsford, New Ash Green, Culverstone Green, Snodland, West Kingdown

Bagshot, Windlesham, Chobham, Addlestone, Byfleet, Ewell, Sutton, Purley, New Addington, Knockholt Pound, Otford, Kemsing, West Malling, Camberley, Frimley, Lightwater, Woking, Knaphill, Pirbright, Send, Ripley, Cobham, Oxshott, Epsom, Banstead, Ashtead, Tadworth, Coulsdon, Warlingham, Biggin Hill, Tatsfield, Caterham, Woldingham, Seal, Ightham, Borough Green, Wrotham, Ditton, Deep Cut, Worplesdon, Leatherhead, Fetcham, Kingswood, Walton on the Hill, Merstham, Westerham, Limpsfield, Sevenoaks, Sevenoaks Weald, Mereworth, Wateringbury

Ash, Onslow Village, Guildford, West Clandon, Horsley, Shere, Gomshall, Dorking, Westcott, North Holmwood, Brockham, Reigate, Redhill, South Nutfield, Oxted, Godstone, South Godstone, Crockham Hill, Marlpit Hill, Shipbourne, West Malling, Godalming, Witley, Milford, Wonersh, Bramley, Rowly, Ockley, Beare Green, Capel, Charlwood, Salfords, Outwood, Edenbridge, Lingfield, Hildenborough, Leigh, Tonbridge, Paddock Wood, Hindhead, Chiddingfold, Elstead, Ewhurst, Cranleigh, Horley, Smallfield, Dormansland, Copthorne, East Grinstead, Fordcombe, Penshurst, Yalding, Hadlow, West Grinstead, Crawley, Ifield, Leith Hill, 294

A1(M), M1, M10, M11, M25, M3, M4, M40, M20, M26, M23, A41(M), A40, 260

Transverse Mercator Projection
© Oxford University Press

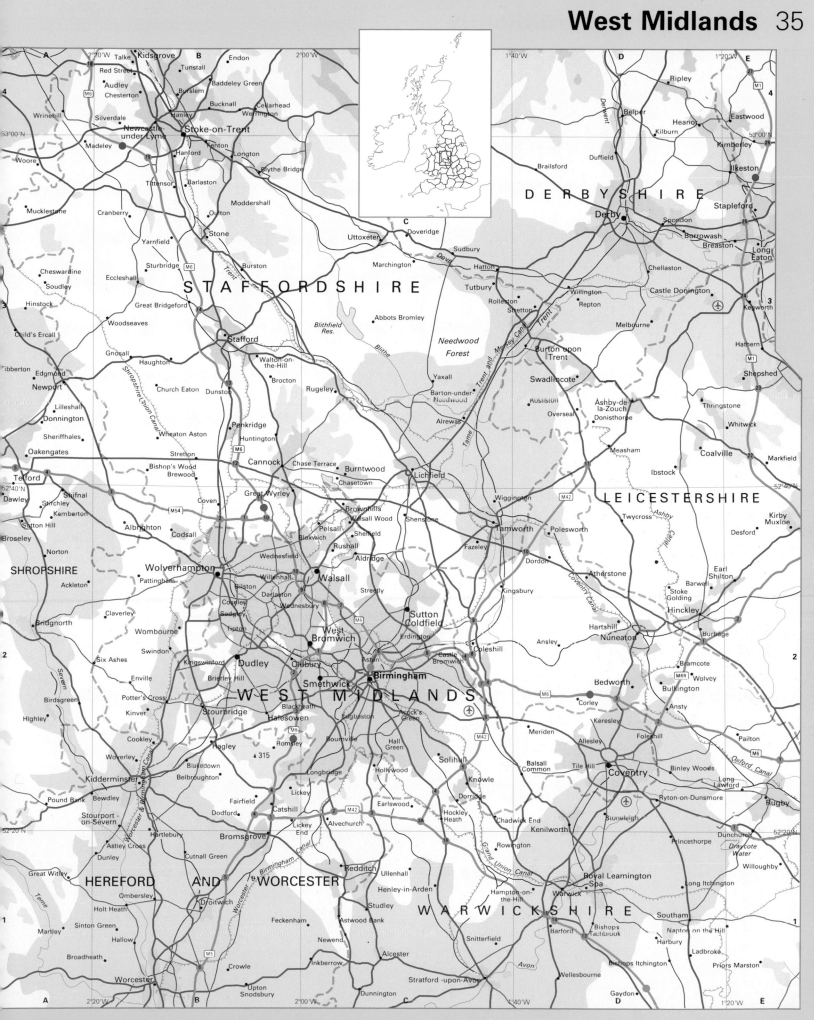

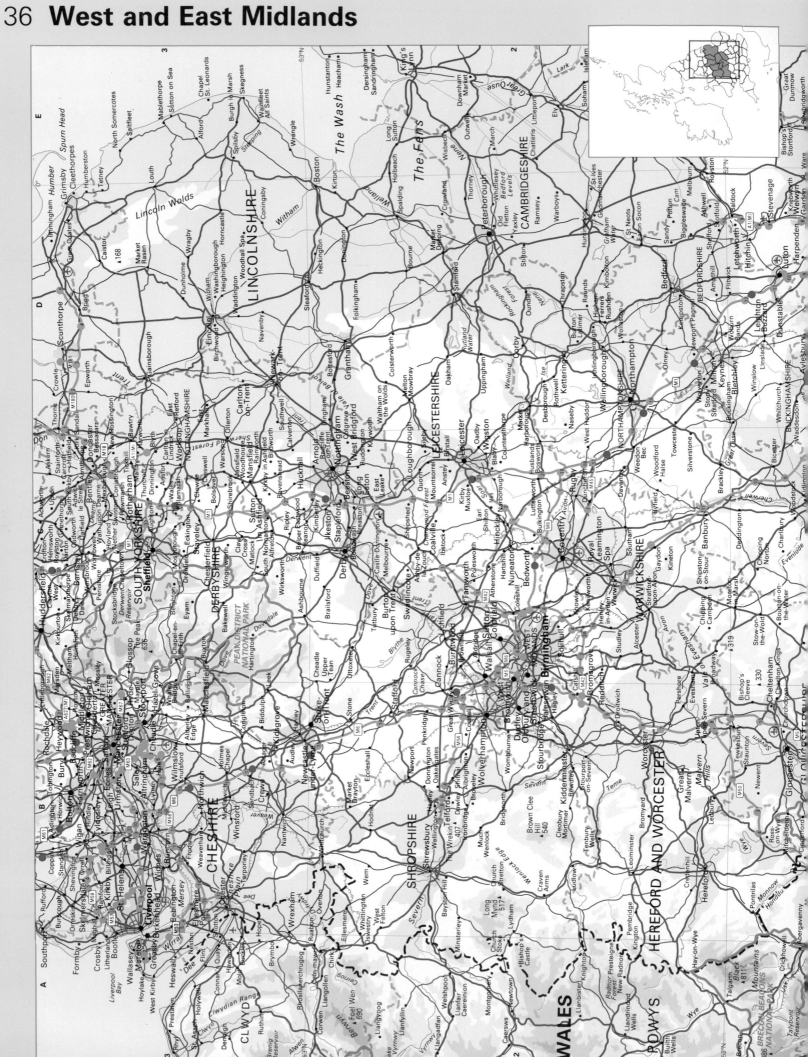

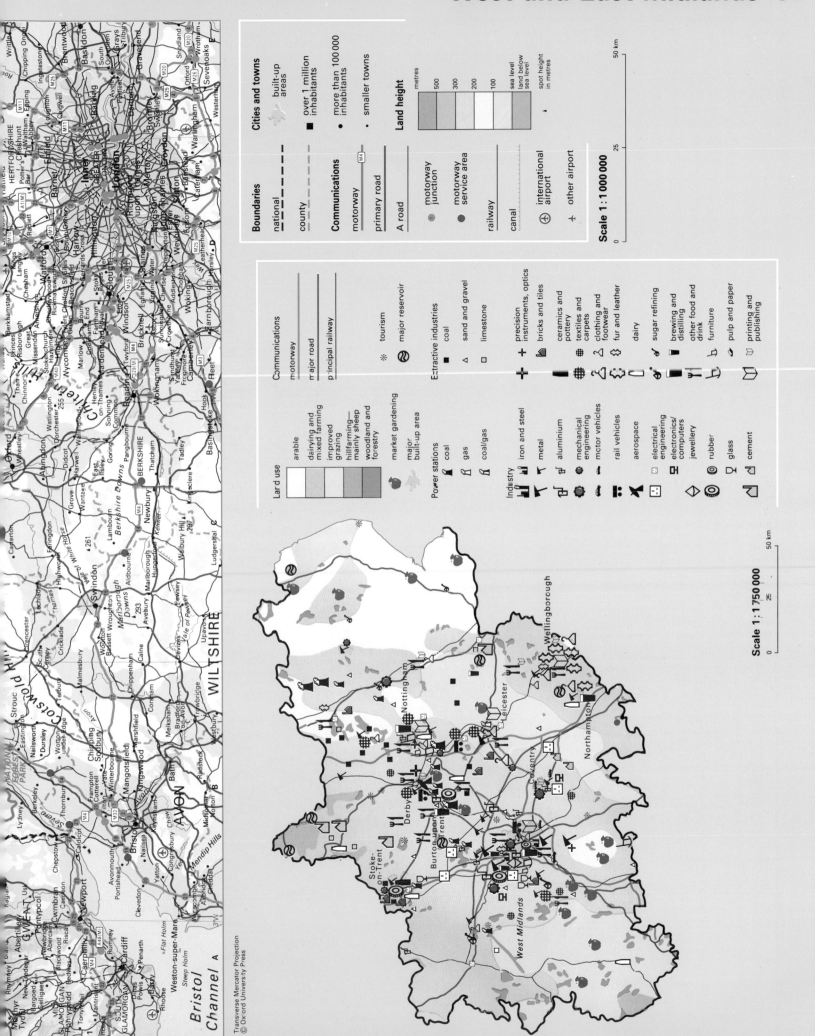

Transverse Mercator Projection
© Oxford University Press

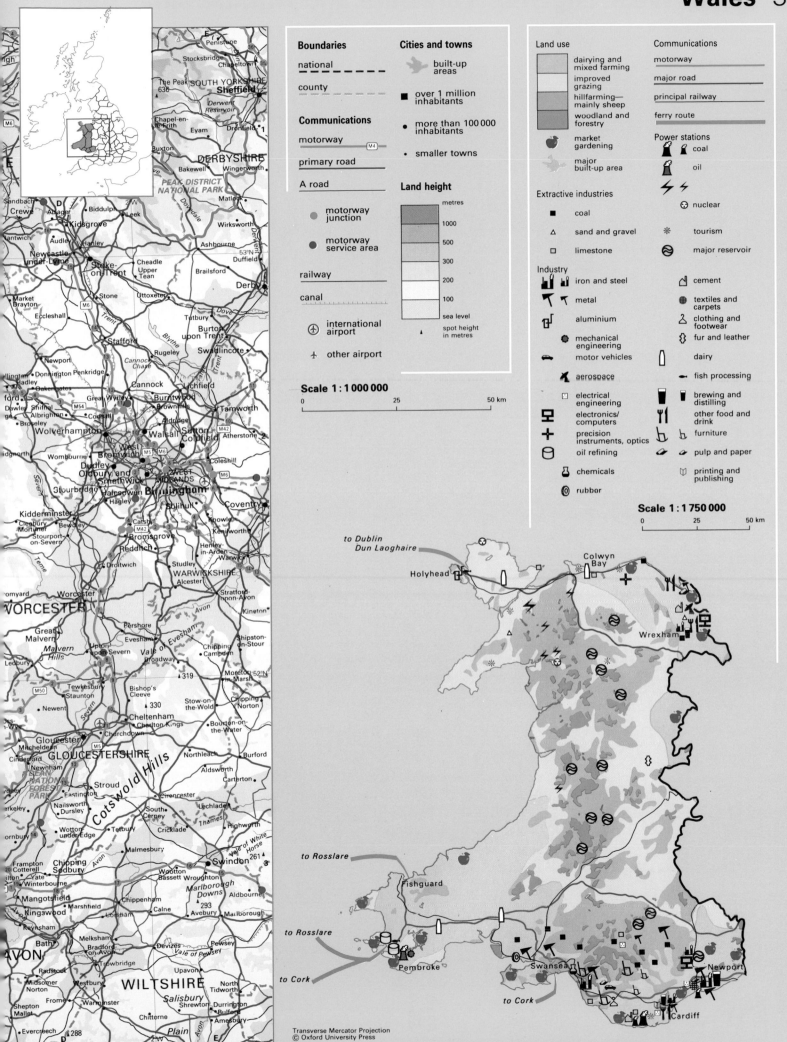

Transverse Mercator Projection
© Oxford University Press

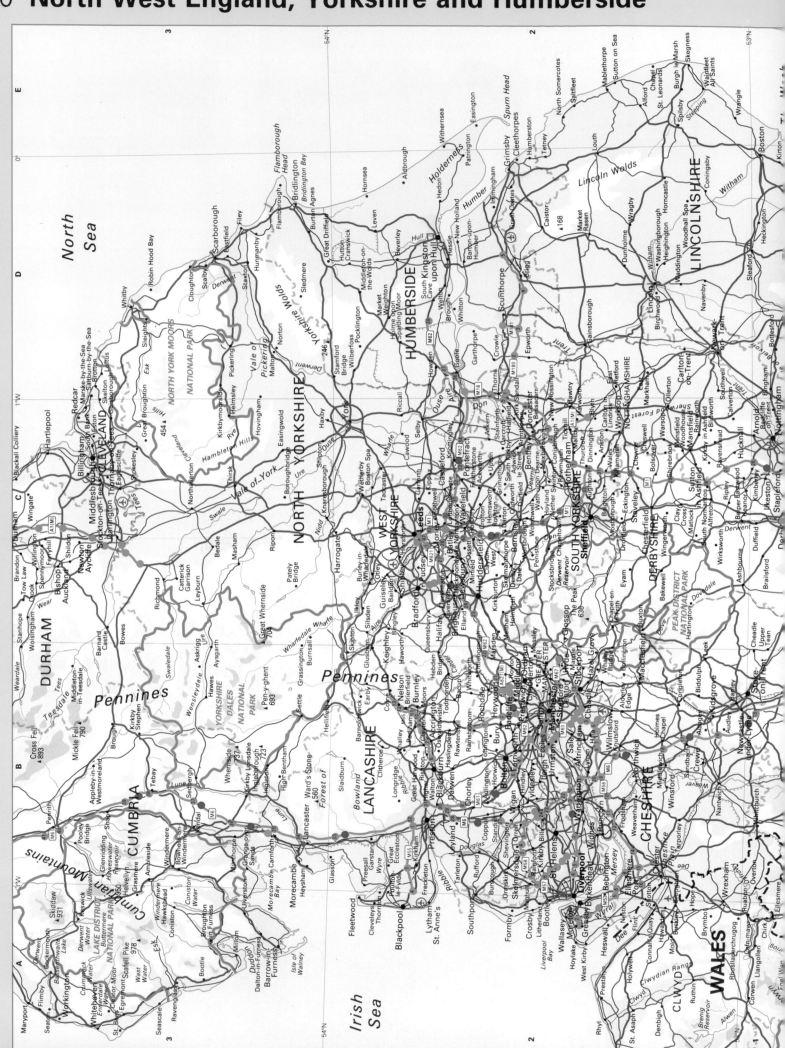

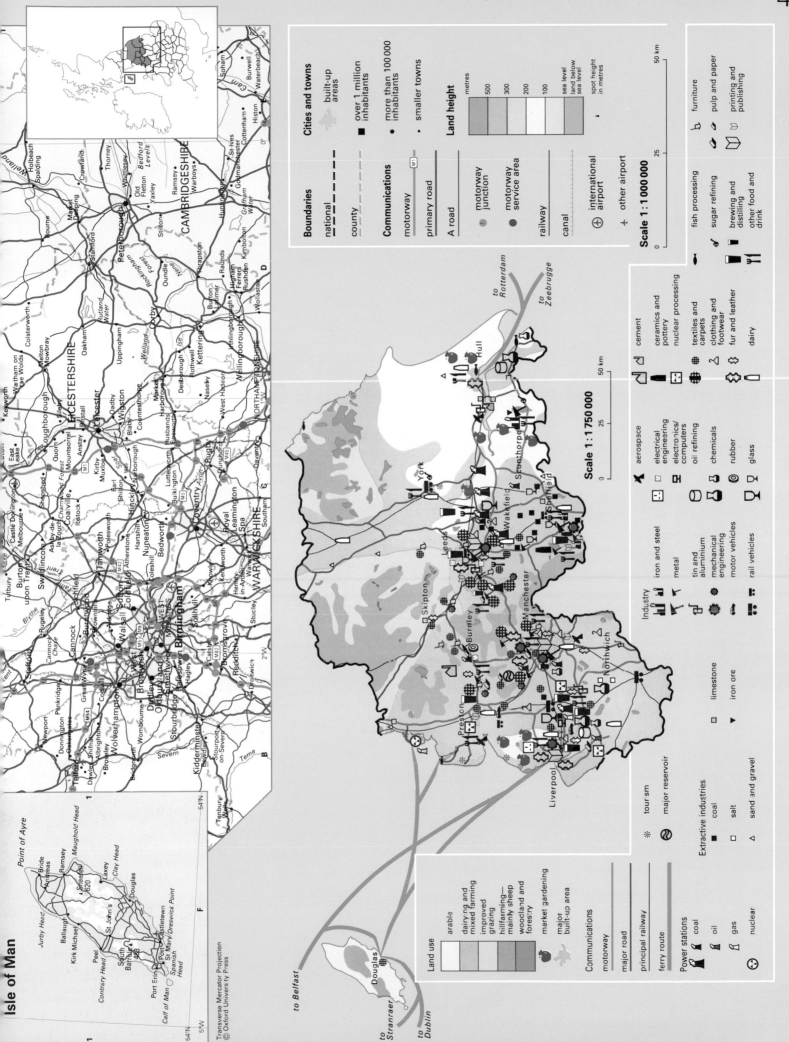

Morecambe Bay

54°00'N
53°40'N
53°20'N

3°00'W 2°40'W 2°20'W 2°00'W

Morecambe
Heysham
Lancaster
Scotforth
Overton
Galgate
Glasson
Cockerham

Torrisholme
Halton
Brookhouse
Ward's Stone 560

Settle
Airton
Long Preston
Hellifield
Stocks Res.

Forest of Bowland

Ribblesdale

Fleetwood
Rossall Pt.
Knott End-on-Sea
Stake Pool
Preesall
Stalmine
Garstang
Cleveleys
Thornton
Poulton-le-Fylde
Great Eccleston
Barton
Blackpool
Great Marton
Kirkham
Broughton
Fulwood
Freckleton
Warton
Lytham St. Anne's
Lytham

Wyre
Calder
Oakenclough
Brock
Longridge
Chipping

LANCASHIRE

Gisburn
Barnoldswick
Earby
Glusburn
Silsden
Colne
Trawden
Nelson
Brierfield
Keighley
Haworth
Oxenhope

Waddington
West Bradford
Clitheroe
Hurst Green
Billington
Whalley
Great Harwood
Clayton-le-Moors
Rishton
Calder
Padiham
Burnley

Leeds & Liverpool Canal

Hebden Water
Hebden Bridge

Preston
Walton-le-Dale
Higher Walton
Blackburn
Oswaldtwistle
Accrington

Samlesbury
Bamber Bridge
Hutton
Much Hoole
Leyland
Hesketh Bank
Beconshall
Tarleton
Banks
Bretherton
Croston
Euxton
Chorley
Charnock Richard
Adlington
Coppull
Standish

Ribble
Longton

Darwen
Haslingden
Rawtenstall
Bacup

Forest of Rossendale

Todmorden
Rochdale Canal
Ripponden
Whitworth
Littleborough
Ramsbottom
Edgworth
Toppings
Tottington
Bradshaw

Southport
Rufford
Scarisbrick
Ainsdale
Burscough Bridge
Newburgh
Ormskirk
Dalton
Skelmersdale
Orrell
Standish
Horwich
Aspull
Shevington
Hindley
Wigan
Ince in Makerfield

Douglas

Bury
Heywood
Rochdale
Milnrow
Shaw
Royton
Middleton
Chadderton
Oldham
Delph
Uppermill
Saddleworth Moor
Marsden
Mossley

Formby
Haskayne
Great Altcar
Aughton
Lydiate
Maghull
Hightown
Crosby
Litherland
Bootle
New Brighton
Wallasey
Moreton
Hoylake
Greasby
West Kirby
Irby
Pensby
Heswall

MERSEYSIDE
Kirkby
Aintree
West Derby
Knowsley
Huyton-with-Roby
Liverpool
Birkenhead
Childwall
Allerton
Halewood
Speke
Widnes
Runcorn

Liverpool Bay
Wirral
Dee

Rainford
Billinge
Ashton in Makerfield
Haydock
St. Helens
Prescot
Whiston
Rainhill
Newton-le-Willows
Golborne
Abram
Leigh
Tyldesley
Atherton
Westhoughton
Walkden
Farnworth
Kearsley
Pendlebury
Swinton
Eccles
Salford
Urmston
Irlam
Stretford
Manchester

Bolton
Little Lever
Radcliffe
Whitefield
Prestwich
Pendleton

GREATER MANCHESTER

Failsworth
Droylsden
Ashton-under-Lyne
Stalybridge
Dukinfield
Audenshaw
Denton
Hyde
Glossop
Hadfield
Bredbury
Romiley
Stockport
Hazel Grove
Marple
New Mills
Whaley Bridge
High Lane
Poynton
Bramhall
Cheadle
Hale
Altrincham
Sale
Partington
Culcheth
Risley
Warrington
Thelwall
Great Sankey
Lymm
Stockton Heath
Mobberley
Wilmslow
Handforth
Knutsford
Alderley Edge
Prestbury
Bollington
Macclesfield

Manchester Ship Canal
Mersey
Weaver
Frodsham
Helsby
Ellesmere Port
Ince
Elton
Burton
Ness
Willaston
Neston
Heswall
Baguilt
Flint
Halkyn
Connah's Quay
Shotton
Queensferry
Blacon
Mancot
Hawarden
Buckley
Mold
Ewloe
Lache
Broughton
Northop

WALES

Delamere Forest
Delamere
Kelsall
Tarvin
Duddon
Tarporley

CHESHIRE

Barnton
Northwich
Lostock Gralam
Weaverham
Hartford
Davenham
Cuddington
Moulton
Winsford
Middlewich
Holmes Chapel
Cranage
Goostrey
Marton
Chelford
Wharton

Trent & Mersey Canal
Macclesfield Canal
Bollin

Shropshire Union Canal
Dee

Ledsham
Dunham-on-the-Hill
Upton
Chester
Duddon

M6 M55 M58 M57 M53 M56 M62 M61 M66 M65 M67 M63 M602 M60 A627(M)

Transverse Mercator Projection
© Oxford University Press

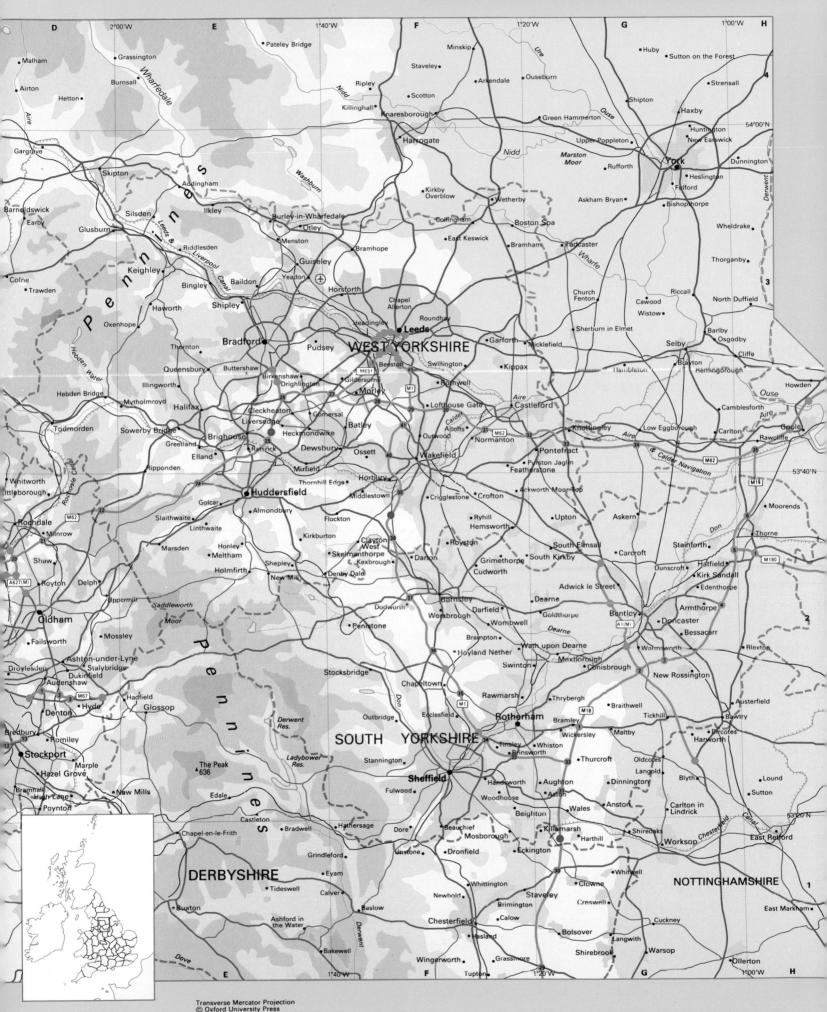

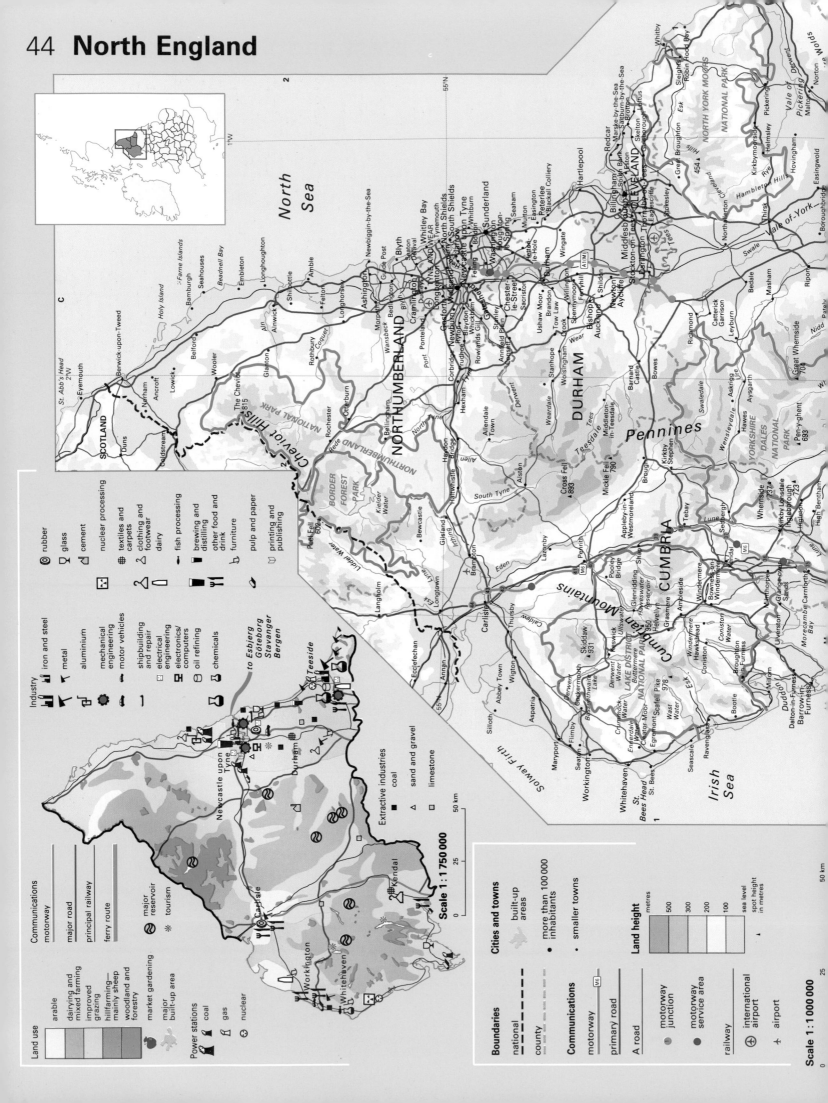

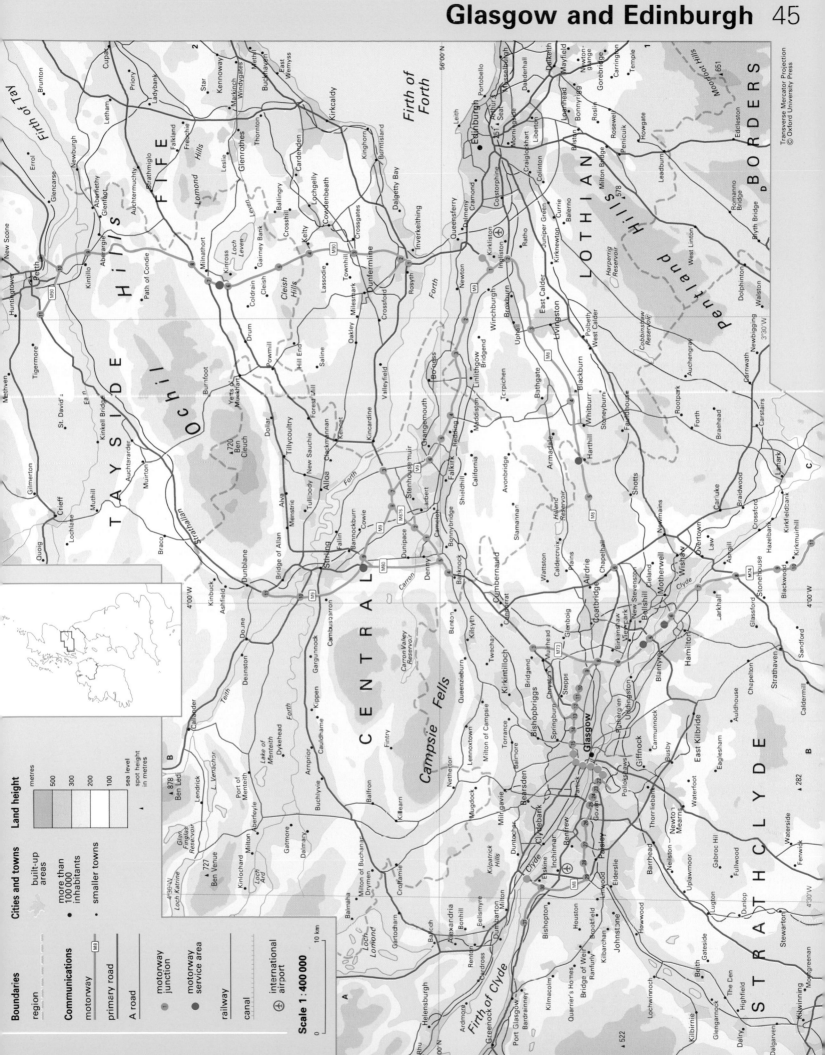

Transverse Mercator Projection
© Oxford University Press

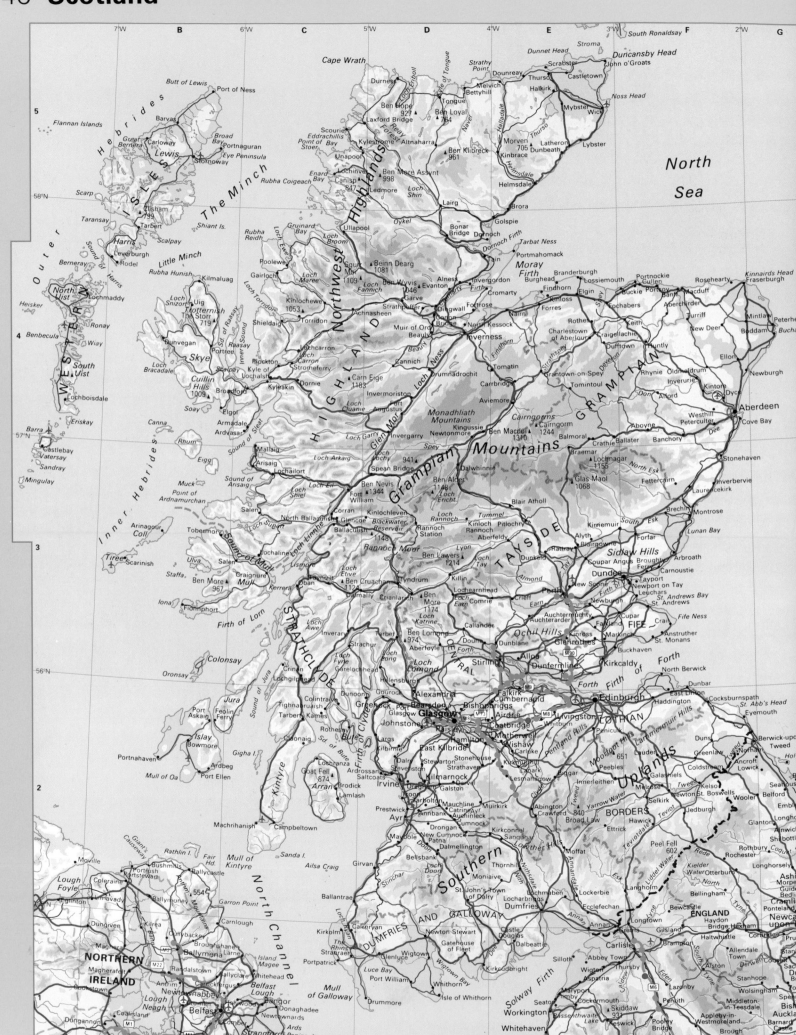

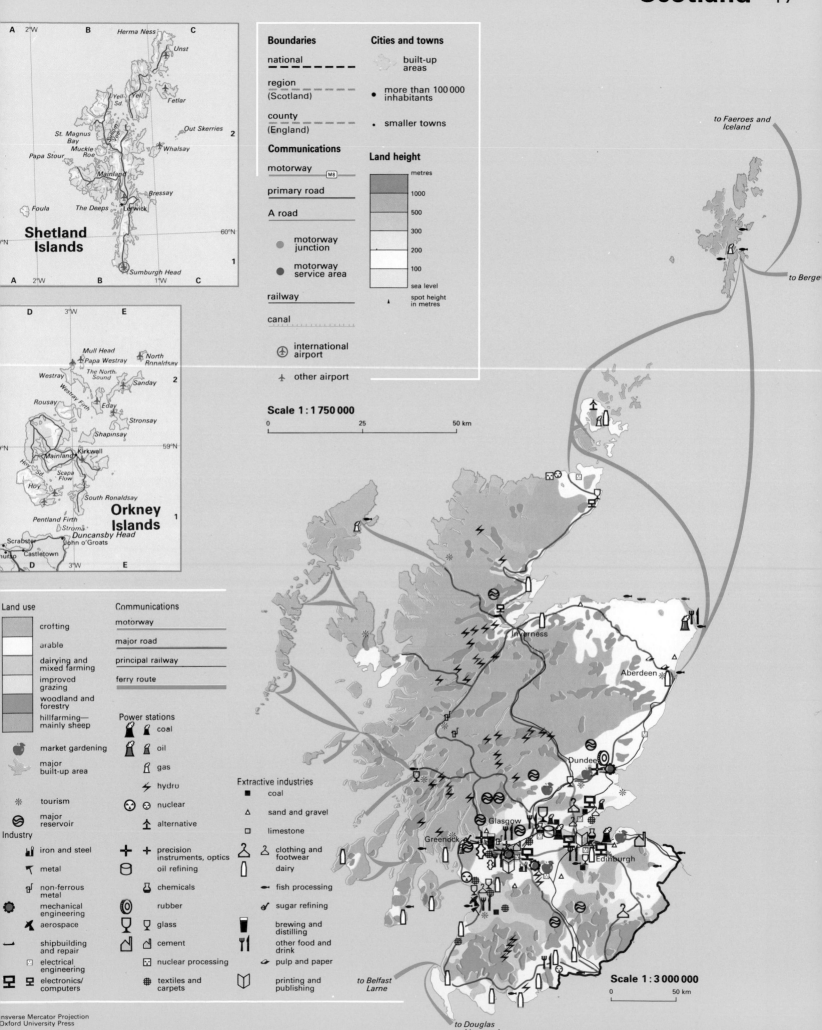

Shetland Islands

A 2°W B Herma Ness C

Unst
Yell Sd. Yell Fetlar
St. Magnus Bay Out Skerries 2
Muckle Roe Whalsay
Papa Stour
Mainland
Bressay
Foula The Deeps Lerwick 60°N
2°W Sumburgh Head 1°W 1

Shetland Islands

Orkney Islands

D 3°W E

Mull Head
Papa Westray North Ronaldsay
Westray The North Sound Sanday 2
Rousay Westray Firth Eday
Stronsay
Shapinsay
Kirkwall 59°N
Mainland
Hoy Sd. Scapa Flow
Hoy South Ronaldsay 1
Pentland Firth
Stroma Duncansby Head
Scrabster John o'Groats
Castletown
D 3°W E

Orkney Islands

Boundaries

- national
- region (Scotland)
- county (England)

Communications

- motorway M8
- primary road
- A road
- ● motorway junction
- ● motorway service area
- railway
- canal
- ⊕ international airport
- ✈ other airport

Cities and towns

- built-up areas
- ● more than 100 000 inhabitants
- · smaller towns

Land height

metres
1000
500
300
200
100
sea level

▲ spot height in metres

Scale 1 : 1 750 000

0 25 50 km

Land use

	crofting
	arable
	dairying and mixed farming
	improved grazing
	woodland and forestry
	hillfarming—mainly sheep

- 🍎 market gardening
- major built-up area
- ✳ tourism
- ⬡ major reservoir

Industry

- iron and steel
- metal
- non-ferrous metal
- ⬢ mechanical engineering
- aerospace
- shipbuilding and repair
- electrical engineering
- electronics/computers

Communications

- motorway
- major road
- principal railway
- ferry route

Power stations

- coal
- oil
- gas
- ⚡ hydro
- ⊙ nuclear
- ⬆ alternative

- ✛ precision instruments, optics
- ⬒ oil refining
- ⚗ chemicals
- ◉ rubber
- glass
- cement
- nuclear processing
- ⊞ textiles and carpets

Extractive industries

- ■ coal
- △ sand and gravel
- ☐ limestone
- clothing and footwear
- dairy
- fish processing
- sugar refining
- brewing and distilling
- other food and drink
- pulp and paper
- printing and publishing

to Faeroes and Iceland

to Bergen

Inverness

Aberdeen

Dundee

Glasgow

Greenock

Edinburgh

to Belfast Larne

to Douglas Liverpool

Scale 1 : 3 000 000

0 50 km

Transverse Mercator Projection
Oxford University Press

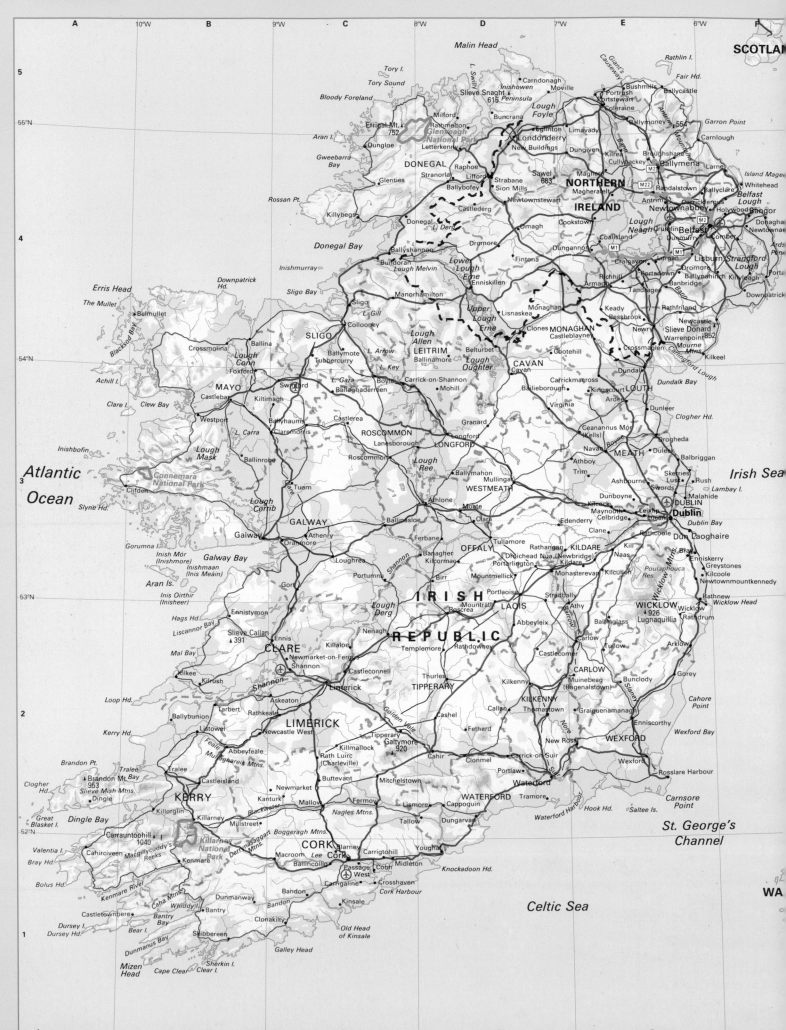

Boundaries

- **— — — —** international
- **— — — —** district (N. Ireland)
- **— — — —** county (Irish Republic)

Communications

- motorway
- primary road
- A road
- ● motorway junction
- railway
- canal
- ⊕ international airport
- ✈ other airport

Cities and towns

- built-up areas
- ● more than 100 000 inhabitants
- ● smaller towns

Land height

metres
1000
500
300
200
100
sea level

▲ spot height in metres

Scale 1 : 1 750 000

0   25   50 km

Transverse Mercator Projection
© Oxford University Press

Boundaries

- **— — — —** county/district

Communications

- motorway M1
- primary road
- A road
- ● motorway junction
- railway
- canal
- ⊕ international airport
- ✈ other airport

Cities and towns

- built-up areas
- ● more than 100 000 inhabitants
- ● smaller towns

Scale 1 : 400 000

0   10 km

Scale 1 : 3 000 000

0   60 km

Land use

	crofting
	arable
	dairying and mixed farming
	hillfarming— mainly sheep

- market gardening
- major built-up area

Extractive industries

- □ limestone

Power stations

- coal
- ◆ peat
- oil
- oil/gas
- ⚡ hydro/pumped storage

Industry

- metal
- non-ferrous metal
- mechanical engineering
- aerospace
- shipbuilding and repair
- electrical engineering
- electronics/ computers
- precision instruments, optics
- jewellery
- oil refining
- chemicals
- rubber
- glass
- cement
- textiles and carpets
- clothing and footwear
- dairy
- fish processing
- sugar refining
- brewing and distilling
- other food and drink
- pulp and paper
- printing and publishing
- ✳ tourism
- major reservoir

Communications

- motorway
- major road
- principal railway
- ferry route

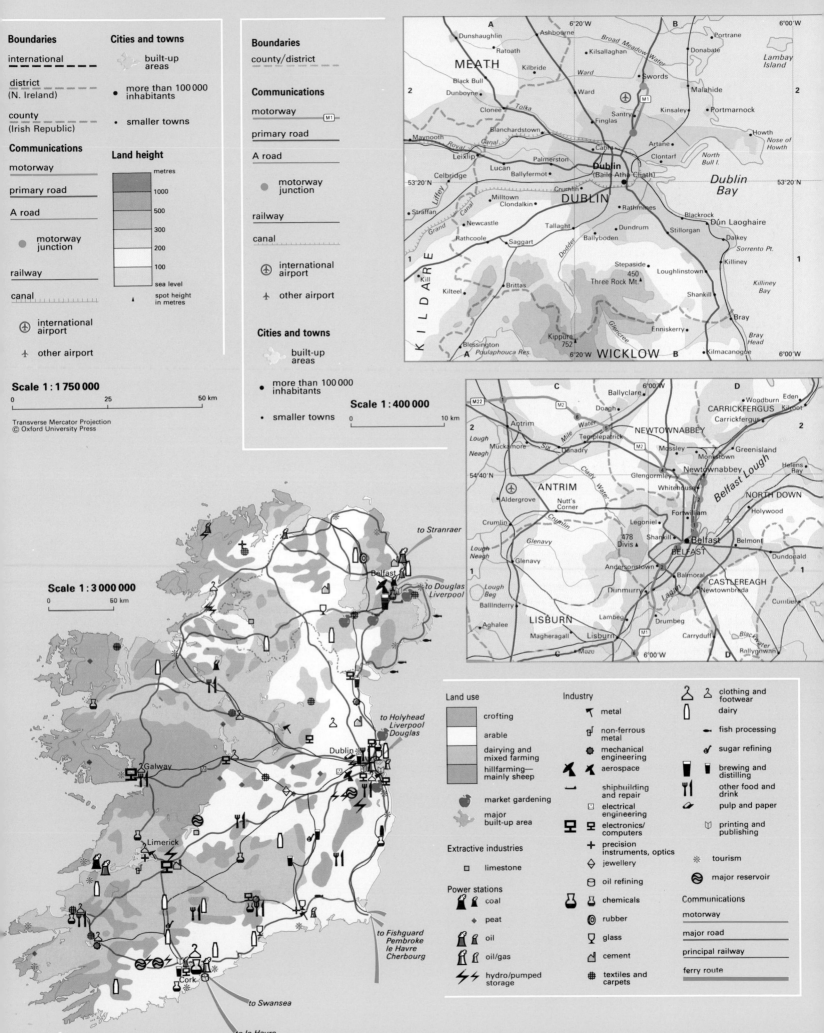

RUSSIAN FEDERATION (RUSSIA)

Moscow

Kiev

U K R A I N E

MOLDOVA
Kishinev

Bucharest

R O M A N I A

B U L G A R I A
Sofiya

TURKEY

SKOPJE
MACEDONIA

Minsk

BELARUS (BYELORUSSIA)

YUGOSLAVIA

ALBANIA
Tiranë

G R E E C E

Athens

Crete

Helsinki

Tallinn
ESTONIA

LATVIA
Riga

LITHUANIA
Vilnius

(RUSSIA)

P O L A N D
Warsaw

SLOVAKIA
Bratislava

Prague
CZECH REP.

Budapest

H U N G A R Y

Zagreb

SLOVENIA

CROATIA

Belgrade
Sarajevo

BOSNIA-
HERZEGOVINA

SAN MARINO

F I N L A N D

S W E D E N

N O R W A Y

Stockholm

Oslo

DENMARK
Copenhagen

Berlin

G E R M A N Y

Bonn

Vienna
AUSTRIA

Vaduz
LIECHTENSTEIN

Ljubljana

I T A L Y

Rome

Sicily

Sardinia
(It.)

ICELAND

Faeroes
Is. (Den.)

SCOTLAND

N.
IRELAND

IRISH
REPUBLIC

Dublin

I. OF MAN

WALES

U N I T E D

K I N G D O M

ENGLAND

London

NETHERLANDS
Amsterdam
The Hague
Brussels
BELGIUM
LUXEMBOURG

Luxembourg

Paris

Strasbourg

Bern
SWITZERLAND

Geneva

F R A N C E

Monaco
MONACO

Corsica
(Fr.)

Channel
Is. (Br.)

Andorra
ANDORRA

S P A I N
Madrid

P O R T U G A L

Lisbon

GIBRALTAR
(U.K.)

Balearic
Is. (Sp.)

Scale 1:350000000

European Organizations

European Union (EU) or Common Market
☐ member

Headquarters: Brussels
European Parliament meets in Strasbourg.
European Court of Justice sits in Luxembourg.

✱ Austria, Finland and Sweden joined the European Union on 1 January 1995

European Free Trade Association (EFTA)
☐ member

Headquarters: Geneva

North Atlantic Treaty Organization (NATO)
☐ member

Headquarters: Brussels

— international boundaries
● national capital
  see note on page 62 about Germany
· other cities

Scale 1:19000000

0   200   400 km

Headquarters of other European and World Organizations

The Hague: International Court of Justice

Geneva: World Health Organization (WHO)

Paris: United Nations Educational, Scientific and
Cultural Organization (UNESCO)

Organization for Economic Co-operation and
Development (OECD)

Rome: Food and Agricultural Organization of the
United Nations (FAO)

Conical Orthomorphic Projection

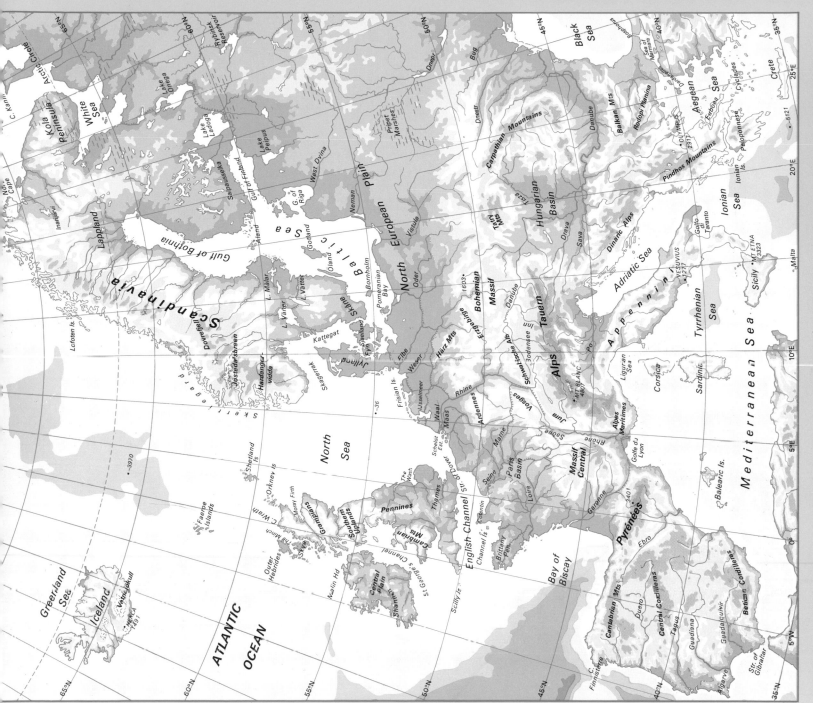

Land height

metres		
3000		
2000		
1000		
500		
300		
200		
100		
sea level land below sea level		

Sea depth

sea level

| 200 | 3000 |
| 4000 | 5000 |

ice cap

marsh

spot height in metres

. –88 sea depths shown as minus numbers

Scale 1:19000000

0   200   400 km

Geological structure

Precambrian
- shields
- underlying platforms

Mountain building
- Caledonian
- Hercynian
- Alpine

Oceans and seas
- continental shelf
- oceanic crust (Atlantic) deep troughs (Mediterranean)
- recent volcanism
- faults
- thrusts
- limit of Quaternary glaciation

Scale 1:56000000

0   400 km

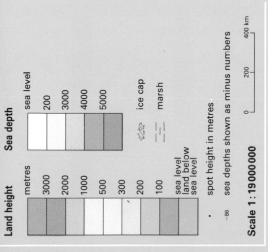

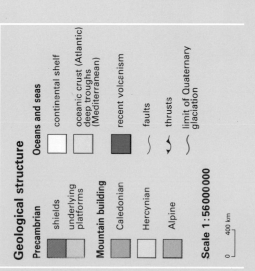

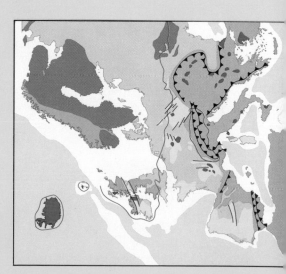

Oxford University Press

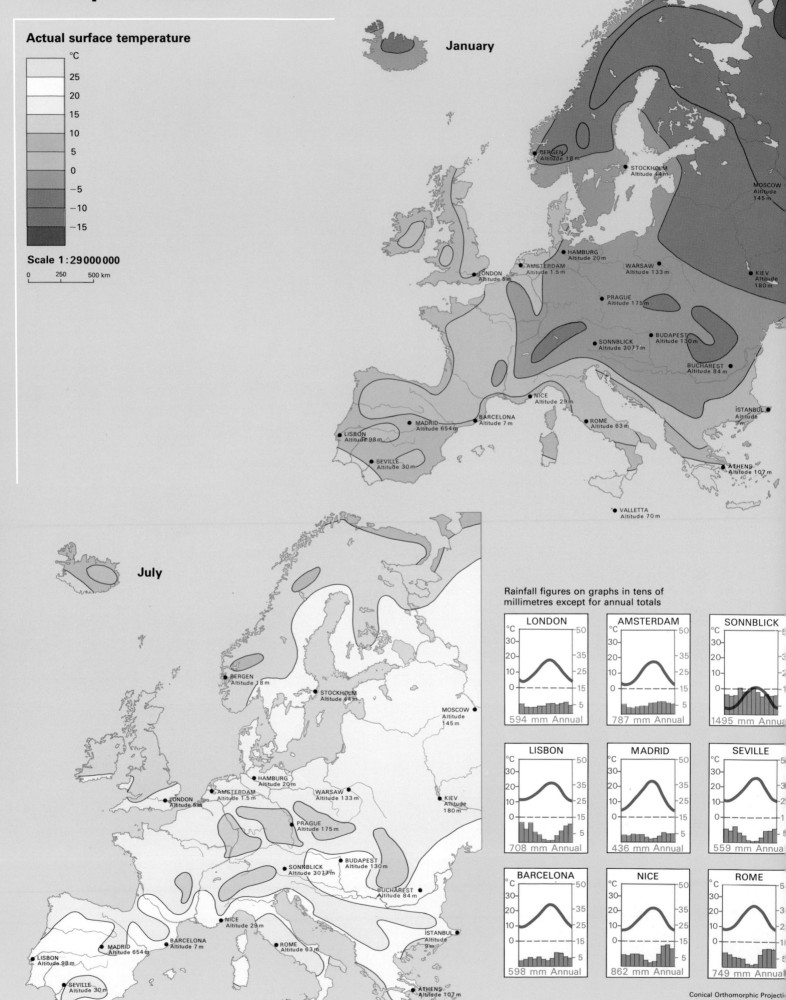

Actual surface temperature

°C
25
20
15
10
5
0
−5
−10
−15

Scale 1:29 000 000

0   250   500 km

January

BERGEN
Altitude 18 m

STOCKHOLM
Altitude 44 m

MOSCOW
Altitude 145 m

HAMBURG
Altitude 20 m

AMSTERDAM
Altitude 1.5 m

WARSAW
Altitude 133 m

KIEV
Altitude 180 m

LONDON
Altitude 5 m

PRAGUE
Altitude 175 m

SONNBLICK
Altitude 3077 m

BUDAPEST
Altitude 130 m

BUCHAREST
Altitude 84 m

NICE
Altitude 29 m

MADRID
Altitude 654 m

BARCELONA
Altitude 7 m

ROME
Altitude 63 m

İSTANBUL
Altitude 9 m

LISBON
Altitude 98 m

SEVILLE
Altitude 30 m

ATHENS
Altitude 107 m

VALLETTA
Altitude 70 m

July

BERGEN
Altitude 18 m

STOCKHOLM
Altitude 44 m

MOSCOW
Altitude 145 m

HAMBURG
Altitude 20 m

LONDON
Altitude 5 m

AMSTERDAM
Altitude 1.5 m

WARSAW
Altitude 133 m

KIEV
Altitude 180 m

PRAGUE
Altitude 175 m

SONNBLICK
Altitude 3077 m

BUDAPEST
Altitude 130 m

BUCHAREST
Altitude 84 m

NICE
Altitude 29 m

MADRID
Altitude 654 m

BARCELONA
Altitude 7 m

ROME
Altitude 63 m

İSTANBUL
Altitude 9 m

LISBON
Altitude 98 m

SEVILLE
Altitude 30 m

ATHENS
Altitude 107 m

VALLETTA
Altitude 70 m

Rainfall figures on graphs in tens of millimetres except for annual totals

LONDON
°C
30
20
10
0
594 mm Annual

AMSTERDAM
°C
30
20
10
0
787 mm Annual

SONNBLICK
°C
30
20
10
0
1495 mm Annual

LISBON
°C
30
20
10
0
708 mm Annual

MADRID
°C
30
20
10
0
436 mm Annual

SEVILLE
°C
30
20
10
0
559 mm Annual

BARCELONA
°C
30
20
10
0
598 mm Annual

NICE
°C
30
20
10
0
862 mm Annual

ROME
°C
30
20
10
0
749 mm Annual

Conical Orthomorphic Projection

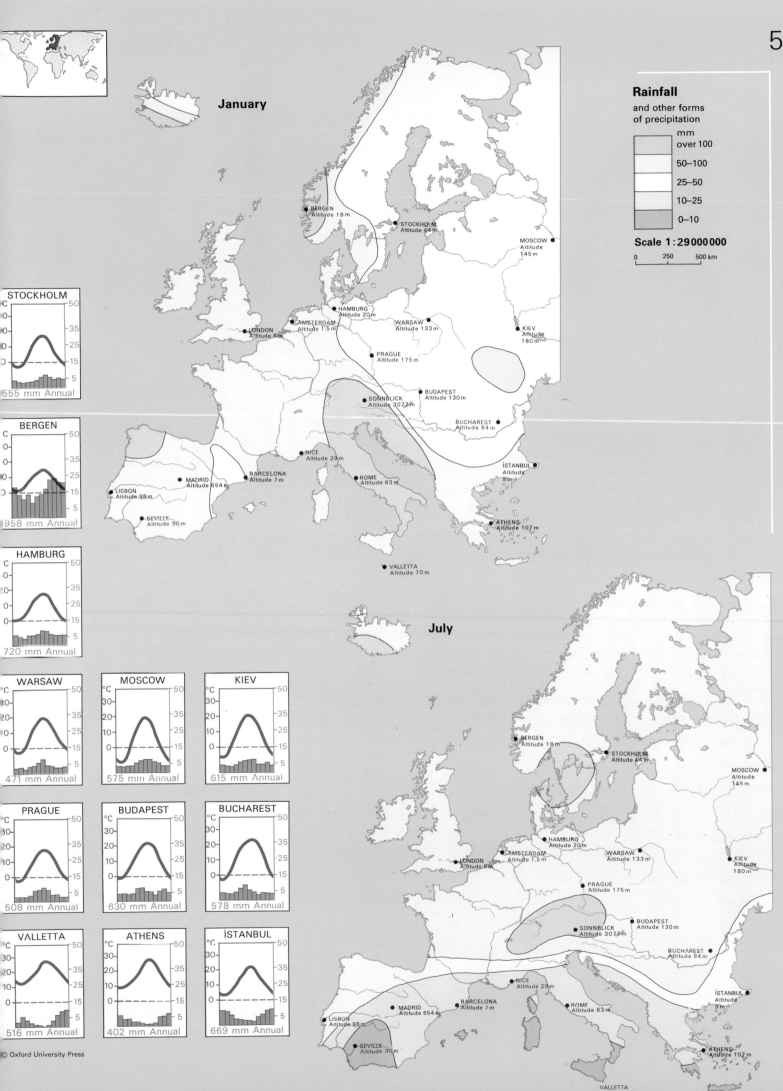

January

Rainfall
and other forms
of precipitation

mm
over 100
50—100
25—50
10—25
0—10

Scale 1:29 000 000

0   250   500 km

July

STOCKHOLM
555 mm Annual

BERGEN
1958 mm Annual

HAMBURG
720 mm Annual

WARSAW
471 mm Annual

MOSCOW
575 mm Annual

KIEV
615 mm Annual

PRAGUE
508 mm Annual

BUDAPEST
630 mm Annual

BUCHAREST
578 mm Annual

VALLETTA
516 mm Annual

ATHENS
402 mm Annual

İSTANBUL
669 mm Annual

© Oxford University Press

31 January 1988, 1526 hours GMT

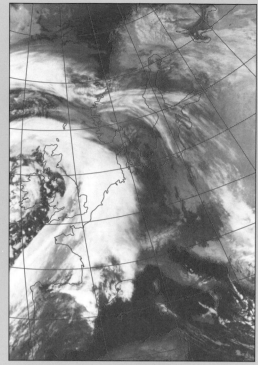

1 February 1988, 0340 hours GMT

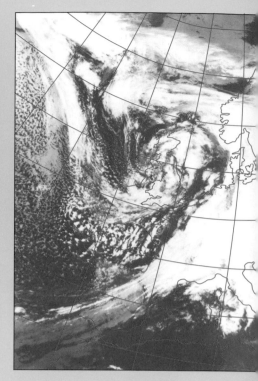

1 February 1988, 1515 hours GMT

Weather summary for the United Kingdom 1 February 1988

Scotland had a period of continuous rain or sleet, with snow in places overnight, the snow principally across higher ground but for a time, snowfall was reported from lower levels. By the end of the night, the weather had turned dry in most places, though heavy rain continued in the far north and extreme east. During the day, as the depression crossed from the southwest, periods of heavy rain developed, with further snow over the mountains.

Across Northern Ireland, England and Wales, heavy overnight rain, with a short period of sleet and snow in the north, had all but cleared by dawn, then the daytime weather was dominated by clusters of heavy, squally showers, these accompanied by hail and thunder. The showers during the morning were most prominent in Wales and the west, but by afternoon, all areas were at risk, with large clusters of heavy showers and squally, stormy winds.

Winds were very strong across England and Wales, with gales or severe gales widespread, with gusts reported widely 45 to 60 knots, and around exposed western and southwestern coasts, gusts above 80 knots, with report of 90 knots from Lands End Coastguard. (Plymouth/Mountbatten reported a gust of 70 knots, the highest February value on record.)

Temperatures were generally above normal, notably so in the southern half of the country, though the mildness was tempered by the strength of the wind.

Cloud amount

○	0	◐	5
◔	1 or less	◕	6
◑	2	◑	7 or more
◕	3	●	8 (oktas)
◐	4		

Weather

= mist

≡ fog

⁏ drizzle

, rain and drizzle

• rain

✳ rain and snow

✲ snow

Air pressure
isobars at 4 mb intervals
——— 1024

Temperature

05 in degrees Celsius

Wind speed (knots)

◎ calm

○— 1–2

○— 3–7

○— 8–12 *for each additional half-feather*

○— 13–17 *add 5 knots*

Fronts

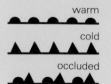

warm

cold

occluded

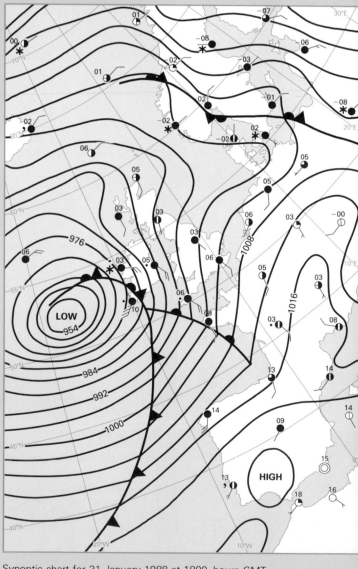

Synoptic chart for 31 January 1988 at 1800 hours GMT

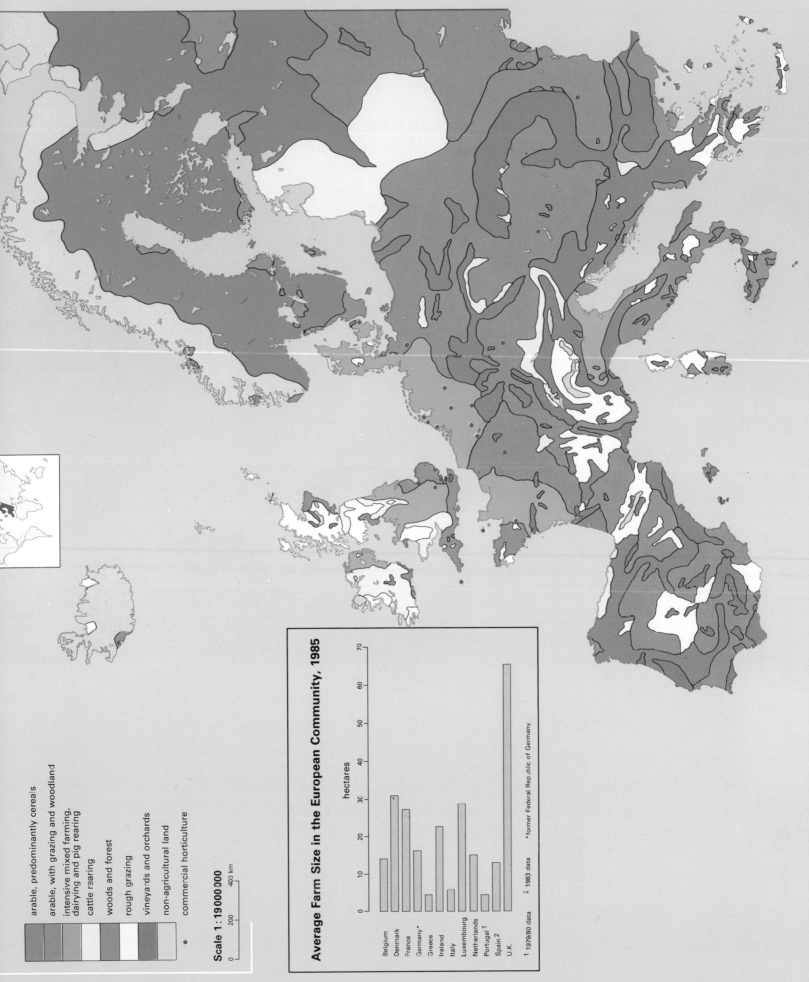

Conical Orthomorphic Projection

Scale 1 : 19 000 000

0   200   400 km

arable, predominantly cereals

arable, with grazing and woodland

intensive mixed farming, dairying and pig rearing

cattle rearing

woods and forest

rough grazing

vineyards and orchards

non-agricultural land

commercial horticulture

Average Farm Size in the European Community, 1985

hectares

Belgium
Denmark
France
Germany*
Greece
Ireland
Italy
Luxembourg
Netherlands
Portugal¹
Spain²
U.K.

70
60
50
40
30
20
10
0

1 1979/80 data   2 1983 data   *former Federal Republic of Germany

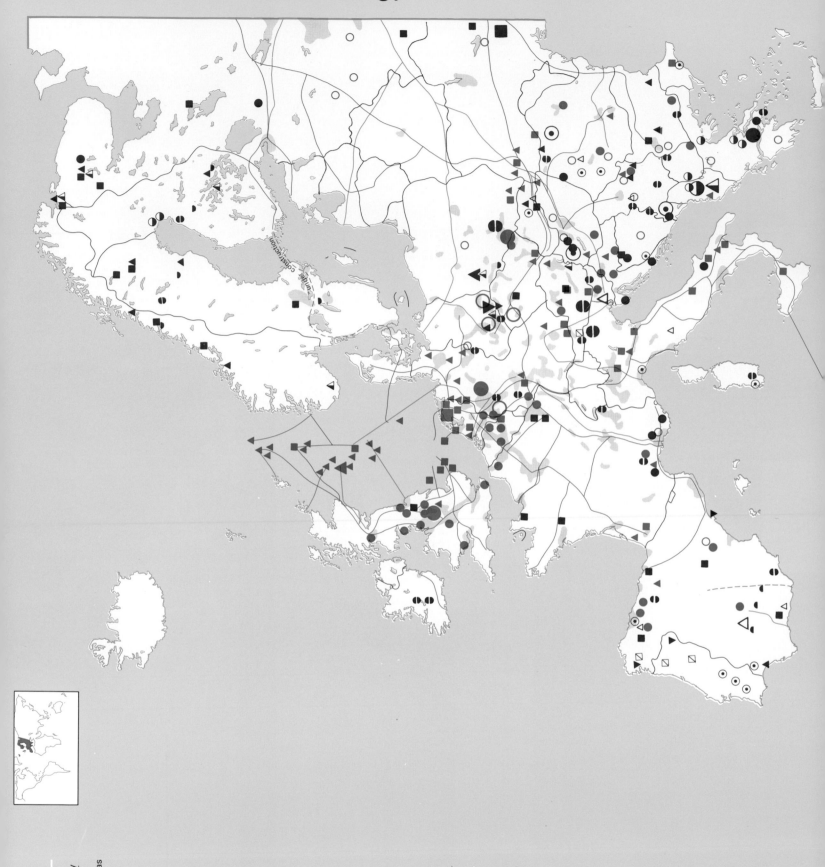

under construction

international boundary

industrial areas

Minerals

iron
copper
manganese
chromium
wolfram
nickel
tin
mercury
lead
zinc
bauxite

Energy

oil
gas
coal
lignite

oil pipeline

gas pipeline

Scale 1 : 19 000 000

0   200   400 km

Conical Orthomorphic Projection

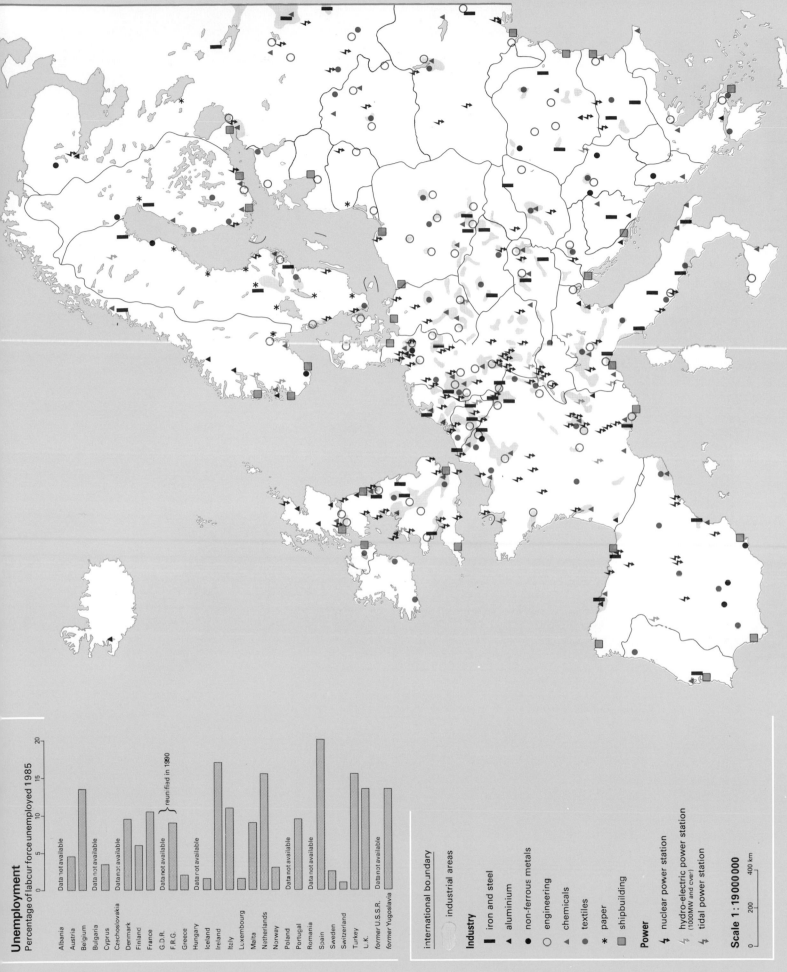

Unemployment
Percentage of labour force unemployed 1985

Albania	Data not available
Austria	
Belgium	
Bulgaria	Data not available
Cyprus	
Czechoslovakia	Data not available
Denmark	
Finland	
France	
G.D.R.	Data not available
F.R.G.	reunified in 1990
Greece	
Hungary	Data not available
Iceland	
Ireland	
Italy	
Luxembourg	
Malta	
Netherlands	
Norway	
Poland	Data not available
Portugal	
Romania	Data not available
Spain	
Sweden	
Switzerland	
Turkey	
U.K.	
former U.S.S.R.	Data not available
former Yugoslavia	

international boundary
industrial areas

Industry
▬ iron and steel
▲ aluminium
● non-ferrous metals
○ engineering
◄ chemicals
● textiles
✳ paper
▣ shipbuilding

Power
⚡ nuclear power station
⚡ hydro-electric power station
(1000MW and over)
⚡ tidal power station

Scale 1 : 19 000 000

0   200   400 km

© Oxford University Press

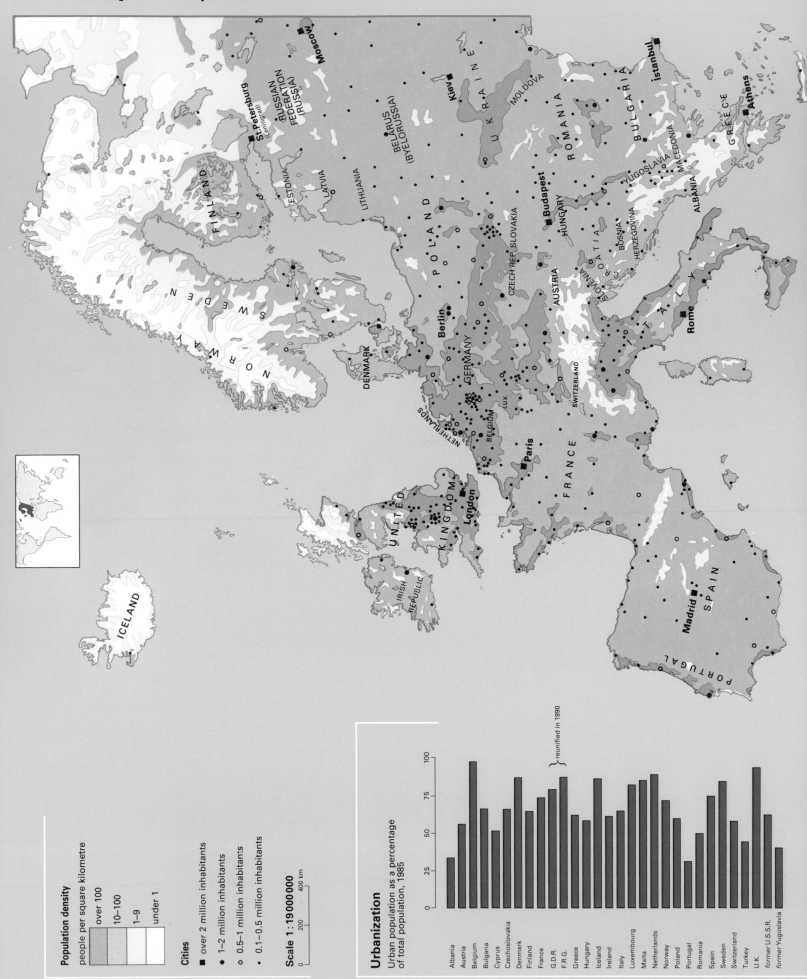

Moscow

RUSSIAN
FEDERATION
(RUSSIA)

St.Petersburg
(Leningrad)

Kiev

U·K·R·A·I·N·E

MOLDOVA

BELARUS
(BYELORUSSIA)

FINLAND

ESTONIA

LATVIA

LITHUANIA

P·O·L·A·N·D

R·O·M·A·N·I·A

B·U·L·G·A·R·I·A

Istanbul

Athens

G·R·E·E·C·E

MACEDONIA

ALBANIA

Budapest

HUNGARY

CZECH REP. SLOVAKIA

YUGOSLAVIA

S·W·E·D·E·N

N·O·R·W·A·Y

Berlin

GERMANY

AUSTRIA

SLOVENIA

C·R·O·A·T·I·A

BOSNIA

HERZEGOVINA

I·T·A·L·Y

Rome

DENMARK

NETHERLANDS

BELGIUM

LUX.

SWITZERLAND

Paris

F·R·A·N·C·E

U·N·I·T·E·D

K·I·N·G·D·O·M

London

IRISH

REPUBLIC

ICELAND

Madrid

S·P·A·I·N

P·O·R·T·U·G·A·L

Population density

people per square kilometre

over 100

10–100

1–9

under 1

Cities

■ over 2 million inhabitants

● 1–2 million inhabitants

○ 0.5–1 million inhabitants

○ 0.1–0.5 million inhabitants

Scale 1:19000000

0   200   400 km

Urbanization

Urban population as a percentage
of total population, 1985

reunified in 1990

Albania		
Austria		
Belgium		
Bulgaria		
Cyprus		
Czechoslovakia		
Denmark		
Finland		
France		
G.D.R.		
F.R.G.		
Greece		
Hungary		
Iceland		
Ireland		
Italy		
Luxembourg		
Malta		
Netherlands		
Norway		
Poland		
Portugal		
Romania		
Spain		
Sweden		
Switzerland		
Turkey		
U.K.		
former U.S.S.R.		
former Yugoslavia		

© Oxford University Press

Conical Orthomorphic Projection

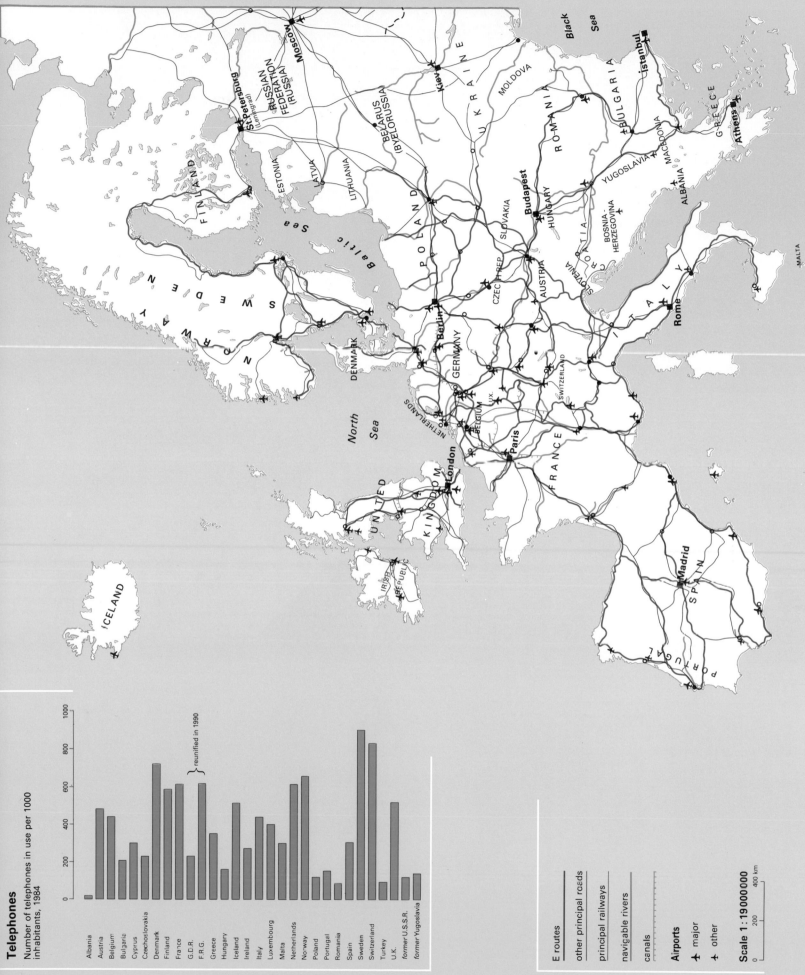

Telephones

Number of telephones in use per 1000
inhabitants, 1984

reunified in 1990

Albania
Austria
Belgium
Bulgaria
Cyprus
Czechoslovakia
Denmark
Finland
France
G.D.R.
F.R.G.
Greece
Hungary
Iceland
Ireland
Italy
Luxembourg
Malta
Netherlands
Norway
Poland
Portugal
Romania
Spain
Sweden
Switzerland
Turkey
U.K.
former U.S.S.R.
former Yugoslavia

E routes
other principal roads
principal railways
navigable rivers
canals

Airports
✈ major
✈ other

Scale 1:19000000
0   200   400 km

Oxford University Press

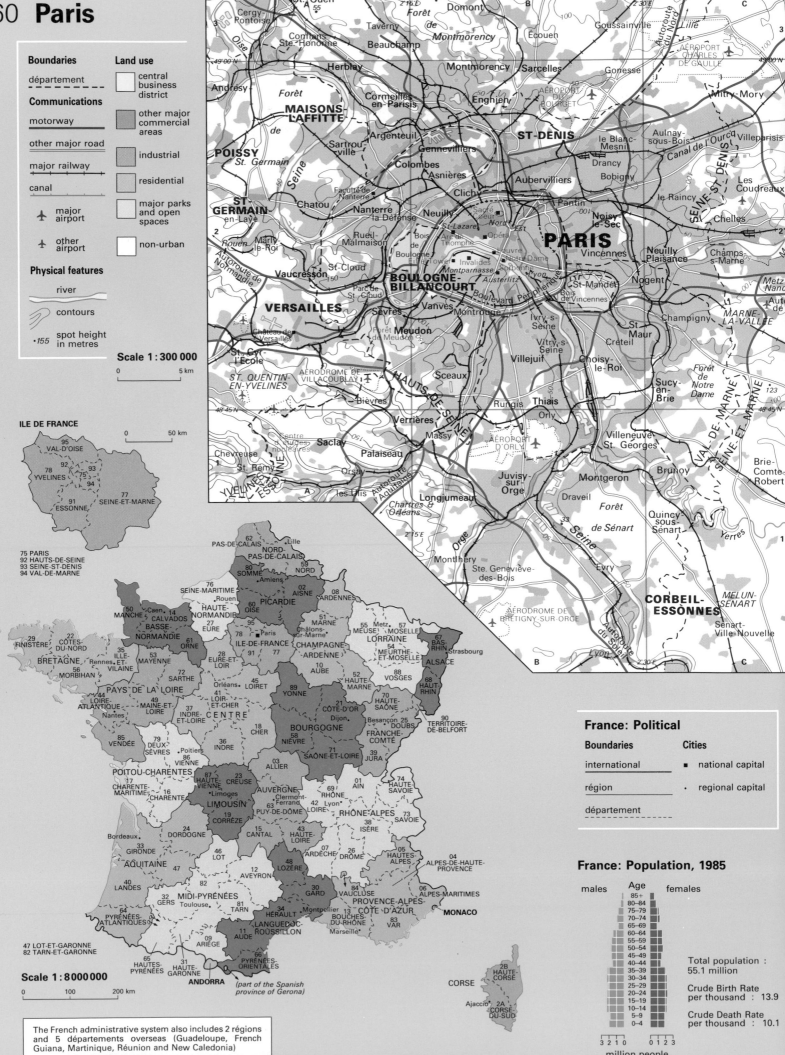

Boundaries

international

Communications

motorway

other major road

railway

canal

✈ major airport

Cities and towns

◓ built-up areas

■ over 1 million
inhabitants

● more than
100 000
inhabitants

• smaller towns

Physical features

marsh

ice cap

Land height

metres	
3000	
2000	
1000	
500	
300	
200	
100	
sea level	
land below sea level	

▲ spot height in metres

Scale 1: 5 000 000

0   50   100 km

Conical Orthomorphic Projection   © Oxford University Press

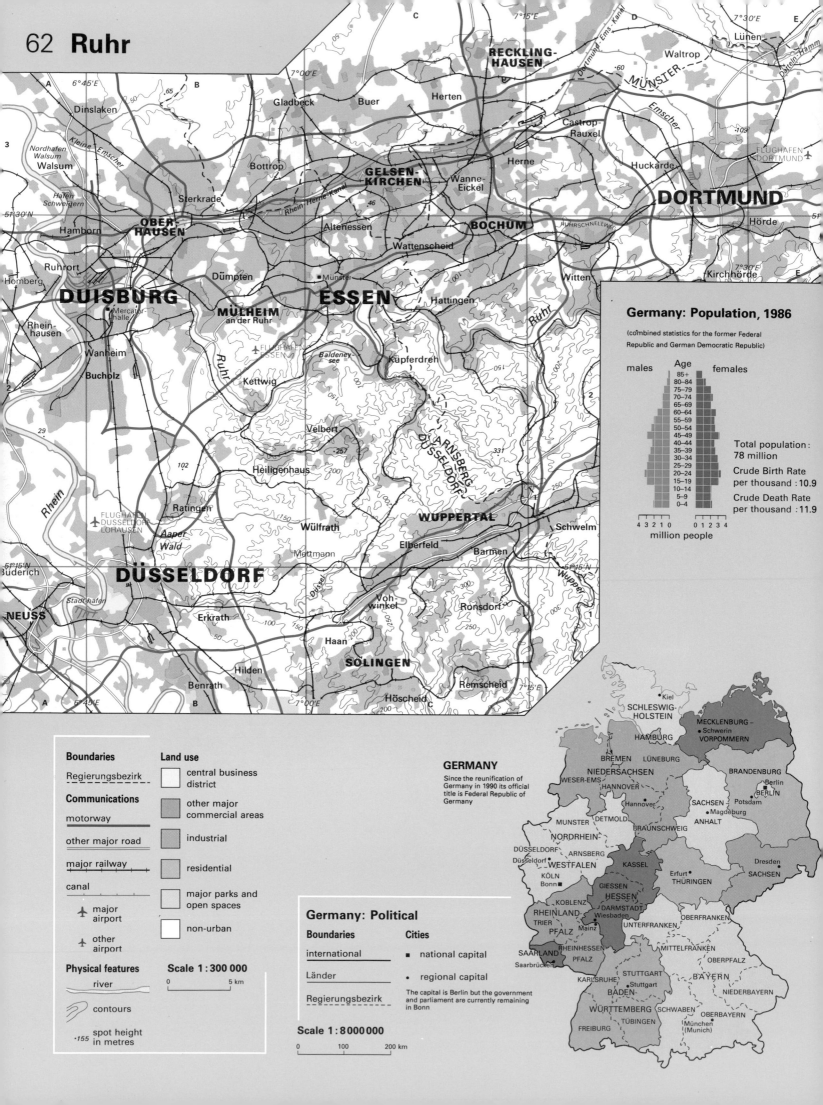

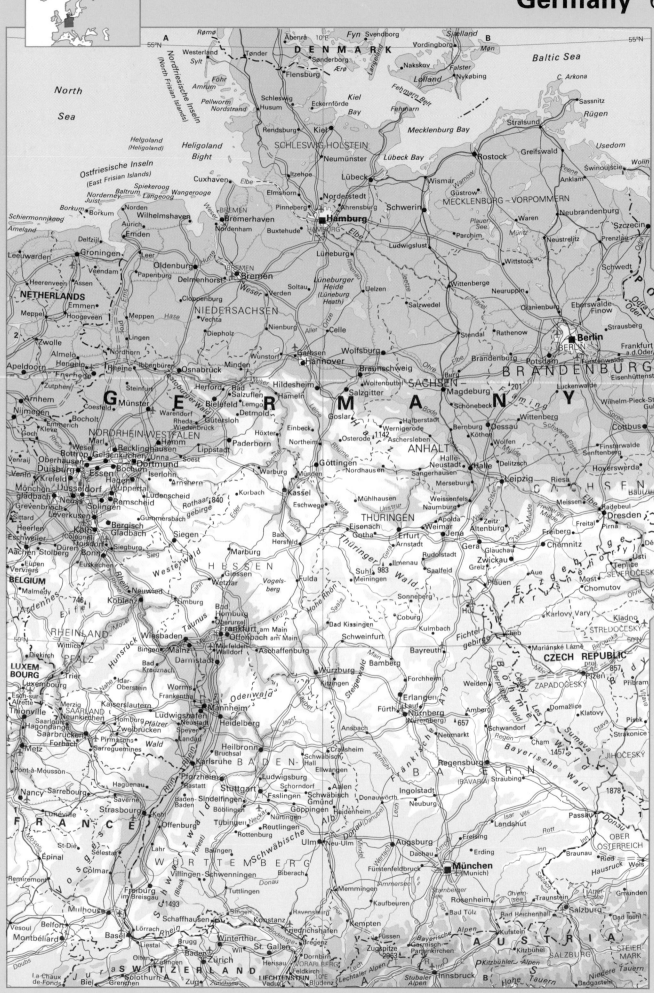

Boundaries

international

internal

Communications

motorway

other major road

railway

canal

✈ major airport

Cities and towns

◁ built-up areas

■ over 1 million
   inhabitants

● more than
   100 000
   inhabitants

· smaller towns

Physical features

marsh

ice cap

Land height

metres

3000

2000

1000

500

300

200

100

sea level

land below
sea level

▲ spot height
   in metres

Scale 1:3 500 000

25   50 km

Benelux: Political

Boundaries | Cities
international | ▪ national capital
région | • provincial capital
province

Scale 1:4 000 000

0   50   100 km

Boundaries
international
internal

Communications
motorway
other major road
railway
canal
✈ major airport

Physical features
marsh

Cities and towns
built-up areas
▪ over 1 million inhabitants
• more than 100 000 inhabitants
• smaller towns

Land height
metres
500
300
200
100
sea level
land below sea level
▲ spot height in metres

Scale 1:2 000 000

0   25   50 km

Conical Orthomorphic Projection

© Oxford University Press

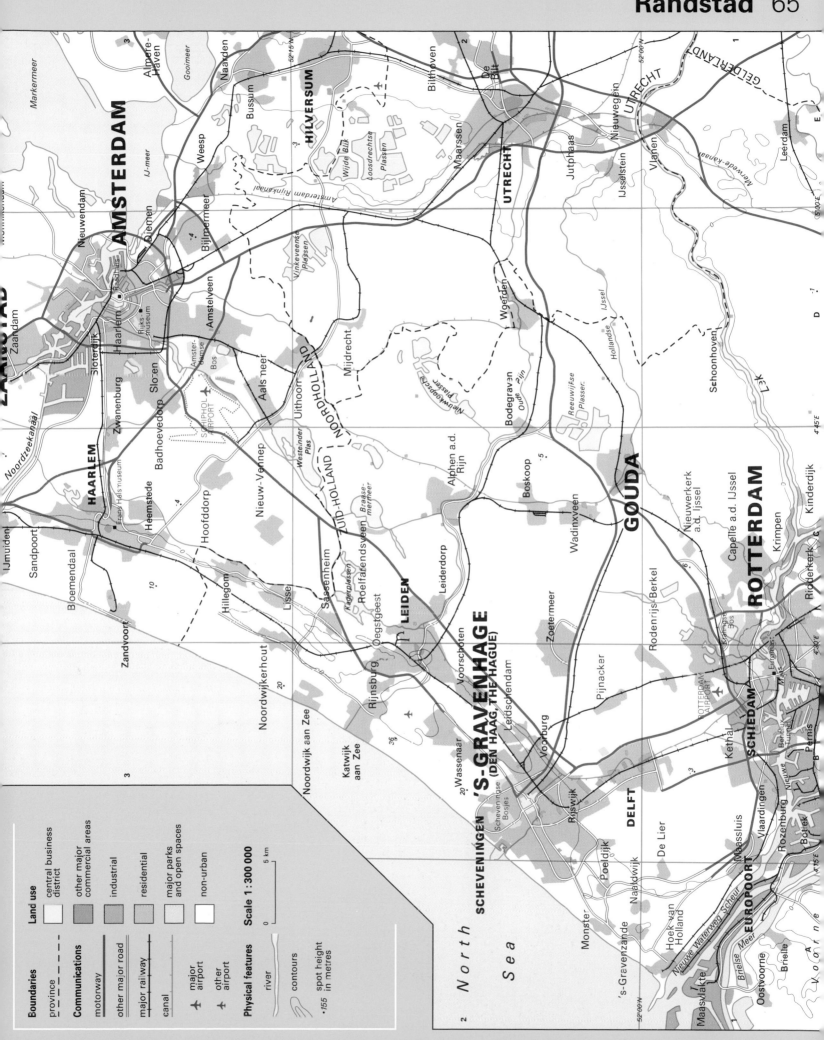

Boundaries

province

Communications

motorway

other major road

major railway

canal

Physical features

river

contours

•155 spot height in metres

Land use

central business district

other major commercial areas

industrial

residential

major parks and open spaces

non-urban

Scale 1 : 300 000

0   5 km

✈ major airport

✈ other airport

AMSTERDAM

HILVERSUM

UTRECHT

HAARLEM

LEIDEN

'S-GRAVENHAGE
(DEN HAAG, THE HAGUE)

SCHEVENINGEN

DELFT

GOUDA

ROTTERDAM

SCHIEDAM

EUROPOORT

Markermeer

Almere-Haven

Gooimeer

Naarden

Bussum

Bilthoven

De Bilt

Nieuwegein

IJsselstein

Vianen

Leerdam

GELDERLAND

Weesp

Nieuwendam

Diemen

Bijlmermeer

Maarssen

UTRECHT

Jutphaas

Merwede-kanaal

Zaandam

Haarlem

Rijks-museum

Amster-damse Bos

Sloterdijk

Zwanenburg

Slofen

Amstelveen

Badhoevedorp

SCHIPHOL AIRPORT

Aalsmeer

Uithoorn

Mijdrecht

NOORD-HOLLAND

Vinkeveense Plassen

Nieuwkoopse Plassen

Woerden

Bodegraven

Oude Rijn

Reeuwijkse Plassen

Hollandse IJssel

Schoonhoven

Lek

IJmuiden

Noordzeekanaal

Sandpoort

Frans Halsmuseum

Heemstede

Bloemendaal

Zandvoort

Hillegom

Lisse

Sassenheim

Nieuw-Vennep

Hoofddorp

Westeinder Plas

ZUID-HOLLAND

Roelofarendsveen

Kagerplassen

Braase-mermeer

Alphen a.d. Rijn

Boskoop

Wadinxveen

Nieuwerkerk a.d. IJssel

Capelle a.d. IJssel

Krimpen

Ridderkerk

Kinderdijk

Noordwijkerhout

Noordwijk aan Zee

Katwijk aan Zee

Rijnsburg

Oegstgeest

Leiderdorp

Voorschoten

Zoetermeer

Leidschendam

Rodenrijs/Berkel

Pijnacker

Kralingse Bos

Maas

Europoort

Wassenaar

Voorburg

Scheveningse Bosjes

Rijswijk

De Lier

Maas

Kethel

Vlaardingen

Benelux Tunnel

Pernis

North Sea

Monster

Naaldwijk

Poeldijk

's-Gravenzande

Hoek van Holland

Rozenburg

Botlek

Maasluis

Nieuwe Waterweg Scheur

Brielle

Oostvoorne

Maasvlakte

Brielse Meer

Voorne

ROTTERDAM AIRPORT

IJ-meer

Amsterdam Rijnkanaal

Wijde Blik

Loosdrechtse Plassen

Bay of Biscay

FRANCE

SPAIN

PORTUGAL

ATLANTIC OCEAN

Mediterranean Sea

ALGERIA

MOROCCO

10°W · 5°W · 5°E

A · B · C

Arcachon · Marmande · Figeac
Mimizan · Agen · Cahors · Millau · Alès
C. Ortegal · Ortigueira · C. de Peñas · Gijón · Mont-de-Marsan · Montauban · Albi · Nîmes
El Ferrol del Caudillo · Luarca · Avilés · Santander · San Sebastián · Dax · Toulouse · Castres · Arles
La Coruña (Corunna) · Oviedo · Mieres · Torrelavega · Bilbao · Biarritz · Bayonne · Pau · Tarbes · Carcassonne · Béziers · Sète
Villalba · Cordillera (Cantabrian Mts.) · Reinosa · Baracaldo · Irún · Tolosa · Lourdes · St-Gaudens · Pamiers · Narbonne · Martigues
C. Finisterre · Lugo · 2321 · Montañas de León · León · Vitoria · Miranda de Ebro · Pamplona · Jaca · ANDORRA · 2921 · Perpignan
Santiago de Compostela · Ponferrada · Logroño · Pirineos · 3404 · 3141 · Andorra la Vella · C. de Creus
Pontevedra · Orense · Benavente · Burgos · Calahorra · Soria · Huesca · Barbastro · Gerona · Figueras
Vigo · Verín · Palencia · Arlanzón · Tarazona · Tudela · Lérida (Lleida) · Manresa · San Feliú de Guixols
Tuy · Minho · Valladolid · Aranda de Duero · Duero · Calatayud · Zaragoza · Tarrasa · Sabadell · Costa Brava
Viana do Castelo · Braga · Bragança · Zamora · Medina del Campo · Segovia · Sigüenza · Daroca · Alcañiz · Hospitalet · Barcelona
Guimarães · Vila Real · Salamanca · 2468 · 2142 · Teruel · Reus · Tarragona
Matosinhos · Porto (Oporto) · Lamego · Sa. de Guadarrama · Cuenca · Vinaroz · C. de Tortosa
Vila Nova de Gaia · Douro · Ávila · Madrid · Guadalajara · Alcalá de Henares · Benicarló
Aveiro · Viseu · Leganés · Móstoles · Getafe · 2019 · 2020 · Castellón de la Plana
Figueira da Foz · Coimbra · 1991 · Sa. de Gredos · Toledo · Aranjuez · Talavera de la Reina · Sagunto · Balearic Islands (Spain)
Leiria · Guarda · Ciudad Rodrigo · Plasencia · Montes de Toledo · Alcázar de San Juan · Valencia · Ciudadela · Mahón
PORTUGAL (Tagus) · Castelo Branco · Cáceres · Trujillo · Villarrobledo · La Mancha · Alcira · Menorca
Tomar · Portalegre · Mérida · Don Benito · Ciudad Real · Albacete · Alcoy · Sóller · Alcudia · Manacor
Santarém · Elvas · Badajoz · Almadén · Manzanares · Almansa · Elda · Palma de Mallorca · Mallorca
Sintra · Cascais · Lisboa (Lisbon) · Évora · Valdepeñas · Puertollano · Hellín · Elche · Alicante · Ibiza · Cabrera
Almada · Barreiro · Setúbal · Jerez de los Caballeros · Zafra · Peñarroya-Pueblonuevo · Sa. de Alcaraz · Murcia · Ibiza · Formentera
Sines · Beja · Aljustrel · Sierra Morena · Andújar · Linares · 2381 · Cartagena
Portimão · Silves · Ayamonte · Nerva · Córdoba · Jaén · Baza · Lorca · Aguilas · C. de Palos
Lagos · Faro · Huelva · Sevilla (Seville) · Utrera · Écija · Lucena · Guadix · Almanzora · C. de Gata
Olhão · Gulf of Cádiz · Las Marismas · Sanlúcar de Barrameda · Loja · Granada · Sierra Nevada 3482 Mulhacén · Almería · Alger (Algiers)
Jerez de la Frontera · Antequera · Ronda · Málaga · Motril · Adra · Boufarik · Blida
Cádiz · San Fernando · El Puerto de Sta. Maria · Marbella · Costa del Sol · Médéa · Tizi Ouzou 2308
Algeciras · La Línea de la Concepción · GIBRALTAR (U.K.) · El Bayadh · Cherchell · Miliana
Tanger (Tangiers) · Ceuta (Sp.) · Strait of Gibraltar · Ech Cheliff · Massif de l'Ouarsenis
Asilah · Tétouan · Melilla (Sp.) · Oran · Arzew · Mostaganem · Ksar El Boukhari · Bougzoul
Larache · Al Hoceima · Nador · Beni Saf · Mohammadia · Mascara · Tiaret · Bou Saâda
Ksar-el-Kebir · Rif Mts. 2455 · Aïn Témouchent · Sidi Bel Abbès
Ouezzane · MOROCCO · ALGERIA · Tlemcen · Saïda · Djelfa
Kénitra · Oujda

Scale 1 : 6 250 000
0 · 50 · 100 km

Boundaries
international

Communications
motorway
other major road
railway
canal

✈ major airport

Cities and towns
built-up areas
■ over 1 million inhabitants
● more than 100 000 inhabitants
• smaller towns

Physical features
seasonal river/lake
marsh

Land height
metres
3000
2000
1000
500
300
200
100
sea level
▲ spot height in metres

Balearic Islands (Spain)

Mediterranean Sea

C. Caballeria · Fornells
Ciudadela · C. de Formentor · C. d'Artrutx · 358 · Alayor · Mahón
Mallorca (Majorca) · Pollensa · C. Freu · Menorca (Minorca)
1445 · Sa. de Alfabia · Sóller · La Puebla · Arta
I. Dragonera · Inca · Sineu · Manacor · 560
Andraitx · Sa. Palma de Mallorca · Felanitx
C. de Cala Figuera · Calvia · Lluchmayor · Campos del Puerto · Santañy · C. de Salinas
Conejera · Cabrera
Ibiza · San Juan Bautista · 409
San Antonio Abad · Sta. Eulalia del Rio
San José · 475 · Ibiza
C. de Barberia · Formentera
San Francisco Javier

Scale 1 : 3 000 000
0 · 25 · 50 km

Conical Orthomorphic Projection
© Oxford University Press

ICELAND

Arctic Circle
Grimsey
925 Siglufjördur · Húsavík
Ísafjördur · Vopnafjördur
Breidha Fjördur · Akureyri · Neskaupstadur
Stykkishólmur · 65°N
Faxaflói · Langjökull Hofsjökull · Pjörsá
Akranes · 2000 Vatnajökull
Reykjavik · Hekla 1491 · Höfn
Keflavik · Hafnarfjördur · Myrdals jökull
Vestmannaeyjar

Boundaries

international
internal

Communications

motorway
other major road
railway
canal
✈ major airport

Cities and towns

■ over 1 million inhabitants
● more than 100 000 inhabitants
· smaller towns

Physical features

marsh
ice cap
▲ spot height in metres

Land height

metres
2000
1000
500
300
200
100
sea level
land below sea level

Scale 1:8 500 000

100 200 km

Modified Conical
Orthomorphic Projection
© Oxford University Press

ARCTIC
OCEAN

Barents Sea

Nordkapp (North Cape)
Hammerfest · Honningsvåg · Berlevåg
Søroya · Lopphavet · Varangerhalvøya · Vardø
Vanna · Lakselv · 1067 · Varangerfjorden · 70°N
Ringvassøy · Alta · 1139 · Jiešjavrre · Teno joki · Poluostrov Rybachiy
Tromsø · Karasjok · 623 · Inarijärvi · Pechenga · Murmansk
Senja · Reisa · 1144 · Enontekiö · 636 · Pudunskoye More · Monchegorsk · 1208
Langøy · Narvik · 1901 · Torneträsk · 807 · Porttipahdan tekojärvi · 555 · Lokan tekojärvi · Ozero Imandra · Apatity
Hinnøya · Torne · Kiruna · Ounasjoki · Kholavyi · Kandalakshskiy Zaliv (White Sea)
Lofoten Is. · Vestfjorden · 2111 · Stora Lulevatten · Gällivare · Sodankylä · Kemijärvi · Ozero Pyazero
Nordfold · 2013 · Jokkmokk · Rovaniemi · Yli-kitka Kuusamo · Muojärvi · Ozero Topozero
Bodø · 1908 · 2021 · Kemi älv · Kalix älv · Övertorneå · Tornio · Kemi · 431 · Kalevala · Ozero Sredneye Kuyto · 65°N
Saltdal · 1754 · 1694 · Boden · Luleå · Pudasjärvi · Kiantajärvi · Ozero Nyuk
1599 · Arctic Circle · Hailuoto · Oulu joki · Oulu järvi · Kuhmo · Ozero Leksozero
Mo-i-Rana · Hornavan · Arjeplog · Pite älv · Piteå · Raahe · Kajaani · 355 · 409
Dønna · Mosjøen · Røssvatnet · 1764 · Uddjaur · Skellefte älv · Skellefteå · Pulkkila · Iisalmi · Pielinen
Vega · Graddis · 1703 · 1588 · Storuman · Lycksele · Vilhelmina · Umeå · Kokkola · Pyhäjärvi · Kuopio · Joensuu
Brønnøysund · Namdalen · Tunnsjøen · Vännäs · Vaasa · Jakobstad · Suvasvesi · Varkaus · Pytäselkä
Kolvereid · Namsos · Hoting · Junsele · Örnsköldsvik · Lappajärvi · Lapua · Keitele · Saimaa · Pyhäselkä
Vikna · Folda · 1337 · Dragan · Hammerdal · Sollefteå · Kasko · Parkano · Näsijärvi · Mikkeli · Imatra · Ludozhskoye Ozero
Frøya · Fosna · Frohavet · Kallsjön · Östersund · Härnösand · Pori · Tampere · Puulavesi · Puruvesi
Hitra · Smøla · Brekstad · Trondheim · Stördal · 1441 · Storsjön · Sundsvall · Rauma · Kouvola · Vyborg
Kristiansund · Trollheimen · 1667 · Berkåk · 1796 · Åsarna · Ljungan · Parnane · Lahti · Salpausselkä · Kotka
Ålesund · Andalsnes · Røros · Östervall · Ytterhogdal · Ljusnan · Hyvinkää · Kronstadt
Måløy · Nordfjord · 2083 · Dovrefjell · Tynset · 1277 · Linsell · Delen · Ljus · Turku · Vantaa · St. Petersburg (Leningrad) · Gatchina
Flora · Jostedalsbreen · 2469 · Dombås · Femund · 1755 · Idre · Vuxnan · Bollnäs · Söderhamn · Åland · Espoo · Helsinki (Helsingfors) · Narva
Sognefjorden · Jotunheimen · Gudbrandsdalen · 887 · Mora · Siljan · Falun · Gävle · Mariehamn · Hangö · Tallinn · Tápa
Bergen · Voss · Lærdalsøyri · Lillehammer · Borlänge · Ludvika · Avesta · Uppsala · Hiiumaa · Haapsalu · Tartu · Ozero Chudskoye
Hardangerfjorden · 1862 · Hamar · Mjøsa · Klöfta · Saaremaa · Kuressaare · Võrtsjärv · Võru · 318 · Pskov
Haugesund · Hardangervidda · Odda · 1660 · Valdres · Oslo · Västerås · Eskilstuna · Mälaren · Pärnu · Valga · Valmiera · Ostrov
Stavanger · Boknafjorden · Setesdal · Telemark · Drammen · Moss · Arvika · Karlstad · Örebro · Stockholm · Södertälje · Nyköping · Mazirbe · Gulf of Riga · Rēzekne
Flekkefjord · Sira · Otra · Bygland · Skien · Porsgrunn · Sarpsborg · Fredrikstad · Uddevalla · Vänern · Katrineholm · Ventspils · Riga · Daugavpils
Mandal · Arendal · Kristiansand · Tønsberg · Skövde · Trollhättan · Vättern · Linköping · Visby · Gotland · Kuldiga · Tukums · Jēkabpils
Skagerrak · Hjørring · Uddevalla · Borås · Mölndal · Jönköping · Sömmen · Vetlanda · Västervik · Liepāja · Saldus · Jelgava · LATVIA
Göteborg · Halmstad · Näsjö · Bolmen · Växjö · Åsnen · Borgholm · Öland · Hanöbukten · Bauska · Panevėžys
Frederikshavn · Ålborg · Viborg · Randers · Limfjorden · Kattegat · Ålmhult · Kalmar · Klaipėda · Šiauliai · Plunge
DENMARK · Århus · Helsingborg · Kristianstad · Karlskrona · Bornholm (Denmark) · LITHUANIA · Kurskiy Zaliv
Ringkøbing Fjord · Horsens · Vejle · Fyn · København (Copenhagen) · Lund · Malmö · Landskrona · Sovetsk · Nemunas
Esbjerg · Kolding · Odense · Roskilde · Sjælland · Sassnitz · Rügen · Sovetsk · Kaunas · Vilnius · BELARUS (BYELORUSSIA)
Nord friesische Inseln · Næstved · Lolland · Nyköbing · Gdynia · Kaliningrad (Russia) · Marijampole · Minsk
Heligoland Bight · Schleswig · Flensburg · Rendsburg · Kiel · Lübeck · Rostock · Stralsund · Pomeranian Bay · Gdańsk · Elbląg · Olsztyn · Ełk · Grodno
Cuxhaven · Neumünster · Wismar · Schwerin · Mecklenburg Bay · POLAND · Szczecin · Płoty
Wilhelmshaven · Bremerhaven · Bremen · Hamburg · GERMANY · Tczew · Malbork
Groningen · NETHERLANDS

North Sea
Norwegian Sea
Baltic Sea
Gulf of Bothnia
Gulf of Finland
Gulf of Riga

ARCTIC OCEAN

RUSSIA (RUSSIAN FEDERATION)
FINLAND
SWEDEN
NORWAY
LAPLAND
ESTONIA

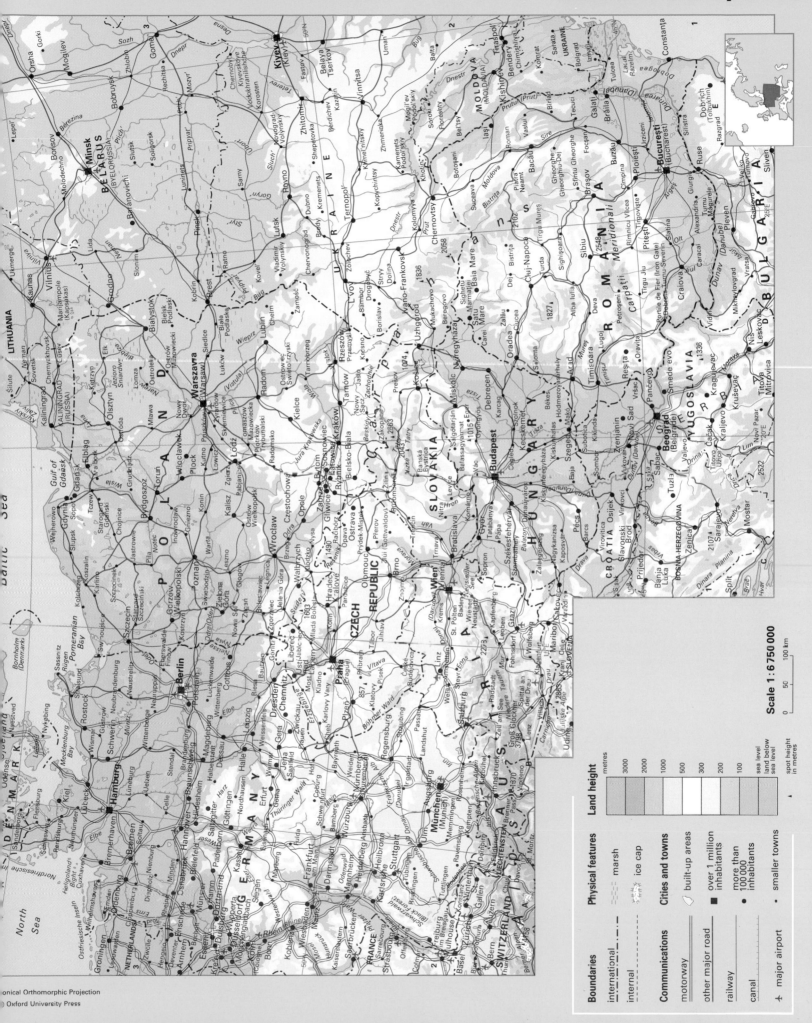

Scale 1 : 6 750 000

0   50   100 km

Boundaries

international

internal

Physical features

marsh

ice cap

Cities and towns

built-up areas

over 1 million inhabitants

more than 100 000 inhabitants

smaller towns

Communications

motorway

other major road

railway

canal

major airport

Land height

metres
3000
2000
1000
500
300
200
100
sea level land below sea level

spot height in metres

Conical Orthomorphic Projection

© Oxford University Press

Boundaries

international
disputed
internal

Communications

motorway
other major road
railway
canal
✈ major airport

Cities and towns

■ over 1 million inhabitants
● more than 100 000 inhabitants
• smaller towns

Scale 1 : 25 000 000

0   250   500 km

Physical features

seasonal river/lake
marsh
salt pan
ice cap
sand dunes

Land height

metres
5000
3000
2000
1000
500
300
200
100
sea level
land below sea level

▲ spot height in metres

Boundaries   city limit/oblast

Land use

central business district
other major commercial areas
industrial
residential
major parks and open spaces
non-urban

Refer to page 83 for complete legend

ICELAND   GREENLAND

Pack ice — average autumn minimum
Pack ice — average spring maximum
Arctic Circle

SPITSBERGEN

Cork   Dublin   IRISH DUBLIN REPUBLIC   Glasgow   Edinburgh   UNITED KINGDOM   Birmingham   London   WALES   FRANCE   Paris   Amsterdam   NETH   Rotterdam   Brussels   Hamburg   Kobenhavn (Copenhagen)   DENMARK   Berlin   GERMANY   Bergen   Oslo   Trondheim   North Cape   Stockholm   SWEDEN   NORWAY   FINLAND   Gulf of Bothnia   Murmansk   Kola Peninsula   White Sea   Arkhangel'sk   Severodvinsk

North Sea   Orkney Is.   Shetland Is.   Faeroes   Baltic Sea   Helsinki   Tallinn   ESTONIA   Riga   LATVIA   LITHUANIA   Kaliningrad   Gdansk   Szczecin   POLAND   Warszawa   Praha   CZECH REP.   SLOVAK REP.   Wien   München   Zürich   CROATIA   Zagreb   Budapest   ROMANIA   Bucuresti   BULGARIA   Sofiya   Beograd   Sarajevo

St. Petersburg   Novgorod   Moskva (Moscow)   Yaroslavl'   Nizhniy Novgorod (Gor'kiy)   Vologda   Perm'   Yekaterinburg (Sverdlovsk)   Kazan'   Ufa   Chelyabinsk   Samara   Ul'yanovsk   Tol'yatti   Saratov   Volgograd   Ural Mountains   Kirov   Izhevsk   Orenburg   Magnitogorsk   Kustanay

BELARUS   Minsk   UKRAINE   Kyyiv (Kiev)   L'viv   Odesa   Dnipropetrovs'k   Donets'k   Kharkiv   Zaporozhzhya   Rostov-na-Donu   Voronezh   Tula   Ryazan'   Tambov   Penza

Black Sea   Istanbul   Ankara   TURKEY   Sevastopol'   Simferopol'   Novorossiysk   Sochi   Sukhumi   Batumi   GEORGIA   Tbilisi   Yerevan   ARMENIA   AZERBAIJAN   Baku   Sumgait   Caspian Sea   Astrakhan'

SYRIA   Baghdad   IRAQ   Al Basrah   KUWAIT   Al Kuwayt   SAUDI ARABIA   IRAN   Tehran   Esfahan   Tabriz   Mashhad   The Gulf   Shiraz   Kerman

KAZAKHSTAN   Aral Sea   UZBEKISTAN   TURKMENISTAN   Ashkhabad   Tashkent   Samarkand   Bukhara   Dushanbe   TAJIKISTAN   AFGHANISTAN   Herat   Kabul   PAKISTAN   Kyzl-Orda   Chimkent

Conical Orthomorphic Projection

Moscow inset

KHIMKI   Khimki–Khovrino   Mitino   Khimki Reservoir   NORTH PORT   TUSHINO   Strogino   Timiryazev Park   Ostankino   Economic Exhibition Grounds   Medvedkovo   Beskudnikovo   BABUSHKIN   Kuybyshev Forest   Cherkizovsky   MOSCOW OBLAST   MOSCOW CITY

MOSKVA (Moscow)   CENTRAL AIRPORT   Khorochevo   Mnevniki   FILI AIRFIELD   WEST PORT   Kremlin   Sokolniki Park   Izmaylovskiy Park   REUTOV   PEROVO

KUNTSEVO   Matveyevskove   Gagarin   Semenovskove   Ochakovo   Gorkiy Park   Moscow University   SOUTH PORT   Kuz'minki   Cheremushki   LYUBLINO

Solntsevo   ORLOVO AIRPORT   Lenino   Chertanovo   Krasny Stroitel   Moskva   Yauza

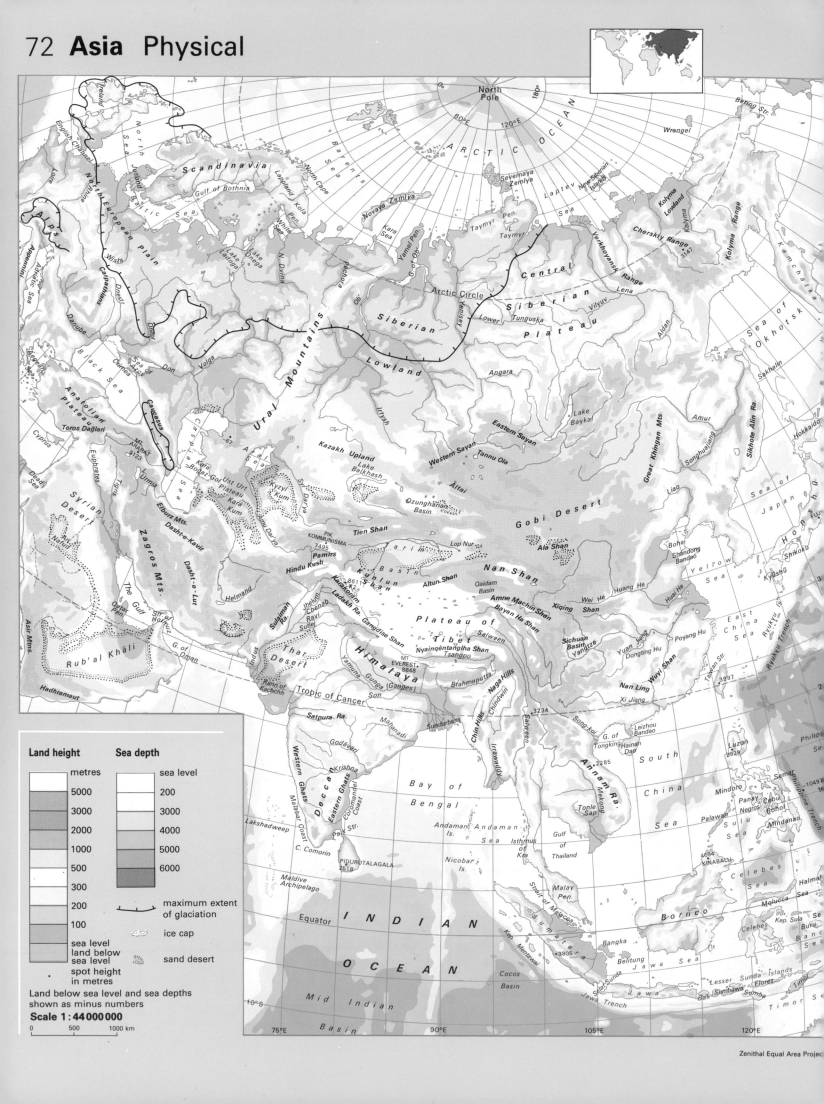

Land height

metres	
5000	
3000	
2000	
1000	
500	
300	
200	
100	
sea level	

land below
sea level

Sea depth

sea level	
200	
3000	
4000	
5000	
6000	

maximum extent
of glaciation

ice cap

sand desert

· spot height
in metres

Land below sea level and sea depths
shown as minus numbers

Scale 1 : 44 000 000

0   500   1000 km

Zenithal Equal Area Project

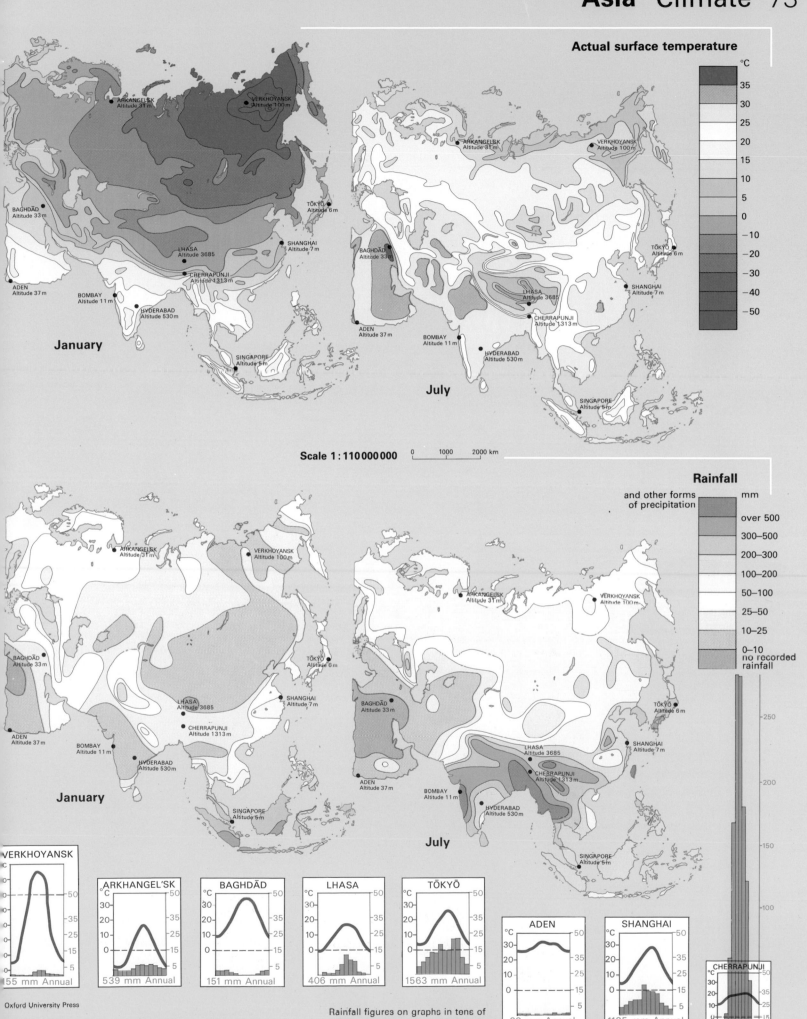

Actual surface temperature

°C
35
30
25
20
15
10
5
0
−10
−20
−30
−40
−50

January

July

Scale 1 : 110 000 000

0   1000   2000 km

Rainfall

and other forms
of precipitation   mm

over 500
300–500
200–300
100–200
50–100
25–50
10–25
0–10
no recorded
rainfall

January

July

VERKHOYANSK

°C
50

35

25

15

5

55 mm Annual

ARKHANGEL'SK
°C   50
30
20   35
10   25
0   15
5

539 mm Annual

BAGHDĀD
°C   50
30
20   35
10   25
0   15
5

151 mm Annual

LHASA
°C   50
30
20   35
10   25
0   15
5

406 mm Annual

TŌKYŌ
°C   50
30
20   35
10   25
0   15
5

1563 mm Annual

ADEN
°C   50
30   35
20
10   25
0   15
5

39 mm Annual

SHANGHAI
°C   50
30
20   35
10   25
0   15
5

1135 mm Annual

CHERRAPUNJI
°C   50
30   35
20
10   25
0   15
5

11437 mm Annual

250

200

150

100

Rainfall figures on graphs in tens of
millimetres except for annual totals

Oxford University Press

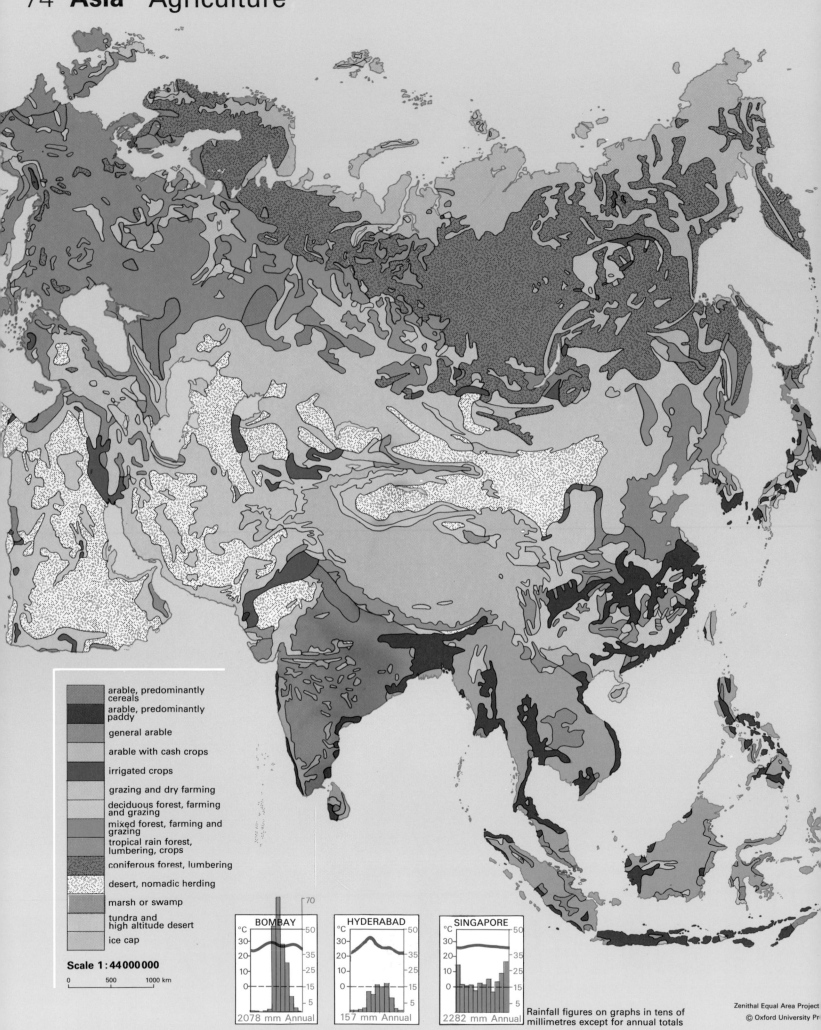

Scale 1:44 000 000

arable, predominantly
cereals

arable, predominantly
paddy

general arable

arable with cash crops

irrigated crops

grazing and dry farming

deciduous forest, farming
and grazing

mixed forest, farming and
grazing

tropical rain forest,
lumbering, crops

coniferous forest, lumbering

desert, nomadic herding

marsh or swamp

tundra and
high altitude desert

ice cap

0   500   1000 km

BOMBAY

2078 mm Annual

HYDERABAD

157 mm Annual

SINGAPORE

2282 mm Annual

Rainfall figures on graphs in tens of
millimetres except for annual totals

Zenithal Equal Area Project

© Oxford University Pr

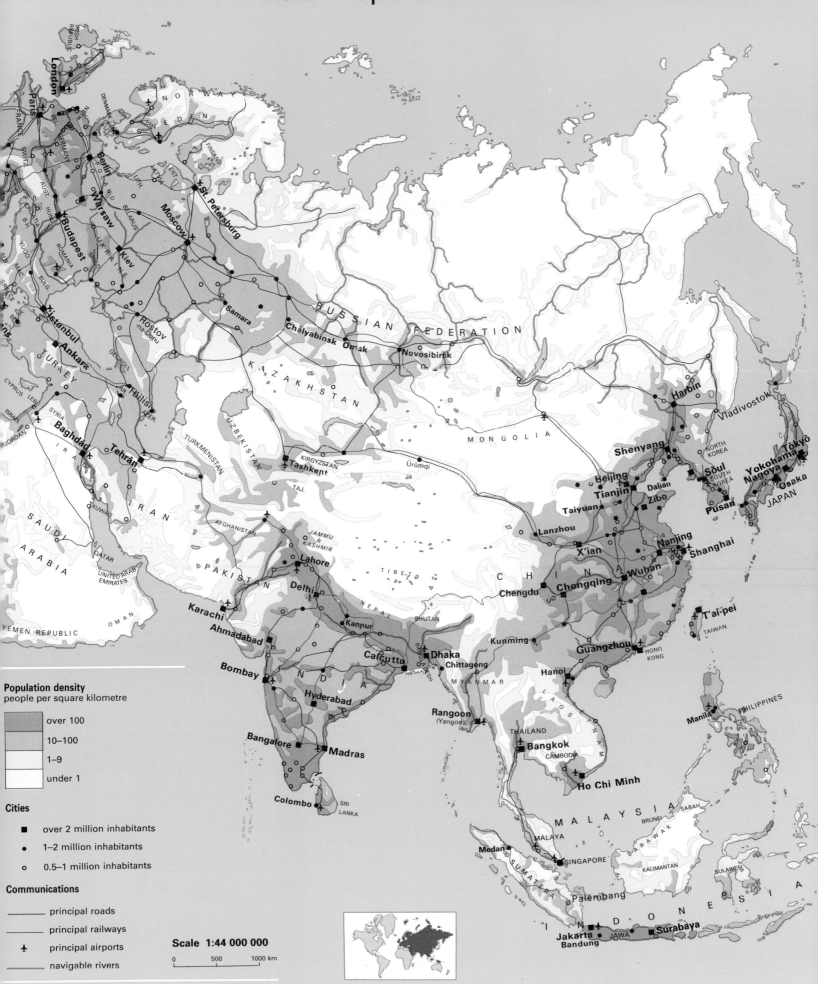

Population density
people per square kilometre

- over 100
- 10–100
- 1–9
- under 1

Cities

- ■ over 2 million inhabitants
- ● 1–2 million inhabitants
- ○ 0.5–1 million inhabitants

Communications

- ——— principal roads
- ——— principal railways
- ✈ principal airports
- ——— navigable rivers

Scale 1:44 000 000

0   500   1000 km

Zenithal Equal Area Projection
Oxford University Press

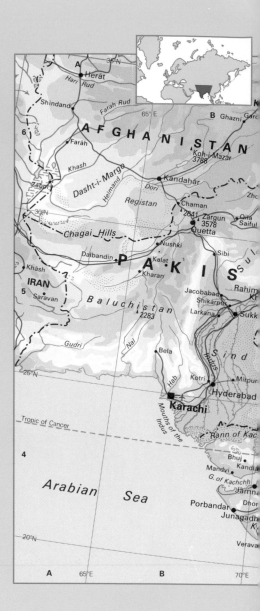

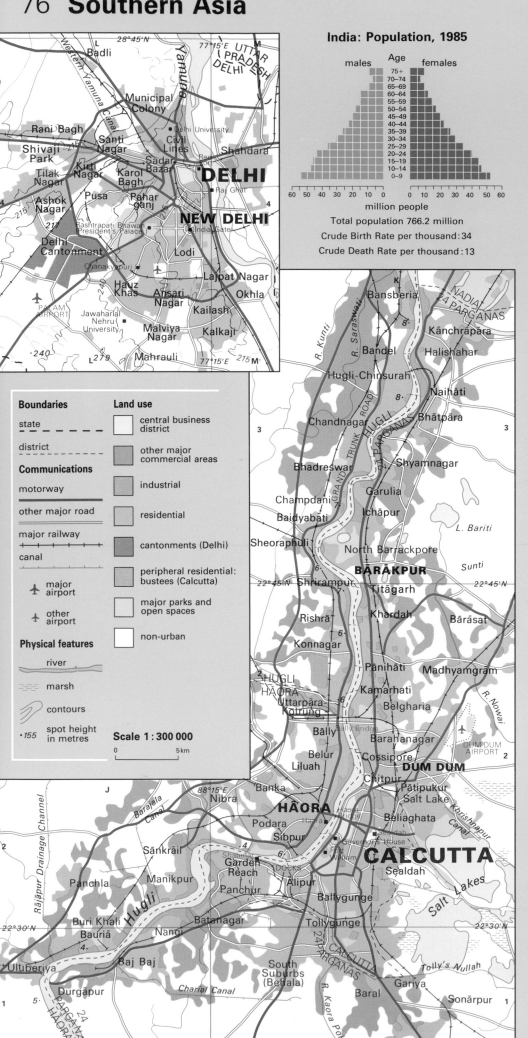

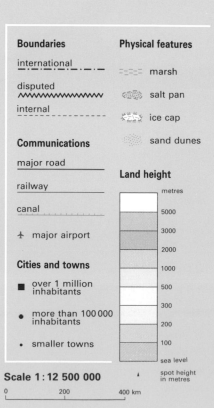

India: Population, 1985

males	Age	females
	75+	
	70–74	
	65–69	
	60–64	
	55–59	
	50–54	
	45–49	
	40–44	
	35–39	
	30–34	
	25–29	
	20–24	
	15–19	
	10–14	
	0–9	

60 50 40 30 20 10 0 0 10 20 30 40 50 60

million people

Total population 766.2 million

Crude Birth Rate per thousand: 34

Crude Death Rate per thousand: 13

Boundaries

state

district

Communications

motorway

other major road

major railway

canal

✈ major airport

✈ other airport

Physical features

river

marsh

contours

•155 spot height in metres

Land use

central business district

other major commercial areas

industrial

residential

cantonments (Delhi)

peripheral residential: bustees (Calcutta)

major parks and open spaces

non-urban

Scale 1 : 300 000

0 ——— 5km

Boundaries

international

disputed

internal

Communications

major road

railway

canal

✈ major airport

Cities and towns

■ over 1 million inhabitants

● more than 100 000 inhabitants

· smaller towns

Physical features

marsh

salt pan

ice cap

sand dunes

Land height

metres
5000
3000
2000
1000
500
300
200
100
sea level

▲ spot height in metres

Scale 1 : 12 500 000

0 ——— 200 ——— 400 km

Israel & Lebanon

Scale 1:4 000 000

0   50   100 km

Conical Orthomorphic Projection

Scale 1:12 500 000

0   125   250 km

© Oxford University Press

Boundaries

international

disputed

internal

Communications

motorway

other major road

railway

canal

✈ major airport

Physical features

seasonal river/lake

marsh

salt pan

ice cap

sand dunes

Land height

	metres
	5000
	3000
	2000
	1000
	500
	300
	200
	100
	sea level
	land below sea level

▲ spot height in metres

Cities and towns

■ over 1 million inhabitants

● more than 100 000 inhabitants

• smaller towns

+ historic sites

Physical features

- ----- seasonal river/lake
- ⋏⋏⋏⋏ marsh
- salt pan
- ice cap
- sand dunes

Boundaries
- ------- international
- ⋏⋏⋏⋏ disputed
- -·-·- internal

Communications
- —— major road
- ┼┼┼┼ railway
- ------ canal

Cities and towns
- ■ over 1 million inhabitants
- ● more than 100 000 inhabitants
- • smaller towns

Land height

metres
5000
3000
2000
1000
500
300
200
100
sea level
land below sea level

▲ spot height in metres

✈ major airport

Scale 1:19 000 000

0   200   400 km

Conical Orthomorphic Projection
© Oxford University Press

Japan

Beijing (China) — inset map

Refer to page 83 for legend

116°15'E · Qinghe · BEIYUAN · Wenyu He · 116°30'E

Yiheyuan · Summer Palace · HAIDIAN · Ditan · Jiuxiaqiao · Dongba · 40°00'N

Kunming Hu · Jin-He · MONGOL EARTH WALL · Agricultural Exhibition Centre

HSI-CHIAO AIRPORT · CITY WALL · Lama Temple

Landianchang · Zoological Garden · Wuluju · Zizhimen · Beihai · Zhonghai · Nanhai

Baiwanzhuang · Gugong Palace Museum (Forbidden City) · Tiananmen · Yun (Grand Canal) · Okushiri-tō

Great Hall of the People · Peking Railway Station

Guang'anmen · **BEIJING (Peking)** · Temple of Heaven

Xizhuang · Yongdingmen

FENGTAI · Luguoqiao

Changxindian · Racecourse Park

NANYUAN · NANYUAN AIRPORT · Majiuqiao

116°15'E · 116°30'E

Japan: Population, 1985

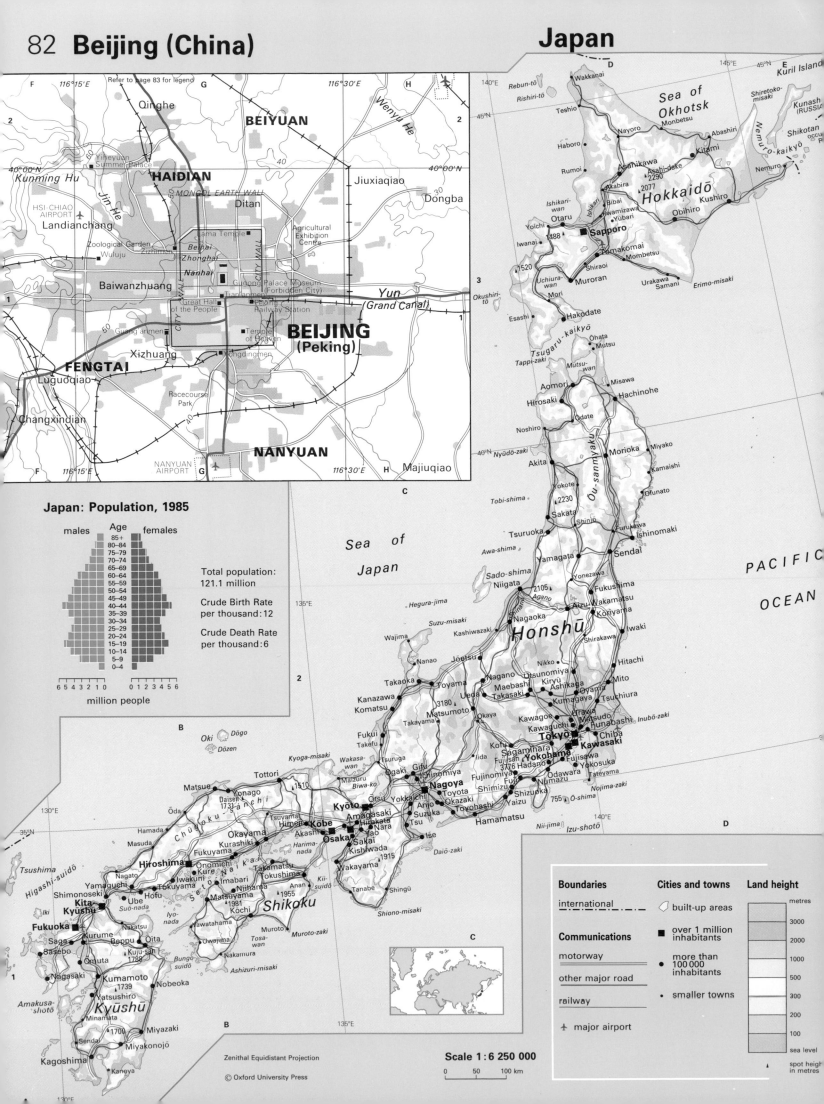

males	Age	females
	85+	
	80–84	
	75–79	
	70–74	
	65–69	
	60–64	
	55–59	
	50–54	
	45–49	
	40–44	
	35–39	
	30–34	
	25–29	
	20–24	
	15–19	
	10–14	
	5–9	
	0–4	

Total population: 121.1 million

Crude Birth Rate per thousand: 12

Crude Death Rate per thousand: 6

6 5 4 3 2 1 0   0 1 2 3 4 5 6
million people

Japan — main map

Sea of Okhotsk

Rebun-tō · Wakkanai · 145°E · 45°N · Kuril Island

Rishiri-tō · Teshio · Nayoro · Monbetsu · Shiretoko-misaki

Haboro · Asahikawa · Abashiri · Kunash (RUSSIA)

Rumoi · Akabira · Asahi-dake 2290 · Kitami · Shikotan

Ishikari-wan · **Hokkaidō** · 2077 · Nemuro-kaikyō

Otaru · Ishikari · Jibai · Iwamizawa · Yūbari · Kushiro

Yoichi · 1488 · Sapporo · Obihiro · Nemuro

Iwanai · Tomakomai · Urakawa · Samani

1520 · Uchiura-wan · Shiraoi · Mombetsu · Erimo-misaki

Esashi · Mori · Muroran

Hakodate

Tsugaru-kaikyō · Ōhata · Mutsu

Tappi-zaki · Mutsu-wan

Aomori · Misawa

Hirosaki · Hachinohe

Ōdate

Noshiro · Morioka · Miyako

40°N · Nyūdō-zaki · Akita · Kamaishi · Ou-sanmyaku · Ōfunato

Tobi-shima · Yokote · 2230 · Shinjo

Sakata · Ishinomaki

Tsuruoka · Furukawa

Awa-shima · Yamagata · Sendai

Sea of Japan · Sado-shima · Niigata · Yonezawa · Fukushima

2105 · Aizu-Wakamatsu · Kōriyama

135°E · Hegura-jima · Agano · Iwaki

Suzu-misaki · Nagaoka · Shirakawa · Hitachi

Wajima · Kashiwazaki · **Honshū** · Mito

Nanao · Jōetsu · Nikko · Utsunomiya

Takaoka · Toyama · Nagano · Kiryū · Ashikaga · Oyama · PACIFIC OCEAN

Kanazawa · Maebashi · Takasaki · Tsuchiura

Komatsu · 3180 · Ueda · Kumagaya · Iwaki

Fukui · Matsumoto · Okaya · Kawagoe · Urawa · Funabashi · Inubō-zaki

Takefu · Takayama · Kōfu · Kawaguchi · Matsudo

Tsuruga · Ogaki · Gifu · Ichinomiya · Sagamihara · **Tokyo** · Chiba

Kyoga-misaki · Wakasa-wan · Fuji-san 3776 · Hadano · **Yokohama** · **Kawasaki**

Tottori · Maizuru · Biwa-ko · Ōtsu · Yokkaichi · Fujinomiya · Fuji · Odawara · Yokosuka · Fujisawa

1510 · Toyota · Shimizu · Numazu · Tateyama

Matsue · Yonago · Nara · Suzuka · Tsu · Shizuoka · 755 · Ō-shima

Ōda · Daisen 1731 · á-n-chi · Tsuyama · Okazaki · Toyohashi · Yaizu · Nojima-zaki

130°E · 35°N · Hamada · Himeji · Akashi · Anjo · Hamamatsu · Izu-shotō

Kyoto · Amagasaki · Hirakata · Ise · Daiō-zaki

Masuda · Okayama · Kurashiki · **Kobe** · Nara · Iao · Nii-jima

Fukuyama · **Osaka** · Sakai · Kishiwada · 1915

Hiroshima · Onomichi · Harima-nada · Wakayama

Tsushima · Nagato · Kure · Imabari · Takamatsu · Kii-suidō · Shiono-misaki

Higashi-suidō · Yamaguchi · Iwakuni · Niihama · Tokushima

Iki · Shimonoseki · Ube · Tokuyama · 1981 · Matsuyama · 1955 · Anan

Kita-Kyushu · Hofu · Iyo-nada · Kōchi · **Shikoku**

Fukuoka · Kurume · Beppu · Ōita · Kawatahama · Muroto · Tosa-wan

Saga · Kuju-san 1788 · Uwajima · Nakamura · Muroto-zaki

Sasebo · Ōmuta · Bungo-suidō · Ashizuri-misaki

Nagasaki · Kumamoto · 1739 · Nobeoka

Amakusa-shotō · Yatsushiro · **Kyūshū**

1700 · Miyazaki

Minamata · Miyakonojō

Kagoshima · Sendai · Kanoya

Legend

Boundaries	Cities and towns	Land height
international ---·---·---	▱ built-up areas	metres
	■ over 1 million inhabitants	3000
Communications		2000
motorway	● more than 100 000 inhabitants	1000
other major road		500
railway	· smaller towns	300
✈ major airport		200
		100
		sea level
		▲ spot height in metres

Zenithal Equidistant Projection

Scale 1 : 6 250 000

0 · 50 · 100 km

© Oxford University Press

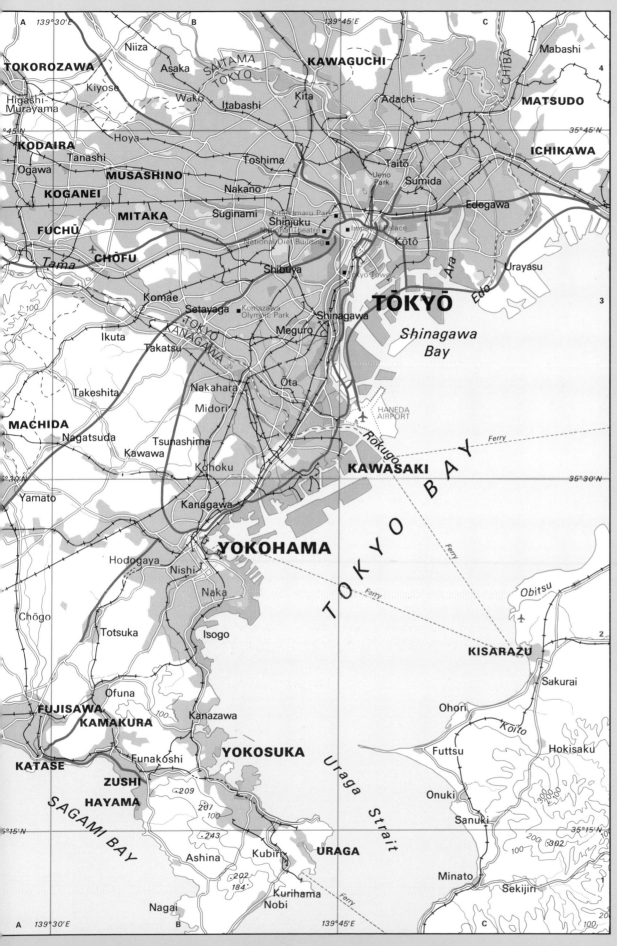

Boundaries
prefecture (Tokyo)

Communications
motorway
other major road
major railway
canal
✈ major airport
✈ other airport

Physical features
~ river
contours
·155 spot height in metres

Land use
central business district
other major commercial areas
industrial
residential
major parks and open spaces
non-urban

Scale 1 : 300 000
0   5km

139°30'E   139°45'E

35°45'N
35°30'N
35°15'N

TOKOROZAWA
Niiza
Asaka
Kiyose
Higashi-Murayama
Wako
Kita
SAITAMA
TOKYO
KAWAGUCHI
Mabashi
MATSUDO
KODAIRA
Hoya
Itabashi
Adachi
CHIBA
Ogawa
Tanashi
Toshima
Taito
ICHIKAWA
MUSASHINO
Nakano
Ueno Park
Sumida
KOGANEI
Suginami
Shinjuku
Edogawa
MITAKA
Kitanomaru Park
National Theatre
Imperial Palace
Kōtō
Urayasu
FUCHŪ
National Diet Building
CHŌFU
Shibuya
Tokyo Tower
Ara
Tama
Komae
Setagaya
Komazawa Olympic Park
Shinagawa
Edo
Ikuta
Meguro
TŌKYŌ
Takatsu
TOKYO
KANAGAWA
Ōta
Shinagawa Bay
Takeshita
Nakahara
Midori
HANEDA AIRPORT
MACHIDA
Nagatsuda
Tsunashima
Kawawa
Rokugo
Ferry
Kōhoku
KAWASAKI
Yamato
Kanagawa
TOKYO BAY
YOKOHAMA
Hodogaya
Nishi
Ferry
Naka
Chōgo
Ferry
Totsuka
Isogo
Obitsu
KISARAZU
Sakurai
Ofuna
FUJISAWA
Kanazawa
KAMAKURA
Ohori
Kōito
Hokisaku
KATASE
Funakoshi
YOKOSUKA
Futtsu
ZUSHI
·209
HAYAMA
·201
Onuki
SAGAMI BAY
·243
Sanuki
Ashina
Kubiri
URAGA
·202
Minato
·184
Nagai
Kurihama
Nobi
Uraga Strait
Sekijiri
Ferry

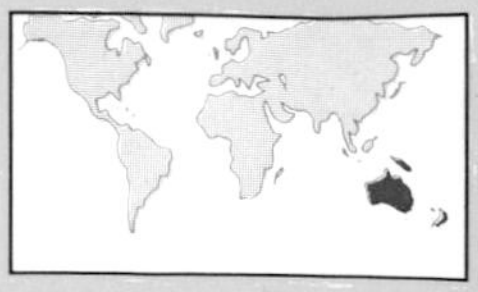

Actual surface temperature

°C
30
25
20
15
10
5
0

July

ALICE SPRINGS
Altitude 584 m

CHARLEVILLE
Altitude 294 m

BRISBANE
Altitude 41 m

DARWIN
Altitude 30 m

KALGOORLIE
Altitude 361 m

PERTH
Altitude 60 m

MELBOURNE
Altitude 35 m

DARWIN
Altitude 30 m

ALICE SPRINGS
Altitude 584 m

CHARLEVILLE
Altitude 294 m

BRISBANE
Altitude 41 m

KALGOORLIE
Altitude 361 m

PERTH
Altitude 60 m

MELBOURNE
Altitude 35 m

January

July

Scale 1 : 60 000 000   0   500   1000 km

Rainfall

and other forms of precipitation

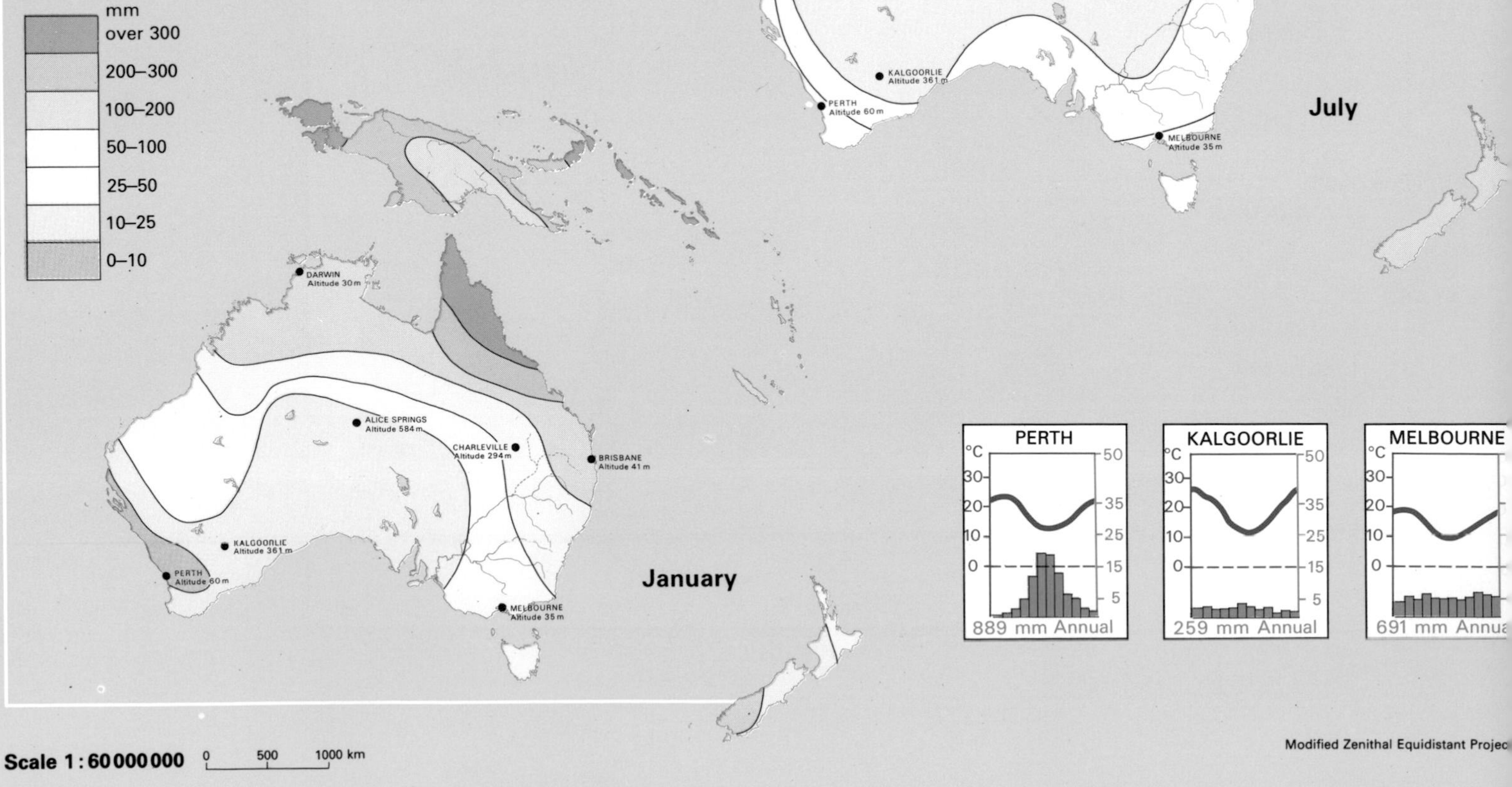

mm
over 300
200–300
100–200
50–100
25–50
10–25
0–10

DARWIN
Altitude 30 m

ALICE SPRINGS
Altitude 584 m

CHARLEVILLE
Altitude 294 m

BRISBANE
Altitude 41 m

KALGOORLIE
Altitude 361 m

PERTH
Altitude 60 m

MELBOURNE
Altitude 35 m

January

PERTH

°C
30
20
10
0

50
35
25
15
5

889 mm Annual

KALGOORLIE

°C
30
20
10
0

50
35
25
15
5

259 mm Annual

MELBOURNE

°C
30
20
10
0

50
35
25
15
5

691 mm Annual

Scale 1 : 60 000 000   0   500   1000 km

Modified Zenithal Equidistant Projection

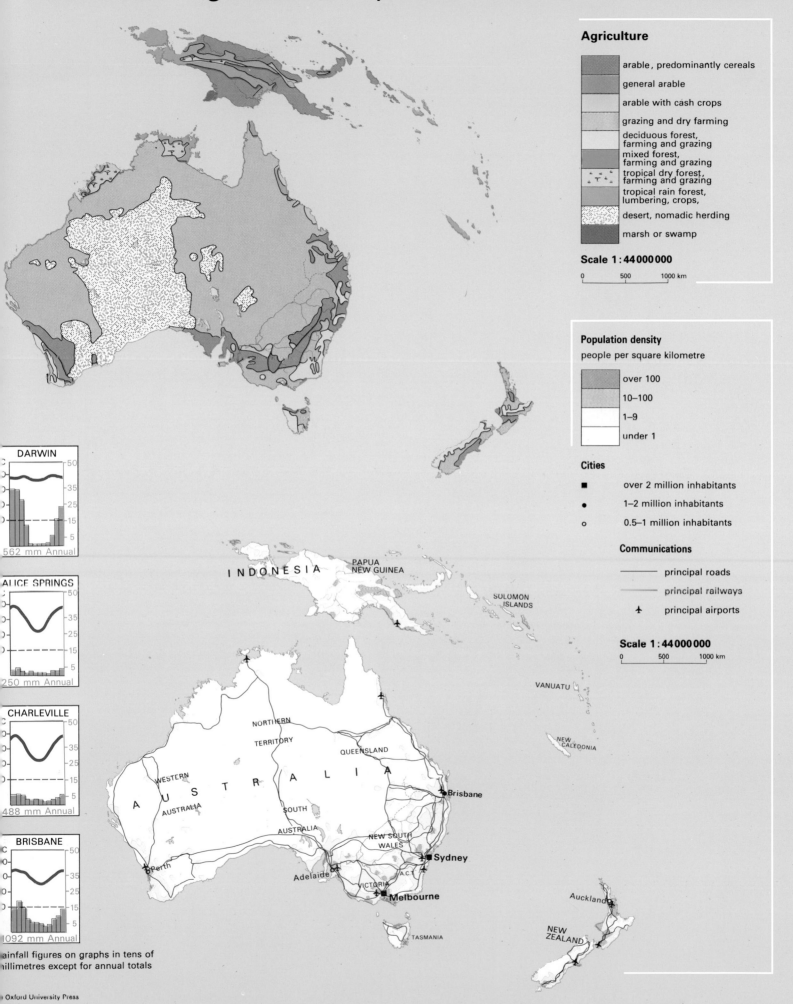

Agriculture

- arable, predominantly cereals
- general arable
- arable with cash crops
- grazing and dry farming
- deciduous forest, farming and grazing
- mixed forest, farming and grazing
- tropical dry forest, farming and grazing
- tropical rain forest, lumbering, crops,
- desert, nomadic herding
- marsh or swamp

Scale 1:44000000

0   500   1000 km

Population density
people per square kilometre

- over 100
- 10–100
- 1–9
- under 1

Cities

- ■ over 2 million inhabitants
- ● 1–2 million inhabitants
- ○ 0.5–1 million inhabitants

Communications

- ──── principal roads
- ──── principal railways
- ✈ principal airports

Scale 1:44000000

0   500   1000 km

DARWIN
562 mm Annual

ALICE SPRINGS
250 mm Annual

CHARLEVILLE
488 mm Annual

BRISBANE
1092 mm Annual

Rainfall figures on graphs in tens of millimetres except for annual totals

Oxford University Press

INDONESIA

PAPUA NEW GUINEA

SOLOMON ISLANDS

VANUATU

NEW CALEDONIA

NORTHERN TERRITORY

QUEENSLAND

WESTERN AUSTRALIA

SOUTH AUSTRALIA

NEW SOUTH WALES

A.C.T.

VICTORIA

A U S T R A L I A

Perth

Adelaide

Melbourne

Sydney

Brisbane

TASMANIA

Auckland

NEW ZEALAND

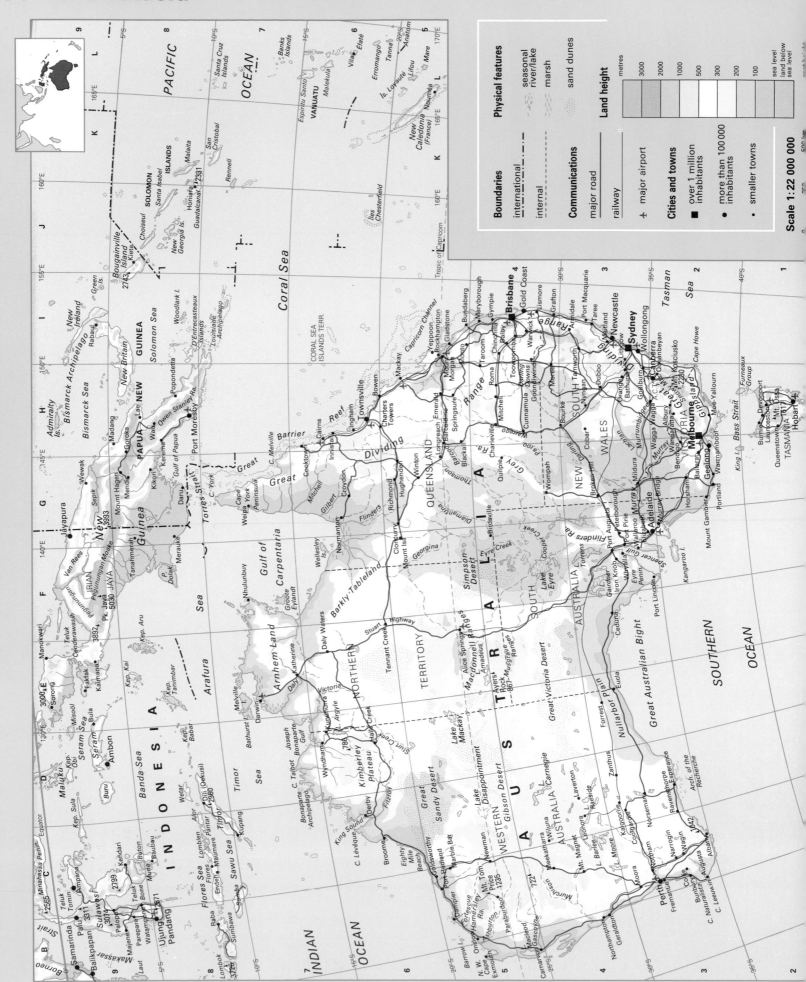

Physical features

seasonal river/lake
marsh
sand dunes

Land height

metres
3000
2000
1000
500
300
200
100
sea level
land below sea level

Boundaries

international
internal

Communications

major road
railway

Cities and towns

+ major airport
■ over 1 million inhabitants
● more than 100 000 inhabitants
· smaller towns

Scale 1:22 000 000

Zenithal Equidistant Projection
© Oxford University Press

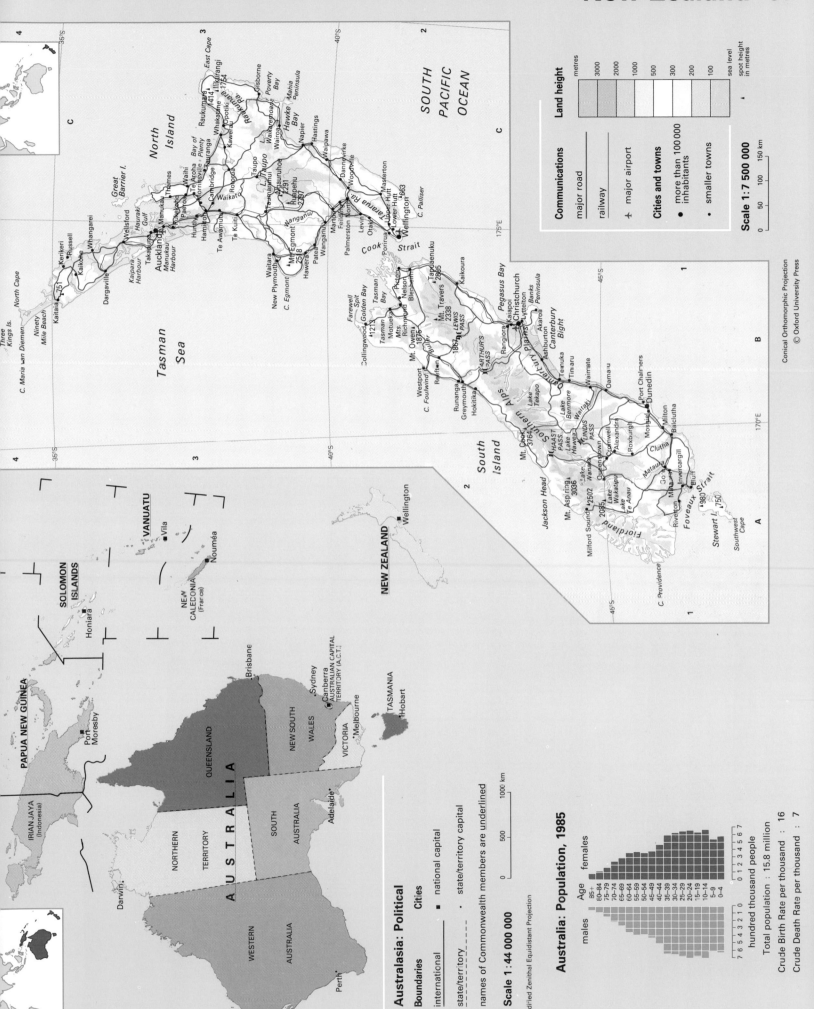

Land height

metres	
3000	
2000	
1000	
500	
300	
200	
100	
sea level	

▲ spot height in metres

Communications

— major road
— railway
✈ major airport

Cities and towns

● more than 100 000 inhabitants
· smaller towns

Scale 1:7 500 000

0 50 100 150 km

Conical Orthomorphic Projection

© Oxford University Press

SOUTH PACIFIC OCEAN

North Island

Tasman Sea

South Island

Australasia: Political

Boundaries — **Cities**
international ■ national capital
state/territory · state/territory capital

names of Commonwealth members are underlined

Scale 1:44 000 000

0 500 1000 km

Modified Zenithal Equidistant Projection

PAPUA NEW GUINEA

IRIAN JAYA (Indonesia)

SOLOMON ISLANDS
Honiara

VANUATU
Vila

NEW CALEDONIA (France)
Nouméa

NEW ZEALAND
Wellington

AUSTRALIA

WESTERN AUSTRALIA
Perth

NORTHERN TERRITORY
Darwin

SOUTH AUSTRALIA
Adelaide

QUEENSLAND
Brisbane

NEW SOUTH WALES
Sydney

AUSTRALIAN CAPITAL TERRITORY (A.C.T.)
Canberra

VICTORIA
Melbourne

TASMANIA
Hobart

Port Moresby

Australia: Population, 1985

Age	
85+	
80–84	
75–79	
70–74	
65–69	
60–64	
55–59	
50–54	
45–49	
40–44	
35–39	
30–34	
25–29	
20–24	
15–19	
10–14	
5–9	
0–4	

males / females

7 6 5 4 3 2 1 0 0 1 2 3 4 5 6 7
hundred thousand people

Total population : 15.8 million
Crude Birth Rate per thousand : 16
Crude Death Rate per thousand : 7

Land height

metres
5000
3000
2000
1000
500
300
200
100
sea level
land below sea level
. spot height in metres

Sea depth

sea level
200
3000
4000
5000
6000

Land below sea level and sea depths shown as minus numbers

sand desert

Scale 1 : 44 000 000

0   500   1000 km

NORTH ATLANTIC OCEAN

Str. of Gibraltar
Madeira Is.
Canary Is.
Haut Atlas
Atlas Sahariern
4165
Grand Erg Occidental
Grand Erg Oriental
Erg Iguidi
C. Blanc
Tanezrouft
Hoggar
C. Vert
Senegal
Fouta Djallon
Niger
Volta
L. Volta
Kainji Res.
Jos Plateau
C. Palmas
Bight of Benin
Gulf of Guinea
Guinea Depression
C. Lopez
Adamawa Mtns.
4095 Sanaga
.2829
Niger Delta
Bight of Bonny
Benue
L. Chad
Chari
Jebel Marra
Bodélé
Tibesti .3415
Sahara Desert
Libyan Desert
Kufrah Oasis
Western Desert
Qattara Depression -133
Nile Delta
Mediterranean Sea
C. Bon
G. of Gabès
Gulf of Sirte
Black Sea
133
Caspian Sea
Tropic of Cancer
An Nafud
Asir Mts.
.3268
C. Guardafui
Bab el Mandab
Danakil
4620.
Atbara
Nubian Desert
Red Sea Hills
Gulf of Suez
Sinai
Red Sea
L. Nasser
White Nile
Blue Nile
Ethiopian Highlands
Ogaden
Shebele
Sudd
Bahr el Ghazal
Bomu
Uele
Oubangui
Sangha
Zaïre (Congo)
Lomami
MT. RUWENZORI 5120
Mitumba Mts
West Rift Valley
East Rift Valley
L. Turkana
L. Kyoga
L. Victoria
Serengeti
5895 KILIMANJARO
L. Tanganyika
Pemba I.
Zanzibar
INDIAN OCEAN
-5340
Equator
Juba
Kasai
L. Mai Ndombe
Lulua
Lualaba
Cuango
L. Bangweula
L. Nyasa (L. Malawi)
Rovuma
Muchinga Mts
Comoro Archipelago
Aldabra Is.
2610.
Angola Plateau
Cunene
Cuito
Zambezi
Kariba L.
Okovango Basin
Makgadikgadi Salt Pan
Limpopo
Mozambique Channel
Madagascar
2658.
Ankarata Mts.
Tropic of Capricorn
Namib Desert
Kalahari Desert
Vaal
Orange
High Veld
Drakensberg 3482.
Gt. Karoo
C. of Good Hope
C. Agulhas
C. St. Francis
Mozambique Depression

SOUTH ATLANTIC OCEAN
Ascension I.
St. Helena
Angola Depression

Africa: Political

⌐ international boundary
· national capital

Names of commonwealth members are underlined

Scale 1 : 80 000 000

0   500   1000 km

MOROCCO
WESTERN SAHARA
MAURITANIA
Nouakchott
ALGERIA
TUNISIA
Alger
Tunis
Tarābulus (Tripoli)
LIBYA
Cairo
EGYPT
CEUTA (Sp.)
Rabat-Salé
Madeira (Port.)
Canary Is. (Sp.)
CAPE VERDE IS.
Praia
Dakar
THE GAMBIA
Banjul
SENEGAL
GUINEA BISSAU
Bissau
GUINEA
Conakry
SIERRA LEONE
Freetown
Monrovia
LIBERIA
Yamoussoukro
CÔTE D'IVOIRE
MALI
Bamako
BURKINA FASO
Ouagadougou
NIGER
Niamey
CHAD
Ndjamena
Khartoum
SUDAN
Asmera
ERITREA
DJIBOUTI
Djibouti
Adīs Abeba
ETHIOPIA
SOMALIA
Mogadishu
NIGERIA
Abuja
GHANA
Accra
BENIN
Lomé
Porto Novo
TOGO
CAMEROON
Yaoundé
Malabo
EQU. GUINEA
São Tomé
SAO TOME AND PRINCIPE
GABON
Libreville
CONGO
Brazzaville
CABINDA (Angola)
ZAÏRE
Kinshasa
CENTRAL AFRICAN REPUBLIC
Bangui
UGANDA
Kampala
KENYA
Nairobi
RWANDA
Kigali
BURUNDI
Bujumbura
TANZANIA
Dodoma
Aldabra Is. (Seychelles)
Luanda
ANGOLA
ZAMBIA
Lusaka
MALAWI
Lilongwe
COMOROS
Moroni
MOZAMBIQUE
Antananarivo
MADAGASCAR
WALVIS BAY (S. Afric.)
Windhoek
NAMIBIA
BOTSWANA
Gaborone
ZIMBABWE
Harare
Pretoria
Maputo
Mbabane
SWAZILAND
REPUBLIC OF SOUTH AFRICA
Maseru
LESOTHO

Zenithal Equal Area Projection

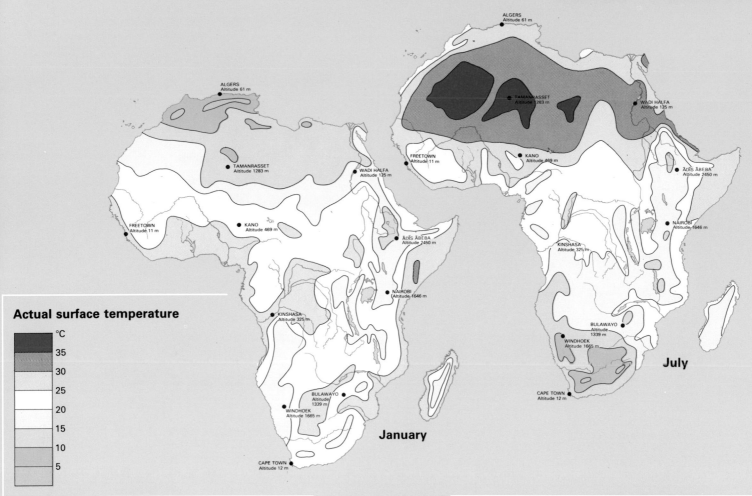

Actual surface temperature

°C
35
30
25
20
15
10
5

July

January

Scale 1 : 80 000 000

0   500   1000 km

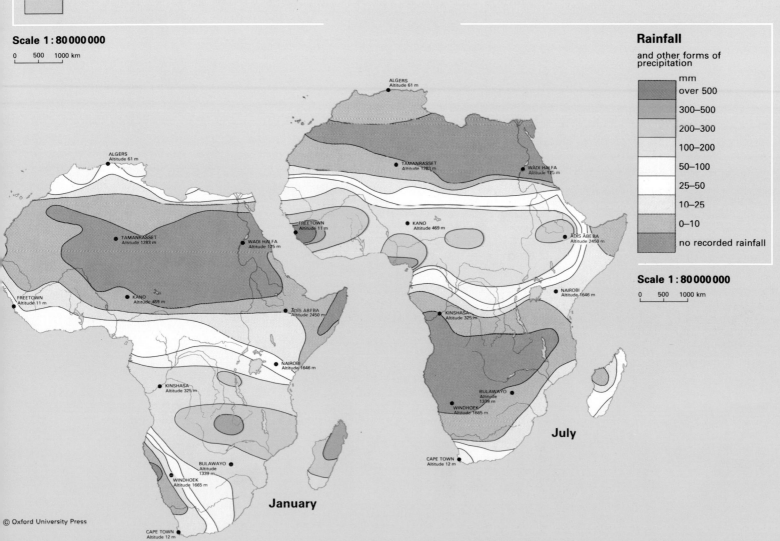

Rainfall

and other forms of
precipitation

mm
over 500
300–500
200–300
100–200
50–100
25–50
10–25
0–10
no recorded rainfall

Scale 1 : 80 000 000

0   500   1000 km

July

January

© Oxford University Press

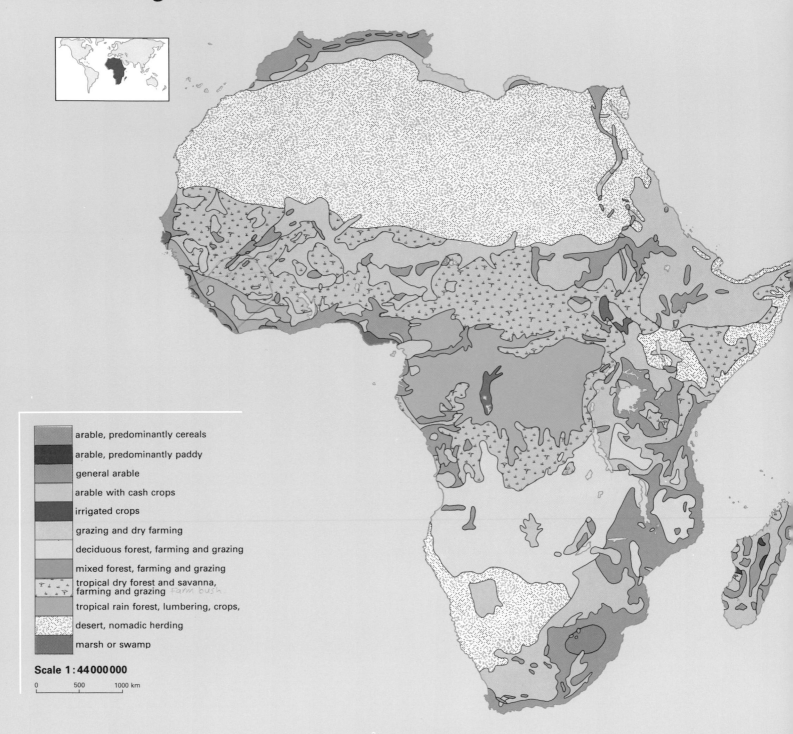

arable, predominantly cereals

arable, predominantly paddy

general arable

arable with cash crops

irrigated crops

grazing and dry farming

deciduous forest, farming and grazing

mixed forest, farming and grazing

tropical dry forest and savanna, farming and grazing *farm bush*

tropical rain forest, lumbering, crops,

desert, nomadic herding

marsh or swamp

Scale 1 : 44 000 000

0   500   1000 km

Tsetse fly

infected areas

Rainfall figures on graphs in tens of millimetres except for annual totals

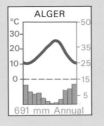

ALGER
691 mm Annual

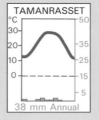

TAMANRASSET
38 mm Annual

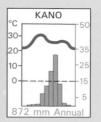

KANO
872 mm Annual

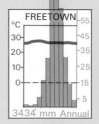

FREETOWN
3434 mm Annual

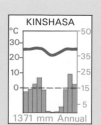

KINSHASA
1371 mm Annual

Zenithal Equal Area Projection

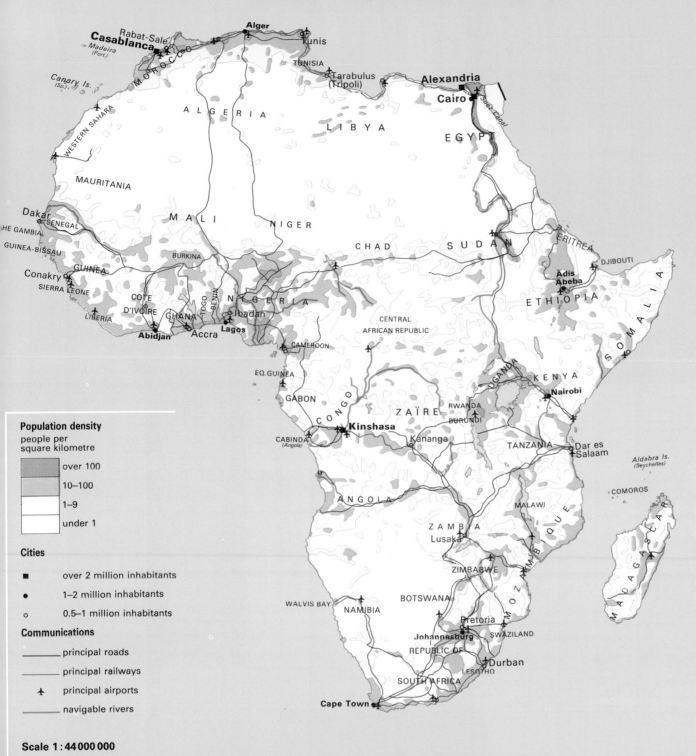

Population density

people per
square kilometre

over 100

10–100

1–9

under 1

Cities

■ over 2 million inhabitants

● 1–2 million inhabitants

○ 0.5–1 million inhabitants

Communications

principal roads

principal railways

✈ principal airports

navigable rivers

Scale 1 : 44 000 000

0   500   1000 km

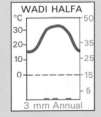

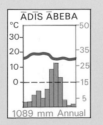

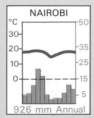

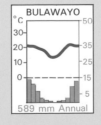

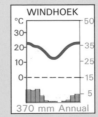

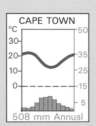

WADI HALFA — 3 mm Annual

ĀDĪS ĀBEBA — 1089 mm Annual

NAIROBI — 926 mm Annual

BULAWAYO — 589 mm Annual

WINDHOEK — 370 mm Annual

CAPE TOWN — 508 mm Annual

Oxford University Press

Legend

Boundaries

international

Communications

major road

major railway

✈ major airport

✈ other airport

Physical features

river

marsh

contours

•155 spot height in metres

Land use

central business district

other major commercial areas

industrial

•.•. craft industry (Ibadan)

residential

self-built housing (Kinshasa)
traditional housing (Brazzaville)
post 1950 housing (Lagos)

older housing
newer (government) housing } Ibadan
newer (privately developed) housing

GRA = Government Residential Area (Ibadan)

major parks and open spaces
(shown only for Brazzaville)

non-urban

Scale 1 : 300 000

0   5 km

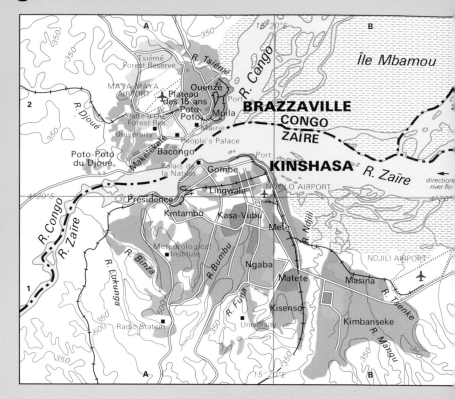

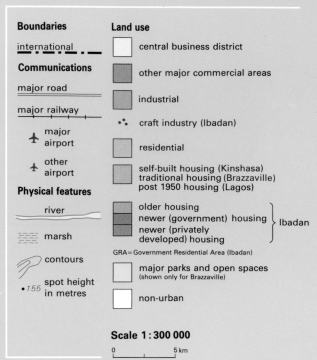

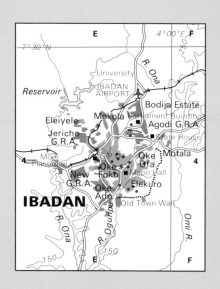

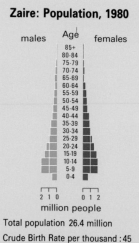

Zaire: Population, 1980

males   Age   females

85+, 80-84, 75-79, 70-74, 65-69, 60-64, 55-59, 50-54, 45-49, 40-44, 35-39, 30-34, 25-29, 20-24, 15-19, 10-14, 5-9, 0-4

2 1 0   0 1 2

million people

Total population 26.4 million

Crude Birth Rate per thousand : 45

Crude Death Rate per thousand : 16

Population growth in selected tropical African cities, 1950–80

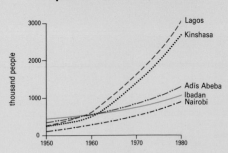

3000

thousand people

2000

1000

0

1950   1960   1970   1980

Lagos
Kinshasa
Adīs Abeba
Ibadan
Nairobi

Nigeria: Population, 1983

males   Age   females

65+, 60-64, 55-59, 50-54, 45-49, 40-44, 35-39, 30-34, 25-29, 20-24, 15-19, 10-14, 5-9, 0-4

16 15 14 13 12 11 10 9 8 7 6 5 4 3 2 1 0   0 1 2 3 4 5 6 7 8 9 10 11 12 13 14 15 16

million people

Total population 92.2 million

Crude Birth Rate per thousand : 50

Crude Death Rate per thousand : 17

Egypt: Population, 1983

males   Age   females

75+, 70-74, 65-69, 60-64, 55-59, 50-54, 45-49, 40-44, 35-39, 30-34, 25-29, 20-24, 15-19, 10-14, 5-9, 0-4

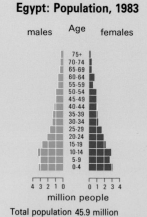

4 3 2 1 0   0 1 2 3 4

million people

Total population 45.9 million

Crude Birth Rate per thousand : 37

Crude Death Rate per thousand : 10

© Oxford University Press

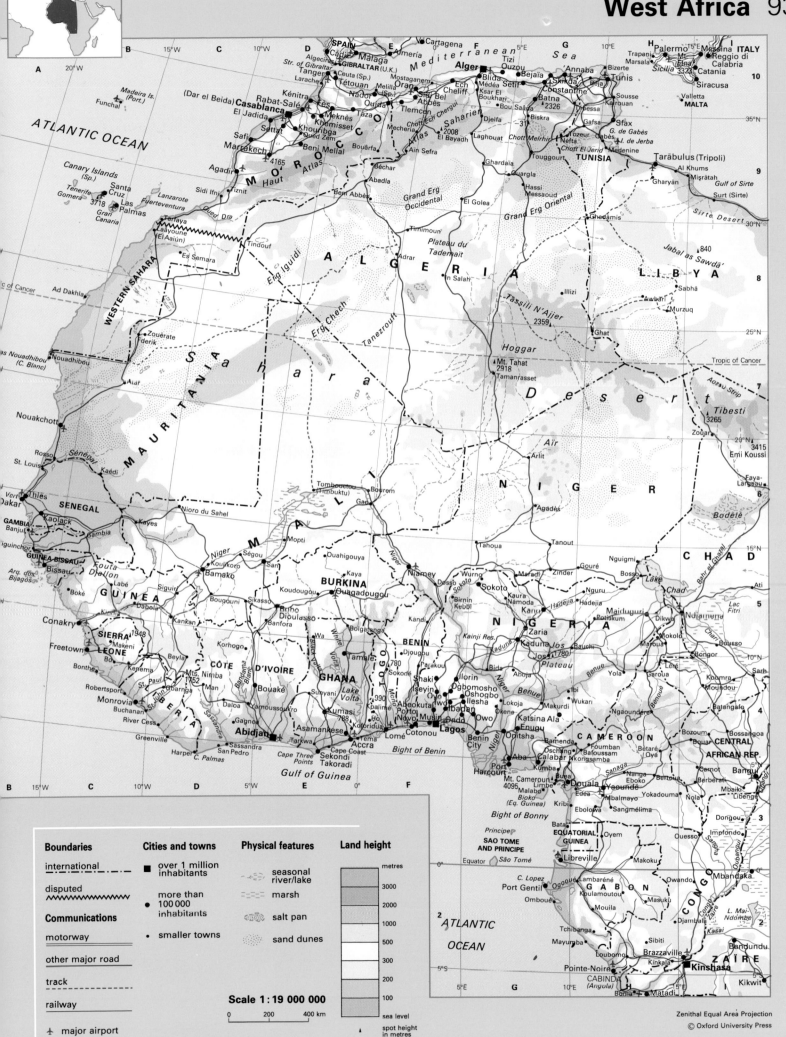

ATLANTIC OCEAN

Madeira Is. (Port.)
Funchal

Canary Islands (Sp.)
Tenerife 3718 Santa Cruz
Gomera Las Palmas
Gran Canaria Fuerteventura
Lanzarote

c of Cancer
Ad Dakhla

as Nouadhibou (C. Blanc)
Nouadhibou

Nouakchott

Rosso St. Louis
Vert Dakar
Thiès
SENEGAL
Kaolack
GAMBIA
Banjul
iguinchor
GUINEA-BISSAU
Bissau
Arq. dos Bijagós
Boké
GUINEA
Labé
Conakry
Kankan
SIERRA LEONE 1948
Makeni
Freetown
Bonthe
Kenema
Robertsport
Monrovia
Buchanan
River Cess
Greenville
Harper C. Palmas
San Pedro

SPAIN
Cartagena Almería
Cádiz Málaga
Algeciras **GIBRALTAR** (U.K.)
Tangier
(Dar el Beida) **Casablanca**
Rabat-Salé Fès Meknès
El Jadida
Khouribga
Safi Settat Oued Zem
Marrakech Beni Mellal
Agadir 4165
Haut Atlas
MOROCCO
Sidi Ifni Tiznit
Tarfaya
Laâyoune (El Aaiún)
Es Semara
WESTERN SAHARA
Zouérate derik
MAURITANIA
Atar
Kaédi
Kayes
Nioro du Sahel
Koulikoro Ségou San
Bamako
Siguiri
Dabola
Kouroussa
Bougouni Sikasso
Banfora
Korhogo
Beyla
Mts. Nimba 1752
Man
CÔTE D'IVOIRE
Daloa
Gagnoa
Sassandra
Yamoussoukro
Bouaké

Mediterranean Sea
Melilla (Sp.)
Oran
Tlemcen
ALGERIA
Béchar Abadla
Erg Iguidi
Erg Chech
Tanezrouft
Tombouctou (Timbuktu)
Bourem
Gao
MALI
Mopti
Ouahigouya
BURKINA
Ouagadougou
Koudougou
Bobo Dioulasso
Bolgatanga
Wa
GHANA
Tamale
Sunyani
Kumasi
Lake Volta
Abidjan
Tarkwa
Accra Tema
Sekondi Takoradi
Cape Three Points
Cape Coast

ITALY
Palermo Messina Reggio di Calabria
Trapani Marsala Mt. Etna 3323 Catania
Bizerte Tunis Siracusa
TUNISIA
Valletta **MALTA**
Sfax
Gafsa
LIBYA
Ghadámis
NIGER
Arlit
Agadès
Tahoua Tanout
Zinder
NIGERIA
Sokoto
Kaduna
Jos
Abuja
Ilorin Oyo Oshogbo
Ibadan
Lagos
Porto Novo Cotonou
Lomé
TOGO
BENIN

Gulf of Guinea
Bight of Benin
Benin City
Port Harcourt
CAMEROON
Mt. Cameroun 4095
Douala Yaoundé
EQUATORIAL GUINEA
Malabo Bioko (Eq. Guinea)
SAO TOME AND PRINCIPE
Principe
São Tomé
Libreville
GABON
Port Gentil
CONGO
Brazzaville
Pointe-Noire
CABINDA (Angola)
ZAIRE
Kinshasa

ATLANTIC OCEAN

Zenithal Equal Area Projection

Boundaries

international

disputed

Communications

motorway

other major road

track

railway

✈ major airport

Cities and towns

■ over 1 million inhabitants

● more than 100 000 inhabitants

· smaller towns

Physical features

seasonal river/lake

marsh

salt pan

sand dunes

Land height

metres
3000
2000
1000
500
300
200
100
sea level

▲ spot height in metres

Scale 1 : 19 000 000

0   200   400 km

Zenithal Equal Area Project

Land height

	metres
	5000
	3000
	2000
	1000
	500
	300
	200
	100
	sea level
	land below sea level
▲	spot height in metres

Physical features

seasonal river/lake
marsh
salt pan
sand dunes

Boundaries

international
disputed
internal
national park

Communications

major road
railway
canal
✈ major airport

Cities and towns

■ over 1 million inhabitants
● more than 100 000 inhabitants
• smaller towns

Scale 1:19 000 000

0   200   400 km

INDIAN

OCEAN

ATLANTIC   OCEAN

ANGOLA

ZAMBIA

TANZANIA

MALAWI

MOZAMBIQUE

ZIMBABWE

BOTSWANA

NAMIBIA

SOUTH AFRICA

MADAGASCAR

COMOROS

Mozambique Channel

Kalahari Desert

Namib Desert

CAPE PROVINCE

TRANSVAAL

ORANGE FREE STATE

NATAL

LESOTHO

SWAZILAND

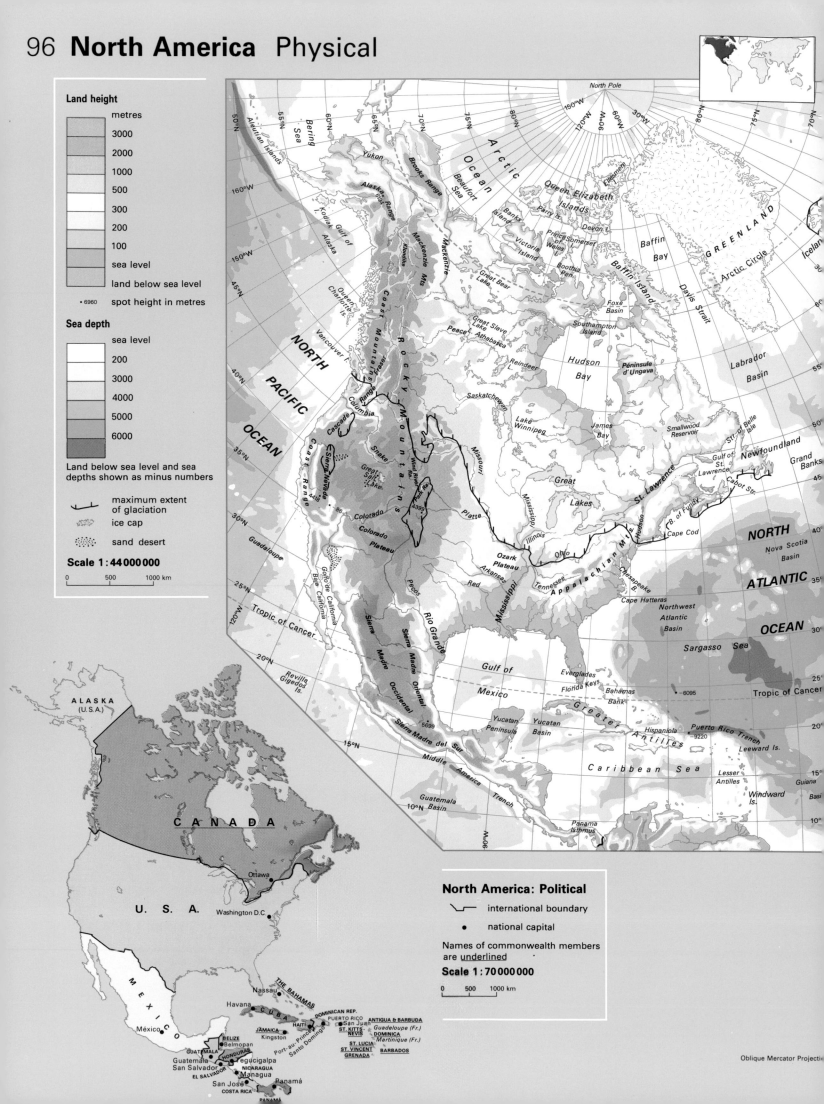

Land height

metres
3000
2000
1000
500
300
200
100
sea level
land below sea level

• 6960 spot height in metres

Sea depth

sea level
200
3000
4000
5000
6000

Land below sea level and sea depths shown as minus numbers

maximum extent of glaciation

ice cap

sand desert

Scale 1:44 000 000

0   500   1000 km

North America: Political

international boundary

• national capital

Names of commonwealth members are underlined

Scale 1:70 000 000

0   500   1000 km

ALASKA (U.S.A.)

C A N A D A

Ottawa

U. S. A.

Washington D.C.

M E X I C O

México

Nassau

THE BAHAMAS

Havana

C U B A

JAMAICA   HAITI

Kingston   Port-au-Prince

DOMINICAN REP.

PUERTO RICO

San Juan

Santo Domingo

ANTIGUA & BARBUDA

ST. KITTS

NEVIS

Guadeloupe (Fr.)

DOMINICA

Martinique (Fr.)

ST. LUCIA

ST. VINCENT

BARBADOS

GRENADA

BELIZE

Belmopan

GUATEMALA

Guatemala

San Salvador

EL SALVADOR

HONDURAS

Tegucigalpa

NICARAGUA

Managua

San José

COSTA RICA

Panamá

PANAMA

Oblique Mercator Projection

Actual surface temperature

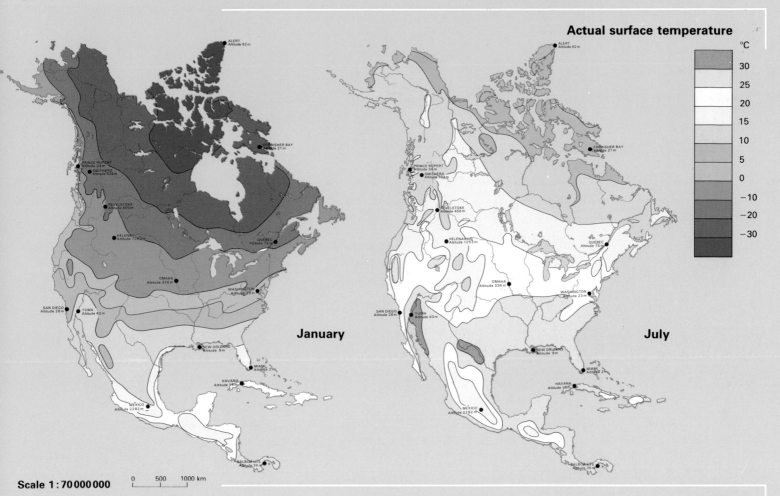

°C
30
25
20
15
10
5
0
−10
−20
−30

January

July

Scale 1 : 70 000 000

0   500   1000 km

Rainfall

and other forms of precipitation

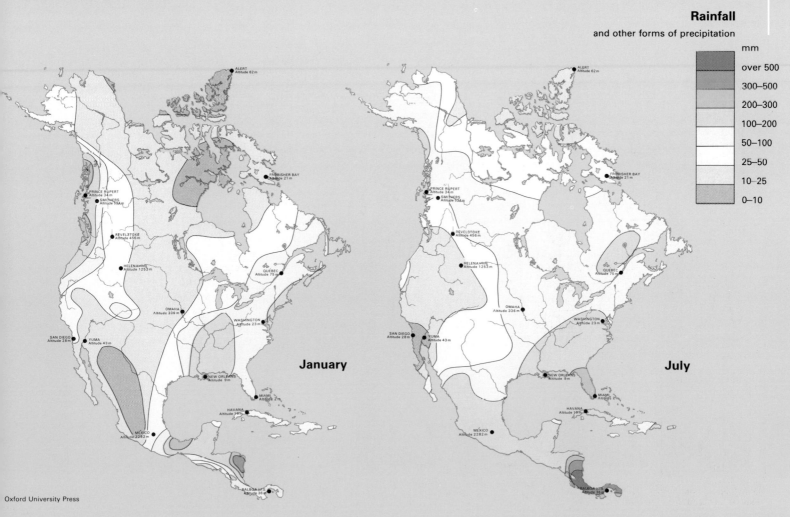

mm
over 500
300–500
200–300
100–200
50–100
25–50
10–25
0–10

January

July

Oxford University Press

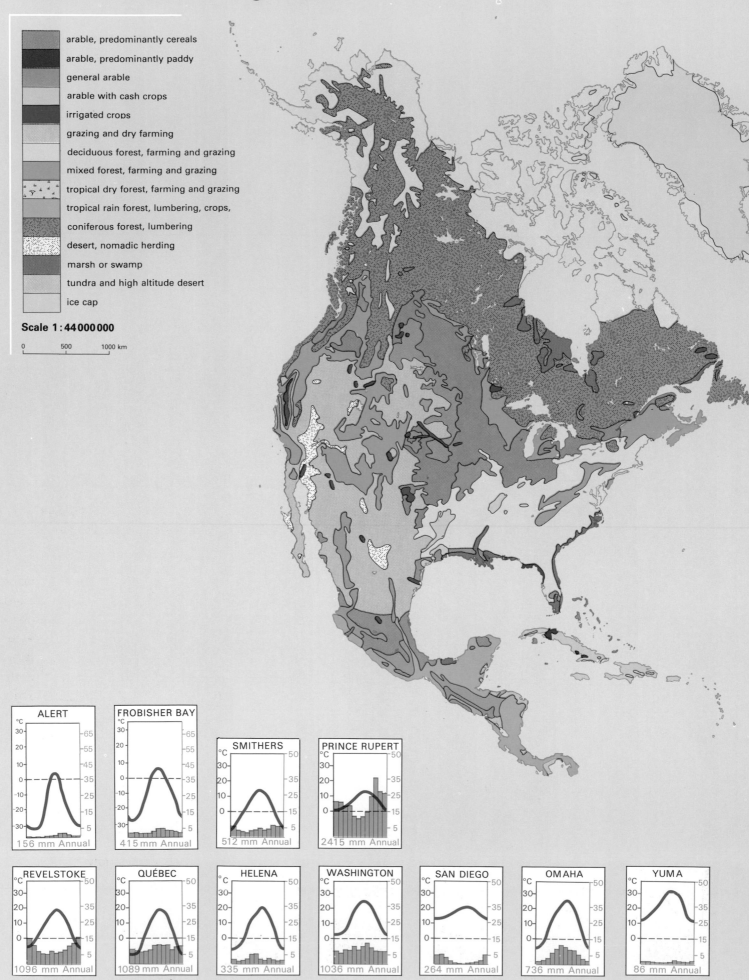

Legend

- arable, predominantly cereals
- arable, predominantly paddy
- general arable
- arable with cash crops
- irrigated crops
- grazing and dry farming
- deciduous forest, farming and grazing
- mixed forest, farming and grazing
- tropical dry forest, farming and grazing
- tropical rain forest, lumbering, crops,
- coniferous forest, lumbering
- desert, nomadic herding
- marsh or swamp
- tundra and high altitude desert
- ice cap

Scale 1 : 44 000 000

0   500   1000 km

ALERT
156 mm Annual

FROBISHER BAY
415 mm Annual

SMITHERS
512 mm Annual

PRINCE RUPERT
2415 mm Annual

REVELSTOKE
1096 mm Annual

QUÉBEC
1089 mm Annual

HELENA
335 mm Annual

WASHINGTON
1036 mm Annual

SAN DIEGO
264 mm Annual

OMAHA
736 mm Annual

YUMA
86 mm Annual

Rainfall figures on graphs in tens of
millimetres except for annual totals

Oblique Mercator Projection

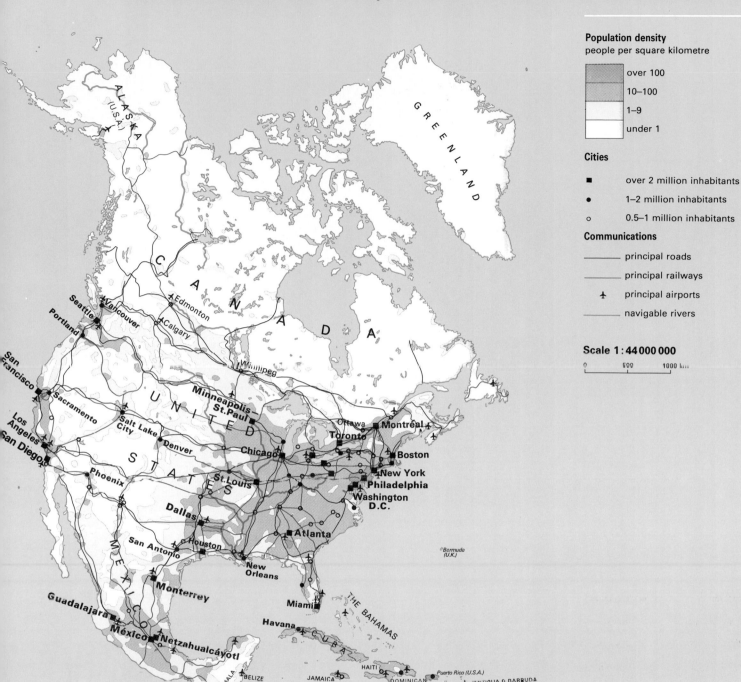

Population density
people per square kilometre

- over 100
- 10–100
- 1–9
- under 1

Cities

- ■ over 2 million inhabitants
- ● 1–2 million inhabitants
- ○ 0.5–1 million inhabitants

Communications

——— principal roads

——— principal railways

✈ principal airports

——— navigable rivers

Scale 1 : 44 000 000

0   500   1000 km

GREENLAND

ALASKA (U.S.A.)

CANADA

UNITED STATES

MEXICO

Seattle Vancouver Edmonton

Portland Calgary

San Francisco Sacramento Winnipeg

Salt Lake City Minneapolis–St.Paul

Los Angeles Denver Ottawa Montréal

San Diego Chicago Toronto Boston

Phoenix St.Louis New York

Dallas Philadelphia Washington D.C.

San Antonio Atlanta

Houston New Orleans

Monterrey Bermuda (U.K.)

Guadalajara Miami THE BAHAMAS

México Netzahualcáyotl Havana CUBA

GUATEMALA BELIZE HAITI Puerto Rico (U.S.A.)

JAMAICA DOMINICAN REPUBLIC ANTIGUA & BARBUDA

HONDURAS ST. KITTS NEVIS DOMINICA

EL SALVADOR ST. LUCIA

NICARAGUA ST. VINCENT BARBADOS

GRENADA

COSTA RICA PANAMA

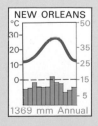

NEW ORLEANS

°C — 50

30 — 35

20 — 25

10 — 15

0 — 5

1369 mm Annual

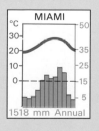

MÉXICO

°C — 50

30 — 35

20 — 25

10 — 15

0 — 5

726 mm Annual

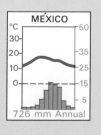

MIAMI

°C — 50

30 — 35

20 — 25

10 — 15

0 — 5

1518 mm Annual

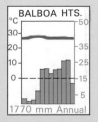

BALBOA HTS.

°C — 50

30 — 35

20 — 25

10 — 15

0 — 5

1770 mm Annual

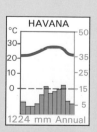

HAVANA

°C — 50

30 — 35

20 — 25

10 — 15

0 — 5

1224 mm Annual

Scale 1:19 000 000

0   200   400 km

Zenithal Equidistant Projection

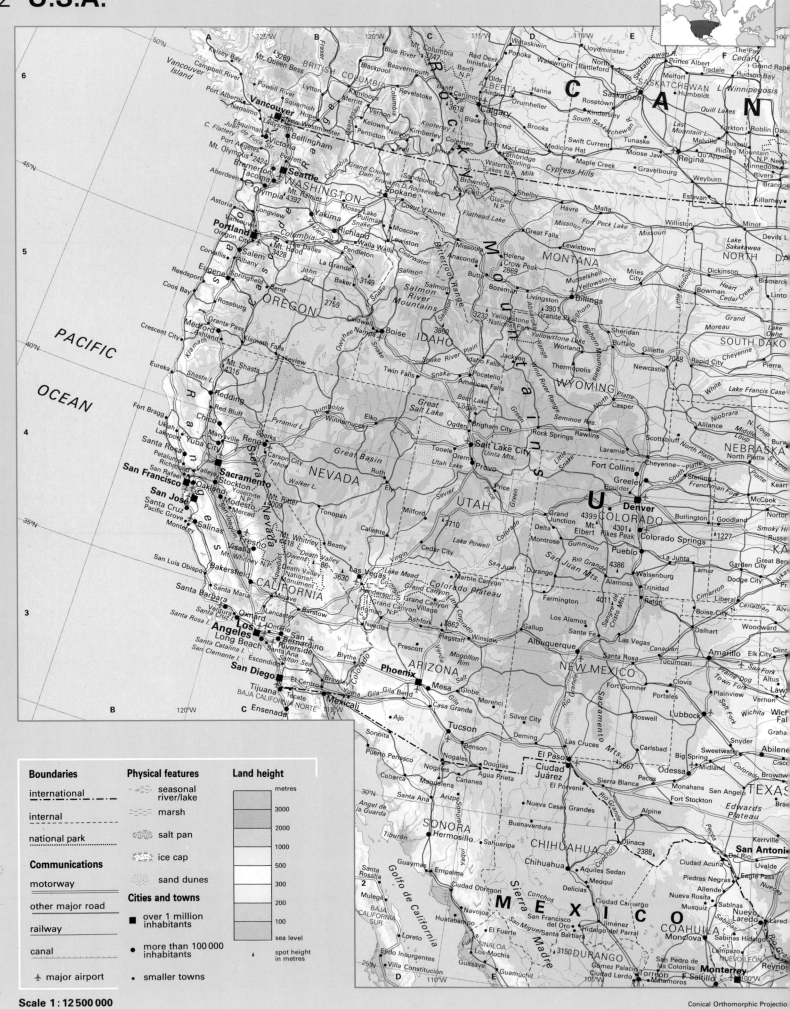

Boundaries

international
internal
national park

Communications

motorway
other major road
railway
canal
✈ major airport

Physical features

seasonal river/lake
marsh
salt pan
ice cap
sand dunes

Cities and towns

■ over 1 million inhabitants
● more than 100 000 inhabitants
• smaller towns
▲ spot height in metres

Land height

| metres |
| 3000 |
| 2000 |
| 1000 |
| 500 |
| 300 |
| 200 |
| 100 |
| sea level |

Scale 1 : 12 500 000

0   125   250 km

Conical Orthomorphic Projection

Boundaries

international

internal

national park

Communications

motorway

other major road

railway

canal

✈ major airport

Cities and towns

◭ built-up areas

■ over 1 million inhabitants

● more than 100 000 inhabitants

• smaller towns

Physical features

seasonal river/lake

marsh

Land height

metres
1000
500
300
200
100
sea level

▴ spot height in metres

Scale 1:6 250 000

0   25   50 km

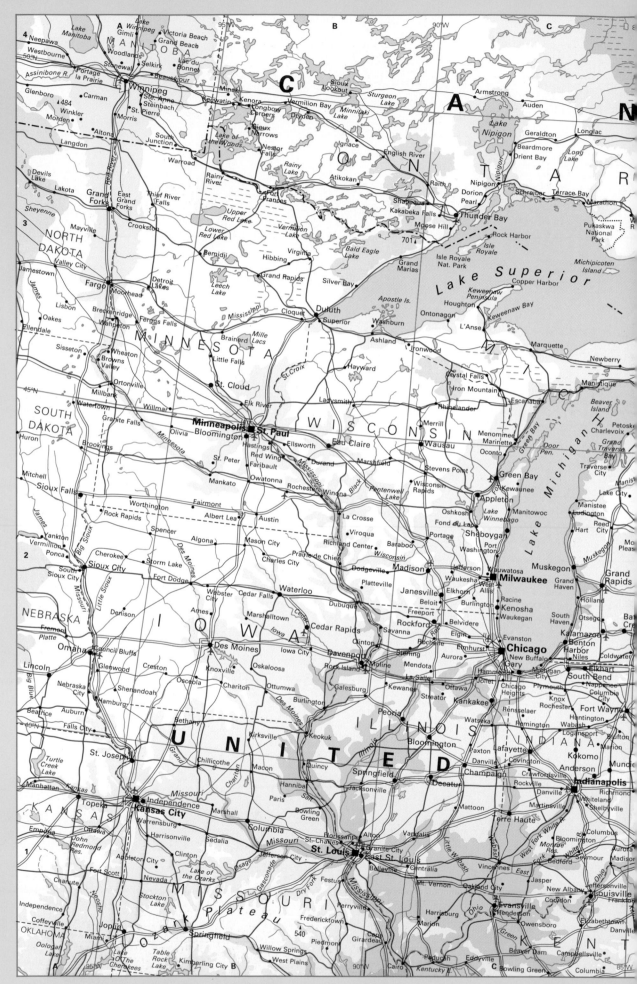

USA: Population, 1985

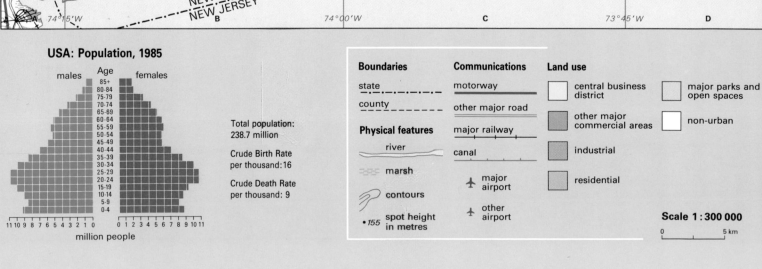

males   Age   females

85+
80-84
75-79
70-74
65-69
60-64
55-59
50-54
45-49
40-44
35-39
30-34
25-29
20-24
15-19
10-14
5-9
0-4

11 10 9 8 7 6 5 4 3 2 1 0   0 1 2 3 4 5 6 7 8 9 10 11

million people

Total population:
238.7 million

Crude Birth Rate
per thousand: 16

Crude Death Rate
per thousand: 9

Boundaries

state
county

Physical features

river
marsh
contours
• 155 spot height in metres

Communications

motorway
other major road
major railway
canal
✈ major airport
✈ other airport

Land use

central business district
other major commercial areas
industrial
residential
major parks and open spaces
non-urban

Scale 1 : 300 000

0   5 km

Pacific Ocean

San Pedro Bay

San Pedro Channel

LOS ANGELES

SAN GABRIEL MOUNTAINS

ANGELES NATIONAL FOREST

STA. MONICA MOUNTAINS

SAN FERNANDO VALLEY

PALOS VERDES HILLS

Van Norman Lake
San Fernando
San Fernando Airport
Sunland
Tujunga
La Crescenta
La Canada
Altadena
Mount Lukens
Big Tujunga Reservoir
Mount Wilson Observatory
Cogswell Reservoir
San Gabriel Reservoir
Morris Reservoir
Van Nuys
Sepulveda Dam Recreational Area
North Hollywood
BURBANK
HOLLYWOOD BURBANK AIRPORT
Brand Park
Devils Gate Reservoir
Rose Bowl
PASADENA
Big Santa Anita Reservoir
Sawpit Canyon Reservoir
Eaton Wash Reservoir
Arcadia
Glendora
Azusa
GLENDALE
Griffith Park
Hollywood Reservoir
Hollywood Bowl
Silver Lake Reservoir
Elysian Park
San Gabriel
Temple City
Santa Fe Flood Control Basin
Baldwin Park
Covina
Stone Canyon Reservoir
Beverly Hills
Franklin Canyon Reservoir
Hollywood
ALHAMBRA
Rosemead
EL MONTE AIRPORT
El Monte
West Covina
LOS ANGELES
Civic Center
West Los Angeles
Monterey Park
East Los Angeles
SANTA MONICA
SANTA MONICA AIRPORT
Culver City
SANTA MONICA FREEWAY
Montebello
Whittier Narrows Dam Reservoir Area
La Puente
POMONA FREEWAY
Marina del Rey
Rio Hondo
Pico-Rivera
Whittier
INGLEWOOD
SOUTH GATE
DOWNEY
LOS ANGELES COUNTY
ORANGE COUNTY
La Habra
LOS ANGELES AIRPORT
NORWALK
Fullerton Reservoir
Hawthorne
Brea Reservoir
Manhattan Beach
COMPTON
COMPTON AIRPORT
Bellflower
FULLERTON
FULLERTON AIRPORT
Lawndale
Gardena
SANTA ANA FREEWAY
Buena Park
TORRANCE
LAKEWOOD
Knott's Berry Farm
ANAHEIM
Redondo Beach
Carson
LONG BEACH AIRPORT
RIVERSIDE FREEWAY
Coyote Creek
TORRANCE AIRPORT
Disneyland
GARDEN GROVE
Orange
San Pedro
LONG BEACH
Westminster
SANTA ANA
Marineland of the Pacific
Sunset Beach
Fountain Valley
Huntington Beach
SAN DIEGO FREEWAY
Santa Ana River

Oxford University Press

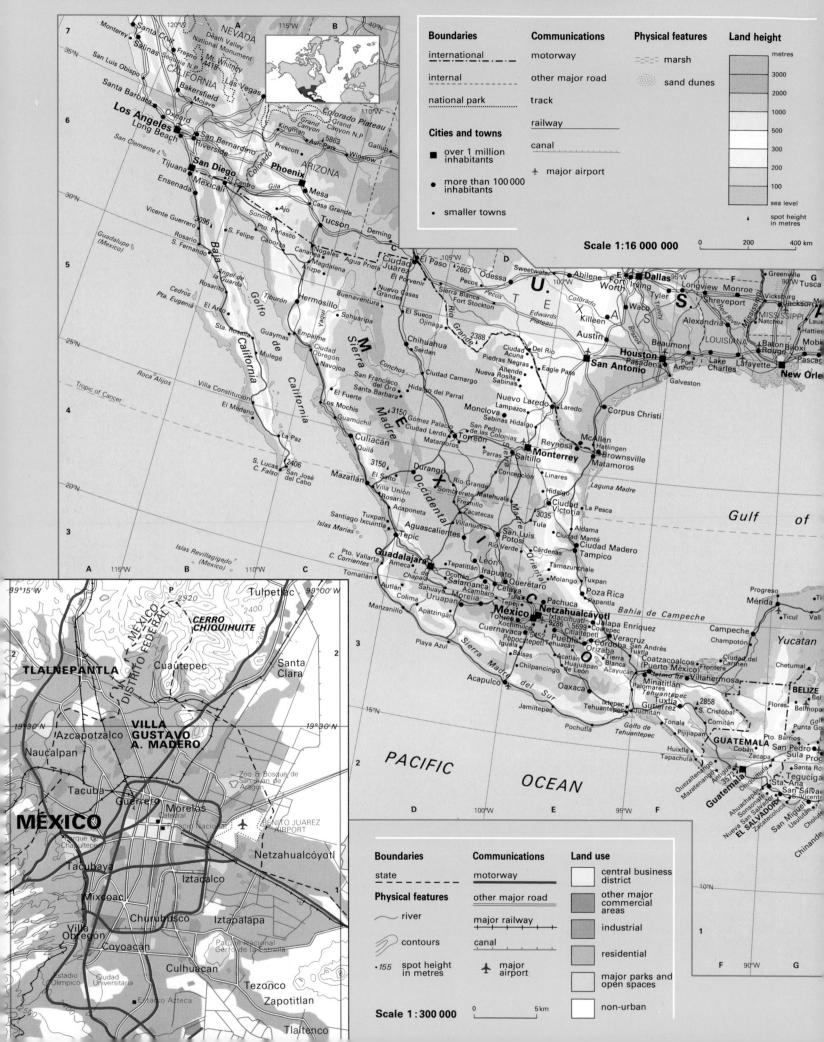

Jamaica

Montego Bay · Falmouth · St. Ann's Bay
Lucea · Brown's Town · Galina Point
Grange Hill · Cambridge · Port Maria
South Negril · Christiana · Ocho Rios · Annotto Bay
Point · Savanna la Mar · Frankfield · Ewarton · Highgate · Buff Bay
Black River · Mandeville · Chapelton · Linstead · Bog Walk · The Blue Mts. · Port Antonio
Santa Cruz · Porus · 2256
May Pen · Spanish Town · Kingston · Bath
Great Pedro Bluff · Old Harbour · Port Royal · Morant Point
Old Harbour Bay · Port Morant
Portland Point · Morant Bay

Scale 1:3 000 000   0   25   50 km

NORTH   ATLANTIC   OCEAN

Tropic of Cancer

THE BAHAMAS
New Providence · Nassau · Eleuthera
Key West · Andros · Cat I. · San Salvador
Straits of Florida · Great Exuma · Long Island
Crooked I. · Mayaguana

West Indies

La Habana (Havana) · Matanzas · Sagua la Grande
Güines · Santa Clara · Morón
Pinar del Río · Cienfuegos · Ciego de Ávila · Nuevitas
La Fé · Trinidad · Camagüey · Holguín
Isla de la Juventud · Bayamo · Guantánamo · Port-de-Paix · Santiago · San Francisco · DOMINICAN · San Juan
2005 · Manzanillo · Santiago de Cuba · Cap Haïtien · 3175 · La Vega · REPUBLIC · Caguas · 1338
Grand Cayman (U.K.) · HAITI · San Pedro · ANTIGUA & BARBUDA
Jérémie · Port-au-Prince · Santo Domingo · La Romana · Ponce · Barbuda
Montego Bay · Les Cayes · Jacmel · 2680 · Baruhona · Mayagüez · PUERTO RICO (U.S.A.) · St. Croix · Codrington
JAMAICA · Hispaniola · ST. KITTS NEVIS · St. John's Antigua
Spanish Town · Kingston · Grande Terre
Guadeloupe (Fr.)
Montserrat (U.K.) · Basse Terre
DOMINICA · Roseau
1397 · Martinique (Fr.)
Fort-de-France
Castries
ST. LUCIA
336
St. Vincent · BARBADOS
Kingstown · Bridgetown
ST. VINCENT & THE GRENADINES
GRENADA
840 · St. George's

Caribbean   Sea

Lesser   Antilles

NICARAGUA
Managua · Laguna de Perlas
Masaya · Pta. del Mono
Granada
L. de Nicaragua
Bluefields

HONDURAS
La Ceiba · Laguna Caratasca · C. Gracias á Dios
Pto. Cabezas
Prinzapolca

Tobago
TRINIDAD & TOBAGO
Port of Spain
Trinidad
San Fernando

ARUBA · Curaçao (Neths.) · Bonaire (Neths.)
Punta Gallinas · Willemstad · Punto Fijo · Pto. Cumarebo · Isla Margarita · La Asunción
Riohacha · Coro · Churuguara · Porlamar · Guiria
Santa Marta · Ciénaga · Golfo de Venezuela · Pto. Cabello · Valencia · Maracay · CARACAS · Carúpano · Caripito
Barranquilla · Valledupar · San Felipe · Los Teques · Petare · Barcelona · Maturín
Cartagena · Sabanalarga · Lago de Maracaibo · Lagunillas · Barquisimeto · La Victoria · Juan de Los Morros · Zaraza · El Tigre · Tucupita
Ariona · Calamar · Maicao · Machiques de · Araure · San Carlos · Calabozo · Valle de la Pascua · Barrancas
Carmen · Maracaibo · Valera · Guanare · Ciudad Guayana · Port Kaituma
Sincelejo · San Carlos del Zulia · Mérida · Trujillo · Barinas · Apure · San Fernando de Apure · Ciudad Bolívar · El Callao
Montería · El Banco del · 5007 · Acarigua · Río Orinoco · Upata
COSTA RICA · Panamá · Colón · Darién · Cordillera · Guasdualito · R. Arauca · La Aurora
San José · Cartago · Golfo de Lorica · Ocaña · San Cristóbal · GUYANA
3432 · Limón · Panama · Balboa · Panamá · COLOMBIA · Cúcuta · VENEZUELA · New Amsterdam · Linden
C. Blanco · Penonomé · Golfo de · El Banco · Bolívar · Georgetown
Puntarenas · David · PANAMA · Panamá · Pamplona · Arauca · Puerto Carreño · Río Paragua · Corriverton
Pto. Armuelles · Santiago · Pen. de Azuero · Yarumal · Bucaramanga · Puerto Ayacucho · BRAZIL
I. de Coiba · Cisneros

nithal Equidistant Projection

Oxford University Press

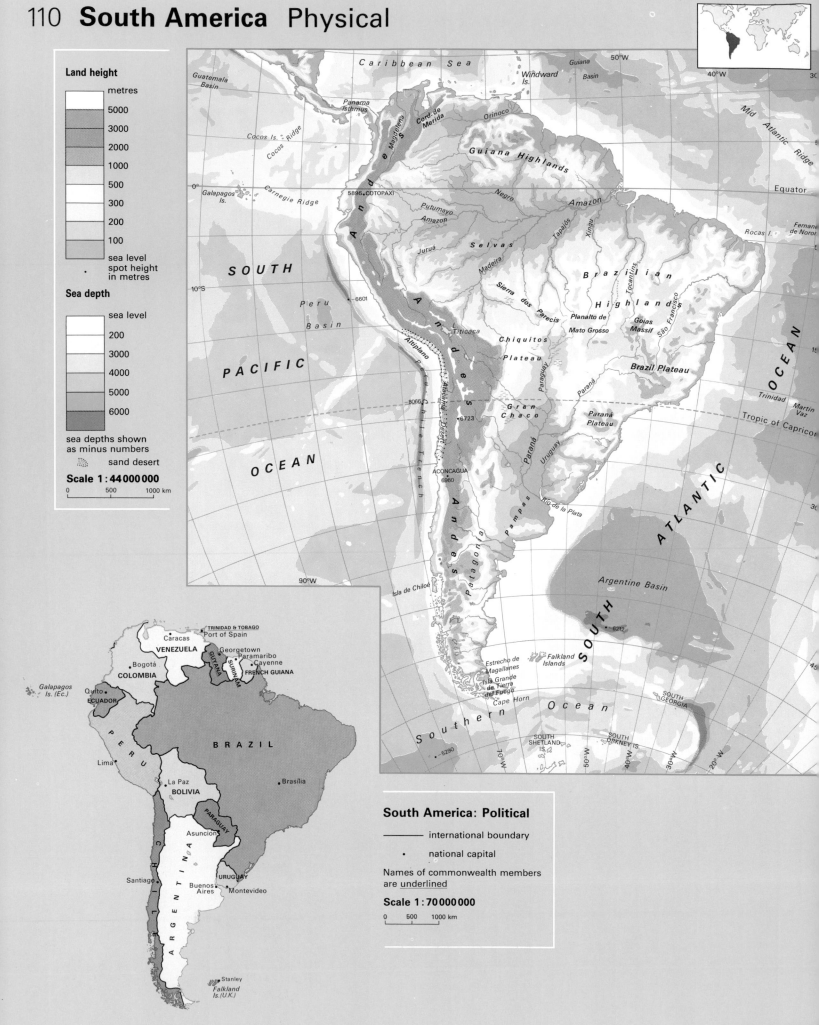

Land height

metres
- 5000
- 3000
- 2000
- 1000
- 500
- 300
- 200
- 100
- sea level
- · spot height in metres

Sea depth

- sea level
- 200
- 3000
- 4000
- 5000
- 6000

sea depths shown as minus numbers

sand desert

Scale 1 : 44 000 000

0   500   1000 km

South America: Political

——— international boundary

· national capital

Names of commonwealth members are underlined

Scale 1 : 70 000 000

0   500   1000 km

Oblique Mercator Project

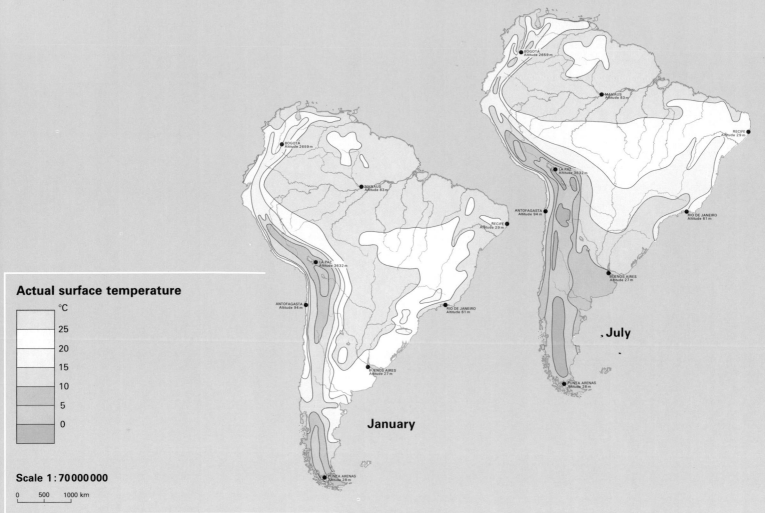

Actual surface temperature

°C
25
20
15
10
5
0

Scale 1 : 70 000 000

0   500   1000 km

January

July

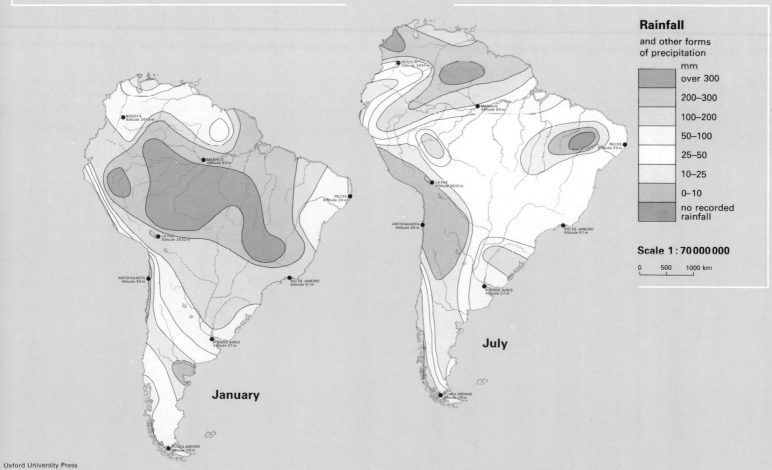

Rainfall

and other forms
of precipitation

mm

over 300
200–300
100–200
50–100
25–50
10–25
0–10
no recorded
rainfall

Scale 1 : 70 000 000

0   500   1000 km

January

July

Oxford University Press

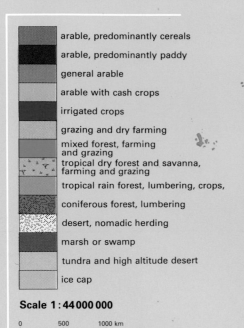

arable, predominantly cereals

arable, predominantly paddy

general arable

arable with cash crops

irrigated crops

grazing and dry farming

mixed forest, farming
and grazing

tropical dry forest and savanna,
farming and grazing

tropical rain forest, lumbering, crops,

coniferous forest, lumbering

desert, nomadic herding

marsh or swamp

tundra and high altitude desert

ice cap

Scale 1 : 44 000 000

0   500   1000 km

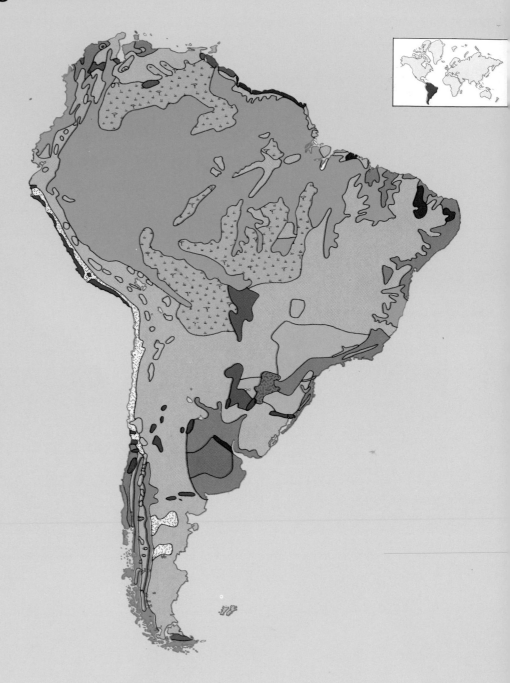

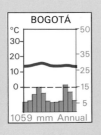

BOGOTÁ

1059 mm Annual

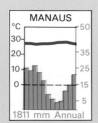

MANAUS

1811 mm Annual

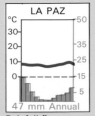

LA PAZ

47 mm Annual

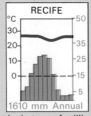

RECIFE

1610 mm Annual

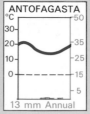

ANTOFAGASTA

13 mm Annual

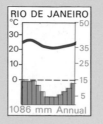

RIO DE JANEIRO

1086 mm Annual

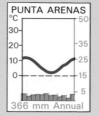

PUNTA ARENAS

366 mm Annual

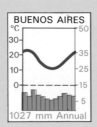

BUENOS AIRES

1027 mm Annual

Rainfall figures on graphs in tens of millimetres
except for annual totals

Oblique Mercator Projec

© Oxford University P

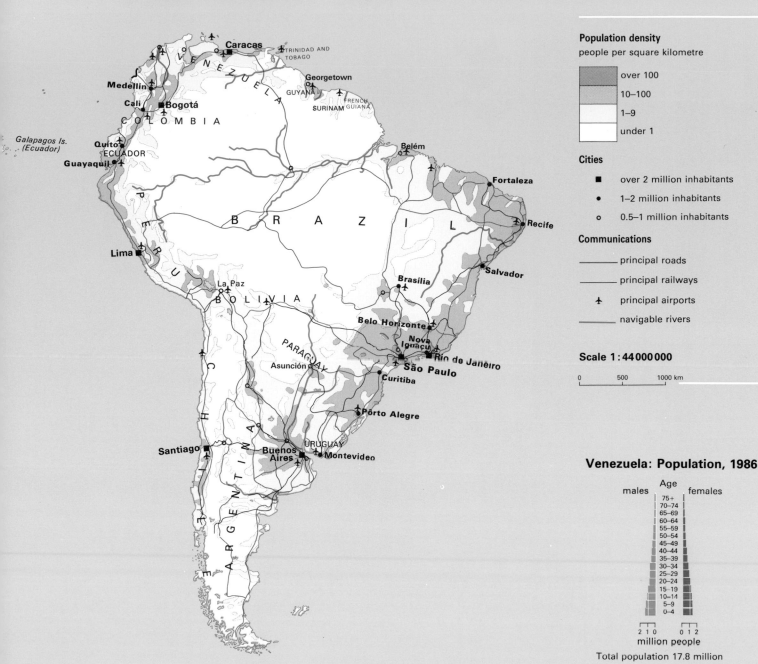

Population density

people per square kilometre

	over 100
	10–100
	1–9
	under 1

Cities

■ over 2 million inhabitants

● 1–2 million inhabitants

○ 0.5–1 million inhabitants

Communications

—— principal roads

—— principal railways

✈ principal airports

—— navigable rivers

Scale 1 : 44 000 000

0   500   1000 km

Venezuela: Population, 1986

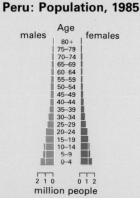

Age
males   females

75+
70–74
65–69
60–64
55–59
50–54
45–49
40–44
35–39
30–34
25–29
20–24
15–19
10–14
5–9
0–4

2 1 0   0 1 2
million people

Total population 17.8 million

Crude Birth Rate per thousand: 32

Crude Death Rate per thousand: 5

Argentina: Population, 1985

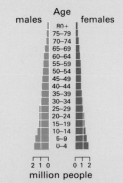

Age
males   females

80+
75–79
70–74
65–69
60–64
55–59
50–54
45–49
40–44
35–39
30–34
25–29
20–24
15–19
10–14
5–9
0–4

2 1 0   0 1 2
million people

Total population 30.6 million

Crude Birth Rate per thousand: 24

Crude Death Rate per thousand: 9

Brazil: Population, 1985

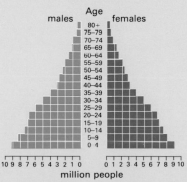

Age
males   females

80+
75–79
70–74
65–69
60–64
55–59
50–54
45–49
40–44
35–39
30–34
25–29
20–24
15–19
10–14
5–9
0–4

10 9 8 7 6 5 4 3 2 1 0   0 1 2 3 4 5 6 7 8 9 10
million people

Total population 135.6 million

Crude Birth Rate per thousand: 30

Crude Death Rate per thousand: 8

Peru: Population, 1985

Age
males   females

80+
75–79
70–74
65–69
60 64
55–59
50–54
45–49
40–44
35–39
30–34
25–29
20–24
15–19
10–14
5–9
0–4

2 1 0   0 1 2
million people

Total population 19.7 million

Crude Birth Rate per thousand: 33

Crude Death Rate per thousand: 10

Oblique Mercator Projection

Oxford University Press

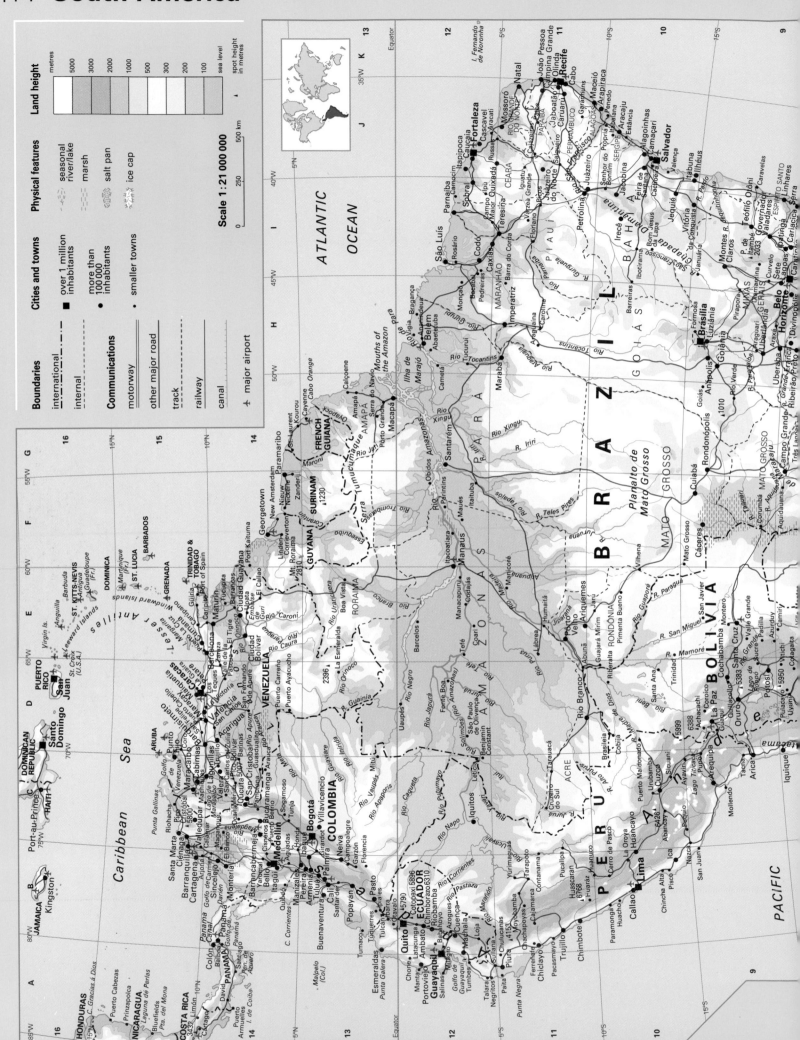

Land height

metres	
5000	
3000	
2000	
1000	
500	
300	
200	
100	
sea level	

spot height in metres

Physical features

seasonal river/lake
marsh
salt pan
ice cap

Cities and towns

■ over 1 million inhabitants
● more than 100 000 inhabitants
• smaller towns

Boundaries

international
internal

Communications

motorway
other major road
track
railway
canal
✈ major airport

Scale 1:21 000 000

0   250   500 km

ATLANTIC OCEAN

PACIFIC

Caribbean Sea

JAMAICA
HONDURAS
NICARAGUA
COSTA RICA
PANAMA
HAITI
DOMINICAN REPUBLIC
PUERTO RICO
COLOMBIA
VENEZUELA
GUYANA
SURINAM
FRENCH GUIANA
ECUADOR
PERU
BOLIVIA
BRAZIL

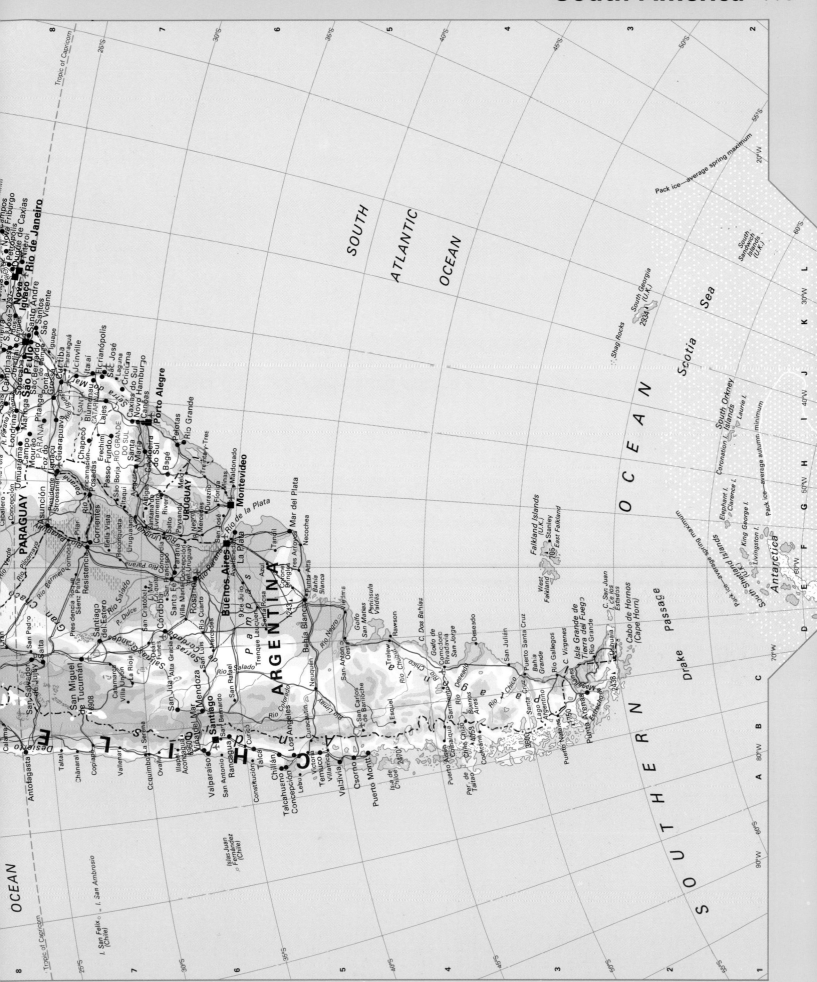

SOUTH ATLANTIC OCEAN

SOUTHERN OCEAN

Pack ice—average spring maximum

Scotia Sea

South Georgia
2934 (U.K.)

South Sandwich Islands (U.K.)

Shag Rocks

South Orkney Islands

Coronation I.
Laurie I.

Elephant I.
Clarence I.

South Shetland Islands
King George I.
Livingston I.

Pack ice—average autumn minimum

Pack ice—average spring maximum

Antarctica

Drake Passage

Falkland Islands (U.K.)

West Falkland
East Falkland
Stanley
105

BRASIL

Nova Friburgo
Petrópolis
Duque de Caxias
Niterói
Rio de Janeiro
Nova Iguaçu
São André
Santos
São Vicente

S. José
Campos
Campinas
São Paulo
Sorocaba
Santa Andre
São Bernardo
Iguape

Londrina
Maringá
Ponta Grossa
Paranaguá
Curitiba
Joinville
Criciúmalópolis
São José
Laguna
Criciúma
Tubarão

PARANÁ
Chapecó
Erechim
RIO GRANDE DO SUL
Novo Hamburgo
Canoas
Porto Alegre
Rio Grande

Presidente
Prudente
Umuarama
Mompo
Foz do Iguaçu
Paranapanema
Itaiaçu
Passo Fundo
Santa Maria
Bagé
Pelotas

PARAGUAY
Caballero
Concepción
Asunción
Pilar

Presidente
Stroessner
Encarnación
Posadas
São Borja
Uruguaiana
Alegrete

Bella Vista
Corrientes
Resistencia
Reconquista

Santana do
Livramento
Rivera
Rosario
Melo
Treinta y Tres

URUGUAY
Salto
Paysandú
Mercedes
Minas
Montevideo
Maldonado

Formosa
Santa Fe
Paraná
Rosario
Buenos Aires
La Plata

Río Verde
Rio Pilcomayo
Rio Bermejo
Pres. dencia Roque
Sáenz Peña

Santiago
del Estero
San Cristóbel
Córdoba

ARGENTINA

San Miguel
de Tucumán
6908
Catamarca
La Rioja
San Juan
Mendoza
Santiago
San Bernardo

Salta
San Salvador
de July
6860

San Luis
Río Cuarto
Villa María
Concepción
Azul
Tandil

Trenque Lauquen
Coronel
Pringles
Bahía Blanca
Punta Alta

Mar del Plata
Necochea

Pampa

Río Colorado
Neuquén
San Antonio
Oeste
Golfo
San Matías

Viedma
Carmen de Patagones

Río Negro

San Carlos
de Bariloche
Esquel

Golfo
San Jorge
Comodoro
Rivadavia

Trelew
Rawson
Península
Valdés

C. Dos Bahías

Deseado
Puerto
Deseado

San Julián
Puerto Santa Cruz
Bahía
Grande

Río Gallegos

C. Vírgenes
Isla Grande de
Tierra del Fuego
2438

Cabo de Hornos
(Cape Horn)

C. San Juan
de los
Estados

Ushuaia
Punta Arenas
Puerto Natales

Lago
Argentino
1750

Lago
Buenos
Aires
3600

CHILE
Antofagasta
Taltal
Chañaral
Copiapó
Vallenar
Huasco

I. San Félix (Chile)
I. San Ambrosio

Ccquimbo
La Serena
Ovalle
Illapel
Aconcagua
6960

Valparaíso
San Antonio
Los Andes
Santiago
Rancagua
San Bernardo

Curicó
Talca
Constitución
Chillán
Concepción
Talcahuano
Lebu
Los Angeles
Victoria
Temuco
Valdivia
Osorno
Puerto Montt

Isla de Chiloé

Puerto Aisén
Coihaique
2970

Islas Juan Fernández (Chile)

Tropic of Capricorn

Transverse Mercator Projection
© Oxford University Press

OCEAN

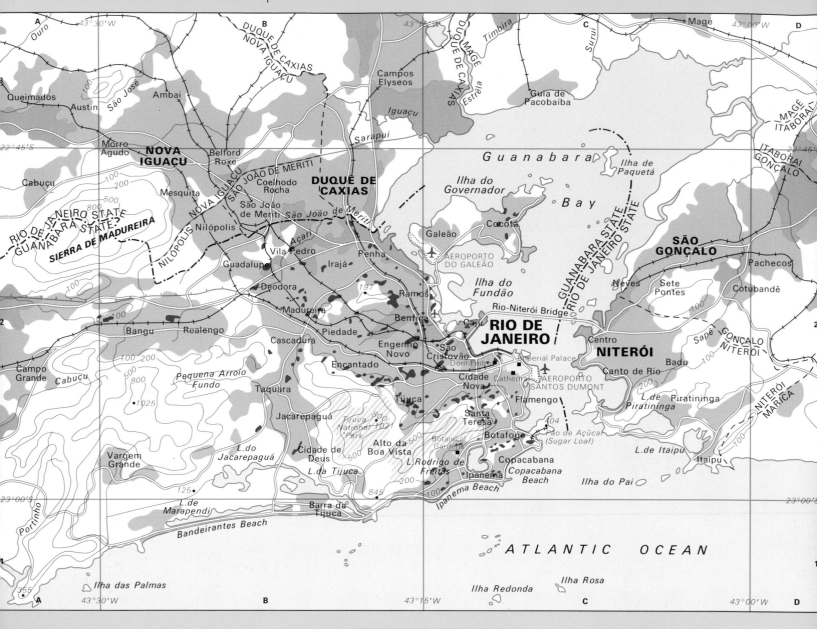

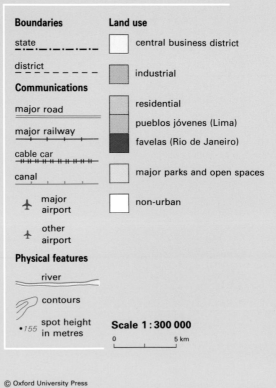

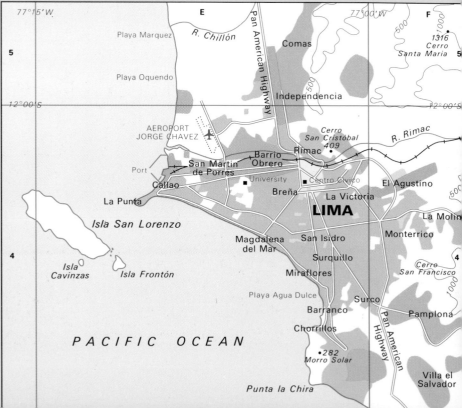

© Oxford University Press

Boundaries

international — ·· — ·· —

disputed ⌇⌇⌇⌇⌇⌇

Communications

✈ major airport (inset only)

Cities and towns

■ over 1 million inhabitants

● more than 100 000 inhabitants

• smaller towns

national capitals are underlined

Physical features

ice cap

Land height

metres
5000
3000
2000
1000
500
300
200
100
sea level
land below sea level

Sea depth

sea level
200
3000
4000
5000
6000

▲ spot height in metres

land below sea level and sea depths shown as minus numbers

Scale 1 : 63 000 000

0   500   1000   1500 km

Falkland Islands (U.K.)

West Falkland
Jason Is.
King George Bay
Queen Charlotte Bay
C. Meredith
George I.

Pebble I.
Mt. Adam 705
San Carlos
Goose Green
Bay of Harbours

C. Dolphin
Macbride Head
Berkeley Sound
Mt. Usborne 681
Port Darwin
Lively I.
Stanley

East Falkland

Scale 1 : 7 500 000

0   100 km

Modified Zenithal Equidistant Projection

© Oxford University Press

Boundaries

international ·–·–·–·–·

Communications

major road*

✈ major airport*

Physical features

🏔 ice cap

🪸 coral reef*

Cities and towns

■ over 1 million inhabitants

● more than 100 000 inhabitants

• smaller towns

national capitals are underlined

Land height

metres	
5000	
3000	
2000	
1000	
500	
300	
200	
100	
sea level	

Sea depth

metres below sea level	
200	
3000	
4000	
5000	
6000	

▲ spot height in metres

sea depths shown as minus numbers

* Island insets only

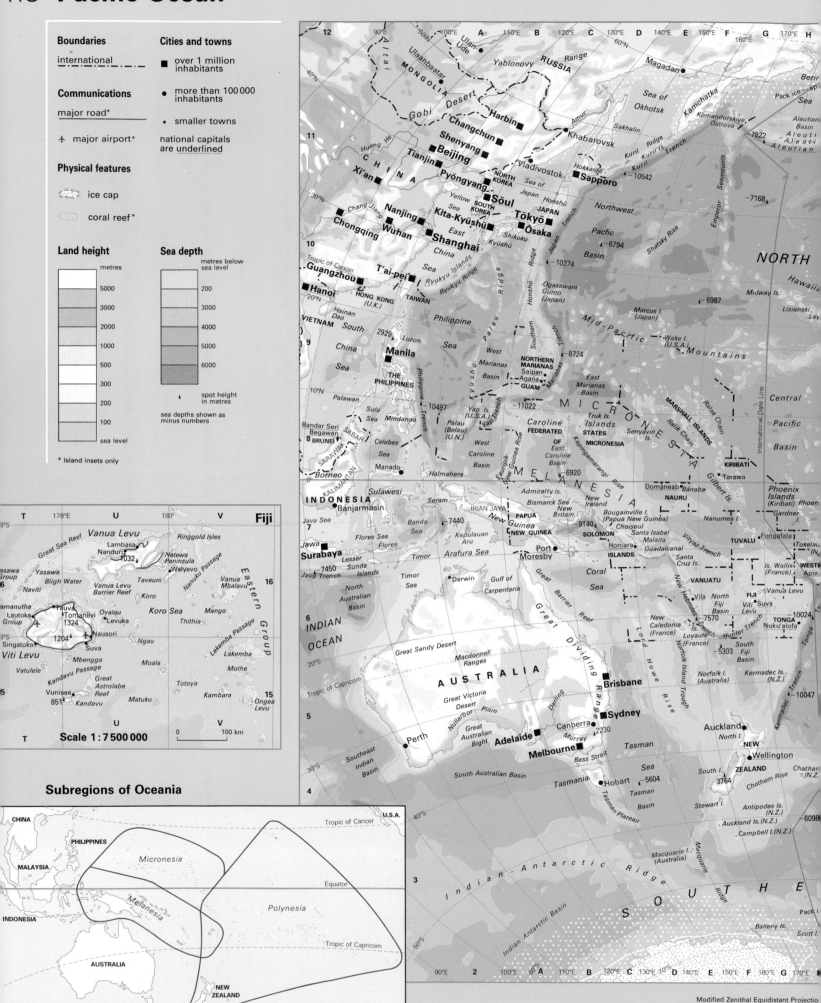

Fiji

Scale 1 : 7 500 000

0   100 km

Subregions of Oceania

Modified Zenithal Equidistant Projection

Scale 1 : 7 500 000

0   100 km

Pacific Ocean

J 160°W K 150°W L 140°W M 130°W N 120°W O 110°W P 100°W Q 90°W 80°W 70°W 13

Arctic Circle

ALASKA
(U.S.A.)
Mt. McKinley
6194
Anchorage   Mt. Logan
5951

CANADA   Canadian   Shield

Great
Slave Lake

Hudson
Bay

Churchill

Rocky

Queen
Charlotte Is.

Vancouver I.   Winnipeg   Great
Vancouver   Minneapolis   Lakes   Toronto   12
Seattle   St. Paul
Chicago   40°N   11

Gorda
Rise   Salt Lake City   Mt. Elbert
4399

UNITED   STATES

San Francisco   Colorado   Mississippi

Los Angeles   Houston   New Orleans   30°N   10

Mendocino Seascarp   Rio Grande

Murray Seascarp   THE   NORTH   60°W
Guadalupe   Miami   BAHAMAS   ATLANTIC
(Mexico)   MEXICO   La Habana   20°N

–6474   Gulf of Mexico   CUBA   OCEAN
Roca   Yucatan   Puerto Rico Trench
Alijos   México   Basin   HAITI   9220 DOMINICAN
–6108   Guadalajara   5452   Cayman Trench   JAMAICA   REPUBLIC   PUERTO RICO
Islands   Acapulco   BELIZE   Kingston   HAITI   (U.S.A.)   Leeward Is.
(U.S.A.)   Middle   GUATEMALA   Venezuelan   ST. LUCIA
Honolulu   –5106   America   Guatemala   –6662   HONDURAS   Caribbean   Basin   BARBADOS
Nihoa   Hawaii   Clarion   East   Trench   EL SALVADOR   Tegucigalpa   Sea   GRENADA   Guyana
Niihau   Ridge   NICARAGUA   Barranquilla   TRINIDAD   Basin
Fracture   Pacific   Managua   Caracas   & TOBAGO
–5298   Zone   Rise   San José   PANAMA   Maracaibo   8
Palmyra Atoll   Clipperton I.   Guatemala   COSTA   Panamá   Orinoco   VENEZUELA   Georgetown
(U.S.A.)   (France)   Basin   RICA   I. del Coco   Medellín   Llanos   Paramaribo   Cayenne
Tabuaaran I.   Clipperton   (Costa Rica)   COLOMBIA   GUYANA   SURINAM   FRENCH
(Kiribati)   Fracture   Zone   Cocos   Bogotá   GUIANA
Kiritimati I.   Ridge   Cali   5750
(Kiribati)   Equator   Islas Galápagos   Carnegie Ridge   Quito   0°

Malden I.   (Ecuador)   6310
Line   ECUADOR   Manaus   Amazonas
Caroline I.   BRAZIL
–6584   Galápagos Rise   PERU   6768
Marquesas   Peru   6601   7
Islands   Chile   Basin   Lima   10°S
(France)   –5469   Trench   6388   Mato Grosso
Tuamotu   La Paz
Archipelago   Titicaca
(France)   Nasca   BOLIVIA   Santa Cruz   Brasília   6
Society Is.   French   Tahiti   Ridge   –8066   6755   Chaco   PARAGUAY
(France)   Polynesia   –6144   Gambier Is.   Oano I.   Easter I.   Easter Island Fracture Zone   Gran   Asunción   Río de
Tubuai Is.   Ducie I.   Salay   I. San   Tropic of Capricorn   Janeiro
(France)   Pitcairn Islands   Gomez   Felix   ARGENTINA   São
Austral Ridge   (U.K.)   (Chile)   (Chile)   PARAGUAY   Paulo   20°S
SOUTH   PACIFIC   OCEAN   –1088   Challenger Fracture   Islas Juan   Valparaíso   Córdoba   Rosario   URUGUAY   Porto
Zone   Fernández   6960   Paraná   Alegre   5
(Chile)   Santiago   Buenos   Montevideo
Chile   Concepción   Chile Basin   Aires
South   Isla de Chiloé   Patagonia
East   Isla   ARGENTINA   30°S
Pacific   Wellington   Argentine
Basin   Basin

Elfanin   Fracture   Pacific   Antarctic   Ridge   Isla Grande de   Falkland Is.   Rio Grande
Zone   Pto.   Tierra del   (N.K.)
Santa Cruz   Fuego
spring maximum   OCEAN   C. de Hornos
N   Antarctic Circle   4
Pack ice — autumn minimum
J 170°W 160°W K 150°W L 140°W M 130°W N 120°W O 110°W P 100°W Q 90°W R 80°W S 70°W T 60°W U 50°W V 40°W W 30°W 20°W

© Oxford University Press   Scale 1 : 63 000 000   0   500   1000   1500 km

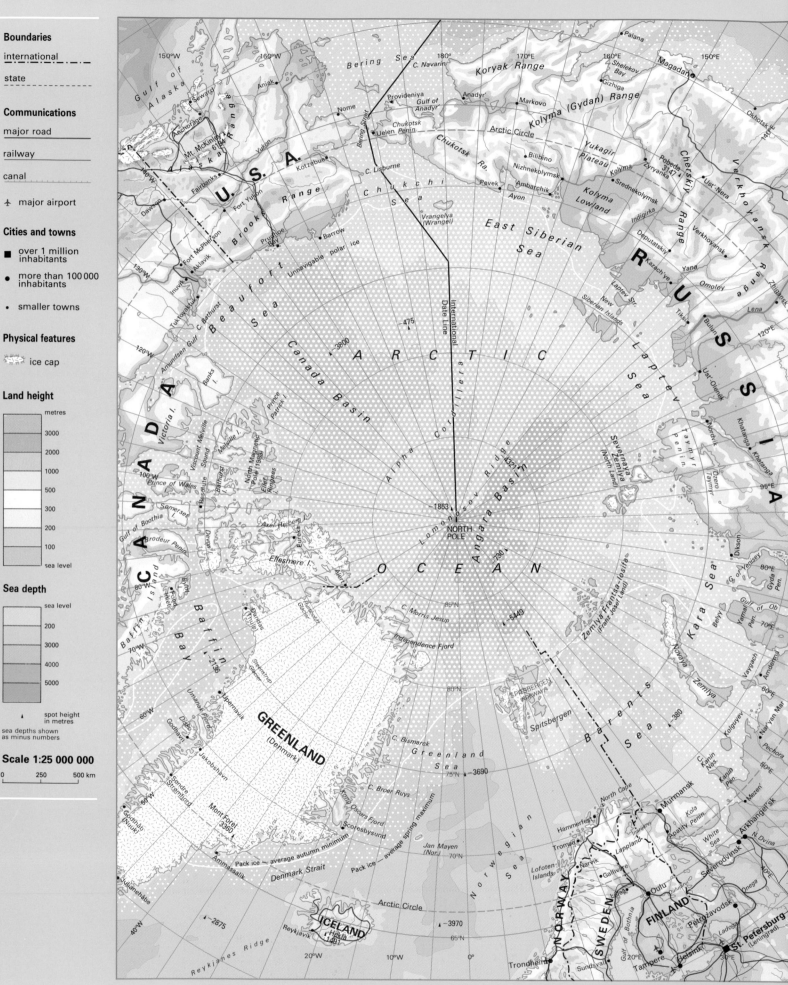

Boundaries

international

state

Communications

major road

railway

canal

✈ major airport

Cities and towns

■ over 1 million inhabitants

● more than 100 000 inhabitants

• smaller towns

Physical features

ice cap

Land height

| metres |
| 3000 |
| 2000 |
| 1000 |
| 500 |
| 300 |
| 200 |
| 100 |
| sea level |

Sea depth

| sea level |
| 200 |
| 3000 |
| 4000 |
| 5000 |

▲ spot height in metres

sea depths shown as minus numbers

Scale 1:25 000 000

0   250   500 km

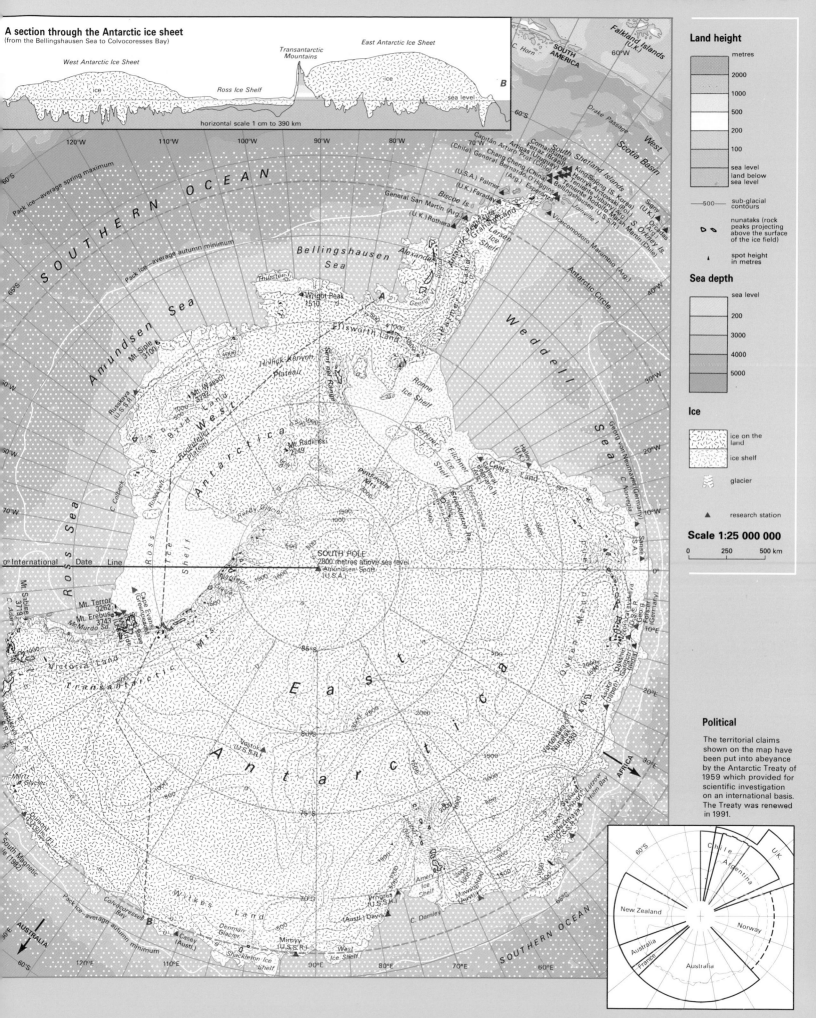

A section through the Antarctic ice sheet
(from the Bellingshausen Sea to Colvocoresses Bay)

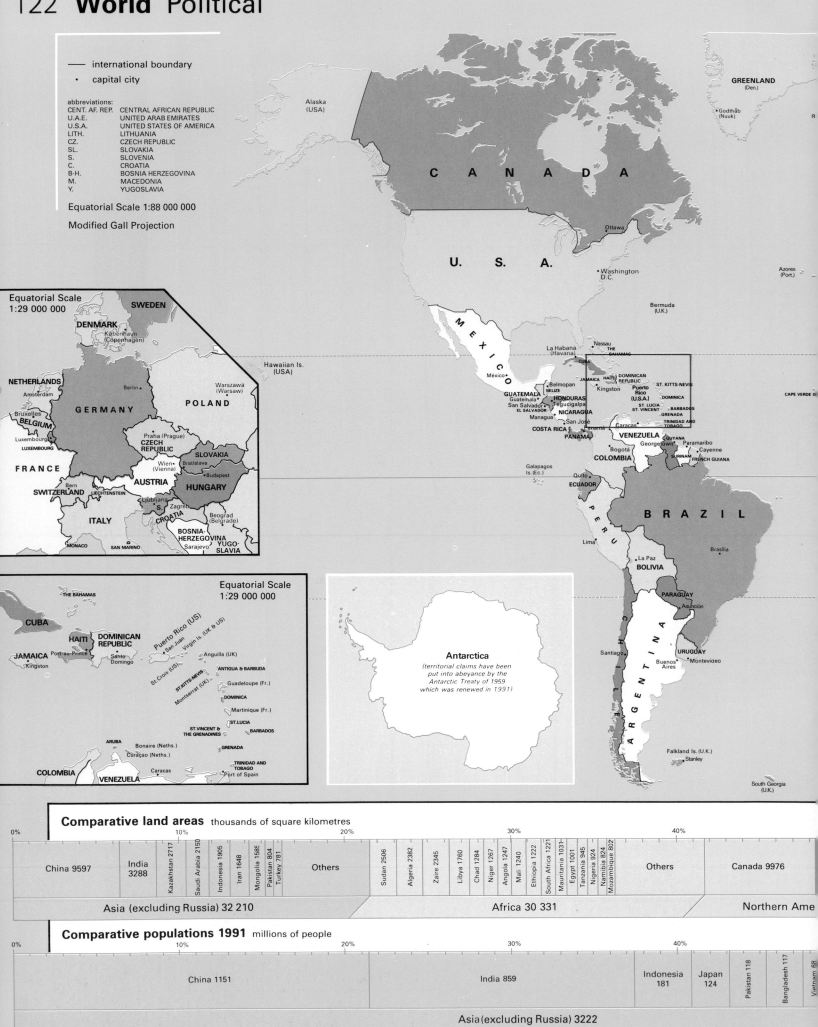

—— international boundary
• capital city

abbreviations:
CENT. AF. REP.   CENTRAL AFRICAN REPUBLIC
U.A.E.   UNITED ARAB EMIRATES
U.S.A.   UNITED STATES OF AMERICA
LITH.   LITHUANIA
CZ.   CZECH REPUBLIC
SL.   SLOVAKIA
S.   SLOVENIA
C.   CROATIA
B-H.   BOSNIA HERZEGOVINA
M.   MACEDONIA
Y.   YUGOSLAVIA

Equatorial Scale 1:88 000 000

Modified Gall Projection

Equatorial Scale
1:29 000 000

Equatorial Scale
1:29 000 000

Antarctica
(territorial claims have been
put into abeyance by the
Antarctic Treaty of 1959
which was renewed in 1991)

Comparative land areas thousands of square kilometres

China 9597 | India 3288 | Kazakhstan 2717 | Saudi Arabia 2150 | Indonesia 1905 | Iran 1648 | Mongolia 1585 | Pakistan 804 | Turkey 781 | Others | Sudan 2506 | Algeria 2382 | Zaire 2345 | Libya 1760 | Chad 1284 | Niger 1267 | Angola 1247 | Mali 1240 | Ethiopia 1222 | South Africa 1221 | Mauritania 1031 | Egypt 1001 | Tanzania 945 | Nigeria 924 | Namibia 824 | Mozambique 802 | Others | Canada 9976

Asia (excluding Russia) 32 210 | Africa 30 331 | Northern Ame

Comparative populations 1991 millions of people

China 1151 | India 859 | Indonesia 181 | Japan 124 | Pakistan 118 | Bangladesh 117 | Vietnam 68

Asia (excluding Russia) 3222

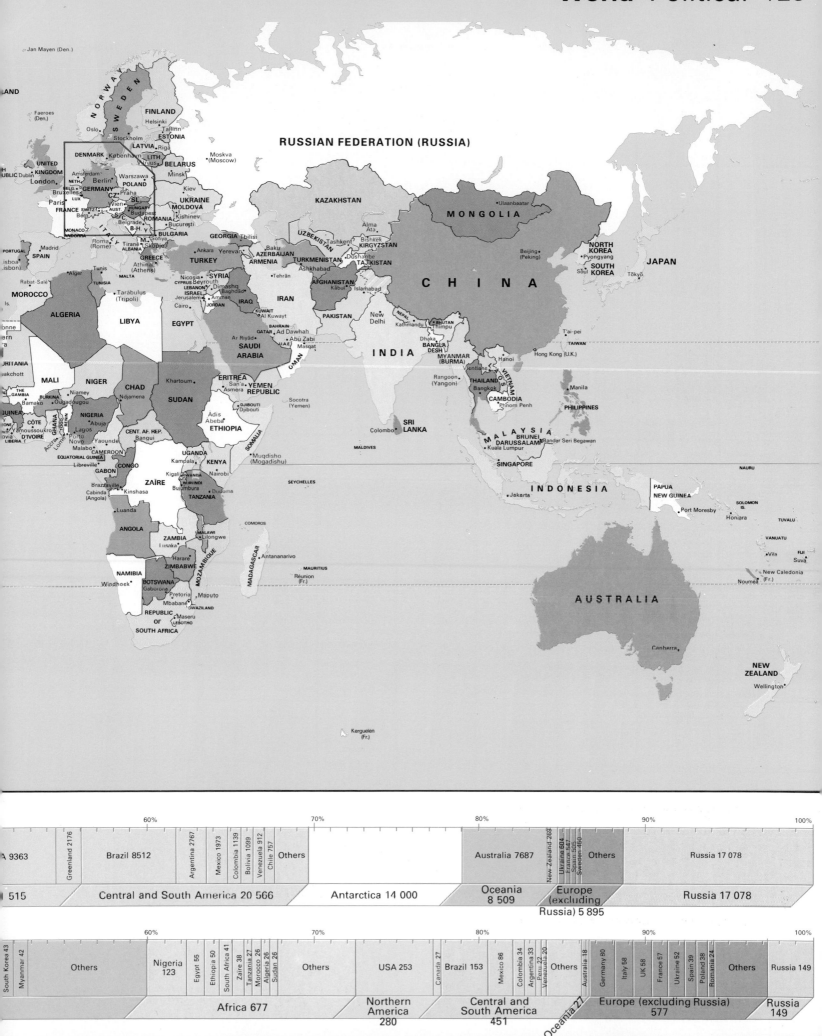

Land height and sea depth

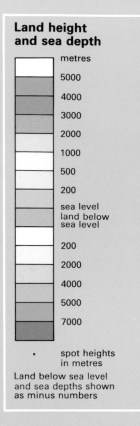

metres
- 5000
- 4000
- 3000
- 2000
- 1000
- 500
- 200

sea level
land below sea level

- 200
- 2000
- 4000
- 5000
- 7000

• spot heights in metres

Land below sea level and sea depths shown as minus numbers

Equatorial Scale 1:88 000 000

Modified Gall Projection

Plate tectonics

The present positions of the major tectonic plates are shown with the white areas representing the smaller plates

Plate boundaries

— lines of shallow focus earthquakes

═ sea ridges which are actively spreading

➤ direction of sea-floor spreading

— major fracture zones

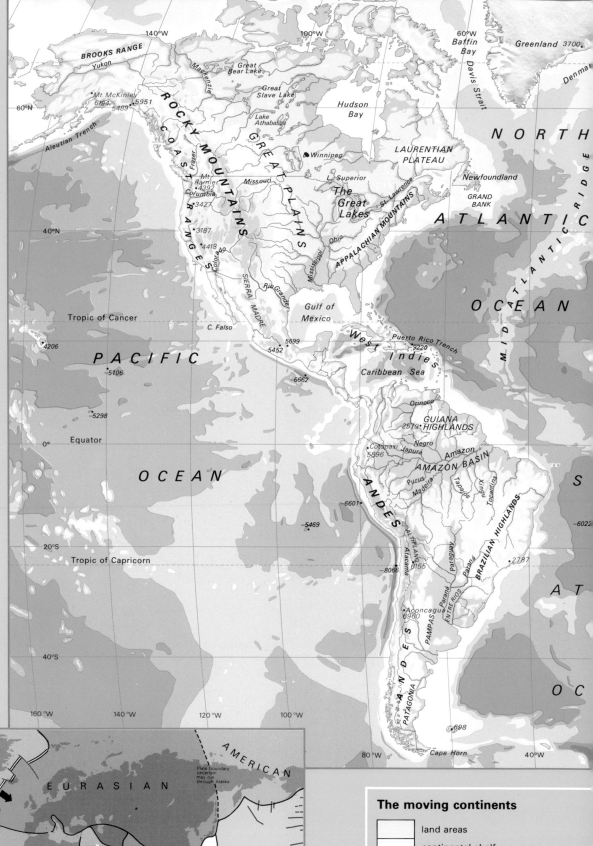

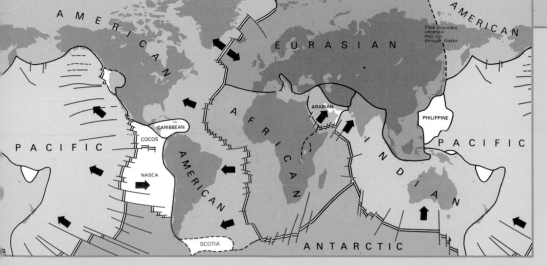

The moving continents

- land areas
- continental shelf
- sea areas
- orogenic belts

········· uncertain coastline

·········· uncertain continental shelf edge

Lines of latitude and longitude indicate position on the globe.

The graticules show how earlier positions of the continents compare with the present

Gall Projection

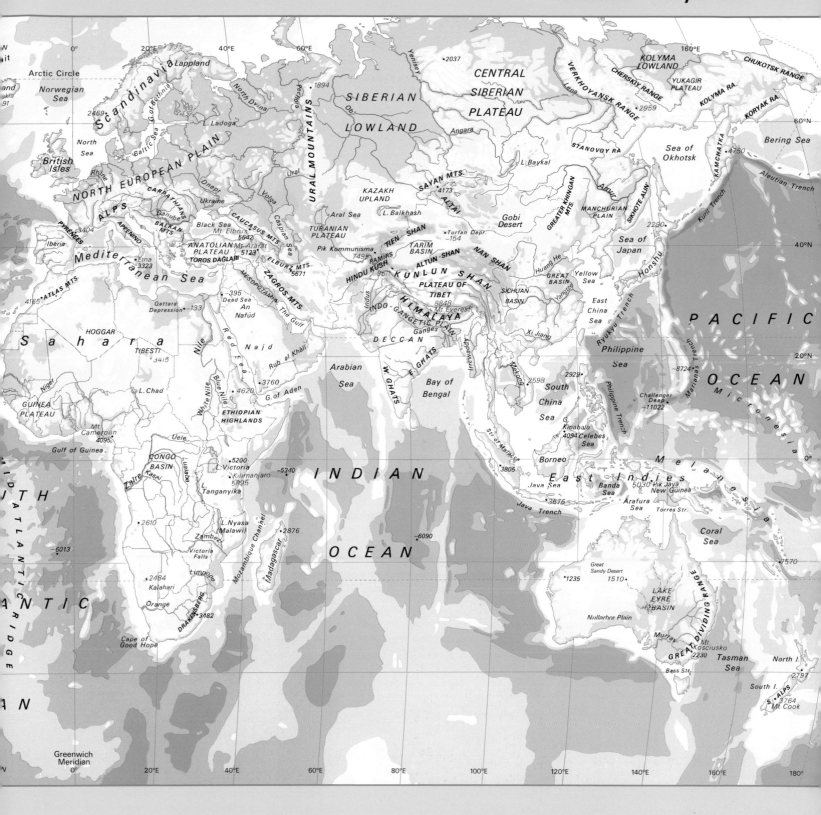

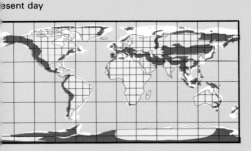

Present day

100 million years ago

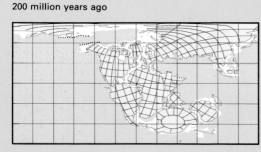

200 million years ago

Oxford University Press

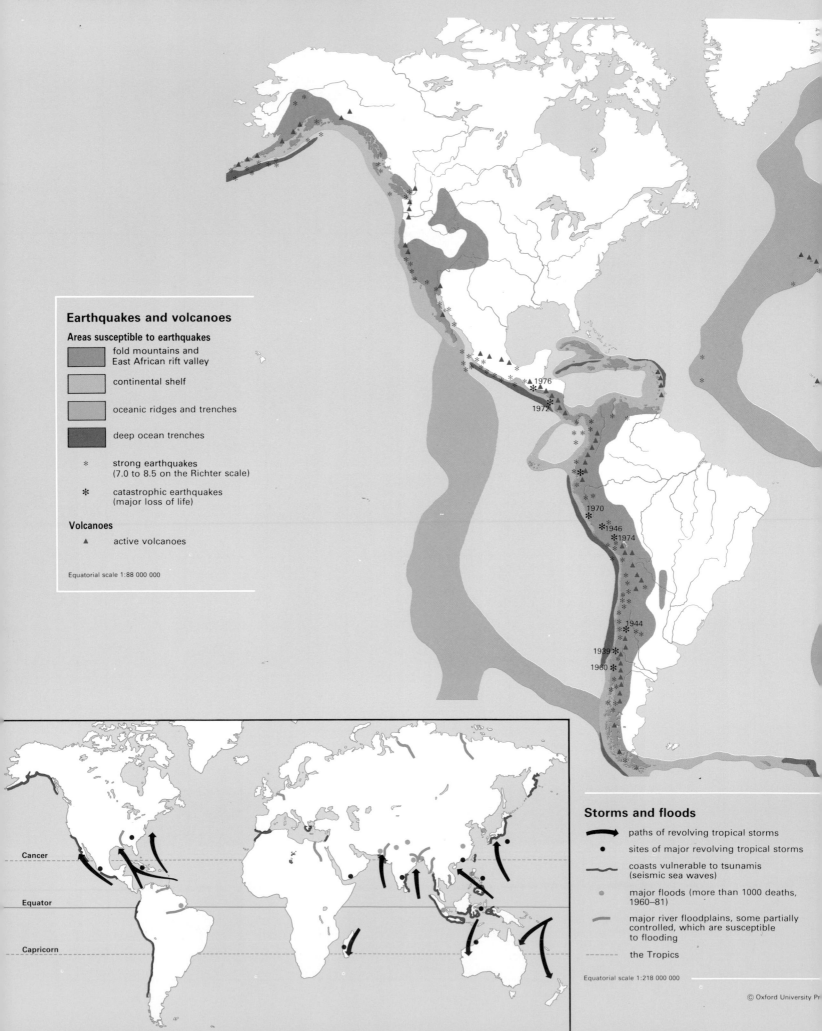

Earthquakes and volcanoes

Areas susceptible to earthquakes

fold mountains and
East African rift valley

continental shelf

oceanic ridges and trenches

deep ocean trenches

* strong earthquakes
(7.0 to 8.5 on the Richter scale)

* catastrophic earthquakes
(major loss of life)

Volcanoes

▲ active volcanoes

Equatorial scale 1:88 000 000

1976
1972
1970
1946
1974
1944
1939
1960

Storms and floods

paths of revolving tropical storms

• sites of major revolving tropical storms

coasts vulnerable to tsunamis
(seismic sea waves)

• major floods (more than 1000 deaths,
1960–81)

major river floodplains, some partially
controlled, which are susceptible
to flooding

the Tropics

Equatorial scale 1:218 000 000

Cancer

Equator

Capricorn

© Oxford University Pr

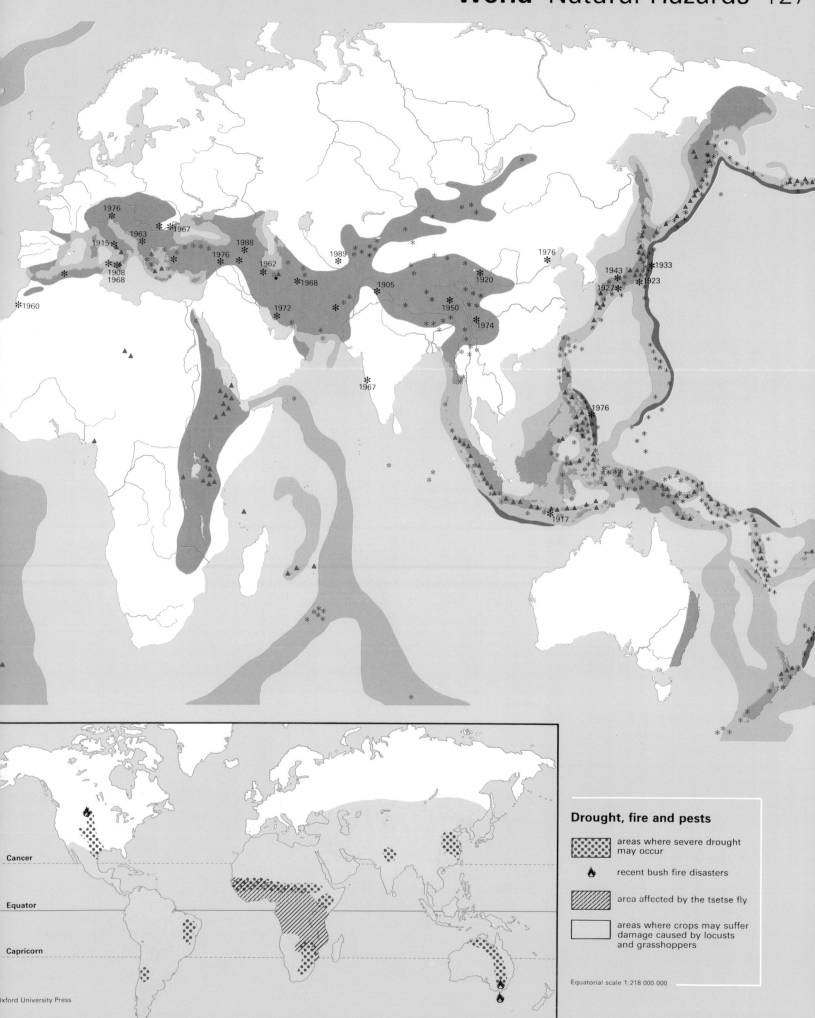

1976
1963 1967
1915 1988
1908 1976 1989 1976
1968 1962 1943 1933
1960 1968 1927 1923
1972 1905 1920
1950
1974
1967
1976
1917

Drought, fire and pests

areas where severe drought
may occur

recent bush fire disasters

area affected by the tsetse fly

areas where crops may suffer
damage caused by locusts
and grasshoppers

Cancer

Equator

Capricorn

Equatorial scale 1:218 000 000

Oxford University Press

Rainfall
and other forms of precipitation

	mm
	over 400
	250–400
	150–250
	50–150
	25–50
	under 25

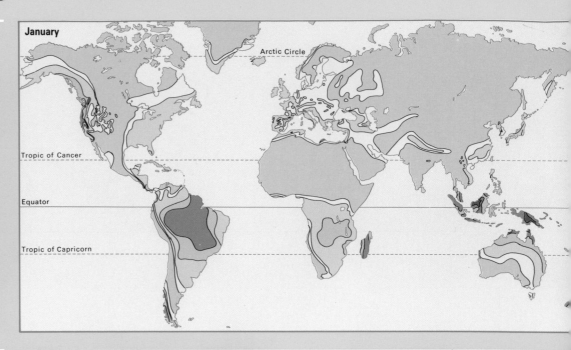

January

Temperature, ocean currents

actual temperature °C

	32
	24
	16
	8
	0
	−8
	−16
	−24

Ocean currents

cold

warm

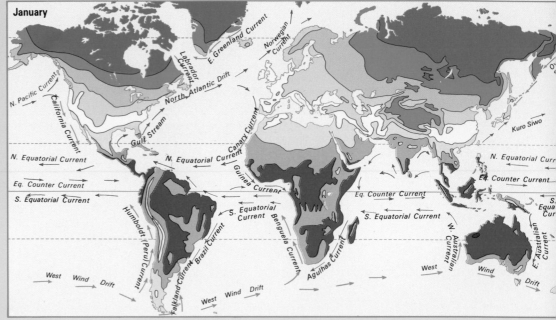

January

Pressure and winds

Pressure reduced to sea level

1035 millibars
1030
1025
1020
1015
1010
1005
1000
 995

H   high pressure cell

L   low pressure cell

Prevailing winds
Arrows fly with the wind:
the heavier the arrow, the
more regular ('constant')
the direction of the wind

January

Equatorial Scale 1:218 000 000

Modified Gall Projection

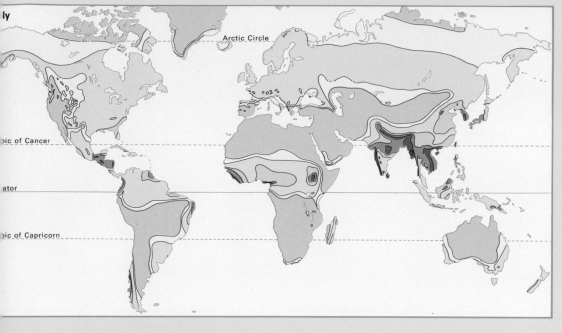

Arctic Circle

pic of Cancer

ator

pic of Capricorn

Tropical revolving storms

temperature 27°C and
over at mean sea level

Northern hemisphere
Maximum frequency August - September

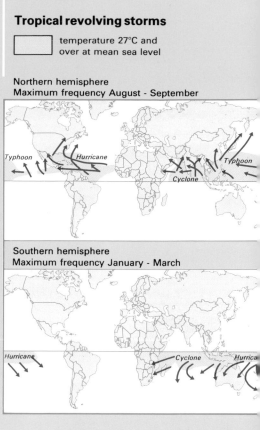

Typhoon — Hurricane — Typhoon
Cyclone

Southern hemisphere
Maximum frequency January - March

Hurricane — Cyclone — Hurrica

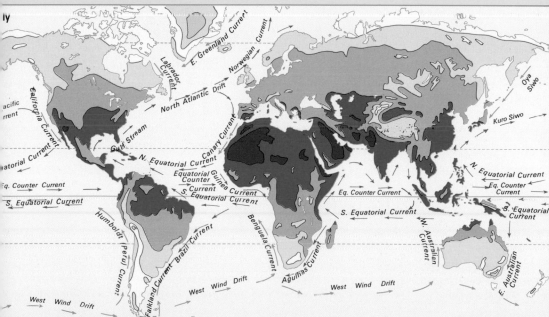

E. Greenland Current
Labrador Current
Norwegian Current
acific rrent — California Current
North Atlantic Drift
Oya Siwo
Kuro Siwo
Gulf Stream
Canary Current
atorial Current — N. Equatorial Current
Equatorial Guinea Current
Equatorial Counter Current
N. Equatorial Current
q. Counter Current
Eq. Counter Current
S. Equatorial Current — S. Equatorial Current
Eq. Counter Current
Eq. Counter Current
Humboldt (Peru) Current
Benguela Current
S. Equatorial Current
Falkland Current
Brazil Current
Agulhas Current
S. Equatorial Current
W. Australian Current
West Wind Drift
West Wind Drift
E. Australian Current
West Wind Drift

Air masses

--- fronts

Arctic

Polar

Temperate

Equatorial

January

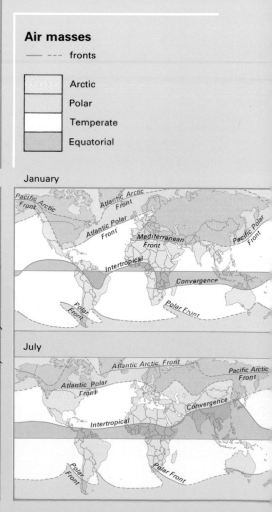

Pacific Arctic Front — Atlantic Arctic Front
Atlantic Polar Front
Mediterranean Front
Pacific Polar Front
Intertropical
Convergence
Polar Front
Polar Front

July

Atlantic Arctic Front — Pacific Arctic Front
Atlantic Polar Front
Convergence
Intertropical
Polar Front

1010
1015
L
L
1015
Westerlies
1015
erlies
1020
Westerlies
1005
1025
L
H
1020
1015
Westerlies
N.E. Trades
1000
L
1015
N.E. Trades
S.W. Monsoon
S.E. Monsoon
N.E. Trades
.E. Trades
S.E. Trades
S.W. Monsoon
1015
S.E. Trades
H
1010
S.E. Monsoon
1020
S.E. Trades
H
(Roaring Forties)
H
1015
1010
Westerlies
Polar
Westerlies
1005
05
00

© Oxford University Press

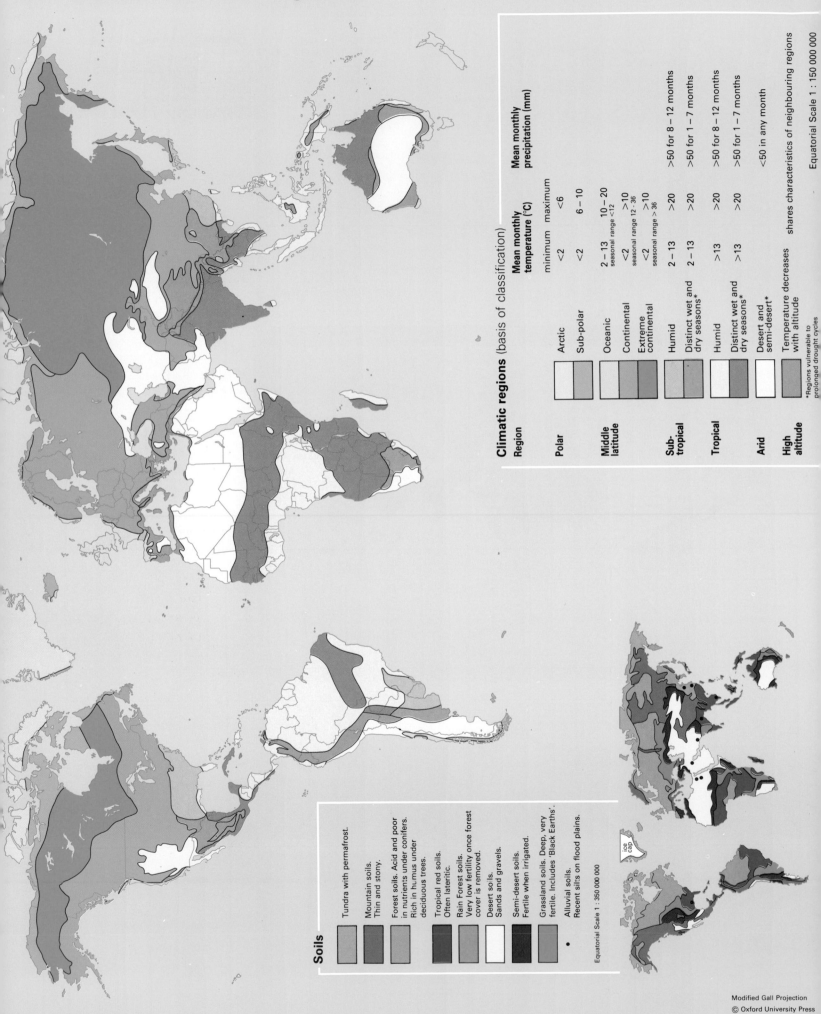

Climatic regions (basis of classification)

Region		Mean monthly temperature (°C)		Mean monthly precipitation (mm)
		minimum	maximum	
Polar	Arctic	<2	<6	
	Sub-polar	<2	6 – 10	
Middle latitude	Oceanic	2 – 13	10 – 20	
		seasonal range <12		
	Continental	<2	>10	
		seasonal range 12 - 36		
	Extreme continental	<2	>10	
		seasonal range > 36		
Sub-tropical	Humid	2 – 13	>20	>50 for 8 – 12 months
	Distinct wet and dry seasons*	2 – 13	>20	>50 for 1 – 7 months
Tropical	Humid	>13	>20	>50 for 8 – 12 months
	Distinct wet and dry seasons*	>13	>20	>50 for 1 – 7 months
Arid	Desert and semi-desert*			<50 in any month
High altitude	Temperature decreases with altitude			shares characteristics of neighbouring regions

*Regions vulnerable to prolonged drought cycles

Equatorial Scale 1 : 150 000 000

Ice cap

Soils

	Tundra with permafrost.
	Mountain soils. Thin and stony.
	Forest soils. Acid and poor in nutrients under conifers. Rich in humus under deciduous trees.
	Tropical red soils. Often lateritic.
	Rain Forest soils. Very low fertility once forest cover is removed.
	Desert soils. Sands and gravels.
	Semi-desert soils. Fertile when irrigated.
	Grassland soils. Deep, very fertile. Includes 'Black Earths'.
•	Alluvial soils. Recent silts on flood plains.

Equatorial Scale 1 : 350 000 000

Modified Gall Projection
© Oxford University Press

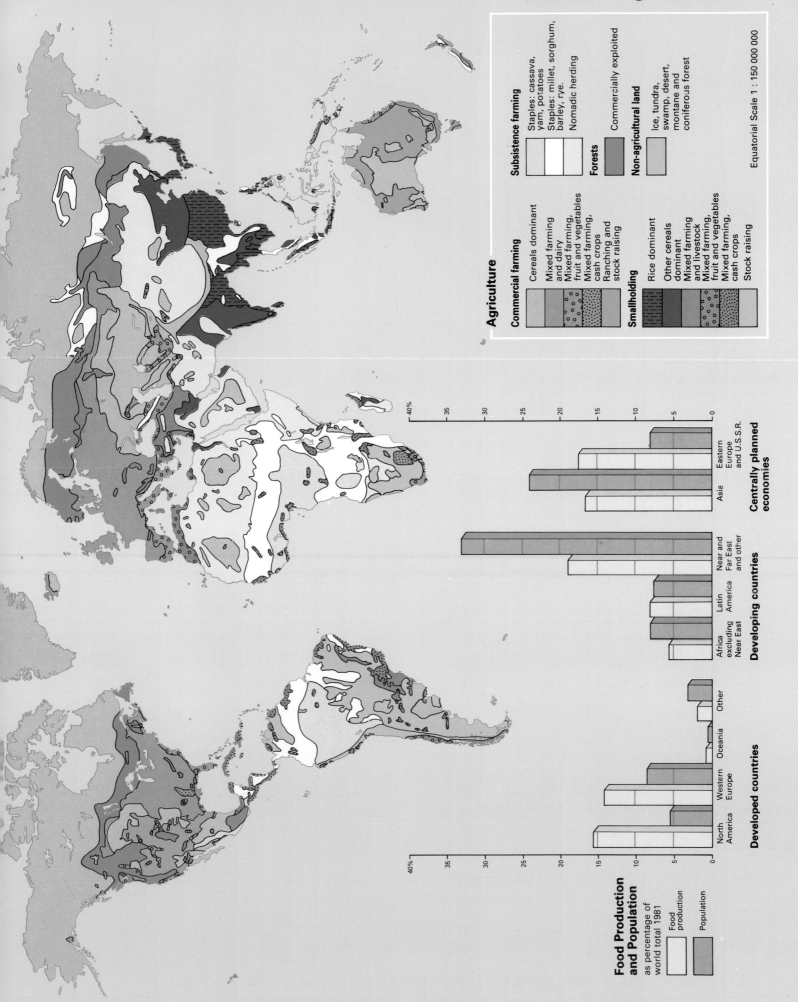

Agriculture

Commercial farming

Cereals dominant

Mixed farming and dairy

Mixed farming, fruit and vegetables

Mixed farming, cash crops

Ranching and stock raising

Smallholding

Rice dominant

Other cereals dominant

Mixed farming and livestock

Mixed farming, fruit and vegetables

Mixed farming, cash crops

Stock raising

Subsistence farming

Staples: cassava, yam, potatoes

Staples: millet, sorghum, barley, rye.

Nomadic herding

Forests

Commercially exploited

Non-agricultural land

Ice, tundra, swamp, desert, montane and coniferous forest

Equatorial Scale 1 : 150 000 000

Food Production and Population

as percentage of world total 1981

Food production

Population

Centrally planned economies

Eastern Europe and U.S.S.R.

Asia

Developing countries

Near and Far East and other

Latin America

Africa excluding Near East

Developed countries

North America

Western Europe

Oceania

Other

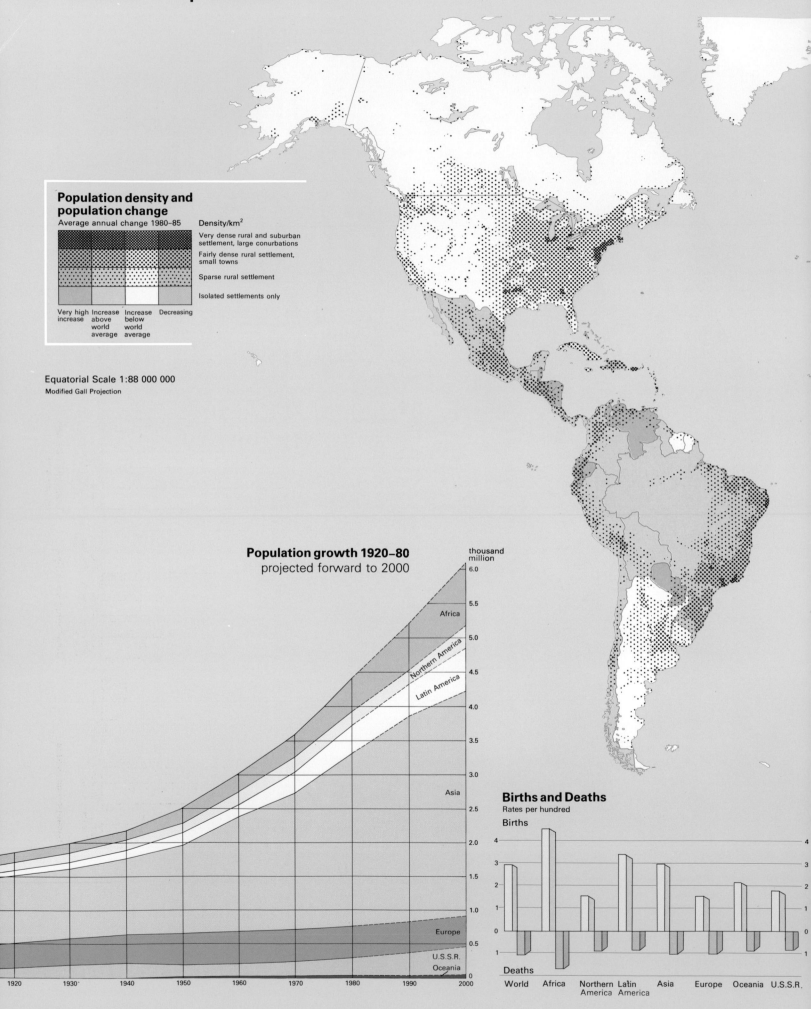

Population density and population change

Average annual change 1980–85

Density/km²

Very dense rural and suburban settlement, large conurbations

Fairly dense rural settlement, small towns

Sparse rural settlement

Isolated settlements only

| Very high increase | Increase above world average | Increase below world average | Decreasing |

Equatorial Scale 1:88 000 000

Modified Gall Projection

Population growth 1920–80
projected forward to 2000

thousand million

6.0
5.5
5.0
4.5
4.0
3.5
3.0
2.5
2.0
1.5
1.0
0.5
0

Africa

Northern America

Latin America

Asia

Europe

U.S.S.R.
Oceania

1920 1930 1940 1950 1960 1970 1980 1990 2000

Births and Deaths
Rates per hundred

Births

4
3
2
1
0

Deaths

1

World   Africa   Northern America   Latin America   Asia   Europe   Oceania   U.S.S.R.

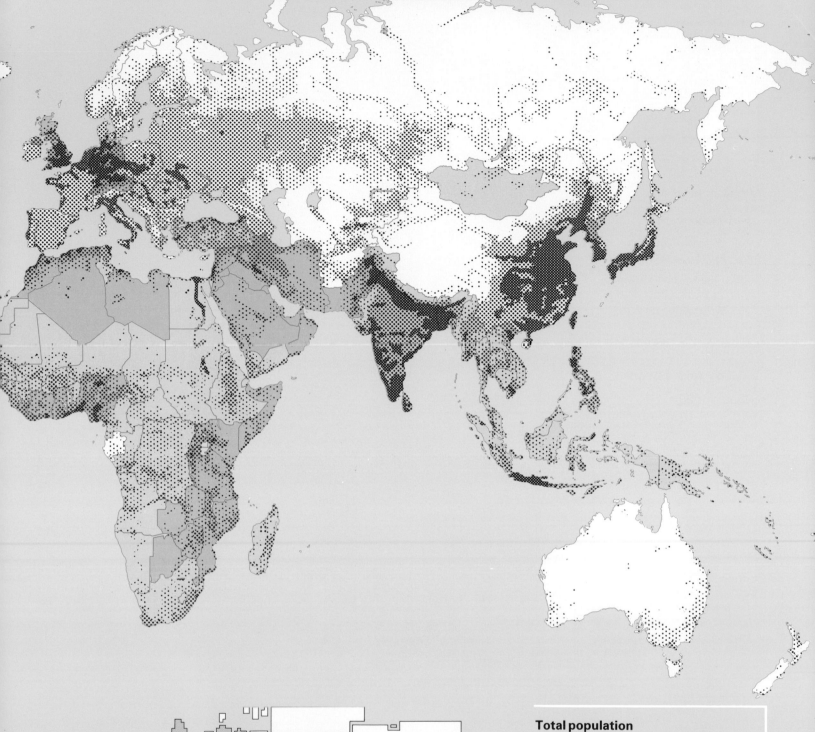

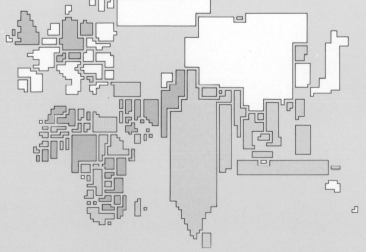

Total population

On this map the size of each country represents the number of people living there, rather than the area of land that the country occupies.

Only those countries with 1 million people living in them are shown. One small square represents 1 million people.

This is Guatemala where six million people live.

Population change

The colours on this map represent the same rates of population increase or decrease shown on the legend to the main map above.

Very high increase - 3 per cent and over

Increase above world average - 1.67 to 3 per cent

Increase below world average - less than 1.67 per cent

Decreasing

Oxford University Press

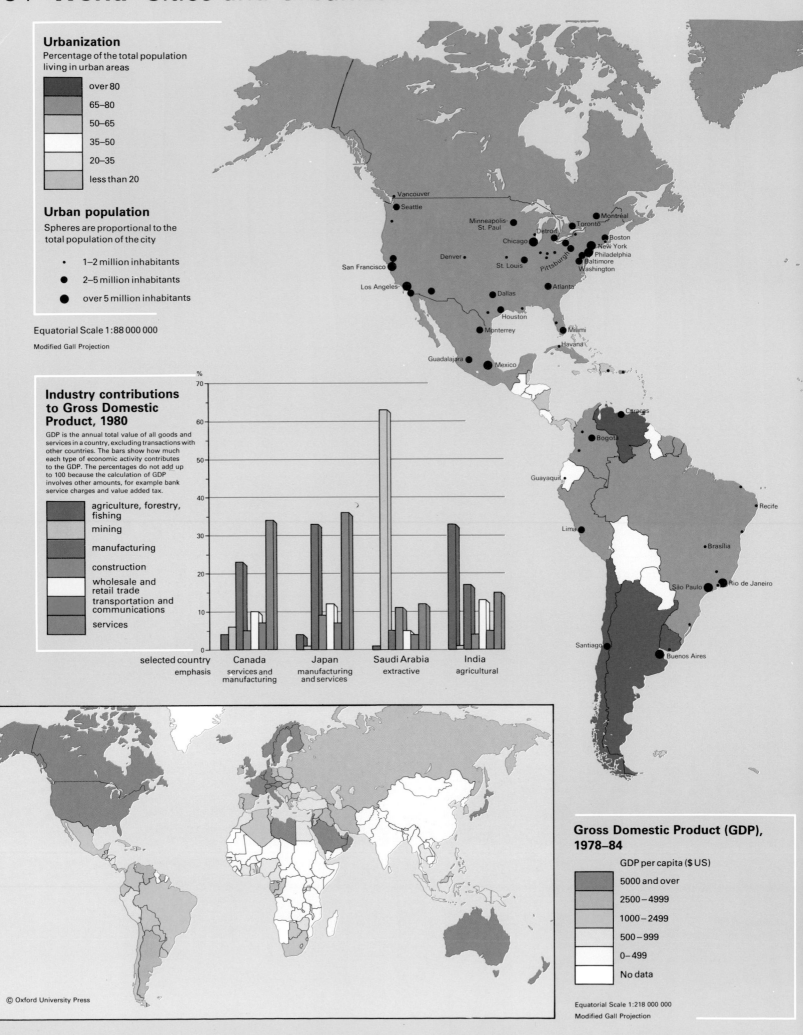

Urbanization

Percentage of the total population living in urban areas

- over 80
- 65–80
- 50–65
- 35–50
- 20–35
- less than 20

Urban population

Spheres are proportional to the total population of the city

- • 1–2 million inhabitants
- ● 2–5 million inhabitants
- ● over 5 million inhabitants

Equatorial Scale 1:88 000 000

Modified Gall Projection

Industry contributions to Gross Domestic Product, 1980

GDP is the annual total value of all goods and services in a country, excluding transactions with other countries. The bars show how much each type of economic activity contributes to the GDP. The percentages do not add up to 100 because the calculation of GDP involves other amounts, for example bank service charges and value added tax.

- agriculture, forestry, fishing
- mining
- manufacturing
- construction
- wholesale and retail trade
- transportation and communications
- services

| selected country emphasis | Canada services and manufacturing | Japan manufacturing and services | Saudi Arabia extractive | India agricultural |

Gross Domestic Product (GDP), 1978–84

GDP per capita ($ US)

- 5000 and over
- 2500–4999
- 1000–2499
- 500–999
- 0–499
- No data

Equatorial Scale 1:218 000 000

Modified Gall Projection

© Oxford University Press

Cities labelled on map: Vancouver, Seattle, Minneapolis-St. Paul, Toronto, Montreal, Detroit, Chicago, Boston, New York, Philadelphia, Baltimore, Washington, Denver, St. Louis, Pittsburgh, San Francisco, Los Angeles, Dallas, Atlanta, Houston, Monterrey, Miami, Havana, Guadalajara, Mexico, Caracas, Bogotá, Guayaquil, Lima, Recife, Brasília, São Paulo, Rio de Janeiro, Santiago, Buenos Aires

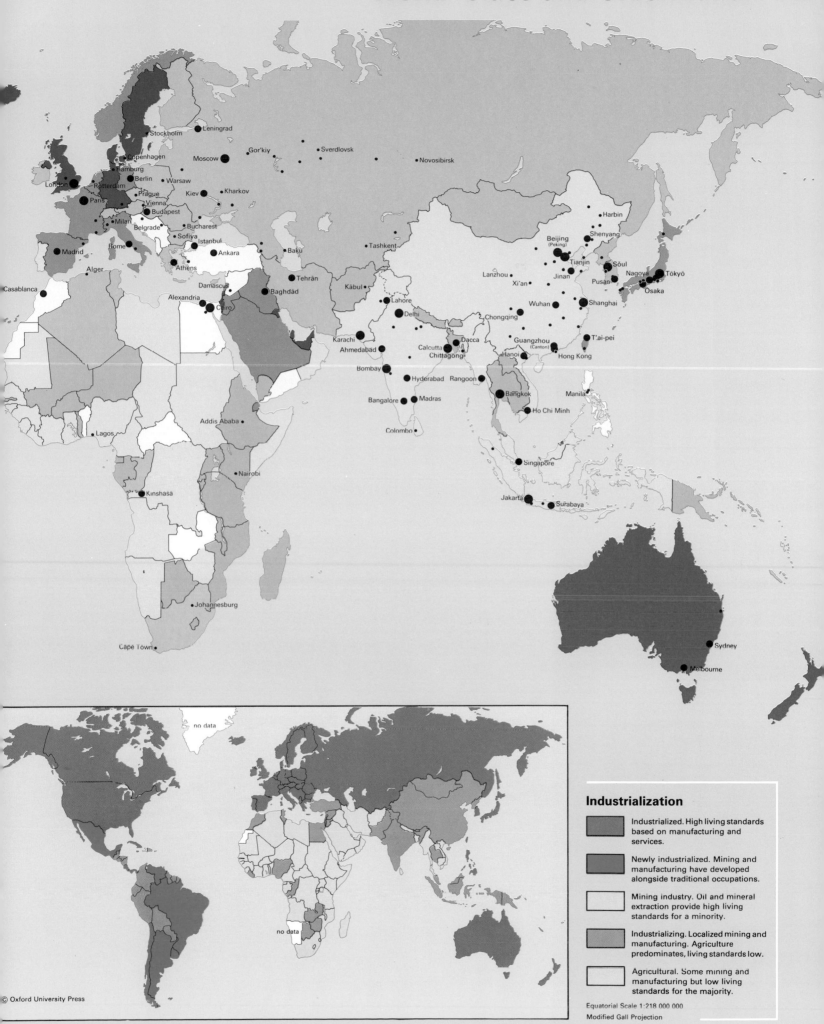

Stockholm · Leningrad
Copenhagen
Hamburg · Moscow · Sverdlovsk · Novosibirsk
Berlin · Warsaw · Gor'kiy
London · Rotterdam · Prague · Kiev · Kharkov
Paris · Vienna
Milan · Budapest · Harbin
Belgrade · Bucharest · Shenyang
Madrid · Rome · Sofiya · Istanbul · Beijing (Peking)
Alger · Athens · Ankara · Baku · Tianjin · Sôul
Casablanca · Tashkent · Lanzhou · Jinan · Nagoya · Tōkyō
Tehrān · Xi'an · Pusan · Osaka
Damascus · Baghdād · Kābul · Wuhan · Shanghai
Alexandria · Cairo · Lahore · Chongqing · T'ai-pei
Karachi · Delhi · Guangzhou (Canton)
Ahmedabad · Calcutta · Dacca · Hong Kong
Chittagong · Hanoi
Bombay · Hyderabad · Rangoon
Bangalore · Madras · Bangkok · Manila
Colombo · Ho Chi Minh
Addis Ababa
Lagos · Singapore
Nairobi
Kinshasa · Jakarta · Surabaya
Johannesburg · Sydney
Cape Town · Melbourne

no data

no data

© Oxford University Press

Industrialization

Industrialized. High living standards based on manufacturing and services.

Newly industrialized. Mining and manufacturing have developed alongside traditional occupations.

Mining industry. Oil and mineral extraction provide high living standards for a minority.

Industrializing. Localized mining and manufacturing. Agriculture predominates, living standards low.

Agricultural. Some mining and manufacturing but low living standards for the majority.

Equatorial Scale 1:218 000 000

Modified Gall Projection

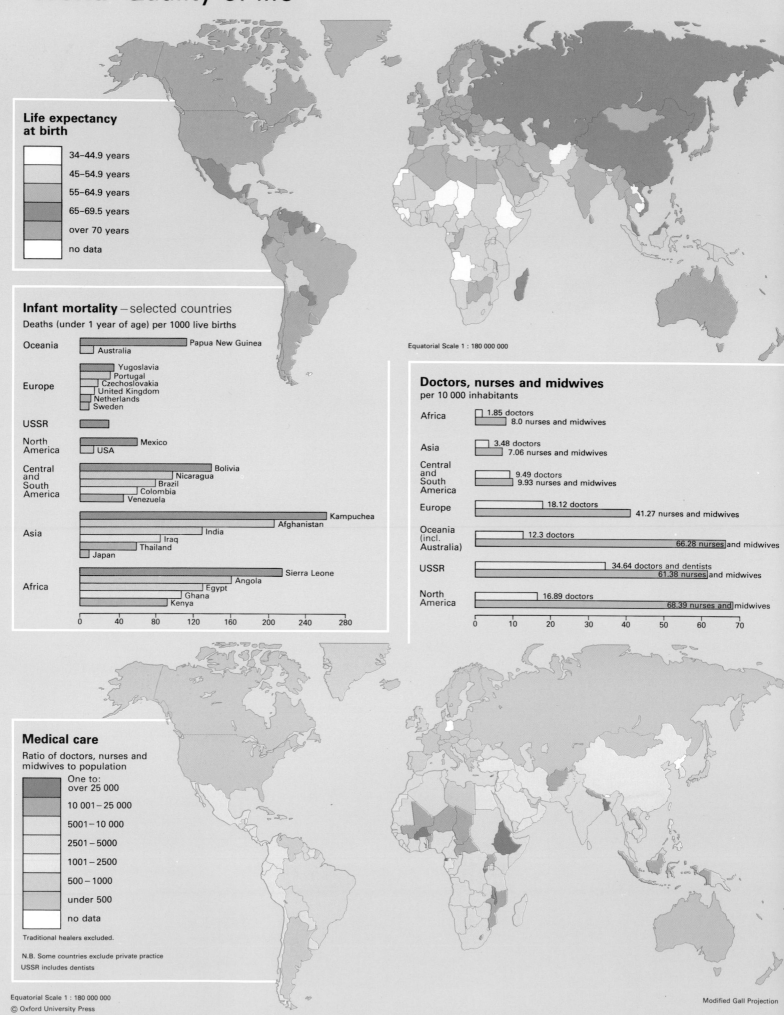

Life expectancy at birth

- 34–44.9 years
- 45–54.9 years
- 55–64.9 years
- 65–69.5 years
- over 70 years
- no data

Infant mortality — selected countries

Deaths (under 1 year of age) per 1000 live births

Oceania
- Papua New Guinea
- Australia

Europe
- Yugoslavia
- Portugal
- Czechoslovakia
- United Kingdom
- Netherlands
- Sweden

USSR

North America
- Mexico
- USA

Central and South America
- Bolivia
- Nicaragua
- Brazil
- Colombia
- Venezuela

Asia
- Kampuchea
- Afghanistan
- India
- Iraq
- Thailand
- Japan

Africa
- Sierra Leone
- Angola
- Egypt
- Ghana
- Kenya

0   40   80   120   160   200   240   280

Equatorial Scale 1 : 180 000 000

Doctors, nurses and midwives

per 10 000 inhabitants

Africa
- 1.85 doctors
- 8.0 nurses and midwives

Asia
- 3.48 doctors
- 7.06 nurses and midwives

Central and South America
- 9.49 doctors
- 9.93 nurses and midwives

Europe
- 18.12 doctors
- 41.27 nurses and midwives

Oceania (incl. Australia)
- 12.3 doctors
- 66.28 nurses and midwives

USSR
- 34.64 doctors and dentists
- 61.38 nurses and midwives

North America
- 16.89 doctors
- 68.39 nurses and midwives

0   10   20   30   40   50   60   70

Medical care

Ratio of doctors, nurses and midwives to population

One to:
- over 25 000
- 10 001 – 25 000
- 5001 – 10 000
- 2501 – 5000
- 1001 – 2500
- 500 – 1000
- under 500
- no data

Traditional healers excluded.

N.B. Some countries exclude private practice

USSR includes dentists

Modified Gall Projection

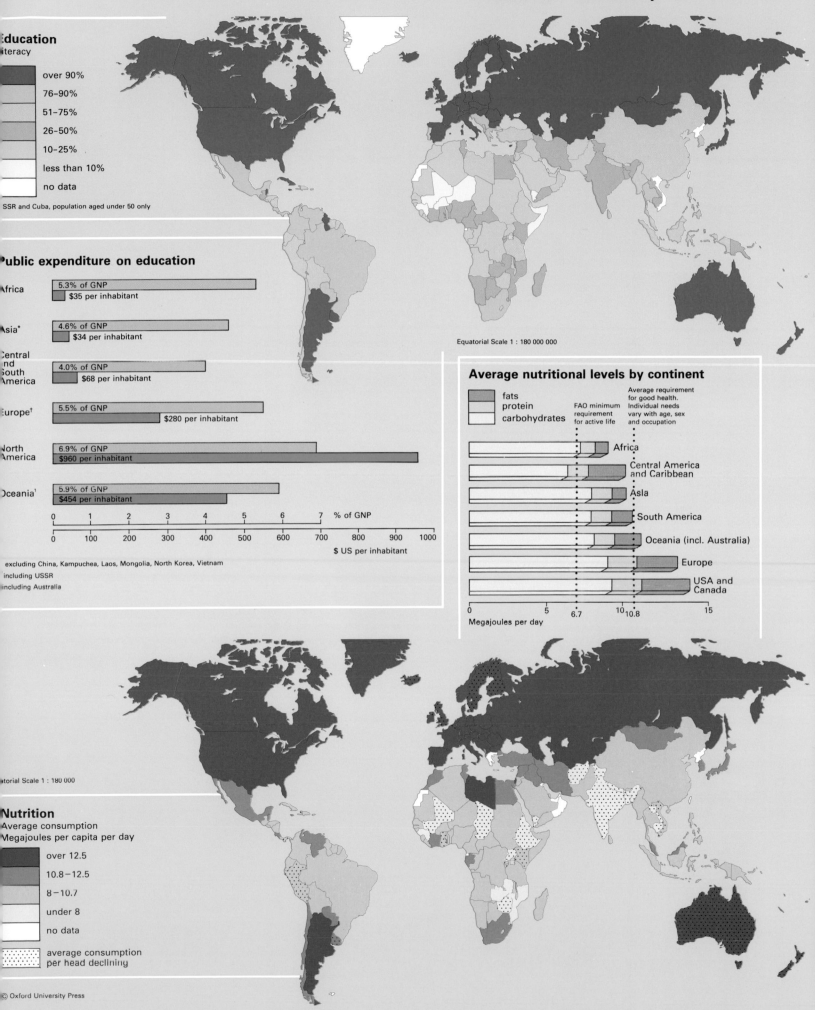

Education
Literacy

- over 90%
- 76–90%
- 51–75%
- 26–50%
- 10–25%
- less than 10%
- no data

USSR and Cuba, population aged under 50 only

Public expenditure on education

Africa
5.3% of GNP
$35 per inhabitant

Asia*
4.6% of GNP
$34 per inhabitant

Central and South America
4.0% of GNP
$68 per inhabitant

Europe†
5.5% of GNP
$280 per inhabitant

North America
6.9% of GNP
$960 per inhabitant

Oceania¹
5.9% of GNP
$454 per inhabitant

0 1 2 3 4 5 6 7 % of GNP

0 100 200 300 400 500 600 700 800 900 1000 $ US per inhabitant

* excluding China, Kampuchea, Laos, Mongolia, North Korea, Vietnam
† including USSR
¹ including Australia

Equatorial Scale 1 : 180 000 000

Average nutritional levels by continent

- fats
- protein
- carbohydrates

FAO minimum requirement for active life

Average requirement for good health. Individual needs vary with age, sex and occupation

- Africa
- Central America and Caribbean
- Asia
- South America
- Oceania (incl. Australia)
- Europe
- USA and Canada

0 5 6.7 10 10.8 15
Megajoules per day

Equatorial Scale 1 : 180 000

Nutrition
Average consumption
Megajoules per capita per day

- over 12.5
- 10.8–12.5
- 8–10.7
- under 8
- no data
- average consumption per head declining

© Oxford University Press

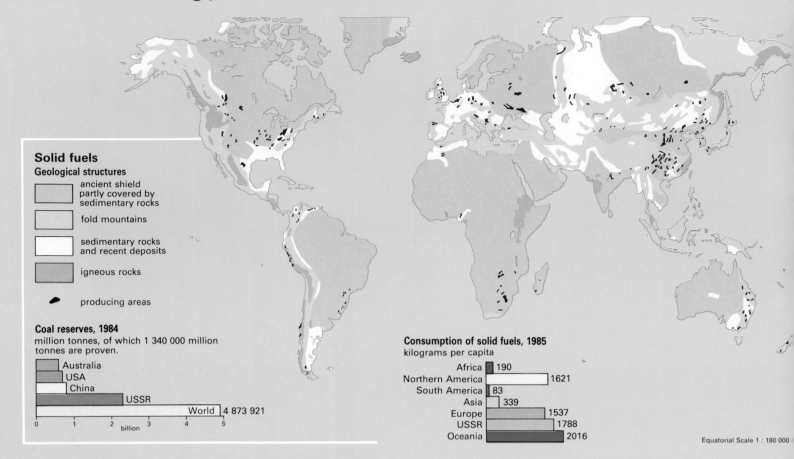

Solid fuels
Geological structures

ancient shield
partly covered by
sedimentary rocks

fold mountains

sedimentary rocks
and recent deposits

igneous rocks

producing areas

Coal reserves, 1984
million tonnes, of which 1 340 000 million
tonnes are proven.

Australia
USA
China
USSR
World   4 873 921

0   1   2   3   4   5
billion

Consumption of solid fuels, 1985
kilograms per capita

Africa	190
Northern America	1621
South America	83
Asia	339
Europe	1537
USSR	1788
Oceania	2016

Equatorial Scale 1 : 180 000

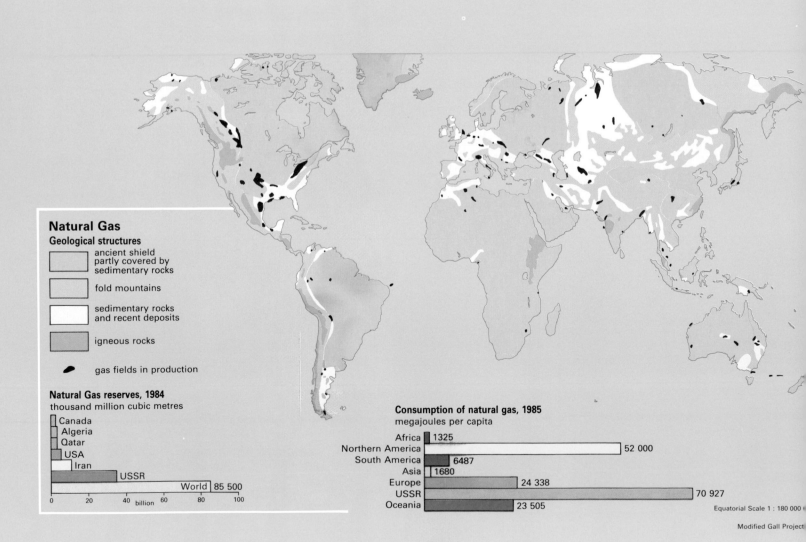

Natural Gas
Geological structures

ancient shield
partly covered by
sedimentary rocks

fold mountains

sedimentary rocks
and recent deposits

igneous rocks

gas fields in production

Natural Gas reserves, 1984
thousand million cubic metres

Canada
Algeria
Qatar
USA
Iran
USSR
World   85 500

0   20   40   60   80   100
billion

Consumption of natural gas, 1985
megajoules per capita

Africa	1325
Northern America	52 000
South America	6487
Asia	1680
Europe	24 338
USSR	70 927
Oceania	23 505

Equatorial Scale 1 : 180 000

Modified Gall Project

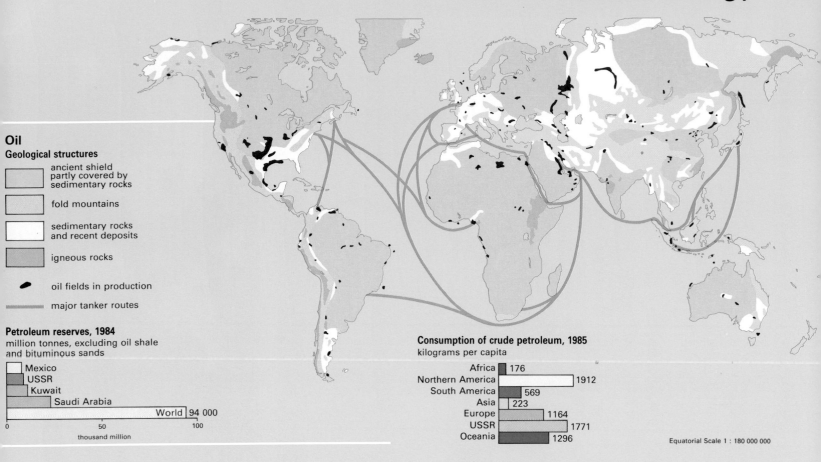

Oil
Geological structures

- ancient shield partly covered by sedimentary rocks
- fold mountains
- sedimentary rocks and recent deposits
- igneous rocks

- oil fields in production
- major tanker routes

Petroleum reserves, 1984
million tonnes, excluding oil shale and bituminous sands

- Mexico
- USSR
- Kuwait
- Saudi Arabia
- World 94 000

0 — 50 — 100
thousand million

Consumption of crude petroleum, 1985
kilograms per capita

- Africa — 176
- Northern America — 1912
- South America — 569
- Asia — 223
- Europe — 1164
- USSR — 1771
- Oceania — 1296

Equatorial Scale 1 : 180 000 000

Electricity
Net installed capacity, 1985
megawatts

- less than 100
- 100–1000
- 1000–5000
- 5000–10 000
- 10 000–50 000
- more than 50 000
- no data

- nuclear power stations

Uranium reserves, 1984
metric tonnes, excluding 1 332 000 estimated reserves

- Canada
- South Africa
- USA
- Australia
- World 2 315 000

0 — 1 — 2 — 3
million

Equatorial Scale 1 : 180 000 000

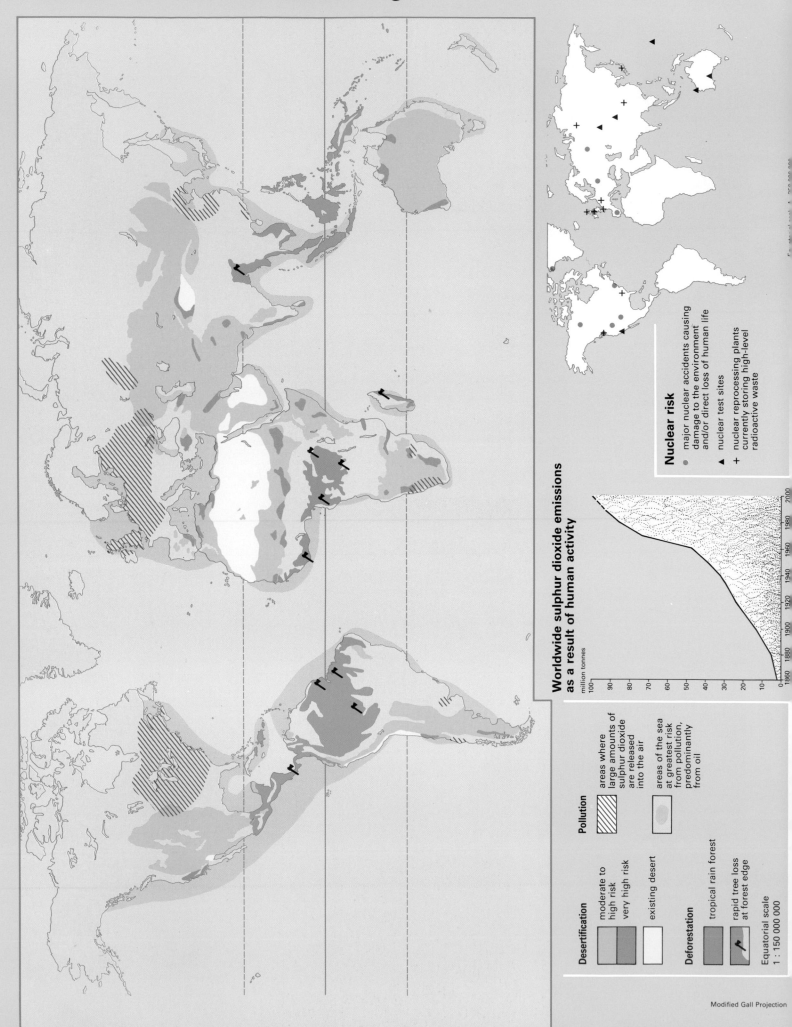

Nuclear risk

● major nuclear accidents causing damage to the environment and/or direct loss of human life

▲ nuclear test sites

+ nuclear reprocessing plants currently storing high-level radioactive waste

Worldwide sulphur dioxide emissions as a result of human activity

million tonnes

Pollution

areas where large amounts of sulphur dioxide are released into the air

areas of the sea at greatest risk from pollution, predominantly from oil

Desertification

moderate to high risk

very high risk

existing desert

Deforestation

tropical rain forest

rapid tree loss at forest edge

Equatorial scale
1 : 150 000 000

Modified Gall Projection

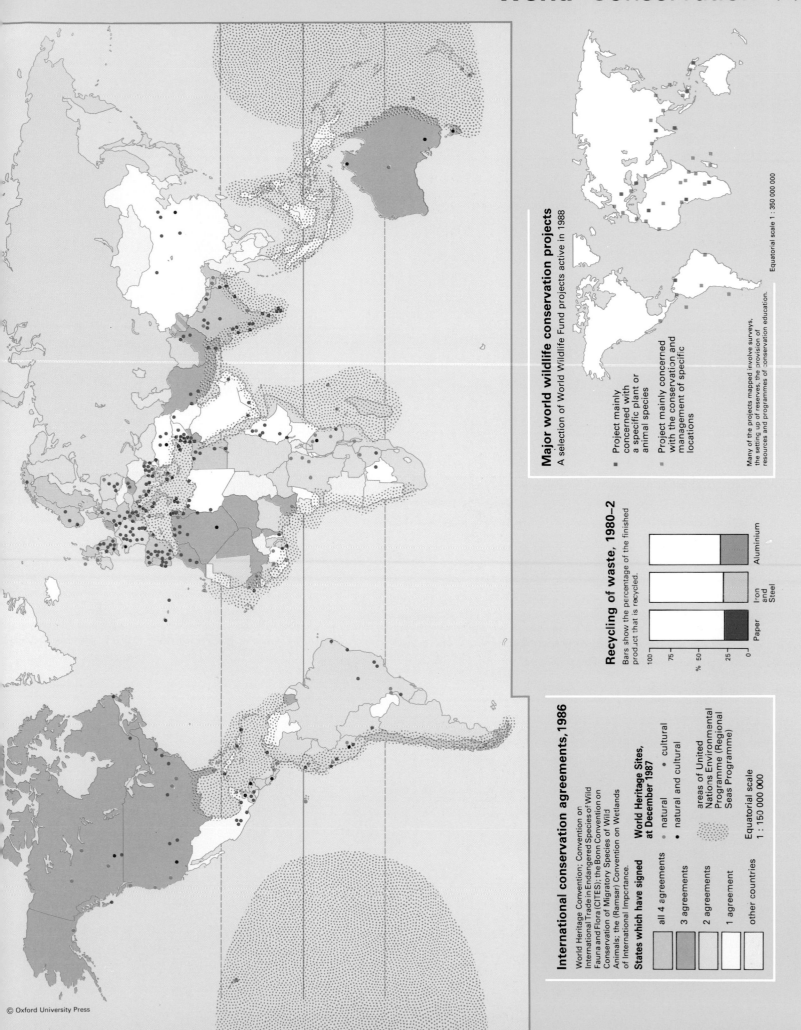

Major world wildlife conservation projects

A selection of World Wildlife Fund projects active in 1988

■ Project mainly concerned with a specific plant or animal species

■ Project mainly concerned with the conservation and management of specific locations

Many of the projects mapped involve surveys, the setting up of reserves, the provision of resources and programmes of conservation education.

Equatorial scale 1 : 350 000 000

Recycling of waste, 1980–2

Bars show the percentage of the finished product that is recycled.

Paper

Iron and Steel

Aluminium

100 75 % 50 25 0

International conservation agreements, 1986

World Heritage Convention; Convention on International Trade in Endangered Species of Wild Fauna and Flora (CITES); the Bonn Convention on Conservation of Migratory Species of Wild Animals; the (Ramsar) Convention on Wetlands of International Importance.

States which have signed

World Heritage Sites, at December 1987

● natural   ● cultural

● natural and cultural

areas of United Nations Environmental Programme (Regional Seas Programme)

☐ all 4 agreements

☐ 3 agreements

☐ 2 agreements

☐ 1 agreement

☐ other countries

Equatorial scale 1 : 150 000 000

© Oxford University Press

Maritime transport

major shipping lanes

● major ports

Air transport

✈ airports handling over 5 million passengers per year

● other airports on major routes

more than 50 direct flights per week

Ground satellite stations

■ space flight centres

✈ Landsat and weather receiving stations

Equatorial Scale 1:88 000 000
Modified Gall Projection

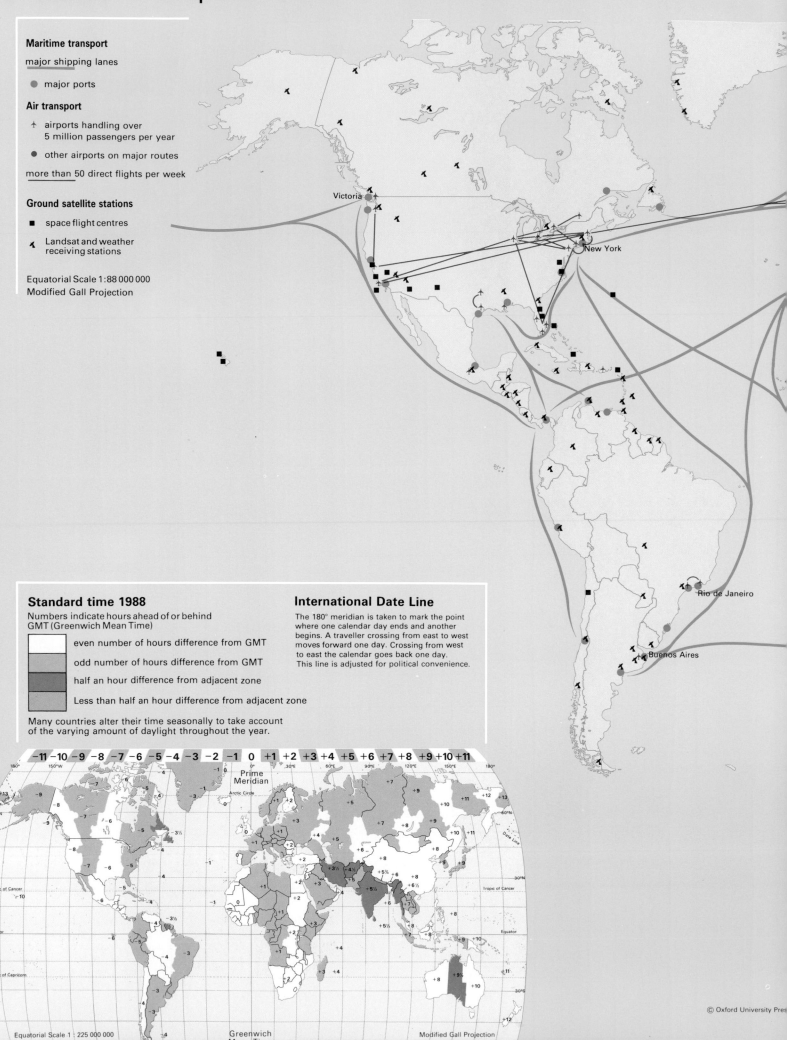

Victoria

New York

Rio de Janeiro

Buenos Aires

Standard time 1988

Numbers indicate hours ahead of or behind GMT (Greenwich Mean Time)

	even number of hours difference from GMT
	odd number of hours difference from GMT
	half an hour difference from adjacent zone
	Less than half an hour difference from adjacent zone

Many countries alter their time seasonally to take account of the varying amount of daylight throughout the year.

International Date Line

The 180° meridian is taken to mark the point where one calendar day ends and another begins. A traveller crossing from east to west moves forward one day. Crossing from west to east the calendar goes back one day. This line is adjusted for political convenience.

−11 −10 −9 −8 −7 −6 −5 −4 −3 −2 −1 0 +1 +2 +3 +4 +5 +6 +7 +8 +9 +10 +11

Prime Meridian

Arctic Circle

Tropic of Cancer

Equator

Tropic of Capricorn

Equatorial Scale 1 : 225 000 000

Greenwich Mean Time

Modified Gall Projection

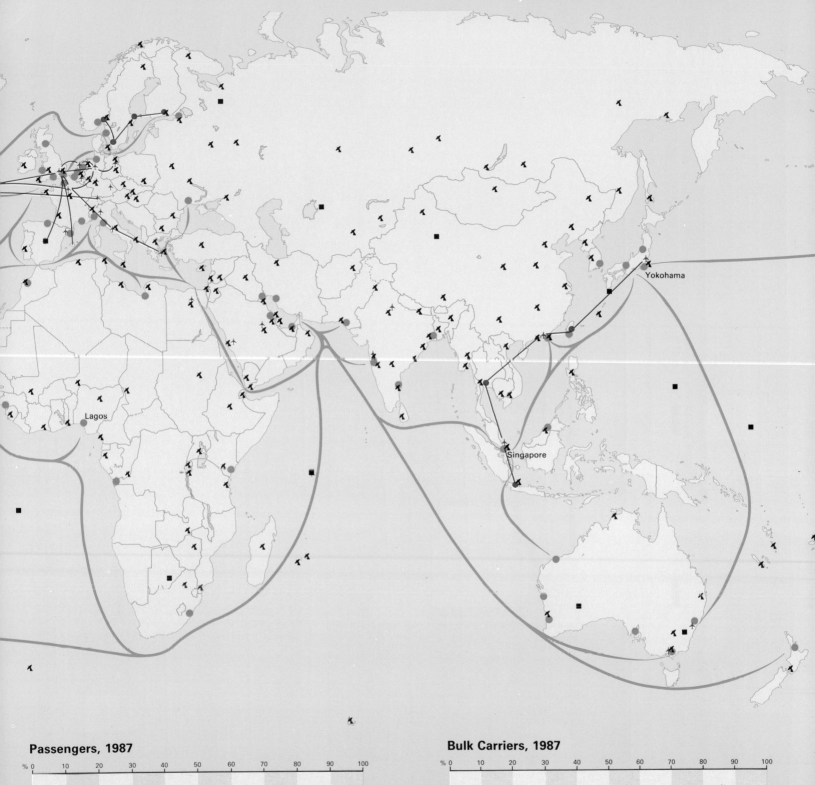

Yokohama

Singapore

Lagos

Passengers, 1987

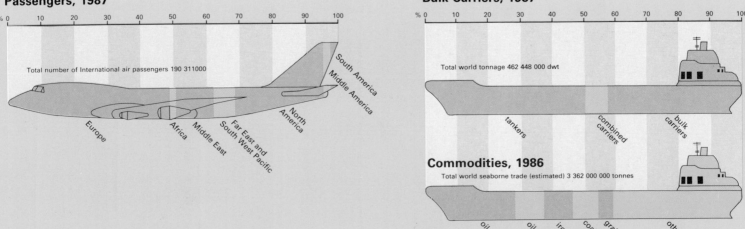

% 0   10   20   30   40   50   60   70   80   90   100

Total number of International air passengers 190 311000

Europe
Africa
Middle East
Far East and
South West Pacific
North America
Middle America
South America

Bulk Carriers, 1987

% 0   10   20   30   40   50   60   70   80   90   100

Total world tonnage 462 448 000 dwt

tankers
combined carriers
bulk carriers

Commodities, 1986

Total world seaborne trade (estimated) 3 362 000 000 tonnes

oil
oil products
iron ore
coal
grain
others

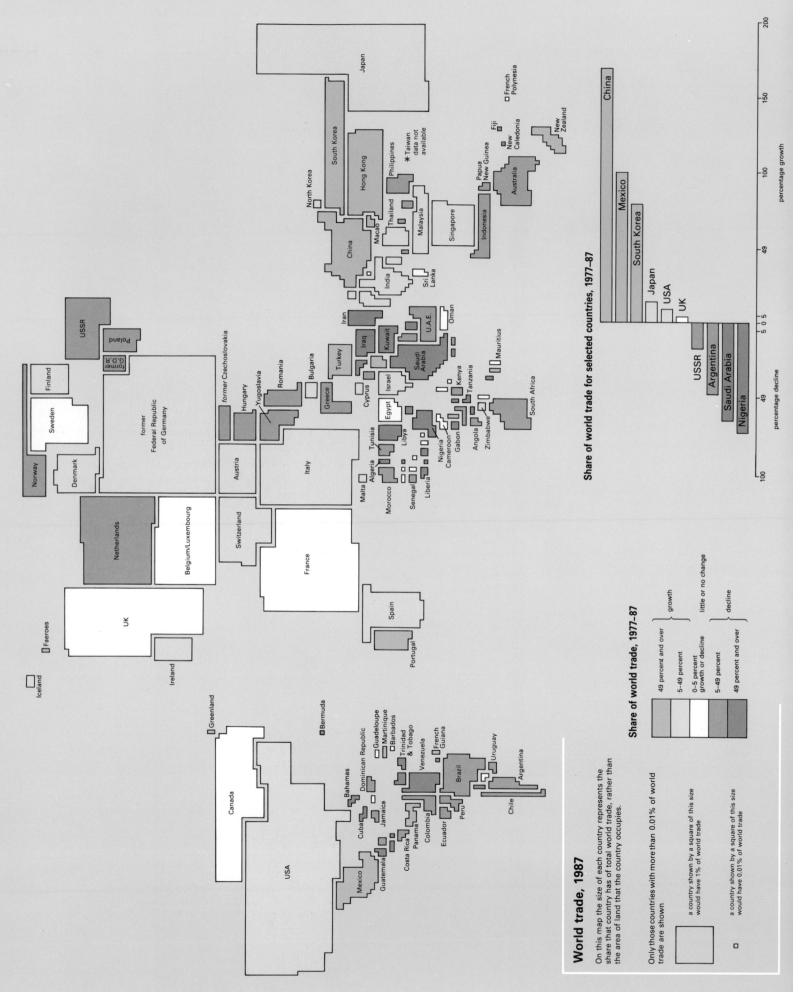

Share of world trade for selected countries, 1977–87

percentage growth

percentage decline

Share of world trade, 1977–87

49 percent and over	growth
5–49 percent	
0–5 percent growth or decline	little or no change
5–49 percent	decline
49 percent and over	

World trade, 1987

On this map the size of each country represents the share that country has of total world trade, rather than the area of land that the country occupies.

Only those countries with more than 0.01% of world trade are shown

a country shown by a square of this size would have 1% of world trade

a country shown by a square of this size would have 0.01% of world trade

© Oxford University Press

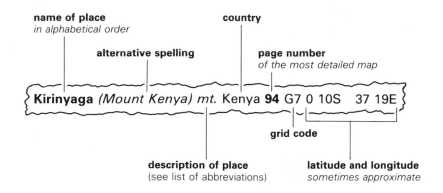

name of place
in alphabetical order

alternative spelling

country

page number
of the most detailed map

Kirinyaga *(Mount Kenya) mt.* Kenya **94** G7 0 10S   37 19E

grid code

description of place
(see list of abbreviations)

latitude and longitude
sometimes approximate

How to use the gazetteer

To find a place on an atlas map use either the grid code or latitude and longitude.

For more information on latitude and longitude look at page 4.

Grid code   ## Latitude and Longitude

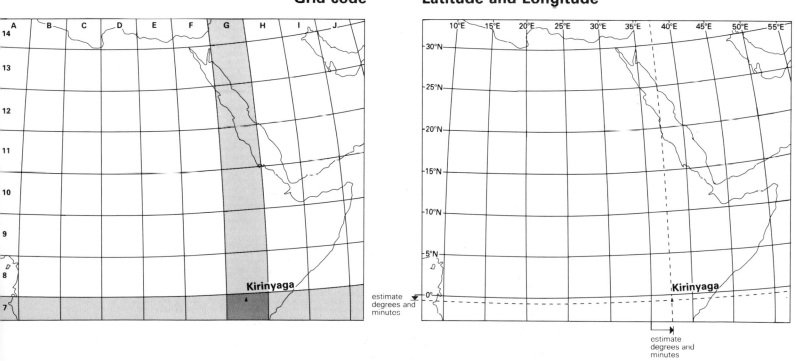

Kirinyaga is in grid square G7

Kirinyaga is at latitude 0 10S longitude 37 19E

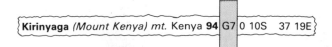

Kirinyaga *(Mount Kenya) mt.* Kenya **94** G7 0 10S   37 19E

Kirinyaga *(Mount Kenya) mt.* Kenya **94** G7 0 10S   37 19E

A

Aa r. France 64 B2 50 50N 2 10E
Aachen Germany 63 A2 50 46N 6 06E
Aalsmeer Netherlands 64 D4 52 16N 4 45E
Aalst Belgium 64 D2 50 57N 4 03E
Aalten Belgium 64 C3 51 56N 6 35E
Aaper Wald hills Germany 62 B2 51 17N 6 50E
Aare r. Switzerland 61 C2 47 00N 7 05E
Aarschot Belgium 64 D2 50 59N 4 50E
Aba Nigeria 93 G4 5 06N 7 21E
Ābādān Iran 79 G5 30 20N 48 15E
Abadla Algeria 93 E9 31 01N 2 45W
Abaetetuba Brazil 114 H12 1 45S 48 54W
Abakan r. Russia 71 K6 52 00N 90 00E
Abakan Russia 71 L6 53 43N 91 25E
Abancay Peru 114 C10 13 37S 72 52W
Abashiri Japan 82 D3 44 02N 144 17E
Abbai (Blue Nile) r. Ethiopia 94 G10 11 00N 37 00E
Abbe, Lake Ethiopia 94 H10 11 00N 44 00E
Abbeville France 61 B3 50 06N 1 51E
Abbeyfeale Limerick Irish Republic 48 B2 52 24N 9 18W
Abbeyleix Laois Irish Republic 48 D2 52 55N 7 20W
Abbey Town Cumbria England 44 A1 54 50N 3 17W
Abbots Bromley Staffordshire England 35 C3 52 49N 1 52W
Abbotsbury Dorset England 31 E2 50 40N 2 36W
Abbots Langley Hertfordshire England 34 B3 51 43N 0 25W
Ábd al Kūrī i. Socotra 79 H1 11 55N 52 20E
Abéché Chad 94 D10 13 49N 20 49E
Åbenrå Denmark 63 A3 55 03N 9 26E
Abeokuta Nigeria 93 F4 7 10N 3 26E
Aberaeron Dyfed Wales 38 B2 52 15N 4 15W
Aberargie Tayside Scotland 45 D2 56 20N 3 23W
Abercarn Gwent Wales 38 C1 51 39N 3 08W
Aberchirder Grampian Scotland 46 F4 57 33N 2 38W
Aberdare Mid Glamorgan Wales 38 C1 51 43N 3 27W
Aberdare National Park Kenya 94 G7 0 30S 37 00E
Aberdaron Gwynedd Wales 38 B2 52 49N 4 43W
Aberdeen Grampian Scotland 46 F4 57 10N 2 04W
Aberdeen Maryland U.S.A. 105 E1 39 31N 76 10W
Aberdeen South Dakota U.S.A. 103 G6 45 28N 98 30W
Aberdeen Washington U.S.A. 102 B6 46 58N 123 49W
Aberdyfi Gwynedd Wales 38 B2 52 33N 4 02W
Aberfeldy Tayside Scotland 46 E3 56 37N 3 54W
Aberffraw Gwynedd Wales 38 B3 53 12N 4 28W
Aberfoyle Central Scotland 45 B2 56 11N 4 23W
Abergavenny Gwent Wales 38 C1 51 50N 3 00W
Abergele Clwyd Wales 38 C3 53 17N 3 34W
Abernethy Tayside Scotland 45 D2 56 20N 3 19W
Aberporth Dyfed Wales 38 B2 52 07N 4 34W
Abersoch Gwynedd Wales 38 B2 52 50N 4 31W
Abertillery Gwent Wales 38 C1 51 45N 3 09W
Aberystwyth Dyfed Wales 38 B2 52 25N 4 05W
Abhā Saudi Arabia 78 F2 18 14N 42 31E
Abidjan Côte d'Ivoire 93 E4 5 19N 4 01W
Abilene Texas U.S.A. 102 G3 32 27N 99 45W
Abingdon Oxfordshire England 32 A2 51 41N 1 17W
Abington Strathclyde Scotland 46 E2 55 29N 3 42W
Abitibi, Lake Canada 105 D3 49 00N 80 00W
Abitibi River r. Ontario Canada 105 D3 50 00N 81 00W
Aboyne Grampian Scotland 46 F4 57 05N 2 50W
Abram Greater Manchester England 42 C2 53 31N 2 36W
Absaroka Range mts. U.S.A. 102 D6 45 00N 110 00W
Abu Dhabi see Abū Z̧abī
Abu Durba Egypt 78 N9 28 29N 33 20E
Abu Hamed Sudan 78 D2 19 32N 33 20E
Abuja Nigeria 93 G4 9 10N 7 11E
Abu Kamal Syria 78 F5 34 29N 40 56E
Abunã Brazil 114 D11 9 41S 65 20W
Abu Tig Egypt 78 D4 27 06N 31 17E
Abū Z̧abī (Abu Dhabi) United Arab Emirates 79 H3 24 28N 54 25E
Acambaro Mexico 108 D4 20 01N 100 42W
Acaponeta Mexico 108 C4 22 30N 105 25W
Acapulco Mexico 108 E3 16 51N 99 56W
Açari r. Brazil 116 B2 22 50S 43 22W
Acarigua Venezuela 114 D14 9 35N 69 12W
Acatlán Mexico 108 E3 18 12N 98 02W
Acayucán Mexico 108 E3 17 59N 94 58W
Accra Ghana 93 E4 5 33N 0 15W
Accrington Lancashire England 42 C3 53 46N 2 21W
Achacachi Bolivia 114 D9 16 01S 68 44W
Achill Island Irish Republic 48 A3 53 55N 10 05W
Achinsk Russia 71 L7 56 20N 90 33E
Achnasheen Highland Scotland 46 C4 57 35N 5 06W
Ackleton Shropshire England 35 A2 52 34N 2 21W
Acklins Island The Bahamas 109 J4 22 30N 74 30W
Ackworth Moor Top tn. West Yorkshire England 43 G2 53 39N 1 20W
Acle Norfolk England 33 D3 52 38N 1 33E
Acock's Green West Midlands England 35 C2 52 26N 1 50W
Aconcagua mt. Argentina 115 C6 32 40S 70 02W
Acre admin. Brazil 114 C11 8 30S 71 30W
Ada Oklhoma U.S.A. 108 G3 34 47N 96 41W
Adachi Japan 83 C4 35 46N 139 48E
Adaga r. Spain 66 B3 40 45N 4 45W
Adamawa Mountains mts. Africa 88 7 00N 13 00E
Adam, Mount Falkland Islands 117 M16 51 36S 60 00W
Adam's Bridge India/Sri Lanka 77 D1 9 10N 79 30E
Adana Turkey 78 E6 37 00N 35 19E
Adapazari Turkey 78 D7 40 45N 30 23E
Adare, Cape Antarctica 121 71 30S 170 24E
Adda r. Italy 61 C2 45 00N 9 00E
Ad Dakhla Western Sahara 93 B7 23 50N 15 58W
Ad Dammām Saudi Arabia 79 H4 26 25N 50 06E
Ad Dawḩah (Doha) Qatar 79 H4 25 15N 51 36E
Ad Dilam Saudi Arabia 79 G3 23 59N 47 06E
Addingham West Yorkshire England 43 E3 53 57N 1 53W
Ad Dir'iyah Saudi Arabia 79 G3 24 45N 46 32E
Addis Ababa see Adis Abeba
Ad Dīwānīyah Iraq 78 F5 32 00N 44 57E
Addlestone Surrey England 34 B2 51 22N 0 31W
Adelaide Australia 86 F3 34 56S 138 36E
Aden Yemen Republic 79 G1 12 50N 45 03E
Aden, Gulf of 79 G1 12 30N 47 30E
Adirondack Mountains New York U.S.A. 105 F2 44 00N 74 00W
Ādīs Ābeba (Addis Ababa) Ethiopia 94 G9 9 03N 38 42E
Adlington Lancashire England 42 C2 53 37N 2 38W
Admiralty Islands Papua New Guinea 86 H9 2 30S 147 00E
Adoni India 77 D3 15 38N 77 16E
Adour r. France 61 A1 43 30N 1 30W
Adra Spain 66 B2 36 45N 3 01W
Adrar Algeria 93 E8 27 51N 0 19W
Adrian Michigan U.S.A. 105 D2 41 55N 84 01W
Adriatic Sea Mediterranean Sea 68 B3 43 00N 15 00E
Adur r. West Sussex England 33 B1 50 55N 0 20W
Adwa Ethiopia 78 E1 14 12N 38 56E
Adwick le Street South Yorkshire England 43 G2 53 34N 1 11W
Aegean Sea Mediterranean Sea 68 D2 39 00N 24 00E
Ærø i. Denmark 63 B2 54 52N 10 20E
AFGHANISTAN 79 J5
Afognak Island i. Alaska U.S.A. 100 E4 58 10N 152 50W
Afyon Turkey 78 D6 38 46N 30 32E
Agadès Niger 93 G6 17 00N 7 56E
Agadir Morocco 93 D9 30 30N 9 40W
Agana Guam 118 E9 13 28N 144 45E
Agano r. Japan 82 C2 37 50N 139 30E
Agartala India 77 G4 23 49N 91 15E
Agawa Ontario Canada 101 S2 47 22N 84 37W
Agboyi Creek r. Nigeria 92 C3 6 37N 3 30E
Agege Nigeria 92 C3 6 41N 3 24E
Agen France 61 B1 44 12N 0 38E
Aghalee Antrim Northern Ireland 49 C1 54 32N 6 16W
Agod G.R.A. Ibadan Nigeria 7 25N 3 58E
Agout r. France 61 B1 43 50N 1 50E
Agra India 77 D5 27 09N 78 00E
Agram Yugoslavia see Zagreb
Agri r. Italy 68 C3 40 00N 16 00E
Agrigento Italy 68 B2 37 19N 13 35E
Agrínion Greece 68 D2 38 38N 21 25E
Agua Prieta Mexico 108 C6 31 20N 109 32W
Aguadas Colombia 114 B14 5 36N 75 30W
Aguadilla Puerto Rico 109 K3 18 27N 67 08W
Aguascalientes Mexico 108 D4 21 51N 102 18W
Agueda r. Spain 66 A3 40 50N 6 50W
Aguilas Spain 66 B2 37 25N 1 35W
Agulhas Basin Indian Ocean 117 K2 45 00S 25 00E
Agulhas, Cape Republic of South Africa 95 D1 34 50S 20 00E
Ahaus Germany 64 G4 52 04N 7 01E
Ahklun Mountains Alaska U.S.A. 100 C4 60 00N 161 00W
Ahmadabad India 77 C4 23 03N 72 40E
Ahmadnagar India 77 C3 19 08N 74 48E
Ahmar Mountains Ethiopia 94 H9 9 00N 41 00E
Ahr r. Germany 64 F2 50 00N 6 00E
Ahrensburg Germany 63 B2 53 41N 10 14E
Ahuachapán El Salvador 108 G2 13 57N 89 49W
Ahvāz Iran 79 G5 31 17N 48 43E
Ailsa Craig i. Scotland 46 C2 55 16N 5 07W
Ain r. France 61 C2 46 30N 5 30E
Aïn Sefra Algeria 93 E9 32 45N 0 35W
Aïr mts. Niger 93 G6 19 10N 8 20E
Ainsdale Merseyside England 42 A2 53 37N 3 03W
Aïn Témouchent Algeria 66 B2 35 18N 1 09W
Aintree Merseyside England 42 B2 53 29N 2 57W
Airdrie Alberta Canada 100 M3 51 20N 114 00W
Airdrie Strathclyde Scotland 45 C1 55 52N 3 59W
Aire r. France 64 D1 49 15N 5 00E
Aire r. North Yorkshire / Humberside England 40 D2 53 40N 1 00W
Aire & Calder Navigation can. England 43 G3 53 40N 1 00W
Aire-sur-l'Adour France 61 A1 43 42N 0 15W
Aire-sur-la-Lys France 64 B2 51 40N 2 25E
Airton North Yorkshire England 43 D4 54 02N 2 09W
Aishihik Yukon Territory Canada 100 H5 62 00N 137 30W
Aisne admin. France 64 C1 49 40N 4 00E
Aisne r. France 61 B2 49 30N 3 00E
Aiviekste r. Latvia 67 F2 57 00N 26 40E
Aix-en-Provence France 61 C1 43 31N 5 27E
Aix-les-Bains France 61 C2 45 41N 5 55E
Aiyion Greece 68 D2 38 15N 22 05E
Aizu-Wakamatsu Japan 82 C2 37 30N 139 58E
Ajaccio Corsica 61 C1 41 55N 8 43E
Ajax Ontario Canada 105 E2 43 48N 79 00W
Ajdābiyā Libya 94 D14 30 46N 20 14E
Ajegunle Nigeria 92 C3 6 24N 3 24E
Ajlūn Jordan 78 O11 32 20N 35 45E
Ajmer India 77 C5 26 29N 74 40E
Akabira Japan 82 D3 43 40N 141 55E
Akaroa New Zealand 87 B2 43 50S 172 59E
Akashi Japan 82 B1 34 39N 135 00E
Aketi Zaïre 94 D8 2 42N 23 51E
Akhelóös r. Greece 68 D2 39 00N 21 00E
Akhisar Turkey 68 E2 38 54N 27 50E
Akimiski Island i. Northwest Territories Canada 101 S3 53 00N 81 00W
Akita Japan 82 D2 39 44N 140 05E
'Akko Israel 78 O11 32 55N 35 04E
Aklavik Northwest Territories Canada 100 I6 68 15N 135 02W
Akobo Sudan 94 F9 7 50N 33 05E
Akola India 77 D4 20 40N 77 05E
Ak'ordat Ethiopia 78 E2 15 26N 37 45E
Akpatok Island i. Northwest Territories Canada 101 V5 60 30N 68 00W
Ákra Akrítas c. Greece 68 D2 36 43N 21 52E
Ákra Kafirévs c. Greece 68 D2 38 10N 24 35E
Ákra Maléa c. Greece 68 D2 36 27N 23 12E
Akranes Iceland 67 H6 64 19N 22 05W
Ákra Taínaron c. Greece 68 D2 36 23N 22 29E
Akron Ohio U.S.A. 105 D2 41 04N 81 31W
Aksum Ethiopia 78 E1 14 10N 38 45E
Aktyubinsk Kazakhstan 70 H6 50 16N 57 13E
Akureyri Iceland 67 I7 65 41N 18 04W
Alabama r. Alabama U.S.A. 103 I3 31 00N 88 00W
Alabama state U.S.A. 103 I3 32 00N 87 00W
Alagoas admin. Brazil 114 J11 9 30S 37 00W
Alagoinhas Brazil 114 J10 12 09S 38 21W
Alagón r. Spain 66 A3 40 00N 6 30W
Alajuela Costa Rica 109 H2 10 00N 84 12W
Alakanuk Alaska U.S.A. 100 C5 62 39N 164 48W
Al'Amārah Iraq 79 G5 31 51N 47 10E
Alamosa Colorado U.S.A. 102 E4 37 28N 105 54W
Åland i. Finland 67 D3 60 15N 20 00E
Alanya Turkey 78 D6 36 32N 32 02E
Al Artāwīyah Saudi Arabia 79 G4 26 31N 45 21E
Ala Shan mts. China F5/F6 40 00N 102 30E
Alaska state U.S.A. 100 D5 63 10N 157 30W
Alaska, Gulf of U.S.A. 100 F4 58 00N 147 00W
Alaska Peninsula Alaska U.S.A. 100 D4 56 30N 159 00W
Alaska Range mts. Alaska U.S.A. 100 E5 62 30N 152 30W
Alatna Alaska U.S.A. 100 E6 66 33N 152 49W
Al 'Ayn United Arab Emirates 79 I3 24 10N 55 43E
Alay Range mts. Asia 70 J3 39 00N 70 00E
Alayor Balearic Islands 66 F4 39 56N 4 08E
Albacete Spain 66 B2 39 00N 1 52W
Alba Iulia Romania 69 D2 46 04N 23 33E
ALBANIA 68 C3
Albany Australia 86 B3 34 57S 117 54E
Albany Georgia U.S.A. 103 J3 31 37N 84 10W
Albany New York U.S.A. 105 F2 42 40N 73 49W
Albany Oregon U.S.A. 102 B5 44 38N 123 07W
Albany River Ontario Canada 101 S3 52 00N 84 00W
Al Başrah Iraq 79 G5 30 30N 47 50E
Al Bayḑā' Libya 94 D14 32 00N 21 30E
Alberche r. Spain 66 B3 40 10N 4 45W
Albert France 61 B2 50 00N 2 40E
Alberta province Canada 100 L3 54 00N 117 30W
Albert-Kanaal can. Belgium 64 D3 51 10N 5 00E
Albert, Lake Uganda/Zaïre 94 F8 2 00N 31 00E
Albert Lea Minnesota U.S.A. 104 B2 43 38N 93 16W
Albertville France 61 C2 45 40N 6 24E
Albi France 61 B1 43 56N 2 08E
Al Bi'r Saudi Arabia 78 P9 28 50N 36 16E
Ålborg Denmark 67 B2 57 05N 9 50E
Albrighton Shropshire England 35 B2 52 38N 2 16W
Albuquerque New Mexico U.S.A. 102 E4 35 05N 106 38W
Al Buraymī Oman 79 I3 24 16N 55 48E
Albury Australia 86 H2 36 03S 146 53E
Alcalá de Henares Spain 66 B3 40 28N 3 22W
Alcamo Italy 68 B2 37 58N 12 58E
Alcañiz Spain 66 B3 41 03N 0 09W
Alcázar de San Juan Spain 66 B2 39 24N 3 12W
Alcester Warwickshire England 35 C1 52 13N 1 52W
Alcira Spain 66 B2 39 10N 0 27W
Alcoy Spain 66 B2 38 42N 0 29W
Alcudia Balearic Islands 66 F4 39 51N 3 06E
Aldabra Islands Indian Ocean 95 I6 9 00S 46 00E
Aldama Mexico 108 E4 22 54N 98 05W
Aldan r. Russia 71 P7 59 00N 132 30E
Aldan Russia 71 O7 58 44N 125 22E
Aldbourne Wiltshire England 31 F3 51 30N 1 37W
Aldbrough Humberside England 40 D2 53 50N 0 06W
Alde r. Suffolk England 33 D3 52 10N 1 30E
Aldeburgh Suffolk England 33 D3 52 09N 1 35E
Aldergrove Antrim North Ireland 49 C1 54 38N 6 09W
Alderley Edge Cheshire England 42 D1 53 18N 2 15W
Alderney i. Channel Islands British Isles 31 G6 49 43N 2 12W
Aldershot Surrey England 33 B2 51 15N 0 47W
Aldridge West Midlands England 35 C2 52 36N 1 55W
Aldsworth Gloucestershire England 31 F3 51 48N 1 46W
Alegrete Brazil 115 F7 29 45S 55 40W
Aleksandrovsk-Sakhalinskiy Russia 71 Q6 50 55N 142 12E
Alençon France 61 B2 48 25N 0 05E
Alenuihaha Channel Hawaiian Islands 119 Y18 20 20N 156 20W
Aleppo see Ḩalab
Alès France 61 B1 44 08N 4 05E
Alessándria Italy 68 A3 44 55N 8 37E
Ålesund Norway 67 B3 62 28N 6 11E
Aleutian Basin Pacific Ocean 118 I13 54 00N 178 00W
Aleutian Islands Alaska U.S.A. 100 A3 54 00N 173 00W
Aleutian Range mts. Alaska U.S.A. 100 D4 56 30N 159 00W
Aleutian Ridge Pacific Ocean 118/119 I13 53 55N 178 00W
Aleutian Trench Pacific Ocean 118/119 I13 50 55N 178 00W
Alexander Archipelago is. Alaska U.S.A. 100 H4 57 00N 137 30W
Alexander Bay tn. Republic of South Africa 95 C2 28 40S 16 30E
Alexander Island Antarctica 121 71 00S 70 00W
Alexandra New Zealand 87 A1 45 14S 169 26E
Alexandria (El Iskandariya) Egypt 78 C5 31 13N 29 55E
Alexandria Louisiana U.S.A. 103 H3 31 19N 92 29W
Alexandria Romania 69 E1 43 59N 25 19E
Alexandria Strathclyde Scotland 45 A1 55 59N 4 36W
Alexandria Virginia U.S.A. 105 E1 38 49N 77 06W
Alexandria Bay tn. New York U.S.A. 105 E2 44 20N 75 55W
Alexandroúpolis Greece 68 E3 40 51N 25 53E
Alfambra r. Spain 66 B3 40 40N 1 00W
Alfiós r. Greece 68 D2 37 00N 22 00E
Alford Grampian Scotland 46 F4 57 13N 2 42W
Alford Lincolnshire England 36 E3 53 17N 0 11E
Alfred Ontario Canada 105 F3 45 33N 74 52W
Alfreton Derbyshire England 36 C3 53 06N 1 23W
Al Fuḩayḩīl Kuwait 79 G4 29 07N 47 02E
Algarve geog. reg. Portugal 51 37 30N 8 00W
Algeciras Spain 66 A2 36 08N 5 27W
Alger (Algiers) Algeria 93 F10 36 50N 3 00E
ALGERIA 93 F8
Alghero Italy 68 A3 40 34N 8 19E
Algiers see Alger
Algona Iowa U.S.A. 104 B2 43 04N 94 11W
Al Hadīthah Iraq 78 F5 34 06N 42 25E
Alhambra California U.S.A. 107 B3 34 05N 118 10W
Al Ḩarīq Saudi Arabia 79 G3 23 34N 46 35E
Al Hasakah Syria 78 F6 36 32N 40 44E
Al Hillah Iraq 78 F5 32 28N 44 29E
Al Hoceima Morocco 66 B2 35 14N 3 56W
Al Hudaydah Yemen Republic 78 F1 14 50N 42 58E
Al Hufūf Saudi Arabia 79 G4 25 20N 49 34E
Aliákmon r. Greece 68 D3 40 00N 22 00E
Alicante Spain 66 B2 38 21N 0 29W
Alice Texas U.S.A. 103 G2 27 45N 98 06W
Alice Springs Australia 86 E5 23 42S 133 52E
Aligarh India 77 D5 27 54N 78 04E
Aling Kangri mt. China 81 B4 32 51N 81 03E
Alipur India 76 K2 22 32N 88 19E
Alivérion Greece 68 D2 38 24N 24 02E
Aliwal North Republic of South Africa 95 E1 30 42S 26 43E
Al Jahrah Kuwait 79 G4 29 22N 47 40E
Al Jawf Libya 94 D12 24 12N 23 18E
Al Jawf Saudi Arabia 78 E4 29 49N 39 52E
Al Jubayl Saudi Arabia 79 G4 26 59N 49 40E
Aljustrel Portugal 66 A2 37 52N 8 10W
Al Khums Libya 94 B14 32 39N 14 16E
Alkmaar Netherlands 64 D4 52 38N 4 44E
Al Kufrah Oasis Libya 94 D12 24 10N 23 15E
Al Kūt Iraq 79 G5 32 30N 45 51E
Al Kuwayt Kuwait 79 G4 29 20N 48 00E
Al Lādhiqīyah Syria 78 E6 35 31N 35 47E
Allahabad India 77 E5 25 27N 81 50E
Allegheny Mountains U.S.A. 105 E1 40 00N 79 00W
Allegheny Reservoir U.S.A. 105 E2 42 00N 79 00W
Allen r. Northumberland England 44 B1 54 58N 2 20W
Allendale Town Northumberland England 44 B1 54 54N 2 15W
Allende Mexico 108 D5 28 22N 100 50W
Allentown Pennsylvania U.S.A. 105 E2 40 37N 75 30W
Alleppey India 77 D1 9 30N 76 22E
Aller r. Germany 63 A2 52 00N 9 00E
Allerton Merseyside England 42 B2 53 23N 2 56W
Allesley West Midlands England 35 D2 52 26N 1 33W
Alliance Nebraska U.S.A. 102 F5 42 08N 102 54W
Allier r. France 61 B2 46 40N 3 00E
Alliston Ontario Canada 105 E2 44 09N 79 51W
Al Līth Saudi Arabia 78 F3 20 10N 40 20E
Alloa Central Scotland 45 C2 56 07N 3 49W
Alma Michigan U.S.A. 105 D2 43 23N 84 40W
Alma Québec Canada 105 F3 48 32N 71 41W
Alma-Ata Kazakhstan 71 J4 43 19N 76 55E
Almada Portugal 66 A2 38 40N 9 09W
Almadén Spain 66 B2 38 47N 4 50W
Al Madīnah Saudi Arabia 78 E3 24 30N 39 35E
Al Manāmah Bahrain 79 H4 26 12N 50 38E
Almansa Spain 66 B2 38 52N 1 06W
Almanzora r. Spain 66 B2 37 15N 2 10W
Al Mayādīn Syria 78 F6 35 01N 40 28E
Almelo Netherlands 64 F4 52 21N 6 40E
Almere Netherlands 64 E4 52 22N 5 12E
Almere-Haven Netherlands 65 E3 52 21N 5 11E
Almería Spain 66 B2 36 50N 2 26W
Älmhult Sweden 67 C2 56 32N 14 10E
Al Miqdādiyah Iraq 78 F5 33 58N 44 58E
Almodôvar Portugal 66 A2 37 31N 8 03W
Almond r. Tayside Scotland 46 E3 56 25N 3 27W
Almondbury West Yorkshire England 43 E2 53 37N 1 48W
Almonte Ontario Canada 105 E3 45 13N 76 12W
Al Mubarraz Saudi Arabia 79 G4 25 26N 49 37E
Al Mukallā Yemen Republic 79 G1 14 34N 49 09E
Al Mukhā Yemen Republic 78 F1 13 20N 43 16E
Aln r. Northumberland England 44 C2 55 30N 1 45W
Alness Highland Scotland 46 D4 57 41N 4 15W
Alnwick Northumberland England 44 C2 55 25N 1 42W
Alor i. Indonesia 80 G2 8 00S 124 30E
Alpena Michigan U.S.A. 105 D3 45 04N 83 27W
Alpes Maritimes mts. France/Italy 61 C1 44 15N 6 45E
Alpha Cordillera ridge Arctic Ocean 120 85 00N 120 00W
Alphen aan den Rijn Netherlands 65 C2 52 08N 4 40E
Alpi Carniche mts. Europe 68 B4 46 00N 13 00E
Alpi Cozie mts. Europe 61 C1 45 00N 7 00E
Alpi Dolomitiche mts. Italy 68 B4 46 00N 12 00E
Alpi Graie mts. Europe 61 C2 45 00N 7 00E
Alpi Lepontine mts. Switzerland 61 C2 46 26N 8 30E
Alpine Texas U.S.A. 102 F3 30 22N 103 40W
Alpi Pennine mts. Switzerland/Italy 61 C2 45 55N 7 30E
Alpi Retiche mts. Switzerland 61 C2 46 25N 9 45E
Alps mts. France / Switzerland / Italy 61 C2 46 00N 7 30E
Al Qunfudhah Saudi Arabia 78 F2 19 09N 41 07E
Alrewas Staffordshire England 35 C3 52 45N 1 43W
Alsager Cheshire England 40 B2 53 06N 2 19W
Alsdorf Germany 64 F2 50 53N 6 10E
Alston Cumbria England 44 B1 54 49N 2 26W
Alta Norway 67 E4 69 57N 23 10E
Altadena California U.S.A. 107 B3 34 12N 118 08W
Altaelv r. Norway 67 E4 69 50N 23 30E
Alta Gracia Argentina 115 E6 31 42S 64 25W
Altai mts. Mongolia 81 D7 47 00N 92 30E
Altamaha r. Georgia U.S.A. 103 J3 32 00N 82 00W
Altamura Italy 68 C3 40 49N 16 34E
Altay China 81 C7 47 48N 88 07E
Altay mts. Russia 71 K6 51 00N 89 00E
Altenburg Germany 63 B2 50 59N 12 27E
Altenessen Germany 62 C2 51 29N 7 02E
Altmühl r. Germany 63 B1 49 00N 10 00E
Altnaharra Highland Scotland 46 D5 58 16N 4 27W
Alto da Boa Vista Brazil 116 B2 22 58S 43 17W
Altofts West Yorkshire England 43 F3 53 42N 1 26W
Alto Molocue Mozambique 95 G4 15 38S 37 42E
Alton Hampshire England 33 B2 51 09N 0 59W
Alton Illinois U.S.A. 104 B1 38 55N 90 10W
Altona Manitoba Canada 104 A3 49 06N 97 35W
Altoona Pennsylvania U.S.A. 105 E2 40 32N 78 23W
Alto Purus, R. Peru 114 C10 10 30S 72 00W
Altrincham Greater Manchester England 42 C2 53 24N 2 21W
Altun Shan mts. China 81 C5 37 30N 86 00E
Altus Oklahoma U.S.A. 102 G3 34 39N 99 21W
Alur Setar Malaysia 80 C5 6 06N 100 23E
Alva Central Scotland 45 C2 56 09N 3 49W
Alva Oklahoma U.S.A. 102 G4 36 48N 98 40W
Alvechurch Hereford & Worcester England 35 C2 52 21N 1 57W
Al Wajh Saudi Arabia 78 E4 26 16N 32 28E
Alwar India 77 D5 27 32N 76 35E
Alwen r. Clwyd Wales 38 C3 53 00N 3 30W
Alyth Tayside Scotland 46 E3 56 37N 3 13W
Amadeus, Lake Australia 86 E5 24 00S 132 30E
Amadi Sudan 94 F9 5 32N 30 20E
Amadjuak Lake Northwest Territories Canada 101 U6 65 00N 71 00W
Amagasaki Japan 82 C1 34 42N 135 23E
Amakusa-shotō is. Japan 82 A1 32 50N 130 05E
Amapá admin. Brazil 114 G13 2 00N 52 30W
Amapá Brazil 114 G13 2 00N 50 50W
Amarillo Texas U.S.A. 102 F4 35 14N 101 50W
Amazon see Rio Amazonas
Amazonas admin. Brazil 114 D12–F12 4 30S 65 00W
Amazon, Mouths of the Brazil 114 H13 1 00N 50 00W
Ambai Brazil 116 B3 22 43S 43 27W
Ambala India 77 D6 30 19N 76 49E
Ambarchik Russia 71 S9 69 39N 162 27E
Ambato Ecuador 114 B12 1 18S 78 39W
Amberg Germany 63 B1 49 26N 11 52E
Amble Northumberland England 44 C2 55 20N 1 34W
Ambleside Cumbria England 44 B1 54 26N 2 58W
Amblève r. Belgium 64 F2 50 22N 6 10E
Ambon Indonesia 80 H3 3 41S 128 10E
Ambovombe Madagascar 95 I2 25 10S 46 06E
Amderma Russia 71 I9 66 44N 61 35E
Amdo China 81 D4 32 22N 91 07E
Ameca Mexico 108 D4 20 34N 104 03W
Ameland i. Netherlands 64 E5 53 28N 5 45E
American Falls tn. Idaho U.S.A. 102 D5 42 47N 112 50W
American Samoa Pacific Ocean 119 J6 15 00S 170 00S
Amersfoort Netherlands 64 E4 52 09N 5 23E
Amersham Buckinghamshire England 34 B3 51 40N 0 38W
Amery Ice Shelf Antarctica 121 70 00S 70 00E
Ames Iowa U.S.A. 104 B2 42 02N 93 33W
Amesbury Wiltshire England 31 F3 51 10N 1 47W
Amfípolis Greece 68 D3 40 48N 23 52E
Amga r. Russia 71 P8 60 00N 130 00E
Amga Russia 71 P8 61 51N 131 59E
Amgun' r. Russia 71 P6 52 00N 137 00E
Amherst Nova Scotia Canada 101 W2 44 09N 76 45W
Amherst Virginia U.S.A. 105 E1 37 35N 79 04W
Amiens France 61 B2 49 54N 2 18E
Amlia Island Alaska U.S.A. 100 A3 52 05N 173 30W
Amlwch Gwynedd Wales 38 B3 53 25N 4 20W
Amman Jordan 78 O10 31 57N 35 56E

Ammanford Dyfed Wales 38 C1 51 48N 3 59W
Ammassalik Greenland 101 BB6 65 45N 37 45W
Ammersee *l.* Germany 63 B1 48 00N 11 00E
Amne Machin Shan *mts.* China 72 35 00N 100 00E
Ampana Indonesia 80 G3 0 54S 121 35E
Amper *r.* Germany 63 B1 48 00N 11 00E
Ampthill Bedfordshire England 34 B4 52 02N 0 30W
Amravati India 77 D4 20 58N 77 50E
Amritsar India 77 D6 31 35N 74 56E
Amroha India 77 D5 28 54N 78 29E
Amrum *i.* Germany 63 A2 54 00N 8 00E
Amstelveen Netherlands 65 D3 52 18N 4 52E
Amsterdam Netherlands 65 D3 52 22N 4 54E
Amsterdam New York U.S.A. 105 F2 42 56N 74 12W
Amsterdam Rijnkanaal *can.* Netherlands 65 E2 51 15N 5 00E
Amstetten Austria 69 B2 48 08N 14 52E
Am Timam Chad 94 D10 10 59N 20 18E
Amudar'ya *(Oxus) r.* Asia 70 I3 38 00N 64 00E
Amund Ringnes Island Northwest Territories Canada 101 P8 78 00W 96 00W
Amundsen Gulf Northwest Territories Canada 100 K7 70 30N 125 00W
Amundsen Sea Southern Ocean 121 72 00S 130 00W
Amundsen-Scott *r.s.* South Pole Antarctica 121 90 00S
Amungen *l.* Sweden 67 D3 61 10N 15 35E
Amur *(Heilong Jiang) r.* Asia 81 K8 52 30N 126 30E
Amursk Russia 71 P6 50 16N 136 55E
Anabar *r.* Russia 71 N10 71 30N 113 00E
Anaconda Montana U.S.A. 102 D6 46 09N 112 56W
Anadyr' *r.* Russia 71 T9 65 00N 175 00E
Anadyr' Russia 71 T8 64 50N 178 00E
Anadyr', Gulf of Russia 71 U8 65 00N 178 00W
Anaheim California U.S.A. 107 C2 33 50N 117 56W
Anai Mudi *mt.* India 77 D2 10 20N 77 15E
Anan Japan 82 B1 33 54N 134 40E
Ananindeua Brazil 114 H12 1 22S 48 20W
Anantapur India 77 D2 14 42N 77 05E
Anápolis Brazil 114 H9 16 19S 48 58W
Anatolian Plateau Turkey 72 39 00N 39 00E
Anatom *i.* Vanuatu 86 L5 20 10S 169 50E
Anchorage Alaska U.S.A. 100 F5 61 10N 150 00W
Ancona Italy 68 B3 43 37N 13 31E
Ancroft Northumberland England 44 B2 55 42N 2 00W
Anda China 81 K7 46 25N 125 20E
Andalsnes Norway 67 B3 62 33N 7 43E
Andaman Islands India 77 G2 12 00N 94 00E
Andaman Sea Indian Ocean 80 B6 12 30N 97 00E
Andenne Belgium 64 E2 50 29N 5 06E
Anderlecht Belgium 64 D2 50 50N 4 20E
Andermatt Switzerland 61 C2 46 38N 8 36E
Anderson Indiana U.S.A. 104 C2 40 05N 85 41W
Anderson *r.* Northwest Territories Canada 100 J6 69 42N 129 01W
Anderson South Carolina U.S.A. 103 J3 34 30N 82 39W
Andes *mts.* South America 114/115 B13–C5
Andhra Pradesh *admin.* India 77 D3 16 00N 79 00E
Andizhan Uzbekistan 70 J4 40 40N 72 12E
Andkhvoy Afghanistan 79 K6 36 58N 65 00E
ANDORRA 66 C3
Andorra la Vella Andorra 66 C3 42 30N 1 30E
Andover Hampshire England 32 A2 51 13N 1 28W
Andraitx Balearic Islands 66 E4 39 35N 2 25E
Andreas Isle of Man British Isles 41 F1 54 22N 4 26W
Andrésy France 60 A2 48 59N 2 03E
Andreyevka Kazakhstan 81 B7 45 50N 80 34E
Andropov *see* Rybinsk
Ándros *i.* Greece 68 D2 37 49N 24 54E
Andros *i.* The Bahamas 109 I4 24 00N 78 00W
Androscoggin River U.S.A. 105 F2 44 00N 70 00W
Androth Island India 77 C2 10 51N 73 41E
Andújar Spain 66 B2 38 02N 4 03W
Andulo Angola 95 C5 11 29S 16 43E
Angara *r.* Russia 71 L7 58 00N 96 00E
Angara Basin Arctic Ocean 120 80 00N
Angarsk Russia 71 M6 52 31N 103 55E
Angel de la Guarda *i.* Mexico 108 B5 29 00N 113 30W
Angeles National Forest California U.S.A. 107 B4 34 15N 118 10W
Ångermanälven *r.* Sweden 67 D3 64 30N 16 15E
Angers France 61 A2 47 29N 0 32W
Angle Dyfed Wales 38 A1 51 41N 5 06W
Anglesey *i.* Gwynedd Wales 38 B3 53 18N 4 25W
Angliers Québec Canada 105 E3 47 33N 79 14W
ANGOLA 95 C5
Angola Basin Atlantic Ocean 117 I5 15 00S 3 00E
Angola Plateau Africa 88 14 00S 17 00E
Angoulême France 61 B2 45 40N 0 10E
Anguilla *i.* Leeward Islands 109 L3 18 14N 63 05W
Anjo Japan 82 C1 34 56N 137 05E
Ankaratra *mt.* Madagascar 95 I4 19 25S 47 12E
Anklam Germany 63 B2 53 52N 13 42E
Ann Arbor Michigan U.S.A. 105 D2 42 18N 83 43W
'Annaba Algeria 93 G10 36 55N 7 47E
An Nabk Saudi Arabia 78 E5 31 21N 37 20E
An Nabk Syria 78 E5 34 02N 36 43E
An Nafud *d.* Saudi Arabia 78 F4 28 20N 40 30E
An Najaf Iraq 78 F5 31 59N 44 19E
Annam Range *hills* Asia 72 15 00N 107 00E
Annan Dumfries & Galloway Scotland 46 E1 54 59N 3 16W
Annan *r.* Dumfries & Galloway Scotland 46 E2 55 15N 3 40W
Annandale *v.* Dumfries & Galloway Scotland 46 E2 55 15N 3 25W
Annapolis Maryland U.S.A. 105 E1 38 59N 76 30W
Annapurna *mt.* Nepal 77 E5 28 34N 83 50E
An Nāsirīyah Iraq 79 G5 31 04N 46 17E
Annbank Strathclyde Scotland 46 D2 55 28N 4 30W
Ann, Cape U.S.A. 105 F2 42 39N 70 37W
Annecy France 61 C2 45 54N 6 07E
Annfield Plain Durham England 44 C1 54 52N 1 45W
Anniston Alabama U.S.A. 103 I3 33 38N 85 50W
Annotto Bay *tn.* Jamaica 109 R8 18 16N 76 47W
Anqing China 81 I4 30 46N 119 40E
Ansari Nagar India 76 L4 28 33N 77 12E
Ansbach Germany 63 B1 49 18N 10 36E
Anshan China 81 J6 41 05N 122 58E
Anshun China 81 G3 26 15N 105 51E
Anstey Leicestershire England 36 C2 52 40N 1 10W
Anston South Yorkshire England 43 G2 53 22N 1 13W
Anstruther Fife Scotland 46 F3 56 14N 2 42W
Ansty Warwickshire England 35 D2 52 26N 1 24W
Antakya Turkey 78 E6 36 12N 36 10E
Antalya Turkey 78 D6 36 53N 30 42E
Antananarivo *(Tananarive)* Madagascar 95 I4 18 52S 47 30E
Antarctica 121
Antarctic Peninsula Antarctica 121 68 00S 65 00W
Antequera Spain 66 B2 37 01N 4 34W
Antibes France 61 C1 43 35N 7 07E
Antigua Guatemala 108 F2 14 33N 90 42W
Antigua *i.* Antigua & Barbuda 109 L3 17 09N 61 49W
ANTIGUA & BARBUDA 109 L3
Antipodes Islands Southern Ocean 118 H3 49 42S 178 50E
Antofagasta Chile 115 C8 23 40S 70 23W
Antrim North Ireland 49 C2 54 43N 6 13W
Antrim Mountains Northern Ireland 48 E4/5 55 00N 6 10W
Antseranana Madagascar 95 I5 12 19S 49 17E
Antwerpen *admin.* Belgium 64 D3 51 20N 4 45E
Antwerpen *(Anvers)* Belgium 64 D3 51 13N 4 25E
Anuradhapura Sri Lanka 77 E1 8 20N 80 25E
Anvers *see* Antwerpen
Anxi China 81 E6 40 32N 95 57E
Anyang China 81 H5 36 04N 114 20E
Anzhero-Sudzhensk Russia 71 K7 56 10N 86 01E
Aomori Japan 82 D3 40 50N 140 43E
Aosta Italy 68 A4 45 43N 7 19E
Aozou Strip Chad 94 C12 23 00N 17 00E
Apapa Nigeria 92 C3 6 22N 3 25E
Aparri The Philippines 80 G7 18 22N 121 40E
Apatity Russia 70 F9 67 32N 33 21E
Apatzingán Mexico 108 D3 19 05N 102 20W
Apeldoorn Netherlands 64 E4 52 13N 5 57E
Apennines *see* Appennini
Apia Western Samoa 118 I6 13 48S 171 45W
Apolda Germany 63 B2 51 02N 11 31E
Apostle Islands Wisconsin U.S.A. 104 B3 47 00N 90 00W
Appalachian Mountains U.S.A. 103 J4 37 00N 82 00W
Appennini *(Apennines) mts.* Italy 68 B3
Appennino Abruzzese *mts.* Italy 68 B3 42 00N 14 00E
Appennino Ligure *mts.* Italy 68 A3 44 30N 9 00E
Appennino Lucano *mts.* Italy 68 C3 40 00N 15 00E
Appennino Tosco-Emiliano *mts.* Italy 68 B3 44 00N 12 00E
Appingedam Netherlands 64 F5 53 18N 6 52E
Appleby-in-Westmoreland Cumbria England 44 B1 53 36N 2 29W
Appledore Devon England 31 C3 51 03N 4 12W
Appleton City Missouri U.S.A. 104 B1 38 10N 94 03W
Appleton Wisconsin U.S.A. 104 C2 44 17N 88 24W
Appomattox Virginia U.S.A. 105 E1 37 21N 78 51W
'Aqaba Jordan 78 O9 29 32N 35 00E
'Aqaba, Gulf of Middle East 78 O9 28 40N 34 40E
Aquidauana Brazil 114 F8 20 27S 55 45W
Ara India 77 E5 25 34N 84 40E
Ara *r.* Japan 83 C3 35 39N 139 51E
Arabian Sea Indian Ocean 79 J2 17 00N 60 00E
Aracaju Brazil 114 J10 10 54S 37 07W
Aracati Brazil 114 J12 4 32S 37 45W
Arad Romania 69 D2 46 10N 21 19E
Arafura Sea Australia/Indonesia 86 E8/F8 10 00S 135 00E
Aragón *r.* Spain 66 B3 42 15N 1 40W
Araguaina Brazil 114 H11 7 16S 48 18W
Araguari Brazil 114 H9 18 38S 48 13W
Arāk Iran 79 G5 34 05N 49 42E
Arakan Yoma *mts.* Myanmar 77 G3 18 00N 94 00E
Araks *(Aras, Araxes) r.* Armenia/Azerbaijan/Turkey/Iran 78 F6 39 30N 45 00E
Aral Sea Asia 70 H5 45 00N 60 00E
Aral'sk Kazakhstan 70 I5 46 56N 61 43E
Aranda de Duero Spain 66 B3 41 40N 3 41W
Aran Fawddwy *mt.* Gwynedd Wales 38 C2 52 47N 3 41W
Aran Island Irish Republic 48 C4/5 55 00N 8 30W
Aran Islands Irish Republic 48 B3 53 10N 9 50W
Aranjuez Spain 66 B3 40 02N 3 37W
Arapiraca Brazil 114 J11 9 45S 36 40W
Ar'ar Saudi Arabia 78 F5 30 58N 41 03E
Araraquara Brazil 115 H8 21 46S 48 08W
Ararat, Mount *see* Bü Ağri Daği
Aras *(Araks, Araxes) r.* Turkey/Azerbaijan/Iran 79 G6 38 40N 46 30E
Arauca Colombia 114 C14 7 04N 70 41W
Araure Venezuela 109 K1 9 36N 69 15W
Araxá Brazil 114 H9 19 37S 46 50W
Araxes *(Araks, Aras) r.* Iran/Azerbaijan/Turkey 79 G6 38 40N 46 30E
Arbil Iraq 78 F6 36 12N 44 01E
Arbroath Tayside Scotland 46 F3 56 34N 2 35W
Arc *r.* France 61 C2 45 15N 6 10E
Arcachon France 61 A1 44 40N 1 11W
Arcadia California U.S.A. 107 B3 34 09N 118 00W
Archipelago Dehalak *is.* Ethiopia 78 F2 15 45N 40 12E
Arctic Bay *tn.* Northwest Territories Canada 101 R7 73 05N 85 20W
Arctic Ocean 120
Ardabīl Iran 79 G6 38 15N 48 18E
Ardbeg Strathclyde Scotland 46 B2 55 39N 6 05W
Ardee Louth Irish Republic 48 E3 53 52N 6 33W
Ardennes *admin.* France 64 D1 49 35N 4 35E
Ardennes *mts.* Belgium 64 E2 50 10N 5 45E
Ardila *r.* Spain 66 A2 38 15N 6 50W
Ardmore Oklahoma U.S.A. 103 G3 34 11N 97 08W
Ardmore Strathclyde Scotland 45 A1 55 59N 4 41W
Ardnamurchan, Point of *c.* Highland Scotland 46 B3 56 44N 6 13W
Ardres France 64 A2 50 51N 1 59E
Ardrossan Strathclyde Scotland 46 D2 55 39N 4 49W
Ards Peninsula Northern Ireland 48 F4 54 25N 5 30W
Ardvasar Highland Scotland 46 C4 57 03N 5 55W
Arendal Norway 67 B2 58 27N 8 56E
Arequipa Peru 114 C9 16 25S 71 32W
Arezzo Italy 68 B3 43 28N 11 53E
Arga *r.* Spain 66 B3 42 30N 1 50W
Argentan France 61 B2 48 45N 0 01W
Argenteuil France 60 A2 48 57N 2 14E
ARGENTINA 115 D5
Argentine Basin Atlantic Ocean 117 D2 42 00S 45 00W
Arges *r.* Romania 69 E1 44 00N 26 00E
Argun *(Ergun He) r.* Asia 81 I8 52 00N 120 00E
Argyle, Lake Australia 86 D6 17 00S 128 30E
Århus Denmark 67 C2 56 15N 10 10E
Arica Chile 114 C9 18 30S 70 20W
Ariège *r.* France 61 B1 42 50N 1 40E
Arinagour Strathclyde Scotland 46 B3 56 37N 6 31W
Aripuanã *r.* Brazil 114 E11 7 00S 60 30W
Ariquemes Brazil 114 E11 9 55S 63 06W
Arisaig Highland Scotland 46 C3 56 51N 5 51W
Arisaig, Sound of Highland Scotland 46 C3 56 50N 5 50W
Arizona *state* U.S.A. 102 D3 34 00N 112 00W
Arizpe Mexico 108 B6 30 20N 110 11W
Arjeplog Sweden 67 D4 66 04N 18 00E
Arjona Colombia 114 B15 10 14N 75 22W
Arkalyk Kazakhstan 70 I6 50 17N 66 51E
Arkansas *r.* U.S.A. 103 H4 35 00N 93 00W
Arkansas *state* U.S.A. 103 H3 34 00N 93 00W
Arkansas City Kansas U.S.A. 103 G4 37 03N 97 02W
Arkendale North Yorkshire England 43 F4 54 02N 1 24W
Arkhangel'sk Russia 70 G8 64 32N 40 40E
Arklow Wicklow Irish Republic 48 E2 52 48N 6 09W
Arkona, Cape Germany 63 B2 54 41N 13 26E
Arlanza *r.* Spain 66 B3 42 00N 3 30W
Arlanzón *r.* Spain 66 B3 42 00N 4 00W
Arles France 61 B1 43 41N 4 38E
Arlit Niger 93 G6 18 50N 7 00E
Arlon Belgium 64 E1 49 41N 5 49E
Armadale Highland Scotland 46 C4 57 05N 5 54W
Armadale Lothian Scotland 45 C1 55 54N 3 42W
Armagh Armagh Northern Ireland 48 E4 54 21N 6 39W
Armavir Russia 70 G5 44 59N 41 10E
Armenia Colombia 114 B13 4 32N 75 40W
ARMENIA 70 G4/G3
Armentières France 61 B3 50 41N 2 53E
Armidale Australia 86 I3 30 32S 151 40E
Armstrong Ontario Canada 104 C4 50 20N 89 02W
Armthorpe South Yorkshire England 43 G2 53 32N 1 03W
Arnhem Netherlands 64 E3 52 00N 5 53E
Arnhem Land *geog. reg.* Australia 86 E7 13 00S 133 00E
Arno *r.* Italy 68 B3 43 00N 10 00E
Arnold Nottinghamshire England 36 C2 53 00N 1 09W
Arnprior Central Scotland 45 B2 56 08N 4 15W
Arnprior Ontario Canada 105 E3 45 26N 76 24W
Arnsberg Germany 63 A2 51 23N 8 03E
Arnstadt Germany 63 B2 50 50N 10 57E
Arquipélago dos Bijagós *is.* Guinea Bissau 93 B5 11 20N 16 40W
Ar Ramādī Iraq 78 F5 33 27N 43 19E
Ar Ramlah Jordan 78 O9 29 28N 35 58E
Arran *i.* Strathclyde Scotland 46 C2 55 35N 5 15W
Ar Raqqah Syria 78 E6 35 57N 39 03E
Arras France 61 B3 50 17N 2 46E
Ar Riyād Saudi Arabia 79 G3 24 39N 46 46E
Arta Balearic Islands 66 E4 39 42N 3 20E
Árta Greece 68 D2 39 10N 20 59E
Artane Dublin Irish Republic 49 B2 53 23N 6 12W
Arthur Ontario Canada 105 D2 43 50N 80 32W
Arthur's Pass New Zealand 87 B2 42 55S 171 34E
Arthur's Seat *sum.* Lothian Scotland 45 D1 55 57N 3 11W
Artigas *r.s.* Antarctica 121 62 11S 58 51W
Artigas Uruguay 115 F6 30 25S 56 28W
Arua Uganda 94 F8 3 02N 30 56E
ARUBA 114 D15 12 30N 70 00W
Arun *r.* West Sussex England 33 B1 51 00N 0 30W
Arunachal Pradesh *admin.* India 77 H5 28 00N 95 00E
Arundel West Sussex England 33 B1 50 51N 0 34W
Arusha Tanzania 94 G7 3 23S 36 40E
Aruwimi *r.* Zaïre 94 E8 2 00N 25 00F
Arvika Sweden 67 C2 59 41N 12 38E
Arzew Algeria 66 B2 35 50N 0 19W
Asahi-dake *mt.* Japan 82 D3 43 42N 142 54E
Asahikawa Japan 82 D3 43 46N 142 23E
Asaka Japan 83 B4 35 47N 139 37E
Asamankese Ghana 93 E4 5 45N 0 45W
Asansol India 77 F4 23 40N 86 59E
Åsarna Sweden 67 C3 62 40N 14 20E
Asbury Park New Jersey U.S.A. 105 F2 40 14N 74 00W
Ascension Island Atlantic Ocean 117 G6 7 57S 14 22W
Aschaffenburg Germany 63 A1 49 58N 9 10E
Aschersleben Germany 63 B2 51 46N 11 28E
Ascoli Piceno Italy 68 B3 42 52N 13 35E
Ascot Berkshire England 34 A2 51 25N 0 41W
Aseb Ethiopia 78 F1 13 01N 42 47E
Asenovgrad Bulgaria 68 D3 42 00N 24 53E
Ash Kent England 33 D2 51 17N 1 16E
Ash Surrey England 34 A1 51 15N 0 44W
Ashbourne Derbyshire England 36 C2 53 01N 1 43W
Ashbourne Meath Irish Republic 49 A2 53 31N 6 24W
Ashburton Devon England 31 D2 50 31N 3 45W
Ashburton New Zealand 87 B2 43 54S 171 46E
Ashburton *r.* Australia 86 B5 22 30S 116 00E
Ashby Canal Leicestershire England 35 D2 52 37N 1 25W
Ashby-de-la-Zouch Leicestershire England 35 D3 52 46N 1 28W
Ashdod Israel 78 O10 31 48N 34 48E
Åsheň *l.* Sweden 67 C2 56 45N 14 40E
Asheville North Carolina U.S.A. 103 J4 35 35N 82 35W
Ashfield Central Scotland 45 C2 56 12N 3 59W
Ashford Kent England 33 C2 51 09N 0 53E
Ashford Surrey England 34 B2 51 26N 0 27W
Ashford in the Water Derbyshire England 43 E1 53 13N 1 43W
Ashfork Arizona U.S.A. 102 D4 35 13N 112 29W
Ashgill Strathclyde Scotland 45 C1 55 44N 3 55W
Ashikaga Japan 82 C2 36 21N 139 26E
Ashina Japan 83 B1 35 13N 139 36E
Ashington Northumberland England 44 C2 55 11N 1 34W
Ashizuri-misaki *c.* Japan 82 B1 32 42N 133 00E
Ashkhabad Turkmenistan 70 H3 37 58N 58 24E
Ashland Kentucky U.S.A. 105 D1 38 28N 82 40W
Ashland Oregon U.S.A. 102 B5 42 14N 122 44W
Ashland Wisconsin U.S.A. 104 B3 46 34N 90 54W
Ashok Nagar India 76 L4 28 38N 77 07E
Ashqelon Israel 78 O10 31 40N 34 35E
Ash Shāriqah United Arab Emirates 79 I4 25 20N 55 20E
Ash Shurayf Saudi Arabia 78 E4 25 50N 39 00E
Ashstead Surrey England 34 C1 51 19N 0 18W
Ashtabula Ohio U.S.A. 105 D2 41 53N 80 47W
Ashton-in-Makerfield Greater Manchester
Ashton-under-Lyne Greater Manchester
Ashwell Hertfordshire England 33 B3 52 03N 0 09W
Asilah Morocco 66 A2 35 32N 6 04W
Asir Mountains Saudi Arabia 88 18 00N 44 00E
Askeaton Limerick Irish Republic 48 C2 52 36N 8 58W
Askern South Yorkshire England 43 G2 53 37N 1 09W
Askham Bryan North Yorkshire England 43 G3 53 55N 1 10W
Askrigg North Yorkshire England 40 B3 54 19N 2 04W
Asmera Eritrea 78 E2 15 20N 38 58E
Asnières France 60 B2 48 55N 2 17E
Aspatria Cumbria England 44 A1 54 46N 3 20W
Aspiring, Mount New Zealand 87 A2 44 23S 168 46E
Aspley Guise Bedfordshire England 34 B4 52 01N 0 37W
Aspull Greater Manchester England 42 C2 53 33N 2 36W
Assam *admin.* India 77 G5 26 20N 92 00E
As Samawah Iraq 79 G5 31 18N 45 18E
Asse Belgium 64 D2 50 55N 4 12E
Assen Netherlands 64 F5 53 00N 6 34E
Assis Brazil 115 G8 22 37S 50 25W
Assisi Italy 68 D3 43 04N 12 37E
As Suq Saudi Arabia 78 F3 21 55N 42 02E
As Suwaydā' Syria 78 P11 32 43N 36 33E
Astārā Russia 79 G6 38 27N 48 53E
Asti Italy 68 A3 44 54N 8 13E
Astipálaia *i.* Greece 68 E2 36 00N 26 00E
Astley Cross Hereford & Worcester England 35 B1 52 19N 2 20W
Aston South Yorkshire England 43 G2 53 22N 1 18W
Aston West Midlands England 35 C2 52 30N 1 54W
Aston Clinton Buckinghamshire England 34 A3 51 48N 0 44W
Astoria Oregon U.S.A. 102 B6 46 12N 123 50W
Astrakhan' Russia 70 G5 46 22N 48 04E
Astwood Bank Hereford & Worcester England 35 C1 52 15N 1 55W
Asuka *r.s.* Antarctica 121 71 32S 24 08E
Asunción Paraguay 115 F7 25 15S 57 40W
Aswa *r.* Uganda 94 F8 3 30N 32 30E
Aswân Egypt 78 D3 24 05N 32 56E
Aswân Dam Egypt 78 D3 23 40N 31 50E
Asyût Egypt 78 D4 27 14N 31 07E
Atacama Desert *see* Desierto de, Atacama
Atar Mauritania 93 C7 20 32N 13 08W
Atbara *r.* Sudan 78 D2 17 28N 34 30E
Atbara Sudan 78 D2 17 42N 34 00E
Atbasar Kazakhstan 70 I6 51 49N 68 18E
Atchison Kansas U.S.A. 103 G4 39 33N 95 09W
Ath Belgium 64 C2 50 38N 3 47E
Athabasca Alberta Canada 100 M3 54 44N 113 15W
Athabasca, Lake Alberta/Saskatchewan Canada 100 N4 59 10N 109 30W
Athabasca River Alberta Canada 100 M4 57 30N 111 00W
Athboy Meath Irish Republic 48 E3 53 37N 6 55W
Athenry Galway Irish Republic 48 C3 53 18N 8 45W
Athens Georgia U.S.A. 103 J3 33 57N 83 24W
Athens Greece *see* Athinai
Athens Ohio U.S.A. 105 D1 39 20N 82 06W
Athens Pennsylvania U.S.A. 105 E2 41 57N 76 31W
Atherstone Warwickshire England 35 D2 52 35N 1 31W
Atherton Greater Manchester England 42 C2 53 31N 2 31W
Athínai *(Athens)* Greece 68 D2 38 00N 23 44E
Athlone Westmeath Irish Republic 48 D3 53 25N 7 56W
Áthos *mt.* Greece 68 D3 40 10N 24 19E
Athy Kildare Irish Republic 48 E2 52 59N 6 59W
Ati Chad 94 C10 13 11N 18 20E
Atikokan Ontario Canada 104 B3 48 45N 91 38W
Atikonak Lake Newfoundland Canada 101 W3 52 40N 64 35W
Atka Island Alaska U.S.A. 100 A3 52 05N 174 40W
Atlanta Georgia U.S.A. 103 J3 33 45N 84 23W
Atlantic City New Jersey U.S.A. 105 F1 39 23N 74 27W
Atlantic-Indian Ridge Atlantic Ocean 117 I1 53 00S 3 00E
Atlantic Ocean 117
Atlas Saharien *mts.* Algeria 93 F9 33 30N 1 00E
Atlin British Columbia Canada 100 I4 59 31N 133 41W
Atlin Lake British Columbia Canada 100 I4 59 31N 133 41W
Atrek *r.* Asia 79 H6 37 00N 54 50E
At Tā'if Saudi Arabia 78 F3 21 15N 40 21E
Attawapiskat Ontario Canada 101 S3 53 00N 82 30W
Attawapiskat River Ontario Canada 101 R3 53 00N 86 00W
Attersee *l.* Austria 63 B1 47 00N 13 00E
Attleborough Norfolk England 33 D3 52 31N 1 01E
Auas Mountains Namibia 95 C3 23 00S 17 00E
Aubagne France 61 C1 43 17N 5 35E
Aube *r.* France 61 B2 48 40N 3 55E
Aubenas France 61 B1 44 37N 4 24E
Aubervilliers France 60 B2 48 55N 2 22E
Auburn Maine U.S.A. 105 F2 44 04N 70 26W
Auburn Nebraska U.S.A. 104 A2 40 22N 95 41W
Auburn New York U.S.A. 105 E2 42 57N 76 34W
Auch France 61 B1 43 40N 0 36E
Auchengray Strathclyde Scotland 45 C1 55 46N 3 37W
Auchterarder Tayside Scotland 45 C2 56 18N 3 43W
Auchtermuchty Fife Scotland 45 D2 56 17N 3 15W
Auckland New Zealand 87 B3 36 55S 174 47E
Auckland Islands Southern Ocean 118 G2 50 35S 116 00E
Aude *r.* France 61 B1 43 00N 2 00E
Auden Ontario Canada 104 C4 50 14N 87 54W
Audenshaw Greater Manchester England 42 D2 53 29N 2 06W
Audley Staffordshire England 36 B3 53 03N 2 20W
Aue Germany 63 B2 50 35N 12 42E
Aughton Lancashire England 42 B2 53 33N 2 55W
Aughton South Yorkshire England 43 G2 53 22N 1 19W
Augsburg Germany 63 B1 48 21N 10 54E
Augusta Australia 86 B3 34 19S 115 09E
Augusta Georgia U.S.A. 103 J3 33 29N 82 00W
Augusta Maine U.S.A. 105 G2 44 17N 69 50W
Auldhouse Strathclyde Scotland 45 B1 55 43N 4 12W
Aulnay-sous-Bois France 60 C2 48 57N 2 31E
Aulne *r.* France 61 A2 48 10N 4 00W
Aurangābād India 77 D3 19 52N 75 22E
Aurich Germany 63 A2 53 28N 7 29E
Aurillac France 61 B1 44 56N 2 26E
Aurora Illinois U.S.A. 104 C2 41 45N 88 20W
Aurora Indiana U.S.A. 104 D1 39 03N 84 55W
Aurora Ontario Canada 105 E2 43 00N 79 28W
Au Sable *r.* Michigan U.S.A. 105 D2 45 00N 84 00W
Austerfield South Yorkshire England 43 G2 53 27N 1 00W
Austin Brazil 116 A3 22 43S 43 31W
Austin Minnesota U.S.A. 104 B2 43 40N 92 58W
Austin Texas U.S.A. 103 G3 30 18N 97 47W
AUSTRALIA 86
Australian Capital Territory *(A.C.T.) admin.* Australia 86 H2 35 00S 144 00E
Austral Ridge Pacific Ocean 119 K5 24 00S 155 30W
AUSTRIA 69 B2
Autlán Mexico 108 D3 19 48N 104 20W
Autun France 61 B2 46 58N 4 18E
Auxerre France 61 B2 47 48N 3 35E
Auyuittuq National Park Northwest Territories
Avallon France 61 B2 47 30N 3 54E
Avebury Wiltshire England 31 F3 51 27N 1 51W
Aveiro Portugal 66 A3 40 38N 8 40W
Aveley Essex England 34 D2 51 30N 0 15E
Avellaneda Argentina 115 F6 34 40S 58 20W
Avesnes-sur-Helpe France 64 C2 50 08N 3 57E
Avesta Sweden 67 D3 60 09N 16 10E
Aveyron *r.* France 61 B1 44 30N 2 05E
Avezzano Italy 68 B3 42 02N 13 26E
Aviemore Highland Scotland 46 E4 57 12N 3 50W
Avignon France 61 B1 43 56N 4 48E
Avila Spain 66 B3 40 39N 4 42W
Avilés Spain 66 A3 43 33N 5 55W
Avon *co.* England 31 E4 51 20N 2 30W

Avon *r.* Avon England **31** E3 51 27N 2 30W
Avon *r.* Devon England **31** D2 50 20N 3 50W
Avon *r.* Warwickshire England **36** C2 52 10N 1 50W
Avonbridge Central Scotland **45** C1 55 56N 3 44W
Avonmouth Avon England **31** E3 51 31N 2 42W
Avranches France **61** A2 48 42N 1 21W
Avre *r.* France **61** B2 48 40N 0 45E
Avre *r.* France **61** B2 49 45N 2 30E
Awali *r.* Lebanon **78** O11 33 35N 35 32E
Awash Ethiopia **94** H9 9 01N 41 10E
Awash *r.* Ethiopia **94** H10 10 00N 40 00E
Awa-shima Japan **82** C2 38 40N 139 15E
Awbārī Libya **94** B13 26 35N 12 46E
Axbridge Somerset England **31** E3 51 18N 2 49W
Axe *r.* Devon/Dorset England **31** E2 50 50N 2 55W
Axe *r.* Somerset England **31** E3 51 11N 2 42W
Axel Heiberg Island Northwest Territories Canada **101** Q8 80 00N 90 00W
Axminster Devon England **31** D2 50 47N 3 00W
Ayaguz Kazakhstan **71** K5 47 59N 80 27E
Ayamonte Spain **66** A2 37 13W 7 24W
Ayan Russia **71** P7 56 29N 138 07E
Ayaviri Peru **114** C10 14 53S 70 35W
Aydin Turkey **68** E2 37 51N 27 51E
Ayers Rock *mt.* Australia **86** E4 25 18S 131 18E
Ayios Nikólaos Greece **68** E2 35 11N 25 43E
Aylesbury Buckinghamshire England **33** B2 51 50N 0 50W
Aylesford Kent England **33** C2 51 18N 0 30E
Aylmer Ontario Canada **105** D2 42 47N 80 58W
Aylmer Québec Canada **105** E3 45 23N 75 51W
Aylsham Kent England **33** D2 51 12N 1 11E
Aylsham Norfolk England **33** D3 52 49N 1 15E
'Aynūnah Saudi Arabia **78** O9 28 06N 35 08E
Ayod Sudan **94** F9 8 08N 31 24E
Ayon *i.* Russia **71** S9 69 55N 168 10E
Ayr *r.* Strathclyde Scotland **46** D2 55 30N 4 10W
Ayr Strathclyde Scotland **46** D2 55 28N 4 38W
Ayre, Point of *c.* Isle of Man British Isles **41** F1 54 25N 4 22W
Aysgarth North Yorkshire England **40** B3 54 17N 2 00W
Ayutthaya Thailand **80** C6 14 20N 100 35E
Azcapotzalco Mexico **108** P1 19 29N 99 11W
AZERBAIJAN **70** G4
Azogues Ecuador **114** B12 2 46S 78 56W
Azores *is.* Atlantic Ocean **117** F10 38 30N 28 00W
Azoum *r.* Chad **94** D10 12 00N 21 00E
Azov, Sea of Asia **70** F5 46 00N 36 00E
Azuero, Peninsula de Panama **109** H1 7 40N 81 00W
Azul Argentina **115** F5 36 46S 59 50W
Azurduy Bolivia **114** E9 20 00S 64 29W
Azusa California U.S.A. **107** C3 34 08N 117 54W
Az Zabadānī Syria **78** P11 33 42N 36 03E
Az Ẓahrān *(Dhahran)* Saudi Arabia **79** H4 26 13N 50 02E

B

Baalbek Lebanon **78** P12 34 00N 36 12E
Baarn Netherlands **64** E4 52 13N 5 16E
Bab el Mandab *sd.* Red Sea **94** H10 12 30N 47 00E
Babahoyo Ecuador **114** B12 1 53S 79 31W
Babar, Kepulauan *is.* Indonesia **80** H2 8 00S 129 30E
Babbacombe Bay Devon England **31** D2 50 30N 3 30W
Babushkin Russia **70** M2 55 55N 37 44E
Babylon *hist. site* Iraq **78** F5 32 33N 44 25E
Bacabal Brazil **114** I12 4 15S 44 45W
Bacău Romania **69** E2 46 33N 26 58E
Back *r.* Northwest Territories Canada **101** P6 66 00N 97 00W
Backbone Ranges *mts.* Northwest Territories Canada **100** J5 63 30N 127 50W
Bacolod The Philippines **80** G6 10 38N 122 58E
Bacongo Congo **92** A2 4 18S 15 15E
Bacup Lancashire England **42** D3 53 43N 2 12W
Badajoz Spain **66** A2 38 53N 6 58W
Badalona Spain **66** C3 41 27N 2 15E
Baddeley Green Staffordshire England **35** B4 53 04N 2 09W
Baden Austria **69** C2 48 01N 16 14E
Baden Switzerland **61** C2 47 28N 8 19E
Baden-Baden Germany **63** A1 48 45N 8 15E
Baden-Württemberg *admin.* Germany **63** A1 48 00N 9 00E
Badgastein Austria **63** B1 47 07N 13 09E
Bad Hersfeld Germany **63** A2 50 53N 9 43E
Badhoevedorp Netherlands **65** D3 52 20N 4 47E
Bad Homburg Germany **63** A2 50 13N 8 37E
Bad Honnef Germany **64** G2 50 38N 7 14E
Bad Ischl Austria **63** B1 47 43N 13 38E
Bad Kissingen Germany **63** B2 50 12N 10 05E
Bad Kreuznach Germany **63** A1 49 51N 7 52E
Badli India **76** L4 28 44N 77 09E
Bad Neuenahr-Ahrweiler Germany **64** G2 50 32N 7 06E
Bad Reichenhall Germany **63** B1 47 43N 12 53E
Bad Salzuflen Germany **63** A2 52 06N 8 45E
Bad Tölz Germany **63** B1 47 45N 11 34E
Badu Brazil **116** C2 22 54S 43 03W
Badulla Sri Lanka **77** E1 6 59N 81 03E
Baffin Bay Canada/Greenland **101** V7 72 00N 65 00W
Baffin Island Northwest Territories Canada **101** S7 68 30N 70 00W
Bafoussam Cameroon **93** H4 5 31N 10 25E
Bāfq Iran **79** I5 31 35N 55 21E
Bagé Brazil **115** G6 31 22W 54 06W
Bagenalstown *see* Muinebeag
Baggy Point Devon England **31** C3 51 09N 4 16W
Baghdād Iraq **78** F5 33 20N 44 26E
Baghlān Afghanistan **79** K6 36 11N 68 44E
Bagshot Surrey England **34** A2 51 22N 0 42W
Baguilt Clwyd Wales **42** A1 53 15N 3 10W
Bahamas Bank Atlantic Ocean **96** 24 00N 77 00W
BAHAMAS, THE **109** I4
Baharampur India **77** F4 24 00N 88 30E
Bahawalpur Pakistan **77** C5 29 24N 71 47E
Bahia *admin.* Brazil **114** I10 12 00S 42 30W
Bahía Blanca Argentina **115** E5 38 45S 62 15W
Bahía Blanca *b.* Argentina **115** E5 39 00S 61 00W
Bahía de Campeche *b.* Mexico **108** E4/F4 20 00N 95 00W
Bahía, Grande *b.* Argentina **115** D2 51 30S 68 00W
Bahraich India **77** E5 27 35N 81 36E
BAHRAIN **79** H4
Bahrain, Gulf of The Gulf **79** H4 25 55N 50 30E
Bahr el Abiad *(White Nile) r.* Sudan **78** D1 14 00N 32 20E
Bahr el Arab *r.* Sudan **94** E10 10 00N 27 30E
Bahr el Azraq *(Blue Nile) r.* Sudan **78** D1 13 30N 33 45E
Bahr el Ghazal *r.* Chad **94** C10 14 00N 16 00E
Bahr el Jebel *(White Nile) r.* Sudan **94** 7 00N 32 00E
Baia Mare Romania **69** D2 47 39N 23 36E
Baicheng China **81** J7 45 37N 122 48E
Baidyabati India **76** K3 22 48N 88 20E
Baie Comeau *tn.* Québec Canada **105** G3 49 12N 68 10W
Baie de la Seine *b.* France **61** A2 49 40N 0 30W
Baie-du-Poste *tn.* Québec Canada **105** F4 50 20N 73 50W
Baie St. Paul *tn.* Québec Canada **105** F3 47 27N 70 30W
Baie Trinité *tn.* Québec Canada **105** G3 49 25N 67 20W
Baildon West Yorkshire England **43** E3 53 52N 1 46W
Baile Atha Cliath *see* Dublin
Bailieborough Cavan Irish Republic **48** E3 53 54N 6 59W
Bailleul France **64** B2 50 44N 2 44E
Baird Mountains Alaska U.S.A. **100** D6 67 30N 160 00W
Baïse *r.* France **61** B1 43 55N 0 25E
Baiwanzhuang China **82** G1 39 55N 116 18E
Baja California *p.* Mexico **108** B5 27 30N 113 00W
Baja Hungary **69** C2 46 11N 18 58E
Baj Baj India **76** J1 22 28N 88 10E
Baker Oregon U.S.A. **102** C5 44 46N 117 50W
Baker Lake Northwest Territories Canada **101** Q5 64 00N 95 00W
Baker Lake *tn.* Northwest Territories Canada **101** P5 64 20N 96 10W
Bakersfield California U.S.A. **102** C4 35 25N 119 00W
Bakewell Derbyshire England **43** E1 53 13N 1 40W
Baku Azerbaijan **70** G4 40 22N 49 53E
Bala Gwynedd Wales **38** C2 52 54N 3 35W
Balaghat India **77** E4 21 48N 80 16E
Balaghat Ra. *mts.* India **77** D3 18 45N 77 00E
Balakovo Russia **70** G6 52 04N 47 46E
Bala, Lake *see* Tegid, Llyn
Balama Mozambique **95** G5 13 19S 38 35E
Bālā Morghāb Afghanistan **79** J6 35 34N 63 20E
Balassagyarmat Hungary **69** C2 48 06N 19 17E
Balaton *l.* Hungary **69** C2 47 00N 17 30E
Balboa Panama **109** I1 8 57N 79 33W
Balbriggan Dublin Irish Republic **48** E3 53 37N 6 11W
Balclutha New Zealand **87** A1 46 16S 169 46E
Balcombe West Sussex England **33** B2 51 04N 0 08W
Bald Eagle Lake Minnesota U.S.A. **104** B3 47 48N 91 32W
Baldeney-see *l.* Germany **62** C2 51 24N 7 02E
Baldock Hertfordshire England **34** C3 51 59N 0 12W
Baldwin Park *tn.* California U.S.A. **107** C3 34 05N 117 59W
Balearic Islands Spain **66** E4
Balerno Lothian Scotland **45** D1 55 53N 3 20W
Balfron Central Scotland **45** B2 56 04N 4 20W
Bali *i.* Indonesia **80** E2/F2 8 00S 115 00E
Balikesir Turkey **78** C6 39 37N 27 51E
Balikpapan Indonesia **80** F3 1 15S 116 50E
Balkan Mountains Europe **51** 42 30N 25 00E
Balkhash *l. see* Ozero Balkhash
Balkhash Kazakhstan **71** J5 46 50N 74 57E
Ballachulish Highland Scotland **46** C3 56 40N 5 10W
Ballaghaderreen Roscommon Irish Republic **48** C3 53 55N 8 36W
Ballantrae Strathclyde Scotland **46** C2 55 06N 5 00W
Ballarat Australia **86** G2 37 36S 143 58E
Ballater Grampian Scotland **46** E4 57 03N 3 03W
Ballaugh Isle of Man England **41** F1 54 18N 4 32W
Balleny Islands Southern Ocean **118** H1 66 30S 164E
Ballina Mayo Irish Republic **48** B4 54 07N 9 09W
Ballinamore Leitrim Irish Republic **48** D4 54 03N 7 47W
Ballinasloe Galway Irish Republic **48** C3 53 20N 8 13W
Ballincollig Cork Irish Republic **48** C1 51 54N 8 35W
Ballinderry Lisburn Northern Ireland **49** C1 54 32N 6 13W
Ballingry Fife Scotland **45** D2 56 09N 3 20W
Ballinrobe Mayo Irish Republic **48** B3 53 37N 9 13W
Balloch Strathclyde Scotland **45** A2 56 00N 4 36W
Bālly India **76** K2 22 38N 88 20E
Ballyboden Dublin Irish Republic **49** B1 53 17N 6 17W
Ballybofey Donegal Irish Republic **48** D4 54 48N 7 47W
Ballybunion Kerry Irish Republic **48** B2 52 31N 9 40W
Ballycastle Northern Ireland **48** E5 55 12N 6 15W
Ballyclare Antrim Northern Ireland **49** C2 54 45N 6 00W
Ballyfermot Dublin Irish Republic **49** A2 53 21N 6 21W
Ballygowan Down Northern Ireland **49** D1 54 30N 5 47W
Ballygunge India **76** K2 22 31N 88 20E
Ballyhaunis Mayo Irish Republic **48** C3 53 46N 8 46W
Ballymahon Longford Irish Republic **48** D3 53 34N 7 45W
Ballymena Antrim Northern Ireland **48** E4 54 52N 6 17W
Ballymoney Northern Ireland **48** E5 55 04N 6 31W
Ballymote Sligo Irish Republic **48** C4 54 06N 8 31W
Ballynahinch Down Northern Ireland **48** F4 54 24N 5 54W
Ballyshannon Donegal Irish Republic **48** C4 54 30N 8 11W
Balmaha Central Scotland **45** A2 56 06N 4 33W
Balmoral Grampian Scotland **46** E4 57 02N 3 13W
Balmoral Northern Ireland **49** D1 54 33N 5 56W
Balmore Strathclyde Scotland **45** B1 55 56N 4 14W
Balsall Common West Midlands England **35** D2 52 23N 1 39W
Balsas Mexico **108** E3 18 00N 99 44W
Balta Ukraine **69** E2 47 58N 29 39E
Baltic Sea Europe **67** D2 55 15N 17 00E
Baltimore Maryland U.S.A. **105** E1 39 18N 76 38W
Baltinglass Wicklow Irish Republic **48** E2 52 55N 6 41W
Baltrum *i.* Germany **63** A2 53 44N 7 23E
Baluchistan *geog. reg.* Pakistan **76** A5/B5 27 30N 65 00E
Bam Iran **79** I4 29 07N 58 20E
Bamako Mali **93** D5 12 40N 7 59W
Bambari Central African Republic **94** D9 5 40N 20 37E
Bamber Bridge *tn.* Lancashire England **42** B3 53 44N 2 40W
Bamberg Germany **63** B1 49 54N 10 54E
Bamburgh Northumberland England **44** C2 55 36N 1 42W
Bamenda Cameroon **93** H4 5 55N 10 09E
Bamingui Bangoran National Park Central African Republic **94** C9 8 00N 20 00E
Bampton Devon England **31** D2 51 00N 3 29W
Banaba *i.* Nauru **118** G7 1 00S 167 00E
Banagher Offaly Irish Republic **48** D3 53 11N 7 59W
Banas *r.* India **77** D5 26 00N 75 00E
Banbridge Down Northern Ireland **48** E4 54 21N 6 16W
Banbury Oxfordshire England **32** A3 52 04N 1 20W
Banchory Grampian Scotland **46** F4 57 30N 2 30W
Bancroft Ontario Canada **105** E3 45 03N 77 52W
Banda India **77** E5 25 28N 80 20E
Banda Aceh Indonesia **80** B5 5 30N 95 20E
Bandama Blanc *r.* Cote d'Ivoire **93** D4 8 00N 5 45W
Bandar Abbās Iran **79** I4 27 12N 56 15E
Bandarbeyla Somalia **94** J9 9 30N 50 50E
Bandar-e Lengeh Iran **79** H4 26 34N 54 52E
Bandar-e Torkeman Iran **79** H6 36 55N 54 01E
Bandar Khomeynī Iran **79** G5 30 40N 49 08E
Bandar Sea Indonesia **80** H2 6 00S 127 00E
Bandar Seri Begawan Brunei **80** F4 4 56N 114 58E
Bandeirantes Beach Brazil **116** B1 23 01S 43 25W
Bandel India **76** K3 22 55N 88 23E
Bandirma Turkey **78** C7 40 21N 27 58E
Bandon Cork Irish Republic **48** C1 51 45N 8 45W
Bandon *r.* Irish Republic **48** C1 51 15N 8 55W
Bandundu Zaïre **95** C7 3 20S 17 24E
Bandung Indonesia **80** D2 6 57S 107 34E
Banff Alberta Canada **100** L3 51 10N 115 34W
Banff Grampian Scotland **46** F4 57 40N 2 33W
Banff National Park Alberta Canada **100** L3 52 00N 116 00W
Banfora Burkina **93** E5 10 36N 4 45W
Bangalore India **77** D2 12 58N 77 35E
Bangassou Central African Republic **94** D8 4 41N 22 48E
Banghāzī *(Benghazi)* Libya **94** D14 32 07N 20 04E
Bangka *i.* Indonesia **80** D3 2 00S 106 30E
Bangkok *(Krung Thep)* Thailand **80** C6 13 44N 100 30E
BANGLADESH **77** F/G4
Bangor Down Northern Ireland **48** F4 54 40N 5 40W
Bangor Gwynedd Wales **38** B3 53 13N 4 08W
Bangor Maine U.S.A. **105** G2 44 49N 68 47W
Bangu Brazil **116** B2 22 53S 43 28W
Bangui Central African Republic **94** C8 4 23N 18 37E
Bangweulu, Lake Zambia **95** E5 11 15S 29 45E
Ban Hat Yai Thailand **80** C5 7 00N 100 28E
Banja Luka Bosnia-Herzegovina **68** C3 44 47N 17 11E
Banjarmasin Indonesia **80** E3 3 22S 114 33E
Banjul The Gambia **93** B5 13 28N 16 39W
Banka India **76** K2 22 36N 88 17E
Banknock Central Scotland **45** C1 55 59N 3 57W
Banks Lancashire England **42** B3 53 41N 2 56W
Banks Island Northwest Territories Canada **100** K7 72 30N 122 30W
Banks Islands Vanuatu **86** L7 13 40S 167 30E
Banks Peninsula New Zealand **87** B2 43 50S 173 10E
Ban Me Thuot Vietnam **80** D6 12 41N 108 02E
Bann *r.* Northern Ireland **48** E4 54 20N 6 10W
Bannockburn Central Scotland **45** C2 56 05N 3 56W
Bannu Pakistan **79** L5 33 00N 70 40E
Bansberia India **76** K3 22 57N 88 23E
Banská Bystrica Slovenska Czechoslovakia **69** C2 48 44N 19 10E
Banstead Surrey England **34** C1 51 19N 0 12W
Banton Strathclyde Scotland **45** B1 55 59N 4 01W
Bantry Cork Irish Republic **48** B1 51 41N 9 27W
Bantry Bay Irish Republic **48** B1 51 35N 9 40W
Banyuwangi Indonesia **80** E2 8 12S 114 22E
Baoding China **81** I5 38 54N 115 26E
Baoji China **81** G4 34 23N 107 16E
Baotou China **81** H6 40 38N 109 59E
Ba'qūbah Iraq **78** F5 33 45N 44 40E
Baraboo Wisconsin U.S.A. **104** C2 43 27N 89 45W
Baracaldo Spain **66** B3 43 17N 2 59W
Barahanagar India **76** K2 22 38N 88 23E
Barahona Dominican Republic **109** J3 18 13N 71 07W
Barajala Canal India **76** J2 22 35N 88 12E
Bārākpur India **76** K3 22 45N 88 22E
Baral India **76** K1 22 27N 88 22E
Baranovichi Belarus **69** E3 53 09N 26 00E
Bārāsat India **76** K2 22 43N 88 26E
Barbacena Brazil **115** I8 21 13S 43 47W
BARBADOS **109** M2
Barbastro Spain **66** C3 42 02N 0 07E
Barbuda *i.* Antigua & Barbuda **109** L3 17 41N 61 48W
Barcaldine Australia **86** H5 23 31S 145 15E
Barcellona Italy **68** C2 38 10N 15 15E
Barcelona Spain **66** C3 41 25N 2 10E
Barcelona Venezuela **114** E15 10 08N 64 43W
Barcelonette France **61** C1 44 24N 6 40E
Barcelos Brazil **114** E12 0 59S 62 58W
Barcoo *r.* Australia **86** G5 23 30S 144 00E
Barcs Hungary **69** C2 45 58N 17 30E
Barddhamān India **77** F4 23 20N 88 00E
Bardrainney Strathclyde Scotland **45** A1 55 55N 4 40W
Barduelv *r.* Norway **67** D4 68 48N 18 22E
Bareilly India **77** D5 28 20N 79 24E
Barents Sea Arctic Ocean **120** 75 00N 40 00E
Barford Warwickshire England **35** D1 52 15N 1 35W
Barga China **77** E6 30 51N 81 20E
Bargoed Mid Glamorgan Wales **38** C1 51 43N 3 15W
Bari Italy **68** C3 41 07N 16 52E
Bariga Nigeria **92** C3 6 32N 3 28E
Barinas Venezuela **114** C14 8 36N 70 15W
Barisal Bangladesh **77** G4 22 41N 90 20E
Bariti, Lake India **76** K3 22 48N 88 26E
Barking Greater London England **34** D2 51 33N 0 06E
Barkly Tableland Australia **86** F6 17 30S 137 00E
Barlaston Staffordshire England **35** B3 52 57N 2 09W
Barlby North Yorkshire England **43** G3 53 48N 1 03W
Bar-le-Duc France **61** C2 48 46N 5 10E
Barlee, Lake Australia **86** B4 28 30S 120 00E
Barletta Italy **68** C3 41 20N 16 17E
Barmen Germany **62** C2 51 16N 7 13E
Barmouth Gwynedd Wales **38** B2 52 43N 4 03W
Barnard Castle Durham England **44** C1 54 33N 1 55W
Barnaul Russia **71** K6 53 21N 83 45E
Barnes Ice Cap Northwest Territories Canada **101** U7 70 10N 74 00W
Barnet Greater London England **34** C2 51 39N 0 12W
Barneveld Netherlands **64** E4 52 08N 5 35E
Barnoldswick Lancashire England **42** D3 53 56N 2 16W
Barnsley South Yorkshire England **43** F2 53 34N 1 28W
Barnstaple Devon England **31** C3 51 05N 4 04W
Barnstaple or **Bideford Bay** Devon England **30/31** C3 51 05N 4 25W
Barnton Cheshire England **42** C1 53 16N 2 33W
Barquisimeto Venezuela **114** D15 10 03N 69 18W
Barra *i.* Western Isles Scotland **46** A4 57 00N 7 25W
Barra da Tijuca Brazil **116** B1 23 00S 43 20W
Barra do Corda Brazil **114** H11 5 30S 45 12W
Barrancabermeja Colombia **114** C14 7 06N 73 54W
Barrancas Venezuela **114** E14 8 45N 62 13W
Barranco Peru **116** E4 12 09S 77 01W
Barranquilla Colombia **114** C15 11 10N 74 50W
Barre Vermont U.S.A. **105** F2 44 13N 72 31W
Barreiras Brazil **114** I10 12 09S 44 58W
Barreiro Portugal **66** A2 38 40N 9 05W
Barrhead Alberta Canada **100** M3 54 10N 114 22W
Barrhead Strathclyde Scotland **45** B1 55 48N 4 24W
Barrie Ontario Canada **105** E2 44 22N 79 42W
Barrio Obrero Peru **116** E4 12 02S 77 04W
Barrow Alaska U.S.A. **100** D7 71 16N 156 50W
Barrow *r.* Irish Republic **48** D2/E2 52 55N 7 00W
Barrow-in-Furness Cumbria England **44** A1 54 07N 3 14W
Barrow Island Australia **86** B5 21 00S 115 00E
Barrow, Point Alaska U.S.A. **100** D7 71 05N 156 00W
Barry South Glamorgan Wales **38** C1 51 24N 3 18W
Barrys Bay *tn.* Ontario Canada **105** E3 45 30N 77 41W
Barstow California U.S.A. **102** C3 34 55N 117 01W
Bartlesville Oklahoma U.S.A. **103** G4 36 44N 95 59W
Barton Lancashire England **42** B3 53 50N 2 45W
Barton Vermont U.S.A. **105** F2 44 44N 72 12W
Barton-le-Clay Bedfordshire England **34** B3 51 58N 0 26W
Barton-under-Needwood Staffordshire England **35** C3 52 45N 1 43W
Barton-upon-Humber Humberside England **40** D2 53 41N 0 27W
Barvas Western Isles Scotland **46** B5 58 22N 6 32W
Barwell Leicestershire England **35** D2 52 32N 1 21W
Basel Switzerland **61** C2 47 33N 7 36E
Basildon Essex England **34** E2 51 34N 0 25E
Basingstoke Hampshire England **32** A2 51 16N 1 05W
Baskatong, Réservoir Québec Canada **105** E3 47 00N 76 00W
Baslow Derbyshire England **43** F1 53 16N 1 37W
Bassas da India *i.* Mozambique Channel **95** H3 22 00S 40 00E
Bassein Myanmar **80** A7 16 46N 94 45E
Bassenthwaite, Lake Cumbria England **44** A1 54 40N 3 13W
Basse Terre *i.* Lesser Antilles **109** L3 16 00N 61 20W
Bastia Corsica France **61** C1 42 41N 9 26E
Bastogne Belgium **64** E2 50 00N 5 43E
Bastrop Louisiana U.S.A. **103** H3 32 49N 91 54W
Bata Equatorial Guinea **93** G3 1 51N 9 49E
Batakan Indonesia **80** E3 4 03S 114 39E
Batala India **77** D6 31 48N 75 17E
Batanagar India **76** K2 22 30N 88 14E
Batan Datuk Malaysia **80** C4 3 58N 100 47E
Batang China **81** E4 30 02N 99 01E
Batangafo Central African Republic **94** C9 7 27N 18 11E
Batangas The Philippines **80** G6 13 46N 121 01E
Batavia New York U.S.A. **105** E2 43 00N 78 11W
Bath Avon England **31** E3 51 23N 2 22W
Bath Jamaica **109** R7 17 57N 76 22W
Batha *r.* Chad **94** C10 13 00N 19 00E
Bathgate Lothian Scotland **45** C1 55 55N 3 39W
Bathurst Australia **86** H3 33 27S 149 35E
Bathurst New Brunswick Canada **101** V2 47 37N 65 40W
Bathurst, Cape Northwest Territories Canada **100** J7 70 31N 127 53W
Bathurst Inlet Northwest Territories Canada **100** N6 66 49N 108 00W
Bathurst Island Australia **86** E7 12 00S 130 00E
Bathurst Island Northwest Territories Canada **101** P8 76 00W 100 00W
Batley West Yorkshire England **43** F3 53 44N 1 37W
Batna Algeria **93** G10 35 34N 6 10E
Baton Rouge Louisiana U.S.A. **103** G3 30 30N 91 10W
Batroûn Lebanon **78** O12 36 16N 35 40E
Battambang Cambodia **80** C6 13 06N 103 13E
Battersea Greater London England **34** C2 51 28N 0 10W
Batticaloa Sri Lanka **77** E1 7 43N 81 42E
Battle East Sussex England **33** C1 50 55N 0 29E
Battle Creek *tn.* Michigan U.S.A. **104** C2 42 20N 85 21W
Battle Harbour *tn.* Newfoundland Canada **101** X3 52 16N 55 36W
Batumi Georgia **70** G4 41 37N 41 36E
Bat Yam Israel **78** O10 32 01N 34 45E
Baubau Indonesia **80** G2 5 30S 122 37E
Bauchi Nigeria **93** G5 10 16N 9 50E
Bauria India **76** J1 22 29N 88 09E
Bauru Brazil **115** H8 22 19S 49 07W
Bautzen Germany **63** B2 51 11N 14 29E
Bavaria *admin.* Germany *see* Bayern
Bawdsey Suffolk England **33** D3 52 01N 1 25E
Bawtry South Yorkshire England **43** G2 53 26N 1 01W
Bayamo Cuba **109** I4 20 23N 76 39W
Bayan Ha Shan *mts.* China **72** 34 00N 100 00E
Bay City Michigan U.S.A. **105** D2 43 35N 83 52W
Bay City Texas U.S.A. **103** G2 28 59N 96 00W
Baydhabo Somalia **94** H8 3 08N 43 34E
Bayerische Alpen *mts.* Germany **63** B1 47 00N 11 00E
Bayerische Wald *geog. reg.* Germany **63** B1 49 00N 13 00E
Bayern *(Bavaria) admin.* Germany **63** B1 49 00N 12 00E
Bayeux France **61** A2 49 16N 0 42W
Baykal, Lake *see* Ozero Baykal
Baykonyr Kazakhstan **70** I5 47 50N 66 03E
Bayonne France **61** A1 43 30N 1 28W
Bayonne New Jersey U.S.A. **106** B1 40 39N 74 07W
Bayreuth Germany **63** B1 49 27N 11 35E
Bay Ridge *tn.* New York U.S.A. **106** C1 40 37N 74 02W
Bayston Hill Shropshire England **36** B2 52 40N 2 48W
Baytown Texas U.S.A. **103** H2 29 43N 94 59W
Baza Spain **66** B2 37 30N 2 45W
Bcharre Lebanon **78** P12 34 15N 36 00E
Beachief South Yorkshire England **43** F1 53 19N 1 30W
Beachy Head *c.* East Sussex England **33** C1 50 44N 0 16E
Beaconsfield Buckinghamshire England **34** B2 51 37N 0 39W
Beadnell Bay Northumberland England **44** C2 55 32N 1 30W
Beaminster Dorset England **31** E2 50 49N 2 45W
Beardmore Ontario Canada **104** C3 49 36N 87 59W
Beardmore Glacier Antarctica **121** 84 00S 170 00E
Beare Green Surrey England **34** C1 51 10N 0 19W
Bear Island Irish Republic **48** B1 51 40N 9 48W
Bear Lake *l.* U.S.A. **102** D5 42 00N 111 20W
Bearsden Strathclyde Scotland **45** B1 55 56N 4 20W
Beatrice Nebraska U.S.A. **104** A2 40 17N 96 45W
Beatty Nevada U.S.A. **102** C4 36 54N 116 45W
Beauchamp France **60** A3 49 00N 2 12E
Beaufort South Carolina U.S.A. **103** J3 32 26N 80 40W
Beaufort Sea Arctic Ocean **120** 72 00N 135 00W
Beaufort West Republic of South Africa **95** D1 32 21S 22 35E
Beaulieu Hampshire England **32** A1 50 49N 1 27W
Beauly Highland Scotland **46** D4 57 29N 4 29W
Beauly *r.* Highland Scotland **46** D4 57 30N 4 40W
Beaumaris Gwynedd Wales **38** B3 53 16N 4 05W
Beaumont Belgium **64** D2 50 14N 4 14E
Beaumont Texas U.S.A. **103** H3 30 04N 94 06W
Beaune France **61** B2 47 02N 4 50E
Beauséjour Manitoba Canada **104** A4 50 04N 96 30W
Beauvais France **61** B2 49 26N 2 05E
Beauval Saskatchewan Canada **100** N4 55 09N 107 35W
Beaver Alaska U.S.A. **100** F6 66 22N 147 30W
Beaver Dam *tn.* Kentucky U.S.A. **104** C1 37 24N 86 52W
Beaver Island Michigan U.S.A. **104** C3 45 00N 85 00W
Beavermouth British Columbia Canada **100** L3 51 30N 117 28W
Bebington Merseyside England **42** B1 53 20N 2 59W
Beccles Suffolk England **33** D3 52 28N 1 34E
Béchar Algeria **93** E9 31 35N 2 17W
Becharof Lake Alaska U.S.A. **100** D4 58 00N 156 30W

Beckley West Virginia U.S.A. 105 D1 37 46N 81 12W
Beconshall Lancashire England 42 B3 53 42N 2 51W
Bedale North Yorkshire England 40 C3 54 17N 1 35W
Bedford Bedfordshire England 33 B3 52 08N 0 29W
Bedford Indiana U.S.A. 104 C1 38 51N 86 30W
Bedford Levels *geog. reg.* Cambridgeshire England 33 B3 52 35N 0 00
Bedfordshire *co.* England 33 B3 52 00N 0 30W
Bedlington Northumberland England 44 C2 55 08N 1 25W
Bedwas Mid Glamorgan Wales 38 C1 51 35N 3 12W
Bedworth Warwickshire England 35 D2 52 29N 1 28W
Beersheba Israel 78 O10 31 15N 34 47E
Beeston Nottinghamshire England 36 C2 52 56N 1 12W
Beeston West Yorkshire England 43 F3 53 46N 1 34W
Beeville Texas U.S.A. 103 G2 28 25N 97 47W
Begna *r.* Norway 67 B3 61 00N 9 00E
Behala *see* South Suburbs
Behbehān Iran 79 H5 30 34N 50 18E
Beht *r.* Morocco 66 A1 34 30N 5 50W
Bei'an China 81 K7 48 16N 126 36E
Beighton South Yorkshire England 43 F2 53 21N 1 21W
Beihai China 81 G2 21 29N 109 10E
Beihai *l.* China 82 G1 39 57N 116 22E
Beijing *(Peking)* China 82 G1 39 55N 116 26E
Beilen Netherlands 64 F4 52 51N 6 31E
Beinn Dearg *mt.* Highland Scotland 46 D4 57 47N 4 56W
Beira Mozambique 95 F4 19 49S 34 52E
Beirut *see* Beyrouth
Beith Strathclyde Scotland 45 A1 55 45N 4 38W
Beiyuan China 82 G2 40 01N 116 25E
Beja Portugal 66 A2 38 01N 7 52W
Béja Tunisia 93 G10 36 52N 9 13E
Bejaïa Algeria 93 G10 36 49N 5 03E
Békes Hungary 69 D2 46 45N 21 09E
Bela Pakistan 76 B5 26 12N 66 20E
BELARUS *(BYELORUSSIA)* 70 E6
Belaya Tserkov Ukraine 69 F2 49 49N 30 10E
Belbroughton Hereford & Worcester England 35 B2 52 23N 2 05W
Belém Brazil 114 H12 1 27S 48 29W
Belfast Antrim Northern Ireland 49 D1 54 35N 5 55W
Belfast Maine U.S.A. 105 G2 44 26N 69 01W
Belfast Lough *est.* Northern Ireland 49 D1/2 54 40N 5 45W
Belford Northumberland England 44 C2 55 36N 1 49W
Belford Roxo Brazil 116 D2 22 46S 43 24W
Belfort France 61 C2 47 38N 6 52E
Belgaum India 77 C3 15 54N 74 36E
Belgharia India 76 K2 22 39N 88 23E
BELGIUM 64 D2
Belgorod Russia 70 F6 50 38N 36 36E
Belgrade *see* Beograd
Beliaghata India 76 K2 22 34N 88 23E
Belitung *i.* Indonesia 80 D3 2 30S 108 00E
BELIZE 108 G3
Belize Belize 108 G3 17 29N 88 10W
Bellac France 61 B2 46 07N 1 04E
Bella Coola British Columbia Canada 100 J3 52 23W 126 46W
Bellary India 77 D3 15 11N 76 54E
Bella Vista Argentina 115 F7 28 31S 59 00W
Belle-Île *i.* France 61 A2 47 20N 3 10W
Belle Isle, Strait of Newfoundland Canada 101 X3 51 00N 57 30W
Belleville Illinois U.S.A. 104 C1 38 31N 89 59W
Belleville Ontario Canada 105 E2 44 10N 77 22W
Bellflower California U.S.A. 107 B2 33 53N 118 08W
Bellingham Northumberland England 44 B2 55 09N 2 16W
Bellingham Washington U.S.A. 102 B6 48 45N 122 29W
Bellingshausen *r.s.* Antarctica 121 62 12S 58 58W
Bellingshausen Sea Southern Ocean 121 71 00S 85 00W
Bellinzona Switzerland 61 C2 46 12N 9 02E
Bello Colombia 114 B14 6 20N 75 41W
Bellsbank Strathclyde Scotland 46 D2 55 19N 4 24W
Bellshill Strathclyde Scotland 45 B1 55 49N 4 02W
Bellsmyre Strathclyde Scotland 45 A1 55 58N 4 33W
Belluno Italy 68 B4 46 08N 12 13E
Belmont Northern Ireland 49 D1 54 36N 5 52W
Belmopan Belize 108 G3 17 13N 88 48W
Belmullet Mayo Irish Republic 48 A4/B4 54 14N 10 00W
Belogorsk Russia 71 O6 50 55N 128 26E
Belo Horizonte Brazil 114 I9 19 54S 43 54W
Beloit Wisconsin U.S.A. 104 C2 42 31N 89 04W
Belovo Russia 81 C8 54 27N 86 19E
Belper Derbyshire England 35 D4 53 01N 1 29W
Belton Norfolk England 33 D3 52 34N 1 40E
Bel'tsy Moldova 69 E2 47 44N 28 41E
Belturbet Cavan Irish Republic 48 D4 54 06N 7 28W
Belur India 76 K2 22 37N 88 20E
Belvidere Illinois U.S.A. 104 C2 42 50N 88 50W
Belvoir, Vale of Leicestershire England 36 D2 52 58N 0 55W
Belyy *i.* Russia 71 J10 73 00N 70 00E
Belyy Yar Russia 71 K7 58 28N 85 03E
Bembézar *r.* Spain 66 A2 38 00N 5 15W
Bembridge Isle of Wight England 32 A1 50 41N 1 05W
Bemidji Minnesota U.S.A. 104 B3 47 29N 94 52W
Ben Alder *mt.* Highland Scotland 46 D3 56 49N 4 28W
Benavente Spain 66 A3 42 00N 5 40W
Benbecula *i.* Western Isles Scotland 46 A4 57 25N 7 20W
Ben Cleuch *mt.* Central Scotland 45 C2 56 11N 3 47W
Ben Cruachan *mt.* Strathclyde Scotland 46 C3 56 26N 5 09W
Bend Oregon U.S.A. 102 B5 44 04N 121 20W
Bendery Moldova 69 E2 46 50N 29 29E
Bendigo Australia 86 G2 36 48S 144 21E
Benevento Italy 68 B3 41 08N 14 46E
Benfica Brazil 116 B2 22 52S 43 16W
Bengal, Bay of Indian Ocean 77 F3/G3 17 00N 88 00E
Bengbu China 81 I4 32 56N 117 27E
Benghazi *see* Banghāzī
Bengkulu Indonesia 80 C3 3 46S 102 16N
Benguela Angola 95 B5 12 34S 13 24E
Ben Hope *mt.* Highland Scotland 46 D5 58 24N 4 37W
Beni Abbès Algeria 93 E9 30 11N 2 14W
Benicarló Spain 66 C3 40 25N 0 25E
Beni Mellal Morocco 93 D9 32 22N 6 29W
BENIN 93 F5
Benin, Bight of W. Africa 93 F4 5 05N 2 30E
Benin City Nigeria 93 G4 6 19N 5 41E
Beni, Rio *r.* Bolivia 114 D10 13 00S 67 30W
Beni Saf Algeria 66 B2 35 28N 1 22W
Beni Suef Egypt 78 D4 29 05N 31 05E
Benjamin Constant Brazil 114 C12 4 23S 69 59W
Ben Klibreck *mt.* Highland Scotland 46 D5 58 14N 4 22W
Ben Lawers *mt.* Tayside Scotland 46 D3 56 33N 4 15W
Ben Ledi *mt.* Central Scotland 45 B2 56 16N 4 20W
Benllech Gwynedd Wales 38 B3 53 19N 4 15W
Ben Lomond *mt.* Central Scotland 46 D3 56 12N 4 38W
Ben Loyal *mt.* Highland Scotland 46 D5 58 24N 4 26W
Ben Macdui *mt.* Grampian Scotland 46 E4 57 04N 3 40W
Ben More *mt.* Central Scotland 46 D3 56 23N 4 31W
Ben More *mt.* Mull Scotland 46 B/C3 56 25N 6 01W
Ben More *mt.* Strathclyde Scotland 46 B3 56 25N 6 02W
Ben More Assynt Highland Scotland 46 D5 58 07N 4 52W
Benmore, Lake New Zealand 87 B2 44 10S 170 20E
Ben Nevis *mt.* Highland Scotland 46 D3 56 48N 5 00W
Bennington Vermont U.S.A. 105 F2 42 54N 73 12W
Bénoué *(Benue) r.* Cameroon 93 H4 8 10N 13 50E
Benrath Germany 62 B1 51 10N 6 53E
Benson Arizona U.S.A. 102 D3 31 58N 110 19W
Bentley South Yorkshire England 43 G2 53 33N 1 09W
Benton Harbor *tn.* Michigan U.S.A. 104 C2 42 07N 86 27W
Benue *(Bénoué) r.* Nigeria 93 G4 8 00N 7 40E
Ben Venue *mt.* Central Scotland 45 B2 56 13N 4 29W
Ben Wyvis *mt.* Highland Scotland 46 D4 57 40N 4 35W
Beograd *(Belgrade)* Serbia Yugoslavia 68 D3 44 50N 20 30E
Beppu Japan 82 B1 33 18N 131 30E
Berat Albania 68 D3 40 43N 19 46E
Berber Sudan 78 D2 18 01N 34 00E
Berbera Somalia 94 I10 10 28N 45 02E
Berbérati Central African Republic 94 C8 4 19N 15 51E
Berck France 61 B3 50 24N 1 35E
Berdichev Ukraine 69 E2 49 54N 28 39E
Beregovo Ukraine 69 D2 48 13N 22 39E
Berezina *r.* Belarus 69 E3 54 00N 29 00E
Berezniki Russia 70 H7 59 26N 56 49E
Berezovo Russia 71 I8 63 58N 65 00E
Bergama Turkey 68 E2 39 08N 27 10E
Bérgamo Italy 68 A4 45 42N 9 40E
Bergen Netherlands 64 D4 52 40N 4 37E
Bergen Norway 67 B3 60 23N 5 20E
Bergenfield New Jersey U.S.A. 106 C2 40 56N 74 00W
Bergen op Zoom Netherlands 64 D3 51 30N 4 17E
Bergerac France 61 B1 44 50N 0 29E
Bergheim Germany 64 F2 50 57N 6 38E
Bergisch Gladbach Germany 63 A2 50 59N 7 10E
Bergues France 64 B2 50 58N 2 26E
Bering Sea Pacific Ocean 100 A4 60 00N 175 00W
Bering Strait Russia/U.S.A. 100 B6 69 00N 169 00W
Berkåk Norway 67 C3 62 48N 10 03E
Berkakit Russia 71 O7 56 36N 124 49E
Berkel *r.* Netherlands 64 F4 52 07N 6 30E
Berkeley Gloucestershire England 31 E3 51 42N 2 27W
Berkeley Sound Falkland Islands 117 M16 51 50S 57 50W
Berkhamsted Hertfordshire England 34 B3 51 46N 0 35W
Berkner Island Antarctica 121 80 00S 45 00W
Berkshire *co.* England 32/33 A2/B2 51 28N 1 00W
Berkshire Downs *hills* Berkshire England 32 A2 51 30N 1 25W
Berlevåg Norway 67 F5 70 50N 29 09E
Berlin *admin.* Germany 63 B2 52 00N 13 00E
Berlin Germany 63 B2 52 32N 13 25E
Berlin New Hampshire U.S.A. 105 F2 44 27N 71 13W
Bermuda *i.* Atlantic Ocean 109 L6 32 50N 64 20W
Bern Switzerland 61 C2 46 57N 7 26E
Bernburg Germany 63 B2 51 49N 11 43E
Berner Alpen *mts.* Switzerland 61 C2 46 25N 7 30E
Berneray *i.* Western Isles Scotland 46 A4 57 45N 7 10W
Berounka *r.* Ceska Czechoslovakia 63 B1 50 00N 14 00E
Berry Head Devon England 31 D2 50 24N 3 29W
Bertoua Cameroon 93 H3 4 34N 13 42E
Berwick Nova Scotia Canada 101 W2 45 03N 64 44W
Berwick Pennsylvania U.S.A. 105 E2 41 04N 76 13W
Berwick-upon-Tweed Northumberland England 44 B2 55 46N 2 00W
Berwyn *r.* Clwyd Wales 38 C2 52 52N 3 25W
Besançon France 61 C2 47 14N 6 02E
Beskidy Zachodnie *mts.* Poland 69 C2–D2 50 00N 20 00E
Beskudnikovo Russia 70 M2 55 54N 37 38E
Bessacarr South Yorkshire England 43 G2 53 30N 1 05W
Bessbrook Northern Ireland 48 E4 54 12N 6 24W
Bétaré Oya Cameroon 93 H4 5 34N 14 09E
Bethany Missouri U.S.A. 104 B2 40 16N 94 02W
Bethel Alaska U.S.A. 100 C5 60 49N 161 49W
Bethersden Kent England 33 C2 51 07N 0 45W
Bethesda Gwynedd Wales 38 B3 53 11N 4 03W
Bethesda Maryland U.S.A. 105 E1 39 00N 77 05W
Bethlehem Jordan 78 O10 31 42N 35 12E
Bethlehem Pennsylvania U.S.A. 105 E2 40 36N 75 22W
Béthune France 61 B3 50 32N 2 38E
Betican Cordilleras *hills* Spain 51 37 00N 3 00W
Betroka Madagascar 95 I3 23 15S 46 07E
Betsiamites Québec Canada 105 G3 48 56N 68 40W
Betsiboka *r.* Madagascar 95 I4 17 00S 46 30E
Bettyhill Highland Scotland 46 D5 58 32N 4 14W
Betws-y-Coed Gwynedd Wales 38 C3 53 05N 3 48W
Beveren Belgium 64 D3 51 13N 4 15E
Beverley Humberside England 40 D2 53 51N 0 26W
Beverly Hills California U.S.A. 107 A3 34 03N 118 22W
Beverwijk Netherlands 64 D4 52 29N 4 40E
Bewcastle Cumbria England 44 B2 55 03N 2 42W
Bewdley Hereford and Worcester England 35 B2 52 22N 2 19W
Bexhill East Sussex England 33 C1 50 50N 0 29E
Bexley Greater London England 34 D2 51 27N 0 09E
Beyla Guinea 93 D4 8 42N 8 39W
Beyrouth *(Beirut)* Lebanon 78 O11 33 52N 35 30E
Beyşehir Gölü *l.* Turkey 78 D6 37 40N 31 43E
Béziers France 61 B1 43 21N 3 13E
Bhadgaon Nepal 77 F5 27 41N 85 26E
Bhadravati India 77 D2 13 54N 75 38E
Bhadreswar India 76 K3 22 50N 88 20E
Bhagalpur India 77 F5 25 14N 86 59E
Bhandara India 77 D4 21 10N 79 41E
Bharatpur India 77 D5 27 14N 77 29E
Bharuch India 77 C4 21 40N 73 02E
Bhatinda India 77 C6 30 10N 74 58E
Bhātpāra India 76 K3 22 52N 88 25E
Bhavnagar India 77 C4 21 46N 72 14E
Bhilwara India 77 C5 25 23N 74 39E
Bhima *r.* India 77 D3 17 00N 77 00E
Bhiwandi India 77 C3 19 21N 73 08E
Bhopal India 77 D4 23 17N 77 28E
Bhubaneshwar India 77 F4 20 13N 85 50E
Bhuj India 76 B4 23 12N 69 54E
Bhusawal India 77 D4 21 01N 75 50E
BHUTAN 77 F/G5
Biała Podlaska Poland 69 D3 52 03N 23 05E
Białystok Poland 69 D3 53 09N 23 10E
Biarritz France 61 A1 43 29N 1 33W
Bibai Japan 82 D3 43 21N 141 53E
Biberach Germany 63 A1 48 06N 9 48E
Bicester Oxfordshire England 32 A2 51 54N 1 09W
Bida Nigeria 93 G4 9 06N 5 59E
Bidar India 77 D3 17 56N 77 35E
Biddeford Maine U.S.A. 105 F2 43 29N 70 27W
Biddulph Staffordshire England 36 B3 53 08N 2 10W
Bideford Devon England 31 C3 51 01N 4 13W
Biebrza *r.* Poland 69 D3 53 00N 22 00E
Biel Switzerland 61 C2 46 27N 8 13E
Bielefeld Germany 63 A2 52 02N 8 32E
Biella Italy 68 A4 45 34N 8 04E
Bielsko-Biała Poland 69 C2 49 50N 19 00E
Bielsk Podlaski Poland 69 D3 52 47N 23 11E
Bièvres France 60 A2 48 45N 2 11E
Biferno *r.* Italy 68 B3 41 00N 14 00E
Biğa Turkey 68 E3 40 13N 27 14E
Big Black *r.* Mississippi U.S.A. 103 H3 33 00N 90 00W
Big Blue *r.* U.S.A. 104 A2 40 00N 96 00W
Bigbury Bay Devon England 31 C2/D2 50 17N 4 00W
Biggar Strathclyde Scotland 46 E2 55 38N 3 32W
Biggin Hill *tn.* Greater London England 34 D1 51 18N 0 04E
Biggleswade Bedfordshire England 33 B3 52 05N 0 17W
Bighorn *r.* U.S.A. 102 E6 45 00N 108 00W
Bighorn Mountains U.S.A. 102 E5 44 00N 108 00W
Big Salmon Yukon Territory Canada 100 I5 61 52N 134 56W
Big Santa Anita Reservoir California U.S.A. 107 B3 34 11N 118 01W
Big Sioux *r.* U.S.A. 104 A2 43 00N 96 00W
Big Spring *tn.* Texas U.S.A. 102 F3 32 15N 101 30W
Big Trout Lake Ontario Canada 101 R3 54 00N 89 00W
Big Tujunga Reservoir California U.S.A. 107 B4 34 19N 118 11W
Bihac Bosnia-Herzegovina 68 C3 44 49N 15 53E
Bihar *admin.* India 77 F4 24 40N 86 00E
Biharamulo Tanzania 94 F7 2 37S 31 20E
Bijapur India 77 D3 16 47N 75 48E
Bijar Iran 79 G6 35 52N 47 39E
Bijlmermeer Netherlands 65 D3 52 19N 4 58E
Bikaner India 77 C5 28 01N 73 22E
Bilaspur India 77 E4 27 51N 82 00E
Bilbao Spain 66 B3 43 15N 2 56W
Bilibino Russia 71 S9 68 00N 166 15E
Billericay Essex England 34 E2 51 38N 0 25E
Billinge Merseyside England 42 B2 53 30N 2 42W
Billingham Cleveland England 44 C1 54 36N 1 17W
Billings Montana U.S.A. 102 E6 45 47N 108 30W
Billingshurst West Sussex England 33 B2 51 01N 0 28W
Billington Bedfordshire England 34 B3 51 54N 0 39W
Billington Lancashire England 42 C3 53 49N 2 24W
Biloxi Mississippi U.S.A. 103 I3 30 24N 88 55W
Bilston Lothian Scotland 45 D1 55 11N 3 52W
Bilston West Midlands England 35 B2 52 34N 2 04W
Bilthoven Netherlands 65 E2 52 08N 5 09E
Binche Belgium 64 D2 50 25N 4 10E
Bingen Germany 63 A1 49 58N 7 55E
Bingham Maine U.S.A. 105 G3 45 03N 69 53W
Bingham Nottinghamshire England 36 D2 52 57N 0 57W
Binghamton New York U.S.A. 105 E2 42 06N 75 55W
Bingley West Yorkshire England 43 E3 53 51N 1 50W
Binley Woods *tn.* Warwickshire England 35 D2 52 25N 1 26W
Bintulu Malaysia 80 E4 3 12N 113 01E
Binza *r.* Zaïre 92 A1 4 23S 15 14E
Bioko *i.* Equatorial Guinea 93 G3 3 00N 8 20E
Birao Central African Republic 94 D10 10 11N 22 49E
Biratnager Nepal 77 F5 26 27N 87 17E
Birchwood Lincolnshire England 36 D3 53 14N 0 33W
Bircotes Nottighamshire England 43 G2 53 25N 1 03W
Birdsgreen Shropshire England 35 A2 52 27N 2 21W
Birdsville Australia 86 F4 25 50S 139 20E
Birjand Iran 79 I5 32 55N 59 10E
Birkenhead Merseyside England 42 A2 53 24N 3 02W
Birkenshaw Strathclyde Scotland 45 B1 55 50N 4 05W
Birkenshaw West Yorkshire England 43 E3 53 46N 1 41W
Birlad Romania 69 E2 46 14N 27 40E
Birmingham Alabama U.S.A. 103 I3 33 30N 86 55W
Birmingham West Midlands England 35 C2 52 30N 1 50W
Birnin Kebbi Nigeria 93 F5 12 30N 4 11E
Birobidzhan Russia 71 P5 48 49N 132 54E
Birr Offaly Irish Republic 48 D3 53 05N 7 54W
Birstall Leicestershire England 36 C2 52 40N 1 08W
Biscay, Bay of Atlantic Ocean 61 A2 45 30N 2 50W
Biscoe Islands Antarctica 121 66 00S 67 00W
Bishkek *(Frunze)* Kirgyzstan 71 J4 42 53N 74 46E
Bishop Auckland Durham England 44 C1 54 40N 1 40W
Bishopbriggs Strathclyde Scotland 45 B1 55 54N 4 14W
Bishop Rock Isles of Scilly England 30 A1 49 52N 6 27W
Bishop's Castle Shropshire England 36 B2 52 29N 3 00W
Bishop's Cleeve Gloucestershire England 31 E3 51 57N 2 04W
Bishop's Itchington Warwickshire England 35 D1 52 14N 2 26W
Bishop's Lydeard Somerset England 31 D3 51 04N 3 12W
Bishop's Stortford Hertfordshire England 34 D3 51 53N 0 09E
Bishop's Tachbrook West Midlands England 35 D1 52 16N 1 33W
Bishopston West Glamorgan Wales 38 B1 51 35N 4 03W
Bishop's Waltham Hampshire England 32 A1 50 58N 1 12W
Bishop's Wood *tn.* Staffordshire England 35 B3 52 41N 2 15W
Bishopthorpe North Yorkshire England 43 G3 53 56N 1 06W
Bishopton Strathclyde Scotland 45 A1 55 54N 4 31W
Biskra Algeria 93 G9 34 50N 5 41E
Bismarck North Dakota U.S.A. 102 F6 46 50N 100 48W
Bismarck Archipelago Papua New Guinea H9/I9 2 30S 149 00E
Bismarck, Cape Greenland 120 77 00N 18 00W
Bismarck Sea Papua New Guinea 86 H9 4 00S 147 30E
Bissau Guinea-Bissau 93 B5 11 52N 15 39W
Bistriţa *r.* Romania 69 E2 47 00N 25 00E
Bistriţa Romania 69 D2 47 08N 24 30E
Bitburg Germany 64 F1 49 58N 6 32E
Bitola Macedonia Yugoslavia 68 D3 41 01N 21 21E
Bitterroot Range *mts.* U.S.A. 102 D6 46 00N 114 00W
Biwa-ko *l.* Japan 82 C2 35 20N 135 20E
Biysk Russia 71 K6 52 35N 85 16E
Bizerte Tunisia 93 G10 37 18N 9 52E
Blaby Leicestershire England 36 C2 52 35N 1 09W
Black *r.* Wisconsin U.S.A. 104 B2 44 00N 91 00W
Blackall Australia 86 H5 24 23S 145 27E
Blackall Colliery Durham England 44 C1 54 43N 1 20W
Black Bull Meath Irish Republic 49 A2 53 27N 6 29W
Blackburn Lancashire England 42 C3 53 45N 2 29W
Blackburn Lothian Scotland 45 C1 55 53N 3 38W
Black Diamond Alberta Canada 100 M3 50 45N 114 12W
Blackdown Hills Devon/Somerset England 31 D2 50 55N 3 10W
Black Forest *see* Schwarzwald
Blackheath West Midlands England 35 B2 52 27N 2 00W
Black Lake *tn.* Québec Canada 105 F3 46 03N 71 21W
Blackmore Vale Dorset England 31 E2 50 55N 2 25W
Black Mountains Powys Wales 38 C1 51 55N 3 10W
Blackpool British Columbia Canada 100 K3 51 33N 120 07W
Blackpool Lancashire England 42 A3 53 50N 3 03W
Black River *tn.* Jamaica 109 Q8 18 02N 77 52W
Blackrock Dublin Irish Republic 49 B1 53 18N 6 11W
Black Sea Europe 70 F4 43 00N 35 00E
Blacksod Bay Irish Republic 48 A4 54 05N 10 00W
Blackstone Virginia U.S.A. 105 E1 37 05N 78 02W
Black Volta *r.* Ghana 93 E4 9 00N 2 40W
Blackwater *r.* Essex England 33 C2 51 45N 0 50E
Blackwater *r.* Irish Republic 48 C2 52 10N 9 05W
Blackwater *r.* Northern Ireland 49 D1 54 30N 5 48W
Blackwater Reservoir Highland Scotland 46 D3 56 41N 4 46W
Blackwell Oklahoma U.S.A. 103 G4 36 47N 97 18W
Blackwood Gwent Wales 38 C1 51 41N 3 13W
Blackwood Strathclyde Scotland 45 C1 55 41N 3 56W
Blacon Cheshire England 42 B1 53 13N 2 56W
Blaenau Ffestiniog Gwynedd Wales 38 C2 52 59N 3 56W
Blaenavon Gwent Wales 38 C1 51 48N 3 05W
Blagoevgrad Bulgaria 68 D3 42 01N 23 05E
Blagoveshchensk Russia 71 O6 50 19N 127 30E
Blaina Gwent Wales 38 C1 51 48N 3 11W
Blair Atholl Tayside Scotland 46 E3 56 46N 3 51W
Blairgowrie Tayside Scotland 46 E3 56 36N 3 21W
Blakedown Hereford & Worcester England 35 B2 52 24N 2 10W
Blakeney Point Norfolk England 33 D3 52 58N 1 00E
Blanc, Cape *see* Ras Nouadhibou
Blanchardstown Dublin Irish Republic 49 A2 53 24N 6 23W
Blandford Forum Dorset England 31 E2 50 52N 2 11W
Blankenberge Belgium 64 C3 51 19N 3 08E
Blantyre Malawi 95 F4 15 46S 35 00E
Blantyre Strathclyde Scotland 45 B1 55 47N 4 06W
Blarney Cork Irish Republic 48 C1 51 56N 8 34W
Blavet *r.* France 61 A2 48 00N 3 10W
Blaxton South Yorkshire England 43 H2 53 30N 0 59W
Blaydon Tyne and Wear England 44 C1 54 58N 1 42W
Blenheim New Zealand 87 B2 41 32S 173 58E
Blenheim Ontario Canada 105 D2 42 20N 81 59W
Blessington Wicklow Irish Republic 49 A1 53 10N 6 32W
Bletchley Buckinghamshire England 34 A3 52 00N 0 46W
Blida Algeria 93 F10 36 30N 2 50E
Blidworth Nottinghamshire England 36 C3 53 09N 1 11W
Blies *r.* Germany 64 G1 49 00N 7 00E
Bligh Water *sd.* Fiji 118 T16 17 00S 178 00E
Blind River *tn.* Ontario Canada 105 D3 46 12N 82 59W
Blind River *tn.* Ontario Canada 101 S2 46 12N 82 59W
Blithe *r.* Staffordshire England 35 C3 52 25N 1 50W
Blithfield Reservoir Staffordshire England 35 C3 52 40N 1 53W
Bloemendaal Netherlands 65 C3 52 24N 4 39E
Bloemfontein Republic of South Africa 95 E2 29 07S 26 14E
Blois France 61 B2 47 36N 1 20E
Bloody Foreland *c.* Irish Republic 48 C5 55 10N 8 15W
Bloomfield New Jersey U.S.A. 106 B2 40 49N 74 10W
Bloomfield New York U.S.A. 106 B1 40 37N 74 10W
Bloomington Illinois U.S.A. 104 C2 40 29N 89 00W
Bloomington Indiana U.S.A. 104 C1 39 10N 86 31W
Bloomington Minnesota U.S.A. 104 B2 44 48N 93 19W
Bloomsburg Pennsylvania U.S.A. 105 E2 41 01N 76 27W
Bloxwich West Midlands England 35 C2 52 37N 2 00W
Bludenz Austria 63 A1 47 10N 9 50E
Bluefield West Virginia U.S.A. 105 D1 37 14N 81 17W
Bluefields Nicaragua 109 H2 12 00N 83 49W
Blue Mountains, The Jamaica 109 R8 18 00N 76 30W
Blue Nile *see* Abbai, Bahr el Azraq
Blue Ridge *mts.* U.S.A. 105 E1 38 00N 78 00W
Bluestone Reservoir West Virginia U.S.A. 105 D1 37 00N 81 00W
Bluff New Zealand 87 A1 46 38S 168 21E
Blufton Indiana U.S.A. 104 C2 40 44N 85 11W
Blumenau Brazil 115 H7 26 55N 49 07W
Blyth Northumberland England 44 C2 55 07N 1 30W
Blyth Nottinghamshire England 43 G2 53 23N 1 03W
Blyth *r.* Northumberland England 44 C2 55 08N 1 45W
Blyth *r.* Suffolk England 33 D3 52 28N 1 30E
Blyth Bridge *tn.* Borders Scotland 45 D1 55 42N 3 24W
Blythe California U.S.A. 102 D3 33 38N 114 35W
Blythe *r.* Staffordshire England 36 C2 52 45N 1 50W
Blythe Bridge Staffordshire England 35 B3 52 57N 2 04W
Bo Sierra Leone 93 C4 7 58N 11 45W
Boa Vista Brazil 114 E13 3 23S 55 30W
Bobcaygeon Ontario Canada 105 E2 44 32N 78 33W
Bobigny France 60 B2 48 55N 2 28E
Böblingen Germany 63 A1 48 41N 9 01E
Bobo Dioulasso Burkina 93 E5 11 11N 4 18W
Bobruysk Belarus 69 E3 53 08N 29 10E
Bocholt Germany 63 A2 51 49N 6 37E
Bochum Germany 62 C2 51 28N 7 11E
Boddam Grampian Scotland 46 G4 57 28N 1 48W
Bode *r.* Germany 63 B2 52 00N 11 00E
Bodegraven Netherlands 65 D2 52 05N 4 45E
Bodélé *dep.* Chad 94 C11 17 00N 17 50E
Boden Sweden 67 E4 65 50N 21 44E
Bodensee *l.* Switzerland 61 C2 47 40N 9 30E
Bodija Estate Ibadan Nigeria 92 E4 7 26N 3 57E
Bodmin Cornwall England 30 C2 50 29N 4 43W
Bodmin Moor Cornwall England 30 C2 50 35N 4 40W
Bodø Norway 67 C4 67 18N 14 26E
Bogalusa Louisiana U.S.A. 103 I3 30 56N 89 53W
Boggeragh Mountains Irish Republic 48 C2 52 00N 8 50W
Bognor Regis West Sussex England 33 B1 50 47N 0 41W
Bogor Indonesia 80 D2 6 34S 106 45E
Bogotá Colombia 114 C13 4 38N 74 05W
Bog Walk Jamaica 109 Q8 18 06N 77 01W
Bo Hai *b.* China 81 I5 38 30N 118 30E
Bohemian Massif *hills* Europe 51 50 00N 15 00E
Böhmer Wald *mts.* Europe 63 B1 49 00N 13 00E
Bohol *i.* The Philippines 80 G5 10 00N 124 00E
Boise Idaho U.S.A. 102 C5 43 38N 116 12W
Boise City Oklahoma U.S.A. 102 F4 36 44N 102 31W
Bokaro India 77 F4 23 46N 85 55E
Boké Guinea 93 C5 10 57N 14 13W
Boknafjorden *fj.* Norway 67 B2 59 20N 6 00E
Boldon Tyne and Wear England 44 C1 54 57N 1 27W

Bolesławiec Poland **69** C3 51 16N 34E
Bolgatanga Ghana **93** E5 10 44N 0 53W
Bolgrad Ukraine **69** E2 45 42N 28 35E
Bolivar, Pico *mt.* Venezuela **114** C14 8 33N 71 03W
BOLIVIA **114** E9
Bollin *r.* Cheshire England **42** D1 53 18N 2 10W
Bollington Cheshire England **42** D1 53 18N 2 06W
Bollnäs Sweden **67** D3 61 20N 16 25E
Bolmen *l.* Sweden **67** C2 56 55N 13 45E
Bologna Italy **68** B3 44 30N 11 20E
Bolsover Derbyshire England **43** G1 53 15N 1 17W
Bolton Greater Manchester England **42** C2 53 35N 2 26W
Bolus Head *c.* Irish Republic **48** A1 51 45N 10 10W
Bolzano Italy **68** B4 46 30N 11 22E
Bom Jesus da Lapa Brazil **114** I10 13 16S 43 23W
Boma Zaïre **95** B6 5 50S 13 03E
Bombay India **77** C3 18 56N 72 51E
Bomu *r.* Central Africa **94** D8 4 50N 24 00E
Bonaire *i.* Lesser Antilles **109** K2 12 15N 68 27W
Bonaparte Archipelago Australia **86** D7 19 00S 126 00E
Bonar Bridge *tn.* Highland Scotland **46** D4 57 53N 4 21W
Bondo Zaïre **94** D8 1 22S 23 54E
Bo'ness Central Scotland **45** C2 56 01N 3 37W
Bongor Chad **94** C10 10 18N 15 20E
Bonhill Strathclyde Scotland **45** A1 55 59N 4 34W
Bonifacio Corsica **61** C1 41 23N 9 10E
Bonn Germany **63** A2 50 44N 7 06E
Bonny, Bight of *b.* W. Africa **93** G3 2 10N 7 30E
Bonnybridge Central Scotland **45** C1 55 59N 3 54W
Bonnyrigg Lothian Scotland **45** D1 55 52N 3 08W
Bonthe Sierra Leone **93** C4 7 32N 12 30W
Boorama Somalia **94** H9 9 56N 43 13E
Boosaaso Somalia **94** I10 11 18N 49 10E
Boothia, Gulf of Northwest Territories Canada **101** R6 69 00N 88 00W
Boothia Peninsula Northwest Territories Canada **101** Q7 70 30N 94 30W
Bootle Cumbria England **44** A1 54 17N 3 23W
Bootle Merseyside England **42** A2 53 28N 3 00W
Borås Sweden **67** C2 57 44N 12 55E
Bordeaux France **61** A1 44 50N 0 34W
Borden Peninsula Northwest Territories Canada **101** S7 73 00N 82 30W
Border Forest Park Northumberland England **44** B2 55 17N 2 30W
Borders *reg.* Scotland **46** F2 55 30N 3 00W
Bordon Camp Hampshire England **33** B2 51 07N 0 53W
Borehamwood Hertfordshire England **34** C2 51 40N 0 16W
Borgholm Sweden **67** D2 56 51N 16 40E
Borislav Ukraine **69** D2 49 18N 23 28E
Borisov Belarus **69** E3 54 09N 28 30E
Borken Germany **64** F3 51 50N 6 52E
Borkum Germany **63** A2 53 35N 6 40E
Borkum *i.* Germany **63** A2 53 00N 6 00E
Borlänge Sweden **67** D3 60 29N 15 25E
Bormida di Spigno *r.* Italy **61** C1 44 17N 8 14E
Borneo *i.* Asia **80** E4 0 00 114 00E
Bornholm *i.* Denmark **67** C2 55 02N 15 00E
Boroughbridge North Yorkshire England **40** C3 54 05N 1 24W
Borough Green Kent England **34** D1 51 17N 0 19E
Borrowash Derbyshire England **35** D3 52 55N 1 24W
Bor Sudan **94** F9 6 18N 31 34E
Borth Dyfed Wales **38** B2 52 29N 4 03W
Borūjerd Iran **79** G5 33 55N 48 48E
Borzya Russia **71** N6 50 24N 116 35E
Boscastle Cornwall England **30** C2 50 41N 4 42W
Boskoop Netherlands **65** C2 52 04N 4 39E
Bosna *r.* Bosnia-Herzegovina **68** C3 45 00N 18 00E
BOSNIA-HERZEGOVINA **68** C3
Bosphorus *sd.* Europe/Asia **51** 41 00N 29 00E
Bossangoa Central African Republic **94** C9 6 27N 17 21E
Bosso Niger **93** H5 13 43N 13 19E
Boston Lincolnshire England **36** D2 52 59N 0 01W
Boston Massachusetts U.S.A. **105** F2 42 20N 71 05W
Boston Mountains Arkansas U.S.A. **103** H4 36 00N 94 00W
Boston Spa West Yorkshire England **43** F3 53 54N 1 21W
Botafogo Brazil **116** C2 22 57S 43 11W
Bothnia, Gulf of Sweden/Finland **67** D3 61 00N 19 10E
Botlek Netherlands **65** B1 51 53N 4 17E
Botley Buckinghamshire England **34** B3 51 43N 0 35W
Botoșani Romania **69** E2 47 44N 26 41E
Botrange *sum.* Belgium **64** F2 50 30N 6 05E
BOTSWANA **95** D3
Bottesford Leicestershire England **36** D2 52 56N 0 48W
Bottrop Germany **62** B3 51 31N 6 55E
Bouaké Côte d'Ivoire **93** D4 7 42N 5 00W
Bouar Central African Republic **94** C9 5 58N 15 35E
Bouârfa Morocco **93** E9 32 30N 1 59W
Boucherville Québec Canada **105** F3 45 00N 73 00W
Boufarik Algeria **66** C2 36 36N 2 54E
Bougainville Island Papua New Guinea **86** J8 6 50S 155 00E
Bougouni Mali **93** D5 11 25N 7 28W
Bougzoul Algeria **66** C2 35 42N 2 51E
Bouillon Belgium **64** E1 49 47N 5 04E
Boulder Colorado U.S.A. **102** E5 40 02N 105 16W
Bouligny France **64** E1 49 16N 5 40E
Boulogne-Billancourt France **60** B2 48 50N 2 15E
Boulogne-sur-Mer France **61** B3 50 43N 1 37E
Bourem Mali **93** E6 16 59N 0 20W
Bourg-en-Bresse France **61** C2 46 12N 5 13E
Bourges France **61** B2 47 05N 2 23E
Bourke Australia **86** H3 30 09S 145 59E
Bourne Lincolnshire England **36** D2 52 46N 0 23W
Bourne End Buckinghamshire England **34** A2 51 34N 0 42W
Bournemouth Dorset England **31** F2 50 43N 1 54W
Bournville West Midlands England **35** C2 52 25N 1 56W
Bourton-on-the-Water Gloucestershire England **31** F3 51 53N 1 46W
Bou Saâda Algeria **93** F10 35 10N 4 09E
Bousso Chad **94** C10 10 32N 16 45E
Bouvet Island Southern Ocean **117** I1 54 26S 3 24E
Bovey *r.* Devon England **31** D2 50 40N 3 50W
Bovey Tracey Devon England **31** D2 50 36N 3 40W
Bovingdon Hertfordshire England **34** B3 51 44N 0 32W
Bowen Australia **86** H6 20 00S 148 10E
Bowes Durham England **44** B1 54 30N 2 01W
Bowland, Forest of *hills* Lancashire England **42** C3 54 00N 2 35W
Bowling Green Kentucky U.S.A. **104** C1 37 00N 86 29W
Bowling Green Missouri U.S.A. **104** B1 39 21N 91 11W
Bowling Green Ohio U.S.A. **105** D2 41 22N 83 40W
Bowman North Dakota U.S.A. **102** F6 46 11N 103 26W
Bowmore Strathclyde Scotland **46** B2 55 45N 6 17W
Bowness-on-Windermere Cumbria England **44** B1 54 22N 2 55W
Boxmeer Netherlands **64** E3 51 39N 5 57E
Boxtel Netherlands **64** E3 51 36N 5 20E
Boyle Roscommon Irish Republic **48** C3 53 58N 8 18W
Boyne *r.* Irish Republic **48** E3 53 40N 6 35W
Boyoma Falls Zaïre **94** E8 0 18N 25 30E
Bozeman Montana U.S.A. **102** D6 45 40N 111 00W
Bozoum Central African Republic **94** C9 6 16N 16 22E
Braase-mermeer *l.* Netherlands **65** C2 52 13N 4 38E
Brabant *admin.* Belgium **64** D2 50 45N 4 30E
Brabourne Lees Kent England **33** D2 51 08N 1 00E
Brač *i.* Croatia **68** C3 43 00N 16 00E
Brackley Northamptonshire England **36** C2 52 02N 1 09W
Bracknell Berkshire England **34** A2 51 26N 0 46W
Braco Tayside Scotland **45** C2 56 16N 3 54W
Bradenton Florida U.S.A. **103** J2 27 29N 82 33W
Bradford Pennsylvania U.S.A. **105** E2 41 57N 78 39W
Bradford West Yorkshire England **43** E3 53 48N 1 45W
Bradford-on-Avon Wiltshire England **31** E3 51 22N 2 15W
Bradshaw Greater Manchester **42** C2 53 36N 2 24W
Bradwell Derbyshire England **43** E1 53 20N 1 45W
Bradwell-on-Sea Essex England **33** C2 51 44N 0 54E
Bradworthy Devon England **31** C2 50 54N 4 24W
Brady Texas U.S.A. **102** G3 31 08N 99 22W
Braehead Strathclyde Scotland **45** C1 55 44N 3 40W
Braemar Grampian Scotland **46** E4 57 01N 3 23W
Braga Portugal **66** A3 41 32N 8 26W
Bragança Brazil **114** H12 1 02S 46 46W
Bragança Portugal **66** A3 41 47N 6 46W
Brahmapur India **77** E3 19 21N 84 51E
Brahmaputra *r.* India **77** G5 26 40N 93 00E
Braidwood Strathclyde Scotland **45** C1 55 42N 3 50W
Brăila Romania **69** E2 45 17N 27 58E
Brailsford Derbyshire England **35** D3 52 59N 1 36W
Braine l'Alleud Belgium **64** D2 50 41N 4 22E
Brainerd Minnesota U.S.A. **104** B3 46 20N 94 10W
Braintree Essex England **33** C2 51 53N 0 32E
Braithwell South Yorkshire England **43** G2 53 27N 1 12W
Bramcote Warwickshire England **35** D2 52 56N 1 15W
Bramhall Greater Manchester England **42** D2 53 23N 2 10W
Bramham West Yorkshire England **43** F3 53 53N 1 21W
Bramhope West Yorkshire England **43** F3 53 53N 1 37W
Bramley South Yorkshire England **43** G2 53 26N 1 15W
Bramley Surrey England **34** B1 51 11N 0 35W
Brampton Cumbria England **44** B1 54 57N 2 43W
Brampton Ontario Canada **105** E2 43 42N 79 46W
Brampton South Yorkshire England **43** F2 53 30N 1 22W
Brandenburg *admin.* Germany **63** B2 53 00N 13 00E
Brandenburg Germany **63** B2 52 25N 12 34E
Branderburgh Grampian Scotland **46** E4 57 43N 3 18W
Brandon Durham England **44** C1 54 46N 1 38W
Brandon Manitoba Canada **101** P2 49 50W 99 57W
Brandon Suffolk England **33** C3 52 27N 0 37E
Brandon Vermont U.S.A. **105** F2 43 47N 73 05W
Brandon Mountain Irish Republic **48** A2 52 10N 10 10W
Brandon Point *c.* Irish Republic **48** A2 52 15N 10 05W
Brantford Ontario Canada **105** D2 43 09N 80 17W
Brasileia Brazil **114** D10 10 59S 68 45W
Brasília Brazil **114** H9 15 45S 47 57W
Brașov Romania **69** E2 45 39N 25 35E
Brasschaat Belgium **64** D3 51 17N 4 30E
Bratislava Slovenska Czechoslovakia **69** C2 48 10N 17 10E
Bratsk Russia **71** M7 56 20N 101 50E
Bratsk Reservoir Russia **71** M7 56 00N 102 00E
Brattleboro Vermont U.S.A. **105** F2 42 51N 75 36W
Braughing Hertfordshire England **34** D3 51 55N 0 01E
Braunau Austria **63** B1 48 16N 13 03E
Braunschweig Germany **63** B2 52 15N 10 30E
Braunton Devon England **31** C3 51 07N 4 10W
Brawley California U.S.A. **102** C3 32 59N 115 30W
Bray Berkshire England **34** A2 51 30N 0 42W
Bray Wicklow Irish Republic **49** B1 53 12N 6 06W
Bray Head *c.* Irish Republic **49** B1 53 12N 6 05W
Bray Head *c.* Irish Republic **48** A1 51 50N 10 15W
Brayton North Yorkshire England **43** G3 53 46N 1 06W
BRAZIL **114** G10
Brazil Basin Atlantic Ocean **117** F5 10 00S 26 00W
Brazilian Highlands Brazil **110** 10 00S 50 00W
Brazil Plateau Brazil **110** 20 00S 45 00W
Brazos *r.* Texas U.S.A. **103** G3 32 00N 97 00W
Brazzaville Congo **92** A2 4 14S 15 14E
Brdy *mts.* Ceska Czechoslovakia **63** B1 49 00N 14 00E
Brea Reservoir California U.S.A. **107** C2 33 54N 117 56W
Breaston Derbyshire England **36** C2 52 56N 1 12W
Brechin Tayside Scotland **46** F3 56 44N 2 40W
Breckenridge Minnesota U.S.A. **104** A3 46 14N 96 35W
Breckland *geog. reg.* Norfolk England **33** C3 52 30N 0 50E
Brecon Powys Wales **38** C1 51 57N 3 24W
Brecon Beacons National Park Powys Wales **38** C2 51 53N 3 30W
Breda Netherlands **64** D3 51 35N 4 46E
Bredbury Greater Manchester England **42** D2 53 25N 2 07W
Bregenz Austria **63** A1 47 31N 9 46E
Breidha Fjördur *b.* Iceland **67** H7 65 15N 23 00W
Brekstad Norway **67** B3 63 50N 9 50E
Bremen *admin.* Germany **63** A2 53 00N 9 00E
Bremen Germany **63** A2 53 05N 8 48E
Bremerhaven Germany **63** A2 53 33N 8 35E
Bremerton Washington U.S.A. **102** B6 47 34N 122 40W
Breña Peru **116** E4 12 04S 77 04W
Brenham Texas U.S.A. **103** G3 30 09N 96 24W
Brenig Reservoir Clwyd Wales **38** C3 53 28N 3 32W
Brenner Pass Austria/Italy **69** B2 47 02N 11 32E
Brent Greater London England **34** C2 51 34N 0 17W
Brentford Greater London England **34** C2 51 29N 0 19W
Brent Pelham Hertfordshire England **34** D3 51 57N 0 05E
Brentwood Essex England **34** D2 51 38N 0 18E
Brescia Italy **68** B4 45 33N 10 13E
Bressay *i.* Shetland Islands Scotland **47** B2 60 08N 1 05W
Brest Belarus **70** E6 52 08N 23 40E
Brest France **61** A2 48 23N 4 30W
Bretherton Lancashire England **42** B3 53 41N 2 48W
Brewerton New York U.S.A. **105** E2 43 15N 76 09W
Brewood Staffordshire England **35** B3 52 41N 2 10W
Brezhnev *see* Naberezhnyye Chelny
Bria Central African Republic **94** D9 6 32N 22 00E
Briançon France **61** C1 44 53N 6 39E
Bricket Wood Hertfordshire England **34** B3 51 43N 0 22W
Bride Isle of Man England **41** F1 54 23N 4 24W
Bridgend Lothian Scotland **45** C1 55 58N 3 32W
Bridgend Mid Glamorgan Wales **38** C1 51 31N 3 35W
Bridgend Strathclyde Scotland **45** B1 55 55N 4 05W
Bridge of Allan *tn.* Central Scotland **45** C2 56 09N 3 58W
Bridge of Weir *tn.* Strathclyde Scotland **45** A1 55 52N 4 35W
Bridgeport Connecticut U.S.A. **105** F2 41 12N 73 12W
Bridgeton New Jersey U.S.A. **105** E1 39 26N 75 14W
Bridgetown Barbados **109** M2 13 06N 59 37W
Bridgnorth Shropshire England **35** A2 52 33N 2 25W
Bridgwater Somerset England **31** D3 51 08N 3 00W
Bridgwater Bay Somerset England **31** D3 51 15N 3 20W
Bridlington Humberside England **40** D3 54 05N 0 12W
Bridlington Bay Humberside England **40** D3 54 03N 0 10W
Bridport Dorset England **31** E2 50 44N 2 46W
Brie-Comte-Robert France **60** C1 48 41N 2 37E
Brielle Netherlands **65** A1 51 54N 4 09E
Brielse Meer *l.* Netherlands **65** A1 51 56N 4 09E
Brienz Switzerland **61** C2 46 46N 8 02E
Brierfield Lancashire England **42** D2 53 50N 2 14W
Brierley Hill *tn.* West Midlands England **35** B2 52 29N 2 07W
Briey France **61** C2 49 15N 5 57E
Brig Switzerland **61** C2 46 19N 8 00E
Brigg Humberside England **40** D2 53 34N 0 30W
Brigham City Utah U.S.A. **102** D5 41 30N 112 02W
Brighouse West Yorkshire England **43** E3 53 42N 1 47W
Brightlingsea Essex England **33** D2 51 49N 1 02E
Brighton East Sussex England **33** B1 50 50N 0 10W
Brighton Beach *tn.* New York U.S.A. **106** C1 40 34N 73 58W
Brignoles France **61** C1 43 25N 6 03E
Brimington Derbyshire England **43** F1 53 16N 1 23W
Bríndisi Italy **68** C3 40 37N 17 57E
Brinsworth South Yorkshire England **43** F2 53 23N 1 22W
Brisbane Australia **86** I4 27 30S 153 00E
Bristol Avon England **31** E3 51 27N 2 35W
Bristol Bay Alaska U.S.A. **100** D4 57 30N 159 00W
Bristol Channel England/Wales **31** D3 51 20N 3 50W
British Columbia *province* Canada **100** J4 56 50N 125 30W
British Mountains U.S.A./Canada **100** G6 65 40N 142 30W
Briton Ferry *tn.* West Glamorgan Wales **38** C1 51 38N 3 49W
Britt Ontario Canada **105** D3 45 46N 80 35W
Brittany Peninsula France **51** 48 00N 4 00W
Brittas Dublin Irish Republic **49** A1 53 14N 6 27W
Brive-la-Gaillarde France **61** B2 45 09N 1 32E
Brixham Devon England **31** D2 50 23N 3 30W
Brixton Greater London England **34** C2 51 28N 0 06W
Brno Ceska Czechoslovakia **69** C2 49 13N 16 40E
Broad Bay Western Isles Scotland **46** B5 58 15N 6 10W
Broadford Highland Scotland **46** C4 57 14N 5 54W
Broadheath Hereford & Worcester England **35** B1 52 12N 2 19W
Broad Law *sum.* Borders Scotland **46** E2 55 30N 3 22W
Broad Meadow Water *r.* Irish Republic **49** B2 53 30N 6 15W
Broadstairs Kent England **33** D2 51 22N 1 27E
Broadstone Dorset England **31** E2 50 45N 2 00W
Broadway Hereford and Worcester England **36** C2 52 02N 1 50W
Brock *r.* Lancashire England **42** B3 53 53N 2 44W
Brockenhurst Hampshire England **32** A1 50 49N 1 34W
Brockham Surrey England **34** C1 51 14N 0 18W
Brockton Massachusetts U.S.A. **105** F2 42 06N 71 01W
Brockville Ontario Canada **105** E2 44 35N 75 44W
Brocton Staffordshire England **35** B3 52 48N 2 03W
Brodeur Peninsula Northwest Territories Canada **101** R7 72 00N 87 30W
Brodick Strathclyde Scotland **46** C2 55 35N 5 09W
Brody Ukraine **69** E3 50 05N 25 08E
Broer Ruys, Cape Greenland **120** 73 30N 20 20W
Broken Hill *tn.* Australia **86** G3 31 57S 141 30E
Bromley Greater London England **34** D2 51 31N 0 01W
Bromsgrove Hereford and Worcester England **35** B1 50 20N 2 03W
Bromyard Hereford and Worcester England **36** B2 52 11N 2 30W
Brønnøysund Norway **67** C4 65 38N 12 15E
Bronx New York U.S.A. **105** F2 40 50N 73 52W
Brookfield Strathclyde Scotland **45** A1 55 51N 4 32W
Brookhouse Lancashire England **42** B4 54 06N 2 42W
Brookings South Dakota U.S.A. **104** A2 44 19N 96 47W
Brooklyn New York U.S.A. **106** C1 40 41N 73 57W
Brookmans Park Hertfordshire England **34** C3 51 43N 0 11W
Brooks Alberta Canada **100** M3 50 35N 111 54W
Brooks Range *mts.* Alaska U.S.A. **100** E6 67 55N 155 00W
Brookville Pennsylvania U.S.A. **105** E2 41 10N 79 06W
Broome Australia **86** C6 17 58S 122 15E
Brora Highland Scotland **46** E5 58 01N 3 51W
Broseley Shropshire England **35** A2 52 37N 2 29W
Brotton Cleveland England **44** D1 54 34N 0 56W
Brough Cumbria England **44** B1 54 32N 2 19W
Brough Humberside England **40** D2 53 44N 0 35W
Broughshane Antrim Northern Ireland **48** E4 54 54N 6 12W
Broughton Buckinghamshire England **34** A4 52 04N 0 42W
Broughton Clwyd Wales **38** C3 53 10N 3 00W
Broughton Lancashire England **42** B3 53 49N 2 44W
Broughton in Furness Cumbria England **44** A1 54 17N 3 13W
Broughty Ferry *tn.* Tayside Scotland **46** F3 56 28N 2 53W
Brown Clee Hill Shropshire England **36** B2 52 27N 2 35W
Brownhills West Midlands England **35** C2 52 39N 1 55W
Browning Montana U.S.A. **102** D6 48 33N 113 00W
Brown's Town Jamaica **109** Q8 18 28N 77 22W
Browns Valley *tn.* Minnesota U.S.A. **104** A3 45 35N 96 50W
Brownsville Texas U.S.A. **103** G2 25 54N 97 30W
Brown Willy *sum.* Cornwall England **30** C2 50 35N 4 36W
Brownwood Texas U.S.A. **102** G3 31 42N 98 59W
Broxburn Lothian Scotland **45** D1 55 57N 3 29W
Bruay-en-Artois France **61** B3 50 29N 2 33E
Bruce Mines *tn.* Ontario Canada **105** D3 46 19N 83 48W
Bruce Peninsula Ontario Canada **105** D3 45 00N 81 20W
Bruchsal Germany **63** A1 49 07N 8 35E
Brue *r.* Somerset England **31** E3 51 10N 2 50W
Bruges *see* Brugge
Brugg Switzerland **66** C2 47 29N 8 13E
Brugge *(Bruges)* Belgium **64** C3 51 13N 3 14E
Brühl Germany **64** F2 50 50N 6 55E
BRUNEI **80** E4
Brunoy France **60** C1 48 40N 2 31E
Brunssum Netherlands **64** E2 50 57N 5 59E
Brunswick Georgia U.S.A. **103** J3 31 09N 81 30W
Brunswick Maine U.S.A. **105** G2 43 55N 69 59W
Brunton Fife Scotland **45** D2 56 23N 3 08W
Brussel *see* Bruxelles
Brussels *see* Bruxelles
Bruton Somerset England **31** E3 51 07N 2 27W
Bruxelles *(Brussel, Brussels)* Belgium **64** D2 50 50N 4 21E
Bryan Texas U.S.A. **103** G3 30 41N 96 24W
Bryansk Russia **70** F6 53 15N 34 09E
Bryher *i.* Isles of Scilly England **30** A1 49 57N 6 21W
Brymbo Clwyd Wales **38** C3 53 05N 3 03W
Brynamman Dyfed Wales **38** C1 51 49N 3 52W
Brynmawr Gwent Wales **38** C1 51 49N 3 11W
Brzeg Poland **69** C3 50 52N 17 27E
Bü Ağri Daği *(Mt. Ararat)* Turkey **78** F6 39 44N 44 15E
Bucaramanga Colombia **114** C14 7 08N 73 10W
Buchanan Liberia **93** C4 5 57N 10 02W
Buchan Ness *c.* Grampian Scotland **46** G4 57 28N 1 47W
Bucharest *see* București
Buchlyvie Central Scotland **45** B2 56 07N 4 18W
Bucholz Germany **62** 51 25N 6 45E
Buckfastleigh Devon England **31** D2 50 29N 3 46W
Buckhaven Fife Scotland **45** D2 56 11N 3 03W
Buckie Grampian Scotland **46** F4 57 40N 2 58W
Buckingham Buckinghamshire England **33** B2 52 00N 1 00W
Buckingham Québec Canada **105** E3 45 35N 75 25W
Buckinghamshire *co.* England **33** B2 51 50N 0 50W
Buckley Clwyd Wales **38** C3 53 10N 3 05W
Bucknall Staffordshire England **35** B4 53 02N 2 09W
Bucksport Maine U.S.A. **105** G2 44 35N 68 47W
București *(Bucharest)* Romania **69** E1 44 25N 26 07E
Budapest Hungary **69** C2 47 30N 19 03E
Bude Cornwall England **30** C2 50 50N 4 33W
Bude Bay Cornwall England **30** C2 50 50N 4 40W
Büderich Germany **62** A1 51 15N 6 20E
Budjala Zaïre **94** C8 2 38N 19 48E
Budleigh Salterton Devon England **31** D2 50 38N 3 20W
Buea Cameroon **93** G3 4 09N 9 13E
Buena Park *tn.* California U.S.A. **107** B2 33 52N 118 02W
Buenaventura Mexico **108** C5 29 50N 107 30W
Buenos Aires Argentina **115** F6 34 40S 58 30W
Buenos Aires, Lake Argentina/Chile **115** C3 47 00S 72 00W
Buer Germany **62** C3 51 35N 7 05E
Buffalo New York U.S.A. **105** E2 42 52N 78 55W
Buffalo Lake Northwest Territories Canada **100** L5 60 40N 115 30W
Buffalo Narrows *tn.* Saskatchewan Canada **100** N4 55 52N 108 28W
Buffalo Wyoming U.S.A. **102** E5 44 21N 106 40W
Buff Bay *tn.* Jamaica **109** R8 18 18N 76 40W
Bug *r.* Europe **69** D3 51 00N 24 00E
Builth Wells Powys Wales **38** C2 52 09N 3 24W
Bujumbura Burundi **95** E7 3 22S 29 19E
Bukachacha Russia **71** N6 53 00N 116 58E
Bukama Zaïre **95** E6 9 13S 25 52E
Bukavu Zaïre **94** E7 2 30S 28 50E
Bukhara Uzbekistan **70** I3 39 47N 64 26E
Bukittinggi Indonesia **80** C3 0 18S 100 20E
Bukoba Tanzania **94** F7 1 19S 31 49E
Bula Indonesia **80** I3 3 07S 130 27E
Bulandshahr India **77** D5 28 30N 77 49E
Bulawayo Zimbabwe **95** E3 20 10S 28 43E
Bulford Wiltshire England **31** F3 51 12N 1 46W
BULGARIA Europe **68** D3
Bulkington Warwickshire England **35** D2 52 28N 1 25W
Bull Shoals Lake U.S.A. **103** H4 36 00N 93 00W
Buller *r.* New Zealand **87** B2 41 50S 172 20E
Bulun Russia **71** O10 70 45N 127 20E
Bumba Zaïre **94** D8 2 10N 22 30E
Bumbu *r.* Zaïre **92** A1 4 22S 15 18E
Bunbury Australia **86** B3 33 20S 115 34E
Bunclody Wexford Irish Republic **48** E2 52 38N 6 40W
Buncrana Donegal Irish Republic **48** D5 55 08N 7 27W
Bundaberg Australia **86** I5 24 50S 152 21E
Bundoran Donegal Irish Republic **48** C4 54 28N 8 17W
Bungay Suffolk England **33** D3 52 28N 1 26E
Bungo-suido *sd.* Japan **82** B1 33 00N 132 30E
Bunia Zaïre **94** F8 1 33N 30 13E
Bura Kenya **94** H7 1 06S 39 58E
Buraydah Saudi Arabia **78** F4 26 20N 43 59E
Burbage Leicestershire England **35** D2 52 31N 1 20W
Burbank California U.S.A. **107** A3 34 10N 118 25W
Burdur Turkey **78** D6 37 44N 30 17E
Bure *r.* Norfolk England **33** D3 52 47N 1 20E
Bureya *r.* Russia **71** P6 52 00N 133 00E
Burford Oxfordshire England **32** A2 51 49N 1 38W
Burg Germany **63** B2 52 17N 11 51E
Burgas Bulgaria **68** E3 42 30N 27 29E
Burgess Hill West Sussex England **33** B1 50 58N 0 08W
Burghead *tn.* Grampian Scotland **46** E4 57 42N 3 30W
Burgh le Marsh Lincolnshire England **36** E3 53 10N 0 15E
Burgos Spain **66** B3 42 21N 3 41W
Burham Beeches Buckinghamshire England **34** B2 51 33N 0 36W
Burhanpur India **77** D4 21 18N 76 08E
Burhou *i.* Channel Islands British Isles **31** G6 49 43N 2 15W
Buri Khali India **76** J2 22 30N 88 10E
BURKINA **93** E5
Burks Falls *tn.* Ontario U.S.A. **105** E3 45 37N 79 25W
Burley in Wharfedale West Yorkshire England **43** E3 53 55N 1 45W
Burlington Colorado U.S.A. **102** F4 39 17N 102 17W
Burlington Iowa U.S.A. **104** B2 40 50N 91 07W
Burlington Ontario Canada **105** E2 43 19N 79 48W
Burlington Vermont U.S.A. **105** F2 44 28N 73 14W
Burlington West Virginia U.S.A. **105** E1 39 20N 78 56W
Burlington Wisconsin U.S.A. **104** C2 42 41N 88 17W
BURMA *see* MYANMAR
Burnfoot Tayside Scotland **45** C2 56 13N 3 37W
Burnham Market Norfolk England **33** C3 52 57N 0 44E
Burnham on Crouch Essex England **33** C2 51 38N 0 49E
Burnham-on-Sea Somerset England **31** D3 51 15N 3 00W
Burnie Australia **86** H1 41 03S 145 55E
Burnley Lancashire England **42** D3 53 48N 2 14W
Burnsall North Yorkshire England **43** E4 54 03N 1 57W
Burntisland *tn.* Fife Scotland **45** D2 56 03N 3 15W
Burntwood Staffordshire England **35** C3 52 40N 1 56W
Burry Port Dyfed Wales **38** D1 51 42N 4 15W
Bursa Turkey **78** C7 40 12N 29 04E
Bur Safâga Egypt **78** D4 26 43N 33 55E
Burscough Bridge *tn.* Lancashire England **42** B2 53 37N 2 51W
Burslem Staffordshire England **35** B4 53 02N 2 12W
Burston Staffordshire England **35** B3 52 52N 2 05W
Burton Cheshire England **42** A1 53 16N 3 02W
Burton Agnes Humberside England **40** D3 54 03N 0 19W
Burton Latimer Northamptonshire England **36** D2 52 22N 0 40W
Burton upon Trent Staffordshire England **35** D3 52 48N 1 36W

Buru *i.* Indonesia **80** H3 3 20S 126 30E
BURUNDI 95 E/F7
Burwell Cambridgeshire England **33** C3 52 16N 0 19E
Burwell Nebraska U.S.A. **102** G5 41 48N 99 09W
Bury Greater Manchester England **42** D2 53 36N 2 17W
Bury St. Edmunds Suffolk England **33** C3 52 15N 0 43E
Busby Strathclyde Scotland **45** B1 55 47N 4 16W
Būshehr Iran **79** H4 28 57N 50 52E
Bushey Hertfordshire England **34** B2 51 39N 0 22W
Bushmills Northern Ireland **48** E5 55 12N 6 32W
Busira *r.* Zaïre **94** C7 1 00S 20 00E
Bussum Netherlands **65** E3 52 16N 5 09E
Busto Arsizio Italy **68** A4 45 37N 8 51E
Buta Zaïre **94** D8 2 49N 24 50E
Butare Rwanda **94** F7 2 35S 29 44E
Bute *i.* Strathclyde Scotland **46** C2 55 50N 5 05W
Bute, Sound of Strathclyde Scotland **46** C2 55 45N 5 10W
Butler Pennsylvania U.S.A. **105** E2 40 51N 79 55W
Buton *i.* Indonesia **80** G3 5 00S 122 40E
Butovo Russia **70** M1 55 30N 37 32E
Butte Montana U.S.A. **102** D6 46 00N 112 31W
Buttermere *l.* Cumbria England **44** A1 54 32N 3 16W
Buttershaw West Yorkshire England **43** E3 53 45N 1 49W
Buttevant Cork Irish Republic **48** C2 52 14N 8 40W
Butt of Lewis *c.* Western Isles Scotland **46** B5 58 30N 6 20W
Butuan The Philippines **80** H5 8 56N 125 31E
Buulobarde Somalia **94** I8 3 50N 45 33E
Buxtehude Germany **63** A2 53 29N 9 42E
Buxton Derbyshire England **43** E1 53 15N 1 55W
Bydgoszcz Poland **69** C3 53 16N 18 00E
BYELORUSSIA *see* BELARUS
Byfield Northamptonshire England **36** C2 52 11N 1 14W
Byfleet Surrey England **34** B1 51 21N 0 29W
Bygland Norway **67** B2 58 50N 7 49E
Bylot Island Northwest Territories Canada **101** T7 73 30N 79 00W
Byrd Land *geog. reg.* Antarctica **121** 77 00S 130 00W
Byrranga Mountains Russia **71** L10 75 00N 100 00E
Bytom Poland **69** C3 50 21N 18 51E

C

Cabanatuan The Philippines **80** G7 15 30N 120 58E
Cabano Québec Canada **105** G3 47 40N 68 56W
Cabimas Venezuela **114** C15 10 26N 71 27W
Cabinda *admin.* Angola **95** B6 5 30S 12 20E
Cabo Brazil **114** J11 8 16S 35 00W
Cabo Blanco *c.* Costa Rica **109** G1 9 36N 85 06W
Cabo Caballeria *c.* Balearic Islands **66** F5 40 05N 4 05E
Cabo Catoche *c.* Mexico **109** G4 21 38N 87 08W
Cabo Corrientes *c.* Colombia **114** B14 5 29N 77 36W
Cabo Corrientes *c.* Mexico **108** C4 20 25N 105 42W
Cabo d'Artrutx Balearic Islands (Spain) **66** E4 39 55N 3 49E
Cabo de Barberia *c.* Balearic Islands **66** D4 38 40N 1 20E
Cabo de Cala Figuera *c.* Balearic Islands **66** E4 39 27N 2 31E
Cabo de Creus *c.* Spain **66** C3 42 19N 3 19E
Cabo de Formentor *c.* Balearic Islands **66** E4 39 58N 3 13E
Cabo de Gata *c.* Spain **66** B2 36 44N 2 10W
Cabo de Hornos *(Cape Horn)* Chile **115** D1 56 00S 67 15W
Cabo de la Nao *c.* Spain **66** C2 38 44N 0 14E
Cabo Delgado *c.* Mozambique **95** H5 10 45S 40 45E
Cabo de Palos *c.* Spain **66** B2 37 38N 0 40W
Cabo de Peñas *c.* Spain **66** A3 43 39N 5 50W
Cabo de Salinas *c.* Balearic Islands **66** E4 39 16N 3 04E
Cabo de São Vicente *c.* Portugal **66** A2 37 01N 8 59W
Cabo de Tortosa *c.* Spain **66** C3 40 44N 0 54E
Cabo Dos Bahías *c.* Argentina **115** D4 45 00S 65 30W
Cabo Espichel *c.* Portugal **66** A2 38 24N 9 13W
Cabo Falso *c.* Mexico **108** B4 22 50N 110 00W
Cabo Finisterre *c.* Spain **66** A3 42 52N 9 16W
Cabo Freu Balearic Islands **66** E4 39 45N 3 27E
Cabo Gracias á Dios *c.* Nicaragua **109** H3 15 00N 83 10W
Cabo Guardafui *see* Raas Caseyr
Cabonga Réservoir Québec Canada **105** E3 47 00N 76 00W
Cabo Orange *c.* Brazil **114** G13 4 25N 51 32W
Cabo Ortegal *c.* Spain **66** A3 43 46N 7 54W
Cabora Bassa Dam Mozambique **95** F4 16 00S 33 00E
Caborca Mexico **108** B6 30 42N 112 10W
Cabo San Juan *c.* Argentina **115** E2 54 45S 63 46W
Cabo Santa Elena *c.* Costa Rica **109** G2 10 54N 85 56W
Cabot Strait Nova Scotia/Newfoundland Canada **101** W2 47 10N 59 30W
Cabo Vírgenes *c.* Argentina **115** D2 52 20S 68 00W
Cabra Dublin Irish Republic **49** B2 53 22N 6 17W
Cabrera *i.* Balearic Islands **66** E4 39 00N 2 59E
Cabuçu Brazil **116** A2 22 46S 43 33W
Cabuçu *r.* Brazil **116** A2 22 55S 43 31W
Cabriel *r.* Spain **66** B2 39 20N 1 15W
Čačak Serbia Yugoslavia **68** D3 43 54N 20 22E
Cáceres Brazil **114** F9 16 05S 57 40W
Cáceres Spain **66** A2 39 29N 6 23W
Cachoeira Brazil **114** J10 12 35S 38 59W
Cachoeira do Sul Brazil **115** G6 30 03S 52 52W
Cachoeiro de Itapemirim Brazil **115** I8 20 51N 41 07W
Caddington Bedfordshire England **34** D3 51 52N 0 27W
Cader Idris *mt.* Gwynedd Wales **38** C2 52 42N 3 54W
Cádiz Spain **66** A2 36 32N 6 18W
Cádiz The Philippines **80** G6 10 57N 123 18E
Cádiz, Gulf of Spain **66** A2 36 30N 7 15W
Caen France **61** A2 49 11N 0 22W
Caerleon Gwent Wales **38** D1 51 37N 2 57W
Caernarfon Gwynedd Wales **38** B3 53 08N 4 16W
Caernarfon Bay Gwynedd Wales **38** B3 53 05N 4 30W
Caerphilly Mid Glamorgan Wales **38** C1 51 35N 3 14W
Caersws Powys Wales **38** C2 52 31N 3 26W
Cagayan de Oro The Philippines **80** G5 8 29N 124 40E
Cágliari Italy **68** A2 39 13N 9 08E
Caguas Puerto Rico **109** K3 18 41N 66 04W
Caha Mountains Irish Republic **48** B1 51 40N 9 40W
Cahir Tipperary Irish Republic **48** D2 52 21N 7 56W
Cahirciveen Kerry Irish Republic **48** A1 51 57N 10 13W
Cahore Point *c.* Wexford Irish Republic **48** E2 52 34N 6 11W
Cahors France **61** B1 44 28N 0 26E
Caicos Passage *sd.* West Indies **109** J4 22 20N 72 30W
Cairngorm *mt.* Grampian Scotland **46** E4 57 07N 3 40W
Cairngorms *mts.* Highland/Grampian Scotland **46** E4 57 10N 3 30W
Cairnryan Dumfries & Galloway Scotland **46** C1 54 58N 5 02W
Cairns Australia **86** H6 16 51S 145 43N
Cairo *(El Qâhira)* Egypt **78** D5 30 03N 31 15E
Cairo Illinois U.S.A. **104** C1 37 01N 89 09W
Caister-on-Sea Norfolk England **33** D3 52 39N 1 44E
Caistor Lincolnshire England **36** D3 53 30N 0 20W
Cajamarca Peru **114** B11 7 09S 78 32W
Cajàzeiras Brazil **114** J11 6 52S 38 31W
Caju Brazil **116** C2 22 53S 43 13W
Cakovec Croatia **68** C4 46 24N 16 26E
Calabar Nigeria **93** G3 4 56N 8 22E
Calahorra Spain **66** B3 49 19N 1 58W
Calais France **61** B3 50 57N 1 52E
Calama Chile **115** D8 22 30S 68 55W
Calamar Colombia **114** C15 10 16N 74 55W
Calamian Group *is.* The Philippines **80** F6 12 00N 120 00E
Calapan The Philippines **80** G6 13 23N 121 10E
Calatayud Spain **66** B3 41 21N 1 39W
Calçoene Brazil **114** G13 2 30N 50 55W
Calcutta India **76** K2 22 30N 88 20E
Caldas da Rainha Portugal **66** A3 39 24N 9 08W
Calder *r.* Lancashire England **42** B3 53 55N 2 43W
Calder *r.* Lancashire England **42** C3 53 48N 2 22W
Calder *r.* West Yorkshire England **43** F3 53 42N 1 29W
Caldercruix Strathclyde Scotland **45** C1 55 53N 3 55W
Caldermill Strathclyde Scotland **45** B1 55 39N 4 08W
Caldew *r.* Cumbria England **44** A1 54 45N 3 00W
Caldey Island Dyfed Wales **38** B1 51 38N 4 42W
Caldicot Gwent Wales **38** D1 51 36N 2 45W
Caldwell Idaho U.S.A. **102** C5 43 39N 116 40W
Caldwell New Jersey U.S.A. **106** A2 40 49N 74 16W
Calf of Man *i.* Isle of Man British Isles **41** F1 54 03N 4 49W
Calgary Alberta Canada **100** M3 51 05N 114 05W
Cali Colombia **114** B13 3 24N 76 30W
Calicut India **77** D2 11 15N 75 45E
Caliente Nevada U.S.A. **102** D4 37 36N 114 31W
California Central Scotland **45** C1 55 58N 3 45W
California *state* U.S.A. **102** C4 35 00N 119 00W
Callan Kilkenny Irish Republic **48** D2 52 33N 7 23W
Callander Central Scotland **45** B2 56 15N 4 13W
Callao Peru **116** E4 12 04S 77 08W
Callington Cornwall England **31** C2 50 30N 4 18W
Calne Wiltshire England **31** F3 51 27N 2 00W
Calow Derbyshire England **43** F1 53 13N 1 24W
Caltanissetta Italy **68** B2 37 29N 14 04E
Calver Derbyshire England **43** F1 53 16N 1 38W
Calverton Nottinghamshire England **36** C3 53 03N 1 05W
Calvi Corsica **61** C1 42 34N 8 44E
Calvia Balearic Islands **66** E4 39 33N 2 29E
Calvinia Republic of South Africa **95** C1 31 25S 19 47E
Cam *r.* Cambridgeshire England **33** C3 52 20N 0 15E
Camaçari Brazil **114** J10 12 44S 38 16W
Camacupa Angola **95** C5 12 03S 17 50E
Camagüey Cuba **109** I4 21 25N 77 55W
Camberley Surrey England **34** A2 51 21N 0 45W
Camblesforth North Yorkshire England **43** G3 53 43N 1 02W
CAMBODIA *(KAMPUCHEA)* **80** C6
Camborne Cornwall England **30** B2 50 12N 5 19W
Cambrai France **61** B3 50 10N 3 14E
Cambrian Mountains Wales **38** C2 52 15N 3 45W
Cambridge Cambridgeshire England **33** C3 52 12N 0 07E
Cambridge Jamaica **109** Q8 18 18N 77 54W
Cambridge Maryland U.S.A. **103** K4 38 34N 76 04W
Cambridge New Zealand **87** C3 37 53S 175 29E
Cambridge Ohio U.S.A. **105** D2 40 02N 81 36W
Cambridge Ontario Canada **105** D2 43 22N 80 20W
Cambridge Bay *tn.* Northwest Territories Canada **101** N6 69 09N 105 00W
Cambridgeshire *co.* England **33** B3 52 30N 0 00
Cambusbarron Central Scotland **45** C2 56 07N 3 59W
Camden Greater London England **34** C2 51 33N 0 10W
Camden New Jersey U.S.A. **105** E1 39 57N 75 06W
Cameia National Park Angola **95** D5 12 00S 22 00E
Camel *r.* Cornwall England **30** C2 5 30N 4 40W
Camelford Cornwall England **30** C2 50 37N 4 41W
Camelon Central Scotland **45** C2 56 00N 3 50W
CAMEROON 93 H4
Cametá Brazil **114** H12 2 12S 49 30W
Camiri Bolivia **114** E8 20 08S 63 33W
Camocim Brazil **114** I12 2 55S 40 50W
Camorta *i.* Nicobar Islands **77** G1 7 30N 93 30E
Campbell Island Southern Ocean **118** G2 52 30S 169 10E
Campbell River *tn.* British Columbia Canada **100** J2 50 00N 125 18W
Campbellsville Kentucky U.S.A. **104** C1 37 20N 85 21W
Campbellton New Brunswick Canada **101** V2 48 00N 66 30W
Campbeltown Strathclyde Scotland **46** C2 55 26N 5 36W
Campeche Mexico **108** F3 19 50N 90 30W
Campina Grande Brazil **114** J11 7 15S 35 50W
Campinas Brazil **115** H8 22 54S 47 06W
Campine *see* Kempen land
Campoalegre Colombia **114** B13 2 49N 75 19W
Campobasso Italy **68** B3 41 33N 14 39E
Campo Grande Brazil **114** G8 20 24S 54 35W
Campo Grande Brazil **116** A2 22 55S 43 33W
Campo Maior Brazil **114** I12 4 50S 42 12W
Campo Mourão Brazil **115** G8 24 01S 52 24W
Campos Brazil **115** I8 21 46S 41 21W
Campos del Puerto Balearic Islands **66** E4 39 26N 3 01E
Campos Elyseos Brazil **116** B3 22 42S 43 16W
Campsie Fells *hills* Central Scotland **45** B2 56 00N 4 15W
Cam Ranh Vietnam **80** C6 11 54N 109 14E
CANADA 101/102
Canada Basin Arctic Ocean **120** 80 00N 140 00W
Canadian *r.* U.S.A. **102** F4 35 00N 104 00W
Canadian Shield *mts.* Canada **119** Q13 50 00N 90 00W
Canakkale Turkey **78** C7 40 09N 26 25E
Canal de l'Ourcq France **60** C2 48 55N 2 32E
Canal des Ardennes France **64** D1 49 50N 4 30E
Canal du Midi France **61** B1 43 20N 2 00E
Cananea Mexico **108** B6 30 59N 110 20W
Canary Basin Atlantic Ocean **117** F9 26 20N 30 00W
Canary Islands Spain **93** B8 28 30N 15 10W
Canaveral, Cape Florida U.S.A. **103** J2 28 28N 80 28W
Canberra Australia **86** H2 35 18S 149 08E
Cangamba Angola **95** C5 13 40S 19 47E
Cangzhou China **81** I5 38 19N 116 54E
Caniapiscau *r.* Québec Canada **101** V4 57 30N 68 40W
Canisp *mt.* Highland Scotland **46** C5 58 07N 5 03W
Canmore Alberta Canada **100** L3 51 07N 115 18W
Canna *i.* Highland Scotland **46** B4 57 05N 6 35W
Cannanore India **77** D2 11 53N 75 23E
Cannes France **61** C1 43 33N 7 00E
Cannich Highland Scotland **46** D4 57 21N 4 46W
Cannington Somerset England **31** D3 51 09N 3 04E
Cannock Staffordshire England **35** B3 52 42N 2 01W
Canôas Brazil **115** G7 28 55S 51 10W
Canso Nova Scotia Canada **101** W2 45 20N 61 00W
Cantabrian Mountains *see* Cordillera Cantabrica
Canterbury Kent England **33** D2 51 17N 1 05E
Canterbury Bight *b.* New Zealand **87** B2 44 00S 172 30E
Canterbury Plains New Zealand **87** B2 43 30S 172 00E
Can Tho Vietnam **80** D6 10 03N 105 46E
Canto de Rio Brazil **116** C2 22 55S 43 06W
Canton Ohio U.S.A. **105** D2 40 48N 81 23W
Canton *see* Guangzhou
Canvey Island *i.* Essex England **33** C2 51 32N 0 33E
Canvey Island *tn.* Essex England **33** C2 51 32N 0 35E
Cap Blanc *see* Ras Nouâdhibou
Cap Bon *c.* Tunisia **68** B2 37 08N 11 00E
Cap Corse *c.* Corsica **61** C1 43 00N 9 21E
Cap d'Ambre *c.* Madagascar **95** I5 12 00S 49 15E
Cap de la Hague *c.* France **61** A2 49 44N 1 56W
Cap de la Madeleine *tn.* Québec Canada **105** F3 46 22N 72 31W
Cap des Trois Fourches *c.* Morocco **66** B2 35 26N 2 57W
Cape Basin Atlantic Ocean **117** I3 36 00S 6 00E
Cape Breton Island Nova Scotia Canada **101** X2 46 45N 60 00W
Cape Charles *tn.* Virginia U.S.A. **105** E1 37 17N 76 01W
Cape Coast *tn.* Ghana **93** E4 5 10N 1 13W
Cape Cod Bay U.S.A. **105** F2 41 00N 70 00W
Cape Dorset *tn.* Northwest Territories Canada **101** T5 64 10N 76 40W
Cape Dyer *m.s.* Northwest Territories Canada **101** W6 66 30N 61 20W
Cape Evans *r.s.* Antarctica **121** 77 38S 166 24E
Cape Girardeau *tn.* Missouri U.S.A. **104** C1 37 19N 89 31W
Capel Surrey England **34** C1 51 10N 0 20W
Capelle aan den IJssel Netherlands **65** C1 51 56N 4 36E
Cape May *tn.* New Jersey U.S.A. **105** F1 38 56N 74 54W
Cape Province *admin.* Republic of South Africa **95** D1 31 00S 22 00E
Cape Rise Indian Ocean **117** J3 42 00S 11 00E
Cape Town Republic of South Africa **95** C1 33 56S 18 28E
Cape Verde Basin Atlantic Ocean **117** E8 11 00N 35 00W
Cape Verde Islands Atlantic Ocean **117** F8 16 00N 24 00W
Cape York Peninsula Australia **86** G7 12 30S 142 30E
Cap Ferret France **61** A1 44 42N 1 16W
Cap Gris Nez *c.* France **64** A2 50 52N 1 35E
Cap-Haïtien Haiti **109** J3 19 47N 72 17W
Capitán Arturo Prat *r.s.* Antarctica **121** 62 30S 59 41W
Capo Carbonara *c.* Italy **68** A2 39 07N 9 33E
Capo Passero *c.* Italy **68** C2 36 42N 15 09E
Capo Santa Maria di Leuca *c.* Italy **68** C2 39 47N 18 22E
Capo San Vito *c.* Italy **68** B2 38 12N 12 43E
Cappoquin Waterford Irish Republic **48** D2 52 08N 7 50W
Capri *i.* Italy **68** B3 40 33N 14 15E
Capricorn Channel Australia **86** I5 23 00S 152 30E
Caprivi Strip Namibia **95** D4 17 30S 27 50E
Cap Ste. Marie *c.* Madagascar **95** I2 25 34S 45 10E
Cap Vert *c.* Senegal **93** B5 14 43N 17 33W
Caracal Romania **69** D1 44 07N 24 18E
Caracas Venezuela **114** D15 10 35N 66 56W
Caratinga Brazil **114** I9 19 50S 42 06W
Caravelas Brazil **114** J9 17 45S 39 15W
Carbondale Pennsylvania U.S.A. **105** E2 41 35N 75 31W
Carcassonne France **61** B1 43 13N 2 21E
Carcroft South Yorkshire England **43** G2 53 35N 1 12W
Carcross Yukon Territory Canada **100** I5 60 11N 134 41W
Cardamon Hills India **77** D1 9 50N 77 00E
Cárdenas Mexico **108** E4 22 00N 99 41W
Cardenden Fife Scotland **45** D2 56 08N 3 15W
Cardiff South Glamorgan Wales **38** C1 51 30N 3 13W
Cardigan Dyfed Wales **38** B2 52 06N 4 40W
Cardigan Bay Wales **38** B2 52 30N 4 30W
Cardross Strathclyde Scotland **45** A1 55 58N 4 38W
Carei Romania **69** D2 47 40N 22 28E
Cariacica Brazil **114** I8 20 15S 40 23W
Caribbean Sea Central America **109** I3 15 00N 75 00W
Caribou Mountains Alberta Canada **100** L4 59 00N 115 30W
Caripito Venezuela **114** E15 10 07N 63 07W
Carleton Place Ontario Canada **105** E3 45 08N 76 09W
Carlingford Lough *b.* Ireland **48** F4 54 05N 6 10W
Carlisle Cumbria England **44** B1 54 54N 2 55W
Carlow Carlow Irish Republic **48** D2 52 50N 6 55W
Carlow *co.* Irish Republic **48** D2 52 40N 6 55W
Carloway Western Isles Scotland **46** B5 58 17N 6 48W
Carlsbad New Mexico U.S.A. **102** F3 32 25N 104 14W
Carlton North Yorkshire England **43** G3 53 43N 1 02W
Carlton in Lindrick Nottinghamshire England **43** G2 53 22N 1 06W
Carlton-on-Trent Nottinghamshire England **36** D3 53 10N 0 48W
Carluke Strathclyde Scotland **45** C1 55 45N 3 51W
Carmacks Yukon Territory Canada **100** H5 62 04N 136 21W
Carman Manitoba Canada **104** A3 49 32N 97 59W
Carmarthen Dyfed Wales **38** B1 51 51N 4 20W
Carmarthen Bay Dyfed Wales **38** B1 51 40N 4 30W
Carmel Church Virginia U.S.A. **105** E1 37 54N 77 25W
Carmel Head Gwynedd Wales **38** B3 53 24N 4 34W
Carmen Colombia **114** B14 9 46N 75 06W
Carmunnock Strathclyde Scotland **45** B1 55 47N 4 15W
Carnarvon Australia **86** A5 24 51S 113 45E
Carndonagh Donegal Irish Republic **48** D5 55 15N 7 15W
Carnedd Llewelyn *mt.* Gwynedd Wales **38** C3 53 10N 3 58W
Carnegie, Lake Australia **86** C4 27 00S 124 00E
Carnegie Ridge Pacific Ocean **119** R7 1 30S 95 00W
Carn Eige *mt.* Highland Scotland **46** C4 57 22N 5 07W
Carnforth Lancashire England **40** B3 54 08N 2 46W
Carnlough Northern Ireland **48** F4 54 59N 5 59W
Car Nicobar *i.* Nicobar Islands **77** G1 9 00N 93 00E
Carnot Central African Republic **94** C8 4 59N 15 56E
Carnoustie Tayside Scotland **46** F3 56 30N 2 44W
Carnsore Point *c.* Wexford Irish Republic **48** E2 52 10N 6 22W
Carnwath Strathclyde Scotland **45** C1 55 43N 3 38W
Carolina Brazil **114** H11 7 20S 47 25W
Caroline Island Pacific Ocean **119** L7 10 00S 150 00W
Caroline Islands Pacific Ocean **118** E8 8 00N 148 00E
Carpathians *mts.* Europe **69** D2 49 00N 22 00E
Carpaţii Meridionali *mts.* Romania **69** D2 45 00N 24 00E
Carpentaria, Gulf of Australia **86** F7 13 30S 138 00E
Carpentras France **61** C1 44 03N 5 03E
Carrauntoohill *mt.* Irish Republic **48** B1 52 00N 9 45W
Carrbridge Highland Scotland **46** E4 57 17N 3 49W
Carrickfergus Antrim Northern Ireland **49** D2 54 43N 5 49W
Carrickmacross Monaghan Irish Republic **48** E3 53 58N 6 43W
Carrick-on-Shannon Leitrim Irish Republic **48** C3 53 57N 8 05W
Carrick-on-Suir Tipperary Irish Republic **48** D2 52 21N 7 25W
Carrigaline Cork Irish Republic **48** C1 51 48N 8 24W
Carrigtohill Cork Irish Republic **48** C1 51 55N 8 16W
Carrington Lothian Scotland **45** D1 55 50N 3 05W
Carrion *r.* Spain **66** B3 42 30N 4 45W
Carron *r.* Central Scotland **45** C2 56 05N 3 55W
Carron Valley Reservoir Central Scotland **45** B2 56 02N 4 05W
Carryduff Down Northern Ireland **49** D1 54 31N 5 53W
Carson California U.S.A. **107** A2 33 49N 118 16W
Carson City Nevada U.S.A. **102** C4 39 10N 119 46W
Carstairs Strathclyde Scotland **45** C1 55 42N 3 42W
Cartagena Colombia **114** B15 10 24N 75 33W
Cartagena Spain **66** B2 37 36N 0 59W
Cartago Costa Rica **109** H1 9 50N 83 52W
Carteret New Jersey U.S.A. **106** B1 40 34N 74 13W
Carterton Oxfordshire England **32** A2 51 45N 1 35W
Cartwright Newfoundland Canada **101** X3 53 40N 57 00W
Caruarú Brazil **114** J11 8 15S 35 55W
Carúpano Venezuela **114** E15 10 39N 63 14W
Casablanca *(Dar el Beida)* Morocco **93** D9 33 39N 7 35W
Casa Grande Arizona U.S.A. **102** D3 32 52N 111 46W
Cascade Range *mts.* North America **102** B6 48 00N 121 00W
Cascadura Brazil **116** B2 22 53S 43 21W
Cascais Portugal **66** A2 38 41N 9 25W
Cascavel Brazil **114** J12 4 10S 38 15W
Caserta Italy **68** B3 41 04N 14 20E
Casey *r.s.* Antarctica **121** 66 17S 77 58E
Cashel Tipperary Irish Republic **48** D2 52 31N 7 53W
Casper Wyoming U.S.A. **102** E5 42 50N 106 20W
Caspian Sea Asia **70** G4 41 00N 50 00E
Cassiar Mountains British Columbia Canada **100** I4 59 15N 129 49W
Cassino Italy **68** B3 41 29N 13 50E
Castellane France **61** C1 43 50N 6 30E
Castellón de la Plana Spain **66** B2 39 59N 0 03W
Castelnaudary France **61** B1 43 18N 1 57E
Castelo Branco Portugal **66** A2 39 50N 7 30W
Castlebar Mayo Irish Republic **48** B3 53 52N 9 17W
Castlebay Western Isles Scotland **46** A3 56 57N 7 28W
Castleblayney Monaghan Irish Republic **48** E4 54 07N 6 44W
Castle Bromwich West Midlands England **35** C2 52 30N 1 45W
Castle Cary Somerset England **31** E3 51 06N 2 31W
Castlecomer Kilkenny Irish Republic **48** D2 52 48N 7 12W
Castleconnell Limerick Irish Republic **48** C2 52 43N 8 30W
Castlederg Northern Ireland **48** D4 54 42N 7 36W
Castle Donington Leicestershire England **35** D3 52 51N 1 19W
Castle Douglas Dumfries & Galloway Scotland **46** E1 54 57N 3 56W
Castleford West Yorkshire England **43** F3 43 44N 1 21W
Castleisland Kerry Irish Republic **48** B2 52 14N 9 27W
Castlerea Roscommon Irish Republic **48** C3 53 46N 8 29W
Castleton Derbyshire England **43** E2 53 21N 1 46W
Castletown Highland Scotland **46** E5 58 35N 3 23W
Castletown Isle of Man British Isles **41** F1 54 04N 4 38W
Castletownbere Cork Irish Republic **48** B1 51 39N 9 55W
Castres France **61** B1 43 30N 2 14E
Castricum Netherlands **64** D4 52 33N 4 40E
Castries St. Lucia **109** L2 14 01N 60 59W
Castrop-Rauxel Germany **62** D3 51 33N 7 18E
Castrovillari Italy **68** C2 39 48N 16 12E
Catamarca Argentina **115** D7 28 28S 65 46W
Catánia Italy **68** C2 37 31N 15 06E
Catanzaro Italy **68** C2 38 54N 16 36E
Cataract, 1st *(R. Nile)* Egypt **78** D3 24 00N 32 45E
Cataract, 2nd *(R. Nile)* Sudan **78** D3 21 40N 31 12E
Cataract, 3rd *(R. Nile)* Sudan **78** D2 19 45N 30 25E
Cataract, 4th *(R. Nile)* Sudan **78** D2 18 40N 32 10E
Cataract, 5th *(R. Nile)* Sudan **78** D2 18 25N 33 52E
Caterham Surrey England **34** C1 51 17N 0 04W
Catford Greater London England **34** D2 51 26N 0 00
Cat Island The Bahamas **109** I4 24 30N 75 30W
Catrine Strathclyde Scotland **46** D2 55 30N 4 20W
Catshill Hereford and Worcester England **35** B2 52 22N 2 03W
Catskill Mountains New York U.S.A. **105** F2 42 00N 74 00W
Catterick Garrison North Yorkshire England **40** C3 54 23N 1 40W
Caucaia Brazil **114** J12 3 44S 38 45W
Caucasus Mountains Asia **70** G4 43 00N 43 00E
Cauldhame Central Scotland **45** B2 56 07N 4 12W
Cavan Cavan Irish Republic **48** D3 53 58N 7 21W
Cavan *co.* Irish Republic **48** D4 54 02N 7 10W
Cawood North Yorkshire England **43** G3 53 50N 1 07W
Caxias Brazil **114** I12 4 53S 43 20W
Caxias do Sul Brazil **115** G7 29 14S 51 10W
Cayenne French Guiana **114** G13 4 55N 52 18W
Cayman Trench Caribbean Sea **119** R9 15 00N 80 00W
Cayuga Lake New York U.S.A. **105** E2 43 00N 77 00W
Cea *r.* Spain **66** A3 42 40N 5 10W
Ceanannus Mór *(Kells)* Meath Irish Republic **48** E3 53 44N 6 53W
Ceara *admin.* Brazil **114** I11/J11 5 30S 40 00W
Cebu *i.* The Philippines **72** 10 30N 123 30E
Cebu The Philippines **80** G6 10 17N 123 56E
Cedar *r.* U.S.A. **104** B2 42 00N 92 00W
Cedar City Utah U.S.A. **102** D4 37 40N 113 04W
Cedar Creek *r.* North Dakota U.S.A. **102** F6 46 00N 102 00W
Cedar Falls *tn.* Iowa U.S.A. **104** B2 42 34N 92 26W
Cedar Grove New Jersey U.S.A. **106** B2 40 51N 74 14W
Cedar Lake Manitoba Canada **101** O3 53 40N 100 30W
Cedar Rapids *tn.* Iowa U.S.A. **104** B2 41 59N 91 39W
Cedros *i.* Mexico **108** A5 28 00N 115 00W
Ceduna Australia **86** E3 32 07S 133 42E
Ceerigaabo Somalia **94** I10 10 40N 47 20E
Cefn-mawr Clwyd Wales **38** C2 52 59N 3 02W
Cegléd Hungary **69** C2 47 10N 19 47E
Ceiriog *r.* Clwyd Wales **38** C2 52 52N 3 10W
Celaya Mexico **108** D4 20 32N 100 48W
Celbridge Kildare Irish Republic **49** A2 53 20N 6 32W
Celebes *see* Sulawesi
Celebes Sea Indonesia **80** G4 3 00N 122 30E
Celje Slovenia **68** C4 46 15N 15 16E
Cellarhead Staffordshire England **35** B4 53 02N 2 04W
Celle Germany **63** B2 52 37N 10 05E
Cemaes Gwynedd Wales **38** B3 53 24N 4 27W
Central *reg.* Scotland **46** D3 56 10N 4 20W
CENTRAL AFRICAN REPUBLIC 94 C9
Central Cordilleras *hills* Spain **51**
Centralia Illinois U.S.A. **104** C1 38 32N 89 08W
Central Pacific Basin Pacific Ocean **118** I9 10 00N 177 00W
Central Plain Ireland **51** 53 30N 8 00W

Coats Island Northwest Territories Canada **101** S5 63 30N 83 00W
Coats Land *geog. reg.* Antarctica **121** 77 00S 25 00W
Coatzacoalcos *(Puerto Mexico)* Mexico **108** F3 18 10N 94 25W
Cobán Guatemala **108** F3 15 28N 90 20W
Cobar Australia **86** H3 31 32S 145 51E
Cobbinshaw Reservoir Lothian Scotland **45** C1 55 48N 3 34W
Cobh Cork Irish Republic **48** C1 51 51N 8 17W
Cobham Surrey England **34** B1 51 20N 0 24W
Cobija Bolivia **114** D10 11 01S 68 45W
Cobourg Ontario Canada **105** E2 43 58N 78 11W
Coburg Germany **63** B2 50 15N 10 58E
Cochabamba Bolivia **114** D9 17 26S 66 10W
Cochin India **77** D1 9 56N 76 15E
Cochrane Chile **115** C3 47 16S 72 33W
Cochrane Ontario Canada **105** D3 49 04N 81 02W
Cockburn Island *i.* Ontario Canada **105** D3 46 00N 83 00W
Cockerham Lancashire England **42** B3 53 59N 2 50W
Cockermouth Cumbria England **44** A1 54 40N 3 21W
Cocksburnspath Borders Scotland **46** F2 55 58N 2 27W
Cocos Basin Indian Ocean **72** 5 00S 96 00E
Cocos Island *see* Isla del Coco
Cocos Ridge Pacific Ocean **119** R8 4 00N 90 00W
Cocota Brazil **116** C2 22 48S 43 11W
Codajás Brazil **114** E12 3 55S 62 00W
Cod, Cape *p.* Massachusetts U.S.A. **105** G2 42 00N 70 00W
Codó Brazil **114** I12 4 28S 43 51W
Codrington Antigua & Barbuda **109** L3 17 43N 61 49W
Codsall Staffordshire England **35** B2 52 37N 2 12W
Coelhodo Rocha Brazil **116** B2 22 46S 43 21W
Coesfeld Germany **63** A2 51 57N 7 10E
Coeur d'Alene Idaho U.S.A. **102** C6 47 40N 116 46W
Coevorden Netherlands **64** F4 52 39N 6 45E
Coffeyville Kansas U.S.A. **104** A1 37 02N 95 37W
Coggeshall Essex England **33** C2 51 52N 0 41E
Coghinhas *r.* Italy **61** C1 40 00N 9 00E
Cognac France **61** A2 45 42N 0 19W
Cogswell Reservoir California U.S.A. **107** C3 34 14N 117 59W
Coihaique Chile **115** C3 45 35S 72 08W
Coimbatore India **77** D2 11 00N 76 57E
Coimbra Portugal **66** A3 40 12N 8 25W
Colbeck, Cape Antarctica **121** 77 00S 150 00W
Colchester Essex England **33** C2 51 54N 0 54E
Cold Lake *tn.* Alberta Canada **100** M3 54 28N 110 15W
Coldrain Tayside Scotland **45** D2 56 12N 3 28W
Coldstream Borders Scotland **46** F2 55 39N 2 15W
Coldwater Michigan U.S.A. **104** C2 41 57N 85 01W
Colebrook New Hampshire U.S.A. **105** F2 44 53N 71 30W
Coleford Gloucestershire England **31** E3 51 48N 2 37W
Coleman Alberta Canada **100** M2 49 38N 114 28W
Coleraine Northern Ireland **48** E5 55 08N 6 40W
Coleshill Warwickshire England **35** C2 52 30N 1 42W
Colima Mexico **108** D3 19 14N 103 41W
Colinton Lothian Scotland **45** D1 55 54N 3 15W
Colintraive Strathclyde Scotland **46** C2 55 56N 5 09W
Coll *i.* Strathclyde Scotland **46** B3 56 40N 6 35W
College Alaska U.S.A. **100** F5 64 54N 147 55W
Collie Australia **86** B3 33 20S 116 06E
Collines de la Puisage *hills* France **61** B2 47 35N 3 18E
Collines de l'Armagnac *hills* France **61** B1 43 30N 0 30E
Collines de Normandie *hills* France **61** A2 48 58N 0 55W
Collines du Perche *hills* France **61** B2 48 30N 0 50E
Collines du Sancerrois *hills* France **61** B2 47 15N 2 30E
Collingham West Yorkshire England **43** F3 53 55N 1 25W
Collingwood New Zealand **87** B2 40 41S 172 41E
Collingwood Ontario Canada **105** D2 44 30N 80 14W
Collooney Sligo Irish Republic **48** C4 54 11N 8 29W
Colmar France **61** C2 48 05N 7 21E
Colne Lancashire England **42** D3 53 52N 2 09W
Colne *r.* Essex England **33** C2 51 53N 0 45E
Coiney Heath Hertfordshire England **34** C3 51 44N 0 14W
Cologne *see* Köln
Colombes France **60** B2 48 55N 2 15E
COLOMBIA **114** C13
Colombo Sri Lanka **77** D1 6 55N 79 52E
Colón Panama **109** I1 9 21N 79 54W
Colonsay *i.* Strathclyde Scotland **46** B3 56 05N 6 15W
Colorado *r.* North America **102** D3 33 00N 114 00W
Colorado *r.* Texas U.S.A. **103** G2 29 00N 96 00W
Colorado *state* U.S.A. **102** E4 39 00N 106 00W
Colorado Plateau Arizona U.S.A. **102** D4 36 00N 111 00W
Colorado Springs *tn.* Colorado U.S.A. **102** F4 38 50N 104 50W
Colsterworth Lincolnshire England **36** D2 52 48N 0 37W
Coltishall Norfolk England **33** D3 52 44N 1 22E
Columbia Kentucky U.S.A. **104** C1 37 05N 85 19W
Columbia Missouri U.S.A. **104** B1 38 58N 92 20W
Columbia *r.* North America **102** B6 46 00N 120 00W
Columbia South Carolina U.S.A. **103** J3 34 00N 81 00W
Columbia City Indiana U.S.A. **104** C2 41 09N 85 20W
Columbia, Mount British Columbia/Alberta Canada **100** L3 52 09N 117 25W
Columbus Georgia U.S.A. **103** J3 32 28N 84 59W
Columbus Indiana U.S.A. **104** C1 39 12N 85 57W
Columbus Mississippi U.S.A. **103** I3 33 30N 88 27W
Columbus Nebraska U.S.A. **103** G5 41 27N 97 21W
Columbus Ohio U.S.A. **105** D2 39 59N 83 03W
Colville *r.* Alaska U.S.A. **100** D6 69 00N 158 00W
Colvocorresses Bay Antarctica **121** 66 00S 120 00E
Colwyn Bay *tn.* Clwyd Wales **38** C3 53 18N 3 43W
Comandante Ferraz *r.s.* Antarctica **121** 62 05S 58 23W
Comas Peru **116** E5 11 57S 77 03W
Combe Martin Devon England **31** C3 51 13N 4 02W
Comber Down Northern Ireland **49** D1 54 33N 5 45W
Comilla Bangladesh **77** G4 23 28N 91 10E
Comitán Mexico **108** F3 16 18N 92 09W
Commonwealth of Independent States *(C.I.S.) see individual member countries:* ARMENIA, AZERBAIJAN, BELARUS, KAZAKHSTAN, KIRGYZSTAN, MOLDOVA, RUSSIA, TAJIKISTAN, TURKMENISTAN, UKRAINE, UZBEKISTAN
Como Italy **68** A4 45 48N 9 05E
Comodoro Rivadavia Argentina **115** D3 45 50S 67 30W
Comorin, Cape India **77** D1 8 04N 77 35E
Comoro Archipelago *is.* Indian Ocean **88** 12 00S 44 00E
COMOROS **95** H5
Compiègne France **61** B2 49 25N 2 50E
Compton California U.S.A. **107** B2 33 55N 118 14W
Conakry Guinea **93** C4 9 30N 13 43W
Concepción Chile **115** C5 36 50S 73 03W
Concepción Mexico **108** D4 24 38N 101 25W
Concepción Paraguay **115** F8 23 22S 57 26W
Concepción del Uruguay Argentina **115** F6 32 30S 58 15W
Conchos *r.* Mexico **108** C5 27 30N 107 00W
Concord New Hampshire U.S.A. **105** F2 43 13N 71 34W
Concordia Argentina **115** F6 31 25S 58 00W
Concordia Kansas U.S.A. **103** G4 39 35N 97 39W
Condom France **61** B1 43 58N 0 23E
Condorrat Strathclyde Scotland **45** B1 55 57N 4 02W
Conduit *r.* Israel **78** O11 32 25N 35 00E
Conecuh *r.* Alabama U.S.A. **103** I3 31 00N 87 00W
Conejera *i.* Balearic Islands **66** E4 39 11N 2 58E
Coney Island New York U.S.A. **106** C1 40 34N 74 00W
Conflans-Ste. Honorine France **60** A3 49 01N 2 09E
Congleton Cheshire England **40** B2 53 10N 2 13W
CONGO **94** C7
Congo *(Zaïre) r.* Congo **94** C7 2 00S 17 00E
Congresbury Avon England **31** E3 51 23N 2 48W
Coningsby Lincolnshire England **36** D3 53 07N 0 10W
Conisbrough South Yorkshire England **43** G2 53 29N 1 13W
Coniston Cumbria England **44** A1 54 22N 3 05W
Coniston Ontario Canada **105** D3 46 29N 80 51W
Coniston Water *l.* Cumbria England **44** A1 54 20N 3 05W
Connah's Quay *tn.* Clwyd Wales **38** C3 53 13N 3 03W
Connecticut *r.* U.S.A. **103** L5 43 00N 72 00W
Connecticut *state* U.S.A. **105** F2 41 00N 73 00W
Connemara National Park Mayo Irish Republic **48** B3 53 30N 9 55W
Conon Bridge *tn.* Highland Scotland **46** D4 57 33N 4 26W
Consett Durham England **44** C1 54 51N 1 49W
Constanţa Romania **69** E1 44 12N 28 40E
Constantine Algeria **93** G10 36 22N 6 40E
Constitución Chile **115** C5 31 05S 57 51W
Contanama Peru **114** B11 7 19S 75 04W
Contrary Head Isle of Man British Isles **41** F1 54 13N 4 45W
Conwy Gwynedd Wales **38** C3 53 17N 3 50W
Conwy *r.* Gwynedd Wales **38** C3 53 00N 3 47W
Cookham Berkshire England **34** A2 51 34N 0 43W
Cook Inlet Alaska U.S.A. **100** E5 60 00N 152 30W
Cook Islands Pacific Ocean **119** K6 19 30S 159 50W
Cookley Hereford & Worcester England **35** B2 52 25N 2 14W
Cook, Mount New Zealand **87** B2 43 37S 170 08E
Cookstown Northern Ireland **48** E4 54 39N 6 45W
Cook Strait New Zealand **87** B2 41 00S 174 30E
Cooktown Australia **86** H6 15 29S 145 15E
Coolgardie Australia **86** C3 31 01S 121 12E
Cooper Creek *r.* Australia **86** F4 28 00S 138 00E
Coosa *r.* U.S.A. **103** I3 33 00N 86 00W
Coos Bay *tn.* Oregon U.S.A. **102** B5 43 23N 124 12W
Cootehill Cavan Irish Republic **48** D4 54 04N 7 05W
Copacabana Brazil **116** C2 22 58S 43 11W
Copacabana Beach Brazil **116** C2 22 59S 43 11W
Copenhagen *see* København
Copiapó Chile **115** C7 27 20S 70 23W
Copper *r.* Alaska U.S.A. **100** F5 60 30N 144 50W
Copper Cliff *tn.* Ontario Canada **105** D3 46 28N 81 05W
Copper Harbor *tn.* Michigan U.S.A. **104** C3 47 28N 87 54W
Coppermine Northwest Territories Canada **100** L6 67 49N 115 12W
Coppermine *r.* Northwest Territories Canada **100** M6 67 00N 114 50W
Coppull Lancashire England **42** B2 53 37N 2 40W
Copthorne West Sussex England **34** C1 51 09N 0 08W
Coquet *r.* Northumberland England **44** C2 55 20N 1 50W
Coquimbo Chile **115** C7 29 57S 71 25W
Coral Ontario Canada **105** D4 50 13N 81 41W
Coral Harbour *tn.* Northwest Territories Canada **101** S5 64 10N 83 15W
Coral Sea Pacific Ocean **86** I7 15 00S 154 00E
Corantijn *r.* Surinam **114** F13 4 30N 57 30W
Corbeil-Essonnes France **60** C1 48 36N 2 29E
Corbridge Northumberland England **44** B1 54 58N 2 01W
Corby Northamptonshire England **36** D2 52 49N 0 32W
Cordillera Cantabrica *(Cantabrian Mountains)* Spain **66** A3 43 00N 5 30W
Cordillera de Mérida *mts.* Venezuela **109** J1 8 00N 72 00W
Córdoba Argentina **115** E6 31 25S 64 11W
Córdoba Mexico **108** E3 18 55N 96 55W
Córdoba Spain **66** B2 37 53N 4 46W
Cordova Alaska U.S.A. **100** F5 60 29N 145 52W
Corfe Castle Dorset England **31** E2 50 38N 2 04W
Corfu *see* Kérkira
Corinth Mississippi U.S.A. **103** I3 34 58N 88 30W
Cork *co.* Irish Republic **48** C1 51 58N 8 40W
Cork Cork Irish Republic **48** C1 51 54N 8 28W
Cork Harbour Irish Republic **48** C1 51 50N 8 10W
Corley Warwickshire England **35** D2 52 28N 1 32W
Çorlu Turkey **68** E3 41 11N 27 48E
Cormeilles-en-Parisis France **60** A2 48 58N 2 11E
Corner Brook *tn.* Newfoundland Canada **101** X2 48 58N 57 58W
Corning New York U.S.A. **105** E2 42 10N 77 04W
Cornwall *co.* England **31** C2 50 25N 4 50W
Cornwall Ontario Canada **105** F3 45 02N 74 45W
Cornwallis Island Northwest Territories Canada **101** O7 74 40N 97 30W
Coro Venezuela **114** D15 11 20N 70 00W
Coroico Bolivia **114** D9 16 09S 67 45W
Coromandel Coast India **77** D2 12 30N 81 30E
Coronation Gulf Northwest Territories Canada **100** M6 68 15N 112 30W
Coronation Island South Orkney Islands **115** H0 61 00S 45 00W
Coronel Pringles Argentina **115** E5 37 56S 61 25W
Corpus Christi Texas U.S.A. **103** G2 27 47N 97 26W
Corran Highland Scotland **46** C3 56 43N 5 14W
Corrientes Argentina **115** F7 27 30S 58 48W
Corrieverton Guyana **114** F14 5 53N 57 10W
Corse *(Corsica) i.* France **61** C1 42 00N 9 00E
Corsham Wiltshire England **31** E3 51 26N 2 11W
Corsica *see* Corse
Corstorphine Lothian Scotland **45** D1 55 57N 3 18W
Corte Corsica **61** C1 42 18N 9 08E
Cortland New York U.S.A. **105** E2 42 36N 76 10W
Çoruh *r.* Turkey **78** F7 40 45N 40 45E
Corumbá Brazil **114** F9 19 00S 57 35W
Corunna *see* La Coruña
Corvallis Oregon U.S.A. **102** B5 44 34N 123 16W
Corwen Clwyd Wales **38** C2 52 59N 3 22W
Corydon Indiana U.S.A. **104** C1 38 12N 86 09W
Coseley West Midlands England **35** B2 52 33N 2 06W
Cosenza Italy **68** C2 39 17N 16 16E
Cossipore India **76** K2 22 37N 88 23E
Costa Blanca *geog. reg.* Spain **66** B2 38 15N 0 20W
Costa Brava *geog. reg.* Spain **66** C3 41 40N 3 50E
Costa del Sol *geog. reg.* Spain **66** B2 36 40N 4 40W
COSTA RICA **109** H1/2
Cotagaita Bolivia **114** D8 20 47S 65 40W
Côteau Québec Canada **105** F3 45 16N 74 16W
Côte D'Azur France **61** C1 43 00N 7 00E
CÔTE D'IVOIRE **93** E4
Côte d'Or *hills* France **61** B2 47 00N 4 30E
Cotentin *p.* France **51** 49 30N 1 30W
Côtes du Nivernais *plat.* France **61** B2 47 15N 3 20E
Cotonou Benin **93** F4 6 24N 2 31E
Cotopaxi *mt.* Ecuador **114** B12 0 40S 78 28W
Cotswold Hills Gloucestershire England **31** E3 51 40N 2 10W
Cottbus Germany **63** B2 51 43N 14 21E
Cottenham Cambridgeshire England **33** C3 52 18N 0 09E
Cotubandê Brazil **116** C2 22 51S 43 00W
Couesnon *r.* France **61** A2 48 30N 1 40W
Coulommiers France **61** B2 48 49N 3 05E
Coulsdon Greater London England **34** C1 51 19N 0 07W
Council Bluffs *tn.* Iowa U.S.A. **104** A2 41 14N 95 54W
Countesthorpe Leicestershire England **36** C2 52 33N 1 09W
Coupar Angus Tayside Scotland **46** E3 56 33N 3 17W
Courtrai *see* Kortrijk
Couvin Belgium **64** D2 50 03N 4 30E
Cove Bay *tn.* Grampian Scotland **46** F4 57 05N 2 05W
Coven Staffordshire England **35** B2 52 39N 2 08W
Coventry West Midlands England **35** D2 52 25N 1 30W
Coverack Cornwall England **30** B2 50 01N 5 05W
Covilhã Portugal **66** A3 40 17N 7 30W
Covina California U.S.A. **107** C3 34 04N 117 53W
Covington Indiana U.S.A. **104** C2 40 10N 87 23W
Covington Kentucky U.S.A. **105** D1 39 04N 84 30W
Cowbridge South Glamorgan Wales **38** C1 51 28N 3 27W
Cowdenbeath Fife Scotland **45** D2 56 07N 3 21W
Cowes Isle of Wight England **32** A1 50 45N 1 18W
Cowie Central Scotland **45** C2 56 05N 3 52W
Cox's Bazar Bangladesh **77** G4 21 25N 91 59E
Coyoacán Mexico **108** P1 19 20N 99 10W
Coyote Creek *r.* California U.S.A. **107** B2 33 50N 118 05W
Craigavon Armagh Northern Ireland **48** E4 54 28N 6 25W
Craigellachie Grampian Scotland **46** E4 57 29N 3 12W
Craiglockhart Lothian Scotland **45** D1 55 55N 3 15W
Craignure Strathclyde Scotland **46** C3 56 28N 5 42W
Crail Fife Scotland **46** F3 56 16N 2 38W
Crailsheim Germany **63** B1 49 09N 10 06E
Craiova Romania **69** D1 44 18N 23 47E
Cramlington Northumberland England **44** C2 55 05N 1 35W
Cramond Lothian Scotland **45** D1 55 59N 3 16W
Cranage Cheshire England **42** C1 53 13N 2 22W
Cranberry Staffordshire England **35** B3 52 55N 2 16W
Cranbourne Berkshire England **34** B2 51 25N 0 40W
Cranbrook Kent England **33** C2 51 06N 0 33E
Cranfield Bedfordshire England **34** B4 52 05N 0 35W
Cranleigh Surrey England **34** B1 51 09N 0 30W
Crathie Grampian Scotland **46** E4 57 02N 3 12W
Craven Arms Shropshire England **36** B2 52 26N 2 50W
Crawford Strathclyde Scotland **46** E2 55 28N 3 40W
Crawfordsville Indiana U.S.A. **104** C2 40 03N 86 54W
Crawley West Sussex England **34** C1 51 07N 0 12W
Crays Hill *tn.* Essex England **34** E2 51 35N 0 27E
Credenhill Hereford and Worcester England **36** B2 52 05N 2 48W
Crediton Devon England **31** D2 50 47N 3 39W
Cree *r.* Saskatchewan Canada **100** N4 58 00N 106 30W
Cree Lake Saskatchewan Canada **100** N4 57 30N 106 30W
Creil France **61** B2 49 16N 2 29E
Cremona Italy **68** B4 45 08N 10 01E
Cres *i.* Croatia **68** B3 45 00N 14 00E
Crescent City California U.S.A. **102** B5 41 46N 124 13W
Creston Iowa U.S.A. **104** B2 41 04N 94 20W
Crestview Florida U.S.A. **103** I3 30 44N 86 34W
Creswell Derbyshire England **43** G1 53 16N 1 12W
Crete *see* Kriti
Créteil France **60** B2 48 47N 2 28E
Crete, Sea of Mediterranean Sea **68** D2 36 00N 25 00E
Creuse *r.* France **61** B2 46 45N 0 45E
Crewe Cheshire England **40** B2 53 05N 2 27W
Crewkerne Somerset England **31** E2 50 53N 2 48W
Crianlarich Central Scotland **46** D4 56 23N 4 37W
Criccieth Gwynedd Wales **38** B2 52 55N 4 14W
Criciúma Brazil **115** H7 28 45S 49 25W
Crickhowell Powys Wales **38** C1 51 53N 3 09W
Cricklade Wiltshire England **31** F3 51 39N 1 51W
Crieff Tayside Scotland **45** C2 56 23N 3 52W
Crigglestone West Yorkshire England **43** F2 53 38N 1 32W
Crimea *see* Krim
Crinan Strathclyde Scotland **46** C3 56 06N 5 35W
CROATIA **68** C4
Crockham Hill *tn.* Kent England **34** D1 51 14N 0 04E
Croftamie Central Scotland **45** B2 56 03N 4 26W
Crofton West Yorkshire England **43** F2 53 39N 1 26W
Cromarty Highland Scotland **46** D4 57 40N 4 02W
Cromarty Firth *est.* Highland Scotland **46** D4 57 40N 4 20W
Cromer Norfolk England **33** D3 52 56N 1 18E
Cromwell New Zealand **87** A1 45 03S 169 14E
Crook Durham England **44** C1 54 43N 1 44W
Crooked Island The Bahamas **109** J4 22 45N 74 10W
Crookston Minnesota U.S.A. **104** A3 47 47N 96 36W
Crosby Merseyside England **42** A2 53 30N 3 02W
Cross Fell *sum.* Cumbria England **44** B1 54 43N 2 29W
Crossford Fife Scotland **45** D2 56 04N 3 30W
Crossford Strathclyde Scotland **45** C1 55 42N 3 54W
Crossgates Fife Scotland **45** D2 56 05N 3 24W
Cross Hands Dyfed Wales **38** B1 51 48N 4 05W
Crosshaven Cork Irish Republic **48** C1 51 48N 8 17W
Crosshill Fife Scotland **45** D2 56 09N 3 18W
Crossmaglen Northern Ireland **48** E4 54 05N 6 37W
Crossmolina Mayo Irish Republic **48** B4 54 06N 9 20W
Croston Lancashire England **42** B2 53 40N 2 47W
Crotone Italy **68** C2 39 05N 17 08E
Crouch *r.* Essex England **33** C2 51 38N 0 42E
Crowborough East Sussex England **33** C2 51 03N 0 09E
Crowland Lincolnshire England **36** D2 52 41N 0 11W
Crowle Hereford & Worcester England **35** B1 52 12N 2 07W
Crowle Humberside England **40** D2 53 37N 0 49W
Crow Peak *mt.* Montana U.S.A. **102** D6 46 19N 111 56W
Crowthorne Berkshire England **33** B2 51 23N 0 49W
Croyde Devon England **31** C3 51 08N 4 15W
Croydon Australia **86** G6 18 10S 142 15E
Croydon Greater London England **34** C2 51 23N 0 06W
Crumlin Dublin Irish Republic **49** B1 53 19N 6 18W
Crumlin Northern Ireland **49** C1 54 37N 6 14W
Crumlin *r.* Northern Ireland **49** C1 54 37N 6 03W
Crummock Water *l.* Cumbria England **44** A1 54 34N 3 18W
Cruzeiro do Sul Brazil **114** C11 7 40S 72 39W
Crymmych Dyfed Wales **38** B1 51 59N 4 40W
Crystal Falls *tn.* Michigan U.S.A. **104** C3 46 06N 88 11W
Crystal Palace Greater London England **34** C2 51 24N 0 04W
Cuando *r.* Southern Africa **95** D4 16 00S 21 30E
Cuango *r.* Angola **95** C6 9 00S 18 30E
Cuanza *r.* Angola **95** C6 9 40S 15 00E
Cuautepec Mexico **108** P2 19 32N 99 08W
CUBA **109** I4
Cubango *r.* Angola **95** C4 17 00S 18 00E
Cuckfield West Sussex England **33** B2 51 00N 0 09W
Cuckney Nottinghamshire England **43** G1 53 15N 1 08W
Cúcuta Colombia **114** C14 7 55N 73 31W
Cuddalore India **77** D2 11 43N 79 46E
Cuddapah India **77** D2 14 30N 78 50E
Cudworth South Yorkshire England **43** F2 53 35N 1 25W
Cuenca Ecuador **114** B12 2 54S 79 00W
Cuenca Spain **66** B3 40 04N 2 07W
Cuernavaca Mexico **108** E3 18 57N 99 15W
Cuffley Hertfordshire England **34** C3 51 47N 0 07W
Cuiabá Brazil **114** F9 15 32S 56 05W
Cuillin Hills Skye Scotland **46** B4 57 15N 6 15W
Cuito *r.* Angola **95** C4 17 30S 19 30E
Culcheth Cheshire England **42** C2 53 27N 2 31W
Culemborg Netherlands **64** E3 51 58N 5 14E
Culhuacan Mexico **108** P1 19 19N 99 06W
Culiacán Mexico **108** C4 24 50N 107 23W
Cullen Grampian Scotland **46** F4 57 41N 2 49W
Cullompton Devon England **31** D2 50 52N 3 24W
Cullybackey Antrim Northern Ireland **48** E4 54 53N 6 21W
Culver City California U.S.A. **107** A3 34 01N 118 24W
Culverstone Green Kent England **34** E2 51 20N 0 21E
Cumaná Venezuela **114** E15 10 29N 64 12W
Cumberland *r.* U.S.A. **103** I4 37 00N 86 00W
Cumberland *tn.* Maryland U.S.A. **105** E1 39 40N 78 47W
Cumberland Peninsula Northwest Territories Canada **101** W6 67 00N 65 00N
Cumberland Plateau U.S.A. **103** I4 36 00N 85 00W
Cumberland Sound Northwest Territories Canada **101** V6 65 30N 66 00W
Cumbernauld Strathclyde Scotland **45** C1 55 57N 4 00W
Cumbria *co.* England **44** B1 54 30N 2 45W
Cumbrian Mountains Cumbria England **44** A1/B1 54 30N 3 00W
Cumnock Strathclyde Scotland **46** D2 55 27N 4 16W
Cunene *r.* Angola / Namibia **95** B4 17 00S 13 30E
Cuneo Italy **68** A3 44 24N 7 33E
Cunnamula Australia **86** H4 28 04S 145 40E
Cupar Fife Scotland **45** D2 56 19N 3 01W
Curaçao *i.* Lesser Antilles **109** K2 12 20N 68 20W
Curacautín Chile **115** C5 38 28S 71 52W
Cure *r.* France **61** B2 47 40N 3 40E
Curicó Chile **115** C5 35 00S 71 15W
Curitiba Brazil **115** H7 25 25S 49 25W
Currie Lothian Scotland **45** D1 55 51N 3 20W
Curvelo Brazil **114** I9 18 45S 44 27W
Cutnall Green Hereford & Worcester England **35** B1 52 18N 2 11W
Cuttack India **77** F4 20 26N 85 56E
Cuxhaven Germany **63** A2 53 52N 8 42E
Cuyahoga Falls *tn.* Ohio U.S.A. **105** D2 41 08N 81 27W
Cuzco Peru **114** C10 13 32S 71 57W
Cwmbran Gwent Wales **38** C1 51 39N 3 00W
Cyclades *see* Kikládhes
Cypress Hills Alberta/Saskatchewan Canada **100** N2 48 40N 108 00W
CYPRUS **78** D5
CZECHOSLOVAKIA *see* CZECH REPUBLIC and SLOVAKIA
CZECH REPUBLIC (CESKA) **69** C2
Częstochowa Poland **69** C3 50 49N 19 07E

D

Dabola Guinea **93** C5 10 48N 11 02W
Dachau Germany **63** B1 48 15N 11 26E
Dadra & Nagar Haveli *admin.* India **77** C4 20 00N 73 00E
Dagenham Greater London England **34** D2 51 33N 0 08E
Dagnall Buckinghamshire England **34** B3 51 50N 0 34W
Da Hinggan Ling *(Greater Khingan Range) mts.* China **81** J7/J8 50 00N 122 00E
Dāhod India **77** C4 22 48N 74 18E
Dahongliutan Kashmir **77** D7 35 55N 79 10E
Dahuk Iraq **78** F6 36 58N 43 01E
Daiō-zaki *c.* Japan **82** C1 34 16N 136 55E
Dairût Egypt **78** D4 27 34N 30 48E
Daisen *mt.* Japan **82** B2 35 23N 133 34E
Dakar Senegal **93** B5 14 38N 17 27W
Dakhla Oasis Egypt **94** E13 26 00N 28 00E
Dakshin Gangotri *r.s.* Antarctica **121** 70 05S 12 00E
Da Lat Vietnam **80** D6 11 56N 108 25E
Dalbandin Pakistan **76** A5 28 56N 64 30E
Dalbeattie Dumfries & Galloway Scotland **46** E1 54 56N 3 49W
Dalby Australia **86** I4 27 11S 151 12E
Dalgarven Strathclyde Scotland **45** A1 55 41N 4 42W
Dalgetty Bay *tn.* Fife Scotland **45** D2 56 03N 3 18W
Dalhart Texas U.S.A. **102** F4 36 05N 102 32W
Dalian China **81** J5 38 53N 121 37S
Dalkeith Lothian Scotland **45** C1 55 51N 3 04W
Dalkey Dublin Irish Republic **49** B1 53 17N 6 06W
Dallas Texas U.S.A. **103** G3 32 47N 96 48W
Dalmally Strathclyde Scotland **46** D3 56 24N 4 58W
Dalmary Central Scotland **45** B2 56 08N 4 23W
Dalmellington Strathclyde Scotland **46** D2 55 19N 4 24W
Dalmeny Lothian Scotland **45** D1 55 58N 3 22W
Daloa Côte d'Ivoire **93** D4 6 56N 6 28W
Dalry Strathclyde Scotland **45** A1 55 43N 4 44W
Dalton Georgia U.S.A. **103** J3 34 46N 84 59W
Dalton Lancashire England **42** B2 53 34N 2 48W
Dalton-in-Furness Cumbria England **44** A1 54 09N 3 11W
Dalwhinnie Highland Scotland **46** D3 56 56N 4 14W
Daly *r.* Australia **86** F7 14 00S 132 00E
Daly Waters *tn.* Australia **86** E0 16 13S 133 20E
Daman India **77** C4 20 25N 72 58E
Damanhûr Egypt **78** D5 31 03N 30 28E
Damascus *see* Dimashq
Damāvand Iran **79** H6 35 47N 52 04E
Damāvand *mt.* Iran **79** H6 35 56N 52 08E
Damba Angola **95** C6 6 44S 15 20E
Damoh India **77** D4 23 50N 79 30E
Dampier Australia **86** B5 20 45S 116 48E
Danakil *geog. reg.* Africa **88** 14 00N 40 00E
Da Nang Vietnam **80** D7 16 04N 108 14E
Danau Toba *l.* Indonesia **80** B4 2 40N 98 50E
Danbury Connecticut U.S.A. **105** F2 41 24N 73 26W
Danbury Essex England **33** C2 51 44N 0 33E
Danderhall Lothian Scotland **45** D1 55 55N 3 06W

93 00E
Duncansby Head *c.* Highland Scotland 46 E5 58 39N 3 02W
Dunchurch Warwickshire England 35 E2 52 20N 1 16W
Dundalk Louth Irish Republic 48 E4 54 01N 6 25W
Dundalk Bay Irish Republic 48 E3 53 55N 6 15W
Dundas Ontario Canada 105 E2 43 16N 79 57W
Dundas *(Ummannaq)* Greenland 101 V8 76 30N 68 58W
Dundee Tayside Scotland 46 E3 56 28N 3 00W
Dundonald Down Northern Ireland 49 D1 54 36N 5 48W
Dundrum Dublin Irish Republic 49 B1 53 17N 6 15W
Dunedin New Zealand 87 B1 45 52S 170 30E
Dunfermline Fife Scotland 45 D2 56 04N 3 29W
Dungannon Northern Ireland 48 E4 54 31N 6 46W
Dungarvan Waterford Irish Republic 48 D2 52 05N 7 37W
Dungeness *c.* Kent England 33 C1 50 55N 0 58E
Dungiven Northern Ireland 48 E4 54 55N 6 55W
Dungloe Donegal Irish Republic 48 C4 54 57N 8 22W
Dunham-on-the-Hill Cheshire England 42 B1 53 15N 2 48W
Dunholme Lincolnshire England 36 D3 53 18N 0 29W
Dunipace Central Scotland 45 C2 56 02N 3 55W
Dunkeld Tayside Scotland 46 E3 56 34N 3 35W
Dunkerque *(Dunkirk)* France 61 B3 51 02N 2 23E
Dunkery Beacon *sum.* Somerset England 31 D3 51 11N 3 35W
Dunkirk New York U.S.A. 105 E2 42 29N 79 21W
Dunkirk *see* Dunkerque
Dún Laoghaire Dublin Irish Republic 49 B1 53 17N 6 08W
Dunleer Louth Irish Republic 48 E3 53 50N 6 24W
Dunley Hereford & Worcester England 35 B1 52 18N 2 19W
Dunlop Strathclyde Scotland 45 A1 55 43N 4 32W
Dunmanus Bay Irish Republic 48 B1 51 30N 9 50W
Dunmanway Cork Irish Republic 48 B1 51 43N 9 06W
Dunmurry Antrim Northern Ireland 49 C1 54 33N 6 00W
Dunnet Head *c.* Highland Scotland 46 E5 58 40N 3 25W
Dunnington North Yorkshire England 43 H3 53 57N 0 59W
Dunnington Warwickshire England 35 C1 52 11N 1 55W
Dunoon Strathclyde Scotland 46 D2 55 57N 4 56W
Duns Borders Scotland 46 F2 55 47N 2 20W
Dunscroft South Yorkshire England 43 G2 53 34N 1 05W
Dunshaughlin Meath Irish Republic 49 A2 53 31N 6 33W
Dunstable Bedfordshire England 34 B3 51 53N 0 32W
Dunster Somerset England 31 D3 51 12N 3 27W
Dunston Staffordshire England 35 B3 52 46N 2 06W
Duntochar Strathclyde Scotland 45 B1 55 55N 4 25W
Dunvegan Highland Scotland 46 B4 57 26N 6 35W
Duque de Caxias Brazil 116 B2 22 46S 43 18W
Durance *r.* France 61 C1 43 50N 5 15E
Durand Wisconsin U.S.A. 104 B2 44 37N 91 56W
Durango Colorado U.S.A. 102 E4 37 16N 107 53W
Durango Mexico 108 D4 24 01N 104 40W
Durant Oklahoma U.S.A. 103 G3 33 59N 96 24W
Durazno Uruguay 115 F6 33 22S 56 31W
Durban Republic of South Africa 95 F2 29 53S 31 00E
Düren Germany 63 A2 50 48N 6 30E
Durgapur India 77 J1 22 47N 87 44E
Durgāpur India 76 J1 22 27N 88 08E
Durg-Bhilai India 77 E4 21 12N 81 20E
Durham *co.* England 44 B1/C1 54 40N 2 00W
Durham Durham England 44 C1 54 47N 1 34W
Durham North Carolina U.S.A. 103 K4 36 00N 78 54W
Durlston Head *c.* Dorset England 31 E2 50 35N 1 57W
Durness Highland Scotland 46 D5 58 33N 4 45W
Durrës Albania 68 C3 41 18N 19 28E
Durrington Wiltshire England 31 F3 51 12N 1 48W
Dursey Head *c.* Irish Republic 48 A1 51 20N 10 10W
Dursey Island Irish Republic 48 A1 51 36N 10 12W
Dursley Gloucestershire England 31 E3 51 42N 2 21W
Dushanbe Tajikistan 70 I3 38 38N 68 51E
Düssel *r.* Germany 62 C1 51 14N 7 01E
Düsseldorf Germany 62 B1 51 13N 6 47E
Dutch Harbor *tn.* Alaska U.S.A. 100 B3 53 55N 166 36W
Duyun China 81 G3 26 16N 107 29E
Dvina, North *see* Severnaya Dvina
Dyce Grampian Scotland 46 F4 57 12N 2 11W
Dyfed *co.* Wales 38 B1 52 00N 4 25W
Dyfi *r.* Powys Wales 38 C2 52 38N 3 50W
Dyfrdwy *r.* Clwyd Wales 38 D2/3 53 00N 2 50W
Dykehead Central Scotland 45 B2 56 09N 4 15W
Dyle *r.* Belgium 64 D2 50 38N 4 35E
Dymchurch Kent England 33 C2 51 02N 1 00E
Dzhambul Kazakhstan 70 J4 42 50N 71 25E
Dzhetygara Kazakhstan 70 I6 52 14N 61 10E
Dzhezkazgan Kazakhstan 70 I5 47 44N 67 42E
Dzhugdzhur Range *mts.* Russia 71 P7 57 00N 137 00E
Dzungarian Basin *see* Junggar Pendi

E

Eagle Alaska U.S.A. 100 G5 64 46N 141 20W
Eagle Lake Maine U.S.A. 105 G3 46 00N 69 00W
Eagle Pass *tn.* Texas U.S.A. 102 F2 28 44N 100 31W
Eaglescliff Cleveland England 44 C1 54 31N 1 22W
Eaglesham Strathclyde Scotland 45 B1 55 44N 4 15W
Ealing Greater London England 34 C2 51 31N 0 18W
Earby Lancashire England 42 D3 53 56N 2 08W
Earls Colne Essex England 33 C2 51 56N 0 42E
Earl Shilton Leicestershire England 35 E2 52 35N 1 18W
Earlswood Warwickshire England 35 C2 52 22N 1 50W
Earn *r.* Tayside Scotland 45 C2 56 45N 3 40W
Easington Durham England 44 C1 54 47N 1 21W
Easington Humberside England 40 E2 53 40N 0 07E
Easingwold North Yorkshire England 40 C3 54 07N 1 11W
East Antarctica *geog. reg.* Antarctica 121
Eastbourne East Sussex England 33 C1 50 46N 0 17E
East Calder Lothian Scotland 45 D1 55 54N 3 27W
East Cape New Zealand 87 C3 37 42S 178 35E
East Caroline Basin Pacific Ocean 118 E8 4 00N 148 00E
East China Sea China/Japan 81 K4 32 00N 126 00E
East Dean East Sussex England 33 C1 50 45N 0 13E
East Dereham Norfolk England 33 C3 52 41N 0 56E
Easter Island Pacific Ocean 119 P5 27 05S 109 20W
Easter Island Fracture Zone Pacific Ocean 119 Q5 24 00S 100 00W
Eastern Ghats *geog. reg.* India 77 D2–E3 15 00N 80 00E
Eastern Group *is.* Fiji 118 V16 17 40S 178 30W
Eastern Sayan *mts.* Russia 71 L6 53 00N 97 30E
East Falkland *i.* Falkland Islands 117 M15 52 00S 58 50W
Eastfield North Yorkshire England 40 D3 54 15N 0 25W
East Fork White River Indiana U.S.A. 104 C1 39 00N 87 00W
East Frisian Islands *see* Ostfriesische Inseln
East Grand Forks Minnesota U.S.A. 104 A3 47 56N 96 59W
East Grinstead West Sussex England 34 C1 51 08N 0 01W
Eastham Merseyside England 42 B1 53 19N 2 58W
East Ilsley Berkshire England 32 A2 51 32N 1 17W
Eastington Gloucestershire England 31 E3 51 45N 2 20W
East Keswick West Yorkshire England 43 F3 53 53N 1 27W
East Kilbride Strathclyde Scotland 45 B1 55 46N 4 10W
East Leake Nottinghamshire England 36 C2 52 50N 1 11W
Eastleigh Hampshire England 32 A1 50 58N 1 22W
East Linton Lothian Scotland 46 F2 55 59N 2 39W
East Liverpool Ohio U.S.A. 105 D2 40 38N 80 36W
East London Republic of South Africa 95 E1 33 00S 27 54E
East Los Angeles California U.S.A. 107 B3 34 02N 118 12W
Eastmain Québec Canada 101 T3 52 10N 78 30W
East Marianas Basin Pacific Ocean 118 F9 13 00N 153 00E
East Markham Nottinghamshire England 43 H1 53 15N 0 54W
Easton Dorset England 31 E2 50 32N 2 26W
Easton Maryland U.S.A. 105 E1 38 46N 76 05W
Easton Pennsylvania U.S.A. 105 E2 40 41N 75 13W
East Pacific Basin Pacific Ocean 119 K9 16 00N 153 00E
East Pacific Ridge Pacific Ocean 119 O5 20 00S 113 00W
East Pacific Rise Pacific Ocean 119 P9 13 00N 103 00W
East Retford Nottinghamshire England 43 H1 53 19N 0 56W
East Rift Valley East Africa 94 G9 6 00N 37 00E
East St. Louis Illinois U.S.A. 104 B1 38 34N 90 04W
East Siberian Sea Arctic Ocean 120 72 00N 165 00E
East Stour *r.* Kent England 33 C2 51 08N 0 55E
East Sussex *co.* England 33 C1 50 55N 0 10E
East Wemyss Fife Scotland 45 D2 56 10N 3 05W
Eastwood Nottinghamshire England 35 E4 53 01N 1 18W
Eaton Bray Befordshire England 34 B3 51 53N 0 36W
Eaton Socon Bedfordshire England 33 B3 52 13N 0 18W
Eaton Wash Reservoir California U.S.A. 107 B3 34 10N 118 05W
Eau Claire *tn.* Wisconsin U.S.A. 104 B2 44 50N 91 30W
Eauripik–New Guinea Rise Pacific Ocean 118 E8 2 00N 142 00E
Ebbw Vale Gwent Wales 38 C1 51 47N 3 12W
Ebensburg Pennsylvania U.S.A. 105 E2 40 28N 78 44W
Eberswalde-Finow Germany 63 B2 52 50N 13 53E
Ebinur Hu *l.* China 81 B6/7 45 00N 83 00E
Ebolowa Cameroon 93 H3 2 56N 11 11E
Ebro *r.* Spain 66 C3 41 00N 0 30E
Ebute Metta Nigeria 92 C3 6 27N 3 28E
Ecclefechan Dumfries & Galloway Scotland 46 E2 55 03N 3 17W
Eccles Greater Manchester England 42 C2 53 29N 2 21W
Ecclesfield South Yorkshire England 43 F2 53 27N 1 27W
Eccleshall Staffordshire England 35 B3 52 52N 2 15W
Ech Cheliff Algeria 93 F10 36 05N 1 15E
Echo Bay *tn.* Northwest Territories Canada 100 L6 65 50N 117 30W
Echternach Luxembourg 64 F1 49 49N 6 25E
Ecija Spain 66 A2 37 33N 5 04W
Eckernförde Germany 63 A2 54 28N 9 50E
Eckington Derbyshire England 43 F1 53 91N 1 21W
Écouen France 60 B3 49 01N 2 22E
ECUADOR 114 B12
Edale Derbyshire England 43 E2 53 22N 1 49W
Edam Netherlands 64 E4 52 30N 5 02E
Eday *i.* Orkney Islands Scotland 47 E2 59 11N 2 47W
Ed Damer Sudan 78 D2 17 37N 33 59E
Ed Debba Sudan 94 F11 18 02N 30 56E
Eddleston Borders Scotland 45 D1 55 43N 3 13W
Eddrachillis Bay Highland Scotland 46 C5 58 25N 5 15W
Eddystone Rocks English Channel 31 C2 50 10N 4 16W
Eddyville Kentucky U.S.A. 104 C1 37 03N 88 02W
Ede Netherlands 64 E4 52 03N 5 40E
Edéa Cameroon 93 H3 3 47N 10 13E
Eden Antrim Northern Ireland 49 D2 54 44N 5 47W
Eden North Carolina U.S.A. 103 K4 36 30N 79 46W
Eden *r.* Cumbria England 44 B1 54 50N 2 45W
Eden *r.* Surrey England 33 B2 51 10N 0 05W
Edenbridge Kent England 34 D1 51 12N 0 04E
Edenderry Offaly Irish Republic 48 D3 53 21N 7 35W
Edenthorpe South Yorkshire England 43 G2 53 33N 1 03W
Eder *r.* Germany 63 A2 51 00N 9 00E
Edgbaston West Midlands England 35 C2 52 26N 1 55W
Edgewood Maryland U.S.A. 105 E1 39 25N 76 18W
Edgmond Shropshire England 35 A3 52 45N 2 25W
Edgware Greater London England 34 C2 51 36N 0 16W
Edgworth Lancashire England 42 C2 53 39N 2 24W
Édhessa Greece 68 D3 40 48N 22 03E
Edinboro Pennsylvania U.S.A. 105 D2 41 53N 80 08W
Edinburgh Lothian Scotland 45 D1 55 57N 3 13W
Edirne Turkey 68 E3 41 40N 26 34E
Edlesborough Buckinghamshire England 34 B3 51 53N 0 35W
Edmonton Alberta Canada 100 M3 53 34N 113 25W
Edmonton Greater London England 34 C2 51 37N 0 04W
Edmundston New Brunswick Canada 105 G3 47 22N 68 20W
Edo *r.* Japan 83 C3 35 38N 139 53E
Edogawa Japan 83 C3 35 41N 139 51E
Edremit Turkey 68 E2 39 34N 27 01E
Edward, Lake Zaïre / Uganda 94 F7 0 30S 29 00E
Edwards Plateau Texas U.S.A. 102 F3 31 00N 100 00W
Eeklo Belgium 64 C3 51 11N 3 34E
Eems *(Ems) est.* Netherlands/F.R.G. 64 F5 53 25N 6 55E
Éfaté *i.* Vanuatu 86 L5 17 30S 168 00E
Eger Hungary 69 D2 47 53N 20 28E
Egham Surrey England 34 B2 51 26N 0 34W
Eglinton Northern Ireland 48 D5 55 01N 7 11W
Egmont, Cape New Zealand 87 B3 39 15S 173 46E
Egmont, Mount New Zealand 87 B3 39 18S 174 05E
Egremont Cumbria England 44 A1 54 29N 3 33W
Egridir Gölü Turkey 78 D6 37 52N 30 51E
EGYPT 78 D4
Eifel *p.* Germany 63 A2 50 00N 7 00E
Eigg *i.* Highland Scotland 46 B3 56 55N 6 10W
Eight Degree Channel Indian Ocean 77 C1 8 00N 73 30E
Eighty Mile Beach Australia 86 C6 19 00S 121 00E
Einbeck Germany 63 A2 51 49N 9 53E
Eindhoven Netherlands 64 E3 51 26N 5 30E
Eisenach Germany 63 B2 50 59N 10 19E
Eisenhüttenstadt Germany 63 B2 52 10N 14 42E
Ekibastuz Kazakhstan 71 J6 51 50N 75 10E
El Aaiún *see* Laayoune
El Agustino Peru 116 F4 12 03S 76 58W
El Arco Mexico 108 B5 28 00N 113 25W
El 'Arish Egypt 78 N10 31 08N 33 48E
Elat Israel 78 O9 29 33N 34 57E
Elâziğ Turkey 78 E6 38 41N 39 14E
El Banco Colombia 114 C14 9 04N 73 59W
Elbasan Albania 68 D3 41 07N 20 05E
El Bayadh Algeria 93 F9 33 40N 1 00E
El Bayadh Algeria 66 C2 36 35N 1 18E
Elbe *(Labe) r.* Europe 63 A2 53 00N 9 00E
Elberfeld Germany 62 C2 51 17N 7 09E
Elbert, Mount Colorado U.S.A. 102 E4 39 05N 106 27W
Elbeuf France 61 B2 49 17N 1 01E
Elbląg Poland 69 C3 54 10N 19 25E
Elburg Netherlands 64 E4 52 27N 5 50E
Elburz Mountains Iran 79 H6 36 15N 51 00E
El Callao Venezuela 114 E14 7 18N 61 48W
El Centro California U.S.A. 102 C3 32 47N 115 33W
Elche Spain 66 B2 38 16N 0 41W
Elda Spain 66 B2 38 29N 0 47W
Elderslie Strathclyde Scotland 45 B1 55 50N 4 29W
El Dorado Arkansas U.S.A. 103 H3 33 12N 92 40W
El Dorado Kansas U.S.A. 103 G4 37 51N 96 52W
Eldoret Kenya 94 G8 0 31N 35 17E
Eleiyele Nigeria 92 E4 7 25N 3 53E
Elekuro Nigeria 92 E4 7 21N 3 57E
Elephant Island South Shetland Islands 115 G0 62 00S 55 00W
Eleuthera *i.* The Bahamas 109 I5 25 05N 76 30W
El Faiyûm Egypt 78 D4 29 19N 30 50E
El Fasher Sudan 94 E10 13 37N 25 22E
El Ferrol del Caudillo Spain 66 A3 43 29N 8 14W
El Fuerte Mexico 108 C5 26 28N 108 35W
Elgin Grampian Scotland 46 E4 57 39N 3 20W
Elgin Illinois U.S.A. 104 C2 42 03N 88 19W
El Gîza Egypt 78 D5 30 01N 31 12E
Elgol Highland Scotland 46 B4 57 09N 6 06W
El Golea Algeria 93 F9 30 35N 2 51E
Elgon, Mount Uganda / Kenya 94 F8 1 07N 34 35E
El Iskandarîya *see* Alexandria
Elista Russia 70 G5 46 18N 44 14E
Elizabeth Australia 86 F3 34 45S 138 39E
Elizabeth City North Carolina U.S.A. 103 K4 36 18N 76 16W
Elizabeth New Jersey U.S.A. 106 B1 40 39N 74 13W
Elizabethtown Kentucky U.S.A. 104 C1 37 41N 85 51W
El Jadida Morocco 93 D9 33 19N 8 35W
El Jafr Jordan 78 P10 30 16N 36 11E
Elk City Oklahoma U.S.A. 102 G4 35 25N 99 26W
El Khârga Egypt 78 D4 25 27N 30 32E
Ełk Poland 69 D3 53 51N 22 20E
Elkhart Indiana U.S.A. 104 C2 41 52N 85 56W
Elkhorn *r.* Nebraska U.S.A. 103 G5 42 00N 98 00W
Elkhorn Wisconsin U.S.A. 104 C2 42 40N 88 34W
Elkins West Virginia U.S.A. 105 E1 38 56N 79 53W
Elko Nevada U.S.A. 102 C5 40 50N 115 46W
Elk River *r.* West Virginia U.S.A. 105 D1 38 00N 81 00W
Elk River *tn.* Minnesota U.S.A. 104 B3 45 19N 93 31W
Elland West Yorkshire England 43 E3 53 41N 1 50W
Ellef Ringnes Island Northwest Territories Canada 101 08 78 30N 102 00W
Ellendale North Dakota U.S.A. 104 A3 46 00N 98 31W
Ellesmere Island Northwest Territories Canada 101 S8 77 30N 82 30W
Ellesmere Port Cheshire England 42 B1 53 17N 2 54W
Ellesmere Shropshire England 36 B2 52 54N 2 54W
Ellis Island New Jersey U.S.A. 106 B1 40 42N 74 02W
Ellon Grampian Scotland 46 F4 57 22N 2 05W
Ellsworth Land *geog. reg.* Antarctica 121 75 00S 80 00W
Ellsworth Maine U.S.A. 105 G2 44 34N 68 24W
Ellsworth Wisconsin U.S.A. 104 B2 44 44N 92 29W
El Mahalla El Kubra Egypt 78 D5 30 59N 31 10E
El Médano Mexico 108 B4 24 35N 111 29W
Elmhurst Illinois U.S.A. 104 C2 41 54N 87 56W
el Milk *r.* Sudan 94 E11 17 00N 29 00E
El Minya Egypt 78 D4 28 06N 30 45E
Elmira New York U.S.A. 105 E2 42 06N 76 50W
El Monte California U.S.A. 107 B3 34 04N 118 01W
Elmshorn Germany 63 A2 53 46N 9 40E
El Muglad Sudan 94 E10 11 01N 27 50E
El Obeid Sudan 94 F10 13 11N 30 10E
El Paso Texas U.S.A. 102 E3 31 45N 106 30W
El Porvenir Mexico 108 C6 31 15N 105 48W
El Puerto de Sta. Maria Spain 66 A2 36 36N 6 14W
El Qâ'hira *see* Cairo
El Qunayţirah Syria 78 O11 33 08N 35 49E
El Reno Oklahoma U.S.A. 103 G4 35 32N 97 57W
El Salto Mexico 108 C4 23 47N 105 22W
EL SALVADOR 108 G2
Elsenham Essex England 34 D3 51 55N 0 14E
Elstead Surrey England 34 A1 51 11N 0 43W
Elstree Hertfordshire England 33 B2 51 39N 0 18W
El Sueco Mexico 108 C5 29 54N 106 22W
El Suweis *(Suez)* Egypt 78 D4 29 59N 32 33E
Eltanin Fracture Zone Pacific Ocean 119 M2 52 00S 135 00W
Eltham Greater London England 34 D2 51 27N 0 03E
El Tigre Venezuela 114 E14 8 44N 64 18W
Elton Cheshire England 42 B1 53 16N 2 49W
El Tûr Egypt 78 N9 28 14N 33 37E
Eluru India 77 E3 16 45N 81 10E
Elvas Portugal 66 A2 38 53N 7 10W
Ely Cambridgeshire England 33 C3 52 24N 0 16E
Ely Nevada U.S.A. 102 D4 39 15N 114 53W
Elyria Ohio U.S.A. 105 D2 41 22N 82 06W
Emāmrūd Iran 79 H6 36 15N 54 59E
Emba *r.* Kazakhstan 70 H5 47 30N 56 00E
Emba Kazakhstan 70 H5 48 47N 58 05E
Embalse de Guri *l.* Venezuela 114 E14 7 30N 62 30W
Embleton Northumberland England 44 C2 55 30N 1 37W
Embrun France 61 C1 44 33N 6 30E
Emden Germany 63 A2 53 23N 7 13E
Emerald Australia 86 H5 23 30S 148 08E
Emi Koussi *mt.* Chad 94 C11 19 52N 18 31E
Emmeloord Netherlands 64 E4 52 43N 5 46E
Emmen Netherlands 64 F4 52 47N 6 55E
Emmerich Germany 63 A2 51 49N 6 16E
Empalme Mexico 108 B5 28 00N 110 49W
Emperor Seamounts Pacific Ocean 118 G12 42 00N 169 00E
Emporia Kansas U.S.A. 104 A1 38 24N 96 10W
Ems *r.* Germany 63 A2 53 00N 7 00E
Emscher *r.* Germany 62 D3 51 35N 7 25E
Emsworth Hampshire England 33 B1 50 51N 0 56W
Enard Bay Highland Scotland 46 C5 58 10N 5 25W
Encantado Brazil 116 B2 22 54S 43 18W
Encarnación Paraguay 115 F7 27 20S 55 50W
Endeh Indonesia 80 G2 8 51S 121 40E
Endicott Mountains Alaska U.S.A. 100 E6 67 35N 154 00W
Endon Staffordshire England 35 B4 53 05N 2 07W
Enfield Greater London England 34 C2 51 39N 0 05W
Engel's Russia 70 G6 51 30N 46 07E
Engenho Novo Brazil 116 B2 22 54S 43 16W
Enggano *i.* Indonesia 80 C2 5 10S 102 40E
Enghien France 60 B2 48 58N 2 19E
England United Kingdom 29 53 00N 2 00W
Englehart Ontario Canada 105 E3 47 50N 79 52W
Englewood New Jersey U.S.A. 106 C2 40 53N 73 58W
English Channel *(La Manche)* U.K./France 61 A2 50 00N 2 30W
English River *tn.* Ontario Canada 104 B3 49 14N 90 58W
Enid Oklahoma U.S.A. 103 G4 36 24N 97 54W
Enkhuizen Netherlands 64 E4 52 42N 5 17E
Enna Italy 68 B2 37 34N 14 16E
En Nahud Sudan 94 E10 12 41N 28 28E
Ennerdale Water *l.* Cumbria England 44 A1 54 31N 3 22W
Ennis Clare Irish Republic 48 C2 52 50N 8 59W
Enniscorthy Wexford Irish Republic 48 E2 52 30N 6 34W
Enniskerry Wicklow Irish Republic 49 B1 53 12N 6 10W
Enniskillen Northern Ireland 48 D4 54 21N 7 38W
Ennistymon Clare Irish Republic 48 B2 52 57N 9 15W
Enns *r.* Austria 69 B2 48 00N 14 00E
Enontekiö Finland 67 E4 68 25N 23 40E
Enschede Netherlands 64 F4 52 13N 6 55E
Ensenada Mexico 108 A6 31 53N 116 38W
Entebbe Uganda 94 F8 0 04N 32 27E
Enugu Nigeria 93 G4 6 20N 7 29E
Enville Staffordshire England 35 B2 52 29N 2 15W
Epe Netherlands 64 E4 52 21N 5 59E
Epernay France 61 B2 49 02N 3 58E
Epinal France 61 C2 48 10N 6 28E
Epping Essex England 34 D3 51 42N 0 08E
Epping Forest Essex England 34 D2 51 40N 0 04E
Epsom Surrey England 34 C1 51 20N 0 16W
Epworth Humberside England 40 D2 53 31N 0 50W
EQUATORIAL GUINEA 93 H3
Erbes Kopf *mt.* Germany 64 G1 49 42N 7 07E
Erding Germany 63 B1 48 17N 11 55E
Erdington West Midlands England 35 C2 52 31N 1 50W
Erebus, Mount Antarctica 121 77 40S 167 20E
Erechim Brazil 115 G7 27 35S 52 15W
Erenhot China 81 H6 43 50N 112 00E
Erft *r.* Germany 64 F2 50 00N 6 00E
Erfurt Germany 63 B2 50 58N 11 02E
Erg Chech *geog. reg.* Algeria 93 E7 24 30N 3 00W
Ergene *r.* Turkey 68 E3 41 00N 27 00E
Erg Iguidi *geog. reg.* Algeria 93 D8 26 00N 6 00W
Ergun He *see* Argun
Erie Pennsylvania U.S.A. 105 D2 42 07N 80 05W
Erie, Lake North America 105 D2 42 00N 82 00W
Erimo-misaki *c.* Japan 82 D3 41 55N 143 13E
Eriskay *i.* Western Isles Scotland 46 A4 57 05N 7 10W
Erith Greater London England 34 D2 51 29N 0 11E
ERITREA (ERTRA) 78 F1
Erkelenz Germany 64 F3 51 05N 6 18E
Erkrath Germany 62 B1 51 13N 6 54E
Erlangen Germany 63 B1 49 36N 11 02E
Ermelo Netherlands 64 E4 52 18N 5 38E
Erode India 77 D2 11 21N 77 43E
Errigal Mountain Irish Republic 48 C5 55 02N 8 07W
Erris Head *c.* Irish Republic 48 A4 54 20N 10 00W
Errol New Hampshire U.S.A. 105 F2 44 47N 71 10W
Errol Tayside Scotland 45 D2 56 23N 3 15W
Erromango *i.* Vanuatu 86 L6 19 00S 169 00E
Er Roseires Sudan 94 F10 11 52N 34 23E
Erskine Strathclyde Scotland 45 B1 55 54N 4 28W
ERTRA *see* ERITREA
Erzgebirge *(Krušnéhory) mts.* Europe 63 B2 50 00N 13 00E
Erzincan Turkey 78 E6 39 44N 39 30E
Erzurum Turkey 78 F6 39 57N 41 17E
Esashi Japan 82 D3 41 54N 140 09E
Esbjerg Denmark 67 B2 55 20N 8 20E
Escanaba Michigan U.S.A. 104 C3 45 47N 87 04W
Escaut *r.* France 64 C2 50 30N 3 28E
Esch-sur-Alzette Luxembourg 64 E1 49 30N 5 59E
Eschwege Germany 63 B2 51 11N 10 03E
Eschweiler Germany 63 A2 50 49N 6 16E
Escondido California U.S.A. 102 C3 33 07N 117 05W
Eşfahān Iran 79 H5 32 41N 51 41E
Esher Surrey England 34 B2 51 22N 0 22W
Esk *r.* Cumbria England 44 A1 54 25N 3 15W
Esk *r.* North Yorkshire England 40 D3 54 30N 0 50W
Esk *r.* Scotland/England 46 E2 55 15N 3 05W
Eskilstuna Sweden 67 D2 59 22N 16 31E
Eskimo Lakes Northwest Territories Canada 100 I6 68 30N 132 30W
Eskimo Point *tn.* Northwest Territories Canada 101 Q5 61 10N 94 15W
Eskişehir Turkey 78 D6 39 46N 30 30E
Esmeraldas Ecuador 114 B13 0 56N 79 40W
Espanola Ontario Canada 105 D3 46 15N 81 46W
Esperance Australia 86 C3 33 49S 121 52E
Esperanza *r.s.* Antarctica 121 63 24S 56 59W
Espirito Santo *admin.* Brazil 114 J9 18 40S 40 00W
Espiritu Santo *i.* Vanuatu 86 L6 15 10S 167 00E
Espoo Finland 67 E3 60 10N 24 40E
Esquel Argentina 115 C4 42 55S 71 20W
Esquimalt British Columbia Canada 100 K2 48 25N 123 29W
Es Semara Western Sahara 93 C8 26 25N 11 30W
Essen Belgium 64 D3 51 28N 4 28E
Essen Germany 62 C2 51 27N 6 57E
Essequibo *r.* Guyana 114 F13 2 30N 58 00W
Essex *co.* England 33 C2 51 46N 0 30E
Esslingen Germany 63 A1 48 45N 9 19E
Estevan Saskatchewan Canada 101 O2 49 09N 103 00W
Estância Brazil 114 J10 11 15S 37 28W
Eston Cleveland England 44 C1 54 34N 1 07W
ESTONIA 67 F2
Estrecho de Magallanes *sd.* Chile 115 C2 53 00S 71 00W
Estrêla *r.* Brazil 116 C3 22 42S 43 14W
Étampes France 61 B2 48 26N 2 10E
Etaples France 61 B3 50 31N 1 39E
Etawah India 77 D5 26 46N 79 01E
ETHIOPIA 94 G9
Ethiopian Highlands Africa 88 8 00N 37 00E
Etna *mt.* Italy 68 C2 37 45N 15 00E
Eton Berkshire England 34 B2 51 31N 0 37W
Etosha National Park Namibia 95 C4 18 30S 16 00E
Etosha Pan *salt l.* Namibia 95 C4 18 30S 16 30E
Ettelbruck Luxembourg 64 F1 49 51N 6 06E
Etten-Leur Netherlands 64 D3 51 34N 4 37E
Ettrick Borders Scotland 46 E2 55 25N 3 05W
Euboea *see* Evvoia
Eucla Australia 86 D3 31 40S 128 51E
Euclid Ohio U.S.A. 105 D2 41 34N 81 33W
Eugene Oregon U.S.A. 102 B5 44 03N 123 04W
Eupen Belgium 64 F2 50 38N 6 02E

Gairney Bank *tn.* Tayside Scotland **45** D2 56 11N 3 24W
Galana *r.* Kenya **94** G7 3 30S 34 30E
Galapagos Islands *see* Islas Galapagos
Galapagos Rise Pacific Ocean **119** R6 12 00S 87 00W
Galashiels Borders Scotland **46** F2 55 37N 2 49W
Galaţi Romania **69** E2 45 27N 28 02E
Galeão Brazil **116** C2 22 49S 43 14W
Galesburg Illinois U.S.A. **104** B2 40 58N 90 22W
Galeton Pennsylvania U.S.A. **105** E2 41 43N 77 39W
Galgate Lancashire England **42** B3 53 59N 2 47W
Galilee, Sea of *see* Tiberias, Lake
Galina Point *c.* Jamaica **109** R8 18 24N 76 58W
Galle Sri Lanka **77** E1 6 01N 80 13E
Gallego *r.* Spain **66** B3 41 55N 0 56W
Galley Head *c.* Irish Republic **48** C1 51 35N 8 55W
Gallipoli Italy **68** C3 40 03N 17 59E
Gallipoli Turkey *see* Gelibolu
Gallipolis Ohio U.S.A. **105** D1 38 49N 82 14W
Gallup New Mexico U.S.A. **102** E4 32 32N 108 46W
Galston Strathclyde Scotland **46** D2 55 36N 4 24W
Galtymore *sum.* Irish Republic **48** C2 52 22N 8 10W
Galty Mountains Irish Republic **48** C2 52 20N 8 10W
Galveston Texas U.S.A. **103** H2 29 17N 94 48W
Galway *co.* Irish Republic **48** C3 53 25N 8 45W
Galway Galway Irish Republic **48** B3 53 16N 9 03W
Galway Bay Irish Republic **48** B3 53 15N 9 15W
Gambell Alaska U.S.A. **100** A5 63 46N 171 45W
Gambia *r.* Senegal **93** C5 13 45N 13 15W
GAMBIA, THE 93 B5
Gambier Islands Pitcairn Islands **119** N5 23 10S 135 00W
Gananoque Ontario Canada **105** E2 44 21N 76 11W
Gand *see* Gent
Gandak *r.* India **77** E5 26 30N 84 30E
Gander Newfoundland Canada **101** Y2 49 00N 54 15W
Ganga *(Ganges) r.* India **77** E4 25 30N 82 00E
Ganga, Mouths of the India **77** F4 21 30N 89 00E
Ganganagar India **77** C5 29 54N 73 56E
Gangdisê Shan *mts.* China **81** B4 31 00N 82 30E
Ganges *see* Ganga
Gangtok India **77** F5 27 20N 88 39E
Ganzhou China **81** H3 25 52N 114 51E
Gao Mali **93** E6 16 19N 0 09W
Gap France **61** C1 44 33N 6 05E
Garanhuns Brazil **114** J11 8 53S 36 28W
Garbsen Germany **63** A2 52 25N 9 36E
Gard *r.* France **61** B1 44 05N 4 20E
Gardena California U.S.A. **107** A2 33 53N 118 19W
Garden City Kansas U.S.A. **102** F4 37 57N 100 54W
Garden City New York U.S.A. **106** D1 40 43N 73 39W
Garden Grove California U.S.A. **107** C2 33 48N 117 52W
Garden Reach India **76** K2 22 32N 88 16E
Gardēz Afghanistan **79** K5 33 37N 69 07E
Gardner Island Pacific Ocean **118** I7 4 40S 174 32W
Garelochhead Strathclyde Scotland **46** D3 56 05N 4 50W
Garfield New Jersey U.S.A. **106** B2 40 52N 74 05W
Garforth West Yorkshire England **43** F3 53 48N 1 22W
Gargrave North Yorkshire England **43** D3 53 59N 2 06W
Gargunnock Central Scotland **45** B2 56 08N 4 05W
Garissa Kenya **94** G7 0 27S 39 39E
Gariya India **76** K1 22 27N 88 23E
Garland Texas U.S.A. **103** G3 32 55N 96 37W
Garmisch-Partenkirchen Germany **63** B1 47 30N 11 05E
Garonne *r.* France **61** A1 44 45N 0 15E
Garoua Cameroon **93** H4 9 17N 13 22E
Garron Point *c.* Northern Ireland **48** E/F5 55 05N 6 00W
Garry Lake Northwest Territories Canada **101** O6 66 20N 100 00W
Garstang Lancashire England **42** B3 53 55N 2 47W
Gartempe *r.* France **61** B2 46 10N 1 10E
Garth Powys Wales **38** C2 52 08N 3 32W
Garthorpe Humberside England **40** D2 53 40N 0 42W
Gartocharn Strathclyde Scotland **45** A2 56 02N 4 32W
Garulia India **76** K3 22 49N 88 23E
Garve Highland Scotland **46** D4 57 37N 4 42W
Gary Indiana U.S.A. **104** C2 41 34N 87 20W
Garyarsa China **77** E6 31 46N 80 21E
Garzón Colombia **114** B13 2 14N 75 37W
Gasconade *r.* Missouri U.S.A. **104** B1 38 00N 92 00W
Gascoyne *r.* Australia **86** A5 25 00S 114 00E
Gasherbrum *mt.* Kashmir **77** D7 35 46N 76 38E
Gaspé Québec Canada **101** W2 48 50N 64 30W
Gastonia North Carolina U.S.A. **103** J4 35 14N 81 12W
Gatchina Russia **67** G2 59 32N 30 05E
Gatehouse of Fleet Dumfries & Galloway Scotland **46** D1 54 53N 4 11W
Gateshead Tyne and Wear England **44** C1 54 58N 1 35W
Gateside Strathclyde Scotland **45** A1 55 44N 4 36W
Gatineau Québec Canada **105** E3 45 29N 75 40W
Gatmore Central Scotland **45** B2 56 08N 4 23W
Gauhati India **77** G5 26 10N 91 45E
Gávdhos *i.* Greece **68** D1 34 00N 24 00E
Gave d'Oloron *r.* France **61** A1 43 15N 0 40W
Gave du Pau *r.* France **61** A1 43 20N 0 30W
Gävle Sweden **67** D3 60 41N 17 10E
Gaya India **77** F4 24 48N 85 00E
Gaydon Warwickshire England **35** D1 52 45N 0 34E
Gaylord Michigan U.S.A. **105** D3 45 02N 84 41W
Gaza Israel **78** O10 31 30N 34 28E
Gaza Strip *territory* Israel **78** O10 31 28N 34 05E
Gaziantep Turkey **78** E6 37 04N 37 21E
Gbarnga Liberia **93** D4 7 02N 9 26W
Gdańsk Poland **69** C3 54 22N 18 41E
Gdańsk, Gulf of Baltic Sea **69** C3 54 00N 19 00E
Gdynia Poland **69** C3 54 31N 18 30E
Gebel el Tîh *p.* Egypt **78** N9 29 30N 33 45E
Gebel Katherina *hill* Egypt **78** O9 28 30N 33 57E
Gebel Mûsa *(Mount Sinai) mt.* Egypt **78** N9 28 32N 33 59E
Gedaref Sudan **78** E1 14 01N 35 24E
Gediz *r.* Turkey **78** C6 38 40N 27 30E
Geel Belgium **64** D3 51 10N 5 00E
Geelong Australia **86** G2 38 10S 144 26E
Gejiu China **81** F2 23 25N 103 05E
Gela Italy **68** B2 37 04N 14 15E
Gelderland *admin.* Netherlands **64** F4 52 05N 0 10E
Geldern Germany **64** F3 51 31N 6 19E
Geldrop Netherlands **64** E3 51 25N 5 34E
Geleen Netherlands **64** E2 50 58N 5 45E
Gelibolu *(Gallipoli)* Turkey **68** E3 40 25N 26 41E
Gelligaer Mid Glamorgan Wales **38** C1 51 39N 3 15W
Gelsenkirchen Germany **62** C3 51 30N 7 05E
Gembloux Belgium **64** D2 50 34N 4 42E
Gemsbok National Park Botswana **95** D2 26 00S 21 00E
Genalē *r.* Ethiopia **94** H9 6 00N 40 00E
Gendringen Netherlands **64** F3 51 53N 6 24E
Geneina Sudan **94** D10 13 27N 22 30E
General Belgrano II *r.s.* Antarctica **121** 77 52S 34 37W
General Bernardo O'Higgins *r.s.* Antarctica **121** 63 19S 57 54W
General San Martin *r.s.* Antarctica **121** 68 08S 67 04W
Geneva New York U.S.A. **105** E2 42 53N 76 59W
Geneva *see* Genève
Geneva, Lake *see* Lac Léman
Genève *(Geneva)* Switzerland **61** C2 46 13N 6 09E
Genil *r.* Spain **66** B2 37 20N 4 45W
Genk Belgium **64** B2 50 58N 5 30E
Gennevilliers France **60** B2 48 56N 2 17E
Genoa *see* Genova
Genova *(Genoa)* Italy **68** A3 44 24N 8 56E
Gent *(Gand)* Belgium **64** C3 51 02N 3 42E
George *r.* Québec Canada **101** V4 58 00N 65 30W
George Island Falkland Islands **117** M15 52 20S 59 45W
Georgetown Delaware U.S.A. **105** E1 38 43N 75 05W
Georgetown Guyana **114** F14 6 46N 58 10W
George Town Malaysia **80** C5 5 30N 100 28E
Georgetown South Carolina U.S.A. **103** K3 33 23N 79 18W
George VI Sound Antarctica **121** 72 00S 67 00W
Georg Forster *r.s.* Antarctica **121** 70 46S 11 50E
GEORGIA 70 G4
Georgia *state* U.S.A. **103** J3 33 00N 83 00W
Georgian Bay Ontario Canada **105** D3 45 00N 81 00W
Georgian S.S.R. *see* Gruzinskaya S.S.R.
Georgina *r.* Australia **86** F5 22 00S 137 00E
Georg von Neumayer *r.s.* Antarctica **121** 70 37S 08 22W
Gera Germany **63** B2 50 51N 12 11E
Gera *r.* Germany **63** B2 50 00N 10 00E
Geraardsbergen Belgium **64** C2 50 47N 3 53E
Geraldton Australia **86** A4 28 49S 114 36E
Geraldton Ontario Canada **104** C3 49 44N 86 59W
GERMANY 63
Gerona Spain **66** C3 41 59N 2 49E
Gerrards Cross Buckinghamshire England **34** B2 51 35N 0 34W
Getafe Spain **66** B3 40 18N 3 44W
Gettysburg Pennsylvania U.S.A. **105** E1 39 50N 77 16W
Ghaghara *r.* India **77** E4 26 20N 83 30E
GHANA 93 E4
Ghanzi Botswana **95** D3 21 42S 21 39E
Ghardaïa Algeria **93** F9 32 20N 3 40E
Gharyān Libya **94** B14 32 10N 13 01E
Ghāt Libya **94** B12 24 58N 10 11E
Ghaziabad India **77** D5 28 39N 77 26E
Ghazni Afghanistan **79** K5 33 33N 68 26E
Gheorghe Gheorghiu-Dej Romania **69** E2 46 17N 26 45E
Ghisonaccia Corsica **61** C1 42 01N 9 24E
Giant's Causeway Northern Ireland **48** E5 55 10N 6 30W
Gibraltar *territory* U.K. **66** A2 36 09N 5 21W
Gibraltar, Strait of Spain/Morocco **66** A2 35 58N 5 30W
Gibson Desert Australia **86** C5 25 00S 123 00E
Gīdolē Ethiopia **94** G9 5 38N 37 28E
Gien France **61** B2 47 41N 2 37E
Giessen Germany **63** A2 50 35N 8 42E
Giffnock Strathclyde Scotland **45** B1 55 49N 4 16W
Gifu Japan **82** C2 35 27N 136 46E
Gigha Isles Strathclyde Scotland **46** C2 55 40N 5 45W
Gigüela *r.* Spain **66** B2 39 40N 3 15W
Gijón Spain **66** A3 43 32N 5 40W
Gila *r.* U.S.A. **102** D3 33 00N 114 00W
Gila Bend Arizona U.S.A. **102** D3 32 56N 112 42W
Gilbert *r.* Australia **86** G6 17 00S 142 30E
Gilbert Islands Pacific Ocean **118** H7 0 00 173 00E
Gildersome West Yorkshire England **43** F3 53 45N 1 37W
Gilfach Goch Mid Glamorgan Wales **38** C1 51 38N 3 30W
Gilgit Kashmir **77** C7 35 54N 74 20E
Gillam Manitoba Canada **101** Q4 56 25N 94 45W
Gillette Wyoming U.S.A. **102** E5 44 18N 105 30W
Gillingham Dorset England **31** E3 51 02N 2 17W
Gillingham Kent England **33** C2 51 24N 0 33E
Gilmerton Tayside Scotland **45** C2 56 23N 3 50W
Gilsland Northumberland England **44** B1 55 00N 2 35W
Gimli Manitoba Canada **104** A4 50 39N 97 00W
Gīnīr Ethiopia **94** H9 7 06N 40 40E
Gippsland *geog. reg.* Australia **86** H2 37 30S 147 00E
Girardot Colombia **114** C13 4 19N 74 47W
Girga Egypt **78** D4 26 17N 31 58E
Gironde *r.* France **61** A2 45 30N 0 45W
Girvan Strathclyde Scotland **46** D2 55 15N 4 51W
Gisborne New Zealand **87** C3 38 41S 178 02E
Gisburn Lancashire England **42** D3 53 57N 2 15W
Giurgiu Romania **69** E1 43 53N 25 58E
Givet France **64** D2 50 08N 4 49E
Gizhiga Russia **71** S8 62 00N 160 34E
Gjirokastër Albania **68** D3 40 05N 20 10E
Gjoa Haven *tn.* Northwest Territories Canada **101** P6 68 39N 96 09W
Glace Bay *tn.* Nova Scotia Canada **101** X2 46 11N 59 58W
Gladbeck Germany **62** B3 51 34N 6 59E
Gladstone Australia **86** I5 23 52S 151 16E
Glåma *r.* Norway **67** C3 60 15N 12 00E
Glanaman Dyfed Wales **38** C1 51 47N 3 55W
Glanton Northumberland England **44** C2 55 26N 1 54W
Glarner Alpen *mts.* Switzerland **61** C2 46 50N 9 00E
Glasgow Strathclyde Scotland **45** B1 55 53N 4 15W
Glas Maol *mt.* Tayside Scotland **46** E3 56 52N 3 22W
Glassford Strathclyde Scotland **45** B1 55 42N 4 02W
Glasson Lancashire England **42** B3 54 00N 2 51W
Glastonbury Somerset England **31** E3 51 09N 2 43W
Glauchau Germany **63** B2 50 48N 12 32E
Glenavy Antrim Northern Ireland **49** C1 54 36N 6 13W
Glenavy *r.* Northern Ireland **49** C1 54 36N 6 03W
Glenboig Strathclyde Scotland **45** B1 55 52N 4 04W
Glenboro Manitoba Canada **104** A3 49 35N 99 20W
Glencarse Tayside Scotland **45** D2 56 23N 3 19W
Glencoe Highland Scotland **46** C3 56 40N 5 04W
Glencree *r.* Wicklow Irish Republic **49** B1 53 09N 6 15W
Glendale California U.S.A. **107** B3 34 09N 118 20W
Glendora California U.S.A. **107** C3 34 07N 117 53W
Glen Finglas Reservoir Central Scotland **45** B2 56 15N 4 25W
Glenfoot Tayside Scotland **45** D2 56 20N 3 20W
Glengarnock Strathclyde Scotland **45** A1 55 44N 4 40W
Glengormley Antrim Northern Ireland **49** D2 54 41N 5 58W
Glen Grove *tn.* New York U.S.A. **106** D2 40 52N 73 38W
Glenluce Dumfries & Galloway Scotland **46** D1 54 53N 4 49W
Glen Mor *v.* Highland Scotland **46** D4 57 10N 4 50W
Glenridding Cumbria England **44** B1 54 33N 2 58W
Glen Ridge New Jersey U.S.A. **106** B2 40 47N 74 13W
Glenrothes Fife Scotland **45** D2 56 12N 3 10W
Glens Falls *tn.* New York U.S.A. **105** F2 43 17N 73 41W
Glenties Donegal Irish Republic **48** C4 54 47N 8 17W
Glenveagh National Park Donegal Irish Republic **48** D5 55 00N 8 00W
Glenwood Iowa U.S.A. **104** A2 41 04N 95 46W
Gliwice Poland **69** C3 50 20N 18 40E
Globe Arizona U.S.A. **102** D3 33 23N 110 48W
Głogów Poland **69** C3 51 40N 16 06E
Glossop Derbyshire England **42** E2 53 27N 1 57W
Gloucester Gloucestershire England **31** E3 51 53N 2 14W
Gloucester Ontario Canada **105** E3 45 16N 75 39W
Gloucestershire *co.* England **31** E3 51 50N 2 20W
Gloversville New York U.S.A. **105** F2 43 03N 74 21W
Glovertown Newfoundland Canada **101** Y2 48 40N 54 03W
Glusburn North Yorkshire England **43** D3 53 55N 2 01W
Glyder Fawr *mt.* Gwynedd Wales **38** B3 53 05N 4 02W
Glyncorrwg West Glamorgan Wales **38** C1 51 41N 3 38W
Glyn Neath West Glamorgan Wales **38** C1 51 46N 3 38W
Gmunden Austria **63** B1 47 56N 13 48E
Gniezno Poland **69** C3 52 32N 17 32E
Gnosall Staffordshire England **35** B3 52 47N 2 15W
Goa, Damān & Diu *admin.* India **77** C3 15 00N 74 00E
Goalpara India **77** G5 26 10N 90 38E
Goat Fell *mt.* Arran Scotland **46** C2 55 39N 5 11W
Gobabis Namibia **95** C3 22 30S 18 58E
Gobi Desert Mongolia **81** E6–G6 48 30N 100 00E
Goch Germany **63** A2 51 40N 6 10E
Godalming Surrey England **34** B1 51 11N 0 37W
Godāvari *r.* India **77** D3/E3 19 00N 80 00E
Goderich Ontario Canada **105** D2 43 43N 81 43W
Godhavn *see* Qeqertarsuaq
Godhra India **77** C4 22 49N 73 40E
Godmanchester Cambridgeshire England **33** B3 52 19N 0 11W
Gods Lake Manitoba Canada **101** Q3 54 40N 94 20W
Godstone Surrey England **34** C1 51 15N 0 04W
Godthåb *(Nuuk)* Greenland **101** Y5 64 10N 51 40W
Godwin Austen *see* K2
Goes Netherlands **64** C3 51 30N 3 54E
Goiânia Brazil **114** H9 16 43S 49 18W
Goiás *admin.* Brazil **114** H10 12 30S 48 00W
Goiás Brazil **114** G9 15 57S 50 07W
Goias Massif *hills* South America **110** 15 00S 53 00W
Gökçeada *i.* Turkey **68** E3 40 00N 25 00E
Golan heights *territory* Israel **78** O11 33 00N 35 50E
Golborne Greater Manchester England **42** C2 53 29N 2 36W
Golcar West Yorkshire England **43** E2 53 39N 1 51W
Gold Coast *tn.* Australia **86** I4 27 59S 153 22E
Golden Bay New Zealand **87** B2 40 40S 173 00E
Golden Vale *v.* Irish Republic **48** C2 52 30N 8 05W
Golders Green Greater London England **34** C2 51 35N 0 13W
Goldsboro North Carolina U.S.A. **103** K4 35 23N 78 00W
Goldsworthy Australia **86** B5 20 20S 119 31E
Goldthorpe South Yorkshire England **43** G2 53 32N 1 19W
Golfe de Gabès *g.* Tunisia **93** H9 34 20N 10 30 E
Golfe de St-Malo *g.* France **61** A2 48 55N 2 30W
Golfe du Lion *g.* France **61** B1 43 10N 4 00E
Golfo de California *g.* Mexico **108** B5 27 00N 111 00W
Golfo de Guayaquil *g.* Ecuador **114** A12 3 00S 81 30W
Golfo de Honduras *g.* Caribbean Sea **108/9** G3 17 00N 87 30W
Golfo de Panamá *g.* Panama **109** I1 8 00N 79 00W
Golfo de San Jorge *g.* Argentina **115** D3 47 00S 66 00W
Golfo de Tehuantepec *g.* Mexico **108** E3/F3 15 30N 95 00W
Golfo de Venezuela *g.* Venezuela **114** C15 12 00N 71 30W
Golfo di Cágliari Italy **68** A2 39 00N 9 00E
Golfo di Catania Italy **68** C2 37 30N 15 20E
Golfo di Gaeta *g.* Italy **68** B3 41 00N 13 00E
Golfo di Genova *g.* Italy **68** A3 44 00N 9 00E
Golfo di Squillace *g.* Italy **68** C2 33 30N 17 00E
Golfo di Táranto *g.* Italy **68** C3 40 00N 17 00E
Golfo di Venèzia Adriatic Sea **68** B4 45 00N 13 00E
Golfo San Matías *g.* Argentina **115** E4 42 00S 64 00W
Golmud China **81** D5 36 22N 94 55E
Golo *r.* Corsica **61** C1 42 30N 9 10E
Golspie Highland Scotland **46** E4 57 58N 3 58W
Gombe Zaire **92** A2 4 19S 15 17E
Gomel' Belarus **70** F6 52 25N 31 00E
Gomera *i.* Canary Islands **93** B8 28 08N 17 14W
Gomersal West Yorkshire England **43** E3 53 43N 1 41W
Gómez Palacio Mexico **108** D5 25 39N 103 30W
Gomshall Surrey England **34** B1 51 13N 0 27W
Gonder Ethiopia **94** G10 12 39N 37 29E
Gondia India **77** E4 21 23N 80 14E
Gonesse France **60** B2 48 59N 2 27E
Good Hope, Cape of Republic of South Africa **95** C1 34 30S 19 00E
Goodland Kansas U.S.A. **102** F4 39 20N 101 43W
Gooimeer *l.* Netherlands **65** E3 52 18N 5 08E
Goole Humberside England **43** H3 43 42N 0 52W
Goondiwindi Australia **86** I4 28 30S 150 17E
Goose Green Falkland Islands **117** M16 51 52S 59 00W
Goostrey Cheshire England **42** D1 53 14N 2 19W
Göppingen Germany **63** A1 48 43N 9 39E
Gora Kamen' *mt.* Russia **71** L9 69 06N 94 59E
Gorakhpur India **77** E5 26 45N 83 23E
Gora Narodnaya *mt.* Russia **71** I9 65 02N 60 01E
Gora Pobeda *mt.* Russia **71** Q9 65 10N 146 00E
Gorda Rise Pacific Ocean **119** M12 43 00N 130 00W
Gordon Landing *tn.* Yukon Territory Canada **100** H5 63 38N 135 27W
Gorē Ethiopia **94** G9 8 10N 35 29E
Gore New Zealand **87** A1 46 06S 168 58E
Gore Bay *tn.* Ontario Canada **105** D3 45 54N 82 28W
Gorebridge Lothian Scotland **45** D1 55 51N 3 02W
Gorey Wexford Irish Republic **48** E2 52 40N 6 18W
Gorgān Iran **79** H6 36 50N 54 29E
Gorinchem Netherlands **64** D3 51 50N 4 59E
Goring Oxfordshire England **32** A2 51 32N 1 09W
Gorizia Italy **68** B4 45 57N 13 37E
Gorki Belarus **69** F3 54 17N 30 59E
Gor'kiy *see* Nizhniy Novgorod
Görlitz Germany **63** B2 51 09N 15 00E
Gormanston Meath Irish Republic **48** E3 53 38N 6 14W
Gorno-Altaysk Russia **81** C8 51 59N 85 56E
Goroka Papua New Guinea **86** H8 6 02S 145 22E
Gorontalo Indonesia **80** G4 0 33N 123 05E
Gorseinon West Glamorgan Wales **38** B1 51 41N 4 02W
Gort Galway Irish Republic **48** C3 53 04N 8 50W
Gorumna Island Irish Republic **48** B3 53 15N 9 55W
Goryn' *r.* Ukraine **69** E3 51 00N 26 00E
Gorzów Wielkopolski Poland **69** C3 52 42N 15 12E
Gosforth Tyne and Wear England **44** C2 55 01N 1 37W
Goslar Germany **63** B2 51 55N 10 25E
Gosport Hampshire England **32** A1 50 48N 1 08W
Gostivar Macedonia Yugoslavia **68** D3 41 47N 20 55E
Göta älv *r.* Sweden **67** C2 58 00N 12 00E
Göteborg Sweden **67** C2 57 45N 12 00E
Gotha Germany **63** B2 50 57N 10 43E
Gotland *i.* Sweden **67** D2 57 30N 18 40E
Göttingen Germany **63** A2 51 32N 9 57E
Gottwaldov *see* Zlúi
Gouda Netherlands **65** C2 52 00N 4 42E
Gough Island Atlantic Ocean **117** H2 40 20S 10 00W
Gouin, Réservoir Québec Canada **105** F3 48 00N 75 00W
Goulburn Australia **86** H3 34 47S 149 43E
Gouré Niger **93** H5 13 59N 10 15E
Gourock Strathclyde Scotland **46** D2 55 58N 4 49W
Goussainville France **60** B3 49 02N 2 28E
Govan Strathclyde Scotland **45** B1 55 51N 4 22W
Governador Valadares Brazil **114** I9 18 51S 41 57W
Govind Ballash Pant Sagar *l.* India 24 00N 83 00E
Gower *p.* West Glamorgan Wales **38** B1 51 35N 4 10W
Gozo *i.* Malta **68** B2 35 00N 14 00E
Grabroc Hill *tn.* Strathclyde Scotland **45** B1 55 44N 4 26W
Gracefield Québec Canada **105** E3 46 05N 76 05W
Grafham Water *l.* Cambridgeshire England **33** B3 52 18N 0 20W
Grafton Australia **86** I4 29 40S 152 56E
Grafton West Virginia U.S.A. **105** D1 39 21N 80 03W
Graham Texas U.S.A. **102** G3 33 07N 98 36W
Graham Island British Columbia Canada **100** I3 53 50N 133 00W
Graham Land *geog. reg.* Antarctica **121** 67 00S 64 00W
Grahamstown Republic of South Africa **95** E1 33 18S 26 32E
Graiguenamanagh Carlow Irish Republic **48** D2 52 32N 6 56W
Grain Kent England **33** C2 51 28N 0 43E
Grampian *reg.* Scotland **46** E4/F4 57 30N 3 00W
Grampian Mountains Scotland **46** D3–E3
Granada Nicaragua **109** G2 11 58N 85 59W
Granada Spain **66** B2 37 10N 3 35W
Granard Longford Irish Republic **48** D3 53 47N 7 30W
Granby Québec Canada **105** F3 45 23N 72 44W
Gran Canaria *i.* Canary Islands **93** B8 28 00N 15 35W
Gran Chaco *geog. reg.* Argentina **115** E8 25 00S 62 30W
Grand *r.* U.S.A. **104** B1 40 00N 94 00W
Grand *r.* South Dakota U.S.A. **102** F6 46 00N 102 00W
Grand Bahama *i.* The Bahamas **109** I5 27 00N 78 00W
Grand Banks Atlantic Ocean **96** 47 00N 47 00W
Grand Beach *tn.* Manitoba Canada **104** A4 50 34N 96 38W
Grand Canal Irish Republic 49 A1 53 18N 6 33W
Grand Canyon U.S.A. **102** D4 36 04N 112 07W
Grand Canyon National Park Arizona/Utah
Grand Canyon Village Arizona U.S.A. **102** D4 36 03N 112 09W
Grand Cayman *i.* Caribbean Sea **109** H3 19 20N 81 15W
Grand Coulee Dam Washington U.S.A. **102** C6 47 59N 118 58W
Grande Cache Alberta Canada **100** L3 53 50N 118 30W
Grand Erg Occidental *geog. reg.* Algeria **93** F9 30 35N 0 30E
Grand Erg Oriental *geog. reg.* Algeria **93** G9 30 15N 6 45E
Grande Rivière de la Baleine *r.* Québec Canada **101** T4 55 15N 77 00W
Grande Terre *i.* Lesser Antilles **109** L3 17 00N 61 40W
Grand Falls *tn.* New Brunswick Canada **101** V2 47 02N 67 46W
Grand Forks North Dakota U.S.A. **104** A6 47 57N 97 05W
Grand Haven Michigan U.S.A. **104** C2 43 04N 86 13W
Grand Island *tn.* Nebraska U.S.A. **103** G5 40 56N 98 21W
Grand Junction Colorado U.S.A. **102** E4 39 04N 108 33W
Grand Lake Newfoundland Canada **101** X2 49 00N 57 20W
Grand Marais Minnesota U.S.A. **104** B3 47 45N 90 20W
Grand Prairie *tn.* Alberta Canada **100** L4 55 10N 118 52W
Grand Rapids *tn.* Manitoba Canada **101** P3 53 12N 99 19W
Grand Rapids *tn.* Michigan U.S.A. **104** C2 42 57N 86 40W
Grand Rapids *tn.* Minnesota U.S.A. **104** B3 47 13N 93 31W
Grand Traverse Bay *b.* Michigan U.S.A. **104** C3 45 00N 85 00W
Grand Union Canal England **34** B3 51 45N 0 35W
Grand Union Canal West Midlands England **35** C/D1 52 18N 1 40W
Grane Norway **67** C4 65 35N 13 25E
Grange Hill *tn.* Jamaica **109** P8 18 19N 78 11W
Grangemouth Central Scotland **45** C2 56 01N 3 44W
Grange-over-Sands Cumbria England **44** B1 54 33N 3 09W
Granite City Illinois U.S.A. **104** B1 38 43N 90 04W
Granite Falls *tn.* Minnesota U.S.A. **104** A2 44 49N 95 31W
Granite Peak Montana U.S.A. **102** E6 45 10N 109 50W
Grantham Lincolnshire England **36** D2 52 55N 0 39W
Grantown-on-Spey Highland Scotland **46** E4 57 20N 3 58W
Grants Pass Oregon U.S.A. **102** B5 42 26N 123 20W
Granville France **61** A2 48 50N 1 35W
Granville Lake Manitoba Canada **101** O4 56 00N 101 00W
Grasmere Cumbria England **44** A1 54 28N 3 02W
Grasse France **61** C1 43 40N 6 56E
Grassington North Yorkshire England **43** D1 54 04N 1 59W
Grassmore Derbyshire England **43** F1 53 11N 1 44W
Gravelbourg Saskatchewan Canada **100** N2 49 53N 106 33W
Gravelines France **64** B2 50 59N 2 08E
Gravenhurst Ontario Canada **105** E2 44 55N 79 22W
Gravesend Kent England **34** E2 51 27N 0 24E
Gravesend New York U.S.A. **106** C1 40 36N 73 58W
Gray France **61** C2 47 27N 5 35E
Grayling Michigan U.S.A. 105 D2 44 40N 84 43W
Grays Essex England **34** D2 51 29N 0 20E
Graz Austria **69** C2 47 05N 15 22E
Greasby Merseyside England **42** A2 53 23N 3 10W
Great Abaco *i.* The Bahamas **109** I5 26 40N 77 00W
Great Altcar Lancashire England **42** A2 53 32N 3 01W
Great Astrolabe Reef Fiji **118** U15 18 45S 178 50E
Great Bardfield Essex England **34** E3 51 57N 0 26E
Great Barrier Island New Zealand **87** C3 35 10S 175 30E
Great Barrier Reef Australia **86** G7–H6 15 00S 146 00E
Great Basin Nevada U.S.A. **102** C4 40 00N 117 00W
Great Bear Lake Northwest Territories Canada **100** K6 66 00N 120 00W
Great Bend Kansas U.S.A. **102** G4 38 22N 98 47W
Great Bernera *i.* Western Isles Scotland **46** B5 58 13N 6 49W
Great Blasket Island Irish Republic **48** A2 52 05N 10 30W
Great Brickhill Bedfordshire England **34** A3 51 57N 0 41W
Great Bridgeford Staffordshire England **35** B3 52 51N 2 10W
Great Broughton North Yorkshire England **40** C3 54 27N 1 10W

Hecate Strait British Columbia Canada **100** I3 53 00N 131 00W
Hechuan China **81** G4 30 02N 106 15E
Heckington Lincolnshire England **36** D2 52 59N 0 18W
Heckmondwike West Yorkshire England **43** E3 53 43N 1 45W
Hedesundafjärdarna *l.* Sweden **67** D3 60 20N 17 00E
Hedge End Hampshire England **32** A1 50 55N 1 18W
Hedon Humberside England **40** D2 53 44N 0 12W
Heemstede Netherlands **65** C3 52 21N 4 37E
Heerenveen Netherlands **64** E4 52 57N 5 55E
Heerhugowaard Netherlands **64** D4 52 40N 4 50E
Heerlen Netherlands **64** E2 50 53N 5 59E
Hefei China **81** I4 31 55N 117 18E
Hegang China **81** L7 47 36N 130 30E
Hegura-jima *i.* Japan **82** C2 37 52N 136 56E
Heidelberg Germany **63** A1 49 25N 8 42E
Heighington Lincolnshire England **36** D3 54 36N 1 37W
Heilbronn Germany **63** A1 49 08N 9 14E
Heiligenhaus Germany **62** B2 52 20N 6 49E
Heilong Jiang *see* Amur
Heiloo Netherlands **64** D4 52 36N 4 43E
Heisker *is.* Western Isles Scotland **46** A4 57 30N 7 40W
Heist op den Berg Belgium **64** D3 51 05N 4 44E
Hekla *mt.* Iceland **67** I6 64 00N 19 41W
Helan Shan *mts.* China **81** G5 38 00N 106 00E
Helchteren Belgium **64** E3 51 03N 5 23E
Helena Montana U.S.A. **102** D6 46 35N 112 00W
Helensburgh Strathclyde Scotland **45** A2 56 01N 4 44W
Helgeland *geog. reg.* Norway **67** C4 65 45N 13 00E
Helgoland *(Heligoland) i.* Germany **63** A2 54 00N 8 00E
Heligoland *see* Helgoland
Heligoland Bight *b.* Germany **63** A2 54 00N 8 00E
Hellendoorn Netherlands **64** 52 23N 6 27E
Hellevoetsluis Netherlands **64** D3 51 49N 4 08E
Hellifield North Yorkshire England **42** D4 54 01N 2 12W
Hellin Spain **66** B2 38 31N 1 43W
Helmand *r.* Afghanistan **79** H5 30 00N 62 30E
Helmond Netherlands **64** E3 51 28N 5 40E
Helmsdale Highland Scotland **46** E5 58 07N 3 40W
Helmsdale *r.* Highland Scotland **46** E5 58 10N 3 50W
Helmsley North Yorkshire England **40** C3 54 14N 1 04W
Helsby Cheshire England **42** B1 53 16N 2 46W
Helsingborg Sweden **67** C2 56 03N 12 43E
Helsingfors *see* Helsinki
Helsinki *(Helsingfors)* Finland **67** E3 60 08N 25 00E
Helston Cornwall England **30** B2 50 05N 5 16W
Helvellyn *mt.* Cumbria England **44** A1 54 32N 3 02W
Hemel Hempstead Hertfordshire England **34** B3 51 46N 0 28W
Hemingbrough North Yorkshire England **43** H3 53 47N 0 59W
Hempstead New York U.S.A. **106** D1 40 41N 73 39W
Hemsworth West Yorkshire England **43** F2 53 38N 1 21W
Henares *r.* Spain **66** B3 40 45N 3 10W
Henderson Kentucky U.S.A. **104** C1 37 49N 87 35W
Henderson Nevada U.S.A. **102** D4 36 01N 115 00W
Hendon Greater London England **34** C2 51 35N 0 14W
Henfield West Sussex England **33** B1 50 56N 0 17W
Hengelo Netherlands **64** F4 52 16N 6 46E
Hengyang China **81** H3 26 58N 112 31E
Henham Essex England **34** D3 51 56N 0 15E
Henley-in-Arden Warwickshire England **35** C1 52 17N 1 46W
Henley-on-Thames Oxfordshire England **33** B2 51 32N 0 56W
Henlow Bedfordshire England **34** C4 52 02N 0 18W
Henrietta Maria, Cape Ontario Canada **101** S4 55 00N 82 30W
Henryetta Oklahoma U.S.A. **103** G4 35 27N 96 00W
Henryk Arctowski *r.s.* Antarctica **121** 62 09S 58 28W
Henzada Myanmar **80** B7 17 36N 95 26E
Herāt Afghanistan **79** J5 34 20N 62 12E
Hérault *r.* France **61** B1 43 50N 3 30E
Herblay France **60** A2 48 59N 2 10E
Hereford Hereford and Worcester England **36** B2 52 04N 2 43W
Hereford and Worcester *co.* England **36** B2 52 10N 2 30W
Herentals Belgium **64** D3 51 11N 4 50E
Herford Germany **63** A2 52 07N 8 40E
Herisau Switzerland **63** A1 47 23N 9 17E
Herm *i.* Channel Islands British Isles **31** G5 49 28N 2 27W
Herma Ness *c.* Shetland Islands Scotland **47** C2 60 50N 0 54W
Hermel Lebanon **78** P12 34 25N 36 23E
Hermon, Mount Lebanon/Syria **78** O11 33 24N 35 50E
Hermosillo Mexico **108** B5 29 15N 110 59W
Herne Germany **62** C3 51 32N 7 12E
Herne Bay *tn.* Kent England **33** D2 51 23N 1 08E
Herning Denmark **67** B2 56 08N 8 59E
Herstal Belgium **64** E2 50 40N 5 38E
Herten Germany **62** C3 51 36N 7 08E
Hertford Hertfordshire England **34** C3 51 48N 0 05W
Hertfordshire *co.* England **33** B2 51 50N 0 05W
Hesketh Bank Lancashire England **42** B3 53 44N 2 52W
Heslington North Yorkshire England **43** G3 53 57N 1 03W
Hessen *admin.* Germany **63** A2 50 00N 9 00E
Hessle Humberside England **40** D2 53 44N 0 26W
Heswall Merseyside England **42** A1 53 19N 3 06W
Hetton North Yorkshire England **43** D4 54 03N 2 04W
Hetton-le-Hole Tyne and Wear England **44** C1 54 50N 1 27W
Hexham Northumberland England **44** B1 54 58N 2 06W
Hextable Kent England **34** D2 51 25N 0 12E
Heysham Lancashire England **42** B4 54 02N 2 54W
Heywood Greater Manchester England **42** D2 53 36N 2 13W
Hibbing Minnesota U.S.A. **104** B3 47 25N 92 55W
Hickory North Carolina U.S.A. **103** J4 35 44N 81 23W
Hidalgo Mexico **108** E4 24 16N 99 28W
Hidalgo del Parral Mexico **108** C5 26 58N 105 40W
Higashi-Murayama Japan **83** A4 35 46N 139 28E
Higash-suidō *sd.* Japan **82** A1 34 10N 130 00E
Higham Kent England **34** E2 51 24N 0 26E
Higham Ferrers Northamptonshire England **36** D2 52 18N 0 36W
High Bentham North Yorkshire England **40** B3 54 08N 2 30W
Higher Walton Lancashire England **42** C3 53 45N 2 37W
Highfield Strathclyde Scotland **45** A1 55 43N 4 41W
Highgate Jamaica **109** R8 18 16N 76 53W
Highland *reg.* Scotland **46** C4
High Lane Greater Manchester England **42** D2 53 22N 2 04W
High Level *tn.* Alberta Canada **100** L4 58 10N 117 20W
Highley Shropshire England **35** A2 52 27N 2 23W
High Point *tn.* North Carolina U.S.A. **103** K4 35 58N 80 00W
High Roding Essex England **34** D3 51 50N 0 19E
Hightown Merseyside England **42** A2 53 32N 3 04W
High Veld *mts.* Republic of South Africa **95** E2 28 00S 28 00E
Highworth Wiltshire England **31** F3 51 38N 1 43W
High Wycombe Buckinghamshire England **34** A2 51 38N 0 46W
Hiiumaa *i.* Estonia **67** E2 58 55N 22 30E
Hilden Germany **62** B1 51 10N 6 56E
Hildenborough Kent England **34** D1 51 13N 0 14E
Hildesheim Germany **63** A2 52 09N 9 58E
Hillegom Netherlands **65** C3 52 18N 4 35E
Hill End Fife Scotland **45** C2 56 08N 3 32W
Hillend Reservoir Strathclyde Scotland **45** C1 55 53N 3 50W
Hillingdon Greater London England **34** B2 51 32N 0 27W
Hillsboro Ohio U.S.A. **105** D1 39 12N 83 37W
Hilo Hawaiian Islands **119** Z17 19 42N 155 04W
Hilversum Netherlands **65** E2 52 14N 5 10E
Himachal Pradesh *admin.* India **77** D6 32 00N 77 30E
Himalaya *mts.* Asia **77** D6–G5
Himeji Japan **82** B1 34 50N 134 40E
Ḥimṣ Syria **78** P12 34 42N 36 40E
Hinckley Leicestershire England **35** D2 52 33N 1 21W
Hindhead Surrey England **34** A1 51 07N 0 44W
Hindley Greater Manchester England **42** C2 53 32N 2 35W
Hindu Kush *mts.* Afghanistan **79** K6 35 00N 70 00E
Hinnøya *i.* Norway **67** D4 68 35N 15 50E
Hinstock Shropshire England **35** A3 52 51N 2 28W
Hirakata Japan **82** C1 34 45N 135 35E
Hirakud Reservoir India **77** E4 21 40N 83 40E
Hirosaki Japan **82** D3 40 34N 140 28E
Hiroshima Japan **82** B1 34 23N 132 27E
Hirson France **61** B2 49 56N 4 05E
Hirwaun Mid Glamorgan Wales **38** C1 51 45N 3 30W
Hisar India **77** D5 29 10N 75 45E
Hispaniola *i.* West Indies **109** J3 18 00N 70 00W
Histon Cambridgeshire England **33** C3 52 15N 0 06E
Hitachi Japan **82** D2 36 35N 140 40E
Hitchin Hertfordshire England **34** C3 51 57N 0 17W
Hitra *i.* Norway **67** B3 63 37N 8 46E
Hjørring Denmark **67** B2 57 28N 9 59E
Ho Ghana **93** F4 6 38N 0 38E
Hobart Australia **86** H1 42 54S 147 18E
Hoboken New Jersey U.S.A. **106** B1 40 44N 74 02W
Hobyo Somalia **94** I9 5 20N 48 30E
Ho Chi Minh Vietnam **80** D6 10 46N 106 43E
Hockcliffe Bedfordshire England **34** B3 51 56N 0 36W
Hockley Essex England **33** C2 51 35N 0 39E
Hockley Heath Warwickshire England **35** C2 52 21N 1 46W
Hodder *r.* Lancashire England **42** C3 53 55N 2 30W
Hoddesdon Hertfordshire England **34** C3 51 46N 0 01W
Hódmezovásárhely Hungary **69** D2 46 26N 20 21E
Hodnet Shropshire England **36** B2 52 51N 2 35W
Hodogaya Japan **83** B2 35 26N 139 36E
Hoek van Holland Netherlands **65** A1 51 59N 4 08E
Hof Germany **63** B2 50 19N 11 56E
Höfn Iceland **67** I6 64 16N 15 10W
Hofsjökull *ice cap* Iceland **67** I6 64 45N 18 45W
Hofu Japan **82** B1 34 02N 131 34E
Hoggar *mts.* Algeria **93** G7 23 45N 6 00E
Hohe Acht *mt.* Germany **64** G2 50 22N 7 00E
Hohe Rhön *hills* Germany **63** A2 50 00N 10 00E
Hohe Tauern *mts.* Austria **63** C1 47 00N 13 00E
Hohhot China **81** H6 40 49N 111 37E
Hokisaku Japan **83** C2 35 18N 139 56E
Hokitika New Zealand **87** B2 42 42S 170 59E
Hokkaidō *i.* Japan **82** D3 43 30N 143 00E
Holbeach Lincolnshire England **36** E2 52 49N 0 01E
Holderness *p.* Humberside England **40** D2 53 45N 0 05W
Holguín Cuba **109** I4 20 54N 76 15W
Holland *tn.* Michigan U.S.A. **104** C2 42 46N 86 06W
Hollandse IJssel *r.* Netherlands **65** D2 52 02N 4 52E
Hollick Kenyon Plateau Antarctica **121** 77 00S 100 00W
Hollywood California U.S.A. **107** A3 34 05N 118 21W
Hollywood Hereford & Worcester England **35** C2 52 23N 1 52W
Hollywood Reservoir California U.S.A. **107** A3 34 07N 118 20W
Holmer Green Buckinghamshire England **34** A2 51 39N 0 42W
Holmes Chapel Cheshire England **42** C1 53 12N 2 22W
Holme upon Spalding Moor Humberside England **40** D2 53 49N 0 46W
Holmfirth West Yorkshire England **43** E2 53 35N 1 46W
Holsteinsborg Greenland **101** Y6 66 55N 53 30W
Holston *r.* U.S.A. **103** J4 37 00N 82 00W
Holsworthy Devon England **30** C2 50 49N 4 21W
Holt Norfolk England **33** D3 52 55N 1 05E
Holt Heath Hereford & Worcester England **35** B1 52 16N 2 16W
Holy Cross Alaska U.S.A. **100** D5 62 10N 159 53W
Holyhead Gwynedd Wales **38** B3 53 19N 4 38W
Holy Island Gwynedd Wales **38** B3 53 16N 4 39W
Holy Island Northumberland England **44** C2 55 41N 1 48W
Holyoke Massachusetts U.S.A. **105** F2 42 12N 72 37W
Holywell Clwyd Wales **38** C3 53 17N 3 13W
Holywood Down Northern Ireland **49** D1 54 38N 5 50W
Homberg Germany **62** A2 51 27N 6 41E
Homburg Germany **63** A1 49 20N 7 20E
Home Bay Northwest Territories Canada **101** V6 69 00N 67 00W
Homer Alaska U.S.A. **100** E4 59 40N 151 37W
Homestead Florida U.S.A. **103** J2 25 29N 80 29W
Honda Colombia **114** C14 5 15N 74 50W
HONDURAS 108/109 G2
Hone Manitoba Canada **101** O4 56 20N 101 15W
Hong Kong *territory* U.K. **81** H2 23 00N 114 00E
Honguedo Passage *(Détroit d'Honguedo) sd.* Québec Canada **101** W2 49 30N 64 20W
Honiara Solomon Islands **80** J8 9 28S 159 57E
Honiton Devon England **31** D2 50 48N 3 13W
Honokaa Hawaiian Islands **119** Z18 20 04N 155 27W
Honolulu Hawaiian Islands **119** Y18 21 19N 157 50W
Honshū *i.* Japan **82** C2 37 15N 139 00E
Hoo Kent England **33** C2 51 26N 0 34E
Hood, Mount Oregon U.S.A. **102** B6 45 24N 121 41W
Hoofddorp Netherlands **65** C3 52 18N 4 41E
Hoofdorp Netherlands **64** D4 52 18N 4 41E
Hoogeveen Netherlands **64** F4 52 43N 6 29E
Hoogezand Netherlands **64** F5 53 10N 6 45E
Hook Hampshire England **33** B2 51 17N 0 58W
Hook Head *c.* Irish Republic **48** E2 52 10N 6 55W
Hoolehua Hawaiian Islands **119** Y18 21 11N 157 06W
Hooper Bay *tn.* Alaska U.S.A. **100** B5 61 29N 166 10W
Hoorn Netherlands **64** E4 52 38N 5 03E
Hope British Columbia Canada **100** K2 49 21N 121 28W
Hope Clwyd Wales **38** C3 53 07N 3 03W
Hopes Advance, Cape Québec Canada **101** V5 61 00N 69 40W
Hopkinsville Kentucky U.S.A. **103** I4 36 50N 87 30W
Hopton-on-Sea Norfolk England **33** D3 52 33N 1 43E
Horbury West Yorkshire England **43** F2 53 41N 1 33W
Hörde Germany **62** D2 51 29N 7 31E
Horley Surrey England **34** C1 51 11N 0 11W
Hormuz, Strait of The Gulf **79** I4 26 35N 56 30E
Hornavan *l.* Sweden **67** D4 66 15N 17 40E
Horn, Cape *see* Cabo de Hornos
Horncastle Lincolnshire England **36** D3 53 13N 0 07W
Hornchurch Greater London England **34** D2 51 34N 0 13E
Hornsea Humberside England **40** D2 53 55N 0 10W
Hornsey Greater London England **34** C2 51 35N 0 08W
Horsens Denmark **67** B2 55 53N 9 53E
Horsforth West Yorkshire England **43** F3 53 51N 1 39W
Horsham Australia **86** G2 36 45S 142 15E
Horsham West Sussex England **33** B2 51 04N 0 21W
Horsley Surrey England **34** B1 51 16N 0 26W
Horwich Greater Manchester England **42** C2 53 37N 2 33W
Höscheid Germany **62** C1 51 08N 7 05E
Hospet India **77** D3 15 16N 76 20E
Hospitalet Spain **66** C3 41 21N 2 06E
Hotan China **81** A5 37 07N 79 57E
Hotan He China **81** B5 37 07N 79 57E
Hoting Sweden **67** D3 64 08N 16 15E
Hot Springs *tn.* Arkansas U.S.A. **103** H3 34 30N 93 02W
Houghton Michigan U.S.A. **104** C3 47 06N 88 34W
Houghton-le-Spring Tyne and Wear England **44** C1 54 51N 1 28W
Houma China **81** H5 35 36N 111 15E
Houma Louisiana U.S.A. **103** H2 29 35N 90 44W
Hounslow Greater London England **34** B2 51 28N 0 21W
Houston Strathclyde Scotland **45** A1 55 52N 4 33W
Houston Texas U.S.A. **103** G2 29 45N 95 25W
Hovd Mongolia **81** D7 48 00N 91 43E
Hove East Sussex England **33** B1 50 49N 0 11W
Hovingham North Yorkshire England **40** D3 54 10N 0 59W
Hövsgöl Nuur *l.* Mongolia **71** M6 51 00N 100 30E
Howar *r.* Sudan **94** D11 17 00N 25 00E
Howden Humberside England **43** H3 53 45N 0 52W
Howe, Cape Australia **86** H2 37 20S 149 59E
Howgate Lothian Scotland **45** D1 55 48N 3 11W
Howth Dublin Irish Republic **49** B2 53 23N 6 04W
Howwood Strathclyde Scotland **45** A1 55 48N 4 34W
Höxter Germany **63** A2 51 47N 9 22E
Hoy *i.* Orkney Islands Scotland **47** D1 58 48N 3 20W
Hoya Japan **83** B3 35 44N 139 34E
Hoyerswerda Germany **63** B2 51 28N 14 17E
Hoylake Merseyside England **42** A2 53 23N 3 11W
Hoyland Nether South Yorkshire England **43** F2 53 30N 1 27W
Hoy Sound Orkney Islands Scotland **47** D1 58 56N 3 20W
Hradec Králové Ceska Czechoslovakia **69** C3 50 13N 15 50E
Hron *r.* Slovenska Czechoslovakia **69** C2 48 00N 18 00E
Hsin-chu Taiwan **81** J2 24 48N 120 59E
Huacho Peru **114** B10 11 05S 77 36W
Huaide China **81** J6 43 30N 124 48E
Huainan China **81** I4 32 41N 117 06E
Huajuápan de Leon Mexico **108** E3 17 50N 97 48W
Huambo Angola **95** C5 12 44S 15 47E
Huancayo Peru **114** B10 12 05S 75 12W
Huang Hai *see* Yellow Sea
Huang He *r.* China **81** F5–H5 38 00N 111 00E
Huangshi China **81** I4 30 13N 115 05E
Huanuco Peru **114** B11 9 55S 76 11W
Huaráz Peru **114** B11 9 33S 77 31W
Huascaran *mt.* Peru **114** B11 9 08S 77 36W
Huashixia China **81** E5 35 13N 99 12E
Huby North Yorkshire England **43** G4 54 05N 1 08W
Huckarde Germany **62** D3 51 33N 7 25E
Hucknall Nottinghamshire England **36** C3 53 02N 1 11W
Huddersfield West Yorkshire England **43** E2 53 39N 1 47W
Hudson *r.* North America **96** 43 00N 74 00W
Hudson Bay *(Baie d'Hudson)* Canada **101** R5 60 00N 89 00W
Hudson Bay *tn.* Saskatchewan Canada **101** O3 52 45N 102 45W
Hudson Strait Northwest Territories/ Québec Canada **101** U5 62 00N 70 00W
Hue Vietnam **80** D7 16 28N 107 35E
Huelva *r.* Spain **66** A2 37 50N 6 30W
Huelva Spain **66** A2 37 15N 6 56W
Huesca Spain **66** B3 42 08N 0 25W
Hughenden Australia **86** G5 20 50S 144 10E
Hugh Town Isles of Scilly England **30** A1 49 55N 6 19W
Hugli *r.* India **76** J2 22 30N 88 14E
Hugli-Chinsurah India **76** K3 22 54N 88 23E
Hugo Oklahoma U.S.A. **103** G3 34 01N 95 31W
Huisne *r.* France **61** B2 48 15N 0 40E
Huixtla Mexico **108** F3 15 09N 92 30W
Huizen Netherlands **64** E4 52 17N 5 15E
Huizhou China **81** H2 23 08N 114 28W
Hull Québec Canada **105** E3 45 26N 75 45W
Hull *r.* Humberside England **40** D2 53 48N 0 20W
Hullbridge Essex England **33** C2 51 37N 0 37E
Hulst Netherlands **64** D3 51 17N 4 03E
Humaitá Brazil **114** E11 7 33S 63 01W
Humber *r.* Humberside England **40** D2 53 40N 0 10W
Humberside *co.* England **40** D2 53 50N 0 40W
Humberston Humberside England **40** D2 53 32N 0 02W
Humboldt *r.* Nevada U.S.A. **102** C5 41 00N 118 00W
Humboldt Saskatchewan Canada **100** N3 52 12N 105 07W
Humboldt Glacier Greenland **120** 79 40N 64 00W
Hungarian Basin Europe **51** 47 00N 20 00E
HUNGARY 69 C2
Hüngnam North Korea **81** K5 39 49N 127 40E
Hunjiang China **81** K6 41 54N 126 23E
Hunmanby North Yorkshire England **40** D3 54 11N 0 19W
Hunsdon Hertfordshire England **34** D3 51 48N 0 03E
Hunsrück *mts.* Germany **63** A1 50 00N 7 00E
Hunstanton Norfolk England **33** C3 52 57N 0 30E
Hunte *r.* Germany **63** A2 53 00N 8 00E
Hunter Trench Pacific Ocean **118** H5 23 00S 175 00E
Huntingdon Cambridgeshire England **33** B3 52 20N 0 12W
Huntingdon Québec Canada **105** F3 45 05N 74 11W
Huntington Indiana U.S.A. **104** C2 40 54N 85 30W
Huntington North Yorkshire England **43** G4 54 01N 1 04W
Huntington Staffordshire England **35** B3 52 43N 2 02W
Huntington West Virginia U.S.A. **105** D1 38 24N 82 26W
Huntington Beach *tn.* California U.S.A. **107** B1 33 40N 118 00W
Huntingtower Tayside Scotland **45** D2 56 24N 3 29W
Huntly Grampian Scotland **46** F4 57 27N 2 47W
Huntly New Zealand **87** C3 37 35S 175 10E
Huntsville Alabama U.S.A. **103** I3 34 44N 86 35W
Huntsville Ontario Canada **105** E3 45 20N 79 14W
Huntsville Texas U.S.A. **103** G3 30 43N 95 34W
Hurghada Egypt **78** D4 27 17N 33 47E
Huron South Dakota U.S.A. **104** A2 44 22N 98 12W
Huron, Lake North America **105** D3 45 00N 83 00W
Hursley Hampshire England **32** A2 51 02N 1 24W
Hurst Green Lancashire England **42** C3 53 50N 2 30W
Hurstpierpoint West Sussex England **33** B1 50 56N 0 11W
Hürth Germany **64** F2 50 52N 6 51E
Húsavík Iceland **67** I7 66 03N 17 17W
Husbands Bosworth Leicestershire England **36** C2 52 27N 1 03W
Husn Jordan **78** O11 32 29N 35 53E
Husum Germany **63** A2 54 29N 9 04E
Hutchinson Kansas U.S.A. **103** G4 38 03N 97 56W
Hutton Lancashire England **42** B3 53 44N 2 46W
Hutton Cranswick Humberside England **40** D2 53 57N 0 27W
Huy Belgium **64** E2 50 32N 5 14E
Huyton-with-Roby Merseyside England **42** B2 53 25N 2 52W
Huzhou China **81** J4 30 56N 120 04E
Hvar *i.* Croatia **68** C3 43 00N 17 00E
Hwange Zimbabwe **95** E4 18 22E 26 29E
Hwange National Park Zimbabwe **95** E4 19 00S 26 00E
Hyde Greater Manchester England **42** D2 53 27N 2 04W
Hyderabad India **77** D3 17 22N 78 26E
Hyderabad Pakistan **76** B5 25 23N 68 24E
Hyères France **61** C1 43 07N 6 08E
Hythe Alberta Canada **100** L4 55 18N 119 33W
Hythe Hampshire England **32** A1 50 51N 1 24W
Hythe Kent England **33** D2 51 05N 1 05E
Hyvinkää Finland **67** E3 60 37N 24 50E

I

Ialomița *r.* Romania **69** E1 44 00N 27 00E
Iași Romania **69** E2 47 09N 27 38E
Ibadan Nigeria **93** F4 7 23N 3 56E
Ibagué Colombia **114** B13 4 25N 75 20W
Ibarra Ecuador **114** B13 0 23N 78 05W
Ibb Yemen Republic **78** F1 14 03N 44 10E
Ibbenbüren Germany **63** A2 52 17N 7 44E
Iberville Québec Canada **105** F3 45 18N 73 15W
Ibi Nigeria **93** G4 8 11N 9 44E
Ibiza Balearic Islands **66** D4 38 54N 1 26E
Ibiza *i.* Balearic Islands **66** D4 39 00N 1 20E
Ibotirama Brazil **114** I10 12 13S 43 12W
Ibrī Oman **79** I3 23 15N 56 35E
Ibstock Leicestershire England **35** D3 52 42N 1 23W
Ica Peru **114** B10 14 02S 75 48W
ICELAND 67 I6
Ichalkaranji India **77** C3 16 40N 74 33E
Ichāpur India **76** K3 22 48N 88 22E
Ichikawa Japan **83** C3 35 44N 139 55E
Ichinomiya Japan **82** C2 35 18N 136 48E
Idaho *state* U.S.A. **102** D5 44 00N 115 00W
Idaho Falls *tn.* Idaho U.S.A. **102** D5 43 30N 112 01W
Idar-Oberstein Germany **63** A1 49 43N 7 19E
Iddo Nigeria **92** C3 6 25N 3 27E
Idfu Egypt **78** D3 24 58N 32 50E
Idre Sweden **67** C3 61 52N 12 45E
Ieper *(Ypres)* Belgium **64** B2 50 51N 2 53E
Ifield West Sussex England **34** C1 51 08N 0 13W
Igarka Russia **71** K9 67 31N 86 33E
Igbobi Nigeria **92** C3 6 32N 3 27E
Ightham Kent England **34** D1 51 17N 0 17E
Iglesias Italy **68** A2 39 19N 8 32E
Ignace Ontario Canada **104** B3 49 26N 91 40W
Iguaçu *r.* Brazil **116** B3 22 44S 43 16W
Iguala Mexico **108** E3 18 21N 99 31W
Iguape Brazil **115** G8 24 37S 47 30W
Iguatu Brazil **114** J11 6 22S 39 20W
Ihosy Madagascar **95** I3 22 23S 46 09E
Iisalmi Finland **67** F3 63 34N 27 08E
IJ-meer *l.* Netherlands **65** E3 52 23N 5 05E
IJmuiden Netherlands **65** C3 52 27N 4 37E
IJssel *r.* Netherlands **64** F4 52 40N 6 10E
IJsselmeer *l.* Netherlands **64** E4 52 50N 5 15E
IJsselstein Netherlands **65** E2 52 00N 5 03E
Ijzer *(Yser) r.* Belgium **64** B3 51 03N 2 50E
Ikaría *i.* Greece **68** E2 37 00N 26 00E
Ikeja Nigeria **92** C3 6 37N 3 25E
Ikela Zaïre **94** D7 1 06S 23 06E
Iki *i.* Japan **82** A1 33 50N 129 40E
Ikoyi Nigeria **92** D3 6 23N 3 32E
Ikuta Japan **83** B3 35 36N 139 34E
Ilagan The Philippines **80** G7 17 07N 121 53E
Ilchester Somerset England **31** E2 51 01N 2 41W
Ilebo Zaïre **95** D7 4 20S 20 35E
Île d'Anticosti *i.* Québec Canada **101** W2 49 20N 62 30W
Île de Groix *i.* France **61** A2 47 38N 3 26W
Île de Jerba *i.* Tunisia **93** H9 33 40N 11 00E
Île de Noirmoutier *i.* France **61** A2 47 00N 2 15W
Île de Ré *i.* France **61** A2 46 10N 1 26W
Île d'Oléron *i.* France **61** A2 45 55N 1 16W
Île d'Ouessant *i.* France **61** A2 48 28N 5 05W
Île d'Yeu *i.* France **61** A2 46 43N 2 20W
Île Mbamou *i.* Congo **92** B2 4 15S 15 25E
Îles Chesterfield *is.* Pacific Ocean **86** J6 19 00S 158 30E
Îles de la Madeleine *is.* Québec Canada **101** W2 48 00N 63 00W
Îles d'Hyères *is.* France **61** C1 43 01N 6 25E
Ilesha Nigeria **93** F4 7 39N 4 38E
Îles Kerkenah *is.* Tunisia **68** B3 34 50N 11 30E
Îles Loyauté *is.* Pacific Ocean **86** L5/L6 21 00S 167 00E
Iles Wallis *is.* Pacific Ocean **118** I6 13 16S 176 15W
Ilford Greater London England **34** D2 51 33N 0 06E
Ilfracombe Devon England **31** C3 51 13N 4 08W
Ilha Bazaruto *i.* Mozambique **95** G3 21 40S 35 30E
Ilha das Palmas *i.* Brazil **116** A1 23 04S 43 30W
Ilha de Marajó *i.* Brazil **114** G12/H12 1 30S 50 00W
Ilha de Paquetá *i.* Brazil **116** C2 22 46S 43 07W
Ilha do Fundão *i.* Brazil **116** C2 22 52S 43 14W
Ilha do Governador *i.* Brazil **116** C2 22 47S 43 13W
Ilha do Pai *i.* Brazil **116** C2 22 59S 43 05W
Ilha Fernando de Noronha, *i.* Brazil **114** K12 3 50S 32 25W
Ilha Redonda *i.* Brazil **116** C1 23 04S 43 11W
Ilha Rosa *i.* Brazil **116** C1 23 04S 43 08W
Ilhéus Brazil **114** J10 14 50S 39 06W

Kaikoura New Zealand **87** B2 42 24S 173 41E
Kailash India **76** L4 28 33N 77 15E
Kailua Hawaiian Islands **119** Z17 19 43N 155 59W
Kainji Reservoir Nigeria **93** F5 10 25N 4 56E
Kaipara Harbour New Zealand **87** B3 36 40S 174 00E
Kairouan Tunisia **93** H10 35 42N 10 01E
Kaiserslautern Germany **63** A1 49 27N 7 47E
Kaitaia New Zealand **87** B3 35 08S 173 18E
Kaiwi Channel Hawaiian Islands **119** Y18 21 20N 157 30W
Kajaani Finland **67** F3 64 14N 27 37E
Kakabeka Falls *tn.* Ontario Canada **104** C3 48 24N 89 40W
Käkināda India **77** E3 16 59N 82 20E
Kaladar Ontario Canada **105** E2 44 39N 77 07W
Kalae *(South Cape)* Hawaiian Islands **119** Z17 18 58N 155 24W
Kalahari Desert Southern Africa **95** D3 23 30S 23 00E
Kalahari Gemsbok National Park Republic of South Africa **95** D2 26 00S 20 30E
Kalámai Greece **68** D2 37 02N 22 07E
Kalamazoo Michigan U.S.A. **104** C2 42 17N 85 36W
Kalambo Falls Tanzania/Zambia **95** F6 8 35S 31 13E
Kalat Pakistan **76** B5 29 01N 66 38E
Kalémié Zaïre **95** E6 5 57S 29 10E
Kalevala Russia **67** G4 65 15N 31 08E
Kalgoorlie Australia **86** C3 30 49S 121 29E
Kaliavesi *l.* Finland **67** F3 63 00N 27 20E
Kalimantan *admin.* Indonesia **80** E3 2 00S 112 00E
Kálimnos *i.* Greece **68** E2 37 00N 26 00E
Kalinin *see* Tver'
Kaliningrad *tn.* Russia **70** E6 54 40N 20 30E
Kaliningrad *admin.* Russia **67** E1 54 50N 21 00E
Kalispell Montana U.S.A. **102** D6 48 12N 114 19W
Kalisz Poland **69** C3 51 46N 18 02E
Kalix älv *r.* Sweden **67** E4 66 40N 22 30E
Kalkajl India **76** M4 28 32N 77 16E
Kallsjön *l.* Sweden **67** C3 63 30N 13 05E
Kalmar Sweden **67** D2 56 39N 16 20E
Kalmthout Belgium **64** D3 51 23N 4 29E
Kalomo Zambia **95** E4 17 02S 26 29E
Kalpeni Island India **77** C2 10 05N 73 15E
Kaluga Russia **70** F6 54 31N 36 16E
Kalutara Sri Lanka **77** D1 6 35N 79 59E
Kama *r.* Russia **70** H7 57 00N 54 00E
Kamaishi Japan **82** D2 39 18N 141 52E
Kamakura Japan **83** B2 35 19N 139 33E
Kamarān *i.* Yemen Republic **78** F2 15 21N 42 40E
Kamarhati India **76** K2 22 40N 88 22E
Kambara *i.* Fiji **118** V15 18 57S 178 58W
Kamchatka *p.* Russia **71** R7 57 30N 160 00E
Kamchatka Bay Russia **71** S7 55 00N 164 00E
Kamchiya *r.* Bulgaria **68** E3 43 00N 27 00E
Kamenets Podol'skiy Ukraine **69** E2 48 40N 26 36E
Kamensk-Ural'skiy Russia **70** I7 56 29N 61 49E
Kames Strathclyde Scotland **46** C2 55 54N 5 15W
Kamet *mt.* India **77** D6 30 55N 79 36E
Kamina Zaïre **95** E6 8 46S 25 00E
Kamloops British Columbia Canada **100** K3 50 39N 120 24W
Kampala Uganda **94** F8 0 19N 32 35E
Kampen Netherlands **64** E4 52 33N 5 55E
Kamp-Lintfort Germany **64** F3 51 30N 6 33E
KAMPUCHEA *see* CAMBODIA
Kamyshin Russia **70** G6 50 05N 45 24E
Kanagawa Japan **83** B2 35 29N 139 38E
Kananga Zaïre **95** D6 5 53S 22 26E
Kanawha *r.* West Virginia U.S.A. **105** D1 38 00N 82 00W
Kanazawa Japan **82** C2 36 35N 136 38E
Kanazawa Japan **83** B2 35 20W 139 37E
Kanbe Myanmar **80** B7 16 15N 95 40E
Kanchipuram India **77** D2 12 50N 79 44E
Känchräpära India **76** K3 22 56N 88 26E
Kandahār Afghanistan **79** K5 31 35N 65 45E
Kandalaksha Russia **70** F9 67 09N 32 31E
Kandavu *i.* Fiji **118** U15 19 10S 178 30E
Kandavu Passage *sd.* Fiji **118** U15 18 50S 178 00E
Kandi Benin **93** F4 11 05N 2 59E
Kandla India **76** B4 23 03N 70 11E
Kandy Sri Lanka **77** E1 7 17N 80 40E
Kane Pennsylvania U.S.A. **105** E2 41 40N 78 48W
Kaneohe Hawaiian Islands **119** Y18 21 25N 157 48W
Kangan Iran **79** H4 27 51N 52 07E
Kangar Malaysia **80** C5 6 28N 100 10E
Kangaroo Island Australia **86** F2 35 50S 137 50E
Kangerlussuaq *(Søndre Strømfjord) tn.* Greenland **101** Y6 67 00N 50 59W
Kangnūng South Korea **81** K5 37 48N 127 52E
Kanin Peninsula Russia **70** G9 68 00N 45 00E
Kankakee Illinois U.S.A. **104** C2 41 08N 87 52W
Kankan Guinea **93** D5 10 22N 9 11W
Kanker India **77** E4 20 17N 81 30E
Kannapolis North Carolina U.S.A. **103** J4 35 30N 80 36W
Kano Nigeria **93** G5 12 00N 8 31E
Kanoya Japan **82** B1 31 22N 130 50E
Kanpur India **77** E5 26 27N 80 14E
Kansas *r.* Kansas U.S.A. **104** A1 39 00N 95 00W
Kansas *state* U.S.A. **102–103** G4 38 00N 98 00W
Kansas City Kansas U.S.A. **104** B1 39 05N 94 37W
Kansas City Missouri U.S.A. **104** B1 39 02N 94 33W
Kansk Russia **71** L7 56 11N 95 48E
Kanturk Cork Irish Republic **48** C2 52 10N 8 55W
Kanye Botswana **95** D3 24 59S 25 19E
Kao-hsiung Taiwan **81** J2 22 36N 120 17E
Kaolack Senegal **93** B5 14 09N 16 08W
Kapaa Hawaiian Islands **119** X19 22 04N 159 20W
Kap Farvel *(Cape Farewell) c.* Greenland **101** AA4 60 00N 44 00W
Kapfenberg Austria **69** C2 47 27N 15 18E
Kapingamarangi Rise Pacific Ocean **118** F8 3 00N 154 00E
Kaposvár Hungary **69** C2 46 21N 17 49E
Kapsukas *see* Marijampole
Kapuskasing Ontario Canada **105** D3 49 25N 82 26W
Kara Bogaz Gol *b.* Turkmenistan **70** H4 42 00N 53 00E
Kara Kum *geog. reg.* Turkmenistan **70** H4–I3 40 00N 60 00E
Kara Sea Russia **71** I11/J10 75 00N 70 00E
Karabük Turkey **78** D7 41 12N 32 36E
Karachi Pakistan **76** B4 24 51N 67 02E
Karaganda Kazakhstan **71** J5 49 53N 73 07E
Karaginskiy *i.* Russia **71** S7 58 00N 164 00E
Karaikkudi India **77** D2 10 04N 78 46E
Karaj Iran **79** H6 35 48N 50 58E
Karak Jordan **78** O10 31 11N 35 42E
Karakoram *mts.* Asia **72** 36 00N 76 00E
Karakoram Pass Kashmir/China **77** D7 35 33N 77 51E
Karama Jordan **78** O10 31 58N 35 34E
Karasburg Namibia **95** C2 28 00S 18 43E
Karasjok Norway **67** F4 69 27N 25 30E
Karbalā' Iraq **78** F5 32 37N 44 03E
Karcag Hungary **69** D2 47 19N 20 53E
Kariba Dam Zambia/Zimbabwe **95** E4 16 31S 28 50E
Kariba, Lake Zambia/Zimbabwe **95** E4 17 00S 28 00E
Karibib Namibia **95** C3 21 59S 15 51E
Karisimbi, Mount Rwanda/Zaïre **94** E7 1 32S 29 27E
Karlino Poland **69** C3 54 02N 15 52E
Karlovac Croatia **68** C4 45 30N 15 34E
Karlovy Vary Ceska Czechoslovakia **69** B3 50 13N 12 52E
Karlskoga Sweden **67** C2 59 19N 14 33E
Karlskrona Sweden **67** D2 56 10N 15 35E
Karlsruhe Germany **63** A1 49 00N 8 24E
Karlstad Sweden **67** C2 59 24N 13 32E
Karnafuli Reservoir Bangladesh **77** 22 30N 92 20E
Karnal India **77** D5 29 41N 76 58E
Karnataka *admin.* India **77** D2 14 40N 75 30E
Karol Bagh India **76** L4 28 39N 77 11E
Kárpathos *i.* Greece **68** E2 35 30N 27 12E
Karpenísion Greece **68** D2 38 55N 21 47E
Kars Turkey **78** F7 40 35N 43 05E
Karsakpay Kazakhstan **70** I5 47 47N 66 43E
Karshi Uzbekistan **79** K6 38 53N 65 45E
Karwar India **77** C2 14 50N 74 09E
Kasai *r.* Angola/Zaïre **95** C7 4 00S 19 00E
Kasama Zambia **95** F5 10 10S 31 11E
Kasaragod India **77** C2 12 30N 74 59E
Kasa-Vubu Zaïre **92** A1 4 21S 15 19E
Kasempa Zambia **95** E5 13 28S 25 48E
Kasese Uganda **94** F8 0 10N 30 06E
Kāshān Iran **79** H5 33 59N 51 35E
Kashi China **81** A5 39 29N 76 02E
Kashiwazaki Japan **82** C2 37 22N 138 33E
Kaskö Finland **67** E3 62 23N 21 10E
Kásos *i.* Greece **68** E2 35 00N 28 00E
Kassala Sudan **78** E2 15 24N 36 30E
Kassel Germany **63** A2 51 18N 9 30E
Kasserine Tunisia **68** A2 35 13N 8 43E
Kastoria Greece **68** D3 40 33N 21 15E
Kaśur Pakistan **77** C6 31 07N 74 30E
Kataba Zambia **95** E4 16 02S 25 03E
Katase Japan **83** A2 35 18N 139 30E
Katchall *i.* Nicobar Is. (India) **77** G1 7 30N 93 30E
Kateríni Greece **68** D3 40 15N 22 30E
Katha Myanmar **81** E2 24 11N 96 20E
Katherine Australia **86** E7 14 29S 132 20E
Kathiawar *p.* India **76/77** C4 21 10N 71 00E
Kathmandu Nepal **77** F5 27 42N 85 19E
Katihar India **77** F5 25 33N 87 34E
Katowice Poland **69** C3 50 15N 18 59E
Katrineholm Sweden **67** D2 58 59N 16 15E
Katsina Ala Nigeria **93** G4 7 10N 9 30E
Kattakurgan Uzbekistan **79** K6 39 54N 66 13E
Kattegat *sd.* Denmark/Sweden **67** C2 57 00N 11 00E
Katwijk aan Zee Netherlands **65** B2 52 12N 4 24E
Kauai *i.* Hawaiian Islands **119** X18 22 00N 159 30W
Kauai Channel Hawaiian Islands **119** X18 21 45N 158 50W
Kaufbeuren Germany **63** B1 47 53N 10 37E
Kaula *i.* Hawaiian Islands **119** W18 21 35N 160 40W
Kaulakahi Channel Hawaiian Islands **119** X18 21 58N 159 50W
Kaunas Lithuania **70** E6 54 52N 23 55E
Kaura Namoda Nigeria **93** G5 12 39N 6 38E
Kavajë Albania **68** C3 41 11N 19 33E
Kavála Greece **68** D3 40 56N 24 25E
Kavaratti Island India **77** C2 10 32N 72 43E
Kawagoe Japan **82** C2 35 55N 139 30E
Kawaguchi Japan **83** B4 35 47N 139 44E
Kawaihae Hawaiian Islands **119** Z18 20 02N 155 50W
Kawasaki Japan **83** C3 35 30N 139 45E
Kawawa Japan **83** B3 35 31N 139 33E
Kawawachikamach *see* Schefferville
Kawerau New Zealand **87** C3 38 03S 176 43E
Kaya Burkina **93** E5 13 04N 1 09W
Kayes Mali **93** C5 14 26N 11 28W
Kayseri Turkey **78** E6 38 42N 35 28E
Kazach'ye Russia **71** P10 70 46N 136 15E
KAZAKHSTAN 70 H5–I5
Kazakh Upland Kazakhstan **71** J5 47 00N 75 00E
Kazan' Russia **70** G7 55 45N 49 10E
Kazanlŭk Bulgaria **68** E3 42 37N 25 23E
Kazatin Ukraine **69** E2 49 41N 28 49E
Kāzerūn Iran **79** H4 29 35N 51 40E
Kazym *r.* Russia **71** I8 63 00N 67 30E
Kéa *i.* Greece **68** D2 37 00N 24 00E
Keady Northern Ireland **48** E4 54 15N 6 42W
Kearney Nebraska U.S.A. **102** G5 40 42N 99 04W
Kearny New Jersey U.S.A. **106** B2 40 45N 74 07W
Kearsley Greater Manchester England **42** C2 53 33N 2 22W
Kecskemét Hungary **69** C2 46 56N 19 43E
Kediri Indonesia **80** E2 7 45S 112 01E
Keele *r.* Northwest Territories Canada **100** J5 64 15N 126 00W
Keene New Hampshire U.S.A. **105** F2 42 55N 72 17W
Keetmanshoop Namibia **95** C2 26 36S 18 08E
Keewatin Ontario Canada **104** B3 49 47N 94 30W
Kefallinia *i.* Greece **68** D2 38 00N 20 00E
Keflavik Iceland **67** H6 64 01N 22 35W
Kegworth Leicestershire England **35** E3 52 50N 1 16W
Kehl Germany **63** A1 48 35N 7 50E
Keighley West Yorkshire England **43** E3 53 52N 1 54W
Keitele *l.* Finland **67** F3 63 10N 26 24E
Keith Grampian Scotland **46** F4 57 32N 2 57W
K'elafo Ethiopia **94** H9 5 37N 44 10E
Kelkit *r.* Turkey **78** E7 40 20N 37 40E
Kells *see* Ceanannus Mór
Kelowna British Columbia Canada **100** L2 49 50N 119 29W
Kelsall Cheshire England **42** B1 53 13N 2 43W
Kelsey Bay *tn.* British Columbia Canada **100** J3 50 22N 125 29W
Kelso Borders Scotland **46** F2 55 36N 2 25W
Kelty Fife Scotland **45** D2 56 08N 3 24W
Kelvedon Essex England **33** C2 51 51N 0 42E
Kemberton Shropshire England **35** A2 52 38N 2 24W
Kemerovo Russia **71** K7 55 25N 86 05E
Kemi Finland **67** E4 65 46N 24 34E
Kemijärvi *l.* Finland **67** F4 66 42N 27 30E
Kemijöki *r.* Finland **67** F4 67 15N 27 45E
Kempenland *(Campine) admin.* Belgium **64** E3 51 08N 15 22E
Kempston Bedfordshire England **33** B3 52 07N 0 30W
Kempten Germany **63** B1 47 44N 10 19E
Kemptville Ontario Canada **105** E3 45 01N 75 39W
Kemsing Kent England **34** D1 51 18N 0 14E
Kenai Alaska U.S.A. **100** E5 60 35N 151 19W
Kendal Cumbria England **44** B1 54 20N 2 45W
Kendalakshskiy Zaliv *(White Sea)* Russia **67** G4 66 55N 32 40E
Kendari Indonesia **80** G3 3 57S 122 36E
Kenema Sierra Leone **93** C4 7 57N 11 11W
Kengtung Myanmar **80** B8 21 16N 99 39E
Kenilworth Warwickshire England **35** D2 52 21N 1 34W
Keningau Malaysia **80** F5 5 21N 116 11E
Kénitra Morocco **93** D9 34 20N 6 34W
Kenmare Kerry Irish Republic **48** B1 51 53N 9 35W
Kenmare River *b.* Irish Republic **48** B1 51 40N 9 00W
Kennebunk Maine U.S.A. **105** F2 43 24N 70 33W
Kennet Fife Scotland **45** C2 56 06N 3 43W
Kennet *r.* Berkshire England **32** A2 51 25N 1 25W
Kennington Kent England **33** C2 51 09N 0 55E
Kennoway Fife Scotland **45** D2 56 12N 3 03W
Kenora Ontario Canada **104** B3 49 47N 94 26W
Kenosha Wisconsin U.S.A. **104** C2 42 34N 87 50W
Kensington & Chelsea Inner London England **34** C2 51 29N 0 10W
Kent *co.* England **33** C2 51 10N 0 45E
Kentford Suffolk England **33** C3 52 16N 0 30E
Kenton Greater London England **34** C2 51 33N 0 16W
Kenton Ohio U.S.A. **105** D2 40 38N 83 38W
Kent Peninsula Northwest Territories Canada **101** N6 68 30N 106 00W
Kentucky *r.* Kentucky U.S.A. **104** D1 38 00N 85 00W
Kentucky *state* U.S.A. **103** I4 37 00N 85 00W
Kentucky Lake Kentucky U.S.A. **104** C1 37 00N 88 00W
KENYA 94 G8
Kenya, Mount *see* Kirinyaga
Keokuk Iowa U.S.A. **104** B2 40 23N 91 25W
Kepulauan Anambas *is.* Indonesia **80** D4 3 00N 106 40E
Kepulauan Aru *is.* Indonesia **80** I2 7 00S 134 00E
Kepulauan Kai *is.* Indonesia **80** I2 5 30S 133 00E
Kepulauan Lingga *is.* Indonesia **80** C3 0 30S 104 00E
Kepulauan Mentawai *is.* Indonesia **80** B3 2 00S 99 00E
Kepulauan Obi *is.* Indonesia **80** H3 1 40S 127 30E
Kepulauan Riau *is.* Indonesia **80** C4 1 00N 104 20E
Kepulauan Sangir *is.* Indonesia **80** H4 2 30N 125 20E
Kepulauan Sula *is.* Indonesia **80** G3/H3 2 00S 125 00E
Kepulauan Talaud *is.* Indonesia **80** H4 4 00N 126 50E
Kepulauan Tanimbar *is.* Indonesia **80** I2 7 30S 132 00E
Kerala *admin.* India **77** D2 10 10N 76 30E
Kerch' Ukraine **70** F5 45 22N 36 27E
Kerema Papua New Guinea **86** H8 7 59S 145 46E
Keren Ethiopia **78** E2 15 46N 38 30E
Keresley West Midlands England **35** D2 52 27N 1 32W
Kerguelen *is.* Indian Ocean **123** 49 30S 69 30E
Kerikeri New Zealand **87** B3 35 12S 173 59E
Kerki Turkmenistan **79** K6 37 53N 65 10E
Kérkira *(Corfu) i.* Greece **68** C2 39 00N 19 00E
Kérkira Greece **68** C2 39 38N 19 55E
Kerkrade Netherlands **64** F2 50 52N 6 04E
Kermadec Islands Pacific Ocean **118** I5 30 00S 178 30W
Kermadec Trench Pacific Ocean **118** I4 33 00S 177 00W
Kermān Iran **79** I5 30 18N 57 05E
Kermānshāh Iran **79** G5 34 19N 47 04E
Kerme Körfezi *b.* Turkey **68** E2 37 00N 27 00E
Kerpen Germany **64** F2 50 52N 6 42E
Kerrera *i.* Strathclyde Scotland **46** C3 56 25N 5 34W
Kerrville Texas U.S.A. **102** G3 30 03N 99 09W
Kerry *co.* Irish Republic **48** B2 52 10N 9 30W
Kerry Head *c.* Irish Republic **48** B2 52 25N 9 55W
Kert *r.* Morocco **66** B2 35 00N 3 30W
Kerulen *r.* Mongolia **81** H7 47 30N 112 30E
Kesagami Lake Ontario Canada **105** D4 50 00N 80 00W
Keşan Turkey **68** E3 40 52N 26 37E
Kessingland Suffolk England **33** D3 52 25N 1 42E
Keswick Cumbria England **44** A1 54 37N 3 08W
Ket' *r.* Russia **71** K7 58 30N 86 30E
Ketapang Indonesia **80** E3 1 50S 109 59E
Ketchikan Alaska U.S.A. **100** I4 55 25N 131 40W
Kethel Netherlands **65** B1 51 56N 4 21E
Ketrzyn Poland **69** D3 54 05N 21 24E
Kettering Northamptonshire England **36** D2 52 24N 0 44W
Kettering Ohio U.S.A. **105** D1 39 42N 84 11W
Kettwig Germany **62** B2 51 22N 6 55E
Kewanee Illinois U.S.A. **104** C2 41 14N 89 56W
Kewaunee Wisconsin U.S.A. **104** C2 44 27N 87 31W
Keweenaw Bay Wisconsin U.S.A. **104** C3 47 00N 88 00W
Keweenaw Peninsula Michigan U.S.A. **104** C3 47 00N 88 00W
Kexbrough South Yorkshire England **43** F2 53 34N 1 32W
Keynsham Avon England **31** E3 51 26N 2 30W
Keyworth Nottinghamshire England **36** C2 52 52N 1 05W
Khabarovsk Russia **71** P5 48 32N 135 08E
Khairpur Pakistan **79** K4 27 30N 68 50E
Khalkidhikí *p.* Greece **68** D3 40 30N 23 00E
Khalkis Greece **68** D2 38 28N 23 36E
Khambhat India **77** C4 22 19N 72 39E
Khambhat, Gulf of India **77** C4 20 30N 72 00E
Khamman India **77** E3 17 16N 80 13E
Khānābad Afghanistan **79** K6 36 42N 69 08E
Khānaqīn Iraq **79** G5 34 22N 45 22E
Khandwa India **77** D4 21 49N 76 23E
Khaniá Greece **68** D2 35 31N 24 01E
Khanty-Mansiysk Russia **71** I8 61 01N 69 00E
Khān Yūnis Israel **78** O10 31 21N 34 18E
Kharagpur India **77** F4 22 23N 87 22E
Kharan Pakistan **76** B5 28 32N 65 26E
Khardah India **76** K2 22 43N 88 23E
Khārg Island Iran **79** H4 29 14N 60 20E
Khar'kov Ukraine **70** F6 50 00N 36 15E
Khartoum Sudan **78** D2 15 33N 32 35E
Khāsh Iran **79** J4 28 14N 61 15E
Khash *r.* Afghanistan **79** J5 31 30N 62 30E
Khashm el Girba Sudan **78** E1 14 59N 35 59E
Khaskovo Bulgaria **68** E3 41 57N 25 32E
Khatanga *r.* Russia **71** M10 72 30N 102 30E
Khatanga Russia **71** M10 71 59N 102 31E
Khemisset Morocco **93** D9 33 50N 6 03N
Kheta *r.* Russia **71** L10 71 30N 95 00E
Khilok *r.* Russia **71** M6 51 00N 107 30E
Khimki Russia **70** L2 55 56N 37 26E
Khimki-Khovrino Russia **70** L2 55 56N 37 30E
Khimki Reservoir Russia **70** L2 55 54N 37 28E
Khíos Greece **68** E2 38 23N 26 07E
Khíos *i.* Greece **68** E2 38 00N 26 00E
Khiva Uzbekistan **70** I4 41 25N 60 49E
Khmel'nitskiy Ukraine **69** E2 49 25N 26 59E
Kholayarvi Russia **67** F4 67 07N 28 50E
Kholmsk Russia **71** Q5 47 02N 142 03E
Khon Kaen Thailand **80** C7 16 25N 102 50E
Khorochevo Russia **70** L2 55 47N 37 30E
Khorog Tajikistan **70** J3 37 22N 71 32E
Khorramābād Iran **79** G5 33 29N 48 21E
Khorramshahr Iran **79** G5 30 25N 48 09E
Khotin Ukraine **69** E2 48 30N 26 31E
Khouribga Morocco **93** D9 32 54N 6 57W
Khrishnapur Canal India **76** K2 22 34N 88 27E
Khulna Bangladesh **77** F4 22 49N 89 34E
Khyber Pass Afghanistan/Pakistan **79** L5 34 00N 71 00E
Kiantajärvi *l.* Finland **67** F4 65 02N 29 00E
Kibombo Zaïre **95** E7 3 58S 25 54E
Kidderminster Hereford and Worcester England **35** B2 52 23N 2 14W
Kidlington Oxfordshire England **32** A2 51 50N 1 17W
Kidsgrove Staffordshire England **35** B4 53 05N 2 14W
Kidwelly Dyfed Wales **38** B1 51 45N 4 18W
Kiel Germany **63** B2 54 20N 10 08E
Kiel Bay Europe **63** B2 54 00N 10 00E
Kielce Poland **69** D3 50 51N 20 39E
Kielder Water *l.* Northumberland England **44** B2 55 10N 2 30W
Kieta Papua New Guinea **86** J8 6 15S 155 37E
Kiev *see* Kiyev
Kigali Rwanda **94** F7 1 56S 30 04E
Kigoma Tanzania **95** E7 4 52S 29 36E
Kii-suidō *sd.* Japan **82** B1 34 00N 134 45E
Kikinda Serbia Yugoslavia **68** D4 45 50N 20 30E
Kikládhes *(Cyclades) is.* Greece **68** D2 37 00N 25 00E
Kikori Papua New Guinea **86** G8 7 25S 144 13E
Kikwit Zaïre **95** C6 5 02S 18 51E
Kilanea Hawaiian Islands **119** X19 22 05N 159 35W
Kilbarchan Strathclyde Scotland **45** A1 55 50N 4 33W
Kilbirnie Strathclyde Scotland **45** A1 55 46N 4 41W
Kilbride Meath Irish Republic **49** A2 53 27N 6 24W
Kilburn Derbyshire England **35** D4 52 59N 1 26W
Kilcock Kildare Irish Republic **48** E3 53 24N 6 40W
Kilcoole Wicklow Irish Republic **48** E3 53 07N 6 04W
Kilcormac Offaly Irish Republic **48** D3 53 10N 7 43W
Kilcullen Kildare Irish Republic **48** E3 53 08N 6 45W
Kildare *co.* Irish Republic **48** E3 53 10N 6 55W
Kildare Kildare Irish Republic **48** E3 53 10N 6 55W
Kilgetty Dyfed Wales **38** B1 51 45N 4 44W
Kilimanjaro *mt.* Tanzania **94** G7 3 04S 37 22E
Kilkee Clare Irish Republic **48** B2 52 41N 9 38W
Kilkeel Northern Ireland **48** E4 54 04N 6 00W
Kilkenny *co.* Irish Republic **48** D2 52 30N 7 10W
Kilkenny Kilkenny Irish Republic **48** D2 52 39N 7 15W
Kilkhampton Cornwall England **30** C2 50 53N 4 29W
Kilkís Greece **68** D3 40 59N 22 52E
Kill Kildare Irish Republic **49** A1 53 15N 6 35W
Killaloe Clare Irish Republic **48** C2 52 48N 8 27W
Killamarsh Derbyshire England **43** G1 53 20N 1 20W
Killarney Kerry Irish Republic **48** B2 52 03N 9 30W
Killarney Manitoba Canada **101** P2 49 12N 99 40W
Killarney National Park Kerry Irish Republic **48** B1 52 10N 9 35W
Killearn Central Scotland **45** B2 56 03N 4 22W
Killeen Texas U.S.A. **103** G3 31 08N 97 44W
Killin Central Scotland **46** D3 56 28N 4 19W
Killiney Dublin Irish Republic **49** B1 53 15N 6 07W
Killinghall North Yorkshire England **43** F3 54 01N 1 34W
Killorglin Kerry Irish Republic **48** B2 52 06N 9 47W
Kilpatrick Hills Strathclyde Scotland **45** B1 55 55N 4 25W
Killybegs Donegal Irish Republic **48** C4 54 38N 8 27W
Killyleagh Down Northern Ireland **48** F4 54 24N 5 39W
Kilmacanogue Wicklow Irish Republic **49** B1 53 10N 6 08W
Kilmacolm Strathclyde Scotland **45** A1 55 54N 4 38W
Kilmallock Limerick Irish Republic **48** C2 52 23N 8 34W
Kilmaluag Highland Scotland **46** B4 57 41N 6 17W
Kilmarnock Strathclyde Scotland **46** D2 55 36N 4 30W
Kilrea Northern Ireland **48** E4 54 57N 6 34W
Kilroot Northern Ireland **49** D2 54 43N 5 46W
Kilrush Clare Irish Republic **48** B2 52 39N 9 30W
Kilsallaghan Dublin Irish Republic **49** B2 53 28N 6 19W
Kilsyth Strathclyde Scotland **45** B1 55 59N 4 04W
Kiltan Island India **77** C2 11 30N 73 00E
Kilteel Kildare Irish Republic **49** A1 53 14N 6 31W
Kiltimagh Mayo Irish Republic **48** C3 53 51N 9 00W
Kilwa Masoko Tanzania **96** G6 8 55S 39 31S
Kilwinning Strathclyde Scotland **45** A1 55 40N 4 42W
Kilyos Turkey **68** E3 41 14N 29 02E
Kimbanseke Zaïre **92** B1 4 24S 15 24E
Kimberley British Columbia Canada **100** L2 49 40N 115 58W
Kimberley Nottinghamshire England **35** E3 53 00N 1 17W
Kimberley Republic of South Africa **95** D2 28 45S 24 46E
Kimberley Plateau Australia **86** D6 17 30S 126 00E
Kimberling City Missouri U.S.A. **104** B1 36 40N 93 25W
Kimbolton Cambridgeshire England **33** B3 52 18N 0 24W
Kinabalu *see* Gunung Kinabalu
Kinbasket Lake British Columbia Canada **100** L3 51 57N 118 02W
Kinbrace Highland Scotland **46** E5 58 15N 3 56W
Kinbuck Central Scotland **45** C2 56 13N 3 57W
Kincardine Fife Scotland **45** C2 56 03N 3 43W
Kincardine Ontario Canada **105** D2 44 11N 81 38W
Kinderdijk Netherlands **65** C1 51 53N 4 39E
Kindersley Saskatchewan Canada **100** N3 51 27N 109 08W
Kindia Guinea **93** C5 10 03N 12 49W
Kindu Zaïre **95** E7 3 00S 25 56E
Kineton Warwickshire England **36** C2 52 10N 1 30W
King George Bay Falkland Islands **117** L16 51 50S 61 00W
King George Island South Shetland Islands **115** F0 62 00S 58 00W
Kinghorn Fife Scotland **45** D2 56 04N 3 11W
King Island Australia **86** G2 40 00S 144 00E
Kingissepp *see* Kuressaare
Kingman Arizona U.S.A. **102** D4 35 12N 114 02W
Kingsbridge Devon England **31** D2 50 17N 3 46W
Kingsbury Warwickshire England **35** C2 52 35N 1 40W
Kingsclere Hampshire England **32** A2 51 20N 1 14W
Kingscourt Cavan Irish Republic **48** E3 53 53N 6 48W
King Sejong *r.s.* Antarctica **121** 62 13S 58 45W
Kingskerswell Devon England **31** D2 50 30N 3 37W
Kings Langley Hertfordshire England **34** B3 51 43N 0 28W
King's Lynn Norfolk England **33** C3 52 45N 0 24E
King Sound Australia **86** C6 16 00S 123 00E
Kings Point *tn.* New York U.S.A. **106** C2 40 49N 73 45W
Kingsport Tennessee U.S.A. **103** J4 36 33N 82 34W
Kingsteignton Devon England **31** D2 50 33N 3 35W
Kingston Jamaica **109** R7 17 58N 76 48W
Kingston New York U.S.A. **105** F2 41 55N 74 00W
Kingston Ontario Canada **105** E2 44 14N 76 30W
Kingston upon Hull Humberside England **40** D2 53 45N 0 20W
Kingston upon Thames Greater London England **34** C2 51 25N 0 18W
Kingstown St. Vincent & The Grenadines **109** L2 13 12N 61 14W
Kingsville Ontario Canada **105** D2 42 02N 82 44W

Kingsville Texas U.S.A. **103** G2 27 32N 97 53W
King's Walden Hertfordshire England **34** C3 51 54N 0 19W
Kingswinford West Midlands England **35** B2 52 29N 2 10W
Kingswood Avon England **31** E3 51 28N 2 30W
Kingswood Surrey England **34** C1 51 17N 0 12W
Kington Hereford and Worcester England **36** A2 52 12N 3 01W
Kingussie Highland Scotland **46** D4 57 05N 4 03W
King William Island Northwest Territories Canada **101** P6 69 00N 97 30W
Kinkala Congo **95** B7 4 18S 14 49E
Kinkell Bridge *tn.* Tayside Scotland **45** C2 56 20N 3 12W
Kinlochard Central Scotland **45** B2 56 12N 4 29W
Kinlochewe Highland Scotland **46** C4 57 36N 5 20W
Kinlochleven Highland Scotland **46** D3 56 42N 4 58W
Kinloch Rannoch Tayside Scotland **46** D3 56 42N 4 11W
Kinloss Grampian Scotland **46** E4 57 38N 3 33W
Kinnairds Head *c.* Grampian Scotland **46** F4 57 40N 2 00W
Kinross Tayside Scotland **45** D2 56 13N 3 27W
Kinsale Cork Irish Republic **48** C1 51 42N 8 32W
Kinsaley Dublin Irish Republic **49** B2 53 25N 6 10W
Kinshasa Zaïre **92** A2 4 18S 15 18E
Kintambo Zaïre **92** A1 4 21S 15 16E
Kintillo Tayside Scotland **45** D2 56 20N 3 24W
Kintore Grampian Scotland **46** F4 57 13N 2 21W
Kintyre *p.* Strathclyde Scotland **46** C2 55 30N 5 35W
Kinver Staffordshire England **35** B2 52 27N 2 14W
Kinzig *r.* Germany **63** A2 50 00N 9 00E
Kiparissiakós Kólpos *g.* Greece **68** D2 37 00N 21 00E
Kipili Tanzania **95** F6 7 30S 30 39E
Kippax West Yorkshire England **43** F3 53 46N 1 22W
Kippen Central Scotland **45** B2 56 08N 4 11W
Kippure *mt.* Irish Republic **49** B1 53 10N 6 20W
Kirby Muxloe Leicestershire England **35** E2 52 38N 1 14W
Kirchhörde Germany **62** D2 51 27N 7 27E
Kirensk Russia **71** M7 57 45N 108 02E
KIRGHIZIA *see* KIRGYZSTAN
KIRGYZSTAN *(KIRGHIZIA)* **70/71** J4
KIRIBATI Pacific Ocean **118** H8
Kirikiri Nigeria **92** C3 6 22N 3 22E
Kirikkale Turkey **78** D6 39 51N 33 32E
Kirinyaga *(Mount Kenya) mt.* Kenya **94** G7 0 10S 37 19E
Kiritimati Island Kiribati **119** K8 2 10N 157 00W
Kirkağaç Turkey **68** E2 39 06N 27 40E
Kirkburton West Yorkshire England **43** E2 53 37N 1 42W
Kirkby Merseyside England **42** B2 53 29N 2 54W
Kirkby in Ashfield Nottinghamshire England **36** C3 53 13N 1 15W
Kirkby Lonsdale Cumbria England **44** B1 54 13N 2 36W
Kirkbymoorside North Yorkshire England **40** C3 54 16N 0 55W
Kirkby Overblow North Yorkshire England **43** F3 53 57N 1 30W
Kirkby Stephen Cumbria England **44** B1 54 28N 2 20W
Kirkcaldy Fife Scotland **45** D2 56 07N 3 10W
Kirkconnel Dumfries & Galloway Scotland **46** D2 55 23N 4 00W
Kirkcudbright Dumfries & Galloway Scotland **46** D1 54 50N 4 03W
Kirkfieldbank Strathclyde Scotland **45** C1 55 41N 3 50W
Kirkham Lancashire England **42** B3 53 47N 2 53W
Kirkintilloch Strathclyde Scotland **45** B1 55 57N 4 10W
Kirkland Lake *tn.* Ontario Canada **105** D3 48 10N 80 02W
Kirklareli Turkey **68** E3 41 45N 27 12E
Kirkliston Lothian Scotland **45** D1 55 58N 3 25W
Kirk Michael Isle of Man British Isles **41** F1 54 17N 4 35W
Kirkmuirhill Strathclyde Scotland **45** C1 55 39N 3 55W
Kirknewton Lothian Scotland **45** D1 55 53N 3 25W
Kirkolm Dumfries & Galloway Scotland **46** C1 54 58N 5 04W
Kirk Sandall South Yorkshire England **43** G2 53 34N 1 04W
Kirksville Missouri U.S.A. **104** B2 40 12N 92 35W
Kirkūk Iraq **78** F6 35 28N 44 26E
Kirkwall Orkney Islands Scotland **47** E1 58 59N 2 58W
Kirov Russia **70** G7 58 00N 49 38E
Kirovabad *see* Gyandzha
Kirovakan Armenia **78** F7 40 49N 44 30E
Kirovograd Ukraine **70** E5 48 31N 32 15E
Kirriemuir Tayside Scotland **46** E3 56 41N 3 01W
Kirti Nagar India **76** L4 28 39N 77 09E
Kirton Lincolnshire England **36** D2 52 56N 0 04W
Kiruna Sweden **67** E4 67 53N 20 15E
Kiryū Japan **82** C2 36 26N 139 18E
Kisangani Zaïre 94 E8 0 33N 25 14E
Kisarazu Japan **83** C2 35 22N 139 55E
Kisenso Zaïre **92** B1 4 24S 15 21E
Kishinev Moldova **70** E5 47 00N 28 50E
Kishiwada Japan **82** C1 34 28N 135 22E
Kiskunfélegyháza Hungary **69** C2 46 42N 19 52E
Kiskunhalas Hungary **69** C2 46 26N 19 29E
Kismaayo Somalia **94** H7 0 25S 42 31E
Kisumu Kenya **94** F7 0 08S 34 47E
Kita Japan **83** B4 35 46N 139 43E
Kita-Kyūshū Japan **82** B1 33 52N 130 49E
Kitami Japan **82** D3 43 51N 143 54E
Kitchener Ontario Canada **105** D2 43 27N 80 30W
Kíthira *i.* Greece **68** D2 36 00N 23 00E
Kíthnos *i.* Greece **68** D2 37 00N 24 00E
Kitimat British Columbia Canada **100** J3 54 05N 128 38W
Kittanning Pennsylvania U.S.A. **105** E2 40 49N 79 31W
Kittery Maine U.S.A. **105** F2 43 05N 70 45W
Kitwe Zambia **95** E5 0 08S 30 30E
Kitzbühel Austria **63** B1 47 27N 12 23E
Kitzbühler Alpen *mts.* Austria **63** B1 47 00N 12 00E
Kitzingen Germany **63** B1 49 45N 10 11E
Kivu, Lake Zaïre / Rwanda **94** E7 2 00S 29 00E
Kiyev *(Kiev)* Ukraine **70** F6 50 25N 30 30E
Klyevskoye Vodokhranilishche *res.* Ukraine **69** F3 51 00N 30 00E
Kiyose Japan **83** B4 35 46N 139 32E
Kizil Irmak *r.* Turkey **78** D7 40 30N 34 00E
Kizyl Arvat Turkmenistan **79** I6 39 00N 56 23E
Kladno Ceska Czechoslovakia **69** B3 50 10N 14 07E
Klagenfurt Austria **69** B2 46 38N 14 20E
Klaipėda Lithuania **70** E7 55 43N 21 07E
Klamath *r.* U.S.A. **102** B5 42 00N 123 00W
Klamath Falls *tn.* Oregon U.S.A. **102** B5 42 14N 121 47W
Klarälven *r.* Sweden **67** C3 60 45N 13 00E
Klatovy Ceska Czechoslovakia **69** B2 49 24N 13 17E
Kleine Emscher *can.* Germany **62** A3 51 35N 6 45E
Klerksdorp Republic of South Africa **95** E2 26 52S 26 39E
Kleve Germany **63** A2 51 47N 6 11E
Kłodzko Poland **69** C3 50 28N 16 40E
Klöfta Norway **67** C3 60 04N 11 06E
Klondike *r.* Yukon Canada **96** 62 00N 135 00W
Kluane National Park Yukon Territory Canada **100** H5 60 30N 139 00W
Klyuchevskaya Sopka *mt.* Russia **71** S7 56 03N 160 38E
Knaphill Surrey England **34** B1 51 19N 0 37W
Knaresborough North Yorkshire England **43** F4 54 00N 1 27W
Knebworth Hertfordshire England **34** C3 51 52N 0 10W
Knighton Powys Wales **38** C2 52 21N 3 03W
Knockadoon Head *c.* Irish Republic **48** D1 51 50N 7 50W
Knockholt Pound Kent England **34** D1 51 19N 0 07E
Knokke-Heist Belgium **64** C3 51 21N 3 19E
Knossós *hist. site* Greece **78** C6 35 18N 25 10E
Knott End-on-Sea Lancashire England **42** B3 53 56N 2 59W
Knottingley West Yorkshire England **43** G3 53 43N 1 14W
Knowle West Midlands England **35** C2 52 23N 1 43W
Knowsley Merseyside England **42** B2 53 26N 2 52W
Knox Indiana U.S.A. **104** C2 41 17N 86 37W
Knoxville Iowa U.S.A. **104** B2 41 26N 93 05W
Knoxville Tennessee U.S.A. **103** J4 36 00N 83 57W
Knutsford Cheshire England **42** C1 53 18N 2 23W
Kōbe Japan **82** C1 34 40N 135 12E
København *(Copenhagen)* Denmark **67** C2 55 43N 12 34E
Koblenz Germany **63** A2 50 21N 7 36E
Kobrin Belarus **69** D3 52 16N 24 22E
Kobuk *r.* Alaska U.S.A. **100** D6 67 00N 157 30W
Koca *r.* Turkey **68** E2 39 00N 27 00E
Koch Bihār India **77** F5 26 18N 89 32E
Kōchi Japan **82** B1 33 33N 133 32E
Kodiak Alaska U.S.A. **100** E4 57 49N 152 30W
Kodiak Island Alaska U.S.A. **100** E4 57 20N 153 40W
Kodiara Japan **83** A3 35 44N 139 28E
Kodok Sudan **94** F9 9 51N 32 07E
Koforidua Ghana **93** E4 6 01N 0 12W
Kofu Japan **82** C2 35 42N 138 34E
Koganei Japan **83** B3 35 42N 139 30E
Kohat Pakistan **77** C6 33 37N 71 30E
Kohima India **77** G5 25 40N 94 08E
Koh-i-Mazar *mt.* Afghanistan **79** K5 32 30N 66 23E
Kohoku Japan **83** B3 35 30N 139 39E
Kohtla-Järve Estonia **67** F2 59 28N 27 20E
Koito *r.* Japan **83** C2 35 20N 139 52E
Kokand Uzbekistan **70** J4 40 33N 70 55E
Kokchetav Kazakhstan **71** I6 53 18N 69 25E
Kokkola Finland **67** E3 63 50N 23 06E
Kokomo Indiana U.S.A. **104** C2 40 30N 86 09W
Koksoak *r.* Québec Canada **101** V4 58 00N 69 00W
Kola Peninsula Russia **70** F9 67 30N 37 30E
Kolar Gold Fields *tn.* India **77** D2 12 54N 78 16E
Kolding Denmark **67** B2 55 29N 9 30E
Kolguyev *i.* Russia **70** G9 69 00N 49 30E
Kolhapur India **77** C3 16 40N 74 20E
Kolín Ceska Czechoslovakia **69** C3 50 02N 15 11E
Köln *(Cologne)* Germany **63** A2 50 56N 6 57E
Kolobrzeg Poland **69** C3 54 10N 15 35E
Kolomyya Ukraine **69** E2 48 31N 25 00E
Kolpashevo Russia **71** K7 58 21N 82 59E
Kolvereid Norway **67** C3 64 53N 11 35E
Kolwezi Zaïre **95** E5 10 45S 25 25E
Kolyma *r.* Russia **71** R9 66 30N 152 00E
Kolyma Lowland Russia **71** R9 69 00N 155 00E
Kolyma *(Gydan)* **Range** *mts.* Russia **71** R8 63 00N 160 00E
Komae Japan **83** B3 35 38N 139 36E
Komandorskiye Ostrova *is.* Russia **118** G13 55 00N 166 30E
Komárno Slovenska Czechoslovakia **69** C2 47 46N 18 05E
Komatsu Japan **82** C2 36 25N 136 27E
Komotiní Greece **68** E3 41 06N 25 25E
Kompong Cham Cambodia **80** D6 11 59N 105 26E
Kompong Chhnang Cambodia **80** C6 12 16N 104 39E
Kompong Som Cambodia **80** C6 11 03N 103 41E
Komrat Moldova **69** E2 46 18N 28 40E
Komsomol'sk-na-Amure Russia **71** P6 50 32N 136 59E
Kondūz Afghanistan **79** K6 36 45N 68 51E
Kong Christian X Island *geog. reg.* Greenland **101** DD8 75 00N 27 30W
Kongolo Zaïre **95** E6 5 20S 27 00E
Kong Oscars Fjord Greenland **101** EE7 72 30N 23 00W
Königswinter Germany **64** G2 50 41N 7 11E
Konin Poland **69** C3 52 12N 18 12E
Konnagar India **76** K2 22 42N 88 20E
Konosha Russia **70** G8 60 58N 40 08E
Konya Turkey **78** D6 37 51N 32 30E
Kootenay Lake British Columbia Canada **100** L3 50 00N 117 15W
Koper Slovenia **68** B4 45 31N 13 44E
Kopychintsy Ukraine **69** E2 49 10N 25 58E
Korbach Germany **63** A2 51 16N 8 53E
Korçë Albania **68** D3 40 38N 20 44E
Korčula *i.* Croatia **68** C3 43 00N 17 00E
Korea Bay China/North Korea **81** J5 39 00N 124 00E
Korea Strait South Korea/Japan **81** K4/L4 33 00N 129 00E
Korhogo Côte d'Ivoire **93** D4 9 22N 5 31W
Korinthiakós Kólpos *g.* Greece **68** D2 38 00N 22 00E
Kórinthos Greece **68** D2 37 56N 22 55E
Kōriyama Japan **82** D2 37 23N 140 22E
Korla China **81** C6 41 48N 86 10E
Koro *i.* Fiji **118** U16 17 20S 179 25E
Koro Sea Fiji **118** U16 17 35S 180 00
Korosten Ukraine **69** E3 51 00N 28 30E
Korsakov Russia **71** Q5 46 36N 142 50E
Kortrijk *(Courtrai)* Belgium **64** C2 50 50N 3 17E
Koryak Range *mts.* Russia **71** T8 62 00N 170 00E
Kos *i.* Greece **68** E2 36 00N 27 00E
Kosciusko, Mount Australia **86** H2 36 28S 148 17E
Košice Slovenska Czechoslovakia **69** D2 48 44N 21 15E
Kosti Sudan **78** D1 13 11N 32 28E
Kostroma Russia **70** G7 57 46N 40 59E
Kostrzyn Poland **69** B3 52 35N 14 40E
Koszalin Poland **69** C3 54 10N 16 10E
Kota India **77** D5 25 11N 75 58E
Kota Baharu Malaysia **80** C5 6 07N 102 15E
Kota Kinabalu Malaysia **80** F5 5 59N 116 04E
Köthen Germany **63** B2 51 46N 11 59E
Kotka Finland **67** F3 60 26N 26 55E
Kotlas Russia **70** G8 61 15N 46 35E
Kōtō Japan **83** C3 35 40N 139 49E
Kotri Pakistan **76** B5 25 22N 68 18E
Kotto *r.* Central African Republic **94** D9 7 00N 22 30E
Kotuy *r.* Russia **71** M9 67 30N 102 00E
Kotzebue Alaska U.S.A. **100** C6 66 51N 162 40W
Kotzebue Sound Alaska U.S.A. **100** C6 66 40N 162 20W
Koudougou Burkina **93** E5 12 15N 2 23W
Koulamoutou Gabon **93** H2 1 12S 12 29E
Koulikoro Mali **93** D5 12 55N 7 31W
Koumra Chad **94** C9 8 56N 17 32E
Kounradskiy Kazakhstan **81** A7 46 58N 74 59E
Kourou French Guiana **114** G14 5 08N 52 37W
Kouvola Finland **67** F3 60 54N 26 45E
Kovel' Ukraine **69** D3 51 12N 24 48E
Koyukuk *r.* Alaska U.S.A. **100** E6 66 00N 154 00W
Kozáni Greece **68** D3 40 18N 21 48E
Kpalimé Togo **93** F4 6 55N 0 44E
Kragujevac Serbia Yugoslavia **68** D3 44 01N 20 55E
Kra, Isthmus of Asia **72** 10 00N 104 00E
Kraków Poland **69** C3 50 03N 19 55E
Kraljevo Serbia Yugoslavia **68** D3 43 44N 20 41E
Kranj Slovenia **68** B4 46 15N 14 20E
Krasnodar Russia **70** F5 45 02N 39 00E
Krasnovodsk Turkmenistan **70** H4 40 01N 53 00E
Krasnoyarsk Russia **71** L7 56 05N 92 46E
Krasny Stroitel Russia **70** M1 55 31N 37 08E
Krefeld Germany **63** A2 51 20N 6 32E
Kremenets Ukraine **69** E3 50 05N 25 48E
Krems Austria **69** C2 48 25N 15 36E
Kribi Cameroon **93** G3 2 56N 9 56E
Krim *(Crimea) p.* Ukraine **70** F5 46 00N 34 00E
Krimpen Netherlands **65** C1 51 54N 4 35E
Krishna *r.* India **77** D3 16 00N 79 00E
Kristiansand Norway **67** B2 58 08N 8 01E
Kristianstad Sweden **67** C2 56 02N 14 10E
Kristiansund Norway **67** B3 63 06N 7 58E
Kríti *(Crete) i.* Greece **68** D1 35 00N 25 00E
Krivoy Rog Ukraine **70** F5 47 55N 33 24E
Krk *i.* Croatia **68** B4 45 00N 14 00E
Kronshtadt Russia **67** F3 60 00N 29 40E
Krosno Poland **69** D2 49 40N 21 46E
Kruger National Park Republic of South Africa **95** F3 24 00S 32 00E
Krugersdorp Republic of South Africa **95** E2 26 06S 27 46E
Krung Thep *see* Bangkok
Kruševac Serbia Yugoslavia **68** D3 43 34N 21 20E
Krušnéhory *see* Erzgebirge
Ksar El Boukhari Algeria **93** F10 35 55N 2 47E
Ksar-el-Kebir Morocco **66** A2 35 04N 5 56W
Kuala Lumpur Malaysia **80** C4 3 08N 101 42E
Kuala Terengganu Malaysia **80** C5 5 20N 103 07E
Kuantan Malaysia **80** C4 3 50N 103 19E
Kubiri Japan **83** B1 35 13N 139 42E
Kuching Malaysia **80** E4 1 32N 110 20E
Kudat Malaysia **80** F5 6 54N 116 47E
Kufstein Austria **63** B1 47 36N 12 11E
Kuhumo Finland **67** F3 64 04N 29 30E
Kuito Angola **95** C5 12 25S 16 56E
Kujū-san *mt.* Japan **82** B1 33 07N 131 14E
Kukës Albania **68** D3 42 05N 20 24E
Kuldiga Latvia **67** E2 56 58N 21 58E
Kulmbach Germany **63** B2 50 06N 11 28E
Kuma *r.* Russia **70** G4 45 00N 45 00E
Kumagaya Japan **82** C2 36 09N 139 22E
Kumairi *(Leninakan)* Armenia **70** G4 40 47N 43 49E
Kumamoto Japan **82** B1 32 50N 130 42E
Kumanovo Macedonia Yugoslavia **68** D3 42 07N 21 40E
Kumasi Ghana **93** E4 6 45N 1 35W
Kumba Cameroon **93** G3 4 39N 9 26E
Kumbakonam India **77** D2 10 59N 79 24E
Kumukahi, Cape Hawaiian Islands **119** Z17 19 30N 154 50W
Kumul *see* Hami
Kunar *r.* Asia **79** L5 35 30N 71 20E
Kunashir *i.* Russia **82** E3 44 30N 146 20E
Kungrad Uzbekistan **70** H4 43 06N 58 54E
Kunlun Shan *mts.* China **81** B5/C5 36 30N 85 00E
Kunming China **81** F3 25 04N 102 41E
Kunming Hu *l.* China **82** G2 40 00N 116 15E
Kunsan South Korea **81** K5 35 57N 126 42E
Kuntsevo Russia **70** L1 55 43N 37 25E
Kununurra Australia **86** D6 15 42S 128 50E
Kuopio Finland **67** F3 62 54N 27 40E
Kupa *r.* Europe **68** C4 45 00N 15 00E
Kupang Indonesia **80** G1 10 13S 123 38E
Kupferdreh Germany **62** C2 51 24N 7 06E
Kura *r.* Azerbaijan **70** G4 41 00N 47 30E
Kurashiki Japan **82** B1 34 36N 133 43E
Kure Japan **82** B1 34 14N 132 32E
Kuressaare *(Kingissepp)* Estonia **67** E2 59 22N 28 40E
Kureyka *r.* Russia **71** L9 67 30N 91 00E
Kurgan Russia **70** I7 55 30N 65 20E
Kuria Muria Islands Oman **79** I2 17 30N 56 00E
Kurihama Japan **83** B1 35 12N 139 41E
Kurikka Finland **67** E3 62 36N 22 25E
Kuril Islands Russia **71** R5/R6 50 00N 155 00E
Kuril Ridge Pacific Ocean **118** F12 47 50N 152 00E
Kuril Trench Pacific Ocean **118** F12 45 40N 154 00E
Kurnool India **77** D3 15 51N 78 01E
Kursk Russia **70** F6 51 45N 36 14E
Kurskiy Zaliv *g.* Russia **69** D4 55 00N 21 00E
Kurume Japan **82** B1 33 20N 130 29E
Kushiro Japan **82** D3 42 58N 144 24E
Kushka Afghanistan **79** J6 35 14N 62 15E
Kuskokwim *r.* Alaska U.S.A. **100** C5 61 30N 160 45W
Kuskokwim Bay Alaska U.S.A. **100** C4 58 50N 164 00W
Kuskokwim Mountains Alaska U.S.A. **100** D5 62 00N 158 00W
Kustanay Kazakhstan **70** I6 53 15N 63 40E
Kütahya Turkey **78** C6 39 25N 29 56E
Kutno Poland **69** C3 52 13N 19 20E
Kuujjuaq Québec Canada **101** V4 58 25N 68 55W
Kuujjuarapik Québec Canada **101** T4 55 15N 77 30W
Kuusamo Finland **67** F4 65 57N 29 15E
Kuvango Angola **95** C5 14 27S 16 20E
KUWAIT **79** G4
Kuybyshev *see* Samara
Kuytun China **81** B6 44 30N 85 00E
Kuzey Anadolu Dağlari *mts.* Turkey **78** E7 41 15N 36 20E
Kuz'minki Russia **70** N1 55 41N 37 45E
Kwangju South Korea **81** K5 35 07N 126 52E
Kwango *r.* Zaïre **95** C6 6 00S 17 00E
Kwe Kwe Zimbabwe **95** E4 18 55S 29 49E
Kwethluk Alaska U.S.A. **100** C5 60 46N 161 34W
Kwigillingok Alaska U.S.A. **100** C4 59 50N 163 10W
Kwilu *r.* Zaïre **95** C6 6 00S 19 00E
Kyaukpyu Myanmar **77** G3 19 27N 93 33E
Kyleakin Highland Scotland **46** C4 57 16N 5 44W
Kyle of Lochalsh Highland Scotland **46** C4 57 17N 5 43W
Kyle of Tongue *b.* Highland Scotland **46** D5 58 40N 4 25W
Kylestrome Highland Scotland **46** C5 58 16N 5 02W
Kyoga, Lake Uganda **94** F8 2 00N 34 00E
Kyoga-misaki *c.* Japan **82** C2 35 48N 135 12E
Kyōto Japan **82** C2 35 02N 135 45E
Kyronjöki *r.* Finland **67** E3 63 00N 21 30E
Kyūshū *i.* Japan **82** B1 32 20N 131 00E
Kyūshū Palau Ridge Pacific Ocean **118** D9 15 00N 135 00E
Kyustendil Bulgaria **68** D3 42 16N 22 40E
Kyzyl Russia **71** L6 51 45N 94 28E
Kyzyl Kum *d.* Asia **70** I4 43 00N 65 00E
Kzyl-Orda Kazakhstan **70** I4 44 52N 65 28E

L

Laascaanood Somalia **94** I9 8 35N 46 55E
La Asunción Venezuela **109** L2 11 06N 63 53W
Laâyoune *(El Aaiún)* Western Sahara **93** C8 27 10N 13 11W
la Baule-Escoublac France **61** A2 47 18N 2 22W
Labé Guinea **93** C5 11 17N 12 11W
Labe *see* Elbe
Labrador *geog. reg.* Newfoundland Canada **101** W3 54 00N 63 00W
Labrador Basin Atlantic Ocean **117** C12 58 00N 50 00W
Labrador City Newfoundland Canada **100** V3 52 54N 66 50W
Labrador Sea Canada/Greenland **101** X4 59 00N 56 00W
Lábrea Brazil **114** E11 7 20S 64 46W
Labytnangi Russia **71** I9 66 43N 66 28E
Lac Alaotra *l.* Madagascar **95** I4 17 30S 54 00E
Lac à l'Eau Claire *l.* Québec Canada **101** U4 56 20N 74 30W
Lac Bienville *l.* Québec Canada **101** U4 55 30N 73 00W
La Canada California U.S.A. **107** B3 34 12N 118 12W
Lac Caniapiscau *l.* Québec Canada **101** V3 54 20N 69 00W
La Ceiba Honduras **109** G3 15 45N 86 45W
la Chaux-de-Fonds Switzerland **61** C2 47 07N 6 51E
la Ciotat France **61** C1 43 10N 5 36E
La Coruña *(Corunna)* Spain **66** A3 43 22N 8 24W
La Cresenta California U.S.A. **107** B3 34 13N 118 14W
La Crosse Wisconsin U.S.A. **104** B2 43 48N 91 04W
Lac de la Forêt d'Orient *l.* France **61** B2 48 15N 4 20E
Lac de Neuchâtel *l.* Switzerland **61** C2 46 45N 6 40E
Lac du Bonnet *tn.* Manitoba Canada **104** A4 50 16N 96 03W
Lac du Der-Chantecoq *l.* France **61** B2 48 35N 4 45E
Lac Fitri *l.* Chad **94** C10 13 00N 17 30E
Lac Joseph *l.* Newfoundland Canada **101** V3 52 30N 65 15W
Lache Cheshire England **42** B1 53 12N 2 54W
Lachlan *r.* Australia **86** H3 33 30S 145 30E
Lachute Québec Canada **105** F3 45 39N 74 21W
Lackawanna New York U.S.A. **105** E2 42 49N 78 49W
Lac la Martre *tn.* Northwest Territories Canada **100** L5 63 00N 117 30W
Lac la Ronge *l.* Saskatchewan Canada **101** N3 54 30N 107 25W
Lac Léman *(Lake Geneva) l.* Switzerland **61** C2 46 20N 6 20E
Lac Mai-Ndombe *l.* Zaïre **94** C7 2 00S 18 20E
Lac Manouané *l.* Québec Canada **105** F4 51 00N 71 00W
Lac Mattagami *l.* Québec Canada **105** E3 50 00N 78 00W
Lac Minto *l.* Québec Canada **101** T4 57 35N 75 00W
Lac Mistassini *l.* Québec Canada **101** U3 51 00N 73 20W
Lac Moero *see* Mweru, Lake
Lacolle Québec Canada **105** F3 45 04 73 22W
Lac Payne *l.* Québec Canada **101** U4 59 25N 74 00W
Lac St.-Jean *l.* Québec Canada **105** F3 48 00N 72 00W
Lac St. Joseph *l.* Ontario Canada **101** Q3 51 30N 91 40W
Lac Seul *l.* Ontario Canada **101** Q3 50 20N 92 00W
Lacul Razelm *l.* Romania **69** E1 45 00N 29 00E
Ladakh Range *mts.* Kashmir **77** D6 34 30N 78 30E
Ladbroke Warwickshire England **35** D1 52 14N 1 23W
la Défense France **60** A2 48 53N 2 14E
Ladoga, Lake *see* Ladozhskoye Ozero
Ladozhskoye Ozero *(Lake Ladoga) l.* Russia **70** F8 61 00N 30 00E
Ladybank Fife Scotland **45** D2 56 17N 3 08W
Ladybower Reservoir Derbyshire England **43** E2 53 23N 1 42W
Ladysmith British Columbia Canada **100** K2 48 57N 123 50W
Ladysmith Republic of South Africa **95** E2 28 34S 29 47E
Ladysmith Wisconsin U.S.A. **104** B3 45 27N 91 07W
Lae Papua New Guinea **86** H8 6 45S 147 00E
Laedalsøyri Norway **67** B3 61 05N 7 15E
La Esmeralda Venezuela **114** D13 3 11N 65 33W
Lafayette Indiana U.S.A. **104** C2 40 25N 86 54W
Lafayette Louisiana U.S.A. **103** G3 30 12N 92 18W
La Fé Cuba **109** H4 22 02N 84 15W
la Flèche France **61** A2 47 42N 0 04W
Lagan *r.* Northern Ireland **49** D1 54 34N 5 58W
Lågen *r.* Norway **67** B3 61 40N 9 45E
Laghouat Algeria **93** F9 33 49N 2 55E
Lago Argentino *l.* Argentina **115** C2 50 10S 72 30W
Lago da Tijuca *l.* Brazil **116** B2 22 59S 43 22W
Lago de Chapala *l.* Mexico **108** D4 20 05N 103 00W
Lago de Itaipu *l.* Brazil **116** C2 22 58S 43 03W
Lago de Maracaibo *l.* Venezuela **114** C14 9 50N 71 30W
Lago de Marapendi *l.* Brazil **116** B1 23 01S 43 24W
Lago de Nicaragua *l.* Nicaragua **109** G2 11 50N 86 00W
Lago de Piratininga *l.* Brazil **116** C2 22 57S 43 05W
Lago de Poopó *l.* Bolivia **114** D9 18 30S 67 20W
Lago di Bolsena *l.* Italy **68** B3 42 00N 12 00E
Lago di Como *l.* Italy **68** A4 46 00N 9 00E
Lago di Garda *l.* Italy **68** B4 45 00N 10 00E
Lago d'Iseo *l.* Italy **61** C2 45 00N 10 00E
Lago do Jacarepaguá *l.* Brazil **116** B2 22 58S 43 23W
Lago Maggiore *l.* Italy **68** A4 46 00N 8 00E
Lago Rodrigo de Freitas *l.* Brazil **116** C2 22 58S 43 13W
Lagos Nigeria **92** C3 6 27N 3 28E
Lagos Portugal **66** A2 37 05N 8 40W
Lagos Island *tn.* Nigeria **92** C3 6 24N 3 28E
Lagos Lagoon Nigeria **92** D3 6 30N 3 33E
Lago Titicaca *l.* Peru/Bolivia **114** C9/D9 16 00S 69 30W
La Grande Oregon U.S.A. **102** C6 45 21N 118 05W
La Grande 2, Réservoir Québec Canada **101** T3 54 00N 77 00W
La Grande 3, Réservoir Québec Canada **101** U3 54 10N 72 30W
La Grande Rivière *r.* Québec Canada **100** U3 59 00N 74 00W
La Grange Georgia U.S.A. **103** I3 33 02N 85 02W
La Guaira Venezuela **114** D15 10 38N 66 55W
Laguna Brazil **115** H7 28 29S 48 45W
Laguna Caratasca *l.* Honduras **109** H3 15 05N 84 00W
Laguna de Perlas *l.* Nicaragua **109** H2 12 30N 83 30W
Laguna Madre *l.* Mexico **108** E4 24 30N 97 30W
Laguna Mar Chiquita *l.* Argentina **115** E6 30 30S 62 30W
Lagunillas Venezuela **114** C15 10 07N 71 16W
La Habana *(Havana)* Cuba **109** H4 23 07N 82 25W
La Habra California U.S.A. **107** C2 33 56N 117 59W
Lahaina Hawaiian Islands **119** Y18 20 23N 156 40W
Lahn *r.* Germany **63** A2 50 00N 8 00E
Lahore Pakistan **77** C6 31 34N 74 22E
Lahr Germany **63** A1 48 21N 7 52E
Lahti Finland **67** F3 61 00N 25 40E

Llangadfan Powys Wales **38** C2 52 41N 3 28W
Llangadog Dyfed Wales **38** C2 51 57N 3 53W
Llangefni Gwynedd Wales **38** B3 53 16N 4 18W
Llangollen Clwyd Wales **38** C2 52 58N 3 10W
Llangurig Powys Wales **38** C2 52 25N 3 36W
Llangynog Powys Wales **38** C2 52 50N 3 25W
Llanharan Mid Glamorgan Wales **38** C1 51 32N 3 28W
Llanidloes Powys Wales **39** C2 52 27N 3 32W
Llanos *geog. reg.* Venezuela **114** D14 7 30N 67 30W
Llanrhystud Dyfed Wales **38** B2 52 18N 4 09W
Llantrisant Mid Glamorgan Wales **38** C1 51 33N 3 23W
Llantwit Major South Glamorgan Wales **38** C1 51 25N 3 39 0W
Llanuwchllyn Gwynedd Wales **38** C2 52 52N 3 41W
Llanwrst Gwynedd Wales **38** C3 53 08N 3 48W
Llanwrtyd Wells Powys Wales **38** C2 52 07N 3 38W
Llanybydder Dyfed Wales **38** B2 52 04N 4 09W
Lleida *see* Lérida
Lleyn Peninsula Gwynedd Wales **38** B2 52 53N 4 30W
Llobregat *r.* Spain **66** C3 42 00N 1 50E
Lloydminster Saskatchewan Canada **100** N3 53 18N 110 00W
Lluchmayor Balearic Islands **66** E4 39 29N 2 53E
Llyn Alaw *l.* Gwynedd Wales **38** B3 53 21N 4 26W
Llyn Celyn *l.* Gwynedd Wales **38** B3 53 04N 4 10W
Llyn Clywedog *l.* Powys Wales **38** C2 52 30N 3 40W
Llyn Tegid *(Lake Bala)* Gwynedd Wales **38** C2 52 53N 3 38W
Llyn Trawsfynydd *l.* Gwynedd Wales **38** C2 52 54N 3 58W
Loanhead Lothian Scotland **45** D1 55 53N 3 09W
Lobatse Botswana **95** E2 25 11S 25 40E
Lobito Angola **95** B5 12 20S 13 34E
Locarno Switzerland **61** C2 46 10N 8 48E
Lochailort *tn.* Highland Scotland **46** C3 56 53N 5 40W
Lochaline *tn.* Highland Scotland **46** C3 56 32N 5 47W
Locharbriggs *tn.* Dumfries & Galloway Scotland **46** E2 55 06N 3 35W
Loch Ard *l.* Central Scotland **45** B2 56 11N 4 28W
Loch Arkaig *l.* Highland Scotland **46** C3 56 58N 5 08W
Loch Awe *l.* Strathclyde Scotland **46** C3 56 15N 5 17W
Lochbuosdale Western Isles Scotland **46** A4 57 09N 7 19W
Loch Bracadale *b.* Highland Scotland **46** B4 57 20N 6 30W
Loch Broom *b.* Highland Scotland **46** C4 57 52N 5 08W
Loch Carron *b.* Highland Scotland **46** C4 57 22N 5 30W
Lochcarron *tn.* Highland Scotland **46** C4 57 24N 5 30W
Loch Cluanie *l.* Highland Scotland **46** C4 57 07N 5 05W
Loch Doon *l.* Strathclyde Scotland **46** D2 55 26N 4 38W
Loch Ell *l.* Highland Scotland **46** C3 56 50N 5 15W
Loch Eriboll *b.* Highland Scotland **46** D5 58 31N 4 41W
Loch Ericht *l.* Scotland **46** D3 56 48N 4 25W
Loches France **61** B2 47 08N 1 00E
Loch Etive *l.* Strathclyde Scotland **46** C3 56 30N 5 10W
Loch Ewe *b.* Highland Scotland **46** C4 57 50N 5 40W
Loch Fannich *l.* Highland Scotland **46** C4/D4 57 40N 5 00W
Loch Fyne *b.* Strathclyde Scotland **46** C3 56 10N 5 05W
Loch Garry *l.* Highland Scotland **46** C4/D4 57 05N 5 00W
Lochgilphead Strathclyde Scotland **46** C3 56 03N 5 26W
Lochinver Highland Scotland **46** C5 58 09N 5 15W
Loch Katrine *l.* Central Scotland **45** A2/B2 56 16N 4 30W
Lochlane Tayside Scotland **45** C2 56 22N 3 52W
Loch Leven *l.* Tayside Scotland **45** D2 56 15N 3 23W
Loch Linnhe *b.* Scotland **46** C3 56 35N 5 25W
Loch Lochy *l.* Highland Scotland **46** D3 56 58N 4 55W
Loch Lomond *l.* Scotland **46** D3 56 10N 4 35W
Loch Long *l.* Strathclyde Scotland **46** D3 56 10N 4 50W
Lochmaben *tn.* Dumfries & Galloway Scotland **46** E2 55 08N 3 27W
Lochmaddy *tn.* Western Isles Scotland **46** A4 57 36N 7 08W
Lochnagar *mt.* Grampian Scotland **46** E3 56 57N 3 16W
Loch Maree *l.* Highland Scotland **46** C4 57 40N 5 30W
Loch Ness *l.* Highland Scotland **46** D4 57 20N 4 30W
Loch Rannoch *l.* Tayside Scotland **46** D3 56 41N 4 18W
Lochranza *tn.* Strathclyde Scotland **46** C2 55 42N 5 18W
Loch Ryan *b.* Scotland **46** C1/C2 55 00N 5 05W
Loch Shiel *l.* Highland Scotland **46** C3 56 45N 5 35W
Loch Shin *l.* Highland Scotland **46** D5 58 05N 4 30W
Loch Snizort *b.* Highland Scotland **46** B4 57 30N 6 30W
Loch Sunart *l.* Highland Scotland **46** C3 56 40N 5 45W
Loch Tay *l.* Tayside Scotland **46** D3 56 31N 4 10W
Loch Torridon *b.* Highland Scotland **46** C4 57 35N 5 46W
Loch Venachor *l.* Central Scotland **45** B2 56 13N 4 18W
Lochwinnoch Strathclyde Scotland **45** A1 55 48N 4 39W
Lockerbie Dumfries & Galloway Scotland **46** E2 55 07N 3 22W
Lockhart Texas U.S.A. **103** G2 29 54N 97 41W
Lock Haven Pennsylvania U.S.A. **105** E2 41 09N 77 28W
Lockport New York U.S.A. **105** E3 43 11N 78 39W
Locks Heath Hampshire England **32** A1 50 52N 1 17W
Lod Israel **78** O10 31 57N 34 54E
Loddon Norfolk England **33** D3 52 32N 1 29E
Lodi India **76** L4 28 35N 77 13E
Łódź Poland **69** C3 51 49N 19 28E
Lofoten Islands Norway **67** C4 68 30N 15 00E
Lofthouse Gate West Yorkshire England **43** F3 53 44N 1 30W
Loftus Cleveland England **44** D1 54 33N 0 53W
Logan Utah U.S.A. **102** D5 41 45N 111 50W
Logan West Virginia U.S.A. **105** D1 37 52N 82 00W
Logan, Mount Yukon Territory Canada **100** G5 60 34N 140 25W
Logansport Indiana U.S.A. **104** C2 40 45N 86 25W
Loghgelly Fife Scotland **45** D2 56 08N 3 19W
Logone *r.* Chad **94** B10 11 00N 15 00E
Logroño Spain **66** B3 42 28N 2 26W
Loir *r.* France **61** B2 47 45N 0 35E
Loire *r.* France **61** A2 47 20N 1 20W
Loja Ecuador **114** B12 3 59S 79 16W
Loja Spain **66** B2 37 10N 4 09W
Lokan tekojärvi *l.* Finland **67** F4 68 00N 27 30E
Lokeren Belgium **64** C3 51 06N 3 59E
Lokoja Nigeria **93** G3 7 49N 6 44E
Lol *r.* Sudan **94** E9 9 00N 28 00E
Lolland *i.* Denmark **67** C1 54 45N 12 20E
Lololda Indonesia **80** H4 1 39N 127 37E
Lomami *r.* Zaïre **95** E6 5 30S 25 30E
Lomblen *i.* Indonesia **80** G2 8 00S 123 30E
Lombok *i.* Indonesia **80** F2 8 29S 116 40E
Lomé Togo **93** F4 6 10N 1 21E
Lomela *r.* Zaïre **94** D7 3 00S 23 00E
Lomela Zaïre **94** D7 2 19S 23 15E
Lomme France **64** B2 50 38N 2 59E
Lommel Belgium **64** E3 51 14N 5 19E
Lomond Hills Tayside/Fife Scotland **45** D2 56 15N 3 15W
Lomonosov Ridge Arctic Ocean **120** 87 00N 60 00W
Lomza Poland **69** D3 53 11N 22 04E
London Ontario Canada **105** D2 42 58N 81 15W
London England United Kingdom **29** K3 51 30N 0 10W
London Colney Hertfordshire England **34** C3 51 44N 0 18W
Londonderry Northern Ireland **48** D4 54 59N 7 19W
Londrina Brazil **115** G8 23 18S 51 13W
Long Beach *beach* New Jersey U.S.A. **105** F1 39 00N 74 00W
Long Beach *tn.* California U.S.A. **107** B2 33 47N 118 15W
Long Beach *tn.* New York U.S.A. **106** D1 40 35N 73 40W
Longbenton Tyne and Wear England **44** C2 55 02N 1 35W
Longbow Corners Ontario Canada **104** B3 49 48N 94 13W
Long Branch New Jersey U.S.A. **103** L5 40 17N 73 59W
Longbridge West Midlands England **35** C2 52 04N 1 58W
Long Crendon Buckinghamshire England **33** A2 51 47N 1 01W
Long Eaton Derbyshire England **35** E3 52 54N 1 15W
Longford *co.* Irish Republic **48** D3 53 40N 7 50W
Longford Longford Irish Republic **48** D3 53 44N 7 47W
Longhorsely Northumberland England **44** C2 55 15N 1 46W
Longhoughton Northumberland England **44** C2 55 26N 1 36W
Long Island New York U.S.A. **105** F2 41 00N 72 00W
Long Island City New York U.S.A. **106** C2 40 46N 73 55W
Long Island The Bahamas **109** J4 23 20N 75 00W
Long Island Sound U.S.A. **105** F2 41 00N 73 00W
Long Itchington Warwickshire England **35** D1 52 17N 1 24W
Longjumeau France **60** B1 48 41N 2 18E
Longlac Ontario Canada **104** C3 49 47N 86 34W
Long Lake Ontario Canada **104** C3 49 00N 87 00W
Long Lawford Warwickshire England **35** E2 52 23N 1 19W
Long Melford Suffolk England **33** C3 52 05N 0 43E
Long Mynd *sum.* Shropshire England **36** B2 52 32N 2 52W
Long Point Ontario Canada **105** D2 42 33N 80 04W
Long Preston North Yorkshire England **42** D4 54 02N 2 15W
Long Range Mountains Newfoundland Canada **101** X3 50 00N 57 00W
Longreach Australia **86** G5 23 30S 144 15E
Longridge Lancashire England **42** C3 53 51N 2 36W
Long Sutton Lincolnshire England **36** E2 52 47N 0 08E
Longton Lancashire England **42** B3 53 44N 2 48W
Longton Staffordshire England **35** B3 52 59N 2 08W
Longtown Cumbria England **44** B2 55 01N 2 58W
Longuyon France **61** C2 49 27N 5 36E
Longview Texas U.S.A. **103** H3 32 30N 94 45W
Longview Washington U.S.A. **105** B6 46 08N 122 56W
Longwy France **61** C2 49 32N 5 46E
Lons-le-Saunier France **61** C2 46 41N 5 33E
Looe Cornwall England **30** C2 51 21N 4 27W
Loop Head *c.* Irish Republic **48** B2 52 30N 9 55W
Loosdrechtse Plassen *l.* Netherlands **65** E2 52 11N 5 04E
Lop Nur *l.* China **81** D6 40 15N 90 20E
Lopez, Cape Gabon **93** G2 0 36S 8 45E
Lopphavet *sd.* Norway **67** E5 70 30N 21 00E
Lorain Ohio U.S.A. **105** D2 41 28N 82 11W
Lorca Spain **66** B2 37 40N 1 41W
Lord Howe Rise Pacific Ocean **118** G5 27 30S 162 00E
Lorica Colombia **109** I1 9 14N 75 50W
Lorient France **61** A2 47 45N 3 21W
Lörrach Germany **63** A1 47 37N 7 40E
Los Alamos New Mexico U.S.A. **102** E4 35 52N 106 19W
Los Angeles California U.S.A. **107** A3 34 00N 118 15W
Los Angeles Chile **115** C5 37 28S 72 23W
Los Angeles River California U.S.A. **107** B2 33 50N 118 13W
Los Mochis Mexico **108** C5 25 48N 109 00W
Losser Netherlands **64** G4 52 16N 7 01E
Lossiemouth Grampian Scotland **46** E4 57 43N 3 18W
Los Teques Venezuela **114** D15 10 25N 67 01W
Lostock Gralam Cheshire England **42** C1 53 16N 2 28W
Lostwithiel Cornwall England **30** C2 50 25N 4 40W
Lot *r.* France **61** B1 44 35N 1 10E
Lothian *reg.* Scotland **46** E2 55 50N 3 20W
Lotta *r.* Russia **67** F4 68 50N 29 00E
Loubomo Congo **95** B7 4 09S 12 47E
Loudéac France **61** A2 48 11N 2 45W
Loudwater Buckinghamshire England **34** A2 51 37N 0 43W
Lough Allen *l.* Irish Republic **48** D4 54 15N 8 00W
Lough Arrow *l.* Irish Republic **48** C4 54 05N 8 15W
Lough Beg *l.* Northern Ireland **49** C1 54 48N 6 16W
Loughborough Leicestershire England **36** C2 52 47N 1 11W
Lough Carra *l.* Irish Republic **48** B3 53 45N 9 15W
Lough Conn *l.* Irish Republic **48** B4 54 05N 9 10W
Lough Corrib *l.* Irish Republic **48** B3 53 10N 9 10W
Lough Derg *l.* Donegal Irish Republic **48** D4 54 35N 7 55W
Lough Derg *l.* Irish Republic **48** C2 52 55N 8 15W
Lough Foyle *b.* Ireland **48** D5 55 10N 7 10W
Lough Gara *l.* Irish Republic **48** C3 53 55N 8 30W
Lough Gill *l.* Irish Republic **48** C4 54 15N 8 25W
Lough Key *l.* Irish Republic **48** C4 54 00N 8 10W
Loughlinstown Dublin Irish Republic **49** B1 53 14N 6 08W
Lough Mask *l.* Irish Republic **48** B3 53 40N 9 30W
Lough Melvin *l.* Ireland **48** C4 54 25N 8 05W
Lough Neagh *l.* Northern Ireland **48** E4 54 35N 6 30W
Loughor *r.* West Glamorgan Wales **38** B1 51 35N 4 25W
Lough Oughter *l.* Irish Republic **48** D4 54 00N 7 30W
Loughrea *tn.* Galway Irish Republic **48** C3 53 12N 8 34W
Lough Ree *l.* Irish Republic **48** D3 53 35N 8 00W
Lough Swilly *b.* Irish Republic **48** D5 55 20N 7 35W
Loughton Essex England **34** D2 51 39N 0 03E
Louisiade Archipelago *is.* Papua New Guinea **86** I7 12 00S 153 00E
Louisiana *state* U.S.A. **103** H3 32 00N 92 00W
Louis Trichardt Republic of South Africa **95** E3 23 01S 29 43E
Louisville Kentucky U.S.A. **104** C1 38 13N 85 48W
Lound Nottinghamshire England **43** H2 53 22N 0 57W
Lourdes France **61** A1 43 06N 0 02W
Louth *co.* Irish Republic **48** E3 53 55N 6 25W
Louth Lincolnshire England **36** D3 53 22N 0 01W
Louvain *see* Leuven
Louviers France **61** B2 49 13N 1 11E
Low Eggborough North Yorkshire England **43** G3 53 43N 0 09W
Lowell Massachusetts U.S.A. **105** F2 42 38N 71 19W
Lower Bay New York U.S.A. **106** B1 40 32N 74 04W
Lower Hutt New Zealand **87** B2 41 12S 174 54E
Lower Lough Erne *l.* Northern Ireland **48** D4 54 25N 7 45W
Lower Nazeing Essex England **34** D3 51 44N 0 01E
Lower Red Lake Minnesota U.S.A. **104** B3 48 00N 95 00W
Lower Tunguska *see* Nizhnyaya Tunguska
Lowestoft Suffolk England **33** D3 52 29N 1 45E
Lowick Northumberland England **44** C2 55 38N 1 58W
Lowicz Poland **69** C3 52 06N 19 55E
Lowther Hills Scotland **46** E2 55 25N 3 45W
Lowville New York U.S.A. **105** E2 43 47N 75 30W
Lualaba *r.* Zaïre **95** E7 4 00S 26 30E
Luanda Angola **95** B6 8 50S 13 15E
Luang Prabang Laos **80** C7 19 53N 102 10E
Luangwa *r.* Zambia **95** F5 12 00S 32 30E
Luanshya Zambia **95** E5 13 09S 28 24E
Luarca Spain **66** A3 43 33N 6 31W
Luau Angola **95** D5 10 42S 22 12E
Lubango Angola **95** B5 14 55S 13 30E
Lubbock Texas U.S.A. **102** F3 33 35N 101 53W
Lübeck Germany **63** B2 53 52N 10 40E
Lübeck Bay Europe **63** B2 54 00N 11 00E
Lubilash *r.* Zaïre **95** D6 4 00S 24 00E
Lublin Poland **69** D3 51 18N 22 31E
Lubumbashi Zaïre **95** E5 11 41S 27 29E
Lucan Dublin Irish Republic **49** A2 53 22N 6 27W
Lucea Jamaica **109** P8 18 26N 78 11W
Luce Bay Dumfries & Galloway Scotland **46** D1 54 47N 4 50W
Lucena Spain **66** B2 37 25N 4 29W
Luckenwalde Germany **63** B2 52 05N 13 11E
Lucknow India **77** E5 26 50N 80 54E
Lucusse Angola **95** D5 12 38S 20 52E
Lüdenscheid Germany **63** A2 51 13N 7 38E
Lüderitz Namibia **95** C2 26 38S 15 10E
Ludgershal Wiltshire England **31** F3 51 16N 1 37W
Ludhiana India **77** D6 30 56N 75 52E
Ludington Michigan U.S.A. **104** C2 43 58N 86 27W
Ludlow Shropshire England **36** B2 52 22N 2 43W
Ludvika Sweden **67** D3 60 08N 15 14E
Ludwigsburg Germany **63** A1 48 54N 9 12E
Ludwigshafen Germany **63** A1 49 29N 8 27E
Ludwigslust Germany **63** B2 53 20N 11 30E
Luena Angola **95** C5 11 47S 19 52E
Lufkin Texas U.S.A. **103** H3 31 21N 94 47W
Luga *r.* Russia **67** F2 59 10N 29 30E
Luga Russia **67** F2 58 42N 29 49E
Lugano Switzerland **61** C2 46 01N 8 57E
Lugansk *(Voroshilovgrad)* Ukraine **70** F5 48 35N 39 20E
Lugnaquillia *mt.* Wicklow Irish Republic **48** E2 52 58N 6 27W
Lugo Spain **66** A3 43 00N 7 33W
Lugoj Romania **69** D2 45 41N 21 57E
Lugton Strathclyde Scotland **45** A1 55 45N 4 32W
Luguoqiao China **82** F1 39 51N 116 13E
Luiana *r.* Angola **95** D4 17 00S 21 00E
Lukens, Mount California U.S.A. **107** B1 34 16N 118 14W
Luków Poland **69** D3 51 57N 22 21E
Lukunga *r.* Zaïre **92** A1 4 23S 15 13E
Luleå Sweden **67** E4 65 35N 22 10E
Lule älv *r.* Sweden **67** E4 66 15N 20 30E
Lüleburgaz Turkey **68** E3 41 25N 27 22E
Lulua *r.* Zaïre **95** D6 9 00S 22 00E
Lumberton North Carolina U.S.A. **103** K3 34 37N 79 03W
Lumbres France **64** B2 50 43N 2 07E
Lunan Bay Tayside Scotland **46** F3 56 39N 2 28W
Lund Sweden **67** C2 55 42N 13 10E
Lundy *i.* Devon England **30** C3 51 11N 4 40W
Lune *r.* Lancashire England **40** B3 54 07N 2 40W
Lüneburg Germany **63** B2 53 15N 10 24E
Lüneburger Heide *(Lüneburg Heath) heath* Germany **63** A2 53 00N 10 00E
Lüneburg Heath *see* Lüneburger Heide
Lünen Germany **62** D3 51 38N 7 31E
Lunenburg Nova Scotia Canada **101** W1 44 23N 64 21W
Lunéville France **61** C2 48 35N 6 30E
Lungue Bungo *r.* Angola/Zambia **95** D5 13 00S 22 00E
Luni *r.* India **77** C5 26 00N 73 00E
Luninets Belarus **69** E3 52 18N 26 50E
Luoshan China **81** H4 32 12N 114 30E
Luoyang China **81** H4 34 47N 112 26E
Lurgan Armagh Northern Ireland **48** E4 54 28N 6 20W
Lurio *r.* Mozambique **95** G5 14 00S 39 00E
Lusaka Zambia **95** E4 15 26S 28 20E
Lusambo Zaïre **95** D7 4 59S 23 26E
Lushun China **81** J5 38 46N 121 15E
Lusk Dublin Irish Republic **48** E3 53 32N 6 10W
Luton Bedfordshire England **34** B3 51 53N 0 25W
Lutsk Ukraine **69** E3 50 42N 25 15E
Lutterworth Leicestershire England **36** C2 52 28N 1 10W
Lützow-Holm Bay Antarctica **121** 69 00S 38 00E
Luuq Somalia **94** H8 2 52N 42 34E
LUXEMBOURG **64** F1
Luxembourg *admin.* Belgium **64** E1 49 55N 5 15E
Luxembourg Luxembourg **64** F1 49 37N 6 08E
Luxor Egypt **78** D4 25 41N 32 24E
Luzern Switzerland **61** C2 47 03N 8 17E
Luzhou China **81** G3 28 55N 105 25E
Luziânia Brazil **114** H9 16 16S 47 57W
Luzon *i.* The Philippines **80** G7 16 30N 121 30E
Luzon Strait China/Philippines **80** G8 20 00N 121 30E
L'vov Ukraine **70** E5 49 50N 24 00E
Lybster Highland Scotland **46** E5 58 18N 3 13W
Lycksele Sweden **67** D3 64 34N 18 40E
Lydd Kent England **33** C1 50 57N 0 55E
Lydham Shropshire England **36** B2 52 31N 2 59W
Lydiate Merseyside England **42** B2 53 33N 2 59W
Lydney Gloucestershire England **31** E3 51 43N 2 32W
Lyme Bay Devon/Dorset England **31** E2 50 40N 2 55W
Lyme Regis Dorset England **31** E2 50 44N 2 57W
Lyminge Kent England **33** D2 51 08N 1 05E
Lymington Hampshire England **32** A1 50 46N 1 33W
Lymm Cheshire England **42** C2 53 23N 2 28W
Lyna *r.* Europe **69** D3 54 00N 20 00E
Lynchburg Virginia U.S.A. **105** E1 37 24N 79 09W
Lyndhurst Hampshire England **32** A1 50 52N 1 34W
Lyne *r.* Cumbria England **44** B2 55 02N 2 40W
Lynher *r.* Cornwall England **30** C2 50 35N 4 25W
Lynmouth Devon England **31** D3 51 15N 3 50W
Lynn Massachusetts U.S.A. **105** F2 42 29N 70 57W
Lynn Lake *tn.* Manitoba Canada **101** O4 56 51N 101 01W
Lynton Devon England **31** D3 51 15N 3 50W
Lyon France **61** B2 45 46N 4 50E
Lyon *r.* Tayside Scotland **46** D3 56 37N 4 05W
Lyons New York U.S.A. **105** E2 43 04N 76 59W
Lys *r.* France **61** B3 50 40N 2 30E
Lytham Lancashire England **42** B3 53 45N 2 59W
Lytham St. Anne's Lancashire England **42** A3 53 45N 3 01W
Lyttelton New Zealand **87** B2 43 36S 172 42E
Lytton British Columbia Canada **100** K3 50 12N 121 34W
Lyublino Russia **70** M1 55 38N 37 44E

M

Ma'ān Jordan **78** O10 30 11N 35 43E
Maanselka *geog. reg.* Finland **67** F4 68 45N 25 10E
Ma'anshan China **81** I4 31 49N 118 32E
Maarssen Netherlands **65** E2 52 07N 5 04E
Maas *r.* Netherlands **64** E3 51 50N 5 32E
Maasmechelen Belgium **64** E2 50 58N 5 40E
Maassluis Netherlands **65** B1 51 56N 4 15E
Maastricht Netherlands **64** E2 50 51N 5 42E
Maasvlakte Netherlands **65** A1 51 57N 4 06E
Mabalane Mozambique **95** F3 23 51S 32 38E
Mabashi Japan **83** C4 35 48N 139 55E
Mablethorpe Lincolnshire England **36** E3 53 21N 0 15E
McAlester Oklahoma U.S.A. **103** G3 34 56N 95 46W
McAllen Texas U.S.A. **103** G2 26 13N 98 15W
Macao *territory* Portugal **81** H2 22 10N 113 40E
Macapá Brazil **114** G13 0 04N 51 04W
Macbride Head Falkland Islands **117** M16 51 25S 57 55W
Macclesfield Cheshire England **42** D1 53 16N 2 07W
Macclesfield Canal England **42** D1 53 19N 2 05W
McClintock Channel Northwest Territories Canada **101** O7 72 00N 102 30W
McComb Mississippi U.S.A. **103** H3 31 13N 90 29W
McCook Nebraska U.S.A. **102** F5 40 13N 100 35W
Macdonnell Ranges *mts.* Australia **86** E5 24 00S 132 30E
Macduff Grampian Scotland **46** F4 57 40N 2 29W
Maceió Brazil **114** J11 9 40S 35 44W
MACEDONIA **68** D3
Macerata Italy **68** B3 43 18N 13 27E
Macgillycuddy's Reeks *mts.* Irish Republic **48** B1 51 55N 9 50W
McGrath Alaska U.S.A. **100** D5 62 58N 155 40W
Machakos Kenya **94** G7 1 32S 27 16E
Machala Ecuador **114** B12 3 20S 79 57W
Machanga Mozambique **95** F3 20 58N 35 01E
Machida Japan **83** A3 35 32N 139 27E
Machilipatnam India **77** E3 16 12N 81 11E
Machiques Venezuela **114** C15 10 04N 72 37W
Machrihanish Strathclyde Scotland **46** C2 55 26N 5 44W
Machynlleth Powys Wales **38** C2 52 35N 3 51W
Mackay Australia **86** H5 21 10S 149 10E
Mackay, Lake Australia **86** D5 22 30S 128 00E
Mckeesport Pennsylvania U.S.A. **105** E2 40 21N 79 52W
Mackenzie *r.* Northwest Territories Canada **100** K5 61 30N 120 00W
Mackenzie Bay Yukon Territory Canada **100** H6 69 45N 137 30W
Mackenzie Mountains Yukon Territory/Northwest Territories Canada **100** I6 66 00N 132 00W
Mackinaw City Michigan U.S.A. **105** D3 45 47N 84 43W
McKinley, Mount Alaska U.S.A. **100** E5 62 02N 151 01W
McKinney Texas U.S.A. **103** G3 33 14N 96 37W
Macleod, Lake Australia **86** A5 24 00S 113 30E
McMurdo *r.s.* Antarctica **121** 77 51S 166 40E
McMurdo Sound Antarctica **121** 75 00S 165 00E
Mâcon France **61** B2 46 18N 4 50E
Macon Georgia U.S.A. **103** J3 32 49N 83 37W
Macon Missouri U.S.A. **104** B1 39 44N 92 27W
McPherson Kansas U.S.A. **103** G4 38 22N 97 41W
Macquarie Islands Southern Ocean **118** F2 54 29S 158 58E
Macquarie Ridge Southern Ocean **118** F2 55 00S 160 00E
Macroom Cork Irish Republic **48** C1 51 54N 8 57W
Mādāba Jordan **78** O10 31 44N 35 48E
MADAGASCAR **95** I3
Madang Papua New Guinea **86** H8 5 14S 145 45E
Madawaska Ontario Canada **105** E3 45 31N 77 59W
Maddiston Central Scotland **45** C1 55 58N 3 42W
Madeira Islands Atlantic Ocean **93** B9 32 45N 17 00W
Madeley Staffordshire England **35** A3 52 39N 2 28W
Madhya *admin.* India **77** D4 23 00N 78 30E
Madhyamgram India **76** K2 22 41N 88 27E
Madīnat ash Sha'b Yemen Republic **79** F1 12 50N 44 56E
Madison Indiana U.S.A. **104** C1 38 46N 85 22W
Madison Wisconsin U.S.A. **104** C2 43 04N 89 22W
Madison Heights *tn.* Virginia U.S.A. **105** E1 37 26N 79 08W
Madium Indonesia **80** E2 7 37S 111 33E
Madoc Ontario Canada **105** E2 44 30N 77 29W
Mado Gashi Kenya **94** G8 0 45N 39 11E
Madras India **77** E2 13 05N 80 18E
Madrid Spain **66** B3 40 25N 3 43W
Madura *i.* Indonesia **80** E2 7 10S 113 30E
Madurai India **77** D1 9 55N 78 07E
Madureira Brazil **116** B2 22 52S 43 21W
Maebashi Japan **82** C2 36 24N 139 04E
Maesteg Mid Glamorgan Wales **38** C1 51 37N 3 40W
Maevantanana Madagascar **95** I4 16 57S 46 50E
Mafia Island Tanzania **95** G6 7 00S 39 00E
Mafikeng Republic of South Africa **95** E2 25 53S 25 39E
Mafraq Jordan **78** P11 32 20N 36 12E
Magadan Russia **71** R7 59 38N 150 50E
Magangué Colombia **114** C14 9 14N 74 46W
Magdalena Mexico **108** B6 30 38N 110 59W
Magdalena del Mar Peru **116** E4 12 06S 77 04W
Magdeburg Germany **63** B2 52 08N 11 37E
Magé Brazil **116** C3 22 40S 43 03W
Magee, Island Northern Ireland **48** F4 54 45N 5 50W
Magelang Indonesia **80** E2 7 28S 110 11E
Maghâgha Egypt **78** D4 28 39N 30 50E
Maghera Northern Ireland **48** E4 54 51N 6 40W
Magherafelt Northern Ireland **48** E4 54 45N 6 36W
Magheragall Northern Ireland **49** C1 54 31N 6 07W
Maghull Merseyside England **42** B2 55 32N 2 57W
Magnitogorsk Russia **70** H6 53 28N 59 06E
Magog Québec Canada **105** F3 45 16N 72 09W
Magwe Myanmar **77** G3 20 08N 94 55E
Mahaded Hills India **77** D4 22 30N 78 30E
Mahajanga Madagascar **95** I4 15 40S 46 20E
Mahanadi *r.* India **77** E4 21 00N 84 00E
Maharashtra *admin.* India **77** C3/D3 19 30N 75 00E
Mahdia Tunisia **68** B2 35 29N 11 03E
Mahia Peninsula New Zealand **87** C3 39 10S 138 00E
Mahón Balearic Islands **66** F4 39 54N 4 15E
Mahrauli India **76** L4 28 30N 77 11E
Maidenhead Berkshire England **34** A2 51 32N 0 44W
Maiden Newton Dorset England **31** E2 50 46N 2 35W
Maidstone Kent England **33** C2 51 17N 0 32E
Maiduguri Nigeria **93** H5 11 53N 13 16E
Maikala Range *mts.* India **77** E4 22 30N 81 30E
Main *r.* Germany **63** A2 50 00N 8 00E
Main Channel Ontario Canada **105** D3 45 00N 82 00W
Mainland *i.* Orkney Islands Scotland **47** D1 59 00N 3 15W
Mainland *i.* Shetland Islands Scotland **47** B2 60 15N 1 20W
Maintirano Madagascar **95** H4 18 01S 44 03E

Mainz Germany **63** A1 50 00N 8 16E
Maiquetia Venezuela **114** D15 10 38N 66 59W
Maisons-Laffitte France **60** A2 48 57N 2 09E
Maitland Australia **86** I3 32 33S 151 33E
Maizuru Japan **82** C2 35 30N 135 20E
Majene Indonesia **80** F3 3 33S 118 59E
Maji Ethiopia **94** G9 6 12N 35 32E
Majiuqiao China **82** H1 39 45N 116 33E
Majorca *see* Mallorca
Makassar Strait Indonesia **80** F3/F4 2 00S 117 30E
Makélékélé Congo **92** A2 4 18S 15 14E
Makeni Sierra Leone **93** C4 8 57N 12 02W
Makgadikgadi Salt Pan Botswana **95** E3 21 00S 26 00E
Makhachkala Russia **70** G4 42 59N 47 30E
Makkah *(Mecca)* Saudi Arabia **78** E3 21 26N 39 49E
Makkovik Newfoundland Canada **101** X4 55 00N 59 10W
Makó Hungary **69** D2 46 11N 20 30E
Makoku Gabon **93** H3 0 38N 12 47E
Makran *geog. reg.* Iran/Pakistan **79** J4 25 55N 61 30E
Makurdi Nigeria **93** G4 7 44N 8 35E
Malabar Coast India **77** C2–D1 74 00E 12 00N
Malabo Equatorial Guinea **93** G3 3 45N 8 48E
Malacca, Strait of Indonesia/Malaysia **80** B5–C4
Málaga Spain **66** B2 36 43N 4 25W
Malahide Dublin Irish Republic **49** B2 53 27N 6 09W
Malaita *i.* Solomon Islands **86** K8 9 00S 161 00E
Malakal Sudan **94** F9 9 31N 31 40E
Malang Indonesia **80** E2 7 59S 112 45E
Malanje Angola **95** C6 9 32S 16 20E
Mälaren *(Lake Mälar) l.* Sweden **67** D2 59 30N 17 00E
Mälar, Lake *see* Mälaren
Malartic Québec Canada **105** E3 48 09N 78 09W
Malatya Turkey **78** E6 38 22N 38 18E
MALAWI **95** F5
Malawi, Lake *see* Nyasa, Lake
Malaya *admin.* Malaysia **80** C4 4 00N 102 30E
Malay Peninsula Asia **72** 5 00N 102 00E
MALAYSIA **80** C5–E5
Mal Bay Irish Republic **48** B2 52 40N 9 30W
Malbork Poland **69** C3 54 02N 19 01E
Maldegem Belgium **64** C3 51 12N 3 27E
Malden Island Pacific Ocean **119** K7 4 03S 154 59W
Maldive Archipelago *is.* Indian Ocean **72** 5 00N 73 00E
MALDIVES **77** C1
Maldon Essex England **33** C2 51 45N 0 40E
Maldonado Uruguay **115** G6 34 57S 54 59W
Malegaon India **77** C4 20 32N 74 38E
Malekula *i.* Vanuatu **86** L6 16 30S 167 20E
Malema Mozambique **95** G5 14 57S 37 25E
Malham North Yorkshire England **43** D4 54 04N 2 09W
MALI **93** E6
Malines *see* Mechelen
Malin Head *c.* Irish Republic **48** D5 55 30N 7 20W
Mallaig Highland Scotland **46** C4 57 00N 5 50W
Mallawi Egypt **78** D4 27 44N 30 50E
Mallorca *(Majorca) i.* Balearic Islands **66** E4 39 50N 2 30E
Mallow Cork Irish Republic **48** C2 52 08N 8 39W
Malmédy Belgium **64** F2 50 26N 6 02E
Malmesbury Republic of South Africa **95** C1 33 28S 18 43E
Malmesbury Wiltshire England **31** E3 51 36N 2 06W
Malmö Sweden **67** C2 55 35N 13 00E
Malone New York U.S.A. **105** F2 44 52N 74 19W
Malonga Zaïre **95** D5 10 26S 23 10E
Måløy Norway **67** B3 61 57N 5 06E
Malpelo *i.* Colombia **114** A13 4 00N 81 35W
MALTA **68** B2
Malta *i.* Mediterranean Sea **68** B2 35 00N 14 00E
Malta Montana U.S.A. **102** E6 48 22N 107 51W
Maltby South Yorkshire England **43** G2 53 26N 1 11W
Malton North Yorkshire England **40** D3 54 08N 0 48W
Maluku *is.* Indonesia **80** H3 1 00S 127 00E
Malvern Hills Hereford and Worcester England **36** B2 52 05N 2 22W
Malviya Nagar India **76** L4 28 32N 77 12E
Mamanutha Group *is.* Fiji **118** T16 17 40S 177 00E
Mamaroneck New York U.S.A. **106** D2 40 57N 73 43W
Mambasa Zaïre **94** E8 1 20N 29 05E
Man Côte d'Ivoire **93** D4 7 31N 7 37W
Manacapuru Brazil **114** E12 3 16S 60 37W
Manacor Balearic Islands **66** E4 39 35N 3 12E
Manado Indonesia **80** G4 1 32N 124 55E
Managua Nicaragua **109** G2 12 06N 86 18W
Manali India **77** D6 32 12N 77 06E
Manaus Brazil **114** F12 3 06S 60 00W
Manchester Connecticut U.S.A. **105** F2 41 47N 72 31W
Manchester Greater Manchester England **42** D2 53 30N 2 15W
Manchester Kentucky U.S.A. **105** D1 37 09N 83 46W
Manchester New Hampshire U.S.A. **105** F2 42 59N 71 28W
Manchester Tennessee U.S.A. **103** I4 35 29N 86 04W
Mancot Clwyd Wales **42** A1 53 12N 3 01W
Mandal Norway **67** B2 58 02N 7 30E
Mandalay Myanmar **81** E2 21 57N 96 04E
Mandeville Jamaica **109** Q8 18 02N 77 31W
Mandvi India **76** B4 22 50N 69 25E
Mandya India **77** D2 12 34N 76 55E
Manfredonia Italy **68** C3 41 37N 15 55E
Mangalore India **77** C2 12 54N 74 51E
Mango *i.* Fiji **118** V16 17 20S 179 20W
Mangoky *r.* Madagascar **95** H3 22 00S 45 00E
Mangotsfield Avon England **31** E3 51 29N 2 31W
Mangu *r.* Zaïre **92** B1 4 25S 15 25E
Mangui China **81** J8 52 05N 122 17E
Manhasset New York U.S.A. **106** D2 40 48N 73 41W
Manhattan Kansas U.S.A. **104** A1 39 11N 96 35W
Manhattan New York U.S.A. **106** C2 40 48N 73 58W
Manhattan Beach *tn.* California U.S.A. **107** A2 33 53N 118 24W
Mania *r.* Madagascar **95** I4 19 30S 50 30E
Manica Mozambique **95** F4 18 56S 32 52E
Manicoré Brazil **114** E11 5 48S 61 16W
Manicouagan Québec Canada **101** V3 50 40N 68 45W
Manicouagan *r.* Québec Canada **105** G4 50 00N 69 00W
Manicouagan, Réservoir Québec Canada **101** V3 51 20N 69 00W
Manikpur India **76** J2 22 32N 88 12E
Manila The Philippines **80** G6 14 37N 120 58E
Manipur *admin.* India **77** G4 24 30N 94 00E
Manipur *r.* Myanmar/India **77** G4 23 30N 93 00E
Manisa Turkey **68** E2 38 36N 27 29E
Manistee Michigan U.S.A. **104** C2 44 14N 86 20W
Manistee *r.* Michigan U.S.A. **104** C2 45 00N 85 00W
Manistique Michigan U.S.A. **104** C3 45 58N 86 17W
Manitoba *province* Canada **101** P4 55 15N 100 00W
Manitoba, Lake Manitoba Canada **101** P3 50 30N 98 15W
Manitoulin Island Ontario Canada **105** D3 46 00N 82 00W
Manitowoc Wisconsin U.S.A. **104** C2 44 04N 87 40W
Maniwaki Québec Canada **105** E3 46 22N 75 58W
Manizales Colombia **114** B13 5 03N 75 32W
Manjra *r.* India **77** D3 18 30N 76 00E
Mankato Minnesota U.S.A. **104** B2 44 10N 94 00W
Mannar Sri Lanka **77** D1 8 58N 79 54E
Mannar, Gulf of India / Sri Lanka 8 30N 79 00E
Mannheim Germany **63** A1 49 30N 8 28E
Manning Alberta Canada **100** L4 56 53N 117 39W
Manningtree Essex England **33** D2 51 57N 1 04E
Manokwari Indonesia **80** I3 0 53S 134 05E
Manorhamilton Leitrim Irish Republic **48** C4 54 18N 8 10W
Manotick Ontario Canada **105** E3 45 10N 75 45W
Manresa Spain **66** C3 41 43N 1 50E
Mansa Zambia **95** E5 11 10S 28 52E
Mansel Island Northwest Territories Canada **101** S5 62 00N 80 00W
Mansfield Nottinghamshire England **36** C3 53 09N 1 11W
Mansfield Ohio U.S.A. **105** D2 40 46N 82 31W
Mansfield Pennsylvania U.S.A. **105** E2 41 47N 77 05W
Mansfield Woodhouse Nottinghamshire England **36** C3 53 10N 1 11W
Manta Ecuador **114** B12 0 59S 80 44W
Mantes-la-Jolie France **61** B2 48 59N 1 43E
Mantova Italy **68** B4 45 10N 10 47E
Manukau Harbour New Zealand **87** B3 37 00S 174 30E
Manyoni Tanzania **95** F6 5 46S 34 50E
Manzanares Spain **66** B2 39 00N 3 23W
Manzanillo Cuba **109** I4 20 21N 77 21W
Manzanillo Mexico **108** D3 19 00N 104 20W
Manzhouli China **81** I7 49 36N 117 28E
Maoming China **81** H2 21 50N 110 56E
Maple Creek *tn.* Saskatchewan Canada **100** N2 49 55N 109 28W
Maputo Mozambique **95** F2 25 58S 32 35E
Marabá Brazil **114** H11 5 23S 49 10W
Maracaibo Venezuela **114** C15 10 44N 71 37W
Maracay Venezuela **114** D15 10 20N 67 28W
Maradi Niger **93** G5 13 29N 7 10E
Marais Poitevin *marsh* France **61** A2 46 22N 1 06W
Maramba *(Livingstone)* Zambia **95** E4 17 50S 25 53E
Maranhão *admin.* Brazil **114** H11 5 20S 46 00W
Marathon Ontario Canada **104** C3 48 44N 86 23W
Marazion Cornwall England **30** B2 50 07N 5 29W
Marbella Spain **66** B2 36 31N 4 53W
Marble Bar *tn.* Australia **86** B5 21 16S 119 45E
Marble Canyon *tn.* Arizona U.S.A. **102** D4 36 50N 111 38W
Marburg Germany **63** A2 50 49N 8 36E
March Cambridgeshire England **33** C3 52 33N 0 06E
Marche-en-Famenne Belgium **64** E2 50 13N 5 21E
Marcus Island Pacific Ocean **118** F10 24 30N 157 30E
Mardan Pakistan **77** C6 34 14N 72 05E
Mar del Plata Argentina **115** F5 38 00S 57 32W
Marden Kent England **33** C2 51 11N 0 30E
Mardin Turkey **78** F6 37 19N 40 43E
Mare *i.* Îles Loyauté **86** L5 22 00S 167 30E
Maresfield East Sussex England **33** C1 51 00N 0 05E
Margai Caka *l.* China **77** F7 35 00N 87 00E
Margam West Glamorgan Wales **38** C1 51 34N 3 44W
Margate Kent England **33** D2 51 24N 1 24E
Maria Elena Chile **115** D8 22 18S 69 40W
Marianas Trench Pacific Ocean **118** E9 16 00N 147 30E
Marian Lake *tn.* Northwest Territories Canada **100** L5 62 55N 115 55W
Mariánské Lázně Ceska Czechoslovakia **63** B1 49 48N 12 45E
Maria van Diemen, Cape New Zealand **87** B4 34 29S 172 39E
Maribor Slovenia **68** C4 46 34N 15 38E
Mariehamn Finland **67** D3 60 05N 19 55E
Mariental Namibia **95** C3 24 36S 17 59E
Marietta Ohio U.S.A. **105** D1 39 26N 81 27W
Marignane France **61** C1 43 25N 5 12E
Marijampole *(Kapsukas)* Lithuania **69** D3 54 31N 23 20E
Marília Brazil **115** G8 22 13S 49 58W
Marina del Rey California U.S.A. **107** A2 33 58N 118 28W
Marinette Wisconsin U.S.A. **104** C3 45 06N 87 38W
Maringá Brazil **115** G8 23 26S 52 02W
Marion Illinois U.S.A. **104** C1 37 42N 88 58W
Marion Indiana U.S.A. **104** C2 40 33N 85 40W
Marion Ohio U.S.A. **105** D2 40 35N 83 08W
Marion, Lake South Carolina U.S.A. **103** J3 33 00N 80 00W
Mariscal Estigarribia Paraguay **115** E8 22 03S 60 35W
Maritsa *r.* Europe **68** E3 41 00N 26 00E
Mariupol *(Zhdanov)* Ukraine **70** F5 47 05N 37 34E
Marjayoun Lebanon **78** O11 33 22N 35 34E
Mark *r.* Belgium **64** D3 51 45N 4 45E
Marka Somalia **94** H8 1 42N 44 47E
Marken *i.* Netherlands **65** E3 52 27N 5 02E
Markermeer *l.* Netherlands **65** E3 52 28N 5 08E
Markerwaard Netherlands **64** E4 52 35N 5 15E
Market Deeping Lincolnshire England **36** D2 52 41N 0 19W
Market Drayton Shropshire England **36** B2 52 54N 2 29W
Market Harborough Leicestershire England **36** D2 52 29N 0 55W
Market Rasen Lincolnshire England **36** D3 53 24N 0 21W
Market Weighton Humberside England **40** D2 53 52N 0 40W
Markfield Leicestershire England **35** E3 52 42N 1 16W
Markha *r.* Russia **71** N8 64 00N 112 30E
Markinch Fife Scotland **45** D2 56 12N 3 09W
Markovo Russia **71** T8 64 40N 170 24E
Markyate Hertfordshire England **34** B3 51 51N 0 28W
Marl Germany **63** A2 51 38N 7 06E
Marlborough Wiltshire England **31** F3 51 26N 1 43W
Marlborough Downs *hills* Wiltshire England **31** F3 51 28N 1 50W
Marlow Buckinghamshire England **33** B2 51 35N 0 48W
Marlpit Hill *tn.* Kent England **34** D1 51 13N 0 04E
Marly-le-Roi France **60** A2 48 52N 2 05E
Marmande France **61** B1 44 30N 0 10E
Marmara, Sea of Turkey **78** C7 15 40N 28 10E
Marne *r.* France **61** B2 49 00N 4 00E
Maroantsetra Madagascar **95** I4 15 23S 49 44E
Maroko Nigeria **92** D3 6 21N 3 32E
Maroni *r.* Surinam **114** G13 4 00N 54 30W
Maroua Cameroon **93** H5 10 35N 14 20E
Marple Greater Manchester England **42** D2 53 24N 2 03W
Marquesas Islands Pacific Ocean **119** M7 10 00S 137 00W
Marquette Michigan U.S.A. **104** C3 46 33N 87 23W
Marrakech Morocco **93** D9 31 49N 8 00W
Marsabit Kenya **94** G8 2 20N 37 59E
Marsala Italy **68** B2 37 48N 12 27E
Marsden West Yorkshire England **43** E2 53 36N 1 55W
Marseille France **61** C1 43 18N 5 22E
Marshall Missouri U.S.A. **104** B1 39 06N 93 11W
MARSHALL ISLANDS **118** G8
Marshalltown Iowa U.S.A. **104** B2 42 05N 92 54W
Marshfield Avon England **31** E3 51 28N 2 19W
Marshfield Wisconsin U.S.A. **104** B2 44 40N 90 11W
Marske-by-the-Sea Cleveland England **44** C1 54 36N 1 01W
Marston Moor North Yorkshire England **43** G3 53 55N 1 15W
Marston Moretaine Bedfordshire England **34** B4 52 04N 0 33W
Marsworth Hertfordshire England **34** A3 51 50N 0 40W
Martaban, Gulf of Myanmar **80** B7 16 00N 97 00E
Martha's Vineyard *i.* Massachusetts U.S.A. **105** F2 41 00N 70 00W
Martigny Switzerland **61** C2 46 07N 7 05E
Martigues France **61** C1 43 24N 5 03E
Martinique *i.* Lesser Antilles **109** L2 14 30N 61 00W
Martin Lake Alabama U.S.A. **103** I3 33 00N 86 00W
Martinsburg West Virginia U.S.A. **105** E1 39 28N 77 59W
Martinsville Indiana U.S.A. **104** C1 39 25N 86 25W
Martinsville Virginia U.S.A. **103** K4 36 43N 79 53W
Martin Vaz *i.* Atlantic Ocean **117** F4 21 00S 27 30W
Martley Hereford & Worcester England **35** A1 52 15N 2 21W
Marton Cheshire England **42** D1 53 12N 2 14W
Marton New Zealand **87** C2 40 04S 175 25E
Marvejols France **61** B1 44 33N 3 18E
Mary U.S.S.R. **70** I3 37 42N 61 54E
Maryborough Australia **86** I4 25 32S 152 36E
Maryland *state* U.S.A. **105** E1 39 00N 77 00W
Maryport Cumbria England **44** A1 54 43N 3 30W
Marysville California U.S.A. **102** B4 39 10N 121 34W
Marysville Ohio U.S.A. **105** D2 40 13N 83 22W
Masada *see* Mezada
Masan South Korea **81** K5 35 10N 128 35E
Masaya Nicaragua **109** G2 11 59N 86 03W
Masbate *i.* The Philippines **80** G6 12 21N 123 36E
Mascara Algeria **66** C2 35 20N 0 09E
Maseru Lesotho **95** E2 29 19S 27 29E
Masham North Yorkshire England **40** C3 54 13N 1 40W
Mashhad Iran **79** I6 36 16N 59 34E
Masina Zaïre **92** B1 4 23S 15 24E
Masindi Uganda **94** F8 1 41N 31 45E
Masīrah *i.* Oman **79** I3 20 25N 58 40E
Mason City Iowa U.S.A. **104** B2 43 10N 93 10W
Masqat Oman **79** I3 23 37N 58 38E
Massachusetts *state* U.S.A. **105** F2 42 00N 72 00W
Massachusetts Bay U.S.A. **105** F2 42 00N 70 00W
Masseik Belgium **64** E3 51 08N 5 48E
Massena New York U.S.A. **105** F2 44 56N 74 57W
Massey Ontario Canada **105** D3 46 13N 82 06W
Massif Central *mts.* France **61** B2 45 00N 3 30E
Massif de la Vanoise *mts.* France **61** C2 45 20N 6 20E
Massif de l'Isola *mts.* Madagascar **95** I3 23 00S 45 00E
Massif de l'Ouarsenis *mts.* Algeria **66** C2 36 00N 2 00E
Massif des Bongos *mts.* Central African Republic **94** D9 9 00N 23 00E
Massif des Ecrins *mts.* France **61** C1 45 00N 6 00E
Massif de Tsaratanana *mts.* Madagascar **95** I5 14 00S 54 00E
Massy France **60** B1 48 44N 2 17E
Masterton New Zealand **87** C2 40 57S 175 39E
Masuda Japan **82** B1 34 42N 131 51E
Masuku Gabon **93** H2 1 40S 13 31E
Masvingo Zimbabwe **95** F3 20 05S 30 50E
Matachel *r.* Spain **66** A2 38 40N 6 00W
Matadi Zaïre **95** B6 5 50S 13 32E
Matagalpa Nicaragua **109** G2 12 52N 85 58W
Matagami Québec Canada **105** E3 49 47N 77 38W
Matale Sri Lanka **77** E1 7 28N 80 37E
Matamoros Mexico **108** D5 25 33N 103 15W
Matamoros Mexico **108** E5 25 50N 97 31W
Matane Québec Canada **105** G3 48 50N 67 31W
Matanzas Cuba **109** H4 23 04N 81 35W
Matara Sri Lanka **77** E1 5 57N 80 32E
Mataram Indonesia **80** F2 8 36S 116 07E
Mataró Spain **66** C3 41 32N 2 27E
Mataura New Zealand **87** A1 46 10S 168 53E
Mataura *r.* New Zealand **87** A1 46 40S 168 50E
Matching Green Essex England **34** D3 51 47N 0 13E
Matehuala Mexico **108** D4 23 40N 100 40W
Matera Italy **68** C3 40 40N 16 37E
Matete Zaïre **92** B1 4 23S 15 21E
Mateur Tunisia **68** A2 37 03N 9 40E
Mathura India **77** D5 27 30N 77 42E
Matlock Derbyshire England **36** C3 53 08N 1 32W
Mato Grosso *admin.* Brazil **114** F10 14 00S 56 00W
Mato Grosso *tn.* Brazil **114** F9 15 05S 59 57W
Mato Grosso do Sul *admin.* Brazil **114** F8/9 20 00S 55 00W
Matopo Hills Zimbabwe **95** E3 21 00S 28 30E
Matosinhos Portugal **66** A3 41 08N 8 45W
Maṭraḥ Oman **79** I3 23 31N 58 18E
Matsudo Japan **83** C4 35 46N 139 54E
Matsue Japan **82** B2 35 29N 133 04E
Matsumoto Japan **82** C2 36 18N 137 58E
Matsuyama Japan **82** B1 33 50N 132 47E
Mattagami River Ontario Canada **105** D3 50 00N 82 00W
Mattawa Ontario Canada **105** E3 46 19N 78 42W
Matterhorn *mt.* Switzerland **61** C2 45 59N 7 39E
Mattice Ontario Canada **105** D3 49 36N 83 16W
Mattoon Illinois U.S.A. **104** C1 39 29N 88 21W
Matuku *i.* Fiji **118** V15 19 11S 179 45E
Maturín Venezuela **114** E14 9 45N 63 10W
Matveyevskoye Russia **70** L1 55 42N 37 30E
Maubeuge France **61** B3 50 17N 3 58E
Maués Brazil **114** F12 3 22S 57 38W
Maughold Head Isle of Man British Isles **41** F1 54 18N 4 19W
Maulden Bedfordshire England **34** B4 52 02N 0 27W
Maumere Indonesia **80** G2 8 35S 122 13E
Mauna Kea *mt.* Hawaiian Islands **119** Z17 19 50N 155 25W
Mauna Loa *vol.* Hawaiian Islands **119** Z17 19 28N 155 35W
MAURITANIA **93** C6
MAURITIUS **123** 20 15S 57 30E
Mawkmai Myanmar **80** B8 20 12N 97 37E
Mawlaik Myanmar **81** D2 23 40N 94 26E
Mawson *r.s.* Antarctica **121** 67 36S 62 52E
Mayaguana *i.* The Bahamas **109** J4 22 30N 72 40W
Mayagüez Puerto Rico **109** K3 18 13N 67 09W
Maybole Strathclyde Scotland **46** D2 55 21N 4 41W
Mayen Germany **64** G2 50 19N 7 14E
Mayenne France **61** A2 48 18N 0 37W
Mayenne *r.* France **61** A2 47 45N 0 50W
Mayfield East Sussex England **33** C2 51 01N 0 16E
Mayfield Lothian Scotland **45** D1 55 52N 3 03W
Maykop Russia **70** G4 44 37N 40 48E
Maynooth Kildare Irish Republic **49** A2 53 23N 6 35W
Mayo *co.* Irish Republic **48** B3 53 55N 9 20W
Mayo Yukon Territory Canada **100** H5 63 34N 135 52W
Mayotte *i.* Indian Ocean **95** I5
May Pen Jamaica **109** Q7 17 58N 77 15W
Maysville Kentucky U.S.A. **105** D1 38 38N 83 46W
Mayumba Gabon **93** H2 3 23S 10 38E
Mayville North Dakota U.S.A. **104** A3 47 30N 97 20W
Mazabuka Zambia **95** E4 15 50S 27 47E
Mazamet France **61** B1 43 29N 2 22E
Mazār-e-Sharif Afghanistan **79** K6 36 42N 67 06E
Mazatenango Guatemala **108** F2 14 31N 91 30W
Mazatlán Mexico **108** C4 23 11N 106 25W
Maze Northern Ireland **49** C1 54 29N 6 07W
Mazirbe Latvia **67** E2 57 40N 22 21E
Mbabane Swaziland **95** F2 26 20S 31 08E
Mbaiki Central African Republic **94** C8 3 53N 18 01E
Mbala Zambia **95** F6 8 50S 31 24E
Mbalmayo Cameroon **93** H3 3 30N 11 31E
Mbandaka Zaïre **94** C8 0 03N 18 28E
Mbengga *i.* Fiji **118** U15 18 24S 178 09E
Mbeya Tanzania **95** F6 8 54S 33 29E
Mbuji-Mayi Zaïre **95** D6 6 10S 23 39E
Mead, Lake U.S.A. **102** D4 36 10N 114 25W
Meadville Pennsylvania U.S.A. **105** D2 41 38N 80 10W
Meaford Ontario Canada **105** D2 44 36N 80 35W
Measham Leicestershire England **35** D3 52 43N 1 29W
Meath *co.* Irish Republic **48** E3 53 35N 6 30W
Meaux France **61** B2 48 58N 2 54E
Mecca *see* Makkah
Mechelen *(Malines)* Belgium **64** D3 51 02N 4 29E
Mecheria Algeria **93** E9 33 31N 0 20W
Mechernich Germany **64** F2 50 35N 6 39E
Mecklenburg Bay Europe **63** B2 54 00N 12 00E
Mecklenburg-Vorpommern *admin.* Germany **63** B2 53 30N 12 30E
Medan Indonesia **80** B4 3 35N 98 39E
Médéa Algeria **93** F10 36 15N 2 48E
Medellín Colombia **114** B14 6 15N 75 36W
Medemblik Netherlands **64** E4 52 47N 5 06E
Medenine Tunisia **93** H9 33 24N 10 25E
Medford Oregon U.S.A. **102** B5 42 20N 122 52W
Medicine Hat Alberta Canada **100** M3 50 03N 110 41W
Medina del Campo Spain **66** B3 41 18N 4 55W
Medinīpur India **77** F4 22 25N 87 24E
Mediterranean Sea **88**
Medvedkovo Russia **70** M2 55 56N 37 08E
Medvezh'yegorsk Russia **70** F8 62 56N 34 28E
Medway *r.* Kent England **33** C2 51 24N 0 40E
Meekatharra Australia **86** B4 26 30S 118 30E
Meerut India **77** D5 29 00N 77 42E
Mēga Ethiopia **94** G8 4 02N 38 19E
Meghalaya *admin.* India **77** G5 25 30N 91 00E
Meguro Japan **83** B3 35 36N 139 43E
Mei Xian China **81** I2 24 19N 116 13E
Meiningen Germany **63** B2 50 34N 10 25E
Meissen Germany **63** B2 51 10N 13 28E
Mejerda *r.* Tunisia **68** A2 36 30N 9 00E
Mek'elē Ethiopia **94** G10 13 32N 39 33E
Meknès Morocco **93** D9 33 53N 5 37W
Mekong *r.* South East Asia **80** C7/D6 16 30N 105 00E
Mekong, Mouths of the Vietnam **80** D5 9 00N 107 00E
Melaka Malaysia **80** C4 2 14N 102 14E
Melanesia *geog. reg.* Pacific Ocean **118** F7
Melbourn Cambridgeshire England **33** C3 52 05N 0 01E
Melbourne Australia **86** H2 37 45S 144 58E
Melbourne Derbyshire England **35** D3 52 49N 1 25W
Melbourne Florida U.S.A. **103** J2 28 04N 80 38W
Melfort Saskatchewan Canada **100** O3 52 52N 104 38W
Melilla *territory* Spain **93** E10 35 17N 2 57W
Melksham Wiltshire England **31** E3 51 23N 2 09W
Mellègue *r.* Tunisia **68** A2 36 00N 8 00E
Melo Uruguay **115** G6 32 22S 54 10W
Melrose Borders Scotland **46** F2 55 36N 2 44W
Meltham West Yorkshire England **43** E2 53 36N 1 52W
Melton Mowbray Leicestershire England **36** D2 52 46N 0 53W
Melun France **61** B2 48 32N 2 40E
Melvich Highland Scotland **46** E5 58 33N 3 55W
Melville Saskatchewan Canada **101** O3 50 57N 102 49W
Melville Bugt *b.* Greenland **101** W8 75 30N 62 30W
Melville, Cape Australia **86** G7 14 08S 144 31E
Melville Hills Northwest Territories Canada **100** K6 69 00N 121 00W
Melville Island Australia **86** E7 11 30S 131 00E
Melville Island Northwest Territories Canada **100** M8 75 30N 112 00W
Melville, Lake Newfoundland Canada **101** X3 53 45N 59 00W
Melville Peninsula Northwest Territories Canada **101** S6 68 00N 84 00W
Memmingen Germany **63** B1 47 59N 10 11E
Memphis *hist. site* Egypt **78** D4 29 52N 31 12E
Memphis Tennessee U.S.A. **103** I4 35 10N 90 00W
Menai Bridge *tn.* Gwynedd Wales **38** B3 53 14N 4 10W
Menai Strait Gwynedd Wales **38** B3 53 14N 4 10W
Mendebo Mountains Ethiopia **94** G9 7 00N 40 00E
Mende France **61** B1 44 32N 3 30E
Menderes *r.* Turkey **78** C6 37 50N 28 10E
Mendi Papua New Guinea **86** G8 6 13S 143 39E
Mendip Hills Somerset England **31** E3 51 18N 2 45W
Mendocino Seascarp Pacific Ocean **119** L12 41 00N 145 00W
Mendota Illinois U.S.A. **104** C2 41 33N 89 09W
Mendoza Argentina **115** D6 32 48S 68 52W
Menen Belgium **64** C2 50 48N 3 07E
Mengdingjie China **81** E2 23 30N 99 03E
Menominee Michigan U.S.A. **104** C3 45 07N 87 37W
Menongue Angola **95** C5 14 36S 17 48E
Menorca *(Minorca) i.* Balearic Islands **66** F4 39 45N 4 15E
Menston West Yorkshire England **43** E3 53 53N 1 44W
Menstrie Central Scotland **45** C2 56 09N 3 52W
Menteith, Lake of Central Scotland **45** B2 56 10N 4 18W
Mentmore Buckinghamshire England **34** A3 51 53N 0 41W
Menton France **61** C1 43 47N 7 30E
Mentor Ohio U.S.A. **103** J5 41 42N 81 22W
Meon *r.* Hampshire England **32** A1/2 51 00N 1 10W
Meppel Netherlands **64** F4 52 42N 6 12E
Meppen Germany **63** A2 52 41N 7 18E
Merauke Indonesia **86** G8 8 30S 140 22E
Merced California U.S.A. **102** B4 37 17N 120 29W
Mercedes Argentina **115** D6 33 41S 65 28W
Mercedes Uruguay **115** F6 34 15S 58 02W
Mere Wiltshire England **31** E3 51 06N 2 16W
Meredith, Cape Falkland Islands **117** L15 52 15S 60 40W
Mereworth Kent England **34** E1 51 16N 0 24E

Mousehole Cornwall England **30** B2 50 04N 5 34W
Moville Donegal Irish Republic **48** D5 55 11N 7 03W
Moyale Kenya **94** G8 3 31N 39 04E
Moyobamba Peru **114** B11 6 04S 76 56W
Mozambique Channel Mozambique/Madagascar **95** H4 18 00S 42 00E
Mozambique Depression Indian Ocean **88** 35 00S 40 00E
MOZAMBIQUE 95 F4
Mozyr' Belarus **69** E3 52 02N 29 10E
Mpanda Tanzania **95** F6 6 21S 31 01E
Mpila Congo **92** A2 4 17S 15 18E
Mtwara Tanzania **95** H5 10 17S 40 11E
Muang Chiang Rai Thailand **80** B7 19 56N 99 51E
Muang Lampang Thailand **80** B7 18 16N 99 30E
Muang Nakhon Sawan Thailand **80** C7 15 42N 100 04E
Muang Phitsanulok Thailand **80** C7 16 50N 100 15E
Much Hadham Hertfordshire England **34** D3 51 52N 0 04E
Much Hoole Lancashire England **42** B3 53 42N 2 48W
Muchinga Mountains Zambia **95** F5 12 30S 32 30E
Much Wenlock Shropshire England **36** B2 52 36N 2 34W
Muck *i.* Highland Scotland **46** B3 56 50N 6 15W
Muckamore Northern Ireland **49** C2 54 42N 6 11W
Muckle Roe *i.* Shetland Islands Scotland **47** B2 60 22N 1 26W
Mucklestone Staffordshire England **35** A3 52 56N 2 25W
Mudanjiang China **81** K6 44 36N 129 42E
Mufulira Zambia **95** E5 12 30S 28 12E
Mugdock Central Scotland **45** B1 55 58N 4 19W
Muğla Turkey **78** C6 37 13N 28 22E
Muhammad Qol Sudan **78** E3 20 53N 37 09E
Mühlhausen Germany **63** B2 51 13N 10 28E
Muinebeag *(Bagenalstown)* Carlow Irish Republic **48** E2 52 41N 6 58W
Muirhead Strathclyde Scotland **45** B1 55 54N 4 04W
Muirkirk Strathclyde Scotland **46** D2 55 31N 4 04W
Muir of Ord Highland Scotland **46** D4 57 31N 4 27W
Muirton Tayside Scotland **45** C2 56 17N 3 44W
Mukachevo Ukraine **69** D2 48 26N 22 45E
Mulde *r.* Germany **63** B2 51 00N 12 00E
Mulegé Mexico **108** B5 26 54N 112 00W
Mulgrave Nova Scotia Canada **101** W2 45 36N 61 25W
Mulhacén *mt.* Spain **66** B2 37 04N 3 19W
Mülheim an der Ruhr Germany **62** B2 51 25N 6 50E
Mulhouse France **61** C2 47 45N 7 21E
Mull *i.* Strathclyde Scotland **46** B3/C3 56 25N 6 00W
Mullaghareirk Mountains Irish Republic **48** D2 52 15N 9 20W
Mullet, The *c.* Irish Republic **48** A4 54 15N 10 05W
Mull Head *c.* Orkney Islands Scotland **47** E2 59 20N 2 58W
Mullingar Westmeath Irish Republic **48** D3 53 32N 7 20W
Mullion Cornwall England **30** B2 50 01N 5 14W
Mull of Galloway *c.* Dumfries & Galloway Scotland **46** D1 54 38N 4 50W
Mull of Kintyre *c.* Strathclyde Scotland **46** C2 55 17N 5 55W
Mull of Oa *c.* Strathclyde Scotland **46** B2 55 35N 6 20W
Multan Pakistan **77** C6 30 10N 71 36E
Muna *i.* Indonesia **80** G3 5 00S 122 30E
München *(Munich)* Germany **63** B1 48 08N 11 35E
Muncie Indiana U.S.A. **104** C2 40 11N 85 22W
Münden Germany **63** A2 51 25N 9 39E
Mundesley Norfolk England **33** D3 52 53N 1 26E
Mundo *r.* Spain **66** B2 38 30N 2 00W
Mungbere Zaïre **94** E8 2 40N 28 25E
Munger India **77** F5 25 24N 86 29E
Munich *see* München
Municipal Colony Delhi India **76** L4 28 42N 77 12E
Münster Germany **63** A2 51 58N 7 37E
Muojärvi *l.* Finland **67** F4 65 52N 29 30E
Muonio älv *r.* Sweden/Finland **67** E4 68 20N 22 00E
Muqdisho *(Mogadishu)* Somalia **94** I8 2 02N 45 21E
Mur *r.* Europe **69** B2 47 00N 14 00E
Murat *r.* Turkey **78** F6 38 50N 40 20E
Murchison *r.* Australia **86** B4 28 00S 117 00E
Murcia Spain **66** B2 37 59N 1 08W
Mureş *r.* Romania **69** D2 46 00N 22 00E
Murfreesboro Tennessee U.S.A. **103** I4 35 50N 86 25W
Murgab *r.* Asia **79** J6 37 00N 62 30E
Müritz *l.* Germany **63** B2 53 00N 12 00E
Murmansk Russia **70** F9 68 59N 33 08E
Murom Russia **70** G7 55 34N 42 04E
Muroran Japan **82** D3 42 21N 140 59E
Muroto-misaki *c.* Japan **82** B1 33 13N 134 11E
Murray *r.* Australia **86** G2/G3 34 00S 142 00E
Murray Bridge *tn.* Australia **86** F2 35 10S 139 17E
Murray Seascarp Pacific Ocean **119** M11 32 00N 138 00W
Murrumbidgee *r.* Australia **86** H3 34 30S 146 30E
Murton Durham England **44** C1 54 49N 1 23W
Murwara India **77** E4 23 49N 80 28E
Murzuq Libya **94** B13 25 55N 13 55E
Muş Turkey **78** F6 38 45N 41 30E
Musashino Japan **83** B3 35 43N 139 35E
Musgrave Ranges *mts.* Australia **86** E4 26 00S 132 00E
Mushin Nigeria **92** C3 6 33N 3 25E
Musin Nigeria **93** F4 6 30N 3 15E
Muskegon Michigan U.S.A. **104** C2 43 13N 86 15W
Muskegon *r.* Michigan U.S.A. **104** C2 43 00N 86 00W
Muskogee Oklahoma U.S.A. **103** G4 35 45N 95 21W
Musselburgh Lothian Scotland **45** D1 55 57N 3 04W
Musselshell *r.* Montana U.S.A. **102** E6 47 00N 108 00W
Mustafa Kemalpaşa Turkey **68** E2 40 03N 28 52E
Mutarara Mozambique **95** G4 17 30S 35 06E
Mutare Zimbabwe **95** F4 18 58N 32 40E
Muthill Tayside Scotland **45** C2 56 20N 3 51W
Mutsu Japan **82** D3 41 18N 141 15E
Mutsu-wan *b.* Japan **82** D3 41 05N 140 40E
Muyun Kum *d.* Kazakhstan **70** I4–J4 44 00N 70 00E
Muzaffarnagar India **77** D5 29 28N 77 42E
Muzaffarpur India **77** F5 26 07N 85 23E
Mwanza Tanzania **95** F7 2 31S 32 56E
Mwaya Tanzania **95** F6 9 33S 33 56E
Mweru, Lake *(Lac Moero)* Zaïre/Zambia **95** E6 8 30S 28 30E
Myanaung Myanmar **77** H3 18 17N 95 19E
MYANMAR *(BURMA)* **80** B7/**81** E2
Myaungmya Myanmar **77** G3 16 33N 94 55E
Mybster Highland Scotland **46** E5 58 27N 3 25W
Myingyan Myanmar **81** E2 21 25N 95 20E
Myitkyina Myanmar **81** E3 25 24N 97 25E
Mymensingh Bangladesh **77** G4 24 45N 90 23E
Mynydd Du *hills* Dyfed Wales **38** C2 51 50N 3 55W
Mynydd Eppynt *hills* Powys Wales **38** C2 52 02N 3 35W
Mynydd Preseli *hills* Dyfed Wales **38** B1 51 58N 4 45W
Mýrdalsjökull *ice cap* Iceland **67** I6 63 40N 19 00W
Mys Chelyuskin *c.* Russia **71** M11 77 44N 103 55E
Mys Kanin Nos *c.* Russia **70** G9 68 38N 43 20E
Mys Navarin *c.* Russia **71** T8 62 17N 179 13E
Mys Olyutorskiy *c.* Russia **71** T7 59 58N 170 25E
Mysore India **77** D2 12 18N 76 37E
Mys Tolstoy *c.* Russia **71** R7 59 00N 155 00E
My Tho Vietnam **80** D6 10 21N 106 21E
Mytholmroyd West Yorkshire England **43** E3 53 43N 1 59W
Mže *r.* Ceska Czechoslovakia **63** B1 49 00N 13 00E
Mzuzu Malawi **95** F5 11 31S 34 00E

N

Naaldwijk Netherlands **65** A2 52 00N 4 10E
Naarden Netherlands **65** E3 52 18N 5 09E
Naas Kildare Irish Republic **48** E3 53 13N 6 39W
Naberezhnyye Chelny *(Brezhnev)* Russia **70** H7 55 42N 52 19E
Nabeul Tunisia **68** B2 36 30N 10 44E
Nablus Jordan **78** O11 32 13N 35 16E
Nabq Egypt **78** O9 28 04N 34 26E
Nacogdoches Texas U.S.A. **103** H3 31 36N 94 40W
Nadiad India **77** C4 22 42N 72 55E
Nador Morocco **93** E10 35 10N 3 00W
Nadym Russia **71** J9 65 25N 72 40E
Naestved Denmark **67** C2 55 14N 11 47E
Naga The Philippines **80** G6 13 36N 123 12E
Naga Hills India/Myanmar **77** G5/H5 26 00N 95 00E
Nagai Japan **83** B1 35 11N 139 37E
Nagaland *admin.* India **77** G5 26 00N 94 30E
Nagano Japan **82** C2 36 39N 138 10E
Nagaoka Japan **82** C2 37 27N 138 50E
Nagasaki Japan **82** A1 32 45N 129 52E
Nagato Japan **82** B1 34 22N 131 11E
Nagatsuda Japan **83** B3 35 31N 139 30E
Nagercoil India **77** D1 8 11N 77 30E
Nagles Mountains Irish Republic **48** C2 52 10N 8 25W
Nagornyy Russia **71** O7 55 57N 124 54E
Nagoya Japan **82** C2 35 08N 136 53E
Nagpur India **77** D4 21 10N 79 12E
Nagqu China **77** G6 31 30N 91 57E
Nagykanizsa Hungary **69** C2 46 27N 17 00E
Nahanni Butte *tn.* Northwest Territories Canada **100** K5 61 30N 123 20W
Nahanni National Park Northwest Territories Canada **100** K5 61 30N 123 20W
Nahariya Israel **78** O11 33 01N 35 05E
Nahe *r.* Germany **63** A1 49 00N 7 00E
Naihati India **76** K3 22 53N 88 27E
Nailsea Avon England **31** E3 51 26N 2 46W
Nailsworth Gloucestershire England **31** E3 51 42N 2 14W
Nain Newfoundland Canada **101** W4 56 30N 61 45W
Nairn Highland Scotland **46** E4 57 35N 3 53W
Nairobi Kenya **94** G7 1 17S 36 50E
Najd *geog. reg.* Saudi Arabia **78** F4 25 40N 42 30E
Najrān Saudi Arabia **78** F2 17 37N 44 40E
Naka Japan **83** B2 35 25N 139 38E
Nakahara Japan **83** B3 35 34N 139 39E
Nakamura Japan **82** B1 33 02N 132 58E
Nakano Japan **83** B3 35 42N 139 40E
Nakatsu Japan **82** B1 33 37N 131 11E
Nakhichevan' Azerbaijan **78** F6 39 12N 45 24E
Nakhodka Russia **71** P4 42 53N 132 54E
Nakhon Ratchasima Thailand **80** C6 15 00N 102 06E
Nakhon Si Thammarat Thailand **80** B5 8 24N 99 58E
Nakina Ontario Canada **101** R3 50 11N 86 43W
Nakskov Denmark **63** B2 54 50N 11 10E
Nakuru Kenya **94** G7 0 16S 36 05E
Nal *r.* Pakistan **76** B5 26 10N 65 30E
Nal'chik Russia **70** G4 43 31N 43 38E
Namangan Uzbekistan **70** J4 40 59N 71 41E
Nam Co *l.* China **77** G6 30 50N 90 30E
Namdalen *geog. reg.* Norway **67** C3 64 40N 12 00E
Nam Dinh 81 G2 20 14N 106 00E
Namib Desert Namibia **95** B3 22 00S 14 00E
Namibe Angola **95** B4 15 10S 12 09E
NAMIBIA 95 C3
Nampa Idaho U.S.A. **102** C5 43 35N 116 34W
Nampula Mozambique **95** G4 15 09S 39 14E
Namsos Norway **67** C3 64 28N 11 30E
Namtu Myanmar **81** E2 23 04N 97 26E
Namur *admin.* Belgium **64** D2 50 10N 4 45E
Namur Belgium **64** D2 50 28N 4 52E
Nanaimo British Columbia Canada **100** K2 49 08N 123 58W
Nanao Japan **82** C2 37 03N 136 58E
Nanchang China **81** I3 28 33N 115 58E
Nanchong China **81** G4 30 54N 106 06E
Nancy France **61** C2 48 42N 6 12E
Nanda Devi *mt.* India **77** E6 30 21N 79 58E
Nānded India **77** D3 19 11N 77 21E
Nanduri Fiji **118** U16 16 26S 179 08E
Nanga Eboko Cameroon **93** H3 4 38N 12 21E
Nangi India **76** J1 22 30N 88 13E
Nanhai *l.* China **82** G1 39 55N 116 22E
Nanjing China **81** I4 32 03N 118 47E
Nan Ling *mts.* China **81** H2/H3 25 00N 112 00E
Nanning China **81** G2 22 50N 108 19E
Nanortalik Greenland **101** Z5 60 10N 45 05W
Nanpan Jiang *r.* China **81** G2 25 00N 106 00E
Nanping China **81** I3 26 40N 118 07E
Nansei-shoto *see* Ryukyu Islands
Nan Shan *mts.* China **72** 38 00N 103 00E
Nanterre France **60** A2 48 53N 2 12E
Nantes France **61** A2 47 14N 1 35W
Nantong China **81** J4 32 06N 121 04E
Nantucket Island Massachusetts U.S.A. **105** G2 41 00N 70 00W
Nantucket Sound Massachusetts U.S.A. **105** F2 41 00N 70 00W
Nantwich Cheshire England **40** B2 53 04N 2 32W
Nant-y-moch Reservoir Dyfed Wales **38** C2 52 30N 3 50W
Nanuku Passage *sd.* Fiji **118** V16 16 40S 179 25W
Nanumea Island Pacific Ocean **118** H7 5 30S 175 40E
Nanyang China **81** H4 33 06N 112 31E
Nanyuan China **82** G1 39 48N 116 23E
Nanyuki Kenya **94** G8 0 01N 37 05E
Napanee Ontario Canada **105** E2 44 15N 74 57W
Napier New Zealand **87** C3 39 29S 176 58E
Naples Florida U.S.A. **103** J2 26 09N 81 48W
Naples *see* Napoli
Napoli *(Naples)* Italy **68** B3 40 50N 14 15E
Napoopoo Hawaiian Islands **119** Z17 19 29N 155 55W
Nappanee Indiana U.S.A. **104** C2 41 27N 86 01W
Napton on the Hill Warwickshire England **35** E1 52 15N 1 24W
Nar *r.* Norfolk England **33** C3 52 40N 0 40E
Nara Japan **82** C1 34 41N 135 49E
Narayanganj Bangladesh **77** G4 23 36N 90 28E
Narberth Dyfed Wales **38** B1 51 48N 4 45W
Narbonne France **61** B1 43 11N 3 00E
Narborough Leicestershire England **36** C2 52 35N 1 11W
Nares Deep Atlantic Ocean **117** C9 26 00N 61 10W
Nares Strait Canada/Greenland **101** U8 78 30N 72 30W
Narew *r.* Europe **69** D3 53 00N 21 00E
Narmada *r.* India **77** C4/D4 22 00N 75 00E
Narrogin Australia **86** B3 32 57S 117 07E
Narsaq Greenland **101** Z5 61 00N 46 00W
Narsarsuaq Greenland **101** Z5 61 10N 45 20W
Narva Estonia **67** F2 59 22N 28 17E
Narvik Norway **67** D4 68 26N 17 25E
Nar'yan Mar Russia **70** H9 67 37N 53 02E
Nasca Ridge Pacific Ocean **119** R5 20 00S 81 00W
Naseby Northamptonshire England **36** D2 52 23N 0 59W
Nashua New Hampshire U.S.A. **105** F2 42 44N 71 28W
Nashville Tennessee U.S.A. **103** I4 36 10N 86 50W
Näsijärvi *l.* Finland **67** E3 61 45N 24 00E
Nasik India **77** C3 20 00N 73 52E
Nassau The Bahamas **109** I5 25 05N 77 20W
Nasser, Lake Egypt **78** D3 22 35N 31 40E
Nässjo Sweden **67** C2 57 40N 14 40E
Natal Brazil **114** J11 5 46S 35 15W
Natal *province* Republic of South Africa **95** F2 29 00S 31 00E
Natashquan Québec Canada **101** W3 50 10N 61 50W
Natchez Mississippi U.S.A. **103** H3 31 32N 91 24W
Natewa Peninsula Fiji **118** V16 16 40S 180 00
Natron, Lake Tanzania **94** G7 2 00S 36 00E
Natuna Besar *i.* Indonesia **80** D4 4 00N 108 00E
Naturaliste, Cape Australia **86** B3 33 32S 115 01E
Naucalpan Mexico **108** P1 19 28N 99 14W
Naumburg Germany **63** B2 51 09N 11 48E
NAURU 118 G7
Nausori Fiji **118** U15 18 01S 178 31E
Navadwip India **77** F4 23 24N 88 23E
Navan Meath Irish Republic **48** E3 53 39N 6 41W
Navenby Lincolnshire England **36** D3 53 06N 0 32W
Naver *r.* Highland Scotland **46** D5 58 25N 4 10W
Navia *r.* Spain **66** A3 43 10N 7 05W
Naviti *i.* Fiji **118** T16 17 08S 177 15E
Navoi Uzbekistan **70** I4 40 04N 65 20E
Navojoa Mexico **108** C5 27 04N 109 28W
Návplion Greece **68** D2 37 34N 22 48E
Navsari India **77** C4 20 58N 73 01E
Náxos *i.* Greece **68** E2 37 00N 25 00E
Nayoro Japan **82** D3 44 21N 142 30E
Nazareth Israel **78** O11 32 41N 35 16E
Nazca Peru **114** C9 14 53S 74 54W
Naze, The *c.* Essex England **33** D2 51 50N 1 20E
Nazilli Turkey **68** E2 37 55N 28 20E
Nazwá Oman **79** I3 22 56N 57 33E
Ndélé Central African Republic **94** D9 8 25N 20 38E
Ndjamena Chad **94** C10 12 10N 14 59E
Ndola Zambia **95** E5 13 00S 28 39E
Neápolis Greece **68** D2 36 31N 23 03E
Neath *r.* West Glamorgan Wales **38** C1 51 40N 3 45W
Neath West Glamorgan Wales **38** C1 51 40N 3 48W
Nebit-Dag Russia **70** H3 39 31N 54 24E
Nebraska *state* U.S.A. **102** F5 42 00N 102 00W
Nebraska City Nebraska U.S.A. **104** A2 40 41N 95 50W
Neckar *r.* Germany **63** A1 48 00N 9 00E
Neckei *i.* Hawaiian Islands **119** J10 23 35N 164 42W
Necochea Argentina **115** F5 38 31S 58 46W
Nederrijn *r.* Netherlands **64** E3 51 58N 5 35E
Needham Market Suffolk England **33** D3 52 09N 1 03E
Needles California U.S.A. **102** D3 34 51N 114 36W
Needles, The *rocks* Isle of Wight England **32** A1 50 39N 1 35W
Needwood Forest *hills* Staffordshire England **35** C3 52 25N 1 45W
Neepawa Manitoba Canada **104** A4 50 14N 99 29W
Nefta Tunisia **93** G9 33 53N 7 50E
Nefyn Gwynedd Wales **38** B2 52 56N 4 32W
Negēlē Ethiopia **94** G9 5 20N 39 35E
Negev *d.* Israel **78** O10 30 50N 30 45E
Negombo Sri Lanka **77** D1 7 13N 79 51E
Negritos Peru **114** A2 4 42S 81 18W
Negros *i.* The Philippines **80** G5 10 00N 123 00E
Nei Mongol Zizhiqu *(Inner Mongolia Autonomous Region) admin.* China **81** G6–I6 42 30N 112 30E
Neijiang China **81** G3 29 32N 105 03E
Neilston Strathclyde Scotland **45** B1 55 47N 4 27W
Neiva Colombia **114** B13 2 58N 75 15W
Nek'emtē Ethiopia **94** G9 9 04N 36 30E
Nellore India **77** D2 14 29N 80 00E
Nelson Forks British Columbia Canada **100** K4 59 30N 124 00W
Nelson Lancashire England **42** D3 53 51N 2 13W
Nelson Manitoba Canada **100** L2 49 29N 117 17W
Nelson New Zealand **87** B2 41 18S 173 17E
Nelson River Manitoba Canada **101** Q4 57 00N 94 00W
Neman *r.* Europe **69** D4 55 00N 22 00E
Nemuro Japan **82** E3 43 22N 145 36E
Nemuro-Kaikyō *sd.* Japan **82** E3 44 00N 146 00E
Nen Jiang *r.* China **81** K8 50 00N 125 00E
Nenagh Tipperary Irish Republic **48** C2 52 52N 8 12W
Nenana Alaska U.S.A. **100** F5 64 35N 149 20W
Nene *r.* Cambridgeshire England **33** C3 52 25N 0 05E
Nenjiang China **81** K7 49 10N 125 15E
Neosho *r.* U.S.A. **104** A1 37 00N 95 00W
NEPAL 77 E5
Nepean Ontario Canada **105** E3 45 16N 75 48W
Nephin Beg Range *mts.* Irish Republic **48** B3/4 54 00N 9 50W
Nerchinsk Russia **71** N6 52 02N 116 38E
Neretva *r.* Europe **68** C3 43 00N 18 00E
Nerva Spain **66** A2 37 41N 6 33W
Neryungri Russia **71** O7 56 39N 124 38E
Nes Netherlands **64** E5 53 27N 5 46E
Neskaupstadur Iceland **67** J7 65 10N 13 43W
Ness Cheshire England **42** A1 53 18N 3 03W
Neste *r.* France **61** B1 43 00N 0 15E
Nestor Falls *tn.* Ontario Canada **104** B3 49 06N 93 55W
Netanya Israel **78** O11 32 20N 34 51E
Nete *r.* Belgium **64** D3 51 06N 4 28E
Nether Stowey Somerset England **31** D3 51 09N 3 10W
NETHERLANDS 64 E4
Netherton Central Scotland **45** B1 55 59N 4 19W
Nettetal Germany **64** F3 51 20N 6 14E
Nettilling Lake Northwest Territories Canada **101** U6 66 30N 71 10W
Netzahualcóyotl Mexico **108** P1 19 24N 99 02W
Neubrandenburg Germany **63** B2 53 33N 13 16E
Neuburg Germany **63** B1 48 44N 11 12E
Neufchâteau Belgium **64** E1 49 51N 5 26E
Neufchâteau France **61** C2 48 21N 5 42E
Neuchâtel Switzerland **61** C2 46 55N 6 56E
Neufchâtel-en-Bray France **61** B2 49 44N 1 26E
Neufchâtel-sur-Aisne France **64** D1 49 27N 4 02E
Neuilly France **60** B2 48 53N 2 17E
Neuilly Plaisance France **60** C2 48 51N 2 31E
Neumarkt Germany **63** B1 49 17N 11 29E
Neumünster Germany **63** A2 54 05N 9 59E
Neunkirchen Germany **63** A1 49 21N 7 12E
Neuquén Argentina **115** D5 38 55S 68 05W
Neuruppin Germany **63** B2 52 56N 12 49E
Neusiedler See *l.* Austria **69** C2 48 00N 16 00E
Neuss Germany **62** A1 51 12N 6 42E
Neustadt Germany **63** A1 49 21N 8 09E
Neustrelitz Germany **63** B2 53 22N 13 05E
Neu-Ulm Germany **63** B1 48 23N 10 01E
Neuwied Germany **63** A2 50 26N 7 28E
Nevada Missouri U.S.A. **104** B1 37 51N 94 22W
Nevada *state* U.S.A. **102** C4 39 00N 118 00W
Nevers France **61** B2 47 00N 3 09E
Neves Brazil **116** C2 22 51S 43 05W
Neviot Egypt **78** O9 28 58N 34 38E
New *r.* U.S.A. **103** J4 37 00N 81 00W
New Addington Greater London England **34** D2 51 21N 0 01E
New Albany Indiana U.S.A. **104** C1 38 17N 85 50W
New Alresford Hampshire England **32** A2 51 06N 1 10W
New Amsterdam Guyana **114** F14 6 18N 57 30W
Newark Bay New Jersey U.S.A. **106** B1 40 40N 74 08W
Newark Delaware U.S.A. **103** K4 39 42N 75 45W
Newark New Jersey U.S.A. **106** B2 40 43N 74 11W
Newark Ohio U.S.A. **105** D2 40 03N 82 25W
Newark-on-Trent Nottinghamshire England **36** D3 53 05N 0 49W
New Ash Green Kent England **34** D2 51 21N 0 18E
New Bedford Massachusetts U.S.A. **105** F2 41 38N 70 55W
New Bern North Carolina U.S.A. **103** K4 35 05N 77 04W
Newberry Michigan U.S.A. **104** C3 46 22N 85 30W
Newbiggin-by-the-Sea Northumberland England **44** C2 55 11N 1 30W
Newbigging Strathclyde Scotland **45** C1 55 42N 3 33W
Newbold Derbyshire England **43** F1 53 15N 1 28W
New Braunfels Texas U.S.A. **103** G2 29 43N 98 09W
Newbridge Gwent Wales **38** C1 51 41N 3 09W
Newbridge *see* Droichead Nua
Newbridge-on-Wye Powys Wales **38** C2 52 13N 3 27W
New Brighton Merseyside England **42** A2 53 27N 3 03W
New Britain Connecticut U.S.A. **105** F2 41 40N 72 47W
New Britain *i.* Papua New Guinea **86** I8 6 10S 150 00E
New Brunswick *province* Canada **101** V2 47 30N 66 00W
New Buffalo Michigan U.S.A. **104** C2 41 48N 86 44W
New Buildings Northern Ireland **48** D4 54 56N 7 21W
Newburg Grampian Scotland **46** G4 57 18N 2 00W
Newburgh Fife Scotland **45** D2 56 21N 3 15W
Newburgh Lancashire England **42** B2 53 35N 2 48W
Newburgh New York U.S.A. **105** F2 41 30N 74 00W
Newburn Tyne and Wear England **44** C1 54 59N 1 43W
Newbury Berkshire England **32** A2 51 25N 1 20W
New Caledonia *i.* Pacific Ocean **86** K5/L5 22 00S 165 00E
Newcastle Australia **86** I3 32 55S 151 46E
Newcastle Down Northern Ireland **48** F4 54 12N 5 54W
Newcastle Dublin Irish Republic **49** A1 53 18N 6 30W
Newcastle Ontario Canada **105** E2 43 55N 78 35W
New Castle Pennsylvania U.S.A. **105** D2 41 00N 80 22W
Newcastle Wyoming U.S.A. **102** E5 43 52N 104 14W
Newcastle Emlyn Dyfed Wales **38** B2 52 02N 4 28W
Newcastle-under-Lyme Staffordshire England **35** B4 53 00N 2 14W
Newcastle-upon-Tyne Tyne and Wear England **44** C1 54 59N 1 35W
Newcastle West Limerick Irish Republic **48** B2 52 27N 9 03W
New Cumnock Strathclyde Scotland **46** D2 55 24N 4 12W
New Deer Grampian Scotland **46** F4 57 30N 2 12W
New Delhi India **76** M4 28 37N 77 14E
New Dorp New York U.S.A. **106** B1 40 34N 74 06W
New Earswick North Yorkshire England **43** G3 53 59N 1 03W
Newend Hereford & Worcester England **35** C1 52 14N 1 55W
Newent Gloucestershire England **31** E3 51 56N 2 24W
New Forest Hampshire England **32** A1 50 50N 1 40W
Newfoundland Basin Atlantic Ocean **117** D11 44 00N 40 00W
Newfoundland *l.* Newfoundland Canada **101** X2 48 15N 57 00W
Newfoundland *province* Canada **101** W3 52 30N 62 30W
New Georgia Islands Solomon Islands **86** J8 8 00S 157 30E
New G.R.A. Ibadan Nigeria **92** E4 7 22N 3 53E
New Guinea *i.* Pacific Ocean **86** G8 6 00S 142 00E
Newham Greater London England **34** D2 51 30N 0 02E
New Hampshire *state* U.S.A. **105** F2 43 00N 72 00W
New Haven Connecticut U.S.A. **105** F2 41 18N 72 55W
Newhaven East Sussex England **33** C1 50 47N 0 03E
New Hebrides Trench Pacific Ocean **118** G6 15 00S 169 00E
New Holland Humberside England **40** D2 53 42N 0 22W
New Hyde Park New York U.S.A. **106** D1 40 44N 73 42W
New Hythe Kent England **34** E1 51 18N 0 27E
New Iberia Louisiana U.S.A. **103** H2 30 00N 91 51W
Newick East Sussex England **33** C1 50 58N 0 01E
New Ireland *i.* Papua New Guinea **86** I9 3 00S 152 00E
New Jersey *state* U.S.A. **105** F1 39 00N 74 00W
New Liskeard Ontario Canada **105** E3 47 31N 79 41W
New London Connecticut U.S.A. **105** F2 41 21N 72 06W
Newlyn Cornwall England **30** B2 50 06N 5 34W
Newmains Strathclyde Scotland **45** C1 55 47N 3 53W
Newman Australia **86** B5 23 20S 119 34E
Newmarket Cork Irish Republic **48** C2 52 13N 9 00W
Newmarket Suffolk England **33** C3 52 15N 0 25E
Newmarket-on-Fergus Clare Irish Republic **48** C2 52 45N 8 53W
New Mexico *state* U.S.A. **102** E3 35 00N 107 00W
New Milford Pennsylvania U.S.A. **105** E2 41 52N 75 44W
New Mill West Yorkshire England **43** E2 53 35N 1 44W
New Mills Derbyshire England **42** D2 53 23N 2 00W
New Milton Hampshire England **32** A1 50 46N 1 40W
Newnham Gloucestershire England **31** E3 51 49N 2 27W
New Orleans Louisiana U.S.A. **103** H2 30 00N 90 03W
New Philadelphia Ohio U.S.A. **105** D2 40 31N 81 28W
New Plymouth New Zealand **87** B3 39 03S 174 04E
Newport Dyfed Wales **38** B2 52 01N 4 50W
Newport Essex England **34** D3 51 58N 0 13E
Newport Gwent Wales **38** D1 51 35N 3 00W
Newport Isle of Wight England **32** A1 50 42N 1 18W
Newport Maine U.S.A. **105** G2 44 50N 69 17W
Newport Rhode Island U.S.A. **105** F2 41 30N 71 19W
Newport Shropshire England **35** A3 52 47N 2 22W
Newport Vermont U.S.A. **105** F2 44 56N 72 18W

Newport News Virginia U.S.A. 105 E1 36 59N 76 26W
Newport on Tay Fife Scotland 46 F3 56 27N 2 56W
Newport Pagnell Buckinghamshire England 33 B3 52 05N 0 44W
New Providence i. The Bahamas 109 I5 25 00N 77 30W
Newquay Cornwall England 30 B2 50 25N 5 05W
New Quay Dyfed Wales 38 B2 52 13N 4 22W
New Radnor Powys Wales 38 C2 52 15N 3 10W
New Rochelle New York U.S.A. 106 C2 40 55N 73 46W
New Romney Kent England 33 C1 50 59N 0 57E
New Ross Wexford Irish Republic 48 E2 52 24N 6 56W
New Rossington South Yorkshire England 43 G2 53 29N 1 04W
Newry Northern Ireland 48 E4 54 11N 6 20W
New Sauchie Central Scotland 45 C2 56 08N 3 41W
New Scone Tayside Scotland 45 D2 56 25N 3 25W
New Siberian Islands Russia 71 Q10 75 00N 145 00E
New South Wales state Australia 86 G3/G4 32 00S 145 00E
New Springville New York U.S.A. 106 B1 40 35N 74 10W
New Stevenston Strathclyde Scotland 45 B1 55 49N 4 01W
Newton Lothian Scotland 45 D1 55 59N 3 25W
Newton Massachusetts U.S.A. 105 F2 42 20N 71 13W
Newton Abbot Devon England 31 D2 50 32N 3 36W
Newton Aycliffe Durham England 44 C1 54 37N 1 34W
Newtongrange Lothian Scotland 45 D1 55 52N 3 04W
Newton-le-Willows Merseyside England 42 C2 53 28N 2 37W
Newton Longville Buckinghamshire England 34 A3 51 58N 0 46W
Newton Mearns Strathclyde Scotland 45 B1 55 45N 4 18W
Newtonmore Highland Scotland 46 D4 57 04N 4 08W
Newton St. Boswells Borders Scotland 46 F2 55 34N 2 40W
Newton Stewart Dumfries & Galloway Scotland 46 D1 54 57N 4 29W
Newtown Powys Wales 38 C2 52 32N 3 19W
Newtownabbey Northern Ireland 49 D2 54 40N 5 54W
Newtownards Down Northern Ireland 48 F4 54 36N 5 41W
Newtownbreda Northern Ireland 49 D1 54 33N 5 54W
Newtownmountkennedy Wicklow Irish Republic 48 E3 53 06N 6 07W
Newtownstewart Northern Ireland 48 D4 54 43N 7 24W
New Tredegar Mid Glamorgan Wales 38 C1 51 44N 3 15W
New Ulm Minnesota U.S.A. 103 H5 44 19N 94 28W
New Westminster British Columbia Canada 100 K2 49 10N 122 58W
New York New York U.S.A. 106 C1 40 40N 73 50W
New York state U.S.A. 105 E2 43 00N 76 00W
NEW ZEALAND 87
Neyland Dyfed Wales 38 B1 51 43N 4 57W
Neyrīz Iran 79 H4 29 14N 54 18E
Neyshābūr Iran 79 I6 36 13N 58 49E
Ngaba Zaïre 92 A1 4 22S 15 19E
Ngami, Lake Botswana 95 D3 21 00S 23 00E
Ngangla Ringco l. China 77 E6 31 40N 83 00E
Nganze Co l. China 77 F6 31 00N 87 00E
Ngaoundéré Cameroon 93 H4 7 20N 13 35E
Ngau i. Fiji 118 U15 18 00S 179 16E
Ngauruhoe mt. New Zealand 87 C3 39 10S 175 40E
Nguigmi Niger 93 H5 14 19N 13 06E
Nguru Nigeria 93 H5 12 53N 10 30E
Nha Trang Vietnam 80 C6 12 15N 109 10E
Nhulunbuy Australia 86 F7 12 30S 136 56E
Niagara Falls tn. New York U.S.A. 105 E2 43 06N 79 04W
Niagara Falls tn. Ontario Canada 105 E2 43 05N 79 06W
Niamey Niger 93 F5 13 32N 2 05E
Niangara Zaïre 94 E8 3 45N 27 54E
Nias i. Indonesia 80 B4 1 30N 97 30E
Nibra India 76 K2 22 35N 88 15E
NICARAGUA 109 G2
Nice France 61 C1 43 42N 7 16E
Nicobar Islands India 77 G1 8 30N 94 00E
Nicosia Cyprus 78 D6 35 11N 33 23E
Nidd r. North Yorkshire England 40 C3 54 02N 1 30W
Nied r. France 64 F1 49 15N 6 30E
Niedere Tauern mts. Austria 63 B1 47 00N 14 00E
Niedersachsen admin. Germany 63 A2 52 00N 9 00E
Nienburg Germany 63 A2 52 38N 9 13E
Niers r. Germany 64 F3 51 00N 6 00E
Nieuwegein Netherlands 65 E2 52 00N 5 05E
Nieuwe Maas r. Netherlands 65 B1 51 54N 4 23E
Nieuwendam Netherlands 65 D3 52 23N 4 57E
Nieuwerkerk aan den IJssel Netherlands 65 C1 51 58N 4 37E
Nieuwe Waterweg Scheur can. Netherlands 65 A1 51 55N 4 10E
Nieuwkoopsche Plassen l. Netherlands 65 D2 52 08N 4 46E
Nieuw Nickerie Surinam 114 F14 5 52N 57 00W
Nieuwpoort Belgium 64 B3 51 08N 2 45E
Nieuw-Vennep Netherlands 65 C3 52 15N 4 39E
NIGER 93 G6
Niger r. Nigeria 93 G4 5 30N 6 15E
Niger Delta Nigeria 88 5 00N 7 00E
NIGERIA 93 G5
Niigata Japan 82 C2 37 58N 139 02E
Niihama Japan 82 B1 33 57N 133 15E
Niihau i. Hawaiian Islands 119 W18 21 50N 160 11W
Nii-jima i. Japan 82 C1 34 20N 139 15E
Niiza Japan 83 B4 35 48N 139 35E
Nijkerk Netherlands 64 E4 52 12N 5 30E
Nijmegen Netherlands 64 E3 51 50N 5 52E
Nikko Japan 82 C2 36 45N 139 37E
Nikolayev Ukraine 70 F5 46 57N 32 00E
Nikolayevsk-na-Amure Russia 71 Q6 53 10N 140 44E
Nikšić Montenegro Yugoslavia 68 C3 42 48N 18 56E
Nile r. Egypt 78 D4 28 30N 30 40E
Nile Delta Egypt 88 31 00N 31 00E
Niles Michigan U.S.A. 104 C2 41 51N 86 15W
Nilgiri Hills India 77 D2 11 00N 76 30E
Nilópolis Brazil 116 B2 22 48S 43 25W
Nîmes France 61 B1 43 50N 4 21E
Nimule Sudan 94 F8 3 35N 32 03E
Ninety Mile Beach New Zealand 87 B4 34 50S 173 00E
Nineveh hist. site Iraq 78 F6 36 24N 43 08E
Ningbo China 81 J3 29 54N 121 33E
Ninh Binh Vietnam 81 G2 20 14N 106 00E
Ninove Belgium 64 D2 50 50N 4 02E
Niobrara r. U.S.A. 102 F5 42 00N 102 00W
Nioro du Sahel Mali 93 D6 15 12N 9 35W
Niort France 61 A2 46 19N 0 27W
Nipigon Ontario Canada 104 C3 49 02N 88 26W
Nipigon r. Ontario Canada 104 C3 49 00N 88 00W
Nipigon, Lake Ontario Canada 104 C3 50 00N 88 00W
Niš Serbia Yugoslavia 68 D3 43 20N 21 54E
Nishi Japan 83 B2 35 26N 139 37E
Niterói Brazil 116 C2 22 54S 43 06W
Nith r. Dumfries & Galloway Scotland 46 E2 55 15N 3 50W
Nithsdale v. Dumfries & Galloway Scotland 46 E2 55 15N 3 50W
Nitra Slovenska Czechoslovakia 69 C2 48 19N 18 04E
Niue i. Pacific Ocean 119 J6 19 02S 169 55W
Nive r. France 61 A1 43 15N 1 15W
Nivelles Belgium 64 D2 50 36N 4 20E
Nizamabad India 77 D3 18 40N 78 05E
Nizhneangarsk Russia 71 M7 55 48N 109 35E
Nizhnekamsk Russia 70 H7 55 38N 51 49E
Nizhnekolymsk Russia 71 S9 68 34N 160 58E
Nizhnevartovsk Russia 71 J8 60 57N 76 40E
Nizhniy Novgorod (Gor'kiy) Russia 70 G7 56 20N 44 00E
Nizhniy Tagil Russia 70 I7 58 00N 59 58E
Nizhnyaya (Lower) Tunguska r. Russia 71 L8/M8 64 00N 94 00E
Nizké Tatry mts. Slovenska Czechoslovakia 69 C2 49 00N 19 00E
Nkongsamba Cameroon 93 G3 4 59N 9 53E
Noatak Alaska U.S.A. 100 C6 67 33N 163 10W
Noatak r. Alaska U.S.A. 100 C6 67 33N 163 10W
Nobeoka Japan 82 B1 32 36N 131 40E
Nobi Japan 83 B1 35 11N 139 41E
Nogales Arizona U.S.A. 102 D3 31 20N 110 56W
Nogales Mexico 108 B6 31 20N 111 00W
Nogent France 60 C2 48 50N 2 30E
Noguera Ribagorzana r. Spain 66 C3 42 25N 0 45E
Noirmont Point c. Jersey Channel Islands 31 G5 49 11N 2 07W
Noisy-le-Sec France 60 B2 48 53N 2 27E
Nojima-zaki c. Japan 82 C1 34 54N 139 54E
Nola Central African Republic 94 C8 3 28N 16 08E
Nome Alaska U.S.A. 100 B5 64 30N 165 30W
Noord Beveland i. Netherlands 64 C3 51 35N 3 45E
Noord-Brabant admin. Netherlands 64 D3 51 29N 5 00E
Noord-Holland admin. Netherlands 64 D4 52 30N 4 45E
Noordoost Polder Netherlands 64 E4 52 47N 5 45E
Noordwijk Netherlands 64 D4 52 15N 4 25E
Noordwijk aan Zee Netherlands 65 B2 52 14N 4 27E
Noordwijkerhout Netherlands 65 B3 52 15N 4 30E
Noordzeekanaal can. Netherlands 65 C3 52 25N 4 45E
Noorvik Alaska U.S.A. 100 C6 66 50N 161 14W
Nord admin. France 64 D2 50 13N 4 03E
Norden Germany 63 A2 53 36N 7 13E
Nordenham Germany 63 A2 53 30N 8 29E
Norderney i. Germany 63 A2 53 00N 7 00E
Norderstedt Germany 63 A2 53 41N 9 58E
Nordfjord fj. Norway 67 B3 62 00N 5 15E
Nordfold Norway 67 D4 67 48N 15 20E
Nordfriesische Inseln (North Frisian Islands) is. Germany 63 A2 54 00N 8 00E
Nordhausen Germany 63 B2 51 31N 10 48E
Nordhorn Germany 63 A2 52 27N 7 05E
Nordkapp (North Cape) c. Norway 67 E5 71 11N 25 40E
Nordrhein-Westfalen admin. Germany 63 A2 52 00N 7 00E
Nordstrand i. Germany 63 A2 54 00N 8 00E
Nordvik Russia 71 N10 74 01N 111 30E
Nore r. Irish Republic 48 D2 52 25N 7 02W
Norfolk co. England 33 C3 52 45N 1 00E
Norfolk Nebraska U.S.A. 103 G5 42 01N 97 25W
Norfolk Virginia U.S.A. 105 E1 36 54N 76 18W
Norfolk Island Pacific Ocean 118 G5 29 05S 167 59E
Norfolk Island Trough Pacific Ocean 118 G5 27 30S 166 00E
Norfolk Lake Arkansas U.S.A. 103 H4 36 00N 92 00W
Norham Northumberland England 44 B2 55 43N 2 10W
Noril'sk Russia 71 K9 69 21N 88 02E
Norman Wells tn. Northwest Territories Canada 100 J6 65 19N 126 46W
Normanton Australia 86 G6 17 40S 141 05E
Normanton West Yorkshire England 43 F3 53 42N 1 25W
Norris Lake Tennessee U.S.A. 103 J4 36 00N 84 00W
Norristown Pennsylvania U.S.A. 105 E2 40 07N 75 20W
Norrköping Sweden 67 D2 58 35N 16 10E
Norseman Australia 86 C3 32 15S 121 47E
North Adams Massachusetts U.S.A. 105 F2 42 42N 73 07W
Northallerton North Yorkshire England 40 C3 54 20N 1 26W
Northam Australia 86 B3 31 40S 116 40E
Northam Devon England 31 C3 51 02N 4 14W
North American Basin Atlantic Ocean 117 C10 34 00N 55 00W
Northampton Australia 86 A4 28 27S 114 37E
Northampton Massachusetts U.S.A. 105 F2 42 19N 72 38W
Northampton Northamptonshire England 36 D2 52 14N 0 54W
Northamptonshire co. England 36 D2 52 20N 1 00W
North Andaman i. Andaman Islands 77 G2 13 00N 93 00E
North Anna r. Virginia U.S.A. 105 E1 38 00N 77 00W
North Australian Basin Indian Ocean 118 B6 14 00S 115 00E
North Baddesley Hampshire England 32 A1 50 58N 1 27W
North Ballaculish Highland Scotland 46 C3 56 42N 5 11W
North Barrackpore India 76 K3 22 46N 88 21E
North Battleford Saskatchewan Canada 100 N3 52 47N 108 19W
North Bay tn. Ontario Canada 105 E3 46 20N 79 28W
North Bergen New Jersey U.S.A. 106 B2 40 46N 74 02W
North Berwick Lothian Scotland 46 F3 56 04N 2 44W
North Bull Island Dublin Irish Republic 49 B2 53 23N 6 08W
North Canadian r. U.S.A. 102 F4 36 00N 100 00W
North Cape New Zealand 87 B4 34 23S 173 04E
North Cape see Nordkapp
North Carolina state U.S.A. 103 K4 36 00N 80 00W
North Channel Ontario Canada 105 D3 46 00N 83 00W
North Cray Kent England 34 D2 51 26N 0 09E
North Dakota state U.S.A. 102 F6 47 00N 102 00W
North Dorset Downs hills Dorset England 31 E2 50 40N 2 30W
North Downs hills Surrey England 33 B3 51 13N 0 30W
North Duffield North Yorkshire England 43 H3 53 48N 0 57W
Northeim Germany 63 A2 51 43N 9 59E
Northern Ireland United Kingdom 48 E4
NORTHERN MARIANAS 118 E9
Northern Territory territory Australia 86 E5/E6 19 00S 132 00E
North Esk r. Tayside Scotland 46 F3 56 50N 2 50W
North European Plain Europe 51 54 00N 20 00E
North Fiji Basin Pacific Ocean 118 H6 18 00S 173 00E
Northfleet Kent England 34 E2 51 27N 0 20E
North Foreland c. Kent England 33 D2 51 23N 1 27E
North Frisian Islands see Nordfriesische Inseln
North Hollywood California U.S.A. 107 A3 34 10N 118 22W
North Holmwood Surrey England 34 B1 51 13N 0 20W
Northiam East Sussex England 33 C1 50 59N 0 36E
North Island New Zealand 87 C3 36 40S 177 00E
North Kessock Highland Scotland 46 D4 57 30N 4 15W
NORTH KOREA 81 K5/6
North Land see Severnaya Zemlya
Northleach Gloucestershire England 31 F3 51 51N 1 50W
North Little Rock Arkansas U.S.A. 103 H3 34 46N 92 16W
North Loup r. Nebraska U.S.A. 102 F5 42 00N 100 00W
Northop Clwyd Wales 42 A1 53 13N 3 08W
North Platte Nebraska U.S.A. 102 F5 41 09N 100 45W
North Platte r. U.S.A. 102 F5 42 00N 103 00W
North Pole Arctic Ocean 120 90 00N
North River tn. Manitoba Canada 101 Q4 58 55N 94 30W
North Ronaldsay i. Orkney Islands Scotland 47 E2 59 23N 2 26W
North Sea Europe 117 I12 55 00N 5 00E
North Shields Tyne and Wear England 44 C2 55 01N 1 26W
North Somercotes Lincolnshire England 36 E3 53 28N 0 08E
North Sound, The Orkney Islands Scotland 47 E2 59 17N 2 45W
North Tawton Devon England 31 D2 50 48N 3 53W
North Tidworth Wiltshire England 31 F3 51 16N 1 40W
North Tyne r. Northumberland England 44 B2 54 05N 2 10W
North Uist i. Western Isles Scotland 46 A4 57 40N 7 15W
Northumberland co. England 44 B2/C2 55 10N 2 00W
Northumberland National Park Northumberland
North Walsham Norfolk England 33 D3 52 50N 1 24E
North Weald Bassett Essex England 34 D3 51 43N 0 10E
North West Cape Australia 86 A5 21 48S 114 10E
North West Christmas Island Ridge Pacific Ocean 119 J8 9 30N 165 00E
Northwestern Atlantic Basin Atlantic Ocean 117 B10 33 00N 70 00W
Northwest Highlands Scotland 46 C4–D5
Northwest Pacific Basin Pacific Ocean 118 F11 35 00N 150 00E
Northwest Territories territory Canada 100–101 M6 65 15N 115 00W
Northwich Cheshire England 42 C1 53 16N 2 32W
North York Moors National Park North Yorkshire England 40 D3 54 22N 0 45W
North Yorkshire co. England 40 C3 54 05N 1 20W
Norton Kansas U.S.A. 102 G4 39 51N 99 53W
Norton North Yorkshire England 40 D3 54 08N 0 48W
Norton Shropshire England 35 A2 52 36N 2 24W
Norton Sound Alaska U.S.A. 100 C5 64 00N 162 30W
Norvegia, Cape Antarctica 121 71 28S 12 25W
Norwalk California U.S.A. 107 B2 33 56N 118 04W
Norwalk Connecticut U.S.A. 105 F2 41 07N 73 25W
NORWAY 67 B3
Norway House Manitoba Canada 101 P3 53 59N 97 50W
Norwegian Basin Arctic Ocean 117 H13 67 00N 0 00
Norwegian Sea Arctic Ocean 120 70 00N 5 00E
Norwich Connecticut U.S.A. 105 F2 41 32N 72 05W
Norwich Norfolk England 33 D3 52 38N 1 18E
Nose of Howth c. Dublin Irish Republic 49 B2 53 23N 6 03W
Noshiro Japan 82 D3 40 13N 140 00E
Nosop r. Southern Africa 95 D2 25 00S 20 30E
Noss Head c. Highland Scotland 46 E5 58 28N 3 04W
Nosy Bé i. Madagascar 95 I5 13 00S 47 00E
Notéc r. Poland 69 C3 53 00N 17 00E
Notre Dame Bay Newfoundland Canada 101 X2 49 40N 55 00W
Notre-Dame du Lac tn. Québec Canada 105 G3 47 38N 68 49W
Nottaway River Québec Canada 105 E4 51 00N 78 00W
Nottingham Nottinghamshire England 36 C2 52 58N 1 10W
Nottingham Island Northwest Territories Canada 101 T5 62 15N 77 30W
Nottinghamshire co. England 36 C3/D3 53 20N 1 00W
Nouadhibou Mauritania 93 B7 20 54N 17 01W
Nouakchott Mauritania 93 B6 18 09N 15 58W
Noumea New Caledonia 86 L5 22 16S 166 26E
Nouzonville France 64 D1 49 49N 4 45E
Nova Friburgo Brazil 115 I8 22 16S 42 34W
Nova Iguaçu Brazil 116 B2 22 45S 43 27W
Novara Italy 68 A4 45 27N 8 37E
Nova Scotia province Canada 101 W1 44 30N 65 00W
Nova Scotia Basin Atlantic Ocean 117 C10 39 00N 55 00W
Novaya Zemlya is. Russia 71 H10 74 00N 55 00E
Novgorod Russia 70 F7 58 30N 31 20E
Novi Pazar Serbia Yugoslavia 68 D3 43 09N 20 29E
Novi Sad Serbia Yugoslavia 68 C4 45 15N 19 51E
Novograd-Volynskiy Ukraine 69 E3 50 34N 27 32E
Novo Hamburgo Brazil 115 G7 29 37S 51 07W
Novokazalinsk Kazakhstan 70 I5 45 48N 62 06E
Novokuznetsk Russia 71 K6 53 45N 87 12E
Novolazarevskaya r.s. Antarctica 121 70 46S 11 50E
Novorossiysk Russia 70 F4 44 44N 37 46E
Novosibirsk Russia 71 K7 55 04N 83 05E
Novyy Port Russia 71 J9 67 38N 72 33E
Novyy Urengoy Russia 71 J9 66 00N 77 20E
Nowai r. India 76 K2 22 39N 88 28E
Nowa Sól Poland 69 C3 51 49N 15 41E
Nowgong India 77 G5 25 03N 79 27E
Nowy Dwor Poland 69 D3 52 27N 20 41E
Nowy Sącz Poland 69 D2 49 39N 20 40E
Nubian Desert Sudan 78 D3 21 00N 33 00E
Nueces r. Texas U.S.A. 102 G2 28 00N 99 00W
Nueltin Lake Northwest Territories Canada 101 P5 60 30N 99 00W
Nueva Rosita Mexico 108 D5 27 58N 101 11W
Nueva San Salvador El Salvador 108 G2 13 40N 89 18W
9 de Julio (Nueve de Julio) tn. Argentina 115 E5 35 28S 60 58W
Nuevitas Cuba 109 I4 21 34N 77 18W
Nuevo Casa Grandes Mexico 108 C6 30 22N 107 53W
Nuevo Laredo Mexico 108 E5 27 30N 99 30W
Nu Jiang (Salween) r. China 77 G6 31 30N 94 00E
Nuku'alofa Tonga 118 I5 21 09S 175 14W
Nukus Uzbekistan 70 H4 42 28N 59 07E
Nullabor Plain Australia 86 D3 32 00S 128 00E
Numazu Japan 82 C2 35 08N 138 50E
Numedal geog. reg. Norway 67 B3 60 40N 9 00E
Nuneaton Warwickshire England 35 D2 52 32N 1 28W
Nunivak Island Alaska U.S.A. 100 B5 60 00N 166 00W
Nunspeet Netherlands 64 E4 52 22N 5 47E
Nuremberg see Nürnberg
Nürnberg (Nuremberg) Germany 63 B1 49 27N 11 05E
Nürtingen Germany 63 A1 48 37N 9 20E
Nuseybin Turkey 78 F6 37 05N 41 11E
Nushki Pakistan 76 B5 29 33N 66 01E
Nutak Newfoundland Canada 101 W4 57 30N 61 59W
Nutt's Corner Northern Ireland 49 C1 54 38N 6 09W
Nuussuaq p. Greenland 101 Y7 70 50N 53 00W
Nyainqêntêngiha Shan mts. China 81 C3–E4 30 00N 90 00E
Nyala Sudan 94 D10 12 01N 24 50E
Nyasa, Lake (Lake Malawi) Southern Africa 95 F5 12 00S 35 00E
Nyíregyháza Hungary 69 D2 47 57N 21 43E
Nykøbing Denmark 67 C1 54 47N 11 53E
Nyköping Sweden 67 D2 58 45N 17 03E
Nyngan Australia 86 H3 31 34S 147 14E
Nyons France 61 C1 44 22N 5 08E
Nysa (Neisse) r. Poland 69 B3 52 00N 14 00E
Nysa Poland 69 C3 50 30N 17 20E
Nyū dō-zaki c. Japan 82 C2 40 00N 139 42E

O

Oadby Leicestershire England 36 C2 52 36N 1 04W
Oahe, Lake U.S.A. 102 F6 45 00N 100 00W
Oahu i. Hawaiian Islands 119 X18 21 30N 158 10W
Oakenclough Lancashire England 42 B3 53 55N 2 42W
Oakengates Shropshire England 35 A3 52 42N 2 28W
Oakes North Dakota U.S.A. 104 A3 46 08N 98 07W
Oakham Leicestershire England 36 D2 42 21N 72 03W
Oak Hill tn. West Virginia U.S.A. 105 D1 37 58N 81 11W
Oakland California U.S.A. 102 B4 37 50N 122 15W
Oakland City Indiana U.S.A. 104 C1 38 21N 87 19W
Oakley Fife Scotland 45 C2 56 05N 3 35W
Oakley Hampshire England 32 A2 51 15N 1 12W
Oak Ridge tn. Tennessee U.S.A. 103 J4 36 02N 84 12W
Oakville Ontario Canada 105 E2 43 27N 79 41W
Oamaru New Zealand 87 B1 45 07S 170 58E
Oano Island Pitcairn Islands 119 N5 23 32S 125 00W
Oaxaca Mexico 108 E3 17 05N 96 41N
Ob' r. Russia 71 I9 65 30N 66 00E
Ob', Gulf of Russia 71 J9 68 00N 74 00E
Oba Ontario Canada 101 S2 48 38N 84 17W
Oban Strathclyde Scotland 46 C3 56 25N 5 29W
Ober Österreich admin. Austria 63 B1 48 00N 14 00E
Oberhausen Germany 62 B2 51 27N 6 50E
Oberpfälzer Wald forest Germany 63 B1 49 00N 12 00E
Oberursel Germany 63 A2 50 12N 8 35E
Obidos Brazil 114 F12 1 52S 55 30W
Obihiro Japan 82 D3 42 56N 143 10E
Obitsu r. Japan 83 C2 35 25N 139 53E
Ocala Florida U.S.A. 103 J2 29 11N 82 09W
Ocaña Colombia 114 C14 8 16N 73 21W
Ocean City Maryland U.S.A. 105 E1 38 21N 75 06W
Ochakovo Russia 70 L1 55 39N 37 30E
Ochil Hills Scotland 45 C2/D2 56 15N 3 30W
Ocho Rios Jamaica 109 Q8 18 24N 77 06W
Ockley Surrey England 34 B1 51 09N 0 22W
Oconto Wisconsin U.S.A. 104 C2 44 55N 87 52W
Ocotlán Mexico 108 D4 20 21N 102 42W
Ōda Japan 82 B2 35 10N 132 29E
Ōdate Japan 82 D3 40 18N 140 32E
Odawara Japan 82 C2 35 15N 139 08E
Odda Norway 67 B3 60 03N 6 34E
Ödemiş Turkey 68 E2 38 11N 27 58E
Odense Denmark 67 C2 55 24N 10 25E
Odenwald mts. Germany 63 A1 49 00N 9 00E
Oder see Odra
Odessa Delaware U.S.A. 105 E1 39 27N 75 40W
Odessa Texas U.S.A. 102 F3 31 50N 102 23W
Odessa Ukraine 70 F5 46 30N 30 46E
Odiel r. Spain 66 A2 37 32N 7 00W
Odra (Oder) r. Europe 69 C3 51 00N 17 00E
Oegstgeest Netherlands 65 B2 52 10N 4 29E
Oekusi (Dili) Indonesia 80 H2 8 35S 125 35E
Ofanto r. Italy 68 C3 41 00N 15 00E
Offaly co. Irish Republic 48 D3 53 15N 7 35W
Offenbach am Main Germany 63 A1 50 06N 8 46E
Offenburg Germany 63 A1 48 29N 7 57E
Ofuna Japan 83 B2 35 21N 139 32E
Ofunato Japan 82 D2 39 04N 141 43E
Ogaden geog. reg. Africa 94 I9 7 00N 51 00E
Ogaki Japan 82 C2 35 22N 136 36E
Ogasawara Guntō i. Pacific Ocean 118 E10 27 30N 143 00E
Ogawa Japan 83 A3 35 43N 135 29E
Ogbomosho Nigeria 93 F4 8 05N 4 11E
Ogden Utah U.S.A. 102 D5 41 14N 111 59W
Ogdensburg New York U.S.A. 105 E2 44 42N 75 31W
Ogilvie Mountains Yukon Territory Canada 100 H6 65 05N 139 00W
Ogoki r. Ontario Canada 101 R3 51 00N 87 00W
Ogooué r. Gabon 93 G2 0 50S 9 50E
Ogun r. Nigeria 92 C3 6 42N 3 29E
Ogunpa r. Nigeria 92 E4 7 19N 3 55E
Ōhata Japan 82 D3 41 22N 141 11E
Ohio r. U.S.A. 104 C1 38 00N 88 00W
Ohio state U.S.A. 105 D2 40 00N 83 00W
Ohori Japan 83 C2 35 20N 139 52E
Ohře r. Ceska Czechoslovakia 63 B2 50 00N 14 00E
Ohre r. Germany 63 B2 52 00N 11 00E
Ohridsko ezero l. Europe 68 D3 41 00N 20 00E
Oil City Pennsylvania U.S.A. 105 E2 41 26N 79 44W
Oise r. France 61 B2 49 10N 2 10E
Ōita Japan 82 B1 33 15N 131 36E
Ojinaga Mexico 108 D5 29 35N 104 26W
Okanagan r. North America 102 C6 49 00N 119 00W
Okara Pakistan 77 C6 30 49N 73 31E
Okavango r. Southern Africa 95 C4 17 50S 20 00E
Okavango Basin Botswana 95 D4 19 00S 23 00E
Okaya Japan 82 C2 36 03N 138 00E
Okayama Japan 82 B1 34 40N 133 54E
Okazaki Japan 82 C1 34 58N 137 10E
Oke Ado Nigeria 92 E4 7 21N 3 55E
Okeechobee, Lake Florida U.S.A. 103 J2 27 00N 81 00W
Oke Foko Nigeria 92 E4 7 22N 3 55E
Okehampton Devon England 31 C2 50 44N 4 00W
Okene Nigeria 93 G4 7 31N 6 14E
Oke Ofa Nigeria 92 E4 7 23N 3 58E
Okha Russia 71 Q6 53 35N 143 01E
Okhla India 76 M4 28 33N 77 16E
Okhotsk Russia 71 Q7 59 20N 143 15E
Okhotsk, Sea of Russia 71 Q7 55 00N 148 00E
Oki is. Japan 82 B2 36 05N 133 00E
Okinawa i. Japan 81 K3 26 30N 128 00E

Oklahoma *state* U.S.A. **103** G4 36 00N 98 00W
Oklahoma City Oklahoma U.S.A. **103** G4 35 28N 97 33W
Oktyabr'skiy Russia **71** R6 52 43N 156 14E
Okushiri-tō *i.* Japan **82** C2 42 15N 139 30E
Öland *i.* Sweden **67** D2 56 45N 51 50E
Olbia Italy **68** A3 40 56N 9 30E
Oldbury West Midlands England **35** C2 52 30N 2 00W
Oldcotes Nottinghamshire England **43** G2 53 24N 1 07W
Old Crow Yukon Territory Canada **100** H6 67 34N 139 43W
Oldenburg Germany **63** A2 53 08N 8 13E
Oldenzaal Netherlands **64** F4 52 19N 6 55E
Old Fletton Cambridgeshire England **33** B3 52 34N 0 14W
Oldham Greater Manchester England **42** D2 53 33N 2 07W
Old Harbour Jamaica **109** Q7 17 56N 77 07W
Old Harbour Bay *tn.* Jamaica **109** Q7 17 54N 77 06W
Old Head of Kinsale *c.* Irish Republic **48** C1 51 40N 8 30W
Oldmeldrum Grampian Scotland **46** F4 57 20N 2 20W
Olds Alberta Canada **100** M3 51 50N 114 06W
Old Town Maine U.S.A. **105** G2 44 55N 68 41W
Old Windsor Berkshire England **34** B2 51 28N 0 35E
Olean New York U.S.A. **105** E2 42 05N 78 26W
Olekma *r.* Russia **71** O7 59 00N 121 00E
Olekminsk Russia **71** O8 60 25N 120 25E
Olenëk *r.* Russia **71** O10 72 00N 122 00E
Olenëk Russia **71** N9 68 28N 112 18E
Olhão Portugal **66** A2 37 01N 7 50W
Ólimbos *(Olympus) mt.* Greece **68** D3 40 05N 22 21E
Olinda Brazil **114** J11 8 00S 34 51W
Olivia Minnesota U.S.A. **104** B2 44 47N 94 58W
Ollerton Nottinghamshire England **43** G1 53 12N 1 00W
Olney Buckinghamshire England **33** B3 52 09N 0 43W
Olomouc Ceska Czechoslovakia **69** C2 49 38N 17 15E
Olongapo The Philippines **80** G6 14 49N 120 17E
Olsztyn Poland **69** D3 53 48N 20 29E
Olt *r.* Romania **69** D1 44 00N 24 00E
Olten Switzerland **61** C2 47 22N 7 55E
Olympia Washington U.S.A. **102** B6 47 03N 122 53W
Olympus *mt.* Cyprus **78** D5 34 55N 32 52E
Olympus *mt.* Greece *see* Ólimbos
Olympus, Mount Washington U.S.A. **102** B6 47 49N 123 42W
Om' *r.* Russia **71** J7 55 00N 79 00E
Omagh Northern Ireland **48** D4 54 36N 7 18W
Omaha Nebraska U.S.A. **104** A2 41 15N 96 00W
OMAN **79** I2
Oman, Gulf of Iran/Oman **79** I3 24 30N 58 30E
Ombersley Hereford & Worcester England **35** B1 52 17N 2 13W
Omboué Gabon **93** G2 1 38S 9 20E
Omdurman Sudan **78** D2 15 37N 32 29E
Omi *r.* Nigeria **92** F4 7 19N 4 01E
Omo *r.* Ethiopia **94** G9 7 00N 37 00E
Omolon *r.* Russia **71** R9 65 00N 160 00E
Omoloy *r.* Russia **71** P9 69 00N 132 00E
Omsk Russia **71** J7 55 00N 73 22E
Ōmuta Japan **82** B1 33 02N 130 26E
Ona *r.* Nigeria **92** E4 7 28N 3 58E
Ondo Nigeria **93** F4 7 05N 4 55E
Onega, Lake *see* Ozero Onezhskoye
Oneonta New York U.S.A. **105** E2 42 28N 75 04W
Ongea Levu *i.* Fiji **118** V15 19 11S 178 28W
Onitsha Nigeria **93** G4 6 10N 6 47E
Onomichi Japan **82** B1 34 25N 33 11E
Onon *r.* Russia/Mongolia **81** H8 51 00N 114 00E
Onslow Australia **86** B5 21 41S 115 12E
Onslow Village Surrey England **34** B1 51 14N 0 36W
Ontario California U.S.A. **102** C3 34 04N 117 38W
Ontario *province* Canada **101** Q3 51 00N 91 00W
Ontario, Lake North America **105** E2 43 00N 78 00W
Ontonagon Michigan U.S.A. **104** C3 46 52N 89 18W
Onuki Japan **83** C2 35 16N 139 51E
Oologah Lake Oklahoma U.S.A. **104** A1 36 00N 95 00W
Oostelijk Flevoland *geog. reg.* Netherlands **64** E4 52 30N 5 40E
Oostende Belgium **64** B3 51 13N 2 55E
Oosterhout Netherlands **64** D3 51 39N 4 52E
Oosterschelde *sd.* Netherlands **64** C3 51 30N 3 58E
Oost-Vlaanderen *admin.* Belgium **64** C3 51 10N 3 45E
Oostvoorne Netherlands **65** A1 51 55N 4 06E
Opala Zaïre **94** D7 0 40S 24 20E
Opava Ceska Czechoslovakia **69** C2 49 58N 17 55E
Opochka Russia **67** F2 56 41N 28 42E
Opole Poland **69** C3 50 40N 17 56E
Oporto *see* Porto
Opotiki New Zealand **87** C3 38 00S 117 18E
Optic Lake *tn.* Manitoba Canada **101** O3 54 47N 101 15W
Oradea Romania **69** D2 47 03N 21 55E
Oradell Reservoir New Jersey U.S.A. **106** B2 40 58N 74 00W
Oran Algeria **93** E10 35 45N 0 38W
Orán Argentina **115** E8 23 07S 64 16W
Orange Australia **86** H3 33 19S 149 10E
Orange California U.S.A. **107** C2 33 43N 117 54W
Orange France **61** B1 44 08N 4 48E
Orange New Jersey U.S.A. **106** B2 40 45N 74 14W
Orange *r.* Southern Africa **95** C2 28 30S 17 30E
Orange Texas U.S.A. **103** H3 30 05N 93 43W
Orangeburg South Carolina U.S.A. **103** J3 33 28N 80 53W
Orange Free State *admin.* Republic of South Africa **95** E2 27 30S 27 30E
Oranienburg Germany **63** B2 52 46N 13 15E
Oranmore Galway Irish Republic **48** C3 53 16N 8 54W
Oraviţa Romania **69** D2 45 02N 21 43E
Orbigo *r.* Spain **66** A3 42 15N 5 45W
Orcadas *r.s.* Antarctica **121** 60 40S 44 44W
Orchies France **64** C2 50 28N 3 15E
Orcia *r.* Italy **68** B3 42 00N 11 00E
Ordzhonikidze *see* Vladikavkaz
Örebro Sweden **67** D2 59 17N 15 13E
Oregon *state* U.S.A. **102** B5 44 00N 120 00W
Oregon City Oregon U.S.A. **102** B6 45 21N 122 36W
Orël Russia **70** F6 52 58N 36 04E
Orem Utah U.S.A. **102** D5 40 20N 111 45W
Orenburg Russia **70** H6 51 50N 55 00E
Orense Spain **66** A3 42 20N 7 52W
Orford Suffolk England **33** D3 52 06N 1 31E
Orford Ness *c.* Suffolk England **33** D3 52 05N 1 34E
Orge *r.* France **60** B1 48 39N 02 19E
Orient Bay *tn.* Ontario Canada **104** C3 49 23N 88 08W
Orihuela Spain **66** B2 38 05N 0 56W
Orillia Ontario Canada **105** E2 44 36N 79 26W
Orissa *admin.* India **77** E4 20 20N 83 00E
Oristano Italy **68** A2 39 54N 8 36E
Orizaba Mexico **108** E3 18 51N 97 08W
Orkney Islands *islands area* Scotland **47** E1 59 00N 3 00W
Orlando Florida U.S.A. **103** J2 28 33N 81 21W
Orléans France **61** B2 47 54N 1 54E
Orly France **60** B1 48 44N 2 24E
Ormskirk Lancashire England **42** B2 53 35N 2 54W
Orne *r.* France **61** A2 48 50N 0 16W
Örnsköldsvik Sweden **67** D3 63 19N 18 45E
Oronsay *i.* Strathclyde Scotland **46** B3 56 00N 6 15W
Orpington Greater London England **34** D2 51 23N 0 05E
Orrell Greater Manchester England **42** B2 53 33N 2 45N
Orsay France **60** A1 48 42N 2 11E
Orsha Belarus **69** F3 54 30N 30 23E
Orsk Russia **70** H6 51 13N 58 35E
Orthez France **61** A1 43 29N 0 46W
Ortigueira Spain **66** A3 43 43N 8 13W
Ortonville Minnesota U.S.A. **104** A3 45 18N 96 28W
Ortze *r.* Germany **63** B2 53 00N 10 00E
Orūmīyeh Iran **78** F6 37 40N 45 00E
Oruro Bolivia **114** D9 17 59S 67 08W
Orwell *r.* Suffolk England **33** D2 52 00N 1 15E
Osage *r.* U.S.A. **104** B1 38 00N 93 00W
Ōsaka Japan **82** C1 34 40N 135 30E
Osceola Iowa U.S.A. **104** B2 41 02N 93 46W
Osgodby North Yorkshire England **43** G3 53 46N 1 01W
Oshawa Ontario Canada **105** E2 43 53N 78 51W
Ō-shima *i.* Japan **82** C1 34 45N 139 25E
Oshkosh Wisconsin U.S.A. **104** C2 44 01N 88 32W
Oshogbo Nigeria **93** F4 7 50N 4 35E
Osijek Croatia **68** C4 45 33N 18 41E
Oskaloosa Iowa U.S.A. **104** B2 41 16N 92 40W
Oslo Norway **67** C2 59 56N 10 45E
Oslofjorden *fj.* Norway **67** C2 59 20N 10 37E
Osmaniye Turkey **78** E6 37 04N 36 15E
Osnabrück Germany **63** A2 52 17N 8 03E
Osorno Chile **115** C4 40 35S 73 14W
Oss Netherlands **64** E3 51 46N 5 31E
Ossa, Mount Australia **86** H1 41 52S 146 04E
Ossett West Yorkshire England **43** F3 53 41N 1 35W
Ostankino Russia **70** M2 55 50N 37 37E
Österdalälven *r.* Sweden **67** C3 61 40N 13 30E
Østerdalen *geog. reg.* Norway **67** C3 62 00N 10 30E
Osterode Germany **63** B2 51 44N 10 15E
Östervall Sweden **67** D3 62 20N 15 20E
Östersund Sweden **67** C3 63 10N 14 40E
Ostfriesische Inseln *(East Frisian Islands) is.* Germany **63** A2 53 00N 7 00E
Ostrava Ceska Czechoslovakia **69** C2 49 50N 18 15E
Ostróda Poland **69** D3 53 42N 19 59E
Ostrołęka Poland **69** D3 53 05N 21 32E
Ostrov Russia **67** F2 57 25N 28 20E
Ostrowiec Swietokrzyski Poland **69** D3 50 58N 21 22E
Ostrów Mazowiecki Poland **69** D3 52 50N 21 51E
Ostrów Wielkopolski Poland **69** C3 51 39N 17 50E
Oswaldtwistle Lancashire England **42** C3 53 44N 2 24W
Oswego New York U.S.A. **105** E2 43 27N 76 31W
Oswestry Shropshire England **36** A2 52 52N 3 03W
Ōta Japan **83** B3 35 34N 139 42E
Otaki New Zealand **87** C2 40 45S 175 09E
Otaru Japan **82** D3 43 14N 140 59E
Otava *r.* Ceska Czechoslovakia **63** B1 49 00N 13 00E
Otavalo Ecuador **114** B13 0 13N 78 15W
Otford Kent England **34** D1 51 19N 0 12E
O'The Cherokees, Lake Oklahoma U.S.A. **104** B1 37 00N 95 00W
Otley West Yorkshire England **43** E3 53 54N 1 41W
Otra *r.* Norway **67** B2 56 17N 7 30E
Otranto Italy **68** C3 40 08N 18 30E
Otranto, Strait of Adriatic Sea **68** C3 40 00N 19 00E
Otsego Michigan U.S.A. **104** C2 42 26N 85 42W
Ōtsu Japan **82** C2 35 00N 135 50E
Ottawa Illinois U.S.A. **104** C2 41 21N 88 51W
Ottawa Kansas U.S.A. **104** A1 38 35N 95 16W
Ottawa Ontario Canada **105** E3 45 25N 75 43W
Ottawa *(Rivière des Outaouais) r.* Ontario/Québec Canada **105** E3 46 00N 77 00W
Ottawa Islands Northwest Territories Canada **101** S4 59 10N 80 25W
Otter *r.* Devon England **31** D2 50 50N 3 10W
Otterburn Northumberland England **44** B2 55 14N 2 10W
Otter Rapids *tn.* Ontario Canada **105** D4 50 12N 81 40W
Ottery *r.* Cornwall England **30** C2 50 40N 4 30W
Ottery St. Mary Devon England **31** D2 50 45N 3 17W
Ottumwa Iowa U.S.A. **104** B2 41 02N 92 26W
Ouachita *r.* U.S.A. **103** H3 34 00N 93 00W
Ouachita Mountains U.S.A. **103** G3 34 00N 95 00W
Ouadda Central African Republic **94** D9 8 09N 22 20E
Ouagadougou Burkina **93** E5 12 20N 1 40W
Ouahigouya Burkina **93** E5 13 31N 2 20W
Ouargla Algeria **93** G9 32 00N 5 16E
Ouassel *r.* Algeria **66** C2 35 30N 2 00E
Oubangui *r.* Africa **94** C8 0 00 17 30E
Oudenaarde Belgium **64** C2 50 50N 3 37E
Oude Rijn *r.* Netherlands **65** D2 52 06N 4 46E
Oudtshoorn Republic of South Africa **95** D1 33 35S 22 12E
Oued Dra *r.* Morocco **68** D1 28 10N 11 00W
Oued Zem Morocco **93** D9 32 55N 6 33W
Ouensé Congo **92** A2 4 16S 15 17E
Ouerrha *r.* Morocco **66** A1 34 00N 6 00W
Ouesso Congo **94** C8 1 38N 16 03E
Ouezzane Morocco **66** A1 34 52N 5 35W
Ouham *r.* Central African Republic **94** C9 7 00N 17 30E
Oujda Morocco **93** E9 34 41N 1 45W
Oulton Staffordshire England **35** B3 52 54N 2 09W
Oulu Finland **67** F3 65 02N 25 27E
Oulujärvi *l.* Finland **67** F3 64 20N 27 00E
Oulujoki *r.* Finland **67** F3 64 50N 26 00E
Ounasjoki *r.* Finland **67** F4 67 00N 25 00E
Oundle Northamptonshire England **36** D2 52 29N 0 29W
Our *r.* Luxembourg/F.R.G. **64** F1 50 00N 6 00E
Ouro *r.* Brazil **116** A3 22 40S 43 32W
Ourthe *r.* Belgium **64** E2 50 20N 5 50E
Ōu-sanmyaku *mts.* Japan **82** D2 39 20N 141 00E
Ouse *r.* East Sussex England **33** C1 50 55N 0 00
Ouse *r.* North Yorkshire England **40** C2 53 40N 1 00W
Ouseburn North Yorkshire England **43** G4 54 04N 1 20W
Oust *r.* France **61** A2 47 50N 2 30W
Out Skerries *is.* Shetland Islands Scotland **47** C2 60 25N 0 46W
Outbridge South Yorkshire England **43** F2 53 26N 1 34W
Outer Hebrides *is.* Western Isles Scotland **46** A4–B5
Outreau France **64** A2 50 42N 1 36E
Outwell Norfolk England **33** C3 52 37N 0 14E
Outwood Surrey England **34** C1 51 13N 0 06W
Outwood West Yorkshire England **43** F3 53 42N 1 30W
Ovalau *i.* Fiji **118** U16 17 40S 178 47E
Ovalle Chile **115** C6 30 33S 71 16W
Overflakkee *i.* Netherlands **64** D3 51 45N 4 10E
Overijssel *admin.* Netherlands **64** F4 52 23N 6 28E
Overseal Derbyshire England **35** D3 52 44N 1 34W
Overton Clwyd Wales **38** D2 52 58N 2 56W
Overton Hampshire England **32** A2 51 15N 1 15W
Overton Lancashire England **42** B4 54 01N 2 53W
Övertorneå Sweden **67** E4 66 22N 23 40E
Overtown Strathclyde Scotland **45** C1 55 45N 3 55W
Oviedo Spain **66** A3 43 21N 5 50W
Owando Congo **94** C7 0 27S 15 44E
Owatonna Minnesota U.S.A. **104** B2 44 06N 93 10W
Owen Falls Dam Uganda **94** F8 0 29N 33 11E
Owen, Mount New Zealand **87** B2 41 33S 172 33E
Owensboro Kentucky U.S.A. **104** C1 37 45N 87 05W
Owens Lake California U.S.A. **102** C4 36 25N 117 56W
Owen Sound Ontario Canada **105** D2 44 34N 80 56W
Owen Sound *tn.* Ontario Canada **101** S1 44 34N 80 56W
Owen Stanley Range *mts.* Papua New Guinea **86** H8 8 00S 147 30E
Owo Nigeria **93** G4 7 10N 5 39E
Owosso Michigan U.S.A. **105** D2 43 00N 84 11W
Owyhee *r.* U.S.A. **102** C5 43 00N 117 00W
Oxenhope West Yorkshire England **43** E3 53 49N 1 57W
Oxford Oxfordshire England **32** A2 51 46N 1 15W
Oxford Canal England **35** E2 52 24N 1 18W
Oxfordshire *co.* England **32** A2 51 45N 1 20W
Oxnard California U.S.A. **102** C3 34 11N 119 10W
Oxshott Surrey England **34** B2 51 20N 0 21W
Oxted Surrey England **34** C1 51 15N 0 01W
Oxus *see* Amudar'ya
Oyama Japan **82** C2 36 18N 139 48E
Oyapock *r.* Brazil **114** G13 3 00N 52 30W
Oyem Gabon **93** H3 1 34N 11 31E
Oykel *r.* Highland Scotland **46** D4 57 58N 4 40W
Oyo Nigeria **93** F4 7 50N 3 55E
Ozark Plateau Missouri U.S.A. **104** B1 37 00N 93 00W
Ozarks, Lake of the Missouri U.S.A. **104** B1 38 00N 93 00W
Ozero Alakol' *salt l.* Kazakhstan **71** K5 46 00N 82 00E
Ozero Balkhash *(Lake Balkhash) l.* Kazakhstan **71** J5 46 00N 75 00E
Ozero Baykal *(Lake Baykal) l.* Russia **71** M6 54 00N 109 00E
Ozero Chany *salt l.* Russia **71** J6 55 00N 77 30E
Ozero Chudskoye *(Lake Peipus) l.* Estonia/Russia **67** F2 58 40N 27 30E
Ozero Imandra *l.* Russia **67** G4 67 45N 33 00E
Ozero Issyk-Kul' *salt l.* Kirgyzstan **71** J4 42 30N 77 30E
Ozero Khanka *l.* Asia **71** P5 45 00N 132 30E
Ozero Leksozero *l.* Russia **67** G3 64 00N 31 20E
Ozero Nyuk *l.* Russia **67** G3 64 30N 31 50E
Ozero Onezhskoye *(Lake Onega) l.* Russia **70** F8 62 00N 40 00E
Ozero Pskovskoye *l.* Estonia/Russia **67** F2 58 00N 28 00E
Ozero Pyazero *l.* Russia **67** G4 66 00N 31 15E
Ozero Sevan *l.* Armenia **78** F7 40 35N 44 00E
Ozero Sredneye Kuyto *l.* Russia **67** G3 65 00N 31 15E
Ozero Taymyr Russia **71** M10 74 00N 102 30E
Ozero Tengiz *salt l.* Russia **70** I6 51 00N 69 00E
Ozero Topozero *l.* Russia **67** G4 65 45N 32 10E
Ozero Zaysan *l.* Kazakhstan **71** K5 48 00N 84 00E
Ozieri Italy **61** C1 40 35N 9 01E

P

Pabjanice Poland **69** C3 51 40N 19 20E
Pabna Bangladesh **77** F4 24 00N 89 15E
Pacasmayo Peru **114** B11 7 27S 79 33W
Pachecos Brazil **116** D2 22 50S 43 00W
Pachuca Mexico **108** E4 20 10N 98 44W
Pacific–Antarctic Ridge Pacific Ocean **119** M2 55 00S 135 00W
Pacific Grove California U.S.A. **102** B4 36 36N 121 56W
Pacific Ocean **118–119**
Padang Indonesia **80** C3 1 00S 100 21E
Paddington Greater London England **34** C3 51 31N 0 12W
Paddock Wood *tn.* Kent England **34** E1 51 11N 0 23E
Paderborn Germany **63** A2 51 43N 8 44E
Padiham Lancashire England **42** D3 53 49N 2 19W
Padilla Bolivia **114** E9 19 18S 64 20W
Padova Italy **68** B4 45 24N 11 53E
Padstow Cornwall England **30** C2 50 33N 4 56W
Paducah Kentucky U.S.A. **104** C1 37 03N 88 36W
Paeroa New Zealand **87** C3 37 21S 175 41E
Pag *i.* Croatia **68** B3 44 00N 15 00E
Pagadian The Philippines **80** G5 7 50N 123 30E
Pahala Hawaiian Islands **119** Z17 19 12N 155 28W
Paharganj India **76** L4 28 38N 77 12E
Paignton Devon England **31** D2 50 26N 3 34W
Päijänne *l.* Finland **67** F3 61 30N 25 25E
Pailton Warwickshire England **35** E2 52 26N 1 17W
Painesville Ohio U.S.A. **105** D2 41 43N 81 15W
Paisley Strathclyde Scotland **45** B1 55 50N 4 26W
Paita Peru **114** A11 5 11S 81 09W
PAKISTAN **76/77** A5–C5
Pakokku Myanmar **81** E2 21 20N 95 05E
Pakse Laos **80** D6 15 07N 105 47E
Palaiseau France **60** A1 48 43N 2 15E
Palana Russia **71** R7 59 05N 159 59E
Palangkaraya Indonesia **80** E3 2 06S 113 55E
Palau *(Belau) i.* Pacific Ocean **118** D8 7 30N 134 30E
Palawan *i.* The Philippines **80** F5/F6 9 00N 114 00E
Palayankottai India **77** D1 8 42N 77 46E
Palembang Indonesia **80** C3 2 59S 104 45E
Palencia Spain **66** B3 41 01N 4 32W
Palermo Italy **68** B2 38 08N 13 23E
Palestine Texas U.S.A. **103** G3 31 45N 95 39W
Palghat India **77** D2 10 46N 76 42E
Palk Strait India **77** D2 10 00N 80 00E
Palliser, Cape New Zealand **87** C2 41 37S 175 16E
Palma de Mallorca Balearic Islands **66** E4 39 35N 2 39E
Palmar Sur Costa Rica **109** H1 8 57N 83 28W
Palmas, Cape Liberia **93** D3 4 25N 7 50W
Palmer Alaska U.S.A. **100** F5 61 35N 149 10W
Palmer *r.s.* Antarctica **121** 64 46S 83 55W
Palmer Land *geog. reg.* Antarctica **121** 72 00S 62 00W
Palmerston Dublin Irish Republic **49** A2 53 22N 6 22W
Palmerston Atoll *is.* Pacific Ocean **119** J6 18 04S 163 10W
Palmerston North New Zealand **87** C2 40 20S 175 39E
Palmira Colombia **114** B13 3 33N 76 17W
Palmyra Atoll *is.* Pacific Ocean **119** K8 5 52N 162 05W
Palomares Mexico **108** E3 17 10N 95 04W
Palopo Indonesia **80** G3 3 01S 120 12E
Palos Verdes Hills California U.S.A. **107** A2 33 46N 118 23W
Palu Indonesia **80** F3 0 54S 119 52E
Pamiers France **61** B1 43 07N 1 36E
Pamirs *mts.* Asia **70** J3 38 00N 74 00E
Pamlico Sound North Carolina U.S.A. **103** K4 35 00N 76 00W
Pampas *geog. reg.* Argentina **115** E5 36 00S 63 00W
Pamplona Colombia **114** C14 7 24N 72 38W
Pamplona Peru **116** F4 12 09S 76 58W
Pamplona Spain **66** B3 42 49N 1 39W
PANAMA **109** H1
Panama Canal Panama **109** I1 9 00N 80 00W
Panama City Florida U.S.A. **103** I3 30 10N 85 41W
Panama Isthmus Central America **96** 9 00N 80 00W
Panamá Panama **109** I1 8 57N 79 30W
Panay *i.* The Philippines **80** G6 11 20N 122 30E
Pančevo Serbia Yugoslavia **68** D3 44 52N 20 40E
Panchla India **76** J2 22 32N 88 08E
Panchur India **76** K2 22 31N 88 15E
Panevėžys Lithuania **69** D4 55 44N 24 24E
Pangbourne Berkshire England **32** A2 51 29N 1 05W
Pangkalpinang Indonesia **80** D3 2 05S 106 09E
Pangnirtung Northwest Territories Canada **101** V6 66 05N 65 45W
Pānihāti India **76** K2 22 41N 88 23E
Panipat India **77** D5 29 24N 76 58E
Pantar *i.* Indonesia **80** G2 8 00S 124 00E
Pantelleria *i.* Italy **68** B2 36 00N 12 00E
Pantin France **60** B2 48 54N 2 25E
Pao de Açúcar *(Sugar Loaf) mt.* Brazil **116** C2 22 57S 43 09W
Papa Hawaiian Islands **119** Z17 19 12N 155 53W
Pápa Hungary **69** C2 47 20N 17 29E
Papantla Mexico **108** E4 20 30N 97 21W
Papa Stour *i.* Shetland Islands Scotland **47** B2 60 20N 1 42W
Papa Westray *i.* Orkney Islands Scotland **47** E2 59 22N 2 54W
Papenburg Germany **63** A2 53 05N 7 25E
Papendrecht Netherlands **64** D3 51 50N 4 42E
Papua, Gulf of Papua New Guinea **86** H8 8 30S 145 00E
PAPUA NEW GUINEA **86** H8
Pará *admin.* Brazil **114** G12 4 30S 52 30W
Paraburdoo Australia **86** B5 23 15S 117 45E
Paracel Islands South China Sea **80** E7 16 40N 112 00E
PARAGUAY **115** F8
Paraíba *admin.* Brazil **114** J11 7 20S 37 10W
Parakou Benin **93** F4 9 23N 2 40E
Paramaribo Surinam **114** F14 5 52N 55 14W
Paramonga Peru **114** B10 10 42S 77 50W
Paramus New Jersey U.S.A. **106** B2 40 55N 74 03W
Parana *admin.* Brazil **115** G8 24 30S 53 00W
Paraná Argentina **115** F6 31 45S 60 30W
Paranaguá Brazil **115** H7 25 32S 48 36W
Paraná Plateau Brazil **110** 25 00S 50 00W
Parbhani India **77** D3 19 16N 76 51E
Parchim Germany **63** B2 53 26N 11 51E
Pardubice Ceska Czechoslovakia **69** C2 50 03N 15 45E
Parepare Indonesia **80** F3 4 00S 119 40E
Parintins Brazil **114** F12 2 38S 56 45W
Paris France **60** B2 48 52N 2 20E
Paris Missouri U.S.A. **104** B1 39 27N 91 59W
Paris Texas U.S.A. **103** G3 33 41N 95 33W
Paris Basin France **51** 48 00N 2 30E
Parish New York U.S.A. **105** E2 43 24N 76 07W
Parkano Finland **67** E3 62 03N 23 00E
Parkersburg West Virginia U.S.A. **105** D1 39 17N 81 33W
Parma Italy **68** B3 44 48N 10 19E
Parma Ohio U.S.A. **105** D2 41 24N 81 44W
Parnaíba Brazil **114** I12 2 58S 41 46W
Parnassós *mt.* Greece **68** D2 38 30N 22 37E
Pärnu Estonia **67** E2 58 28N 24 30E
Paroo *r.* Australia **86** G4 27 00S 144 00E
Páros *i.* Greece **68** E2 37 00N 25 00E
Parras Mexico **108** D5 25 30N 102 11W
Parrett *r.* Somerset England **31** E3 51 05N 3 00W
Parry, Cape Northwest Territories Canada **100** K7 70 08N 124 34W
Parry Islands Northwest Territories Canada **101** N8 75 15N 109 00W
Parry Sound *tn.* Ontario Canada **105** D3 45 21N 80 03W
Parthenay France **61** A2 46 39N 0 14W
Partick Strathclyde Scotland **45** B1 55 52N 4 18W
Partington Greater Manchester England **42** C2 53 26N 2 26W
Pasadena California U.S.A. **107** B3 34 10N 118 09W
Pasadena Texas U.S.A. **103** G2 29 42N 95 14W
Pascagoula Mississippi U.S.A. **103** I3 30 21N 88 32W
Pas-de-Calais *admin.* France **64** A2 50 45N 2 00E
Pas de Calais *sd. see* Strait of Dover
Passage de la Déroute *sd.* Channel Islands / France **31** G6–H5 49 30N 2 00W
Passage West *tn.* Cork Irish Republic **48** C1 51 52N 8 20W
Passaic New Jersey U.S.A. **106** B2 40 50N 74 08W
Passaic River New Jersey U.S.A. **106** B2 40 46N 74 09W
Passau Germany **63** B1 48 35N 13 28E
Passo Fundo Brazil **115** G7 28 16S 52 20W
Pasto Colombia **114** B13 1 12N 77 17W
Patagonia *geog. reg.* Argentina **115** C2–D4 48 00S 70 00W
Patan India **77** C4 23 51N 72 11E
Patan Nepal **77** F5 27 40N 85 20E
Patchogue New York U.S.A. **105** F2 40 46N 73 01W
Patea New Zealand **87** C3 39 45S 174 29E
Pate Island Kenya **94** H7 2 05S 41 05E
Pateley Bridge *tn.* North Yorkshire England **43** E4 54 05N 1 45W
Paterson New Jersey U.S.A. **106** B2 40 55N 74 08W
Pathankot India **77** D6 32 16N 75 43E
Path of Condie Tayside Scotland **45** D2 56 17N 3 28W
Patiala India **77** D6 30 21N 76 27E
Pātipukur India **76** K2 22 36N 88 24E
Patna India **77** F5 25 37N 85 12E
Patna Strathclyde Scotland **46** D2 55 20N 4 30W
Patos Brazil **114** J11 6 55S 37 15W
Pátrai Greece **68** D2 38 14N 21 44E
Pattingham Staffordshire England **35** B2 52 36N 2 16W
Pau France **61** A1 43 18N 0 22W
Paungde Myanmar **77** H3 18 30N 95 30E
Pavia Italy **68** A4 45 12N 9 09E
Pavlodar Kazakhstan **71** J6 52 21N 76 59E
Pawtucket Massachusetts U.S.A. **105** F2 41 53N 71 23W
Paxton Illinois U.S.A. **104** C2 40 28N 88 07W
Payne, Lake Québec Canada **101** U4 59 00N 74 00W
Paysandú Uruguay **115** F6 32 21S 58 05W
Pazardzhik Bulgaria **68** D3 42 10N 24 20E
Peacehaven East Sussex England **33** C1 50 47N 0 01E
Peace River British Columbia/Alberta Canada **100** L4 57 30N 117 00W
Peace River *tn.* Alberta Canada **100** L4 56 15N 117 18W
Peak District National Park Derbyshire England **36** C3 53 12N 1 50W
Peake Deep Atlantic Ocean **117** F11 43 00N 20 05W
Peak, The *mt.* Derbyshire England **43** E2 53 24N 1 51W
Pearl Ontario Canada **104** C3 48 41N 88 39W

Pearl *r.* Mississippi U.S.A. **103** H3 32 00N 90 00W
Pearl Harbor Hawaiian Islands **119** X18 21 22N 158 00W
Pebble Island Falkland Islands **117** M16 51 20S 59 40W
Peć Serbia Yugoslavia **68** D3 42 40N 20 19E
Pechenga Russia **67** G4 69 28N 31 04E
Pechora *r.* Russia **70** H9 66 00N 52 00E
Pechora Russia **70** H9 65 14N 57 18E
Pecos *r.* U.S.A. **102** F3 30 00N 102 00W
Pecos Texas U.S.A. **102** F3 31 25N 103 30W
Pécs Hungary **69** C2 46 04N 18 15E
Pedreiras Brazil **114** I12 4 32S 44 40W
Pedro Juan Caballero Paraguay **115** F8 22 30S 55 44W
Peebles Borders Scotland **46** E2 55 39N 3 12W
Peekskill New York U.S.A. **105** F2 41 18N 73 56W
Peel Isle of Man England **41** F1 54 14N 4 42W
Peel *r.* Yukon Territory Canada **100** H6 66 00N 135 00W
Peel Fell *sum.* Scotland/England **46** F2 55 17N 2 35W
Peel Sound Northwest Territory Canada **101** P7 73 50N 95 55W
Peene *r.* Germany **63** B2 53 00N 14 00E
Pegasus Bay New Zealand **87** B2 43 00S 173 00E
Pegu Myanma **80** B7 17 18N 96 31E
Pegunungan Barisan *mts.* Indonesia **80** C3 2 30S 102 00E
Pegunungan Maoke *mts.* Indonesia **86** F9 4 00S 137 30E
Pegunungan Muller *mts.* Indonesia **80** E4 1 00N 113 40E
Pegunungan Schwaner *mts.* Indonesia **80** E3 1 00S 112 00E
Pegunungan Van Rees *mts.* Indonesia **86** F9 2 30S 138 00E
Pegu Yoma *mts.* Myanmar **77** H3 19 00N 96 00E
Peipus, Lake *see* Ozero Chudskoye
Pekalongan Indonesia **80** D2 6 54S 109 37E
Pekanbaru Indonesia **80** C4 0 33N 101 30E
Peking *see* Beijing
Pelee Point Ontario Canada **105** D2 41 45N 82 39W
Pelican Point Namibia **95** B3 22 54S 14 25E
Pelješac *i.* Croatia **68** C3 43 00N 17 00E
Pellworm *i.* Germany **63** A2 54 00N 8 00E
Pelly Lake Northwest Territories Canada **101** O6 65 10N 102 30W
Peloponnese *see* Pelopónnisos
Pelopónnisos *(Peloponnese) geog. reg.* Greece **68** D2 37 00N 22 00E
Pelotas Brazil **115** G6 31 45S 52 20W
Pelsall West Midlands England **35** C2 52 38N 1 58W
Pematangsiantar Indonesia **80** B4 2 59N 99 01E
Pemba Mozambique **95** H5 13 00S 40 30E
Pemba Island Tanzania **95** G6 5 30S 39 50E
Pemba National Park Zaïre **95** E6 9 00S 26 30E
Pembridge Hereford and Worcester England **36** B2 52 14N 2 53W
Pembroke Dyfed Wales **38** B1 51 41N 4 55W
Pembroke Ontario Canada **105** E3 45 49N 77 08W
Pembroke Dock Dyfed Wales **38** B1 51 42N 4 56W
Pembrokeshire Coast National Park Dyfed Wales **38** A1 51 50N 5 25W
Pembury Kent England **33** C2 51 08N 0 19E
Peñarroya-Pueblonuevo Spain **66** A2 38 19N 5 16W
Penarth South Glamorgan Wales **38** C1 51 27N 3 11W
Pencoed Mid Glamorgan Wales **38** C1 51 31N 3 30W
Pendlebury Greater Manchester England **42** D2 53 32N 2 21W
Pendleton Oregon U.S.A. **102** C6 45 40N 118 46W
Penedo Brazil **114** J10 10 16S 36 33W
Penha Brazil **116** B2 22 49S 43 17W
Penicuik Lothian Scotland **45** D1 55 50N 3 14W
Península de Taitao *p.* Chile **115** C3 46 30N 75 00W
Péninsule d'Ungava *p.* Québec Canada **101** U5 60 00N 74 00W
Penistone South Yorkshire England **43** F2 53 32N 1 37W
Penketh Cheshire England **40** B2 53 23N 2 40W
Penkridge Staffordshire England **35** B3 52 44N 2 07W
Penmaenmawr Gwynedd Wales **38** C3 53 16N 3 54W
Penner *r.* India **77** D2 14 30N 77 30E
Pennines *hills* North West England **40** B3
Pennsylvania *state* U.S.A. **105** E2 41 00N 78 00W
Penonomé Panama **109** H1 8 30N 80 20W
Penrhyndeudraeth Gwynedd Wales **38** B2 52 56N 4 04W
Penrith Cumbria England **44** B1 54 40N 2 44W
Penryn Cornwall England **30** B2 50 09N 5 06W
Pensacola Florida U.S.A. **103** I3 30 26N 87 12W
Pensacola Mountains Antarctica **121** 84 00S 60 00W
Pensby Merseyside England **42** A2 53 21N 3 06W
Penshurst Kent England **34** D1 51 11N 0 11E
Pensilva Cornwall England **30** C2 50 30N 4 25W
Pentenwell Lake Wisconsin U.S.A. **104** C2 44 00N 90 00W
Penticton British Columbia Canada **100** L2 49 29N 119 38W
Pentland Firth *sd.* Scotland **47** C1 58 45N 3 10W
Pentland Hills Scotland **45** D1 55 45N 3 30W
Pen-y-ghent *sum.* North Yorkshire England **40** B3 54 10N 2 14W
Penygroes Gwynedd Wales **38** B3 53 04N 4 17W
Penza Russia **70** G6 53 11N 45 00E
Penzance Cornwall England **30** B2 50 07N 5 33W
Peoria Illinois U.S.A. **104** C2 40 43N 89 38W
Pequena Arroio Fundo *r.* Brazil **116** B2 22 54S 43 24W
Pereira Colombia **114** B13 4 47N 75 46W
Perhojöki *r.* Finland **67** E3 63 30N 24 00E
Peribonca River Québec Canada **105** F3 49 00N 71 00W
Périgueux France **61** B2 45 12N 0 44E
Perm' Russia **70** H7 58 01N 56 10E
Pernambuco *admin.* Brazil **114** J11 8 00S 37 30W
Pernik Bulgaria **68** D3 42 36N 23 03E
Pernis Netherlands **65** B1 51 53N 4 23E
Péronne France **61** B2 49 56N 2 57E
Perovo Russia **70** N1 55 44N 37 46E
Perpignan France **61** B1 42 42N 2 54E
Perranporth Cornwall England **30** B2 50 20N 5 09W
Perros-Guirec France **61** A2 48 49N 3 27W
Perryville Missouri U.S.A. **104** C1 37 43N 87 52W
Pershore Hereford and Worcester England **36** B2 52 07N 2 05W
Perth Australia **86** B3 31 58S 115 49E
Perth Ontario Canada **105** E2 44 54N 76 15W
Perth Tayside Scotland **45** D2 56 24N 3 28W
Perth Amboy New Jersey U.S.A. **106** 40 31N 74 17W
PERU **114** B10
Peru Basin Pacific Ocean **119** Q6 18 00S 95 00W
Peru-Chile Trench Pacific Ocean **119** S6 13 00S 87 00W
Perugia Italy **68** B3 43 07N 12 23E
Peruwelz Belgium **64** C2 50 30N 3 35E
Pesaro Italy **68** B3 43 54N 12 54E
Pescara Italy **68** B3 42 27N 14 13E
Peshawar Pakistan **77** C6 34 01N 71 40E
Pessac France **61** A1 44 49N 0 37W
Petah Tiqwa Israel **78** O11 32 05N 34 53E
Petaluma California U.S.A. **102** B4 38 13N 122 39W
Pétange Luxembourg **64** E1 49 33N 5 53E
Petare Venezuela **114** D15 10 31N 66 50W
Petauke Zambia **95** F5 14 15S 31 20E
Peterborough Australia **86** F3 33 00S 138 51E
Peterborough Cambridgeshire England **33** B3 52 35N 0 15W
Peterborough Ontario Canada **105** E2 44 19N 78 20W
Peterculter Grampian Scotland **46** F4 57 05N 2 16W
Peterhead Grampian Scotland **46** G4 57 30N 1 46W
Peterlee Durham England **44** C1 54 46N 1 19W
Petersburg Alaska U.S.A. **100** I4 56 49N 132 58W
Petersburg Virginia U.S.A. **105** E1 37 14N 77 24W
Petersfield Hampshire England **33** B2 51 00N 0 56W
Petitot *r.* British Columbia Canada **100** K4 59 40N 122 30W
Petoskey Michigan U.S.A. **104** D3 45 22N 84 59W
Petra *hist. site.* Jordan **78** O10 30 19N 35 26E
Petrolina Brazil **114** I11 9 22S 40 30W
Petropavlovsk Kazakhstan **71** I6 54 53N 69 13E
Petropavlovsk-Kamchatskiy Russia **71** R6 53 03N 158 43E
Petrópolis Brazil **115** I8 22 30S 43 06W
Petroşeni Romania **69** D2 45 25N 23 22E
Petrozavodsk Russia **70** F8 61 46N 34 19E
Petworth West Sussex England **33** B1 50 59N 0 38W
Pevek Russia **71** T9 69 41N 170 19E
Pevensey East Sussex England **33** C1 50 49N 0 20E
Pewsey Wiltshire England **31** F3 51 21N 1 46W
Pewsey, Vale of Wiltshire England **31** F3 51 20N 1 50W
Pfälzer Wald *mts.* Germany **63** A1 49 00N 8 00E
Pforzheim Germany **63** A1 48 53N 8 41E
Phenix City Alabama U.S.A. **103** I3 32 28N 85 01W
Philadelphia Pennsylvania U.S.A. **105** E1 40 00N 75 10W
Philippeville Belgium **64** D2 50 12N 4 33E
Philippine Sea Pacific Ocean **118** C10 21 00N 130 00E
PHILIPPINES, THE **80** G7–H5
Philippine Trench Pacific Ocean **118** C9 12 00N 127 00E
Philip Smith Mountains Alaska U.S.A. **100** F6 68 20N 148 00W
Phillipsburg New Jersey U.S.A. **105** E2 40 41N 75 12W
Phnom Penh Cambodia **80** C6 11 35N 104 55E
Phoenix Arizona U.S.A. **102** D3 33 30N 112 03W
Phoenix Island Pacific Ocean **118** I7 3 30S 174 30W
Phoenix Islands Kiribati **118** I7 4 40S 177 30W
Phongsali Laos **81** F2 21 40N 102 06E
Phuket Thailand **80** B5 7 52N 98 22E
Piacenza Italy **68** A3 45 03N 9 41E
Piatra Neamt Romania **69** E2 46 53N 26 23E
Piauí *admin.* Brazil **114** I11 7 30S 43 00W
Pickering North Yorkshire England **40** D3 54 14N 0 46W
Pickering Ontario Canada **105** E2 43 48N 79 11W
Pickering, Vale of North Yorkshire England **40** D3 54 10N 0 45W
Pickle Lake Ontario Canada **101** Q3 52 30N 90 00W
Pico Cristóbal *mt.* Colombia **114** C15 10 53N 73 48W
Pico de Itambé *mt.* Brazil **114** I9 18 23S 43 21W
Pico-Rivera California U.S.A. **107** B2 33 59N 118 06W
Picos Brazil **114** I11 7 05S 41 24W
Picton New Zealand **87** B2 41 17S 174 02E
Picton Ontario Canada **105** E2 44 01N 77 09W
Pidurutalagala *mt.* Sri Lanka **77** E1 7 01N 80 45E
Piedade Brazil **116** B2 22 53S 43 19W
Piedmont Missouri U.S.A. **104** B1 37 09N 90 42W
Piedras Negras Mexico **108** D5 28 40N 100 32W
Pielinen *l.* Finland **67** F3 63 20N 29 40E
Pierre South Dakota U.S.A. **102** F5 44 23N 100 20W
Pietermaritzburg Republic of South Africa **95** F2 29 36S 30 24E
Pietersburg Republic of South Africa **95** E3 23 54S 29 23E
Pijijiapan Mexico **108** F3 15 42N 93 12W
Pijnacker Netherlands **65** B2 52 00N 4 27E
Pikangikum Lake Ontario Canada **101** Q3 52 15N 94 00W
Pikes Peak Colorado U.S.A. **102** E4 38 50N 105 03W
Pik Kommunizma *mt.* Tajikistan **70** J3 38 59N 72 01E
Pik Pobedy *mt.* Kirgyzstan **71** J4 42 25N 80 15E
Piła Poland **69** C3 53 09N 16 44E
Pilar Paraguay **115** F7 26 51S 58 20W
Pilgrims Hatch Essex England **34** D2 51 38N 0 17E
Pilica *r.* Poland **69** D3 52 00N 21 00E
Pimenta Bueno Brazil **114** E10 11 40S 61 14W
Pinang *i.* Malaysia **80** C5 5 30N 100 20E
Pinar del Rio Cuba **109** H4 22 24N 83 42W
Pindhos *mts.* Greece **68** D2 40 00N 21 00E
Pine Bluff Arkansas U.S.A. **103** H3 34 13N 92 00W
Pingdingshan China **81** H4 33 50N 113 20E
P'ing-tung Taiwan **81** J2 22 40N 120 30E
Pingxiang China **81** H3 27 35N 113 46E
Piniós *r.* Greece **68** D2 39 00N 22 00E
Pink Mountain *tn.* British Columbia Canada **100** K4 57 10N 122 36W
Pinneberg Germany **63** A2 53 40N 9 49E
Pinsk Belarus **70** E6 52 08N 26 01E
Piombino Italy **68** B3 42 56N 10 32E
Piotrków Trybunalski Poland **69** C3 51 27N 19 40E
Piraiévs Greece **68** D2 37 57N 23 42E
Pirapora Brazil **114** I9 17 20S 44 54W
Piratininga Brazil **116** C2 22 56S 43 04W
Pirbright Surrey England **34** B1 51 18N 0 39W
Pirgos Greece **68** D2 37 40N 21 27E
Pirgos Greece **68** E2 35 00N 25 10E
Pirineos *(Pyrénées) mts.* Spain/France **66** C3 42 50N 0 30E
Pirin Planina *mts.* Bulgaria **68** D3 41 00N 23 00E
Pirmasens Germany **63** A1 49 12N 7 37E
Pirna Germany **63** B2 50 58N 13 58E
Pisa Italy **68** B3 43 43N 10 24E
Pisco Peru **114** B10 13 46S 76 12W
Písek Ceska Czechoslovakia **69** B2 49 18N 14 10E
Pistoia Italy **68** B3 43 56N 10 55E
Pitanga Brazil **115** G8 24 45S 51 43W
Pitcairn Islands Pacific Ocean **119** N5 25 04S 130 06W
Piteå Sweden **67** E4 65 19N 21 30E
Pite älv *r.* Sweden **67** D4 66 45N 17 20E
Piteşti Romania **69** D1 44 51N 24 51E
Pitlochry Tayside Scotland **46** E3 56 43N 3 45W
Pitti Island India **77** C2 11 00N 73 00E
Pittsburgh Pennsylvania U.S.A. **105** E2 40 26N 80 00W
Pittsfield Massachusetts U.S.A. **105** F2 42 27N 73 15W
Piura Peru **114** A11 5 15S 80 38W
Pjörsá *r.* Iceland **67** I6 64 15N 19 00W
Placentia Bay Newfoundland Canada **101** X2 46 50N 55 00W
Plains Strathclyde Scotland **45** C1 55 53N 3 55W
Plainview Texas U.S.A. **102** F3 34 12N 101 43W
Planalto de Mato Grosso *geog. reg.* Brazil **114** F10 13 00S 56 00W
Plasencia Spain **66** A3 40 02N 6 05W
Plateau de Langres *hills* France **61** B2 47 40N 4 55E
Plateau des 15 ans *tn.* Congo **92** A2 4 16S 15 16E
Plateau du Barrois *hills* France **61** C2 48 30N 5 15E
Plateau du Tchigaï *plat.* Niger **94** B12 20 30N 15 00E
Plateau du Tademaït *plat.* Algeria **93** F8 28 45N 2 00E
Plateaux du Limousin *hills* France **61** B2 45 45N 1 15E
Platte *r.* U.S.A. **102** F5 41 00N 100 00W
Platteville Wisconsin U.S.A. **104** B2 42 44N 90 29E
Plattsburgh New York U.S.A. **105** F2 44 42N 73 29W
Plauen Germany **63** B2 50 29N 12 08E
Plauer See *l.* Germany **63** B2 53 00N 12 00E
Playa Agua Dulce *beach* Peru **116** E4 12 08S 77 02W
Playa Azul Mexico **108** D3 18 00N 102 24W
Playa Conchán *beach* Peru **116** E4 12 13S 77 01W
Playa Marquez *beach* Peru **116** E5 11 57S 77 08W
Playa Oquendo *beach* Peru **116** E5 11 59S 77 08W
Plenty, Bay of New Zealand **87** C3 37 30S 117 00E
Plessisville Québec Canada **105** F3 46 14N 71 46W
Pleven Bulgaria **68** D3 43 25N 24 40E
Płock Poland **69** C3 52 32N 19 40E
Plockton Highland Scotland **46** C4 57 20N 5 40W
Ploieşti Romania **69** E1 44 57N 26 01E
Płoty Poland **69** C3 53 48N 15 14E
Plovdiv Bulgaria **68** D3 42 08N 24 45E
Plunge Lithuania **69** D4 55 52N 21 49E
Plym *r.* Devon England **31** C2 50 28N 4 05W
Plymouth Devon England **31** C2 50 23N 4 10W
Plymouth Indiana U.S.A. **104** C2 41 20N 86 19W
Plympton Devon England **31** C2 50 23N 4 03W
Plymstock Devon England **31** C2 50 21N 4 07W
Plynlimon *mt.* Dyfed Wales **38** C3 52 28N 3 47W
Plyussa *r.* Russia **67** F2 58 40N 28 15E
Plzeň Ceska Czechoslovakia **69** B2 49 45N 13 25E
Po *r.* Italy **68** B4 45 00N 11 00E
Pocatello Idaho U.S.A. **102** D5 42 53N 112 26W
Pochutla Mexico **108** E3 15 45N 96 30W
Pocklington Humberside England **40** D2 53 56N 0 46W
Pocomoke City Maryland U.S.A. **105** E1 38 04N 75 35W
Podara India **76** K2 22 34N 88 17E
Podkamennaya (Stony) **Tunguska** *r.* Russia **71** L8/M8 62 00N 95 00E
Podol'sk Russia **70** F7 55 23N 37 32E
P'ohang South Korea **81** K5 36 00N 129 26E
Pohénégamook Québec Canada **105** G3 47 28N 69 17W
Pointe-à-Pitre Lesser Antilles **109** L3 16 14N 61 32W
Pointe au Baril Station *tn.* Ontario Canada **105** D3 45 36N 80 23W
Point Hope *tn.* Alaska U.S.A. **100** B6 68 20N 166 50W
Point-Noire *tn.* Congo **95** B7 4 46S 11 53E
Poissy France **60** A2 48 56N 2 03E
Poitiers France **61** B2 46 35N 0 20E
Pokhara Nepal **77** E5 28 14N 83 58E
POLAND **69** C3
Polbeth Lothian Scotland **45** C1 55 53N 3 32W
Polegate East Sussex England **33** C1 50 50N 0 15E
Polesworth Warwickshire England **35** D2 52 44N 1 36W
Poles'ye *geog. reg.* Belarus **70** E6 53 00N 27 30E
Poles'ye Pripyat' *(Pripet Marshes) marsh* Belarus **70** E6 52 00N 27 00E
Poliyiros Greece **68** D3 40 23N 23 25E
Pollachi India **77** D2 10 38N 77 00E
Pollensa Balearic Islands **66** E4 39 52N 3 01E
Pollokshaws Strathclyde Scotland **45** B1 55 49N 4 19W
Polotsk Belarus **69** E4 55 30N 28 43E
Polperro Cornwall England **30** C2 50 19N 4 31W
Poltava Ukraine **70** F5 49 35N 34 35E
Poluostrov Rybachiy *p.* Russia **67** G4 69 50N 32 35E
Polynesia *geog. reg.* Pacific Ocean **119** J4–L9
Pomeranian Bay Baltic Sea **69** B3 54 00N 14 00E
Ponca Nebraska U.S.A. **104** A2 42 35N 96 42W
Ponca City Oklahoma U.S.A. **103** G4 36 41N 97 04W
Ponce Puerto Rico **109** K3 18 01N 66 36W
Pondicherry India **77** D2 11 59N 79 50E
Pondine Dyfed Wales **38** B1 51 34N 4 35W
Pond Inlet *tn.* Northwest Territories Canada **101** T7 72 40N 77 59W
Ponferrada Spain **66** A3 42 33N 6 35W
Ponoka Alberta Canada **100** M3 52 42N 113 33W
Pont *r.* Northumberland England **44** C2 55 02N 1 55W
Ponta da Marca *c.* Angola **95** B4 16 33S 11 43E
Ponta das Salinas *c.* Angola **95** B5 12 50S 12 54E
Ponta Grossa Brazil **115** G7 25 07S 50 09W
Pont-à-Mousson France **61** C2 48 55N 6 03E
Ponta Porã Brazil **115** F8 22 27S 55 39W
Pontardawe West Glamorgan Wales **38** C1 51 44N 3 52W
Pontardulais West Glamorgan Wales **38** B1 51 43N 4 02W
Pontchartrain, Lake Louisiana U.S.A. **103** H3 30 00N 90 00W
Pontefract West Yorkshire England **43** G3 53 42N 1 18W
Ponteland Northumberland England **44** C2 55 03N 1 44W
Ponte Leccia Corsica **61** C1 42 28N 9 12E
Ponterwyd Dyfed Wales **38** C2 52 25N 3 50W
Pontevedra Spain **66** A3 42 25N 8 39W
Pontiac Michigan U.S.A. **105** D2 42 39N 83 18W
Pontianak Indonesia **80** D3 0 05S 109 16E
Pontivy France **61** A2 48 04N 2 58W
Pontrilas Hereford and Worcester England **36** B1 51 57N 2 53W
Pontycymer Mid Glamorgan Wales **38** C1 51 36N 3 35W
Pontypool Gwent Wales **38** C1 51 43N 3 02W
Pontypridd Mid Glamorgan Wales **38** C1 51 37N 3 22W
Poole Dorset England **31** F2 50 43N 1 59W
Poolewe Highland Scotland **46** C4 57 45N 5 37W
Pooley Bridge *tn.* Cumbria England **44** B1 54 38N 2 49W
Pool Malebo *l.* Zaïre **95** C7 5 00S 17 00E
Popayán Colombia **114** B13 2 27N 76 32W
Poperinge Belgium **64** B2 50 52N 2 44E
Poplar Bluff *tn.* Missouri U.S.A. **103** H4 36 16N 90 25W
Popocatepetl *mt.* Mexico **108** E3 19 02N 98 38W
Popondetta Papua New Guinea **86** H8 8 45S 148 15E
Porbandar India **76** B4 21 40N 69 40E
Porcupine *r.* U.S.A./Canada **100** G6 67 15N 144 00W
Pordenone Italy **68** B4 45 58N 12 39E
Pori Finland **67** E3 61 28N 21 45E
Porirua New Zealand **87** B2 41 08S 174 52E
Porlamar Venezuela **109** L2 11 01N 63 54W
Porlock Somerset England **31** D3 51 14N 3 36W
Poronaysk Russia **71** Q5 49 13N 143 05E
Porsangen *fj.* Norway **67** F5 70 40N 25 30E
Porsgrunn Norway **67** B2 59 10N 9 40E
Portadown Armagh Northern Ireland **48** E4 54 26N 6 27W
Portaferry Down Northern Ireland **48** F4 54 23N 5 33W
Portage la Prairie Manitoba Canada **104** A3 49 58N 98 20W
Portage Wisconsin U.S.A. **104** C2 43 33N 89 29W
Port Alberni British Columbia Canada **100** K2 49 11N 124 49W
Portalegre Portugal **66** A2 39 17N 7 25W
Portales New Mexico U.S.A. **102** F3 34 12N 103 20W
Port Alfred Québec Canada **101** U2 48 20N 70 54W
Port Angeles Washington U.S.A. **102** B6 48 06N 123 26W
Port Antonio Jamaica **109** R8 18 10N 76 27W
Portarlington Laois / Offaly Irish Republic **48** D3 53 10N 7 11W
Port Arthur Texas U.S.A. **103** H2 29 55N 93 56W
Port Askaig Strathclyde Scotland **46** B2 55 51N 6 07W
Port Augusta Australia **86** F3 32 30S 137 27E
Port-au-Prince Haiti **109** J3 18 33N 72 20W
Port Austin Michigan U.S.A. **105** D2 44 04N 82 59W
Port Blair Andaman Islands **77** G2 11 40N 92 44E
Port Chalmers New Zealand **87** B1 45 48S 170 38E
Port Colborne Ontario Canada **105** E2 42 53N 79 16W
Port Darwin Falkland Islands **117** M16 51 51S 58 55W
Port-de-Paix Haiti **109** J3 19 56N 72 52W
Port Dinorwic Gwynedd Wales **38** B3 53 11N 4 13W
Port Elgin Ontario Canada **105** D2 44 25N 81 23W
Port Elizabeth Republic of South Africa **95** E1 33 58S 25 36E
Port Ellen Strathclyde Scotland **46** B2 55 39N 6 12W
Port Erin Isle of Man British Isles **41** F1 54 05N 4 45W
Port Gentil Gabon **93** G2 0 40S 8 50E
Port Glasgow Strathclyde Scotland **45** A1 55 56N 4 41W
Port Harcourt Nigeria **93** G3 4 43N 7 05E
Port Hardy British Columbia Canada **100** J3 50 41N 127 30W
Port Hawkesbury Nova Scotia Canada **101** W2 45 36N 61 22W
Porthcawl Mid Glamorgan Wales **38** C1 51 29N 3 43W
Port Hedland Australia **86** B5 20 24S 118 36E
Porthleven Cornwall England **30** B2 50 30N 5 21W
Porthmadog Gwynedd Wales **38** B2 52 55N 4 08W
Port Hope Ontario Canada **105** E2 43 58N 78 18W
Port Huron Michigan U.S.A. **105** D2 42 59N 82 28W
Portile de Fier *(Iron Gate) gorge* Romania / Yugoslavia **69** D1 44 00N 22 00E
Portimão Portugal **66** A2 37 08N 8 32W
Portinho *r.* Brazil **116** A1 23 01S 43 33W
Port Isaac Cornwall England **30** C2 50 35N 4 49W
Portishead Avon England **31** E3 51 30N 2 46W
Port Jervis New York U.S.A. **105** F2 41 22N 74 40W
Port Kaituma Guyana **114** F14 7 44N 59 53W
Portland Australia **86** G2 38 21S 141 38E
Portland Bill *c.* Dorset England **31** E2 50 31N 2 27W
Portland Maine U.S.A. **105** F2 43 41N 70 18W
Portland Oregon U.S.A. **102** B6 45 32N 122 40W
Portland Point *c.* Jamaica **109** Q7 17 42N 77 11W
Portland, Isle of Dorset England **31** E2 50 33N 2 27W
Portlaoise Laois Irish Republic **48** D3 53 02N 7 17W
Portlaw Waterford Irish Republic **48** D2 52 17N 7 19W
Port Lincoln Australia **86** F3 34 43S 135 49E
Port Macquarie Australia **86** I3 31 28S 152 25E
Portmahomack Highland Scotland **46** E4 57 49N 3 50W
Port Maria Jamaica **109** R8 18 22N 76 54W
Portmarnock Dublin Irish Republic **49** B2 53 26N 6 08W
Port Morant Jamaica **109** R7 17 53N 76 20W
Port Moresby Papua New Guinea **86** H8 9 30S 147 07E
Portnaguran Western Isles Scotland **46** B5 58 17N 6 13W
Portnahaven Strathclyde Scotland **46** B2 55 41N 6 31W
Portnockie Grampian Scotland **46** F4 57 42N 2 54W
Port Nolloth Republic of South Africa **95** C2 29 17S 16 51E
Porto *(Oporto)* Portugal **66** A3 41 09N 8 37W
Porto Alegre Brazil **115** G6 30 03S 51 10W
Porto Amboim Angola **95** B5 10 47S 13 43E
Portobello Lothian Scotland **45** D1 55 58N 3 07W
Port of Menteith Central Scotland **45** B2 56 11N 4 18W
Port of Ness Western Isles Scotland **46** B5 58 29N 6 13W
Port of Spain Trinidad and Tobago **109** L2 10 38N 61 31W
Pôrto Grande Brazil **114** G13 0 43N 51 23W
Porto Novo Benin **93** F4 6 30N 2 47E
Porto Tórres Italy **61** C1 40 51N 8 24E
Porto-Vecchio Corsica **61** C1 41 35N 9 16E
Pôrto Velho Brazil **114** E11 8 45S 63 54W
Portoviejo Ecuador **114** A12 1 07S 80 28W
Portpatrick Dumfries & Galloway Scotland **46** C1 54 51N 5 07W
Port Perry Ontario Canada **105** E2 44 06N 78 58W
Port Pirie Australia **86** F3 33 11S 138 01E
Portrane Dublin Irish Republic **49** B2 53 29N 6 06W
Portreath Cornwall England **30** B2 50 16N 5 17W
Portree Highland Scotland **46** B4 57 24N 6 12W
Port Royal Jamaica **109** R7 17 55N 76 52W
Portrush Northern Ireland **48** E5 55 12N 6 40W
Port Said Egypt **78** D5 31 17N 32 18E
Port St. Mary Isle of Man British Isles **41** F1 54 04N 4 44W
Portsmouth Hampshire England **32** A1 50 48N 1 05W
Portsmouth New Hampshire U.S.A. **105** F2 43 03N 70 47W
Portsmouth Ohio U.S.A. **105** D1 38 45N 82 59W
Portsmouth Virginia U.S.A. **105** E1 36 50N 76 20W
Portsoy Grampian Scotland **46** F4 57 41N 2 41W
Port Stanley Ontario Canada **105** D2 42 40N 81 14W
Portstewart Northern Ireland **48** E5 55 11N 6 43W
Port Sudan Sudan **78** E2 19 38N 37 07E
Port Talbot West Glamorgan Wales **38** C1 51 36N 3 47W
Porttipahdan tekojärvi *l.* Finland **67** F4 68 15N 26 00E
PORTUGAL **66** A2
Portumna Galway Irish Republic **48** C3 53 06N 8 13W
Port Washington New York U.S.A. **106** D2 40 50N 73 41W
Port Washington Wisconsin U.S.A. **104** C2 43 23N 87 54W
Port William Dumfries & Galloway Scotland **46** D1 54 46N 4 35W
Porus Jamaica **109** Q8 18 02N 77 25W
Posadas Argentina **115** F7 27 27S 55 50W
Potenza Italy **68** C3 40 38N 15 48E
Potiskum Nigeria **93** H5 11 40N 11 03E
Potomac River U.S.A. **105** E1 38 00N 77 00W
Poto-Poto Congo **92** A2 4 16S 15 17E
Poto-Poto du Djoué Congo **92** A2 4 18S 15 13E
Potosí Bolivia **114** D9 19 34S 65 45W
Potsdam Germany **63** B2 52 24N 13 04E
Potsdam New York U.S.A. **105** F2 44 40N 75 01W
Potten End Hertfordshire England **34** B3 51 46N 0 31W
Potter's Bar Hertfordshire England **34** C3 51 42N 0 11W
Potter's Cross Staffordshire England **35** B2 52 27N 2 12W
Potton Bedfordshire England **33** B3 52 08N 0 14W
Poughkeepsie New York U.S.A. **105** F2 41 43N 73 56W
Poulaphouca Reservoir Wicklow Irish Republic **48** E3 53 10N 6 30W
Poulton-le-Fylde Lancashire England **42** B3 53 51N 3 00W
Pound Bank Hereford & Worcester England **35** A2 52 21N 2 24W
Poverty Bay New Zealand **87** C3 38 40S 178 00E
Povungnituk Québec Canada **101** T4 59 45N 77 20W

Powell, Lake U.S.A. 102 D4 37 00N 110 00W
Powell River *tn.* British Columbia Canada 100 K2 49 54N 124 34W
Powmill Tayside Scotland 45 C2 56 09N 3 35W
Powys *co.* Wales 38 C2 52 10N 3 30W
Poyang Hu *l.* China 81 I3 29 00N 116 30E
Poynton Cheshire England 42 D2 53 21N 2 07W
Poza Rica Mexico 108 E4 20 34N 97 26W
Poznań Poland 69 C3 52 25N 16 53E
Pradesh *admin.* India 77 E5 26 00N 81 00E
Prague *see* Praha
Praha *(Prague)* Ceska Czechoslovakia 69 B3 50 06N 14 26E
Prairie de Chien *tn.* Wisconsin U.S.A. 104 B2 43 02N 91 08W
Prairie Dog Town Fork *r.* U.S.A. 102 F3 34 00N 101 00W
Prato Italy 68 B3 43 53N 11 06E
Pratt Kansas U.S.A. 102 G4 37 40N 98 45W
Prawle Point *c.* Devon England 31 D2 50 12N 3 44W
Preesall Lancashire England 42 B3 53 55N 2 57W
Prenzlau Germany 63 B2 53 19N 13 52E
Přerov Ceska Czechoslovakia 69 C2 49 28N 17 30E
Prescot Merseyside England 42 B2 53 26N 2 48W
Prescott Arizona U.S.A. 102 D3 34 34N 112 28W
Prescott Ontario U.S.A. 105 E2 44 43N 75 33W
Presidence Zaïre 92 A1 4 20S 15 14E
Presidencia Roque Sáenz Peña Argentina 115 E7 26 45S 60 30W
Presidente Prudente Brazil 115 G8 22 09S 51 24W
Presidente Stroessner Paraguay 115 G7 25 32S 54 34W
Prešov Slovenska Czechoslovakia 69 D2 49 00N 21 10E
Presque Isle Maine U.S.A. 105 G3 46 42N 68 01W
Prestatyn Clwyd Wales 38 C3 53 20N 3 24W
Prestbury Cheshire England 42 D1 53 16N 2 07W
Presteigne Powys Wales 38 C2 52 17N 3 00W
Preston Lancashire England 42 B3 53 46N 2 42W
Preston Brook *tn.* Cheshire England 42 B1 53 19N 2 41W
Prestwich Greater Manchester England 42 D2 53 32N 2 17W
Prestwick Strathclyde Scotland 46 D2 55 30N 4 37W
Prestwood Buckinghamshire England 34 A3 51 42N 0 43W
Pretoria Republic of South Africa 95 E2 25 45S 28 12E
Préveza Greece 68 D2 38 59N 20 45E
Příbram Ceska Czechoslovakia 69 B2 49 42N 14 01E
Price *r.* Utah U.S.A. 102 D4 39 00N 110 00W
Price Utah U.S.A. 102 D4 39 35N 110 49W
Prieska Republic of South Africa 95 D2 29 40S 22 45E
Prijedor Bosnia-Herzegovina 68 C3 45 00N 16 41E
Prilep Macedonia Yugoslavia 68 D3 41 20N 21 32E
Prince Albert Saskatchewan Canada 100 N3 53 13N 105 45W
Prince Albert National Park Saskatchewan Canada 100 N3 54 00N 106 00W
Prince Albert Sound Northwest Territories Canada 100 L7 175 15N 117 30W
Prince Charles Island Northwest Territories Canada 101 T6 67 40N 77 00W
Prince Edward Island *province* Canada 101 W2 46 30N 63 00W
Prince George British Columbia Canada 100 K3 53 55N 122 49W
Prince of Wales Island Alaska U.S.A. 100 I4 56 00N 132 00W
Prince of Wales Island Northwest Territories Canada 101 P7 73 00N 98 00W
Prince of Wales Strait Northwest Territories Canada 100 L7 71 00N 119 50W
Prince Patrick Island Northwest Territories Canada 100 K8 77 00N 120 00W
Prince Regent Inlet Northwest Territories Canada 101 Q7 72 40N 91 00W
Prince Rupert British Columbia Canada 100 I3 54 09N 130 20W
Princes Risborough Buckinghamshire England 33 B2 51 44N 0 51W
Princethorpe Warwickshire England 35 D1 52 20N 1 24W
Princetown Devon England 31 D2 50 33N 3 59W
Prince William Sound Alaska U.S.A. 100 F5 61 00N 147 30W
Principe *i.* Gulf of Guinea 93 G3 1 37N 7 27E
Prinzapolca Nicaragua 109 H2 13 19N 83 35W
Priors Marston Warwickshire England 35 E1 52 13N 1 17W
Priory Fife Scotland 45 D2 56 17N 3 05W
Pripet Marshes *see* Poles'ye Pripyat'
Pripyat' *r.* Europe 69 E3 52 00N 28 00E
Prispansko ezero *l.* Europe 68 D3 41 00N 21 00E
Priština Serbia Yugoslavia 68 D3 42 39N 21 10E
Privas France 61 B1 44 44N 4 36E
Prizren Serbia Yugoslavia 68 D3 42 12N 20 43E
Probilov Islands Alaska U.S.A. 100 B4 57 20N 168 00W
Probolinggo Indonesia 80 E2 7 45S 113 09E
Proddatur India 77 D2 14 45N 78 34E
Progres *r.s.* Antarctica 121 69 24S 76 24E
Progreso Honduras 108 G3 15 20N 87 50W
Progreso Mexico 108 G4 21 20N 89 40W
Prokop'yevsk Russia 71 K6 53 55N 86 45E
Prome Myanmar 80 B7 18 50N 95 14E
Propriá Brazil 114 J10 10 15S 36 51W
Propriano Corsica 61 C1 41 40N 8 54E
Providence Rhode Island U.S.A. 105 F2 41 50N 71 25W
Providence, Cape New Zealand 87 A1 46 01S 166 28E
Provideniya Russia 71 U8 64 30N 173 11E
Provincetown Massachusetts U.S.A. 105 F2 42 04N 70 11W
Provins France 61 B2 48 34N 3 18E
Provo Utah U.S.A. 102 D5 40 15N 111 40W
Prudhoe Northumberland England 44 C1 54 58N 1 51W
Prudhoe Bay *tn.* Alaska U.S.A. 100 F7 70 05N 148 20W
Prüm Germany 64 F2 50 12N 6 25E
Prüm *r.* Germany 64 F2 50 00N 6 00E
Pruszków Poland 69 D3 52 10N 20 47E
Prutul *(Prut)* *r.* Romania 69 E2 47 00N 28 00E
Prýdek-Místek Ceska Czechoslovakia 69 C2 49 42N 18 20E
Przemyśl Poland 69 D2 49 48N 22 48E
Przheval'sk Kirgyzstan 71 J4 42 31N 78 22E
Pskov Russia 67 F2 57 48N 28 26E
Ptich' *r.* Belarus 69 E3 53 00N 28 00E
Ptich' Belarus 69 E3 52 15N 28 49E
Pucallpa Peru 114 C11 8 21S 74 33W
Puckeridge Hertfordshire England 34 D3 51 53N 0 01E
Pudasjärvi Finland 67 F4 65 25N 26 50E
Puddletown Dorset England 31 E2 50 45N 2 21W
Pudsey West Yorkshire England 43 E3 53 48N 1 40W
Pudunskoye More *l.* Russia 67 G4 68 45N 31 15E
Puebla Mexico 108 E3 19 03N 98 10W
Pueblo Colorado U.S.A. 102 F4 38 17N 104 38W
Puerta Eugenia *c.* Mexico 108 A5 27 50N 115 05W
Puerto Aisén Chile 115 C3 45 27S 72 58W
Puerto Armuelles Panama 109 H1 8 19N 82 51W
Puerto Ayacucho Venezuela 114 D14 5 39N 67 32W
Puerto Barrios Guatemala 108 G3 15 41N 88 32W
Puerto Berrio Colombia 114 C14 6 28N 74 28W
Puerto Cabello Venezuela 114 D15 10 29N 68 02W
Puerto Cabezas Nicaragua 109 H2 14 02N 83 24W
Puerto Carreño Colombia 114 D14 6 08N 69 27W
Puerto Cortés Honduras 108 G3 15 50N 87 55W
Puerto de Morelos Mexico 109 G4 20 49N 86 52W
Puerto La Cruz Venezuela 114 E15 10 14N 64 40W
Puertollano Spain 66 B2 38 41N 4 07W
Puerto Maldonado Peru 114 D10 12 37S 69 11W
Puerto Mexico *see* Coatzacoalcos
Puerto Montt Chile 115 C4 41 28S 73 00W
Puerto Natales Chile 115 C2 51 41S 72 15W
Puerto Peñasco Mexico 108 B6 31 20N 113 35W
Puerto Princesa The Philippines 80 F5 9 46N 118 45E
PUERTO RICO 109 K3
Puerto Rico Trench Atlantic Ocean 117 B9 21 00N 65 00W
Puerto Santa Cruz Argentina 115 D2 50 03S 68 35W
Puerto Vallarta Mexico 108 C4 20 36N 105 15W
Pukekohe New Zealand 87 B3 37 12S 174 56E
Pula Croatia 68 B3 44 52N 13 52E
Pulacayo Bolivia 114 D8 20 25S 66 41W
Pulau Dolak *i.* Indonesia 86 F8 8 00S 138 00E
Pulau Pulau Batu *is.* Indonesia 80 B3 0 20S 98 00E
Pulborough West Sussex England 33 B1 50 58N 0 30W
Pulkkila Finland 67 F3 64 16N 25 50E
Pullman Washington U.S.A. 102 C6 46 46N 117 09W
Pumsaint Dyfed Wales 38 C2 52 03N 3 58W
Puncak Jaya *mt.* Indonesia 86 F9 4 05S 137 09E
Pune India 77 C3 18 34N 73 58E
Punjab *admin.* India 77 D6 30 40N 75 30E
Puno Peru 114 C9 15 53S 70 03W
Punta Alta Argentina 115 E5 38 50S 62 00W
Punta Arenas Chile 115 C2 53 10S 70 56W
Punta del Mono *c.* Nicaragua 109 H2 11 36N 83 37W
Punta Galera *c.* Ecuador 114 A13 0 49N 80 03W
Punta Gallinas *c.* Colombia 114 C15 12 27N 71 44W
Punta Gorda Belize 108 G3 16 10N 88 45W
Punta la Chira *c.* Peru 116 E4 12 12S 77 04W
Punta Negra *c.* Peru 114 A11 6 06S 81 09W
Puntarenas Costa Rica 109 10 00N 84 50W
Punto Fijo Venezuela 114 C15 11 50N 70 16W
Puquio Peru 114 C10 14 44S 74 07W
Pur *r.* Russia 71 J9 66 30N 77 30E
Purbeck, Isle of Dorset England 31 E2 50 38N 2 05W
Purfleet Essex England 34 D2 51 29N 0 14E
Puri India 77 F3 19 49N 85 54E
Purley Greater London England 34 C2 51 21N 0 07W
Purmerend Netherlands 64 D4 52 30N 4 56E
Purnia India 77 F5 25 47N 87 28E
Pursat Cambodia 80 C6 12 27N 103 40E
Purston Jaglin West Yorkshire England 43 F3 53 41N 1 21W
Purus *r.* Brazil 114 E11 7 00S 65 00W
Puruvesi *l.* Finland 67 F3 61 50N 29 30E
Pusa India 76 L4 28 38N 77 10E
Pusan South Korea 81 K5 35 05N 129 02E
Putao Myanmar 77 H5 27 22N 97 27E
Putney Greater London England 34 C2 51 28N 0 14W
Putoran Mountains Russia 71 L9 68 00N 95 00E
Puttalam Sri Lanka 77 D1 8 02N 79 50E
Putten Netherlands 64 E4 52 15N 5 36E
Puttenham Surrey England 34 A1 51 13N 0 40W
Putumayo *r.* Colombia/Peru 114 C12 2 30S 72 30W
Puulavesi *l.* Finland 67 F3 61 50N 26 40E
Puy de Sancy *mt.* France 61 B2 45 32N 2 48E
Pwllheli Gwynedd Wales 38 B2 52 53N 4 25W
Pyasina *r.* Russia 71 K10 71 00N 90 00E
Pyatigorsk Russia 70 G4 44 04N 43 06E
Pyhäjärvi Finland 67 F3 63 41N 26 00E
Pyhäjärvi *l.* Finland 67 E3 61 00N 22 20E
Pyhäjärvi *l.* Finland 67 F3 61 50N 30 00E
Pyinmana Myanmar 80 B7 19 45N 96 12E
Pyle West Glamorgan Wales 38 C1 51 32N 3 42W
Pyŏngyang North Korea 81 K5 39 00N 125 47E
Pyramid Lake Nevada U.S.A. 102 C5 40 00N 119 00W
Pyramids *hist. site* Egypt 78 D4 29 50N 30 50E
Pyrénées *(Pirineos)* *mts.* France/Spain 66 C3 42 50N 0 30E
Pytäselkä *l.* Finland 67 F3 62 20N 29 30E

Q
Qaidam Basin *see* Qaidam Pendi
Qaidam Pendi *(Qaidam Basin)* China 81 D5/E5 37 30N 94 00E
Qamdo China 77 H6 31 11N 97 18E
Qasr-e-Shīrīn Iraq 79 G5 34 32N 45 35E
Qasr Farâfra Egypt 94 E13 27 03N 28 00E
QATAR 79 H4
Qatar Peninsula Middle East 72 25 00N 53 00E
Qatrāna Jordan 78 P10 31 14N 36 03E
Qattara Depression Egypt 94 E13 24 00N 27 30E
Qazvīn Iran 79 G6 36 16N 50 00E
Qena Egypt 78 D4 26 08N 32 42E
Qeqertarsuaq *(Godhavn)* Greenland 101 Y6 69 18N 53 40W
Qezi'ot Israel 78 O10 30 53N 34 28E
Qiemo China 81 C5 38 08N 85 33E
Qila Saifullah Pakistan 76 B6 30 42N 68 30E
Qilian Shan *mts.* China 81 E5 39 00N 98 00E
Qingdao China 81 J5 36 04N 120 22E
Qinghai Hu *l.* China 81 37 00N 100 00E
Qinghe China 82 G2 40 01N 116 20E
Qingjiang China 81 I4 33 35N 119 02E
Qinhuangdao China 81 I5 39 55N 119 37E
Qin Ling *mts.* China 81 G4 34 00N 107 30E
Qionghai China 81 H1 19 17N 110 30E
Qiqihar China 81 J7 47 23N 124 00E
Qogir Feng *see* K2 *mt.*
Qom Iran 79 H5 34 39N 50 57E
Qomishēh Iran 79 H5 32 01N 51 55E
Quabbin Reservoir Massachusetts U.S.A. 105 F2 42 00N 72 00W
Quang Ngai Vietnam 80 D7 15 09N 108 50E
Quantock Hills Somerset England 31 D3 51 05N 3 15W
Quanzhou China 81 I2 24 53N 118 36E
Qu'Appelle Saskatchewan Canada 100 O3 50 33N 103 54W
Quarrier's Homes Strathclyde Scotland 45 A1 55 53N 4 36W
Queanbeyan Australia 86 H2 35 24S 149 17E
Québec *province* Canada 101 T3 50 00N 75 00W
Québec Québec Canada 105 F3 46 50N 71 15W
Queen Bess, Mount British Columbia Canada 100 K3 51 13N 124 35W
Queenborough Kent England 33 C2 51 26N 0 45E
Queen Charlotte British Columbia Canada 100 I3 53 18N 132 04W
Queen Charlotte Bay Falkland Islands 117 L16 51 50S 61 30W
Queen Charlotte Islands British Columbia Canada 100 I3 53 00N 132 30W
Queen Charlotte Sound British Columbia Canada 100 J3 52 10N 130 00W
Queen Elizabeth Islands Northwest Territories Canada 101 N8 77 30N 105 00W
Queen Maud Gulf Northwest Territories Canada 101 O6 68 00N 101 00W
Queen Maud Land *geog. reg.* Antarctica 121 73 00S 10 00E
Queens New York U.S.A. 106 C1 40 44N 73 54W
Queensbury West Yorkshire England 43 E3 53 46N 1 50W
Queensferry Clwyd Wales 42 A1 53 12N 3 01W
Queensferry Lothian Scotland 45 D1 55 59N 3 21W
Queensland *state* Australia 86 G5 23 00S 143 00E
Queenstown Australia 86 H1 42 07S 145 33E
Queenstown New Zealand 87 A2 45 03S 168 41E
Queenzieburn Strathclyde Scotland 45 B1 55 58N 4 04W
Queimados Brazil 116 A3 22 43S 43 33W
Quelimane Mozambique 95 G4 17 53S 36 51E
Quelpart *see* Cheju do
Quendon Essex England 34 D3 51 57N 0 12E
Querétaro Mexico 108 D4 20 38N 100 23W
Quesnel British Columbia Canada 100 K3 53 03N 122 31W
Quetta Pakistan 76 B6 30 15N 67 00E
Quezaltenango Guatemala 108 F2 14 50N 91 30W
Quezon City The Philippines 80 G6 14 39N 121 02E
Quibala Angola 95 B5 10 48S 14 59E
Quibdó Colombia 114 B14 5 40N 76 38W
Quiberon France 61 A2 47 29N 3 07W
Quilá Mexico 108 C4 24 26N 107 11W
Quillacollo Bolivia 114 D9 17 26S 66 16W
Quill Lakes Saskatchewan Canada 100 O3 52 03N 104 12W
Quilon India 77 D1 8 53N 76 38E
Quilpie Australia 86 G4 26 35S 144 14E
Quimper France 61 A2 48 00N 4 06W
Quincy Illinois U.S.A. 104 B1 39 55N 91 22W
Quincy Massachusetts U.S.A. 105 F2 42 17N 71 00W
Quincy-sous-Sénart France 60 C1 48 40N 2 33E
Qui Nhon Vietnam 80 D6 13 47N 109 11E
Quito Ecuador 114 B12 0 14S 78 30W
Quixadá Brazil 114 J12 4 57S 39 04W
Quoig Tayside Scotland 45 C2 56 23N 3 55W
Quorn Leicestershire England 36 C2 52 45N 1 10W
Qus Egypt 78 D4 25 53N 32 48E
Quseir Egypt 78 D4 26 04N 34 15E

R
Raahe Finland 67 E3 64 42N 24 30E
Raalte Netherlands 64 F4 52 23N 6 16E
Raasay *l.* Highland Scotland 46 B4 57 25N 6 05W
Raasay, Sound of Highland Scotland 46 B4 57 30N 6 05W
Raas Caseyr *(Cabo Guardafui)* *c.* Somalia 94 J10 11 49N 51 15E
Raba Indonesia 80 F2 8 27S 118 45E
Rabat-Salé Morocco 93 D9 34 02N 6 51W
Rabaul Papua New Guinea 86 I9 4 13S 152 11E
Rach Gia Vietnam 80 D5 9 55N 105 05E
Racibórz Poland 69 C3 50 05N 18 10E
Racine Wisconsin U.S.A. 104 C2 42 42N 87 50W
Radcliffe Greater Manchester England 42 D2 53 34N 2 20W
Radcliffe on Trent Nottinghamshire England 36 C2 52 57N 1 03W
Radebeul Germany 63 B2 51 06N 13 41E
Radford Virginia U.S.A. 103 J4 37 07N 80 34W
Radlett Hertfordshire England 34 C3 51 41N 0 19W
Radlinski, Mount Antarctica 121 82 30S 105 00W
Radnor Forest *mts.* Powys Wales 38 C2 52 15N 3 10W
Radom Poland 69 D3 51 26N 21 10E
Radom Sudan 94 D9 9 58N 24 53E
Radomsko Poland 69 C3 51 04N 19 25E
Radstadt Austria 69 B2 47 23N 13 20E
Radstock Avon England 31 E3 51 18N 2 28W
Raeside, Lake Australia 86 C4 29 00S 122 00E
Rafah Egypt 78 O10 31 18N 34 15E
Rafsanjān Iran 79 I5 30 25N 56 00E
Raglan Gwent Wales 38 D1 51 47N 2 51W
Ragusa Italy 68 B2 36 56N 14 44E
Rahimyar Khan Pakistan 76 B5 28 22N 70 20E
Raichur India 77 D3 16 15N 77 20E
Raigarh India 77 E4 21 53N 83 28E
Rainford Merseyside England 42 B2 53 30N 2 48W
Rainham Greater London England 34 D2 51 31N 0 12E
Rainhill Merseyside England 42 B2 53 26N 2 46W
Rainier, Mount Washington U.S.A. 102 B6 46 52N 121 45W
Rainworth Nottinghamshire England 36 C3 53 08N 1 08W
Rainy Lake Ontario Canada 104 B3 49 00N 93 00W
Rainy River *tn.* Ontario Canada 104 B3 48 44N 94 33W
Raipur India 77 E4 21 16N 81 42E
Raith Ontario Canada 104 C3 48 51N 89 56W
Rajahmundry India 77 E3 17 01N 81 52E
Rajapalaiyam India 77 D1 9 26N 77 36E
Rajasthan *admin.* India 77 C5 26 30N 73 00E
Rajkot India 77 C4 21 18N 70 53E
Rājpur India 76 K1 22 25N 88 25E
Rajshahi Bangladesh 77 F4 24 24N 88 40E
Raleigh North Carolina U.S.A. 103 K4 35 46N 78 39W
Ramat Gan Israel 78 O11 32 04N 34 48E
Rame Head *c.* Cornwall England 31 C2 50 19N 4 13W
Ramos Brazil 116 B2 22 51S 43 16W
Rampur India 77 D6 31 26N 77 37E
Rampur India 77 D5 28 50N 79 05E
Ramree *i.* Myanmar 77 G3 9 00N 93 30E
Ramsbottom Greater Manchester England 42 D2 53 39N 2 19W
Ramsey Cambridgeshire England 33 B3 52 27N 0 07W
Ramsey Isle of Man British Isles 41 F1 54 19N 4 23W
Ramsey Island Dyfed Wales 38 A1 51 53N 5 20W
Ramsgate Kent England 33 D2 51 20N 1 25E
Ramtha Jordan 78 O11 32 34N 36 00E
Rancagua Chile 115 C6 34 10S 70 45W
Ranchi India 77 F4 23 22N 85 20E
Randalstown Antrim Northern Ireland 48 E4 54 45N 6 19W
Randers Denmark 67 C2 56 28N 10 03E
Ranfurly Strathclyde Scotland 45 A1 55 52N 4 35W
Rangiora New Zealand 87 B2 43 18S 172 38E
Rangoon *(Yangon)* Myanmar 80 B7 16 47N 96 10E
Rangpur Bangladesh 77 F5 24 45N 89 21E
Rani Bagh India 76 L4 28 41N 77 06E
Raniganj India 77 F4 23 35N 87 07E
Rankin Inlet *tn.* Northwest Territories Canada 101 Q5 62 45N 92 05W
Rannoch Moor Scotland 46 D3 56 35N 4 50W
Rannoch Station Tayside Scotland 46 D3 56 42N 4 34W
Rann of Kachchh *geog. reg.* India / Pakistan 76 B4/C4 24 00N 69 00E
Raphoe Donegal Irish Republic 48 D4 54 52N 7 36W
Rapid City South Dakota U.S.A. 102 F5 44 06N 103 14W
Rappahannock River Virginia U.S.A. 105 E1 38 00N 77 00W
Ras al Ḥadd *c.* Oman 79 I3 22 31N 59 45E
Ras Dashen Terara *mt.* Ethiopia 78 E1 13 15N 38 27E
Ras Fartak *c.* Yemen Republic 79 H2 15 20N 52 12E
Rasht Iran 79 G6 37 18N 49 38E
Ras Lanuf Libya 94 C14 30 31N 18 34E
Ra's Madrakah *c.* Oman 79 I2 18 58N 57 50E
Ras Nouadhibou *(Cap Blanc)* *c.* Mauritania 93 B7 20 53N 17 01W
Rastatt Germany 63 A1 48 51N 8 13E
Rasto *geog. reg.* Sweden 67 E4 68 40N 21 00E
Ratak Chain *is.* Pacific Ocean 118 H9 10 00N 172 30E
Rat-Buri Thailand 80 B6 13 30N 99 50E
Rathangan Kildare Irish Republic 48 D3 53 12N 6 59W
Rathcoole Dublin Irish Republic 49 A1 53 17N 6 28W
Rathdowney Laois Irish Republic 48 D2 52 50N 7 34W
Rathdrum Wicklow Irish Republic 48 E2 52 56N 6 13W
Rathenow Germany 63 B2 52 37N 12 21E
Rathfriland Northern Ireland 48 E4 54 14N 6 10W
Rathkeale Limerick Irish Republic 48 C2 52 32N 8 56W
Rathlin Island Northern Ireland 48 E5 55 20N 6 10W
Rath Luirc *(Charleville)* Cork Irish Republic 48 C2 52 21N 8 41W
Rathmelton Donegal Irish Republic 48 D5 55 02N 7 38W
Rathmines Dublin Irish Republic 49 B1 53 19N 6 15W
Rathnew Wicklow Irish Republic 48 E2 53 00N 6 05W
Ratho Lothian Scotland 45 D1 55 56N 3 23W
Ratingen Germany 62 B2 51 18N 6 50E
Ratlam India 77 D4 23 18N 75 06E
Ratnapura Sri Lanka 77 E1 6 41N 80 25E
Ratno Ukraine 69 D3 51 40N 24 32E
Ratoath Meath Irish Republic 49 A2 53 31N 6 24W
Raton New Mexico U.S.A. 102 F4 36 54N 104 27W
Rattray Tayside Scotland 46 E3 56 36N 3 20W
Raukumara *mt.* New Zealand 87 C3 37 45S 178 09E
Raukumara Range *mts.* New Zealand 87 C3 38 00S 178 00E
Rauma Finland 67 E3 61 09N 21 30E
Raunds Northamptonshire England 36 D2 52 21N 0 33W
Raurkela India 77 E4 22 16N 85 01E
Ravenglass Cumbria England 44 A1 54 21N 3 24W
Ravenna Italy 68 B3 44 25N 12 12E
Ravensburg Germany 63 A1 47 47N 9 37E
Ravenshead Nottinghamshire England 36 C3 53 40N 1 10W
Ravensthorpe Australia 86 C3 33 34S 120 01E
Ravi *r.* Pakistan 77 C6 31 00N 73 00E
Rawalpindi Pakistan 77 C6 33 40N 73 08E
Rawcliffe Humberside England 43 H3 53 42N 0 58W
Rawlins Wyoming U.S.A. 102 E5 41 46N 107 16W
Rawmarsh South Yorkshire England 42 F2 53 27N 1 21W
Rawson Argentina 115 E4 43 15S 65 06W
Rawtenstall Lancashire England 42 D3 53 42N 2 18W
Rayleigh Essex England 33 C2 51 36N 0 36E
Raymondville Texas U.S.A. 103 G2 26 30N 97 48W
Razgrad Bulgaria 68 E3 43 31N 26 33E
Reading Berkshire England 33 B2 51 28N 0 59W
Reading Pennsylvania U.S.A. 105 E2 40 20N 75 55W
Realengo Brazil 116 B2 22 53S 43 25W
Rebun-to *i.* Japan 82 D4 45 25N 141 04E
Recherche, Archipelago *is.* Australia 86 C3 35 00S 122 50E
Rechitsa Belarus 69 F3 52 21N 30 24E
Recife Brazil 114 J11 8 06S 34 53W
Recklinghausen Germany 62 C3 51 37N 7 11E
Reconquista Argentina 115 F7 29 08S 59 38W
Recovery Glacier Antarctica 121 81 00S 25 00W
Red Bluff California U.S.A. 102 B5 40 11N 122 16W
Redbourn Hertfordshire England 34 B3 51 48N 0 24W
Redbridge Greater London England 34 D2 51 34N 0 05E
Redcar Cleveland England 44 C1 54 37N 1 04W
Red Deer Alberta Canada 100 M3 52 15N 113 48W
Redding California U.S.A. 102 B5 40 35N 122 24W
Redding Central Scotland 45 C1 55 59N 3 41W
Redditch Hereford and Worcester England 35 C1 52 19N 1 56W
Redhill Surrey England 34 C1 51 14N 0 11W
Redon France 61 A2 47 39N 2 05W
Redondo Beach *tn.* California U.S.A. 107 A2 33 51N 118 24W
Red River North America U.S.A. 104 A3 48 00N 97 00W
Red River U.S.A. 103 H3 32 00N 93 00W
Redruth Cornwall England 30 B2 50 13N 5 14W
Red Sea Middle East 78 O8 36 15E 34 20E
Red Sea Hills Africa 88 27 00N 33 00E
Red Street Staffordshire England 35 B4 53 04N 2 16W
Red Wing Minnesota U.S.A. 104 B2 44 33N 92 31W
Reed City Michigan U.S.A. 104 C2 43 54N 85 31W
Reedsport Oregon U.S.A. 102 B5 43 42N 124 05W
Reedy Glacier Antarctica 121 85 00S 140 00W
Reefton New Zealand 87 B2 42 05S 171 51E
Reepham Norfolk England 33 D3 52 46N 1 07E
Reeuwijkse Plassen *l.* Netherlands 65 D2 52 05N 4 45E
Regen *r.* Germany 63 B1 49 00N 12 00E
Regensburg Germany 63 B1 49 01N 12 07E
Reggio di Calabria Italy 68 C2 38 06N 15 39E
Reggio nell 'Emilia Italy 68 B3 44 42N 10 37E
Regina Saskatchewan Canada 100 O3 50 30N 104 38W
Registan *geog. reg.* Afghanistan 79 J5 30 30N 65 00E
Rehovot Israel 78 O10 31 54N 34 46E
Reigate Surrey England 34 C1 51 14N 0 13W
Reims France 61 B2 49 15N 4 02E
Reindeer Lake Saskatchewan/Manitoba Canada 101 O4 57 30N 102 30W
Reinosa Spain 66 B3 43 01N 4 09W
Reisa *r.* Norway 67 E4 69 40N 21 30E
Reitdiep *r.* Netherlands 64 F5 53 40N 6 20E
Relizane Algeria 66 C2 35 44N 0 35E
Rembang Indonesia 80 E2 6 45S 111 22E
Remington Indiana U.S.A. 104 C2 40 46N 87 09W
Remiremont France 63 A1 48 01N 6 35E
Remscheid Germany 62 C1 51 10N 7 11E
Rendsburg Germany 63 A2 54 19N 9 39E

Renfrew Ontario Canada **105** E3 45 28N 76 44W
Renfrew Strathclyde Scotland **45** B1 55 53N 4 24W
Renkum Netherlands **64** E3 51 58N 5 44E
Rennell *i.* Solomon Islands **86** K7 11 45S 160 15E
Rennes France **61** A2 48 06N 1 40W
Reno Nevada U.S.A. **102** C4 39 32N 119 49W
Rensselaer Indiana U.S.A. **104** C2 40 57N 87 09W
Renton Strathclyde Scotland **45** A1 55 58N 4 35W
Repton Derbyshire England **35** D3 52 50N 1 32W
REPUBLIC OF SOUTH AFRICA 95 D2
Resistencia Argentina **115** F7 27 28S 59 00W
Reşiţa Romania **69** D2 45 16N 21 55E
Resolute Northwest Territories Canada **101** Q7 74 40N 95 00W
Rethel France **61** B2 49 31N 4 22E
Réthimnon Greece **68** D2 35 23N 24 28E
Réunion *i.* Indian Ocean **123** 21 00S 55 30E
Reus Spain **66** C3 41 10N 1 06E
Reutlingen Germany **63** A1 48 30N 9 13E
Reutov Russia **70** N2 55 46N 37 47E
Revelstoke British Columbia Canada **100** L3 51 02N 118 12W
Revin France **64** D1 49 57N 4 39E
Rewa India **77** E4 24 32N 81 18E
Reykjanes Ridge Atlantic Ocean **117** E12 57 00N 33 00W
Reykjavík Iceland **67** H6 64 09N 21 58W
Reynosa Mexico **108** E5 26 05N 98 18W
Rēzekne Latvia **67** F2 56 30N 27 22E
Rhayader Powys Wales **38** C2 52 18N 3 30W
Rheda-Wiedenbrück Germany **63** A2 51 51N 8 17E
Rheden Netherlands **64** F4 52 01N 6 02E
Rhein *(Rhin, Rijn, Rhine) r.* Germany **61** C3 50 30N 7 00E
Rheinbach Germany **64** F2 50 37N 6 57E
Rheine Germany **63** A2 52 17N 7 26E
Rheinhausen Germany **62** A2 51 23N 6 41E
Rhein-Herne-Kanal *can.* Germany **62** B2 51 30N 7 00E
Rheinland-Pfalz *admin.* Germany **63** A2 50 00N 7 00E
Rhin *(Rhein, Rijn, Rhine) r.* France **61** C2 48 05N 7 30E
Rhine *see* Rhin, Rhein, Rijn
Rhinelander Wisconsin U.S.A. **104** C3 45 39N 89 23W
Rhins, The *p.* Dumfries & Galloway Scotland **46** C1 54 50N 5 00W
Rhode Island *state* U.S.A. **105** F2 41 00N 71 00W
Rhodes *see* Ródhos
Rhondda Mid Glamorgan Wales **38** C1 51 40N 3 30W
Rhône *r.* France **61** B1 43 55N 4 40E
Rhoose South Glamorgan Wales **38** C1 51 26N 3 22W
Rhosllanerchrugog Clwyd Wales **38** C3 53 01N 3 04W
Rhosneigr Gwynedd Wales **38** B3 53 14N 4 31W
Rhossili West Glamorgan Wales **38** B1 51 34N 4 17W
Rhu Strathclyde Scotland **45** A2 56 01N 4 47W
Rhum *i.* Highland Scotland **46** B4 57 00N 6 20W
Rhume *r.* Germany **63** B2 51 00N 10 00E
Rhyl Clwyd Wales **38** C3 53 19N 3 29W
Rhymney Mid Glamorgan Wales **38** C1 51 46N 3 18W
Rhynie Grampian Scotland **46** F4 57 19N 2 50W
Ribble *r.* Lancashire England **42** B3 53 44N 2 56W
Ribblesdale *v.* North Yorkshire England **42** D4 54 00N 2 18W
Ribeirão Prêto Brazil **114** H8 21 09S 47 48W
Riberalta Bolivia **114** D10 10 59S 66 06W
Riccall North Yorkshire England **43** G3 53 51N 1 04W
Richhill Armagh Northern Ireland **48** E4 54 22N 6 33W
Richibucto New Brunswick Canada **101** V2 46 42N 64 54W
Richland Center Wisconsin U.S.A. **104** B2 43 22N 90 24W
Richland Washington U.S.A. **102** C6 46 17N 119 17W
Richmond Australia **86** G5 20 45S 143 05E
Richmond California U.S.A. **102** B4 37 56N 122 20W
Richmond Indiana U.S.A. **104** D1 39 50N 84 51W
Richmond Kentucky U.S.A. **105** D1 37 45N 84 19W
Richmond New York U.S.A. **106** B1 40 36N 74 10W
Richmond New Zealand **87** B2 41 20S 173 10E
Richmond North Yorkshire England **40** C3 54 24N 1 44W
Richmond Virginia U.S.A. **105** E1 37 34N 77 27W
Richmond upon Thames Greater London England **34** C2 51 28N 0 19W
Richmond Valley New York U.S.A. **106** B1 40 31N 74 13W
Rickmansworth Hertfordshire England **34** B2 51 38N 0 29W
Ridderkerk Netherlands **65** C1 51 53N 4 36E
Riddlesden West Yorkshire England **43** E3 53 54N 1 51W
Ridgewood New Jersey U.S.A. **106** B2 40 58N 74 08W
Ried Austria **63** B1 48 13N 13 29E
Riesa Germany **63** B2 51 18N 13 18E
Rieti Italy **68** B3 42 24N 12 51E
Rif Mountains Morocco **66** A2 35 00N 5 00W
Riga Lativia **67** E2 56 53N 24 08E
Riga, Gulf of Latvia/Estonia **67** E2 57 30N 23 30E
Rijeka Croatia **68** B4 45 20N 14 27E
Rijn *(Rhin, Rhein, Rhine) r.* Netherlands **64** F3 51 53N 6 05E
Rijnsburg Netherlands **65** B2 52 11N 4 27E
Rijssen Netherlands **64** F4 52 18N 6 31E
Rijswijk Netherlands **65** B2 52 02N 4 19E
Rímac Peru **116** E4 12 02S 77 02W
Rimini Italy **68** B3 44 03N 12 34E
Rîmnicu Vîlcea Romania **69** D2 45 06N 24 21E
Rimouski Québec Canada **105** G3 48 27N 68 32W
Ringgold Isles Fiji **118** V16 16 10S 179 50W
Ringkøbing Fjord Denmark **67** B2 56 00N 8 00E
Ringvassøy *i.* Norway **67** D4 69 55N 19 10E
Ringwood Dorset England **32** A1 50 51N 1 47W
Rio Amazonas *r.* Brazil **114** G12 2 00S 53 00W
Río Apaporis *r.* Colombia **114** C13 1 00N 72 30W
Río Apure *r.* Venezuela **114** D14 7 40N 68 00W
Rio Aquidauana *r.* Brazil **114** F9 20 00S 56 00W
Rio Araguaia *r.* Brazil **114** H11 7 20S 49 00W
Río Arauca *r.* Venezuela **114** D14 7 10N 68 30W
Riobamba Ecuador **114** B12 1 44S 78 40W
Río Bermejo Argentina **115** E7 25 00S 61 00W
Rio Branco *r.* Brazil **114** E13 0 00 62 00W
Rio Branco *tn.* Brazil **114** D11 9 59S 67 49W
Río Caqueta *r.* Colombia **114** C12 0 05S 72 30W
Río Caroni *r.* Venezuela **114** E14 7 00N 62 30W
Río Caura *r.* Venezuela **114** E14 6 00N 64 00W
Río Chico *r.* Argentina **115** D4 45 00S 67 30W
Río Chico *r.* Argentina **115** D3 49 00S 70 00W
Río Chillón *r.* Peru **116** E5 11 57S 77 07W
Río Chubut *r.* Argentina **115** D4 43 30S 67 30W
Río Colorado *r.* Argentina **115** D5 37 30S 69 00W
Río Corrientes *r.* Peru **114** B12 2 30S 76 30W
Río Cuarto *tn.* Argentina **115** E6 33 08S 64 20W
Rio de Janeiro *admin.* Brazil **115** I8 22 00S 42 30W
Rio de Janeiro *tn.* Brazil **116** C2 22 53S 43 17W
Río de la Plata *r.* Uruguay / Argentina **115** F5 35 00S 57 00W
Rio de Para *r.* Brazil **114** H12 1 00S 48 00W
Río Deseado *r.* Argentina **115** D3 47 00S 68 00W
Río Dulce *r.* Argentina **115** E7 29 00S 63 00W
Río Gallegos *tn.* Argentina **115** D2 51 35S 68 10W
Río Grande *r.* Bolivia **114** E9 18 00S 65 00W
Rio Grande *r.* Brazil **114** G8 20 00S 50 00W
Río Grande *r.* Mexico / U.S.A. **108** D5/D6 30 00N 104 00W
Río Grande *tn.* Argentina **115** D2 53 45S 67 46W
Rio Grande *tn.* Brazil **115** G6 32 03S 52 08W
Río Grande *tn.* Mexico **108** D4 23 50N 103 02W
Rio Grande do Norte *admin.* Brazil **114** J11 6 00S 37 00W
Rio Grande do Sul *admin.* Brazil **115** G7 28 00N 52 30W
Rio Grande Rise Atlantic Ocean **117** E3 32 00S 36 00W
Río Guainía *r.* Colombia / Venezuela **114** D13 2 30N 67 30W
Río Guaporé *r.* Brazil / Bolivia **114** E10 13 00S 62 00W
Río Guaviare *r.* Colombia **114** C13 3 00N 70 00W
Rio Gurgueia *r.* Brazil **114** I11 9 00S 44 00W
Rio Gurupi *r.* Brazil **114** H12 4 00S 47 00W
Riohacha Colombia **114** C15 11 34N 72 58W
Rio Hondo *r.* California U.S.A. **107** B3 34 00N 118 07W
Rio Iguaçu *r.* Brazil **115** G7 26 00S 51 00W
Río Inírida *r.* Colombia **114** C13/D13 2 30N 70 00W
Rio Japurá *r.* Brazil **114** D12 2 00S 67 30W
Rio Jari *r.* Brazil **114** G13 2 00N 54 00W
Rio Jequitinhonha *r.* Brazil **114** I9 16 00S 41 00W
Rio Juruá *r.* Brazil **114** D12 4 30S 67 00W
Rio Juruena *r.* Brazil **114** F11 10 00S 57 40W
Rio Madeira *r.* Brazil **114** E11 6 00S 61 30W
Río Madre de Dios *r.* Bolivia **114** D10 12 00S 68 00W
Río Magdalena *r.* Colombia **114** C14 8 00N 73 30W
Río Mamoré *r.* Bolivia **114** E9 15 00S 65 00W
Río Marañón *r.* Peru **114** B12 4 50S 77 30W
Río Meta *r.* Colombia **114** C14 6 00N 71 00W
Río Napo *r.* Peru **114** C12 2 30S 73 30W
Río Negro *r.* Argentina **115** E5 40 00S 65 00W
Rio Negro *r.* Brazil **114** D12 0 05S 67 00W
Río Negro *r.* Uruguay **115** F6 33 00S 57 30W
Río Orinoco *r.* Venezuela **114** E14 8 00N 64 00W
Río Paraguá *r.* Bolivia **114** E10 14 00S 61 30W
Río Paragua *r.* Venezuela **114** E14 6 00N 63 30W
Río Paraguay *r.* Paraguay / Argentina **115** F7 26 30S 58 00W
Río Paraná *r.* Paraguay / Argentina **115** F7 27 00S 56 00W
Rio Paranaiba *r.* Brazil **114** H9 18 00S 49 00W
Rio Pardo *r.* Brazil **114** J9 15 10S 40 00W
Rio Parnaíba *r.* Brazil **114** I11 7 30S 45 00W
Río Parana Panema *r.* Brazil **115** G8 22 30S 52 00W
Río Pastaza *r.* Peru **114** B12 2 30S 77 00W
Río Pilcomayo *r.* Paraguay / Argentina **115** F8 24 00S 60 00W
Río Rimac *r.* Peru **116** F4 12 01S 76 58W
Río Salado *r.* Argentina **115** E7 28 30S 62 30W
Río Salado *r.* Argentina **115** D5 35 00S 66 30W
Río San Miguel *r.* Bolivia **114** E9 15 00S 63 30W
Rio São Francisco *r.* Brazil **114** J11 8 30S 39 00W
Rio Solimões *r.* Brazil **114** D12 3 30S 69 00W
Rio Tapajós *r.* Brazil **114** F11 6 30S 57 00W
Rio Taquari *r.* Brazil **114** F9 18 00S 57 00W
Río Tefé *r.* Brazil **114** D12 4 30S 65 30W
Rio Teles Pires *r.* Brazil **114** F11 8 00S 57 00W
Rio Tocantins *r.* Brazil **114** H12 3 00S 49 00W
Rio Trombetas *r.* Brazil **114** F13 1 30N 57 00W
Río Ucayali *r.* Peru **114** C11 6 00S 74 00W
Rio Uraricuera *r.* Brazil **114** E13 3 00N 62 30W
Río Uruguay *r.* Uruguay / Argentina **115** F6 32 00S 57 40W
Río Vaupés *r.* Colombia **114** C13 1 30N 72 00W
Río Verde *r.* Paraguay **115** F8 23 20S 60 00W
Rio Verde *tn.* Brazil **114** G9 17 50S 50 55W
Río Verde *tn.* Mexico **108** D4 21 58N 100 00W
Rio Xingu *r.* Brazil **114** G12 2 30S 52 30W
Río Yavari *r.* Peru/Brazil **114** C12 5 00S 72 30S
Ripley Derbyshire England **35** D4 53 03N 1 24W
Ripley North Yorkshire England **43** F4 54 03N 1 34W
Ripley Surrey England **34** B1 51 18N 0 29W
Ripley West Virginia U.S.A. **105** D1 38 49N 81 44W
Ripon North Yorkshire England **40** C3 54 08N 1 31W
Ripponden West Yorkshire England **43** E3 53 41N 1 57W
Risca Gwent Wales **38** C1 51 37N 3 07W
Rishiri-tō *i.* Japan **82** D4 45 10N 141 20E
Rishra India **76** K2 22 43N 88 19E
Rishton Lancashire England **42** C3 53 47N 2 24W
Risley Cheshire England **42** C2 53 26N 2 32W
Ritter, Mount California U.S.A. **102** C4 37 40N 119 15W
Rivera Uruguay **115** F6 30 52S 55 30W
River Cess *tn.* Liberia **93** D4 5 28N 9 32W
Riverhead New York U.S.A. **105** F2 40 55N 72 40W
Rivers *tn.* Manitoba Canada **101** O3 50 02N 100 14W
Riverside California U.S.A. **102** C3 33 59N 117 22W
Riverton Manitoba Canada **101** P3 51 00N 97 00W
Riverton New Zealand **87** A1 46 21S 168 02E
Rivière aux Feuilles *r.* Québec Canada **101** U4 57 45N 73 00W
Rivière aux Outardes *r.* Québec Canada **105** G4 50 00N 69 00W
Rivière-du-Loup *tn.* Québec Canada **105** G3 47 49N 69 32W
Roanne France **61** B2 46 02N 4 05E
Roanoke *r.* Virginia U.S.A. **105** D1 37 00N 80 00W
Roanoke Virginia U.S.A. **105** E1 37 15N 79 58W
Robertsport Liberia **93** C4 6 45N 11 22W
Roberval Québec Canada **105** F3 48 31N 72 16W
Robin Hood Bay *tn.* North Yorkshire England **40** D3 54 25N 0 33W
Roblin Manitoba Canada **101** O3 51 15N 101 20W
Robson, Mount British Columbia Canada **100** L3 53 08N 118 18W
Roca Alijos *is.* Mexico **108** A4 24 59N 115 49W
Rocas Island Atlantic Ocean **110** 3 50S 33 50W
Rochdale Greater Manchester England **42** D2 53 38N 2 09W
Rochdale Canal England **42** D3 53 40N 2 05W
Rochefort France **61** A2 45 57N 0 58W
Rochelle Illinois U.S.A. **104** C2 41 55N 89 05W
Rochester Indiana U.S.A. **104** C2 41 03N 86 13W
Rochester Kent England **33** C2 51 24N 0 30E
Rochester Minnesota U.S.A. **104** B2 44 01N 92 27W
Rochester New York U.S.A. **105** E2 43 12N 77 37W
Rochester Northumberland England **44** B2 55 16N 2 16W
Rochford Essex England **33** C2 51 36N 0 43E
Rock *r.* U.S.A. **104** C2 42 00N 89 00W
Rock Rapids *tn.* Iowa U.S.A. **104** A2 43 25N 96 10W
Rock Springs *tn.* Wyoming U.S.A. **102** E5 41 35N 109 13W
Rockall Bank Atlantic Ocean **117** G12 58 00N 15 00W
Rockaway Beach New York U.S.A. **106** C1 40 33N 73 55W
Rockaway Inlet New York U.S.A. **106** C1 40 34N 73 56W
Rockefeller Plateau Antarctica **121** 79 00S 140 00W
Rockford Illinois U.S.A. **104** C2 42 16N 89 06W
Rockhampton Australia **86** I5 23 22S 150 32E
Rock Harbor *tn.* Michigan U.S.A. **104** C3 48 08N 88 30W
Rock Hill South Carolina U.S.A. **103** J3 34 55N 81 01W
Rockingham Forest *hills* Northamptonshire England **36** D2 52 30N 0 30W
Rock Island *tn.* Illinois U.S.A. **104** B2 41 30N 90 34W
Rockland Maine U.S.A. **105** G2 44 06N 69 08W
Rockville Center New York U.S.A. **106** D1 40 40N 73 38W
Rockville Indiana U.S.A. **104** C1 39 45N 87 15W
Rocky Mount *tn.* North Carolina U.S.A. **103** K4 35 56N 77 48W
Rocky Mountains U.S.A./Canada **100** K4–N1
Rocroi France **64** D1 49 56N 4 31E
Rodel Western Isles Scotland **46** B4 57 41N 7 05W
Rodenrijs-Berkel Netherlands **65** B1 51 59N 4 29E
Rodez France **61** B1 44 21N 2 34E
Rodhós Greece **68** E2 36 26N 28 14E
Ródhos *(Rhodes) i.* Greece **68** E2 36 00N 28 00E
Roding *r.* Essex England **33** C2 51 45N 0 15E
Rodopi Planina *mts.* Bulgaria **68** D3 41 00N 25 00E
Roelofarendsveen Netherlands **65** C2 52 11N 4 38E
Roer *r.* Netherlands **64** F3 51 10N 6 03E
Roermond Netherlands **64** F3 51 12N 6 00E
Roes Welcome Sound Northwest Territories Canada **101** R5 63 30N 87 30W
Roeselare Belgium **64** C2 50 57N 3 08E
Rogers City Michigan U.S.A. **105** D3 45 24N 83 50W
Rokugo *r.* Japan **83** C3 35 31N 139 46E
Rolla Missouri U.S.A. **103** H4 37 56N 91 55W
Rolleston Staffordshire England **35** C3 52 51N 1 39W
Roma Australia **86** H4 26 32S 148 46E
Roma *(Rome)* Italy **68** B3 41 53N 12 30E
Roman Romania **69** E2 46 56N 26 56E
ROMANIA 69 D2
Romannobridge Borders Scotland **45** D1 55 44N 3 20W
Romans-sur-Isère France **61** C2 45 03N 5 03E
Rome Georgia U.S.A. **103** I3 34 01N 85 02W
Rome New York U.S.A. **105** E2 43 13N 75 28W
Rome *see* Roma
Romford Greater London England **34** D2 51 35N 0 11E
Romiley Greater Manchester England **42** D2 53 24N 2 09W
Romney Marsh Kent England **33** C2 51 03N 0 58E
Rømø *i.* Denmark **63** A3 55 00N 8 00E
Romorantin-Lanthenay France **61** B2 47 22N 1 44E
Romsey Hampshire England **32** A1 50 59N 1 30W
Romsley Hereford & Worcester England **35** B2 52 25N 2 03W
Rona *i.* Western Isles Scotland **29** F11 59 10N 5 50W
Ronay *i.* Western Isles Scotland **46** A4 57 30N 7 11W
Ronda Spain **66** A2 36 45N 5 10W
Rondônia *admin.* Brazil **114** E10 11 30S 63 00W
Rondonópolis Brazil **114** G9 16 29S 54 37W
Ronne Ice Shelf Antarctica **121** 77 00S 60 00W
Ronsdorf Germany **62** C1 51 13N 7 13E
Ronse Belgium **64** C2 50 45N 3 36E
Roosendaal Netherlands **64** D3 51 32N 4 28E
Roosevelt Island Antarctica **121** 79 00S 160 00W
Rootpark Strathclyde Scotland **45** C1 55 46N 3 40W
Roraima *admin.* Brazil **114** E13 2 30N 62 30W
Rosario Argentina **115** E6 33 00S 60 40W
Rosário Brazil **114** I12 3 00S 44 15W
Rosario Mexico **108** C4 23 00N 105 51W
Rosario Mexico **108** A6 30 02N 115 46W
Rosarito Mexico **108** B5 28 38N 114 02W
Roscoff France **61** A2 48 43N 3 59W
Roscommon *co.* Irish Republic **48** C3 53 45N 8 10W
Roscommon Roscommon Irish Republic **48** C3 53 38N 8 11W
Roscrea Tipperary Irish Republic **48** D2 52 57N 7 47W
Roseau Dominica **109** L3 15 18N 61 23W
Roseburg Oregon U.S.A. **102** B5 43 13N 123 21W
Rosehearty Grampian Scotland **46** F4 57 42N 2 07W
Roselle New Jersey U.S.A. **106** A1 40 40N 74 16W
Rosemead California U.S.A. **107** B3 34 03N 118 07W
Rosenheim Germany **63** B1 47 51N 12 09E
Rosetown Saskatchewan Canada **100** N3 51 34N 107 59W
Rosewell Lothian Scotland **45** D1 55 51N 3 08W
Roskilde Denmark **67** C2 55 39N 12 07E
Roslin Lothian Scotland **45** D1 55 51N 3 11W
Rosliston Derbyshire England **35** D3 52 45N 1 38W
Ross Ice Shelf Antarctica **121** 80 00S 180 00
Ross River *tn.* Yukon Territory Canada **100** I5 62 02N 132 28W
Rossal Point *c.* Lancashire England **42** A3 53 56N 3 04W
Rossan Point *c.* Irish Republic **48** C4 54 40N 8 50W
Rossano Italy **68** C2 39 35N 16 38E
Rossendale, Forest of *hills* Lancashire England **42** D3 53 45N 2 15W
Rossiyskaya S.F.S.R. *(Russian Soviet Federated Socialist Republic) rep.* Russia **71** J8–M8
Rosslare Harbour *tn.* Wexford Irish Republic **48** E2 52 15N 6 22W
Rosso Mauritania **93** B6 16 29N 15 53W
Ross-on-Wye Hereford and Worcester England **36** B1 51 55N 2 35W
Røssvatnet *mt.* Sweden **67** D4 66 00N 15 10E
Rostock Germany **63** B2 54 06N 12 09E
Rostov-na-Donu Russia **70** F5 47 15N 39 45E
Roswell New Mexico U.S.A. **102** F3 33 24N 104 33W
Rosyth Fife Scotland **45** D2 56 03N 3 26W
Rothaar-gebirge *mts.* Germany **63** A2 51 00N 8 00E
Rothbury Northumberland England **44** C2 55 19N 1 55W
Rother *r.* Kent/East Sussex England **33** C2 51 00N 0 40E
Rother *r.* West Sussex England **33** B1 51 00N 0 50W
Rothera *r.s.* Antarctica **121** 67 34S 68 07W
Rotherham South Yorkshire England **43** F2 53 26N 1 20W
Rothes Grampian Scotland **46** E4 57 31N 3 13W
Rothesay Strathclyde Scotland **46** C2 55 51N 5 03W
Rothwell Northamptonshire England **36** D2 52 25N 0 48W
Rothwell West Yorkshire England **43** F3 53 45N 1 29W
Rotorua New Zealand **87** C3 38 07S 176 17E
Rott *r.* Germany **63** B1 48 00N 13 00E
Rottenburg Germany **63** A1 48 28N 12 03E
Rotterdam Netherlands **65** C1 51 54N 4 28E
Rottingdean East Sussex England **33** B1 50 48N 0 04W
Roubaix France **61** B3 50 42N 3 10E
Rouen France **61** B2 49 26N 1 05E
Roundhay West Yorkshire England **43** F3 53 48N 1 30W
Rousay *i.* Orkney Islands Scotland **47** D2 59 10N 3 00W
Rouyn-Noranda Québec Canada **105** E3 48 15N 79 00W
Rovaniemi Finland **67** F4 66 29N 25 40E
Rovigo Italy **68** B4 45 04N 11 47E
Rovno Ukraine **70** E6 50 39N 26 10E
Rovuma *(Ruvuma) r.* Mozambique **95** G5 11 30S 38 00E
Rowington Warwickshire England **35** C2 52 19N 1 42W
Rowlands Gill Tyne and Wear England **44** C1 54 54N 1 45W
Rowly Surrey England **34** B1 51 10N 0 31W
Roxas The Philippines **80** G6 11 36N 122 45E
Roxburgh New Zealand **87** A1 45 34S 169 21E
Royal Canal Irish Republic **49** A2 53 22N 6 39W
Royal Leamington Spa Warwickshire England **35** D1 52 18N 1 31W
Royal Tunbridge Wells Kent England **33** C2 51 08N 0 16E
Royan France **61** A2 45 38N 1 02W
Roydon Essex England **34** D3 51 46N 0 03E
Royston Cambridgeshire England **33** B2 52 03N 0 01W
Royston South Yorkshire England **43** F2 53 37N 1 27W
Royton Greater Manchester England **42** D2 53 34N 2 08W
Rozel Jersey Channel Islands **31** G5 49 14N 2 03W
Rozenburg Netherlands **65** A1 51 54N 4 15E
Râs Banâs *c.* Egypt **78** E3 23 58N 35 50E
Râs Ghârib Egypt **78** N9 28 22N 33 04E
Râs Kasar *c.* Sudan **78** E2 18 02N 38 33E
Râs Muhammed *c.* Egypt **78** O8 27 44N 34 15E
R.S.F.S.R. *see* Rossiyskaya S.F.S.R.
Ruabon Clwyd Wales **38** C2 52 59N 3 02W
Ruaha National Park Tanzania **95** F6 7 00S 35 00E
Ruapehu *mt.* New Zealand **87** C3 39 18S 176 36E
Rub' Al Khālī *d.* Saudi Arabia **79** G2 19 30N 48 00E
Rubha Coigeach *c.* Highland Scotland **46** C5 58 06N 5 26W
Rubha Hunish *c.* Highland Scotland **46** B4 57 40N 6 20W
Rubha Reidh *c.* Highland Scotland **46** C4 57 50N 5 55W
Rubtsovsk Russia **71** K6 51 34N 81 11E
Ruby Alaska U.S.A. **100** D5 64 41N 155 35W
Ruddington Nottinghamshire England **36** C2 52 54N 1 09W
Rudnyy Kazakhstan **70** I6 53 00N 63 05E
Rudolstadt Germany **63** B2 50 44N 11 20E
Rueil-Malmaison France **60** A2 48 52N 2 12E
Rufford Lancashire England **42** B2 53 39N 2 49W
Rufforth North Yorkshire England **43** G3 53 57N 1 07W
Rufiji *r.* Tanzania **95** G6 7 30S 38 40E
Rugby Warwickshire England **35** E2 52 23N 1 15W
Rugeley Staffordshire England **35** C3 52 46N 1 55W
Rügen *i.* Germany **63** B1 54 00N 14 00E
Ruhr *r.* Germany **63** A2 51 00N 7 00E
Ruhrort Germany **62** A2 51 27N 6 44E
Ruislip Greater London England **34** B2 51 35N 0 25W
Rukwa, Lake Tanzania **95** F6 8 00S 33 00E
Rumford Maine U.S.A. **105** F2 44 33N 70 34W
Rumney South Glamorgan Wales **38** C1 51 30N 3 10W
Rumoi Japan **82** D3 43 57N 141 40E
Runanga New Zealand **87** B2 42 24S 171 12E
Runcorn Cheshire England **42** B2 53 20N 2 44W
Rungis France **60** B2 48 45N 2 22E
Rupel *r.* Belgium **64** D3 51 05N 4 20E
Rur *r.* Germany **64** F2 51 00N 6 00E
Ruse Bulgaria **68** E3 43 50N 25 59E
Rush Dublin Irish Republic **48** E3 53 32N 6 06W
Rushall West Midlands England **35** C2 52 37N 1 57W
Rushden Northamptonshire England **36** D2 52 17N 0 36W
Rusk Texas U.S.A. **103** G3 31 49N 95 11W
Russas Brazil **114** J12 4 56S 38 02W
Russell Kansas U.S.A. **102** G4 38 54N 98 51W
Russell Manitoba Canada **101** O3 50 47N 101 17W
Russell New Zealand **87** B3 35 16S 174 10E
RUSSIA 71 J8–M8
Russkaya *r.s.* Antarctica **121** 74 46S 136 51W
Rustavi Georgia **78** G7 41 34N 45 03E
Ruston Louisiana U.S.A. **103** H3 32 32N 92 39W
Ruth Nevada U.S.A. **102** D4 39 16N 114 59W
Rutherglen Strathclyde Scotland **45** B1 55 50N 4 12W
Ruthin Clwyd Wales **38** C3 53 07N 3 18W
Rutland Vermont U.S.A. **105** F2 43 37N 72 59W
Rutland Water *l.* Leicestershire **36** D2 52 40N 0 37W
Rutog China **81** A4 33 27N 79 43E
Ruvuma *(Rovuma) r.* Tanzania **95** G5 11 30S 38 00E
Ruwenzori National Park Rwanda **94** E7 0 30S 29 30E
Ruwenzori, Mount *mt.* Uganda/Zaïre **88** 0 23N 29 54E
Ružomberok Slovenska Czechoslovakia **69** C2 49 04N 19 15E
RWANDA 94 F7
Ryazan' Russia **70** F6 54 37N 39 43E
Rybach'ye *see* Issyk-Kul'
Rybinsk *(Andropov)* Russia **70** F7 58 03N 38 50E
Rybinskoye Vodakhranilishche *res.* Russia **70** F7 59 00N 38 00E
Rybnik Poland **69** C3 50 07N 18 30E
Ryde Isle of Wight England **32** A1 50 44N 1 10W
Rye East Sussex England **33** C1 50 57N 0 44E
Rye New York U.S.A. **106** D2 40 58N 73 41W
Rye *r.* North Yorkshire England **40** C3 54 15N 1 10W
Ryhill West Yorkshire England **43** F2 53 38N 1 25W
Ryton-on-Dunsmore Warwickshire England **35** D2 52 22N 1 26W
Ryukyu Islands *(Nansei-shoto)* Japan **81** K3 27 30N 127 30E
Ryukyu Ridge Pacific Ocean **118** C10 25 50N 128 00E
Ryukyu Trench Pacific Ocean **72** 25 00N 128 00E
Rzeszów Poland **69** D3 50 04N 22 00E

S

Saale *r.* Germany **63** B2 50 00N 10 00E
Saale *r.* Germany **63** B2 52 00N 11 00E
Saalfeld Germany **63** B2 50 39N 11 22E
Saar *r.* Germany **64** F1 49 00N 6 00E
Saarbrücken Germany **63** A1 49 15N 6 58E
Saaremaa *i.* Estonia **67** E2 58 20N 22 00E
Saarland *admin.* Germany **63** A1 49 00N 6 00E
Saarlouis Germany **63** A1 49 19N 6 45E
Šabac Serbia Yugoslavia **68** C3 44 45N 19 41E
Sabadell Spain **66** C3 41 33N 2 07E
Sabah *state* Malaysia **80** F5 5 00N 117 30E
Sabaloka Cataract (River Nile) Sudan **78** D2 16 19N 32 40E
Sabanalarga Colombia **109** J2 10 38N 74 55W
Sabhā Libya **94** B13 27 02N 14 26E
Sabi *r.* Zimbabwe / Mozambique **95** F3 20 30S 33 00E
Sabinas Mexico **108** D5 27 50N 101 09W
Sabinas Hidalgo Mexico **108** D5 26 33N 100 10W
Sabine *r.* U.S.A. **103** H3 30 00N 94 00W
Sabine, Mount Antarctica **121** 72 00S 169 00W
Sabkhet el Bardawîl *l.* Egypt **78** N10 31 10N 33 35E
Sable, Cape Florida U.S.A. **103** J2 25 08N 80 07W
Sable Island Nova Scotia Canada **101** X1 43 57N 60 00W
Sabor *r.* Portugal **66** A3 41 22N 6 50W
Sabyā Saudi Arabia **78** F2 17 07N 42 39E
Sabzevār Iran **79** I6 36 15N 57 38E
Sachsen *admin.* Germany **63** B2 52 30N 11 30E

Sachsen-Anhalt *admin.* Germany **63** B2 51 00N 13 00E
Saclay France **60** A1 48 43N 2 09E
Sacramento California U.S.A. **102** B4 38 32N 121 30W
Sacramento Mountains U.S.A. **102** E3 33 00N 105 00W
Sacriston Durham England **44** C1 54 50N 1 38W
Sadar Bazar India **76** L4 28 39N 77 12E
Saddleworth Moor England **43** E2 53 30N 1 55W
Sadiya India **77** H5 27 49N 95 38E
Sado *r.* Portugal **66** A2 38 15N 8 30W
Sado-shima *i.* Japan **82** C2 38 20N 138 30E
Saffron Walden Essex England **33** C3 52 01N 0 15E
Safi Morocco **93** D9 32 20N 9 17W
Saga Japan **82** B1 33 16N 130 18E
Sagaing Myanmar **77** H4 21 55N 95 56E
Sagami Bay Japan **83** B2 35 15N 139 32E
Sagamihara Japan **82** C2 35 34N 139 22E
Sagar India **77** D4 23 50N 78 44E
Saggart Dublin Irish Republic **49** A1 53 16N 6 26W
Saginaw Michigan U.S.A. **105** D2 43 25N 83 54W
Saginaw Bay Michigan U.S.A. **105** D2 44 00N 84 00W
Sagua la Grande Cuba **109** H4 22 48N 80 06W
Saguenay River Québec Canada **105** F3 48 00N 71 00W
Sagunto Spain **66** B2 39 40N 0 17W
Sahara Desert North Africa **93** E7
Saharanpur India **77** D5 29 58N 77 33E
Sahiwal Pakistan **77** C6 30 41N 73 11E
Sahuaripa Mexico **108** C5 29 00N 109 13W
Sahuayo Mexico **108** D4 20 05N 102 42W
Saïda Algeria **66** C1 34 50N 0 10E
Saïda *(Sidon)* Lebanon **78** O11 33 32N 35 22E
Saidpur Bangladesh **77** F5 25 48N 89 00E
Saikhoa Ghat India **77** H5 27 46N 95 38E
Saimaa *l.* Finland **67** F3 61 15N 27 45E
St. Abb's Head *c.* Borders Scotland **46** F2 55 55N 2 09W
Ste. Agathe des Monts Québec Canada **105** F3 46 03N 74 19W
St. Agnes Cornwall England **30** B2 50 18N 5 13W
St. Agnes *i.* Isles of Scilly England **30** A1 49 54N 6 21W
St. Albans Hertfordshire England **34** B3 51 46N 0 21W
St. Albans *or* **St. Aldhelm's Head** *c.* Dorset
St. Albans Vermont U.S.A. **105** F2 44 49N 73 07W
St.-Amand-les-Eaux France **64** C2 50 27N 3 26E
St. Andrews Bay Fife Scotland **46** F3 56 20N 2 35W
St. Andrews Fife Scotland **46** F3 56 20N 2 48W
Ste. Anne de Beaupré Québec Canada **105** F3 47 02N 70 58W
Sainte-Anne-des-Monts Québec Canada **101** V2 49 07W 66 29W
Ste. Anne Manitoba Canada **104** A3 49 40N 96 40W
St. Ann's Bay *tn.* Jamaica **109** Q8 18 26N 77 12W
St. Ann's Head *c.* Dyfed Wales **38** A1 51 41N 5 10W
St. Anthony Newfoundland Canada **101** X3 51 24N 55 37W
St. Asaph Clwyd Wales **38** C3 53 15N 3 26W
St. Aubin Jersey Channel Islands **31** G5 49 12N 2 10W
St. Augustine Florida U.S.A. **103** J2 29 54N 81 19W
St. Austell Cornwall England **30** C2 50 20N 4 48W
St. Bees Cumbria England **44** A1 54 29N 3 35W
St. Bees Head *c.* Cumbria England **44** A1 54 31N 3 39W
St. Blazey Cornwall England **30** C2 50 22N 4 43W
St. Bride's Bay Dyfed Wales **38** A1 51 50N 5 15W
St-Brieuc France **61** A2 48 31N 2 45W
St. Catharines Ontario Canada **105** E2 43 10N 79 15W
St. Catherine's Point *c.* Isle of Wight England **32** A1 50 34N 1 18W
St.-Chamond France **61** B2 45 29N 4 32E
St. Charles Missouri U.S.A. **104** B1 38 48N 91 29W
St. Clair River North America **105** D2 43 00N 82 00W
St. Clair, Lake North America **105** D2 43 00N 82 00W
St. Clears Dyfed Wales **38** B1 51 50N 4 30W
St-Cloud France **60** A2 48 51N 2 11E
St. Cloud Minnesota U.S.A. **104** B3 45 34N 94 10W
St. Columb Major Cornwall England **30** C2 50 26N 4 56W
St. Croix *i.* West Indies **109** L3 22 45N 65 00W
St. Croix *r.* North America **104** B3 46 00N 93 00W
St. Cyr-l'École France **60** A2 48 47N 2 03E
St. David's Dyfed Wales **38** A1 51 54N 5 16W
St. Davids Tayside Scotland **45** C2 56 22N 3 41W
St. David's Head *c.* Dyfed Wales **38** A1 51 55N 5 19W
St-Denis France **60** B2 48 57N 2 22E
St.-Dié France **61** C2 48 17N 6 57E
St.-Dizier France **61** B2 48 38N 5 58E
St. Elias, Mount U.S.A./Canada **100** G5 60 12N 140 57W
St.-Étienne France **61** B2 45 26N 4 23E
St. Fabien Québec Canada **105** G3 48 19N 68 51W
St.-Félicien Québec Canada **105** F3 48 38N 72 29W
Ste.-Foy Québec Canada **105** F3 46 47N 71 18W
St. Francis *r.* U.S.A. **103** H4 35 00N 90 00W
St. Francis, Cape Republic of South Africa **88** 34 13S 24 51E
St. Gallen Switzerland **61** C2 47 25N 9 23E
St.-Gaudens France **61** B1 43 07N 0 44E
Ste. Geneviève-des-Bois France **60** B1 48 38N 2 19E
Saint George *i.* Alaska/U.S.A. **100** B4 56 34N 169 31W
St. George New York U.S.A. **106** B1 40 48N 74 06W
St. George's Grenada **109** L2 12 04N 61 44W
St. Georges Québec Canada **105** F3 46 08N 70 40W
St. George's Channel British Isles **48** E2 52 00N 6 00W
St.-Germain-en-Laye France **61** B2 48 53N 2 04E
St.-Germain-en-Laye France **60** A2 48 54N 2 04E
St.-Ghislain Belgium **64** C2 50 27N 3 49E
St.-Girons France **61** B1 42 59N 1 08E
St. Govan's Head *c.* Dyfed Wales **38** B1 51 36N 4 55W
St. Helena Bay Republic of South Africa **95** C1 32 00S 17 30E
St. Helena *i.* Atlantic Ocean **117** H5 15 58S 5 43W
St. Helens Merseyside England **42** B2 53 28N 2 44W
St. Helier Jersey Channel Islands **31** G5 49 12N 2 07W
St.-Hubert Belgium **64** E2 50 02N 5 22E
St. Hyacinthe Québec Canada **105** F3 45 38N 72 57W
St. Ignace Michigan U.S.A. **105** D3 45 53N 84 44W
St. Ives Cambridgeshire England **33** B3 52 20N 0 05W
St. Ives Cornwall England **30** B2 50 12N 5 29W
St. Jean de Dieu Québec Canada **105** G3 48 00N 69 05W
St.-Jean-de-Luz France **61** A1 43 23N 1 39W
St. Jean Port Joli Québec Canada **63** F3 47 13N 70 16W
St. Jean Québec Canada **105** F3 45 18N 73 16W
St. Jerôme Québec Canada **105** F3 45 47N 74 01W
Saint John New Brunswick Canada **101** V2 45 16N 66 03W
St. John *r.* Liberia **93** D4 6 30N 9 40W
Saint John *r.* North America **103** M6 46 00N 69 00W
St. John's Antigua & Barbuda **109** L3 17 08N 61 50W
St. John's Isle of Man British Isles **41** F1 54 12N 4 40W
St. John's Newfoundland Canada **101** Y2 47 34N 52 41W
St. John's Town of Dalry Dumfries & Galloway Scotland **46** D2 55 07N 4 10W
St. Joseph Island Ontario Canada **105** D3 46 00N 84 00W
St. Joseph Missouri U.S.A. **104** B1 39 45N 94 51W
St. Just Cornwall England **30** B2 50 07N 5 41W
St. Keverne Cornwall England **30** B2 50 03N 5 06W
ST. KITTS-NEVIS **109** L3
St. Laurent French Guiana **114** G14 5 29N 54 03W
St. Laurent *r.* Canada/U.S.A. *see* St. Lawrence
St. Lawrence *(St. Laurent) r.* Canada/U.S.A. **105** G3 48 00N 69 00W
St. Lawrence, Gulf of Canada **101** W2 49 00N 62 30W
St. Lawrence Island Alaska U.S.A. **100** B5 63 15N 169 50W
St. Lawrence Seaway North America **105** E2 44 00N 76 00W
St. Leonard New Brunswick Canada **105** G3 47 10N 67 55W
St. Leonards Dorset England **31** F2 50 50N 1 50W
St-Lô France **61** A2 49 07N 1 05W
St. Louis Missouri U.S.A. **104** B1 38 40N 90 15W
St. Louis Senegal **93** B6 16 01N 16 30W
ST. LUCIA **109** L2
St. Magnus Bay Shetland Islands Scotland **47** B2 60 25N 1 35W
St.-Malo France **61** A2 48 39N 2 00W
St-Mandé France **60** B2 48 50N 2 26E
St. Margaret's at Cliffe Kent England **33** D2 51 10N 1 23E
Ste. Marie Québec Canada **105** F3 46 26N 71 00W
St. Martin Guernsey Channel Islands **31** G5 49 13N 2 03W
St. Martins *i.* Isles of Scilly England **30** A1 49 58N 6 17W
St. Mary Jersey Channel Islands **31** G5 49 14N 2 10W
St. Marys *i.* Isles of Scilly England **30** A1 49 55N 6 18W
St. Marys Ohio U.S.A. **105** D2 40 32N 84 22W
St. Matthew Island Alaska U.S.A. **100** A5 60 30N 172 30W
St. Maur France **60** B2 48 48N 2 30E
St. Mawes Cornwall England **30** B2 50 09N 5 01W
St. Moritz Switzerland **66** C2 46 30N 9 51E
St.-Nazaire France **61** A2 47 17N 2 12W
St. Neots Cambridgeshire England **33** B2 52 14N 0 17W
St.-Niklaas Belgium **64** D3 51 10N 4 09E
St.-Omer France **61** B3 50 45N 2 15E
St. Ouen France **60** A3 49 03N 2 07E
St. Pacôme Québec Canada **105** G3 47 24N 69 58W
St. Pascal Québec Canada **105** G3 47 32N 69 48W
St. Paul Minnesota U.S.A. **104** B2 45 00N 93 10W
Saint Paul Alaska U.S.A. **100** A4 57 05N 170 18W
St. Paul *r.* Liberia **93** C4 7 10N 10 05W
St. Paul Rocks Atlantic Ocean **117** F7 0 23N 29 23W
St. Peter Minnesota U.S.A. **104** B2 44 21N 93 58W
St. Peter Port Guernsey Channel Islands **31** G5 49 27N 2 32W
St. Petersburg *(Leningrad, Sankt-Peterburg)* Russia **70** F7 59 55N 30 25E
St. Pierre Manitoba Canada **104** A3 49 28N 96 58W
Saint-Pierre & Miquelon *is.* Atlantic Ocean **101** X2 47 00N 56 20W
St. Pölten Austria **69** C2 48 13N 15 37E
St-Quentin France **61** B2 49 51N 3 17E
St. Remy France **60** A1 48 42N 2 04E
St. Siméon Québec Canada **105** G3 47 50N 69 55W
St. Stephen New Brunswick Canada **101** V2 45 12N 67 18W
St. Thomas *i.* West Indies **109** K3 18 00N 65 30W
St. Thomas Ontario Canada **105** D2 42 46N 81 12W
St-Tropez France **61** C1 43 16N 6 39E
St.-Truiden Belgium **64** E2 50 49N 5 11E
St.-Vieth Belgium **64** F2 50 15N 6 07E
ST. VINCENT AND THE GRENADINES **109** L2
St. Vincent *i.* St. Vincent and The Grenadines **109** L2 13 15N 61 12W
St. Wendel Germany **64** G1 49 28N 7 10E
St.-Yvieix-la-Perche France **61** B2 45 31N 1 12E
Saintes France **61** A2 45 44N 0 38W
Saipan Northern Marianas **118** E9 15 12N 145 43E
Sakai Japan **82** C1 34 35N 135 28E
Sākākah Saudi Arabia **78** F4 29 59N 40 12E
Sakakawea, Lake North Dakota U.S.A. **102** F6 48 00N 103 00W
Sakarya *r.* Turkey **78** D6 40 05N 30 15E
Sakata Japan **82** C2 38 55N 139 51E
Sakhalin *i.* Russia **71** Q6 50 00N 143 00E
Sakhalin Bay Russia **71** Q6 54 00N 141 00E
Sakurai Japan **83** C2 35 21N 139 55E
Sala y Gomez *i.* Pacific Ocean **119** P5 26 28S 105 28W
Salālah Oman **79** H2 17 00N 54 04E
Salamanca Mexico **108** D4 20 34N 101 12W
Salamanca Spain **66** A3 40 58N 5 40W
Salcombe Devon England **31** D2 50 13N 3 47W
Saldus Latvia **67** E2 56 38N 22 30E
Sale Greater Manchester England **42** D2 53 26N 2 19W
Salekhard Russia **71** I9 66 33N 66 35E
Salem India **77** D2 11 38N 78 08E
Salem Massachusetts U.S.A. **105** F2 42 32N 70 53W
Salem Oregon U.S.A. **102** B5 44 57N 123 01W
Salen Highland Scotland **46** C3 56 43N 5 47W
Salen Strathclyde Scotland **46** C3 56 31N 5 57W
Salerno Italy **68** B3 40 40N 14 46E
Salford Greater Manchester England **42** D2 53 30N 2 16W
Salfords Surrey England **34** C1 51 12N 0 10W
Salgótarján Hungary **69** C2 48 05N 19 47E
Salgueiro Brazil **114** J11 8 04S 39 05W
Salihli Turkey **68** E2 38 29N 28 08E
Salima Malawi **95** F5 13 45S 34 29E
Salina Kansas U.S.A. **103** G4 38 53N 97 36W
Salinas California U.S.A. **102** B4 36 39N 121 40W
Salinas Ecuador **114** A12 2 15S 80 58W
Salinas Grandes *l.* Argentina **115** D6/E7 30 00S 65 00W
Saline Fife Scotland **45** C2 56 07N 3 36W
Salisbury Maryland U.S.A. **105** E1 38 22N 75 37W
Salisbury North Carolina U.S.A. **103** J4 35 20N 80 30W
Salisbury Wiltshire England **31** F3 51 05N 1 48W
Salisbury Island Northwest Territories Canada **101** T5 63 10N 77 20W
Salisbury Plain Wiltshire England **31** F3 51 10N 1 55W
Salmon Idaho U.S.A. **102** D6 45 11N 113 55W
Salmon *r.* Idaho U.S.A. **102** C6 45 00N 116 00W
Salmon River Mountains Idaho U.S.A. **102** C6 45 00N 115 00W
Salo Finland **67** E3 60 23N 23 10E
Salon-de-Provence France **61** C1 43 38N 5 06E
Salonta Romania **69** D2 46 49N 21 40E
Salpausselka *geog. reg.* Finland **67** F3 61 40N 26 00E
Salt Jordan **78** O11 32 03N 35 44E
Salt *r.* Arizona U.S.A. **102** D3 34 00N 110 00W
Salt *r.* Missouri U.S.A. **104** B1 39 00N 91 00W
Salta Argentina **115** D8 24 46S 65 28W
Saltash Cornwall England **31** C2 50 24N 4 12W
Saltburn-by-the-Sea Cleveland England **44** D1 54 35N 0 58W
Saltcoats Strathclyde Scotland **46** D2 55 38N 4 47W
Saltdal Norway **67** D4 67 06N 15 25E
Saltdean East Sussex England **33** B1 50 49N 0 02W
Saltee Islands Wexford Irish Republic **48** E2 52 07N 6 36W
Salten *geog. reg.* Norway **67** D4 67 05N 15 00E
Saltfleet Lincolnshire England **36** E3 53 26N 0 10E
Salt Fork *r.* Texas U.S.A. **102** F3 33 00N 101 00W
Salt Fork *r.* Texas/Oklahoma U.S.A. **102** F4 35 00N 100 00W
Saltillo Mexico **108** D5 25 30N 101 00W
Salt Lake City Utah U.S.A. **102** D5 40 45N 111 55W
Salt Lake *tn.* India **76** K2 22 35N 88 23E
Salto Uruguay **115** F6 31 27S 57 50W
Salton Sea *l.* California U.S.A. **102** C3 33 00N 116 00W
Salvador Brazil **114** J10 12 58S 38 29W
Salween *r.* China *see* Nu Jiang
Salween *r.* Myanmar **80** B8 21 00N 98 30E
Salzach *r.* Europe **63** B1 48 00N 13 00E
Salzburg *admin.* Austria **63** B1 47 00N 13 00E
Salzburg Austria **63** B1 47 48N 13 03E
Salzgitter Germany **63** B2 52 13N 10 20E
Salzwedel Germany **63** B2 52 51N 11 10E
Samani Japan **82** D3 42 07N 142 57E
Samar *i.* The Philippines **80** G6 12 30N 125 00E
Samara *(Kuybyshev)* Russia **70** H6 53 10N 50 10E
Samarinda Indonesia **80** F3 0 30S 117 09E
Samarkand Uzbekistan **70** I3 39 40N 66 57E
Sāmarrā' Iraq **78** F5 34 13N 43 52E
Sambalpur India **77** E4 21 28N 84 04E
Sambor Ukraine **69** D2 49 31N 23 10E
Sambre *r.* France **64** C2 50 15N 4 00E
Samlesbury Lancashire England **42** C3 53 46N 2 38W
Sámos *i.* Greece **68** E2 37 00N 26 00E
Samothráki *i.* Greece **68** E3 40 00N 25 00E
Samsun Turkey **78** E7 41 17N 36 22E
San Mali **93** D5 13 21N 4 57W
San'ā Yemen Republic **78** F2 15 23N 44 14E
Sanae *r.s.* Antarctica **121** 70 18S 02 25E
Sanaga *r.* Cameroon **93** H3 4 30N 12 20E
Sanak Island Alaska U.S.A. **100** C3 54 26N 162 40W
Sanandaj Iran **79** G6 35 18N 47 01E
San Andrés Tuxtla Mexico **108** E3 18 28N 95 15W
San Angelo Texas U.S.A. **102** F3 31 28N 100 28W
San Antonio Abad Balearic Islands **66** D4 38 59N 1 19E
San Antonio Chile **115** C6 33 35S 71 39W
San Antonio Oeste Argentina **115** E4 40 45S 64 58W
San Antonio *r.* Texas U.S.A. **103** G2 29 00N 97 00W
San Antonio Texas U.S.A. **102** G2 29 25N 98 30W
San Bernardino California U.S.A. **102** C3 34 07N 117 18W
San Bernardo Chile **115** C6 33 37S 70 45W
San Carlos Falkland Islands **117** M16 51 00S 58 50W
San Carlos The Philippines **80** G6 10 30N 123 29E
San Carlos The Philippines **80** G7 15 59N 120 22E
San Carlos Venezuela **114** D14 9 39N 68 35W
San Carlos de Bariloche Argentina **115** C4 41 11S 71 23W
San Carlos del Zulia Venezuela **114** C14 9 01N 71 58W
San Clemente Island California U.S.A. **102** C3 32 55N 118 30W
San Cristóbal Argentina **115** E6 30 20S 61 14W
San Cristobal *i.* Solomon Islands **86** K7 11 00S 162 00E
San Cristóbal Mexico **108** F3 16 45N 92 40W
San Cristobal Venezuela **114** C14 7 46N 72 15W
Sanda Island Strathclyde Scotland **46** C2 55 18N 5 35W
Sandakan Malaysia **80** F5 5 52N 118 04E
Sanday *i.* Orkney Islands Scotland **47** E2 59 15N 2 30W
Sandbach Cheshire England **40** B2 53 09N 2 22W
Sandford Strathclyde Scotland **45** B1 55 39N 4 02W
Sandhurst Berkshire England **33** B2 51 21N 0 48W
San Diego California U.S.A. **102** C3 32 45N 117 10W
Sandoway Myanmar **77** G3 18 28N 94 20E
Sandown Isle of Wight England **32** A1 50 39N 1 09W
Sandpoint *tn.* Idaho U.S.A. **102** C6 48 17N 116 34W
Sandray *i.* Western Isles Scotland **46** A3 56 53N 7 30W
Sandringham Norfolk England **33** C3 52 50N 0 31E
Sandspit British Columbia Canada **100** I3 53 14N 131 50W
Sandusky Ohio U.S.A. **105** D2 41 27N 82 42W
Sandwich Kent England **33** D2 51 17N 1 20E
Sandy Bedfordshire England **33** B3 52 08N 0 18W
Sandy Lake Ontario Canada **101** Q3 52 45N 93 00W
San Felipe Mexico **108** B6 31 03N 114 52W
San Felipe Venezuela **114** D15 10 25N 68 40W
San Feliú de Guixols Spain **66** C3 41 47N 3 02E
San Fernando California U.S.A. **107** A1 34 17N 118 27W
San Fernando de Apure Venezuela **114** D14 7 53N 67 15W
San Fernando Mexico **108** A5 29 59N 115 10W
San Fernando Spain **66** A2 36 28N 6 12W
San Fernando Trinidad and Tobago **109** L2 10 16N 61 28W
Sanford Florida U.S.A. **103** J2 28 49N 81 17W
San Francisco Argentina **115** E6 31 29S 62 06W
San Francisco California U.S.A. **102** B4 37 45N 122 27W
San Francisco del Oro Mexico **108** C5 26 52N 105 50W
San Francisco Dominican Republic **109** J3 19 19N 70 15W
San Francisco Javier Balearic Islands **66** D4 38 43N 1 26E
San Gabriel California U.S.A. **107** B3 34 06N 118 06W
San Gabriel Mountains California U.S.A. **107** B4 34 18N 118 05W
San Gabriel Reservoir California U.S.A. **107** C3 34 12N 117 52W
San Gabriel River California U.S.A. **107** B2 33 58N 118 06W
Sangar Russia **71** O8 64 02N 127 30E
Sangerhausen Germany **63** B2 51 29N 11 18E
Sangha *r.* Africa **94** C8 2 00N 17 00E
Sangli India **77** C3 16 55N 74 37E
Sangmélima Cameroon **93** H3 2 57N 11 56E
Sangre de Cristo Mountains New Mexico U.S.A. **102** E4 37 00N 105 00W
San Isidro Peru **116** E4 12 06S 77 02W
San Javier Bolivia **114** E9 16 22S 62 38W
San Joaquin *r.* California U.S.A. **102** B4 37 00N 120 00W
San José Balearic Islands **66** D4 38 55N 1 18E
San Jose California U.S.A. **102** B4 37 20N 121 55W
San José Costa Rica **109** H1 9 59N 84 04W
San José del Cabo Mexico **108** C4 23 01N 109 40W
San José Uruguay **115** F6 34 27S 56 40W
San Juan Argentina **115** D6 31 33S 68 31W
San Juan Bautista Balearic Islands **66** D4 39 05N 1 31E
San Juán Peru **114** B9 15 22S 75 07W
San Juan Puerto Rico **109** K3 18 29N 66 08W
San Juan *r.* U.S.A. **102** D4 37 00N 110 00W
San Julián Argentina **115** D3 49 17S 67 45W
Sānkrāil India **76** J2 22 33N 88 14E
Sankt-Peterburg *see* St. Petersburg
Sankuru *r.* Zaïre **95** D7 4 00S 23 30E
Sanlúcar de Barrameda Spain **66** A2 36 46N 6 21W
San Lucas Mexico **108** C4 22 50N 109 52W
San Luis Argentina **115** D6 33 20S 66 23W
San Luis Obispo California U.S.A. **102** B4 35 16N 120 40W
San Luis Potosí Mexico **108** D4 22 10N 101 00W
San Marcos Texas U.S.A. **103** G2 29 54N 97 57W
SAN MARINO **68** B3 44 00N 12 00E
San Martin de Porres Peru **116** E4 12 03S 77 07W
Sanmenxia China **81** H4 34 46N 111 17E
San Miguel de Tucumán Argentina **115** D7 26 47S 65 15W
San Miguel El Salvador **108** G2 13 28N 88 10W
Sanming China **81** I3 26 16N 117 35E
San Pablo The Philippines **80** G6 14 03N 121 19E
San Pedro Argentina **115** E8 24 12S 64 55W
San Pedro California U.S.A. **107** A2 33 45N 118 19W
San Pedro Bay California U.S.A. **107** B1 33 43N 118 12W
San Pedro Channel California U.S.A. **107** A1 33 43N 118 22W
San Pedro Côte d'Ivoire **93** D3 4 45N 6 37W
San Pedro de las Colonias Mexico **108** D5 25 50N 102 59W
San Pedro Dominican Republic **109** K3 18 30N 69 18W
San Pedro Sula Honduras **108** G3 15 26N 88 01W
Sanquhar Dumfries & Galloway Scotland **46** E2 55 22N 3 56W
San Rafael California U.S.A. **102** B4 37 58N 122 30W
San Rafael Argentina **115** D6 34 35S 68 24W
San Remo Italy **68** A3 43 48N 7 46E
San Salvador El Salvador **108** G2 13 40N 89 10W
San Salvador *i.* The Bahamas **109** J4 24 00N 74 32W
San Salvador de Jujuy Argentina **115** D8 24 10S 65 48W
San Sebastián Spain **66** B3 43 19N 1 59W
San Severo Italy **68** C3 41 41N 15 23E
Sant' Antioco Italy **68** A2 39 04N 8 27E
Santa Ana River California U.S.A. **107** C2 33 46N 117 54W
Santa Ana Bolivia **114** D10 13 46S 65 37W
Santa Ana California U.S.A. **107** C2 33 44N 117 54W
Santa Ana El Salvador **108** G2 14 00N 89 31W
Santa Barbara California U.S.A. **102** C3 33 29N 119 01W
Santa Barbara Mexico **108** C5 26 48N 105 50W
Santa Catalina Island California U.S.A. **102** C3 33 25N 118 25W
Santa Catarina *admin.* Brazil **115** G7 27 00S 51 00W
Santa Clara Cuba **109** I4 22 25S 79 58W
Santa Clara Mexico **108** P2 19 32N 99 03W
Santa Cruz *r.* Argentina **115** D2 50 00S 70 00W
Santa Cruz Bolivia **114** E9 17 50S 63 10W
Santa Cruz California U.S.A. **102** B4 36 58N 122 03W
Santa Cruz Canary Islands **93** B8 28 28N 16 15W
Santa Cruz Jamaica **109** Q8 18 03N 77 43W
Santa Cruz Island California U.S.A. **102** C3 34 00N 119 40W
Santa Cruz Islands Solomon Islands **86** L7 11 00S 167 00E
Santa Eulalia del Rio Balearic Islands **66** D4 38 59N 1 33E
Santa Fé Argentina **115** E6 31 35S 60 50W
Santa Fe New Mexico U.S.A. **102** E4 35 41N 105 57W
Santa Isabel *i.* Solomon Islands **86** J8 7 30S 158 30E
Santa Maria Brazil **115** G7 29 45S 53 40W
Santa Maria California U.S.A. **102** B3 34 56N 120 25W
Santa Marta Colombia **114** C15 11 18N 74 10W
Santa Monica California U.S.A. **107** A3 34 00N 118 25W
Santa Monica Mountains California U.S.A. **107** A3 33 07N 118 27W
Santa Rosa Argentina **115** E5 36 37S 64 17W
Santa Rosa California U.S.A. **102** B4 38 26N 122 43W
Santa Rosa Honduras **108** G2 14 48N 88 43W
Santa Rosa New Mexico U.S.A. **102** F3 34 56N 104 42W
Santa Rosa Island California U.S.A. **102** B3 34 00N 120 05W
Santa Rosalía Mexico **108** B5 27 20N 112 20W
Santa Teresa Brazil **116** C2 22 57S 43 12W
Santa Teresa Gallura Italy **61** C1 41 14N 9 12E
Santana do Livramento Brazil **115** F6 30 52S 55 30W
Santander Colombia **114** B13 3 00N 76 25W
Santander Spain **66** B3 43 28N 3 48W
Santañy Balearic Islands **66** E4 39 22N 3 07E
Santarém Brazil **114** G12 2 26S 54 41W
Santarém Portugal **66** A2 39 14N 8 40W
Santi Nagar India **76** L4 28 40N 77 10E
Santiago Chile **115** C6 33 30S 70 40W
Santiago Dominican Republic **109** J3 19 30N 70 42W
Santiago Panama **109** H1 8 08N 80 59W
Santiago de Compostela Spain **66** A3 42 52N 8 33W
Santiago de Cuba Cuba **109** I4 20 00N 75 49W
Santiago del Estero Argentina **115** E7 27 47S 64 15W
Santiago Ixcuintla Mexico **108** C4 21 50N 105 11W
Santo Andre Brazil **115** H8 23 39S 46 29W
Santo Domingo Dominican Republic **109** K3 18 30N 69 57W
Santos Brazil **115** H8 23 56S 46 22W
Santpoort Netherlands **65** C3 52 25N 4 39E
Santry Dublin Irish Republic **49** B2 53 24N 6 15W
Sanuki Japan **83** C2 35 15N 139 53E
San Vicente El Salvador **108** G2 13 38N 88 42W
São Bernardo do Campo Brazil **115** H8 23 45S 46 34W
São Borja Brazil **115** F7 28 35S 56 01W
São Cristovão Brazil **116** C2 22 54S 43 14W
São Gonçalo Brazil **116** C2 22 49S 43 03W
São João de Meriti Brazil **116** B2 22 47S 43 22W
São João de Meriti *r.* Brazil **116** B2 22 48S 43 20W
São José Brazil **115** H7 27 35S 48 40W
São José do Rio Prêto Brazil **114** H8 20 50S 49 20W
São José dos Campos Brazil **115** H8 23 07S 45 52W
São José *r.* Brazil **116** B3 22 43S 43 29W
São Luís Brazil **114** I12 2 34S 44 16W
São Paulo *admin.* Brazil **114** G8/H8 21 30S 50 00W
São Paulo Brazil **115** H8 23 33S 46 39W
São Paulo de Olivença Brazil **114** D12 3 34S 68 55W
São Tomé *i.* Gulf of Guinea **93** G3 0 25N 6 35E
SÃO TOMÉ AND PRINCIPE **93** G3
São Vicente Brazil **115** H8 23 57S 46 23W
Saône *r.* France **61** B2 46 28N 4 55E
Sapê *r.* Brazil **116** C2 22 53S 43 03W
Sappemeer Netherlands **64** F5 53 10N 6 47E
Sapporo Japan **82** D3 43 05N 141 21E
Saqqez Iran **79** G6 36 14N 46 15E
Sarajevo Bosnia-Herzegovina **68** C3 43 52N 18 26E
Sarakhs Iran **79** J6 36 32N 61 07E
Saranac Lake *tn.* New York U.S.A. **105** F2 44 19N 74 10W
Saransk Russia **70** G6 54 12N 45 10E
Sarapul *r.* Brazil **116** B3 22 44S 43 17W
Sarasota Florida U.S.A. **103** J2 27 20N 82 32W
Sarata Ukraine **69** E2 46 00N 29 40E
Saratov Russia **70** G6 51 30N 45 55E
Saravan Iran **79** J4 27 25N 62 17E

Sarawak *state* Malaysia 80 E4 2 30N 112 30E
Sarcelles France 60 B2 48 59N 2 22E
Sardegna *(Sardinia) i.* Italy 68 A3 40 00N 9 00E
Sardindida Plain Kenya 94 G8/9 2 00N 40 00E
Sardinia *see* Sardegna
Sar-e Pol Afghanistan 79 K6 36 13N 65 55E
Sargasso Sea Atlantic Ocean 117 B9 27 00N 66 00W
Sargodha Pakistan 77 C6 32 01N 72 40E
Sarh Chad 94 C9 9 08N 18 22E
Sarīr Calanscio *d.* Libya 94 D13 26 00N 22 00E
Sark *i.* Channel Islands British Isles 31 G5 49 26N 2 22W
Sarmiento Argentina 115 D3 45 38S 69 08W
Sarnia Ontario Canada 105 D2 42 57N 82 24W
Sarny Ukraine 69 E3 51 21N 26 31E
Saronikós Kólpos *g.* Greece 68 D2 38 00N 23 00E
Sarpsborg Norway 67 C2 59 17N 11 06E
Sarrebourg France 61 C2 48 43N 7 03E
Sarreguemines France 61 C2 49 06N 6 55E
Sartène Corsica 61 C1 41 37N 8 58E
Sarthe *r.* France 61 A2 47 45N 0 30W
Sartrou-ville France 60 A2 48 56N 2 11E
Sasebo Japan 82 A1 33 10N 129 42E
Saskatchewan *province* Canada 100 N3 53 50N 109 00W
Saskatchewan *r.* Canada 96 54 00N 103 00W
Saskatoon Saskatchewan Canada 100 N3 52 10N 106 40W
Sassandra Côte d'Ivoire 93 D3 4 58N 6 08W
Sassandra *r.* Côte d'Ivoire 93 D4 5 50N 6 55W
Sassari Italy 68 A3 40 43N 8 34E
Sassenheim Netherlands 65 C2 52 13N 4 31E
Sassnitz Germany 63 B2 54 32N 13 40E
Satna India 77 E4 24 33N 80 50E
Satpura Range *mts.* India 77 C4/D4 21 40N 75 00E
Sattahip Thailand 80 C6 12 36N 100 56E
Satu Mare Romania 69 D2 47 48N 22 52E
SAUDI ARABIA 78 F3
Sauer *(Sûre) r.* Europe 64 F1 49 45N 6 30E
Sault Ste. Marie Michigan U.S.A. 105 D3 46 29N 84 22W
Sault Ste. Marie Ontario Canada 105 D3 46 32N 84 20W
Saumur France 61 A2 47 16N 0 05W
Saundersfoot Dyfed Wales 38 B1 51 43N 4 43W
Saurimo Angola 95 D6 9 39S 20 24E
Sava *r.* Europe 68 C3 45 00N 19 00E
Savanna Illinois U.S.A. 104 B2 42 06N 90 07W
Savannah Georgia U.S.A. 103 J3 32 04N 81 07W
Savannah *r.* U.S.A. 103 J3 33 00N 82 00W
Savannakhet Laos 80 C7 16 34N 104 45E
Savanna la Mar Jamaica 109 P8 18 13N 78 08W
Saverne France 63 A1 48 45N 7 22E
Savona Italy 68 A3 44 18N 8 28E
Sawahlunto Indonesia 80 C3 0 41S 100 52E
Sawbridgeworth Hertfordshire England 34 D3 51 50N 0 09E
Sawel *mt.* Northern Ireland 48 D4 54 49N 7 02W
Sawpit Canyon Reservoir California U.S.A. 107 B3 34 10N 117 59W
Sawston Cambridgeshire England 33 C3 52 07N 0 10E
Sawu Sea Indonesia 80 G2 9 30S 122 00E
Saxmundham Suffolk England 33 D3 52 13N 1 29E
Saxthorpe Norfolk England 33 D3 52 50N 1 09E
Sayabec Québec Canada 105 G3 48 35N 67 41W
Sayanogorsk Russia 71 L6 53 00N 91 26E
Saylac Somalia 94 H10 11 21N 43 30E
Saynshand Mongolia 81 G7 44 58N 111 10E
Say'ūn Yemen Republic 79 G2 15 59N 48 44E
Scafell Pike *mt.* Cumbria England 44 A1 54 27N 3 14W
Scalby North Yorkshire England 40 D3 54 18N 0 27W
Scalpay *i.* Highland Scotland 46 B4 57 15N 6 00W
Scalpay *i.* Western Isles Scotland 46 B4 57 52N 6 40W
Scandinavia *geog. reg.* Europe 51 65 00N 15 00E
Scapa Flow *sd.* Orkney Islands Scotland 47 D1 58 55N 3 00W
Scarborough North Yorkshire England 40 D3 54 17N 0 24W
Scarinish Strathclyde Scotland 46 B3 56 29N 6 48W
Scarisbrick Lancashire England 42 B2 53 37N 2 57W
Scarp *i.* Western Isles Scotland 46 A5 58 02N 7 08W
Scarsdale New York U.S.A. 106 C2 40 59N 73 49W
Sceaux France 60 B2 48 46N 2 18E
Schaerbeek Belgium 64 D2 50 52N 4 22E
Schaffhausen Switzerland 61 C2 47 42N 8 38E
Schagen Netherlands 64 D4 52 47N 4 47E
Schefferville *(Kawawachikamach)* Québec Canada 101 V3 54 50N 67 00W
Schelde *(Sheldt) r.* Belgium 64 D3 51 15N 4 16E
Scheldt *see* Schelde
Scheldt Estuary Europe 51 51 30N 3 30E
Schenectady New York U.S.A. 105 F2 42 48N 73 57W
Scheveningen Netherlands 65 B2 52 06N 4 18E
Schiedam Netherlands 65 B1 51 55N 4 25E
Schiermonnikoog *i.* Netherlands 64 E5 53 28N 6 10E
Schleswig Germany 63 A2 54 32N 9 34E
Schleswig-Holstein *admin.* Germany 63 A2 54 00N 10 00E
Schönebeck Germany 63 B2 52 01N 11 45E
Schoonhoven Netherlands 65 D1 51 56N 4 51E
Schorndorf Germany 63 A1 48 48N 9 33E
Schoten Belgium 64 D3 51 15N 4 30E
Schouwen *i.* Netherlands 64 D3 51 40N 3 50E
Schreiber Ontario Canada 104 C3 48 48N 87 17W
Schwäbische Alb *mts.* Germany 63 A1 48 00N 9 00E
Schwäbisch Gmünd Germany 63 A1 48 49N 9 48E
Schwäbisch Hall Germany 63 A1 49 07N 9 45E
Schwandorf Germany 63 B1 49 20N 12 07E
Schwarze Elster *r.* Germany 63 B2 52 00N 13 00E
Schwarzwald *(Black Forest) mts.* Germany 63 A1 47 00N 8 00E
Schwarzwälder Hochwald *mts.* Germany 64 F1 49 00N 7 00E
Schwedt Germany 63 B2 53 04N 14 17E
Schweinfurt Germany 63 B2 50 03N 10 16E
Schwelm Germany 62 D2 51 17N 7 18E
Schwerin Germany 63 B2 53 38N 11 25E
Schwyz Switzerland 61 C2 47 02N 8 34E
Scilly, Isles of Cornwall England 30 A1 49 56N 6 20W
Scioto *r.* Ohio U.S.A. 105 D1 40 00N 83 00W
Scoresbysund *sd.* Greenland 101 EE7 70 30N 22 45W
Scoresbysund *tn.* Greenland 120 70 30N 22 00W
Scotforth Lancashire England 42 B4 54 02N 2 48W
Scotia Ridge Antarctica 117 C1 53 00S 50 00W
Scotia Sea Antarctica 117 C1 56 30N 50 00W
Scotland United Kingdom 46/47
Scott Base *r.s.* Antarctica 121 77 51S 166 45E
Scott Island Southern Ocean 118 H1 66 35S 180 00
Scotton North Yorkshire England 43 F4 54 03N 1 32W
Scottsbluff Nebraska U.S.A. 102 F5 41 52N 103 40W
Scourie Highland Scotland 46 C5 58 20N 5 08W
Scrabster Highland Scotland 46 E5 58 37N 3 34W
Scranton Pennsylvania U.S.A. 105 E2 41 25N 75 40W
Scunthorpe Humberside England 40 D2 53 35N 0 39W
Seaford East Sussex England 33 C1 50 46N 0 06E
Seaham Durham England 44 C1 54 50N 1 20W
Seahouses Northumberland England 44 C2 55 35N 1 38W
Seal Kent England 34 D1 51 17N 0 14E
Sealdah India 76 K2 22 32N 88 22E
Seal River *r.* Manitoba Canada 101 P4 59 10N 97 00W
Seascale Cumbria England 44 A1 54 24N 3 29W
Seaton Cumbria England 44 A1 54 40N 3 30W
Seaton Devon England 31 D2 50 43N 3 05W
Seaton Delaval Northumberland England 44 C2 55 04N 1 31W
Seattle Washington U.S.A. 102 B6 47 35N 122 20W
Sebkra Sidi-el-Hani *salt l.* Tunisia 35 30N 10 00E
Sedalia Missouri U.S.A. 104 B1 38 42N 93 15W
Sedan France 61 B2 49 42N 4 57E
Sedbergh Cumbria England 44 B1 54 20N 2 31W
Sedgley West Midlands England 35 B2 52 33N 2 08W
Ségou Mali 93 D5 13 28N 6 18W
Segovia Spain 66 B3 40 57N 4 07W
Segre *r.* Spain 66 C3 42 00N 1 10E
Segura *r.* Spain 66 B2 38 10N 1 30W
Seine *r.* France 61 B2 49 15N 1 15E
Sekijiri Japan 83 C1 35 12N 139 55E
Sekondi Takoradi Ghana 93 E3 4 59N 1 43W
Selat Sunda *sd.* Indonesia 80 D2 6 00S 106 00E
Selborne Hampshire England 33 B2 51 06N 0 56W
Selby North Yorkshire England 43 G3 53 48N 1 04N
Seldovia Alaska U.S.A. 100 E4 59 29N 151 45W
Selemdzha *r.* Russia 71 P6 52 30N 132 00E
Selenga *(Selenge) r.* Russia/Mongolia 81 G8 51 00N 106 00E
Selenge *(Selenga) r.* Mongolia/Russia 81 F7 49 00N 102 00E
Sélestat France 61 B2 48 16N 7 28E
Selima Oasis Sudan 94 E12 21 22N 29 19E
Selkirk Borders Scotland 46 F2 55 33N 2 50W
Selkirk Manitoba Canada 104 A4 50 10N 96 52W
Selma Alabama U.S.A. 103 I3 32 24N 87 01W
Selsey West Sussex England 33 B1 50 44N 0 48W
Selsey Bill *p.* West Sussex England 33 B1 50 43N 0 48W
Sélune *r.* France 61 A2 48 40N 1 15W
Selvas *geog. reg.* South America 110 7 00S 65 00W
Selwyn Mountains British Columbia Canada 100 I5 63 00N 131 00W
Semarang Indonesia 80 E2 6 58S 110 29E
Semenovskoye Russia 70 M1 55 39N 37 32E
Seminoe Reservoir Wyoming U.S.A. 102 E5 42 00N 106 00W
Seminole Oklahoma U.S.A. 103 G4 35 15N 96 40W
Semipalatinsk Kazakhstan 71 K6 50 26N 80 16E
Semnān Iran 79 H6 35 30N 53 25E
Semois *r.* Belgium 64 E1 49 40N 5 30E
Senart-Ville-Nouvelle France 60 C1 48 36N 2 35E
Send Surrey England 34 B1 51 17N 0 32W
Sendai Japan 82 D2 38 16N 140 52E
Sendai Japan 82 B1 31 50N 130 17E
Seneca Lake New York U.S.A. 105 E2 43 00N 77 00W
SENEGAL 93 C5
Sénégal *r.* Senegal / Mauritania 93 C6 16 45N 14 45W
Senftenberg Germany 63 B2 51 31N 14 01E
Senhor do Bonfim Brazil 114 I10 10 28S 40 11W
Senja *i.* Norway 67 D4 69 15N 17 20E
Senlis France 61 B2 49 12N 2 35E
Sennar Sudan 78 D1 13 31N 33 38E
Sennar Dam Sudan 78 D1 13 20N 33 45E
Sennen Cornwall England 30 B2 50 03N 5 42W
Sennybridge Powys Wales 38 C1 51 57N 3 34W
Sens France 61 B2 48 12N 3 18E
Sentinel Range *mts.* Antarctica 121 78 00S 87 00W
Senyavin Islands Pacific Ocean 118 G8 7 00N 161 30E
Seoul *see* Sŏul
Sepik *r.* Papua New Guinea 86 G9 4 00S 142 30E
Sept-Îles *tn.* Québec Canada 101 V3 50 10N 66 00W
Sequoia National Park California U.S.A. 108 A7 36 30N 118 30W
Seraing Belgium 64 E2 50 37N 5 31E
Seram *i.* Indonesia 80 H3 2 50S 129 00E
Seram Sea Indonesia 80 H3/I3 2 30S 130 00E
Serang Indonesia 80 D2 6 07S 106 09E
Serbia *admin.* Yugoslavia 68 D3 44 00N 21 00E
Serdan Mexico 108 C5 28 40N 105 57W
Seremban Malaysia 80 C4 2 42N 101 54E
Serengeti National Park Tanzania 94 F7 2 30S 35 00E
Serenje Zambia 95 F5 13 12S 30 15E
Sergiev Posad *(Zagorsk)* Russia 70 F7 56 20N 38 10E
Sergino Russia 71 I8 62 30N 65 40E
Sergipe *admin.* Brazil 114 J10 11 00S 38 00W
Seria Brunei 80 E4 4 39N 114 23E
Serian Malaysia 80 E4 1 10N 110 35E
Serov Russia 70 I7 59 42N 60 32E
Serowe Botswana 95 E3 22 25S 26 44E
Serra Brazil 114 I9 20 06S 40 16W
Serra do Mar *mts.* Brazil 115 H7 27 30S 49 00W
Serra do Navio Brazil 114 G13 1 00N 52 05W
Sérrai Greece 68 D3 41 03N 23 33E
Serrania de Cuenca *mts.* Spain 66 B3 40 30N 2 15W
Serra Tumucumaque *mts.* Brazil 114 F13/G13 2 00N 55 00W
Serre *r.* France 64 C1 49 40N 3 52E
Setagaya Japan 83 B3 35 37N 139 38E
Sète France 61 B1 43 25N 3 43E
Sete Lagoas Brazil 114 I9 19 29S 44 15W
Sete Pontes Brazil 116 C2 22 51S 43 04W
Setesdal *geog. reg.* Norway 67 B2 59 30N 7 10E
Sétif Algeria 93 G10 36 11N 5 24E
Setit *r.* Sudan 78 E1 14 20N 36 15E
Seto-Naikai *sd.* Japan 82 B1 34 00N 132 30E
Settat Morocco 93 D9 33 04N 7 37W
Settle North Yorkshire England 42 D4 54 04N 2 16W
Setúbal Portugal 66 A2 38 31N 8 54W
Sevastopol' Ukraine 70 F4 44 36N 33 31E
Sevenoaks Kent England 34 D1 51 16N 0 12E
Sevenoaks Weald Kent England 34 D1 51 41N 0 11E
Severn *r.* England / Wales 36 A2–B1
Severnaya *(North)* **Donets** *r.* Asia 70 F5 49 00N 37 00E
Severnaya *(North)* **Dvina** *r.* Asia 70 G8 63 00N 43 00E
Severnaya Sos'va *r.* Russia 70 I8 62 30N 62 00E
Severnaya Zemlya *(North Land) is.* Russia 71 L12 80 00N 95 00E
Severn River *r.* Ontario Canada 101 R4 55 10N 89 00W
Severočeský *admin.* Ceska Czechoslovakia 63 B2 50 00N 14 00E
Severodvinsk Russia 70 F8 64 35N 39 50E
Sevier *r.* Utah U.S.A. 102 D4 39 00N 113 00W
Sevilla *(Seville)* Spain 66 A2 37 24N 5 59W
Seville *see* Sevilla
Sèvre *r.* France 61 A2 47 00N 1 10W
Sèvres France 60 A2 48 49N 2 13E
Seward Alaska U.S.A. 100 F5 60 05N 149 34W
Seward Peninsula Alaska U.S.A. 100 B6 65 20N 165 00W
SEYCHELLES 123 4 30S 55 30E
Seymchan Russia 71 R8 62 54N 152 26E
Seymour Indiana U.S.A. 104 C1 38 57N 85 55W
Sézanne France 61 B2 48 44N 3 44E
Sfax Tunisia 93 H9 34 45N 10 43E
Sfîntu Gheorghe Romania 69 E2 45 51N 25 48E
's-Gravenhage *(Den Haag, The Hague)* Netherlands 65 B2 52 05N 4 16E
's-Gravenzande Netherlands 65 A1 52 00N 4 08E
Sgurr Mor *mt.* Highland Scotland 46 C4 57 42N 5 03W
Shabaqua Ontario Canada 104 C3 48 35N 89 54W
Shache China 81 A5 38 27N 77 16E
Shackleton Ice Shelf Antarctica 121 66 00S 100 00E
Shackleton Range *mts.* Antarctica 121 81 00S 20 00W
Shaftesbury Dorset England 31 E3 51 01N 2 12W
Shag Rocks South Atlantic Ocean 115 I2 53 00S 42 00N
Shah Alam Malaysia 80 C4 3 02N 101 31E
Shahdara India 76 M4 28 40N 77 17E
Shahdol India 77 E4 23 19N 81 26E
Shahjahanpur India 77 D5 27 53N 79 55E
Shaki Nigeria 93 F4 8 39N 3 25E
Shalford Surrey England 34 B1 51 13N 0 35W
Shamokin Pennsylvania U.S.A. 105 E2 40 45N 76 34W
Shandong Bandao *p.* China 72 37 30N 120 00E
Shangani *r.* Zimbabwe 95 E4 19 00S 29 00E
Shanghai China 81 J4 31 06N 121 22E
Shangqiu China 81 I4 34 27N 115 07E
Shangrao China 81 I3 28 28N 117 54E
Shangshui China 81 H4 33 36N 114 38E
Shankill Dublin Irish Republic 49 B1 53 14N 6 07W
Shankill Northern Ireland 49 D1 54 37N 5 57W
Shanklin Isle of Wight England 32 A1 50 38N 1 10W
Shannon Clare Irish Republic 48 C2 52 41N 8 55W
Shannon *r.* Irish Republic 48 C3 53 30N 9 00W
Shantou China 81 I2 23 23N 116 39E
Shaoguan China 81 H2 24 54N 113 33E
Shaoxing China 81 J4 30 02N 120 35E
Shaoyang China 81 H3 27 10N 111 25E
Shap Cumbria England 44 B1 54 32N 2 41W
Shapinsay *i.* Orkney Islands Scotland 47 E2 59 03N 2 51W
Shaqrā' Saudi Arabia 79 G4 25 18N 45 15E
Sharon Pennsylvania U.S.A. 105 D2 41 16N 80 30W
Shashi China 81 H4 30 16N 112 20E
Shasta Lake California U.S.A. 102 B5 40 45N 122 20W
Shasta, Mount California U.S.A. 102 B5 41 25N 122 12W
Shatsky Rise Pacific Ocean 118 G11 34 00N 160 00E
Shaw Greater Manchester England 42 D2 53 35N 2 06W
Shawinigan Québec Canada 101 U2 46 33N 72 45W
Shebelē *r.* Ethiopia / Somalia 94 H9 6 00N 44 00E
Sheberghān Afghanistan 79 K6 36 41N 65 45E
Sheboygan Wisconsin U.S.A. 104 C2 43 46N 87 44W
Sheering Essex England 34 D3 51 48N 0 11E
Sheerness Kent England 33 C2 51 27N 0 45E
Sheffield South Yorkshire England 43 F2 53 23N 1 30W
Shefford Bedfordshire England 34 C4 52 02N 0 20W
Shelburne Nova Scotia Canada 101 V1 43 47N 65 20W
Shelburne Ontario Canada 105 D2 44 05N 80 13W
Shelby Montana U.S.A. 102 D6 48 30N 111 52W
Shelbyville Indiana U.S.A. 104 C1 39 31N 85 46W
Shelekhov Bay Russia 71 R8 60 00N 157 00E
Shelfield West Midlands England 35 C2 52 37N 1 55W
Shelikof Strait Alaska U.S.A. 100 E4 57 30N 155 00W
Shenandoah Iowa U.S.A. 104 A2 40 48N 95 22W
Shenandoah *r.* Virginia U.S.A. 105 E1 39 00N 78 00W
Shenandoah Mountains U.S.A. 105 E1 39 00N 79 00W
Shenley Hertfordshire England 34 C3 51 43N 0 17W
Shenstone Staffordshire England 35 C2 52 39N 1 50W
Shenyang China 81 J6 41 50N 123 26E
Shenzhen China 81 H2 22 31N 114 08W
Sheoraphuli India 76 K3 22 46N 88 20E
Shepetovka Ukraine 69 E3 50 12N 27 01E
Shepley West Yorkshire England 43 E2 53 36N 1 42W
Shepperton Surrey England 34 B2 51 23N 0 28W
Sheppey, Isle of Kent England 33 C2 51 25N 0 50E
Shepshed Leicestershire England 35 E3 52 47N 1 18W
Shepton Mallet Somerset England 31 E3 51 12N 2 33W
Sherborne Dorset England 31 E2 50 57N 2 31W
Sherbrooke Québec Canada 105 F3 45 24N 71 54W
Sherburn in Elmet North Yorkshire England 43 G3 53 48N 1 15W
Shere Surrey England 34 B1 51 13N 0 28W
Sheridan Wyoming U.S.A. 102 E5 44 48N 106 57W
Sheriffhales Shropshire England 35 A3 52 42N 2 21W
Sheringham Norfolk England 33 D3 52 57N 1 12E
Sherkin Island Irish Republic 48 B1 51 28N 9 25W
's-Hertogenbosch Netherlands 64 E3 51 41N 5 19E
Sherwood Forest Nottinghamshire England 36 C3 53 15N 1 00W
Shetland Islands *islands area* Scotland 47 B1 60 00N 1 15W
Shevchenko Kazakhstan 70 H4 43 37N 51 11E
Shevington Greater Manchester England 42 B2 53 34N 2 42W
Sheyenne *r.* North Dakota U.S.A. 104 A3 47 00N 98 00W
Shiant *is.* Western Isles Scotland 46 B4 57 55N 6 20W
Shibuya Japan 83 B3 35 39N 139 42E
Shieldaig Highland Scotland 46 C4 57 31N 5 39W
Shieldhill Central Scotland 45 C1 55 58N 3 46W
Shifnal Shropshire England 35 A2 52 41N 2 22W
Shihezi China 81 C6 44 19N 86 10E
Shijiazhuang China 81 H5 38 04N 114 28E
Shikarpur Pakistan 76 B5 27 58N 68 42E
Shikoku *i.* Japan 82 B1 33 40N 134 00E
Shikotan *i.* Japan 82 E3 43 47N 148 45E
Shilbottle Northumberland England 44 C2 55 23N 1 42W
Shildon Durham England 44 C1 54 38N 1 39W
Shiliguri India 77 F5 26 42N 88 30E
Shilka *r.* Russia 71 N6 52 30N 117 30E
Shillington Bedfordshire England 34 B3 51 59N 0 22W
Shillong India 77 G5 25 34N 91 53E
Shimizu Japan 82 C2 35 01N 138 29E
Shimoga India 77 D2 13 56N 75 31E
Shimonoseki Japan 82 B1 33 59N 130 58E
Shinagawa Japan 83 B3 35 37N 139 44E
Shinagawa Bay Japan 83 C3 35 36N 139 50E
Shinano *r.* Japan 82 C2 37 40N 139 00E
Shīndand Afghanistan 79 J5 33 16N 62 05E
Shingū Japan 82 C1 33 42N 136 00E
Shinjō Japan 82 D2 38 45N 140 18E
Shinjuku Japan 83 B3 35 41N 139 42E
Shinyanga Tanzania 95 F7 3 40S 33 25E
Shiono-misaki *c.* Japan 82 C1 33 28N 135 47E
Shipbourne Kent England 34 D1 51 15N 0 17E
Shipki Pass India 77 D6 31 50N 78 50E
Shipley West Yorkshire England 43 E3 53 50N 1 47W
Shipston-on-Stour Warwickshire England 36 C2 52 04N 1 37W
Shipton North Yorkshire England 43 G4 54 01N 1 09W
Shirakawa Japan 82 D2 37 07N 140 11E
Shiraoi Japan 82 D3 42 34N 141 19E
Shīrāz Iran 79 H4 29 38N 52 34E
Shirebrook Derbyshire England 43 G1 53 13N 1 13W
Shireoaks Nottinghamshire England 43 G1 53 19N 1 11W
Shiretoko-misaki *c.* Japan 82 E3 44 24N 145 20E
Shishmaref Alaska U.S.A. 100 B6 66 15N 166 11W
Shivaji Park *tn.* India 76 L4 28 40N 77 07E
Shizuishan China 81 G5 39 04N 106 22E
Shizuoko Japan 82 C1 34 59N 138 24E
Shkodër Albania 68 C3 42 03N 19 01E
Shkumbin *r.* Albania 68 C3 41 00N 20 00E
Shomolu Nigeria 92 C3 6 34N 3 26E
Shoreham-by-Sea West Sussex England 33 B1 50 49N 0 16W
Shotton Clwyd Wales 38 C3 53 12N 3 02W
Shotts Strathclyde Scotland 45 C1 55 49N 3 48W
Shreveport Louisiana U.S.A. 103 H3 32 30N 93 46W
Shrewsbury Shropshire England 36 B2 52 43N 2 45W
Shrewton Wiltshire England 31 F3 51 12N 1 55W
Shrirampur India 76 K3 22 45W 88 21E
Shropshire *co.* England 36 B2 52 45N 2 40W
Shropshire Union Canal England 35 B3 52 43N 2 17W
Shuangliao China 81 J6 43 30N 123 29E
Shuangyashan China 81 L7 46 42N 131 20E
Shumagin Islands Alaska U.S.A. 100 D4 55 00N 159 00W
Shumen Bulgaria 68 E3 43 17N 26 55E
Shunde China 81 H2 22 50N 113 16E
Shuqrā Yemen Republic 79 G1 13 23N 45 44E
Shwebo Myanmar 81 E2 24 26N 97 05E
Shyamnagar India 76 K3 22 50N 88 24E
Sialkot Pakistan 77 C6 32 29N 74 35E
Šiauliai Lithuania 67 E2 55 51N 23 20E
Šibenik Croatia 68 C3 43 45N 15 55E
Siberian Lowland Russia 72 60 00N 80 00E
Sibi Pakistan 76 B5 29 31N 67 54E
Sibiti Congo 95 B7 3 40S 13 24E
Sibiu Romania 69 D2 45 46N 24 09E
Sible Hedingham Essex England 33 C2 51 58N 0 35E
Sibolga Indonesia 80 B4 1 42N 98 48E
Sibpur India 76 K2 22 34N 88 19E
Sibu Malaysia 80 E4 2 18N 111 49E
Sibut Central African Republic 94 C9 5 46N 19 06E
Sichuan Basin *see* Sichuan Pendi
Sichuan Pendi *(Sichuan Basin)* China 81 F4/G4 32 00N 107 00E
Sicilian Channel *sd.* Mediterranean Sea 68 B2 37 00N 12 00E
Sicily *i.* Italy 68 B2 37 00N 14 00E
Sicuani Peru 114 C10 14 21S 71 13W
Sidcup Greater London England 34 D2 51 26N 0 07E
Sidi Barrani Egypt 94 E14 31 38N 25 58E
Sidi Bel Abbès Algeria 93 E10 35 15N 0 39W
Sidi Ifni Morocco 93 C8 29 24N 10 12W
Sidlaw Hills Tayside Scotland 46 E3 56 30N 3 10W
Sidmouth Devon England 31 D2 50 41N 3 15W
Sidney Lanier, Lake Georgia U.S.A. 103 J3 34 00N 84 00W
Sidon *see* Saïda
Siedlce Poland 69 D3 52 10N 22 18E
Sieg *r.* Germany 63 A2 50 00N 8 00E
Siegburg Germany 63 A2 50 48N 7 13E
Siegen Germany 63 A2 50 52N 8 02E
Siena Italy 68 B3 43 19N 11 19E
Sierra Blanca *tn.* Texas U.S.A. 102 E3 31 10N 105 22W
Sierra da Estrêla *mts.* Portugal 66 A3 40 17N 8 00W
Sierra de Alcaraz *mts.* Spain 66 B2 38 30N 2 30W
Sierra de Alfabia *mts.* Balearic Islands 66 E4 39 30N 2 45E
Sierra de Gata *mts.* Spain 66 A3 40 15N 6 40W
Sierra de Gredos *mts.* Spain 66 A3 40 18N 5 20W
Sierra de Guadarrama *mts.* Spain 66 B3 40 45N 4 00W
Sierra del Cadi *mts.* Spain 66 C3 42 20N 1 30E
Sierra de Madureira *mts.* Brazil 116 A2 23 30N 43 30W
Sierra de Maracaju *mts.* Brazil 114 F8–G9 20 00S 55 00W
Sierra de Segura *mts.* Spain 66 B2 38 00N 2 45W
Sierra dos Parecis *hills* Brazil 110 7 00S 60 00W
SIERRA LEONE 93 C4
Sierra Madre del Sur *mts.* Mexico 108 D3/E3 17 30N 100 00W
Sierra Madre Occidental *mts.* Mexico 108 C5–D4 26 00N 107 00W
Sierra Madre Oriental *mts.* Mexico 108 D5–E4 23 30N 100 00W
Sierra Morena *mts.* Spain 66 B2 38 05N 5 50W
Sierra Nevada *mts.* Spain 66 B2 37 30N 3 20W
Sierra Nevada *mts.* U.S.A. 102 C4 37 00N 119 00W
Sierras de Cordoba *mts.* Argentina 115 D6/E6 32 30S 65 00W
Sighetu Marmaţiei Romania 69 D2 47 56N 23 53E
Sighişoara Romania 69 D2 46 12N 24 48E
Siglufjördur Iceland 67 I7 66 09N 18 55W
Signy *r.s.* South Orkney Islands 121 60 43S 45 36W
Sigüenza Spain 66 B3 41 04N 2 38W
Siguiri Guinea 93 D5 11 28N 9 07W
Sikar India 77 D5 27 33N 75 12E
Sikasso Mali 93 D5 11 18N 5 38W
Sikhote-Alin' *mts.* Russia 71 P5 45 00N 137 00E
Sikkim *admin.* India 77 F5 27 30N 88 30E
Sil *r.* Spain 66 A3 42 25N 7 05W
Silchar India 77 G4 24 49N 92 47E
Sileby Leicestershire England 36 C2 52 44N 1 05W
Silifke Turkey 78 D6 36 22N 33 57E
Siling Co *l.* China 77 F6 31 45N 88 50E
Silistra Bulgaria 68 E3 44 06N 27 17E
Siljan *l.* Sweden 67 D3 60 55N 14 50E
Silloth Cumbria England 44 A1 54 52N 3 23W
Silsden West Yorkshire England 43 E3 53 55N 1 56W
Silver Bay *tn.* Minnesota U.S.A. 104 B3 47 15N 91 17W
Silver City New Mexico U.S.A. 102 E3 32 47N 108 16W
Silverdale Staffordshire England 35 B4 53 01N 2 16W
Silver Lake Reservoir California U.S.A. 107 A3 34 05N 118 16W
Silverstone Northamptonshire England 36 C2 52 06N 1 02W
Silverton Devon England 31 D2 50 48N 3 30W
Silves Portugal 66 A2 37 11N 8 26W
Simanggang Malaysia 80 E4 1 10N 111 32E
Simcoe Ontario Canada 105 D2 42 50N 80 19W
Simcoe, Lake Ontario Canada 105 E2 44 23N 79 18W
Simeulue *i.* Indonesia 80 B4 2 40N 96 00E
Simferopol' Ukraine 70 F4 44 57N 34 05E

0 55W
Stoke Poges Buckinghamshire England **34** B2 51 33N 0 35W
Stoke-on-Trent Staffordshire England **35** B4 53 00N 2 10W
Stokesley North Yorkshire England **40** C3 54 28N 1 11W
Stolberg Germany **63** A2 50 45N 6 15E
Stondon Massey Essex England **34** D3 51 41N 0 17E
Stone Staffordshire England **35** B3 52 54N 2 10W
Stone Canyon Reservoir California U.S.A. **107** A3 34 07N 118 27W
Stonehaven Grampian Scotland **46** F3 56 38N 2 13W
Stonehouse Strathclyde Scotland **45** C1 55 43N 3 59W
Stoneleigh Warwickshire England **35** D2 52 21N 1 31W
Stonewall Manitoba Canada **104** A4 50 08N 97 20W
Stoneyburn Lothian Scotland **45** C1 55 51N 3 37W
Stony Rapids *tn.* Saskatchewan Canada **100** N4 59 14N 105 48W
Stony Stratford Buckinghamshire England **33** B3 52 04N 0 52W
Stony Tunguska *see* Podkamennaya Tunguska
Stora Lulevattern *l.* Sweden **67** D4 67 20N 19 00E
Størdal Norway **67** C3 63 18N 11 48E
Støren Norway **67** C3 63 03N 10 16E
Storm Lake *tn.* Iowa U.S.A. **104** A2 42 39N 95 11W
Stornoway Western Isles Scotland **46** B5 58 12N 6 23W
Storr, The *mt.* Highland Scotland **46** B4 57 30N 6 11W
Storrington West Sussex England **33** B1 50 55N 0 28W
Storsjön *l.* Sweden **67** C3 63 10N 14 10E
Storuman Sweden **67** D4 65 05N 17 10E
Stotfold Bedfordshire England **34** C4 52 01N 0 15W
Stour *r.* Dorset England **31** E2 50 55N 2 15W
Stour *r.* Kent England **33** D2 51 10N 1 10E
Stour *r.* Suffolk / Essex England **33** C2 51 58N 0 55E
Stourbridge West Midlands England **35** B2 52 27N 2 09W
Stourport-on-Severn Hereford and Worcester
Stowmarket Suffolk England **33** D3 52 11N 1 00E
Stow-on-the-Wold Gloucestershire England **31** F3 51 56N 1 44W
Strabane Northern Ireland **48** D4 54 49N 7 27W
Strachur Strathclyde Scotland **46** C3 56 10N 5 04W
Stradbally Laois Irish Republic **48** D2 53 00N 7 08W
Straffan Kildare Irish Republic **49** A1 53 18N 6 37W
Straits of Florida *sd.* Florida U.S.A. **103** J1 25 00N 80 00W
Strakonice Ceska Czechoslovakia **63** B1 49 16N 13 54E
Stralsund Germany **63** B2 54 18N 13 06E
Strangford Lough *l.* Northern Ireland **48** F4 54 25N 5 45W
Stranorlar Donegal Irish Republic **48** D4 54 48N 7 46W
Stranraer Dumfries & Galloway Scotland **46** C1 54 55N 5 02W
Strasbourg France **61** C2 48 35N 7 45E
Stratford Ontario Canada **105** D2 43 22N 81 00W
Stratford-upon-Avon Warwickshire England **35** C1 52 12N 1 41W
Strathallan *v.* Tayside Scotland **45** C2 56 30N 3 50W
Strathaven Strathclyde Scotland **45** B1 55 41N 4 05W
Strathclyde *reg.* Scotland **46** C3 56 10N 5 30W
Strathmiglo Fife Scotland **56** D2 56 17N 3 16W
Strathpeffer Highland Scotland **46** D4 57 35N 4 33W
Strathspey *v.* Scotland **46** E4 57 25N 3 30W
Strathy Point *c.* Highland Scotland **46** D5 58 35N 4 02W
Stratton Cornwall England **30** C2 50 50N 4 31W
Straubing Germany **63** B1 48 53N 12 35E
Strausberg Germany **63** B2 52 34N 13 53E
Streatham Greater London England **34** C2 51 26N 0 07W
Streatley Bedfordshire England **34** B3 51 57N 0 27W
Streator Illinois U.S.A. **104** C2 41 07N 88 53W
Stredočeský *admin.* Ceska Czechoslovakia **63** B2 50 00N 14 00E
Street Somerset England **31** E3 51 03N 2 45W
Streetly West Midlands England **35** C2 52 34N 1 52W
Strensall North Yorkshire England **43** G4 54 02N 1 03W
Stretford Greater Manchester England **42** D2 53 27N 2 19W
Stretto di Messina *sd.* Italy **68** C2 38 00N 15 00E
Stretton Cheshire England **40** B2 53 21N 2 35W
Stretton Staffordshire England **35** D3 52 50N 1 39W
Stretton Staffordshire England **35** B3 52 42N 2 09W
Strimón *r.* Greece **68** D3 41 00N 23 00E
Strogino Russia **70** L2 55 49N 37 26E
Stroma *i.* Scotland **46** E5 58 40N 3 08W
Stromboli *mt.* Italy **68** C2 38 48N 15 15E
Stromeferry Highland Scotland **46** C4 57 21N 5 34W
Stronsay *i.* Orkney Islands Scotland **47** E2 59 07N 2 37W
Strood Kent England **34** E2 51 24N 0 28E
Stroud Gloucestershire England **31** E3 51 45N 2 12W
Stroudsburg Pennsylvania U.S.A. **105** E2 41 00N 75 12W
Struma *r.* Bulgaria **68** D3 42 00N 23 00E
Strumble Head *c.* Dyfed Wales **38** A2 52 02N 5 04W
Stryy Ukraine **69** D2 49 16N 23 51E
Stuart Highway *rd.* Australia **86** E5/E6 20 00S 135 00E
Stubaler Alpen *mts.* Austria **63** B1 47 00N 11 00E
Stubbington Hampshire England **32** A1 50 49N 1 13W
Studley Warwickshire England **35** C1 52 16N 1 52W
Stung Treng Cambodia **80** D6 13 31N 105 59E
Stura di Demonte *r.* Italy **61** C1 44 00N 7 00E
Sturbridge Staffordshire England **35** B3 52 52N 2 15W
Sturgeon Falls *tn.* Ontario Canada **105** E3 46 22N 79 57W
Sturgeon Lake Ontario Canada **104** B4 50 00N 91 00W
Sturgeon Landing Saskatchewan Canada **101** O3 54 18N 101 49W
Sturminster Newton Dorset England **31** E2 50 56N 2 19W
Sturt Creek *r.* Australia **86** D6 18 00S 127 30E
Stuttgart Germany **63** A1 48 47N 9 12E
Stykkishólmur Iceland **67** H7 65 05N 22 44W
Styr' *r.* Ukraine **69** E3 51 00N 25 00E
Suakin Sudan **78** E2 19 08N 37 17E
Słubice Poland **63** B2 52 20N 14 35E
Subotica Serbia Yugoslavia **68** C4 46 04N 19 41E
Suceava Romania **69** E2 47 37N 26 18E
Sucre Bolivia **114** D9 19 05S 65 15W
Sucy-en-Brie France **60** C2 48 46N 2 31E
SUDAN **94** D2
Sudbury Derbyshire England **35** C3 52 53N 1 44W
Sudbury Ontario Canada **105** D3 46 30N 81 01W
Sudbury Suffolk England **33** C3 52 02N 0 44E
Sudd *swamp* Africa **88** 7 00N 30 00E
Sudety Reseniky *mts.* Europe **69** C3 50 00N 16 00E
Sudr Egypt **78** N9 29 40N 32 42E
Sue *r.* Sudan **94** E9 7 00N 28 00E
Suez *see* El Suweis
Suez Canal Egypt **78** D5 30 20N 32 20E
Suez, Gulf of Egypt **78** N9 28 20N 33 15E
Suffolk *co.* England **33** C3 52 10N 1 00E
Sugar Loaf *see* Pao de Açúcar
Suginami Japan **83** B3 35 41N 139 40E
Sühbaatar Mongolia **81** G8 50 10N 106 14E
Suhl Germany **63** B2 50 37N 10 43E
Suir *r.* Irish Republic **48** D2 52 15N 7 05W
Sukabumi Indonesia **80** D2 6 55S 106 50E
Sukhona *r.* Russia **70** G8 60 00N 45 00E
Sukhumi Georgia **70** G4 43 01N 41 01E
Sukkertoppen Greenland **101** Y6 65 25N 53 00W
Sukkur Pakistan **76** B5 27 42N 68 54E
Sulaiman Range *mts.* Pakistan **76** B5–C6 30 00N 70 00E
Sulawesi *(Celebes) i.* Indonesia **80** F3/G3 2 30S 120 30E
Sulaymānīyah Iraq **79** G6 35 32N 45 27E
Sullana Peru **114** A12 4 52S 80 39W
Sullom Voe *b.* Shetland Islands Scotland **47** B2 60 27N 1 20W
Sultanpur India **77** E5 26 15N 82 04E
Sulu Archipelago *is.* The Philippines **80** G5 5 30N 121 00E
Sulu Sea Malaysia/The Philippines **80** F5/G5 8 00N 120 00E
Sumatera *i.* Indonesia **80** B4–C3 1 00N 101 00E
Sumba *i.* Indonesia **80** F2/G2 10 00S 120 00E
Sumbawa *i.* Indonesia **80** F2 8 00S 117 30E
Sumburgh Head *c.* Shetland Islands Scotland **47** B1 59 51N 1 16W
Sumgait Azerbaijan **70** G4 40 35N 49 38E
Sumida Japan **83** C3 35 42N 139 49E
Summit Lake *tn.* British Columbia Canada **100** K4 58 45N 124 45W
Sumy Ukraine **70** F6 50 55N 34 49E
Sunbury Pennsylvania U.S.A. **105** E2 40 52N 76 47W
Sunbury Surrey England **34** B2 51 24N 0 25W
Sunch'ŏn South Korea **81** K4 34 56N 127 28E
Sundarbans *geog. reg.* Southern Asia **72** 23 00N 90 00E
Sunderland Tyne and Wear England **44** C1 54 55N 1 23W
Sundsvall Sweden **67** D3 62 22N 17 20E
Sunland California U.S.A. **107** A4 34 15N 118 17W
Sunningdale Berkshire England **34** B2 51 24N 0 37W
Sunset Beach *tn.* California U.S.A. **107** B1 33 43N 118 04W
Suntar Russia **71** N8 62 10N 117 35E
Sunyani Ghana **93** E4 7 22N 2 18W
Suō-nada *b.* Japan **82** B1 33 50N 131 30E
Superior Wisconsin U.S.A. **104** B3 46 42N 92 05W
Superior, Lake North America **104** C3 47 00N 88 00W
Słupsk Poland **69** C3 54 28N 17 00E
Sūr Oman **79** I3 22 34N 59 32E
Surabaya Indonesia **80** E2 7 14S 112 45E
Surakarta Indonesia **80** E2 7 32S 110 50E
Surat India **77** C4 21 10N 72 54E
Surat Thani Thailand **80** B5 9 09N 99 20E
Surbiton Greater London England **34** C2 51 24N 0 19W
Surco Peru **116** E4 12 08S 77 00W
Sûre *(Sauer) r.* Europe **64** F1 49 45N 6 30E
Surendranagar India **77** C4 22 44N 71 43E
Surgut Russia **71** J8 61 13N 73 20E
SURINAM **114** F13
Surquillo Peru **116** E4 12 07S 77 02W
Surrey *co.* England **33** B2 51 15N 0 30W
Surt *(Sirte)* Libya **94** C14 31 13N 16 35E
Surui *r.* Brazil **116** C3 22 40S 43 08W
Surulere Nigeria **92** C3 6 30N 3 25E
Susitna *r.* Alaska U.S.A. **100** E5 62 10N 150 15W
Susquehanna River U.S.A. **105** E2 40 00N 77 00W
Susuman Russia **71** Q8 62 46N 148 08E
Sutlej *r.* Pakistan **77** C6 30 00N 73 00E
Sutton Greater London England **34** C2 51 22N 0 12W
Sutton Québec Canada **105** F3 45 05N 72 36W
Sutton Coldfield West Midlands England **35** C2 52 34N 1 48W
Sutton Hill *tn.* Shropshire England **35** A2 52 38N 2 06W
Sutton in Ashfield Nottinghamshire England **36** C3 53 08N 1 15W
Sutton Nottinghamshire England **43** H2 53 11N 0 49W
Sutton on Sea Lincolnshire England **36** E3 53 19N 0 17E
Sutton on the Forest North Yorkshire England **43** G4 54 04N 1 06W
Suva Fiji **118** U15 18 08S 178 25E
Suvasvesi *l.* Finland **67** F3 62 40N 28 10E
Suzhou China **81** J4 31 21N 120 40E
Suzuka Japan **82** C1 34 52N 136 37E
Suzu-misaki *c.* Japan **82** C2 37 30N 137 21E
Svendborg Denmark **63** B3 55 04N 10 38E
Sverdlovsk *see* Yekaterinburg
Svobodnyy Russia **71** O6 51 24N 128 05E
Swadlincote Derbyshire England **35** D3 52 46N 1 33W
Swaffham Norfolk England **33** C3 52 39N 0 41E
Swale *r.* Kent England **33** C2 51 20N 0 50E
Swale *r.* North Yorkshire England **40** C3 54 15N 1 30W
Swaledale *v.* North Yorkshire England **40** B3 54 25N 2 05W
Swanage Dorset England **31** E2 50 37N 1 58W
Swanley Kent England **34** D2 51 24N 0 12E
Swanscombe Kent England **34** D2 51 26N 0 18E
Swansea West Glamorgan Wales **38** C1 51 38N 3 57W
Swansea Bay West Glamorgan Wales **38** C1 51 35N 3 55W
SWAZILAND **95** F2
SWEDEN **67** C2
Sweetwater *tn.* Texas U.S.A. **102** F3 32 27N 100 25W
Swellendam Republic of South Africa **95** D1 34 01S 20 26E
Swiebodzin Poland **69** C3 52 15N 15 31E
Swift Current *tn.* Saskatchewan Canada **100** N3 50 17N 107 49W
Swillington West Yorkshire England **43** F3 53 47N 1 25W
Swindon Staffordshire England **35** B2 52 30N 2 12W
Swindon Wiltshire England **31** F3 51 34N 1 47W
Swinford Mayo Irish Republic **48** C3 53 57N 8 57W
Swinoujście Poland **69** B3 53 55N 14 18E
Swinton Greater Manchester England **42** C2 53 31N 2 21W
Swinton South Yorkshire England **43** G2 53 30N 1 19W
SWITZERLAND **61** C2
Swords Dublin Irish Republic **49** B2 53 28N 6 13W
Sydney Australia **86** I3 33 55S 151 10E
Sydney Nova Scotia Canada **101** W2 46 10N 60 10W
Syktyvkar Russia **70** H8 61 42N 50 45E
Sylhet Bangladesh **77** G4 24 53N 91 51E
Sylt *i.* Germany **63** A2 54 00N 8 00E
Syowa *r.s.* Antarctica **121** 69 00S 39 35E
Syracuse New York U.S.A. **105** E2 43 03N 76 10W
Syr-Dar'ya *r.* Asia **70** I4 43 00N 66 30E
SYRIA **78** E6
Syrian Desert Middle East **78** E5 32 30N 39 20E
Syzran' Russia **70** G6 53 10N 48 29E
Szczecin Poland **69** B3 53 25N 14 32E
Szczecinek Poland **69** C3 53 42N 16 41E
Szeged Hungary **69** D2 46 15N 20 09E
Székesfehérvár Hungary **69** C2 47 11N 18 22E
Szolnok Hungary **69** D2 47 10N 20 10E
Szombathely Hungary **69** C2 47 14N 16 38E

T

Ţabas Iran **79** I5 33 37N 56 54E
Taber Alberta Canada **100** M2 49 48N 112 09W
Table Rock Lake Missouri U.S.A. **104** B1 36 38N 93 17W
Tábor Ceska Czechoslovakia **69** B2 49 25N 14 39E
Tabora Tanzania **95** F7 5 01S 32 48E
Tabrīz Iran **79** G6 38 05N 46 18E
Tabuaeran Island Kiribati **119** K8 4 00N 158 10E
Tabūk Saudi Arabia **78** E4 28 33N 36 36E
Tacloban The Philippines **80** G6 11 15N 125 01E
Tacna Peru **114** C9 18 00S 70 15W
Tacoma Washington U.S.A. **102** B6 47 16N 122 30W
Tacuba Mexico **108** P1 19 27N 99 11W
Tacubaya Mexico **108** P1 19 24N 99 11W
Tadcaster North Yorkshire England **43** G3 53 53N 1 16W
Tadley Hampshire England **32** A2 51 21N 1 08W
Tadmur Syria **78** E5 34 40N 38 10E
Tadoussac Québec Canada **105** G3 48 09N 69 43W
Tadworth Surrey England **34** C1 51 18N 0 14W
Taegu South Korea **81** K5 35 52N 128 36E
Taejŏn South Korea **81** K5 36 20N 127 26E
Taff *r.* South Glamorgan Wales **38** C1 51 30N 3 15W
Tafila Jordan **78** O10 30 52N 35 36E
Tafna *r.* Algeria **66** B2 35 00N 2 00W
Taganrog Russia **70** F5 47 14N 38 55E
Tagus *see* Tejo
Tahat, Mount Algeria **93** G7 23 18N 5 33E
Tahiti *i.* French Polynesia **119** L6 17 30S 148 30W
Tahoe, Lake U.S.A. **102** C4 39 00N 120 00W
Tahoua Niger **93** G5 14 57N 5 19E
Tahta Egypt **78** D4 26 47N 31 31E
Tai'an China **81** I5 36 15N 117 10E
T'ai-chung Taiwan **81** J2 24 09N 120 40E
Tain Highland Scotland **46** D4 57 48N 4 04W
T'ai-nan Taiwan **81** J2 23 01N 120 14E
T'ai-pei Taiwan **81** J3 25 05N 121 32E
Taitō Japan **83** C3 35 43N 139 48E
TAIWAN **81** J2
Taiwan Strait Taiwan / China **81** I2–H3 24 00N 119 30E
Taiyuan China **81** H5 37 50N 112 30E
Ta'izz Yemen Republic **78** F1 13 35N 44 02E
TAJIKISTAN **70** I3/J3
Tajo *(Tejo) r.* Spain / Portugal **66** A2 40 30N 2 00W
Tak Thailand **80** B7 16 51N 99 08E
Takada Japan **82** C2 37 06N 138 16E
Takamatsu Japan **82** B1 34 20N 134 01E
Takaoka Japan **82** C2 36 47N 137 00E
Takapuna New Zealand **87** B3 36 48S 174 47E
Takasaki Japan **82** C2 36 20N 139 00E
Takatsu Japan **83** B3 35 35N 139 37E
Takayama Japan **82** C2 36 09N 137 16E
Takefu Japan **82** C2 35 54N 136 10E
Takeley Essex England **34** D3 51 52N 0 15E
Takeo Cambodia **80** C6 11 00N 104 46E
Takeshita Japan **83** B3 35 33N 139 32E
Takla Lake British Columbia Canada **100** J4 55 30N 125 40W
Takla Landing British Columbia Canada **100** J4 55 28N 125 58W
Talara Peru **114** A12 4 38S 81 18W
Talavera de la Reina Spain **66** B2 39 58N 4 50W
Talbot, Cape Australia **86** D7 13 49S 126 42E
Talca Chile **115** C5 35 28S 71 40W
Talcahuano Chile **115** C5 36 40S 73 10W
Taldy-Kurgan Kazakhstan **71** J5 45 02N 78 23E
Talgarth Powys Wales **38** C1 52 00N 3 15W
Talke Staffordshire England **35** B4 53 04N 2 16W
Tall Kalakh Syria **78** P12 34 45N 36 17E
Tallaght Dublin Irish Republic **49** A1 53 17N 6 21W
Tallahassee Florida U.S.A. **103** J3 30 26N 84 19W
Tallinn Estonia **67** E2 59 22N 24 48E
Tallow Waterford Irish Republic **48** D2 52 05N 8 00W
Talodi Sudan **94** F10 10 40N 30 25E
Taltal Chile **115** C7 25 26S 70 33W
Talybont Dyfed Wales **38** C2 52 29N 3 59W
Talybont Reservoir Powys Wales **38** C1 51 50N 3 25W
Tama *r.* Japan **83** B3 35 40N 139 30E
Tamabo Range *mts.* Malaysia **80** F4 4 00N 115 30E
Tamale Ghana **93** E4 9 26N 0 49W
Tamanrasset Algeria **93** G7 22 50N 5 28E
Tamar *r.* Devon / Cornwall England **31** C2 50 35N 4 15W
Tambov Russia **70** G6 52 44N 41 28E
Tambre *r.* Spain **66** A3 42 55N 8 50W
Tame *r.* Staffordshire England **36** C2 52 40N 1 45W
Tâmega *r.* Portugal **66** A3 41 40N 7 45W
Tamil Nadu *admin.* India **77** D2 12 00N 78 30E
Tampa Florida U.S.A. **103** J2 27 58N 82 38W
Tampere Finland **67** E3 61 32N 23 45E
Tampico Mexico **108** E4 22 18N 97 52W
Tamworth Australia **86** I3 31 07S 150 57E
Tamworth Staffordshire England **35** D2 52 39N 1 40W
Tana *r.* Kenya **94** G7 1 00S 39 50E
Tana, Lake Ethiopia **94** G10 12 20N 37 20E
Tanabe Japan **82** C1 33 43N 135 22E
Tanafjord *fj.* Norway **67** F5 71 00N 28 15E
Tanahmerah Indonesia **86** G8 6 08N 140 18E
Tanana Alaska U.S.A. **100** E6 65 11N 152 10W
Tanana *r.* Alaska U.S.A. **100** G5 63 00N 143 00W
Tananarive *see* Antananarivo
Tanashi Japan **83** B3 35 43N 139 31E
Tandil Argentina **115** F5 37 18S 59 10W
Tandragee Armagh Northern Ireland **48** E4 54 22N 6 25W
Tanezrouft *admin.* Algeria **93** E7 24 00N 0 30W
Tanga Tanzania **95** G6 5 07S 39 05E
Tanganyika, Lake East Africa **95** F6 7 00S 30 00E
Tanger *(Tangiers)* Morocco **66** A2 35 48N 5 45W
Tanggula Shan *mts.* China **81** D4 32 30N 92 30E
Tangiers *see* Tanger
Tangra Yumco *l.* China **77** F6 31 00N 86 15E
Tangshan China **81** I5 39 37N 118 05E
Tanjungkarang Telukbetung Indonesia **80** D2 5 22S 105 18E
Tanna *i.* Vanuatu **86** L6 19 30S 169 00E
Tannu Ola *mts.* Russia **71** L6 51 00N 92 30E
Tanout Niger **93** G6 15 05N 8 50E
Tanta Egypt **78** D5 30 48N 31 00E
TANZANIA **95** F6
Taolañaro Madagascar **95** I2 25 01S 47 00E
Tapa Estonia **67** F2 59 16N 25 50E
Tapachula Mexico **108** F2 14 54N 92 15W
Tāpi *r.* India **77** D4 21 30N 76 30E
Taplow Buckinghamshire England **34** A2 51 32N 0 41W
Tappi-zaki *c.* Japan **82** D3 41 14N 140 21E
Tapti *r.* India **77** C4 21 30N 74 30E
Tapuaenuku *mt.* New Zealand **87** B2 42 00S 173 39E
Taquara Brazil **116** B2 22 55S 43 22W
Ţarābulus *(Tripoli)* Libya **94** B14 32 54N 13 11E
Tarakan Indonesia **80** F4 3 20N 117 38E
Taransay *i.* Western Isles Scotland **46** A4 57 55N 7 00W
Táranto Italy **68** C3 40 28N 17 15E
Tarapoto Peru **114** B11 6 31S 76 23W
Tararua Range *mts.* New Zealand **87** C2 41 00S 175 30E
Tarauacá Brazil **114** C11 8 06S 70 45W
Tarawa Kiribati **118** H8 1 30N 173 00E
Tarazona Spain **66** B3 41 54N 1 44W
Tarbat Ness *c.* Highland Scotland **46** E4 57 50N 3 45W
Tarbert Kerry Irish Republic **48** B2 52 32N 9 23W
Tarbert Strathclyde Scotland **46** C2 55 52N 5 26W
Tarbert Western Isles Scotland **46** B4 57 54N 6 49W
Tarbes France **61** B1 43 14N 0 05E
Tarbet Strathclyde Scotland **46** D3 56 12N 4 43W
Tarbolton Strathclyde Scotland **46** D2 55 31N 4 29W
Taree Australia **86** I3 31 54S 152 26E
Tarfaya Morocco **93** C8 27 58N 12 55W
Tarija Bolivia **114** D8 21 33S 64 45W
Tarim Basin *see* Tarim Pendi
Tarim He *r.* China **81** B6 41 00N 82 00E
Tarim Pendi *(Tarim Basin)* China **81** B5/C5 39 00N 84 00E
Tarko-Sale Russia **71** J8 64 55N 77 50E
Tarkwa Ghana **93** E4 5 16N 1 59W
Tarleton Lancashire England **42** B3 53 41N 2 50W
Tarn *r.* France **61** B1 44 05N 1 40E
Tarnobrzeg Poland **69** D3 50 35N 21 40E
Tarnów Poland **69** D2 50 01N 20 59E
Taro *r.* Italy **61** C1 44 00N 9 00E
Taroom Australia **86** H4 25 39S 149 50E
Tarporley Cheshire England **42** B1 53 10N 2 40W
Tarragona Spain **66** C3 41 07N 1 15E
Tarrasa Spain **66** C3 41 34N 2 00E
Tarsus Turkey **78** D6 36 52N 34 52E
Tartary, Gulf of Russia **71** Q5/Q6 50 00N 141 00E
Tartu Estonia **67** F2 58 20N 26 44E
Tartus Syria **78** E5 34 55N 35 52E
Tarvin Cheshire England **42** B1 53 12N 2 46W
Tashauz Turkmenistan **70** H4 41 49N 59 58E
Tashkent Uzbekistan **70** I4 41 16N 69 13E
Tasman Basin Pacific Ocean **118** F3 46 00S 154 00E
Tasman Bay New Zealand **87** B2 41 00S 173 20E
Tasmania *state* Australia **86** H1 43 00S 147 00E
Tasman Mountains New Zealand **87** B2 41 20S 172 30E
Tasman Plateau Southern Ocean **118** E3 48 00S 147 00E
Tasman Sea Pacific Ocean **118** F4 40 00S 155 00E
Tassili N'Ajjer Algeria **93** G8 26 00N 6 20E
Tatabánya Hungary **69** C2 47 31N 18 25E
Tateyama Japan **82** C1 34 59N 139 50E
Tatnam, Cape Manitoba Canada **101** Q4 57 25N 91 00W
Tatry *mts.* Europe **69** C2 49 00N 20 00E
Tatsfield Surrey England **34** D1 51 18N 0 02E
Tauber *r.* Germany **63** A1 49 00N 9 00E
Tauern *mts.* Europe **52** 47 30N 12 00E
Taumarunui New Zealand **87** C3 38 53S 175 16E
Taunton Massachusetts U.S.A. **105** F2 41 54N 71 06W
Taunton Somerset England **31** D3 51 01N 3 06W
Taunus *mts.* Germany **63** A2 50 00N 8 00E
Taupo New Zealand **87** C3 38 42S 176 06E
Taupo, Lake New Zealand **87** C3 38 50S 175 55E
Tauranga New Zealand **87** C3 37 42S 176 11E
Tauva Fiji **118** T16 17 31S 177 53E
Tavda *r.* Russia **70** I7 58 00N 64 00E
Taverham Norfolk England **33** D3 52 41N 1 10E
Taverny France **60** A3 49 01N 2 13E
Taveuni *i.* Fiji **118** U16 16 40S 180 00
Tavignano *r.* Corsica **61** C1 42 05N 9 40E
Tavira Portugal **66** A2 37 07N 7 39W
Tavistock Devon England **31** C2 50 33N 4 08W
Tavoy Myanmar **80** B6 14 02N 98 12E
Tavy *r.* Devon England **31** C2 50 35N 4 05W
Taw *r.* Devon England **31** D2 50 58N 3 55W
Tawas City Michigan U.S.A. **105** D2 44 16N 83 33W
Tawau Malaysia **80** F4 4 16N 117 54E
Tay *r.* Scotland **46** E3 56 30N 3 25W
Taymā' Saudi Arabia **78** E4 27 37N 38 30E
Taymyr Peninsula Russia **71** M11/L10 75 00N 100 00E
Taynuilt Strathclyde Scotland **46** C3 56 25N 5 14W
Tayport Fife Scotland **46** F3 56 27N 2 53W
Tayshet Russia **71** L7 55 56N 98 01E
Tayside *reg.* Scotland **46** E3 56 35N 3 40W
Taz *r.* Russia **71** K9 67 00N 82 00E
Taza Morocco **93** E9 34 16N 4 01W
Tbilisi Georgia **70** G4 41 43N 44 48E
Tchibanga Gabon **93** H2 2 49S 11 00E
Tczew Poland **69** C3 54 05N 18 46E
Te Anau, Lake New Zealand **87** A1 45 30S 168 00E
Te Aroha New Zealand **87** C3 37 32S 175 43E
Te Awamutu New Zealand **87** C3 38 00S 175 20E
Tebay Cumbria England **44** B1 54 26N 2 35W
Te Kuiti New Zealand **87** C3 38 20S 175 10E
Tébessa Algeria **93** G10 35 21N 8 06E
Tecuci Romania **69** E2 45 50N 27 27E
Tedzhen *r.* Turkmenistan/Iran **79** J6 37 00N 61 00E
Tees *r.* Northern England **44** C1 54 30N 1 25W
Teesdale *v.* Durham England **44** B1 54 40N 2 15W
Tefé Brazil **114** E12 3 24S 64 45W
Tegal Indonesia **80** D2 6 52S 109 07E
Tegucigalpa Honduras **108** G2 14 05N 87 14W
Tehrān Iran **79** H6 35 40N 51 26E
Tehuacán Mexico **108** E3 18 30N 97 26W
Tehuantepec Mexico **108** E3 16 21N 95 13W
Teifi *r.* Dyfed Wales **38** B2 52 03N 4 15W
Teign *r.* Devon England **31** D2 50 42N 3 50W
Teignmouth Devon England **31** D2 50 33N 3 30W
Teith *r.* Central Scotland **45** B2 56 30N 4 15W
Tejo *(Tagus, Tajo) r.* Portugal **66** A2 39 30N 8 15W
Tekapo, Lake New Zealand **87** B2 43 30S 170 30E
Tekezē *r.* Ethiopia **78** E1 13 48N 38 05E
Tekirdağ Turkey **68** E3 40 59N 27 31E
Tel *r.* India **77** E4 20 30N 83 30E
Tela Honduras **108** G3 15 46N 87 25W
Tel Aviv-Yafo Israel **78** O11 32 05N 34 46E
Telegraph Creek *tn.* British Columbia Canada **100** I4 57 56N 131 11W
Telemark *geog. reg.* Norway **67** B2 59 42N 8 00E
Telford Shropshire England **35** A2 52 42N 2 28W
Teller Alaska U.S.A. **100** B6 65 12N 166 23W
Teluk Bone *b.* Indonesia **80** G3 4 00S 121 00E
Teluk Cenderawasih *b.* Indonesia **86** F9 2 30S 135 30E
Teluk Tomini *b.* Indonesia **80** G3 1 00S 121 00E
Tema Ghana **93** E4 5 41N 0 00
Teme *r.* Hereford and Worcester England **36** B2 52 15N 2 25W
Temirtau Kazakhstan **71** J6 50 05N 72 55E
Témiscaming Québec Canada **105** E3 46 44N 79 05W
Tempio Pausania Italy **68** A3 40 54N 9 07E

Temple Lothian Scotland **45** D1 55 49N 3 05W
Temple Texas U.S.A. **103** G3 31 06N 97 22W
Temple City California U.S.A. **107** B3 34 06N 118 02W
Templemore Tipperary Irish Republic **48** D2 52 48N 7 50W
Templepatrick Northern Ireland **49** C2 54 42N 6 06W
Temse Belgium **64** D3 51 08N 4 13E
Temuco Chile **115** C5 38 45S 72 40W
Temuka New Zealand **87** B2 44 12S 171 16E
Tenali India **77** E3 16 13N 80 36E
Tenbury Wells Shropshire England **36** B2 52 19N 2 35W
Tenby Dyfed Wales **38** B1 51 41N 4 43W
Ten Degree Channel Andaman / Nicobar Islands **77** G1 10 00N 93 00E
Tenerife *i.* Canary Islands **93** B8 28 15N 16 35W
Teniente Jubany *r.s.* Antarctica **121** 62 14S 58 40W
Teniente Rodolfo Marsh Martín *r.s.* Antarctica **121** 62 12S 58 54W
Tennant Creek *tn.* Australia **86** E6 19 31S 134 15E
Tennessee *r.* U.S.A. **103** I4 35 00N 88 00W
Tennessee *state* U.S.A. **103** I4 35 00N 87 00W
Tenojoki *r.* Finland/Norway **67** F4 69 50N 26 10E
Tenterden Kent England **33** C2 51 05N 0 41E
Teófilo Otôni Brazil **114** I9 17 52S 41 31W
Tepatitlán Mexico **108** D4 20 50N 102 46W
Tépeji Mexico **108** E3 19 55N 99 21W
Tepic Mexico **108** D4 21 30N 104 51W
Teplice Ceska Czechoslovakia **63** B2 50 40N 13 49E
Ter *r.* Spain **66** C3 41 55N 2 30E
Teramo Italy **68** B3 42 40N 13 43E
Teresina Brazil **114** I11 5 09S 42 46W
Termez Uzbekistan **70** I3 37 15N 67 15E
Termim Imerese Italy **68** B2 37 59N 13 42E
Ternate Indonesia **80** H4 0 48N 127 23E
Terneuzen Netherlands **64** C3 51 20N 3 50E
Terni Italy **68** B3 42 34N 12 39E
Ternopol' Ukraine **69** E2 49 35N 25 39E
Terpeniya Bay Russia **71** Q5 48 00N 144 00E
Terrace British Columbia Canada **100** J3 54 31N 128 32W
Terrace Bay *tn.* Ontario Canada **104** C3 48 47N 87 06W
Terracina Italy **68** B3 41 17N 13 15E
Terre Haute Indiana U.S.A. **104** C1 39 27N 87 24W
Terror, Mount Antarctica **121** 77 30S 168 30E
Terschelling *i.* Netherlands **64** E5 53 22N 5 20E
Teruel Spain **66** B3 40 21N 1 06W
Teseney Ethiopia **70** E2 15 10N 36 40E
Teshio Japan **82** D3 44 53N 141 46E
Teslin Yukon Territory Canada **100** I5 60 10N 132 42W
Teslin Lake Yukon Territory Canada **100** I4 59 50N 132 25W
Test *r.* Hampshire England **32** A2 51 05N 1 30W
Testa del Gargano *c.* Italy **68** C3 41 00N 16 00E
Tetbury Gloucestershire England **31** E3 51 39N 2 10W
Tete Mozambique **95** F4 16 10S 33 35E
Teterev *r.* Ukraine **69** E3 50 00N 29 00E
Tetney Lincolnshire England **36** D3 53 30N 0 01W
Tétouan Morocco **93** D10 35 34N 5 22W
Tetovo Macedonia Yugoslavia **68** D3 42 00N 20 59E
Teutoburger Wald *hills* Germany **63** A2 52 00N 8 00E
Teviot *r.* Borders Scotland **46** F2 55 00N 2 10W
Teviotdale *v.* Borders Scotland **46** F2 55 25N 3 00W
Tewin Hertfordshire England **34** C3 51 49N 0 09W
Tewkesbury Gloucestershire England **31** E3 51 59N 2 09W
Texarkana Arkansas U.S.A. **103** H3 33 28N 94 02W
Texas *state* U.S.A. **102** F3 31 00N 100 00W
Texel *i.* Netherlands **64** D5 53 05N 4 45E
Texoma, Lake U.S.A. **103** G3 34 00N 97 00W
Tezonco Mexico **108** P1 19 19N 99 04W
THAILAND 80 C7
Thailand, Gulf of South East Asia **80** C6 12 00N 101 30E
Thakhek Laos **80** C7 17 22N 104 50E
Thame Oxfordshire England **33** B2 51 45N 0 59W
Thame *r.* Buckinghamshire England **33** B2 51 45N 0 55W
Thames New Zealand **87** C3 37 08S 175 35E
Thames *r.* England **32/33** A2–C2
Thane India **77** C3 19 14N 73 02E
Thanh Hoa Vietnam **80** D7 19 49N 105 48E
Thanjavur India **77** D2 10 46N 79 09E
Thar Desert India **77** C5 27 30N 72 00E
Thásos *i.* Greece **68** D3 40 00N 24 00E
Thatcham Berkshire England **32** A2 51 25N 1 15W
Thaxted Essex England **34** E3 51 57N 0 20E
Thayetmyo Myanmar **80** B7 19 20N 95 10E
Thebes *hist. site* Egypt **78** D4 25 41N 32 40E
The Bronx New York U.S.A. **106** C2 40 50N 73 55W
The Dalles Oregon U.S.A. **102** B6 45 36N 121 10W
The Den Strathclyde Scotland **45** A1 55 43N 4 40W
The Everglades *swamp* Florida U.S.A. **103** J2 26 00N 81 00W
The Mumbles West Glamorgan Wales **38** B1 51 35N 3 59W
The Pas Manitoba Canada **101** O3 53 49N 101 14W
Thelon *r.* Northwest Territories Canada **101** O5 64 40N 102 30W
Thelwall Cheshire England **42** C2 53 23N 2 31W
Thermaïkós Kólpos *g.* Greece **68** D3 40 00N 22 50E
Thermopolis Wyoming U.S.A. **102** E5 43 39N 108 12W
Thessalon Ontario Canada **105** D3 46 15N 83 34W
Thessaloníki Greece **68** D3 40 38N 22 58E
Thetford Norfolk England **33** C3 52 25N 0 45E
Thetford Mines *tn.* Québec Canada **105** F3 46 06N 71 18W
Theydon Bois Essex England **34** D3 51 40N 0 05E
Thiais France **60** B2 48 45N 2 24E
Thief River Falls *tn.* Minnesota U.S.A. **104** A3 48 12N 96 48W
Thiers France **61** B2 45 51N 3 33E
Thiès Senegal **93** B5 14 49N 16 52W
Thika Kenya **94** G7 1 03S 37 05E
Thimphu Bhutan **77** F5 27 32N 89 43E
Thionville France **61** C2 49 22N 6 11E
Thíra *i.* Greece **68** E2 36 00N 25 00E
Thirsk North Yorkshire England **40** C3 54 14N 1 20W
Thithia *i.* Fiji **118** V16 17 45S 179 20W
Thívai Greece **68** D2 38 19N 23 19E
Tholen *i.* Netherlands **64** D3 51 33N 4 05E
Thomastown Kilkenny Irish Republic **48** D2 52 31N 7 08W
Thomasville Georgia U.S.A. **103** J3 30 50N 83 59W
Thompson Manitoba Canada **101** P4 55 45N 97 54W
Thomson *r.* Australia **86** G5 24 00S 143 30E
Thorganby North Yorkshire England **43** H3 53 28N 0 11W
Thornaby-on-Tees Cleveland England **44** C1 54 34N 1 18W
Thornbury Avon England **31** E3 51 37N 2 32W
Thorne South Yorkshire England **43** H2 53 37N 0 58W
Thorney Cambridgeshire England **33** B3 52 37N 0 07W
Thornhill Dumfries & Galloway Scotland **46** E2 55 15N 3 46W
Thornhill Edge West Yorkshire England **43** F2 53 41N 1 38W
Thornliebank Strathclyde Scotland **45** B1 55 47N 4 19W
Thornton Fife Scotland **45** D2 56 10N 3 09W
Thornton Lancashire England **42** B3 53 53N 3 00W
Thornton West Yorkshire England **43** E3 53 47N 1 52W
Thornwood Common Essex England **34** D3 51 43N 0 07E
Thorpe-le-Soken Kent England **33** D2 51 52N 1 10E
Thouars France **61** A2 46 59N 0 13W
Thrapston Northamptonshire England **36** D2 52 24N 0 32W
Three Kings Islands New Zealand **87** B4 34 00S 172 30E
Three Mile Bay *tn.* New York U.S.A. **105** E2 44 04N 76 12W
Three Points, Cape Ghana **93** E3 4 43N 2 06W
Three Rock Mountain Dublin Irish Republic **49** B1 53 14N 6 14W
Thringstone Leicestershire England **35** D3 52 44N 1 22W
Thrybergh South Yorkshire England **43** G2 53 27N 1 18W
Thuin Belgium **64** D2 50 21N 4 18E
Thule Greenland **101** V8 77 30N 69 00W
Thun Switzerland **61** C2 46 46N 7 38E
Thunder Bay *tn.* Ontario Canada **104** C3 48 27N 89 12W
Thurcroft South Yorkshire England **43** G2 53 24N 1 16W
Thüringen *admin.* Germany **63** B2 50 30N 11 00E
Thüringer Wald *hills* Germany **63** B2 50 00N 10 00E
Thurles Tipperary Irish Republic **48** D2 52 41N 7 49W
Thursby Cumbria England **44** A1 54 51N 3 03W
Thurso Highland Scotland **46** E5 58 35N 3 32W
Thurso *r.* Highland Scotland **46** E5 58 15N 3 35W
Thurston Island *i.* Antarctica **121** 72 00S 100 00W
Tianjin China **81** I5 39 08N 117 12E
Tianshui China **81** G4 34 25N 105 58E
Tiaret Algeria **66** C2 35 20N 1 20E
Tibberton Shropshire England **35** A3 52 47N 2 28W
Tiber *r.* Italy **68** B3 42 00N 12 00E
Tiberias Israel **78** O11 32 48N 35 32E
Tiberias, Lake *(Sea of Galilee) l.* Israel **78** O11 32 45N 35 30E
Tibesti *mts.* Chad **94** C12 21 00N 17 00E
Tibet Autonomous Region *see* Xizang Zizhiqu
Tibet, Plateau of Asia **72** 33 00N 90 00E
Tiburón *i.* Mexico **108** B5 28 30N 112 30W
Ticehurst East Sussex England **33** C2 51 02N 0 24E
Ticino *r.* Italy / Switzerland **61** C2 45 00N 9 00E
Tickhill South Yorkshire England **43** G2 53 26N 1 06W
Ticul Mexico **108** G4 20 22N 89 31W
Tideswell Derbyshire England **43** E1 53 17N 1 46W
Tiel Netherlands **64** E3 51 53N 5 26E
Tielt Belgium **64** C3 51 00N 3 20E
Tienen Belgium **64** D2 50 48N 4 56E
Tien Shan *(Tyan-Shan') mts.* China **71** J4 41 00N 76 00E
Tierra Blanca Mexico **108** E3 18 28N 96 21W
Tierra del Fuego *see* Isla Grande de Tierra del Fuego
Tietar *r.* Spain **66** A3 40 07N 5 15W
Tiffin Ohio U.S.A. **105** D2 41 07N 83 11W
Tigermore Tayside Scotland **45** C2 56 24N 3 32W
Tighnabruaich Strathclyde Scotland **46** C2 55 56N 5 14W
Tigris *r.* Iraq **79** G5 32 00N 46 00E
Tijuana Mexico **108** A6 32 29N 117 10W
Tijuca Brazil **116** B2 22 56S 43 16W
Tikrīt Iraq **78** F5 34 36N 43 42E
Tiksi Russia **71** O10 71 40N 128 45E
Tilak Nagar India **76** L4 28 38N 77 07E
Tilburg Netherlands **64** E3 51 34N 5 05E
Tilbury Essex England **34** E2 51 28N 0 23E
Tile Hill West Midlands England **35** D2 52 24N 1 31W
Tillsonburg Ontario Canada **105** D2 42 53N 80 44W
Tillycoultry Central Scotland **45** C2 56 09N 3 45W
Timaru New Zealand **87** B2 44 23S 171 14E
Timbira *r.* Brazil **116** C3 22 40S 43 12W
Timimoun Algeria **93** F8 29 15N 0 14E
Timişoara Romania **69** D2 45 45N 21 15E
Timişul *r.* Romania / Yugoslavia **69** D2 45 00N 21 00E
Timmins Ontario Canada **101** S2 48 30N 81 20W
Timor *i.* Indonesia **80** G2/H2 9 00S 125 00E
Timor Sea Australia / Indonesia **80** H1/H2 10 00S 128 00E
Tindouf Algeria **93** D8 27 42N 8 10W
Tinos *i.* Greece **68** E2 37 00N 25 00E
Tinsley South Yorkshire England **43** F2 53 25N 1 24W
Tintagel Cornwall England **30** B2 50 40N 4 45W
Tintagel Head *c.* Cornwall England **30** C2 50 41N 4 46W
Tipperary *co.* Irish Republic **48** C2/D2 52 30N 8 00W
Tipperary Tipperary Irish Republic **48** C2 52 29N 8 10W
Tipton West Midlands England **35** B2 52 32N 2 05W
Tiptree Essex England **33** C2 51 49N 0 45E
Tiranë Albania **68** C3 41 20N 19 49E
Tiraspol' Moldova **69** E2 46 50N 29 38E
Tiraz Mountains Namibia **95** C2 25 30S 16 30E
Tiree *i.* Strathclyde Scotland **46** B3 56 30N 6 55W
Tîrgovişte Romania **69** E1 44 56N 25 27E
Tîrgu Jiu Romania **69** D1 45 03N 23 18E
Tîrgu Mureş Romania **69** D2 46 33N 24 34E
Tirol *admin.* Austria **63** B1 47 00N 11 00E
Tirso *r.* Italy **68** A2 40 00N 9 00E
Tiruchchirāppalli India **77** D2 10 50N 78 41E
Tirunelveli India **77** D1 8 45N 77 43E
Tirupati India **77** D2 13 39N 79 25E
Tiruppur India **77** D2 11 05N 77 20E
Tisdale Saskatchewan Canada **100** O3 52 51N 104 01W
Tisza *r.* Hungary / Yugoslavia **69** D2 46 00N 20 00E
Titāgarh India **76** K2 22 44N 88 22E
Titograd Montenegro Yugoslavia **68** C3 42 28N 19 17E
Titov Veles Serbia Yugoslavia **68** D3 41 43N 21 49E
Titova Mitrovica Serbia Yugoslavia **68** D3 42 54N 20 52E
Titovo Užice Serbia Yugoslavia **68** C3 43 52N 19 50E
Tittensor Staffordshire England **35** B3 52 57N 2 12W
Tiverton Devon England **31** D2 50 55N 3 29W
Tiverton Rhode Island U.S.A. **105** F2 41 38N 71 13W
Tivoli Italy **68** D3 41 58N 12 48E
Tizimím Mexico **108** G4 21 10N 88 09W
Tizi Ouzou Algeria **93** F10 36 44N 4 05E
Tiznit Morocco **93** D8 29 43N 9 44W
Tlalnepantla Mexico **108** P2 19 32N 99 12W
Tlaltenco Mexico **108** P1 19 17N 99 01W
Tlemcen Algeria **93** E9 34 53N 1 21W
Toad River *tn.* British Columbia Canada **100** J4 59 00N 125 10W
Toamasina Madagascar **95** I4 18 10S 49 23E
Tobago *i* Trinidad and Tobago **109** L2 11 15N 60 40W
Tobermory Ontario Canada **105** D3 45 15N 81 39W
Tobermory Strathclyde Scotland **46** B3 56 37N 6 05W
Tobi-shima *i.* Japan **82** C2 39 12N 139 32E
Tobol *r.* Russia **71** I7 56 00N 66 00E
Tobol'sk Russia **71** I7 58 15N 68 12E
Tocopilla Chile **115** C8 22 05S 70 10W
Toddington Bedfordshire England **34** B3 51 57N 0 32W
Todmorden West Yorkshire England **43** D3 53 43N 2 05W
TOGO 93 F4
Tokelau Islands Pacific Ocean **118** I7 9 00S 168 00W
Tokorozawa Japan **83** A4 35 47N 139 28E
Tokushima Japan **82** B1 34 03N 134 34E
Tokuyama Japan **82** B1 34 04N 131 48E
Tōkyō Japan 83 C3 35 40N 139 45E
Tokyo Bay Japan **83** C2 35 25N 139 45E
Tolbukhin Bulgaria **68** E3 43 34N 27 51E
Toledo Ohio U.S.A. **105** D2 41 40N 83 35W
Toledo Spain **66** B2 39 52N 4 02W
Toliara Madagascar **95** H3 23 20S 43 41E
Tolka *r.* Dublin Irish Republic **49** B2 53 23N 6 19W
Tollygunge India **76** K2 22 30N 88 19E
Tolosa Spain **66** B3 43 09N 2 04W
Toluca Mexico **108** E3 19 20N 99 40W
Tol'yatti Russia **70** G6 53 32N 49 24E
Tomakomai Japan **82** D3 42 39N 141 33E
Tomaniivi *mt.* Fiji **118** U16 17 37S 178 01E
Tomar Portugal **66** A2 39 36N 8 25W
Tomaszów Mazowiecka Poland **69** C3 51 33N 20 00E
Tomatin Highland Scotland **46** E4 57 20N 3 59W
Tomatlán Mexico **108** C3 19 54N 105 18W
Tombigbee *r.* U.S.A. **103** I3 32 00N 88 00W
Tombouctou Mali **93** E6 16 49N 2 59W
Tombua Angola **95** B4 15 49S 11 53E
Tomintoul Grampian Scotland **46** E4 57 14N 3 22W
Tom Price, Mount Australia **86** B5 22 49S 117 51E
Tomsk Russia **71** K7 56 30N 85 05E
Tonala Mexico **108** F3 16 08N 93 41W
Tonawanda New York U.S.A. **105** E2 43 01N 78 54W
Tonbridge Kent England **34** D1 51 12N 0 16E
Tønder Denmark **63** A2 54 57N 8 53E
TONGA 118 I5
Tonga Trench Pacific Ocean **118** I5 20 00S 173 00W
Tongchuan China **81** G5 35 05N 109 02E
Tongeren Belgium **64** E2 50 47N 5 28E
Tonghai China **81** F2 24 07N 102 45E
Tonghua China **81** K6 41 42N 125 45E
Tongking, Gulf of Vietnam/China **80** D7 19 00N 107 00E
Tongling China **81** I4 30 58N 117 48N
Tongue Highland Scotland **46** D5 58 28N 4 25W
Tonle Sap *l.* Cambodia **80** C6 13 00N 104 00E
Tonopah Nevada U.S.A. **102** C4 38 05N 117 15W
Tønsberg Norway **67** C2 59 16N 10 25E
Tonyrefail Mid Glamorgan Wales **38** C1 51 36N 3 25W
Tooele Utah U.S.A. **102** D5 40 32N 112 18W
Toowoomba Australia **86** I4 27 35S 151 54E
Topeka Kansas U.S.A. **104** A1 39 02N 95 41W
Toppings Greater Manchester England **42** C2 53 38N 2 27W
Topsham Devon England **31** D2 50 42N 3 27W
Tor Bay *b.* Devon England **31** D2 50 27N 3 30W
Torbalı Turkey **68** E2 38 07N 27 08E
Torbay *tn.* *see* Torquay *or* Paignton
Tordesillas Spain **66** A3 41 30N 5 00W
Torhout Belgium **64** C3 51 04N 3 06E
Torino *(Turin)* Italy **68** A4 45 04N 7 40E
Tormes *r.* Spain **66** A3 41 03N 5 58W
Torne älv *r.* Sweden **67** E4 67 03N 23 02E
Torne-träsk *l.* Sweden **67** D4 68 14N 19 40E
Torngat Mountains *(Monts Torngat)* Newfoundland/ Québec Canada **101** W4 59 00N 64 15W
Tornio Finland **67** E4 65 50N 24 10E
Toronto Ontario Canada **105** E2 43 42N 79 25W
Tororo Uganda **94** F8 0 42N 34 12E
Toros Dağlari *mts.* Turkey **78** D6 37 10N 33 10E
Torpichen Lothian Scotland **45** C1 55 56N 3 39W
Torpoint *tn.* Cornwall England **31** C2 50 22N 4 11W
Torquay Devon England **31** D2 50 28N 3 30W
Torrance California U.S.A. **107** A2 33 50N 118 20W
Torrance Strathclyde Scotland **45** B1 55 56N 4 11W
Torre del Greco Italy **68** B3 40 46N 14 22E
Torrelavega Spain **66** B3 43 21N 4 03W
Torrens, Lake Australia **86** F3 31 00S 137 50E
Torreón Mexico **108** D5 25 34N 103 25W
Torres Strait Australia **86** G7/G8 10 00S 142 30E
Torridge *r.* Devon England **31** C2 50 55N 4 05W
Torridon Highland Scotland **46** C4 57 33N 5 31W
Torrington Connecticut U.S.A. **105** F2 41 48N 73 08W
Torrisholme Lancashire England **42** B4 54 05N 2 50W
Tortosa Spain **66** C3 40 49N 0 31E
Toruń Poland **69** C3 53 01N 18 35E
Tory Island Irish Republic **48** C5 55 16N 8 14W
Tory Sound Irish Republic **48** C5 55 15N 8 05W
Tosa-wan *b.* Japan **82** B1 33 20N 133 40E
Toshima Japan **83** B3 35 43N 139 41E
Totland Isle of Wight England **32** A1 50 40N 1 32W
Totnes Devon England **31** D2 50 25N 3 41W
Totoya *i.* Fiji **118** V15 18 56S 179 50W
Totsuka Japan **83** B2 35 23N 139 32E
Tottenham Greater London England **34** C2 51 35N 0 05W
Tottington Greater Manchester England **42** C2 53 37N 2 20W
Totton Hampshire England **32** A1 50 56N 1 29W
Tottori Japan **82** B2 35 32N 134 12E
Touggourt Algeria **93** G9 33 08N 6 04E
Toul France **61** C2 48 41N 5 54E
Toulon France **61** C1 43 07N 5 55E
Toulouse France **61** B1 43 33N 1 24E
Toungoo Myanmar **80** B7 18 57N 96 26E
Tourcoing France **61** B3 50 44N 3 10E
Tournai Belgium **64** C2 50 36N 3 24E
Tours France **61** B2 47 23N 0 42E
Towcester Northamptonshire England **36** D2 52 08N 1 00W
Tower Hamlets Greater London England **34** C3 51 30N 0 02W
Tow Law *sum.* Durham England **44** C1 54 45N 1 49W
Townhill Fife Scotland **45** D2 56 05N 3 27W
Townsville Australia **86** H6 19 13S 146 48E
Toyama Japan **82** C2 36 42N 137 14E
Toyohashi Japan **82** C1 34 46N 137 22E
Toyota Japan **82** C2 35 05N 137 09E
Tozeur Tunisia **93** G9 33 55N 8 07E
Trâblous *(Tripoli)* Lebanon **78** O12 34 27N 35 50E
Trabzona Turkey **78** E7 41 00N 39 43E
Tracy Québec Canada **105** F3 45 59N 73 04W
Trail British Columbia Canada **100** L2 49 04N 117 39W
Tralee Kerry Irish Republic **48** B2 52 16N 9 42W
Tralee Bay Irish Republic **48** B2 52 20N 9 55W
Tramore Waterford Irish Republic **48** D2 52 10N 7 10W
Transantarctic Mountains Antarctica **121** 77 00S 147 00E
Transvaal *province* Republic of South Africa **95** E3 24 30S 28 00E
Trápani Italy **68** B2 38 02N 12 32E
Traunstein Germany **63** B1 47 52N 12 39E
Travers, Mount New Zealand **87** B2 42 01S 172 47E
Traverse City Michigan U.S.A. **104** C2 44 46N 85 38W
Trawden Lancashire England **42** D3 53 51N 2 08W
Trawsfynydd Gwynedd Wales **38** C2 52 54N 3 55W
Tredegar Gwent Wales **38** C1 51 47N 3 16W
Tregaron Dyfed Wales **38** C2 52 13N 3 55W
Tregony Cornwall England **30** C2 50 16N 4 55W
Treinta-y-Tres Uruguay **115** G6 33 16S 54 17W
Trelew Chile **115** D4 43 13S 65 15W
Tremadog Bay Gwynedd Wales **38** B2 52 54N 4 15W
Trenčín Slovenska Czechoslovakia **69** C2 48 53N 18 00E
Trenque Lauquen Argentina **115** E5 35 56S 62 43W
Trent *r.* Midlands England **36** C2–D3
Trent & Mersey Canal England **35** C3 52 25N 1 40W
Trento Italy **68** B4 46 04N 11 08E
Trenton New Jersey U.S.A. **105** F2 40 15N 74 43W
Trenton Ontario Canada **105** E2 44 07N 77 34W
Trepassey Newfoundland Canada **101** Y2 46 45N 53 20W
Tres Arroyos Argentina **115** E5 38 26S 60 17W
Tresco *i.* Isles of Scilly England **30** A1 49 57N 6 20W
Três Lagoas Brazil **114** G8 20 46S 51 43W
Treviso Italy **68** B4 45 40N 12 15E
Trevose Head *c.* Cornwall England **30** B2 50 33N 5 01W
Trichur India **77** D2 10 32N 76 14E
Trier Germany **63** A1 49 45N 6 39E
Trieste Italy **68** B4 45 39N 13 47E
Tríkkala Greece **68** D2 39 33N 21 46E
Trim Meath Irish Republic **48** E3 53 34N 6 47W
Trincomalee Sri Lanka **77** E1 8 34N 81 13E
Trindade *i.* Atlantic Ocean **117** F4 20 30S 29 20W
Tring Hertfordshire England **34** B3 51 48N 0 40W
TRINIDAD AND TOBAGO 109 L2
Trinidad Bolivia **114** E10 14 46S 64 50W
Trinidad Colorado U.S.A. **102** F4 37 11N 104 31W
Trinidad Cuba **109** H4 21 48N 80 00W
Trinidad *i.* Trinidad and Tobago **109** L2 11 00N 61 30W
Trinity *r.* U.S.A. **103** G3 32 00N 96 00W
Trinity Islands Alaska U.S.A. **100** E4 56 45N 154 15W
Tripoli Lebanon *see* Trâblous
Tripoli Libya *see* Tarābulus
Trípolis Greece **68** D2 37 31N 22 22E
Tripura Mizoram *admin.* India **77** G4 23 40N 92 30E
Tristan da Cunha *i.* Atlantic Ocean **117** G3 37 15S 12 30W
Trivandrum India **77** D1 8 30N 76 57E
Trnava Slovenska Czechoslovakia **69** C2 48 23N 17 35E
Troisdorf Germany **63** A2 50 49N 7 09E
Trois-Pistoles Québec Canada **105** G3 48 08N 69 10W
Trois Rivières *tn.* Québec Canada **105** F3 46 21N 72 34W
Trollhättan Sweden **67** C2 58 17N 12 20E
Trollheimen *mts.* Norway **67** B3 63 00N 9 00E
Tromsø Norway **67** D4 69 42N 19 00E
Trondheim Norway **67** C3 63 36N 10 23E
Trondheimsfjorden *fj.* Norway **67** C3 63 40N 10 30E
Troon Strathclyde Scotland **46** D2 55 32N 4 40W
Trotternish *p.* Skye Scotland **46** B4 57 00N 6 00W
Trout Lake Northwest Territories Canada **100** K5 61 00N 121 30W
Trouville France **61** B2 49 22N 0 05E
Trowbridge Wiltshire England **31** E3 51 20N 2 13W
Troy Alabama U.S.A. **103** I3 31 49N 86 00W
Troy *hist. site* Turkey **78** C6 39 55N 26 17E
Troy New York U.S.A. **105** F2 42 43N 73 43W
Troyes France **61** B2 48 18N 4 05E
Trujillo Peru **114** B11 8 06S 79 00W
Trujillo Spain **66** A2 39 28N 5 53W
Trujillo Venezuela **114** C14 9 20N 70 38W
Truk Islands Caroline Islands **118** F8 7 30N 152 30E
Truro Cornwall England **30** B2 50 16N 5 03W
Truro Nova Scotia Canada **101** W2 45 24N 63 18W
Truyère *r.* France **61** B1 44 55N 2 47E
Tsangpo *see* Yarlung Zangbo Jiang
Tsavo National Park Kenya **94** G7 3 30S 38 00E
Tselinograd Kazakhstan **71** J6 51 10N 71 28E
Tsenke *r.* Zaïre **92** B1 4 24S 15 26E
Tshane Botswana **95** D3 24 05S 21 54E
Tshuapa *r.* Zaïre **94** D7 1 00S 23 00E
Tsiéme *r.* Congo **92** A2 4 15S 15 17E
Tsu Japan **82** C1 34 41N 136 30E
Tsuchiura Japan **82** D2 36 05N 140 11E
Tsugaru-kaikyō *sd.* Japan **82** D3 41 30N 140 30E
Tsumeb Namibia **95** C4 19 13S 17 42E
Tsunashima Japan **83** B3 35 31N 139 38E
Tsuruga Japan **82** C2 35 40N 136 05E
Tsuruoko Japan **82** C2 38 42N 139 50E
Tsushima *i.* Japan **82** A1 34 30N 129 20E
Tsuyama Japan **82** B2 35 04N 134 01E
Tua *r.* Portugal **66** A3 41 20N 7 30W
Tuam Galway Irish Republic **48** C3 53 31N 8 50W
Tuamotu Archipelago *is.* Pacific Ocean **119** M6 15 00S 145 00W
Tuamotu Ridge Pacific Ocean **119** L6 19 00S 144 00W
Tubbercurry Sligo Irish Republic **48** C4 54 03N 8 43W
Tübingen Germany **63** A1 48 32N 9 04E
Tubize Belgium **64** D2 50 42N 4 12E
Tubruq Libya **94** D14 32 05N 23 59E
Tubuai Islands Pacific Ocean **119** L5 23 23S 149 27W
Tuchitua Yukon Territory Canada **100** J5 61 20N 129 00W
Tucson Arizona U.S.A. **102** D3 32 15N 110 57W
Tucumcari New Mexico U.S.A. **102** F4 35 11N 103 44W
Tucupita Venezuela **114** E14 9 02N 62 04W
Tucuruí Brazil **114** H12 3 42S 49 44W
Tudela Spain **66** B3 42 04N 1 37W
Tudweiliog Gwynedd Wales **38** B2 52 55N 4 39W
Tugaske Saskatchewan Canada **100** N3 50 54N 106 15W
Tujunga California U.S.A. **107** A3 34 14N 118 16W
Tuktoyaktuk Northwest Territories Canada **100** I6 69 24N 133 01W
Tukums Latvia **67** E2 56 58N 23 10E
Tula Mexico **108** E4 23 00N 99 41W
Tula Mexico **108** E4 20 01N 99 21W
Tula Russia **70** F6 54 11N 37 38E
Tuloan Ecuador **114** B3 0 50N 77 48W
Tulcea Romania **69** E2 45 10N 28 50E
Tulkarm Jordan **78** O11 32 19N 35 02E
Tullamore Offaly Irish Republic **48** D3 53 16N 7 30W
Tulle France **61** B2 45 16N 1 46E
Tullibody Central Scotland **45** C2 56 06N 3 47W
Tullow Carlow Irish Republic **48** D2 52 48N 6 44W
Tuloma *r.* Russia **67** G4 69 00N 32 00E
Tulpetlac Mexico **108** P2 19 21N 99 02W
Tulsa Oklahoma U.S.A. **103** G4 36 07N 95 58W
Tuluá Colombia **114** B13 4 05N 76 12W
Tulun Russia **71** M6 54 32N 100 35E
Tumaco Colombia **114** B13 1 51N 78 46W
Tumbes Peru **114** A12 3 37S 80 27W
Tumkur India **77** D2 13 20N 77 06E
Tummel *r.* Tayside Scotland **46** D3/E3 56 38N 4 00W
Tunduru Tanzania **95** G5 11 08S 27 21E

Vindhya Range *mts.* India **77** C4 23 00N 75 00E
Vineland New Jersey U.S.A. **105** E1 39 29N 75 02W
Vinh Vietnam **80** D7 18 42N 105 41E
Vinkeveense Plassen *l.* Netherlands **65** D2 52 15N 4 51E
Vinkovci Croatia **68** C4 45 16N 18 49E
Vinnitsa Ukraine **70** E5 49 11N 28 30E
Vipiteno Italy **68** B4 46 54N 11 27E
Virgin *r.* U.S.A. **102** D4 37 00N 114 00W
Virginia *state* U.S.A. **103** K4 38 00N 77 00W
Virginia Beach *tn.* Virginia U.S.A. **103** K4 36 51N 75 59W
Virginia Cavan Irish Republic **48** D3 53 49N 7 04W
Virginia Minnesota U.S.A. **104** B3 47 30N 92 28W
Virginia Water *tn.* Surrey England **34** B2 51 24N 0 34W
Virgin Islands West Indies **109** L3 18 00N 64 30W
Viroqua Wisconsin U.S.A. **104** B2 43 33N 90 54W
Virovitica Croatia **68** C4 45 50N 17 25E
Virton Belgium **64** E1 49 34N 5 32E
Vis *i.* Croatia **68** C3 43 00N 16 00E
Visalia California U.S.A. **102** C4 36 20N 119 18W
Visby Sweden **67** D2 57 32N 18 15E
Viscount Melville Sound Northwest Territories Canada **101** N7 74 10N 105 00W
Viseu Portugal **66** A3 40 40N 7 55W
Vishakhapatnam India **77** E3 17 42N 83 24E
Vistula *see* Wisła
Vitebsk Belarus **70** F7 55 10N 30 14E
Viterbo Italy **68** B3 42 24N 12 06E
Vitichi Bolivia **114** D8 20 14S 65 22W
Viti Levu *i.* Fiji **118** T15 18 10S 177 55E
Vitim *r.* Russia **71** N7 58 00N 113 00E
Vitim Russia **71** N7 59 28N 112 35E
Vitória Brazil **114** I8 20 20S 40 18W
Vitoria Spain **66** B3 42 51N 2 40W
Vitória da Conquista Brazil **114** I10 14 53S 40 52W
Vitry-le-François France **61** B2 48 44N 4 36E
Vitry-sur-Seine France **60** B2 48 47N 2 24E
Vityaz Trench Pacific Ocean **118** G7 9 30S 170 00E
Vivi *r.* Russia **71** L9 61 00N 96 00E
Vize *i.* Russia **71** J11 79 30N 77 00E
Vizianagaram India **77** E3 18 07N 83 30E
Vlaardingen Netherlands **65** B1 51 54N 4 20E
Vladikavkaz *(Ordzhonikidze)* Russia **70** G4 43 02N 44 43E
Vladimir Russia **70** G7 56 08N 40 25E
Vladimir Volynskiy Ukraine **69** D3 50 51N 24 19E
Vladivostok Russia **71** P4 43 09N 131 53E
Vlanen Netherlands **65** E1 51 59N 5 05E
Vlieland *i.* Netherlands **64** D5 53 16N 5 00E
Vlissingen Netherlands **64** C3 51 27N 3 35E
Vlorë Albania **68** C3 40 29N 19 29E
Vltava *r.* Ceska Czechoslovakia **69** B2 49 00N 14 00E
Vogelsberg *mts.* Germany **63** A2 50 00N 9 00E
Vohwinkel Germany **62** C1 51 13N 7 05E
Voi Kenya **94** G7 3 23S 38 35E
Volendam Netherlands **64** E4 52 30N 5 04E
Volga *r.* Russia **70** G5/G6 50 00N 45 00E
Volgodonsk Russia **70** G5 47 35N 42 08E
Volgograd Russia **70** G5 48 45N 44 30E
Volksrust Republic of South Africa **95** F2 27 22S 29 54E
Vologda Russia **70** F7 59 10N 39 55E
Vólos Greece **68** D2 39 22N 22 57E
Volta Redonda Brazil **115** I8 22 31S 44 05W
Volta, Lake Ghana **93** E4 7 30N 0 30W
Volturno *r.* Italy **68** B3 41 00N 14 00E
Volzhskiy Russia **70** G5 48 48N 44 45E
Voorburg Netherlands **65** B2 52 04N 4 22E
Voorne *geog. reg.* Netherlands **65** A1 51 53N 4 08E
Voorschoten Netherlands **65** B2 52 07N 4 27E
Voorst Netherlands **64** F4 52 10N 6 10E
Vopnafjördur Iceland **67** J7 65 46N 14 50W
Vorarlberg *admin.* Austria **63** A1 47 00N 10 00E
Vorderrhein *r.* Switzerland **61** C2 46 45N 9 15E
Vordingborg Denmark **63** B3 55 01N 11 55E
Voríai Sporadhes *is.* Greece **68** D2 39 00N 24 00E
Vorkuta Russia **71** I9 67 27N 64 00E
Voronezh Russia **70** F6 51 40N 39 13E
Voroshilovgrad *see* Lugansk
Vørterkaka Nunatak *mt.* Antarctica **121** 71 45S 32 00E
Võrtsjärv *l.* Estonia **67** F2 58 15N 26 10E
Võru Estonia **67** F2 57 46N 26 52E
Vosges *mts.* France **61** C2 48 10N 6 50E
Voss Norway **67** B3 60 38N 6 25E
Vostochnyy Russia **71** P4 42 52N 132 56E
Vostok *r.s.* Antarctica **121** 78 27S 106 51E
Vouga *r.* Portugal **66** A3 40 45N 8 15W
Vouziers France **64** D1 49 25N 4 41E
Voxnan Sweden **67** D3 61 22N 15 39E
Vrangelya *(Wrangel) i.* Russia **71** T10 71 30N 180 00
Vranje Serbia Yugoslavia **68** D3 42 33N 21 54E
Vratsa Bulgaria **68** D3 43 12N 23 32E
Vrbas *r.* Bosnia-Herzegovina **68** C3 44 00N 17 00E
Vršac Serbia Yugoslavia **68** D4 45 07N 21 19E
Vryburg Republic of South Africa **95** D2 26 57S 24 44E
Vught Netherlands **64** E3 51 40N 5 18E
Vukovar Croatia **68** C4 45 19N 19 01E
Vung Tau Vietnam **80** D6 10 21N 107 04E
Vunisea Fiji **118** U15 19 04S 178 09E
Vyatka *r.* Russia **70** G7 58 00N 50 00E
Vyborg Russia **67** F3 60 45N 28 41E
Vychegda *r.* Russia **70** H8 62 00N 52 00E
Vyrnwy *r.* Powys Wales **38** C2 52 41N 3 25W
Vyrnwy, Lake Powys Wales **38** C2 52 47N 3 30W

W

Wa Ghana **93** E5 10 07N 2 28W
Waal *r.* Netherlands **64** E3 51 50N 5 07E
Waalwijk Netherlands **64** E3 51 42N 5 04E
Wabana Newfoundland Canada **101** Y2 47 40N 52 58W
Wabash Indiana U.S.A. **104** C2 40 47N 85 48W
Wabash *r.* U.S.A. **104** C1 39 00N 87 00W
Wabowden Manitoba Canada **101** P3 54 57N 98 38W
Wabush Lake *tn.* Newfoundland Canada **101** V3 52 45N 00 30W
Waco Texas U.S.A. **103** G3 31 33N 97 10W
Waddeneilanden *(West Frisian Islands)* Netherlands **64** E5 53 25N 5 15E
Waddenzee *sea* Netherlands **64** E5 53 15N 5 15E
Waddesdon Buckinghamshire England **33** B2 51 51N 0 56W
Waddington Lancashire England **42** C3 53 54N 2 24W
Waddington Lincolnshire England **36** D3 53 10N 0 32W
Waddington, Mount British Columbia Canada **100** J3 51 22N 125 14W
Wadebridge Cornwall England **30** C2 50 32N 4 50W
Wadhurst East Sussex England **33** C2 51 04N 0 21E
Wādī al Masīlah *r.* Yemen Republic **79** H2 16 00N 50 00E
Wadi Araba *r.* Israel **78** O10 30 30N 35 10E
Wadi el'Arish *r.* Egypt **78** N10 30 05N 33 50E
Wadi Halfa Sudan **78** D3 21 55N 31 20E
Wadinxveen Netherlands **65** C2 52 02N 4 39E
Wad Medani Sudan **78** D1 14 24N 33 30E
Waesch, Mount Antarctica **121** 77 00S 127 30W
Wageningen Netherlands **64** E3 51 58N 5 40E
Wager Bay Northwest Territories Canada **101** R6 66 00N 89 00W
Wagga Wagga Australia **86** H2 35 07S 147 24E
Wagin Australia **86** B3 33 20S 117 15E
Wah Pakistan **77** C6 33 50N 72 44E
Waha Libya **94** C13 28 10N 19 57E
Wahiawa Hawaiian Islands **119** X18 21 35N 158 05W
Wahpeton North Dakota U.S.A. **104** A3 46 16N 96 36W
Waialua Hawaiian Islands **119** X18 21 35N 158 08W
Waigeo *i.* Indonesia **80** I3 0 00 131 00E
Waihi New Zealand **87** C3 37 22S 175 51E
Waikaremoana, Lake New Zealand **87** C3 38 50S 178 40E
Waikato New Zealand **87** C3 38 00S 175 30E
Wailuku Hawaiian Islands **119** Y18 20 54N 156 30W
Waimate New Zealand **87** B2 44 45S 171 03E
Wainfleet All Saints Lincolnshire England **36** E3 53 06N 0 15E
Wainwright Alaska U.S.A. **100** D7 70 39N 160 10W
Wainwright Alberta Canada **100** M3 52 49N 110 52W
Waipawa New Zealand **87** C3 39 48S 176 36E
Wairoa New Zealand **87** C3 39 03S 177 25E
Waitaki *r.* New Zealand **87** B2 44 30S 170 30E
Waitara New Zealand **87** B3 38 59S 174 13E
Wajima Japan **82** C2 37 23N 136 53E
Wajir Kenya **94** G8 1 46N 40 05E
Wakasa-wan *b.* Japan **82** C2 35 40N 135 30E
Wakatipu, Lake New Zealand **87** A1 45 00S 168 50E
Wakayama Japan **82** C1 34 12N 135 10E
Wake Island Pacific Ocean **118** G10 19 18N 166 36E
Wakefield Rhode Island U.S.A. **105** F2 41 26N 71 30W
Wakefield West Yorkshire England **43** F3 53 42N 1 29W
Wakkanai Japan **82** D4 45 26N 141 43E
Wako Japan **83** B4 35 46N 139 37E
Wałbrzych Poland **69** C3 50 48N 16 19E
Walcheren *i.* Netherlands **64** C3 51 30N 3 30E
Waldorf Maryland U.S.A. **105** E1 38 38N 76 56W
Wales South Yorkshire England **43** G2 53 21N 1 17W
Wales United Kingdom **38**
Wales Alaska U.S.A. **100** B6 65 38N 168 09W
Walkden Greater Manchester England **42** C2 53 32N 2 24W
Walker Lake Nevada U.S.A. **102** C4 38 40N 110 40W
Walkern Hertfordshire England **34** C3 51 55N 0 07W
Walkerton Ontario Canada **105** D2 44 08N 81 10W
Wallaceburg Ontario Canada **105** D2 42 34N 82 22W
Wallaroo Australia **86** F3 33 57S 137 36E
Wallasey Merseyside England **42** A2 53 26N 3 03W
Walla Walla Washington U.S.A. **102** C6 46 05N 118 18W
Wallingford Oxfordshire England **32** A2 51 37N 1 08W
Wallsend Tyne and Wear England **44** C2 55 00N 1 31W
Walmer Kent England **33** D2 51 13N 1 24E
Walney, Isle of Cumbria England **44** A1 54 05N 3 15W
Walsall West Midlands England **35** C2 52 35N 1 58W
Walsall Wood *tn.* West Midlands England **35** C2 52 37N 1 56W
Walsenburg Colorado U.S.A. **102** F4 37 36N 104 48W
Walston Strathclyde Scotland **45** D1 55 42N 3 30W
Walsum Germany **62** A3 51 32N 6 41E
Waltham Abbey Essex England **34** D3 51 41N 0 00
Waltham Forest *tn.* Greater London England **34** C2 51 35N 0 00
Waltham on the Wolds Leicestershire England **36** D2 52 49N 0 49W
Walton-le-Dale Lancashire England **42** B3 53 45N 2 41W
Walton-on-Thames Surrey England **34** B2 51 24N 0 25W
Walton-on-the-Hill Staffordshire England **35** B3 52 47N 2 04W
Walton on the Hill Surrey England **34** C1 51 17N 0 15W
Walton on the Naze Essex England **33** D2 51 51N 1 16E
Waltrop Germany **62** D3 51 37N 7 25E
Walvis Bay *tn.* Namibia **95** B3 22 59S 14 31E
Walvis Ridge Atlantic Ocean **117** I4 30 00S 3 00E
Walyevo Fiji **118** V16 17 35S 179 58W
Wamba *r.* Zaïre **95** C6 6 30S 17 30E
Wanaka, Lake New Zealand **87** A2 44 30S 169 00E
Wandsworth Greater London England **34** C2 51 27N 0 11W
Wanganui New Zealand **87** C3 39 56S 175 02E
Wanganui *r.* New Zealand **87** C3 39 30S 175 00E
Wangaratta Australia **86** H2 36 22S 146 20E
Wangerooge *i.* Germany **63** A2 53 47N 7 54E
Wanheim Germany **62** B2 51 23N 6 45E
Wanne-Eickel Germany **62** C3 51 31N 7 09E
Wansbeck *r.* Northumberland England **44** C2 55 10N 1 50W
Wanstead Greater London England **34** D2 51 34N 0 02E
Wantage Oxfordshire England **32** A2 51 36N 1 25W
Wanxian China **81** G4 30 54N 108 20E
Warangal India **77** D3 18 00N 79 35E
Warboys Cambridgeshire England **33** B3 52 24N 0 06W
Warburg Germany **63** A2 51 28N 9 10E
Ward Dublin Irish Republic **49** B2 53 26N 6 20W
Ward *r.* Dublin Irish Republic **49** B2 53 28N 6 19W
Ward's Stone *hill* Lancashire England **42** C4 54 03N 2 38W
Ware British Columbia Canada **100** J4 57 26N 124 41W
Ware Hertfordshire England **34** C3 51 49N 0 02W
Waregem Belgium **64** C2 50 53N 3 26E
Wareham Dorset England **31** E2 50 41N 2 07W
Waremme Belgium **64** E2 50 42N 5 15E
Waren Germany **63** B2 53 32N 12 42E
Warendorf Germany **63** A2 51 57N 8 00E
Warlingham Surrey England **34** C1 51 19N 0 04W
Warminster Wiltshire England **31** E3 51 13N 2 12W
Warmsworth South Yorkshire England **43** G2 53 30N 1 10W
Warnow *r.* Germany **63** B2 53 00N 12 00E
Warrego *r.* Australia **86** H4 27 30S 146 00E
Warren Michigan U.S.A. **105** D2 42 30N 83 02W
Warren Ohio U.S.A. **105** D2 41 15N 80 49W
Warren Pennsylvania U.S.A. **105** E2 41 52N 79 09W
Warrenpoint *tn.* Northern Ireland **48** E4 54 06N 6 15W
Warrensburg Missouri U.S.A. **104** B1 38 46N 93 44W
Warrington Cheshire England **42** C2 53 24N 2 37W
Warrnambool Australia **86** G2 38 23S 142 03E
Warroad Minnesota U.S.A. **104** A3 48 54N 95 20W
Warsaw *see* Warszawa
Warsop Nottinghamshire England **43** G1 53 13N 1 10W
Warszawa *(Warsaw)* Poland **69** D3 52 15N 21 00E
Warta *r.* Poland **69** C3 52 00N 17 00E
Warton Lancashire England **42** B3 53 46N 2 54W
Waruha *r.* India **77** D4 20 30N 79 00E
Warwick Australia **86** I4 28 12S 152 00E
Warwick Rhode Island U.S.A. **105** F2 41 42N 71 23W
Warwick Warwickshire England **35** D1 52 17N 1 34W
Warwickshire *co.* England **36** C2 52 15N 1 40W
Wasaga Beach *tn.* Ontario Canada **105** D2 44 31N 80 02W
Wash, The *b.* Lincolnshire England **36** E2 52 55N 0 10E
Washburn *r.* North Yorkshire England **43** E3 53 56N 1 40W
Washburn Wisconsin U.S.A. **104** B3 46 41N 90 53W
Washingborough Lincolnshire England **36** D3 53 14N 0 28W
Washington District of Columbia U.S.A. **105** E1 38 55N 77 00W
Washington Pennsylvania U.S.A. **105** D2 40 11N 80 16W
Washington *state* U.S.A. **102** B6 47 00N 120 00W
Washington Tyne and Wear England **44** C1 54 54N 1 31W
Wasmes Belgium **64** C2 50 25N 3 51E
Wassenaar Netherlands **65** B2 52 07N 4 23E
Wast Water *l.* Cumbria England **44** A1 54 26N 3 18W
Watampone Indonesia **80** G3 4 33S 120 20E
Watchet Somerset England **31** D3 51 12N 3 20W
Waterbeach Cambridgeshire England **33** C3 52 16N 0 11E
Waterbury Connecticut U.S.A. **105** F2 41 33N 73 03W
Waterbury Vermont U.S.A. **105** F2 44 21N 72 46W
Waterfoot Strathclyde Scotland **45** B1 55 46N 4 18W
Waterford *co.* Irish Republic **48** D2 52 10N 7 30W
Waterford Harbour Irish Republic **48** D2 52 10N 7 00W
Waterford Waterford Irish Republic **48** D2 52 15N 7 06W
Wateringbury Kent England **34** E1 51 16N 0 26E
Waterloo Belgium **64** D2 50 43N 4 24E
Waterloo Iowa U.S.A. **104** B2 42 30N 92 20W
Waterlooville Hampshire England **32** A1 50 53N 1 02W
Waterside Strathclyde Scotland **45** B1 55 21N 4 28W
Watertown New York U.S.A. **105** E2 43 57N 75 56W
Watertown South Dakota U.S.A. **104** A2 44 54N 97 08W
Waterville Maine U.S.A. **105** G2 44 34N 69 41W
Watford Hertfordshire England **34** B2 51 39N 0 24W
Wath upon Dearne South Yorkshire England **43** F2 53 31N 1 21W
Watkins Glen *tn.* New York U.S.A. **105** E2 42 23N 76 53W
Watlington Oxfordshire England **33** A2 51 39N 1 01W
Watseka Illinois U.S.A. **104** C2 40 46N 87 45W
Watson Lake *tn.* Yukon Territory Canada **100** J5 60 07N 128 49W
Watten France **64** B2 50 50N 2 13E
Wattenscheid Germany **62** C3 51 27N 7 07E
Watton Norfolk England **33** C3 52 34N 0 50E
Watton at Stone Hertfordshire England **34** C3 51 52N 0 07W
Wattrelos Belgium **64** C2 50 40N 3 14E
Wattston Strathclyde Scotland **45** C1 55 54N 3 56W
Wau Papua New Guinea **86** H8 7 22S 146 40E
Wau Sudan **94** E9 7 40N 28 04E
Waukegan Illinois U.S.A. **104** C2 42 21N 87 52W
Waukesha Wisconsin U.S.A. **104** C2 43 01N 88 14W
Wausau Wisconsin U.S.A. **104** C2 44 58N 89 40W
Wauwatosa Wisconsin U.S.A. **104** C2 43 04N 88 02W
Waveney *r.* Suffolk / Norfolk England **33** D3 52 30N 1 30E
Wavre Belgium **64** D2 50 43N 4 37E
Wawa Ontario Canada **105** D3 48 04N 84 49W
Waycross Georgia U.S.A. **103** J3 31 12N 82 22W
Wayne New Jersey U.S.A. **106** A2 40 55N 74 15W
Waynesboro Virginia U.S.A. **105** E1 38 04N 78 54W
Weald, The *geog. reg.* Kent England **33** C2 51 05N 0 25E
Wear *r.* Durham England **44** C1 54 40N 1 50W
Weardale *v.* Durham England **44** B1 54 55N 2 10W
Weaver *r.* Cheshire England **42** C1 53 17N 2 40W
Weaverham Cheshire England **42** C1 53 16N 2 35W
Webster City Iowa U.S.A. **104** B2 42 30N 93 50W
Weddell Island Falkland Islands **117** L16 51 55S 61 30W
Weddell Sea Southern Ocean **121** 71 00S 40 00W
Wedmore Somerset England **31** E3 51 14N 2 49W
Wednesbury West Midlands England **35** B2 52 34N 2 00W
Wednesfield West Midlands England **35** B2 52 36N 2 04W
Weedon Beck Northamptonshire England **36** C2 52 14N 1 05W
Weert Netherlands **64** E3 51 15N 5 42E
Weesp Netherlands **65** E3 52 19N 5 02E
Wei He *r.* China **81** G4 34 00N 106 00E
Weiden Germany **63** B1 49 40N 12 10E
Weifang China **81** I5 36 44N 119 10E
Weimar Germany **63** B2 50 59N 11 20E
Weipa Australia **86** G7 12 35S 141 56E
Weirton West Virginia U.S.A. **103** J5 40 24N 80 37W
Weisse Elster *r.* Germany **63** B2 51 00N 12 00E
Weissenfels Germany **63** B2 51 12N 11 58E
Weisswasser *tn.* Germany **63** B2 51 31N 14 38E
Wejherowo Poland **69** C3 54 36N 18 12E
Welham Green Hertfordshire England **34** C3 51 44N 0 12W
Welland Ontario Canada **105** E2 45 59N 79 14W
Welland *r.* East Midlands England **36** D2 52 50N 0 00
Wellesbourne Warwickshire England **35** D1 52 12N 1 35W
Wellesley Islands Australia **86** F6 16 30S 139 00E
Wellingborough Northamptonshire England **36** D2 52 19N 0 42W
Wellington Kansas U.S.A. **103** G4 37 17N 97 25W
Wellington New Zealand **87** B2 41 17S 174 47E
Wellington Shropshire England **36** B2 52 43N 2 31W
Wellington Somerset England **31** D2 50 59N 3 15W
Wells Somerset England **31** E3 51 13N 2 39W
Wellsboro Pennsylvania U.S.A. **105** E2 41 45N 77 18W
Wellsford New Zealand **87** B3 36 16S 174 32E
Wells-next-the-Sea Norfolk England **33** C3 52 58N 0 51E
Wels Austria **63** B1 48 10N 14 02E
Welshpool Powys Wales **38** C2 52 40N 3 09W
Welton Humberside England **40** D2 54 47N 3 00W
Welwyn Hertfordshire England **34** C3 51 50N 0 13W
Welwyn Garden City Hertfordshire England **34** C3 51 48N 0 13W
Wem Shropshire England **36** B2 52 51N 2 44W
Wembley Greater London England **34** C2 51 33N 0 18W
Wendover Buckinghamshire England **34** A3 51 46N 0 46W
Wenlock Edge *hills* Shropshire England **36** B2 52 30N 2 45W
Wensleydale *v.* North Yorkshire England **40** B3 54 20N 2 20W
Wensum *r.* Norfolk England **33** D3 52 45N 1 10E
Wenyu He *r.* China **82** H2 40 02N 116 32E
Wenzhou China **81** J3 28 02N 120 40E
Wernigerode Germany **63** B2 51 51N 10 48E
Werra *r.* Germany **63** B2 51 00N 10 00E
Werrington Staffordshire England **35** B4 53 02N 2 06W
Wertach *r.* Germany **63** B1 48 00N 10 00E
Wesel Germany **63** A2 51 39N 6 37E
Weser *r.* Germany **63** A2 53 00N 8 00E
West Allis Wisconsin U.S.A. **104** C2 43 01N 88 00W
West Antarctica *geog. reg.* Antarctica **121** 80 00S 120 00W
West Bank *territory* Israel **78** O11 32 00N 35 00E
West Bengal *admin.* India **77** F4 22 00N 88 00E
West Berlin *see* Berlin, West
Westbourne Manitoba Canada **104** A4 50 08N 98 33W
West Bradford Lancashire England **42** C3 53 54N 2 24W
West Bridgford Nottinghamshire England **36** C2 52 56N 1 08W
West Bromwich West Midlands England **35** C2 52 31N 1 59W
Westbrook *tn.* Maine U.S.A. **105** F2 43 41N 70 22W
Westbury Wiltshire England **31** E3 51 16N 2 11W
West Calder Lothian Scotland **45** C1 55 51N 3 35W
West Caroline Basin Pacific Ocean **118** D8 3 00N 136 00E
West Chester Pennsylvania U.S.A. **105** E1 39 58N 75 37W
West Clandon Surrey England **34** B1 51 16N 0 30W
Westcot Surrey England **34** B1 51 13N 0 22W
West Covina California U.S.A. **107** C3 34 04N 117 56W
West Derby Merseyside England **42** B2 53 26N 2 55W
West Drayton Greater London England **34** B2 51 30N 0 28W
West Dvina *see* Zap Dvina
Westeinder Plas *l.* Netherlands **65** C2 52 15N 4 44E
Westerham Kent England **34** D1 51 16N 0 05E
Westerland Germany **63** A2 54 54N 8 19E
Western Australia *state* Australia **86** C4/C5 25 00S 117 00E
Western Desert Egypt **88** 30 00N 30 00E
Western Ghats *mts.* India **77** C3/C2 15 30N 74 00E
Western Isles *islands area* Scotland **46** A4–B5
WESTERN SAHARA **93** C7
WESTERN SAMOA **118/119** I6
Western Sayan *mts.* Russia **71** L6 52 30N 92 30E
Western Yamuna Canal India **76** L4 28 40N 77 08E
Westerschelde *sd.* Netherlands **64** C3 51 20N 3 45E
Westerwald *geog. reg.* Germany **63** A2 50 00N 8 00E
West European Basin Atlantic Ocean **117** G11 47 00N 18 00W
West Falkland *i.* Falkland Islands **117** L16 51 00S 60 40W
West Felton Shropshire England **36** B2 52 49N 2 58W
Westfield Massachusetts U.S.A. **105** F2 42 07N 72 45W
West Fork White River Indiana U.S.A. **104** C1 39 00N 87 00W
West Frisian Islands *see* Waddeneilanden
West Glamorgan *co.* Wales **38** C1 51 45N 3 55W
West Haddon Northamptonshire England **36** C2 52 20N 1 04W
West Ham Greater London England **34** D2 51 32N 0 01E
Westhill Grampian Scotland **46** F4 57 11N 2 16W
Westhoughton Greater Manchester England **42** C2 53 34N 2 32W
West Ice Shelf Antarctica **121** 66 00S 85 00E
West Indies *is.* **Caribbean Sea** **109** K4 22 00N 69 00W
West Kingsdown Kent England **34** D2 51 20N 0 16E
West Kirby Merseyside England **42** A2 53 22N 3 10W
West Linton Borders Scotland **45** D1 55 46N 3 22W
West Los Angeles California U.S.A. **107** A3 34 02N 118 25W
West Malling Kent England **34** E1 51 18N 0 25E
West Marianas Basin Pacific Ocean **118** D9 16 00N 137 30E
Westmeath *co.* Irish Republic **48** D3 53 30N 7 30W
West Memphis Arkansas U.S.A. **103** H4 35 09N 90 11W
West Mersea Essex England **33** C2 51 47N 0 55E
West Midlands *admin.* England **35** B2–D2 52 28N 1 40W
Westminster California U.S.A. **107** C2 33 45N 117 59W
Westminster Inner London England **34** C2 51 30N 0 09W
Weston West Virginia U.S.A. **105** D1 39 03N 80 28W
Weston-super-Mare Avon England **31** E3 51 21N 2 59W
West Palm Beach *tn.* Florida U.S.A. **103** J2 26 42N 80 05W
Westport Connecticut U.S.A. **105** F2 41 09N 73 22W
Westport Mayo Irish Republic **48** B3 53 48N 9 32W
Westport New Zealand **87** B2 41 46S 171 38E
West Plains *tn.* Missouri U.S.A. **104** B1 36 44N 91 51W
Westray *i.* Orkney Islands Scotland **47** D2 59 18N 3 00W
Westray Firth *sd.* Orkney Islands Scotland **47** D2 59 15N 3 00W
West Rift Valley Africa **88** 0 00 30 00E
West Scotia Basin Southern Ocean **121** 58 00S 52 00W
West Siberian Lowland Russia **71** J7/J8 60 00N 75 00E
West Sussex *co.* England **33** B1 51 00N 0 25W
West Terschelling Netherlands **64** E5 53 22N 5 13E
West Thurrock Essex England **34** D2 51 29N 0 17E
West Virginia *state* U.S.A. **105** D1 39 00N 81 00W
West-Vlanderen *admin.* Belgium **64** B3 51 10N 3 00E
Westward Ho! Devon England **31** C3 51 02N 4 15W
West Wittering West Sussex England **33** B1 50 47N 0 54W
West Yorkshire *admin.* England **43** F3 53 50N 1 30W
Wetar *i.* Indonesia **80** H2 7 30S 126 30E
Wetaskiwin Alberta Canada **100** M3 52 57N 113 20W
Wetherby West Yorkshire England **43** F3 53 56N 1 23W
Wetzlar Germany **63** A2 50 33N 8 30E
Wevelgem Belgium **64** C2 50 48N 3 12E
Wewak Papua New Guinea **86** G9 3 35S 143 35E
Wexford *co.* Irish Republic **48** E2 52 25N 6 35W
Wexford Wexford Irish Republic **48** E2 52 20N 6 27W
Wexford Bay Irish Republic **48** E2 52 25N 6 10W
Wey *r.* Surrey England **33** B2 51 18N 0 30W
Weybridge Surrey England **34** B2 51 22N 0 28W
Weyburn Saskatchewan Canada **100** O2 49 39N 103 51W
Weymouth Dorset England **31** E2 50 37N 2 25W
Weymouth Massachusetts U.S.A. **105** F2 42 14N 70 58W
Whakatane New Zealand **87** C3 37 56S 177 00E
Whaley Bridge Derbyshire England **42** E1 53 20N 1 59W
Whalley Lancashire England **42** C3 53 50N 2 24W
Whalsay *l.* Shetland Islands Scotland **47** C2 60 22N 0 59W
Whangarei New Zealand **87** B3 35 43S 174 20E
Wharfe *r.* North Yorkshire England **40** C2 53 50N 1 15W
Wharfedale *v.* North Yorkshire England **40** C3 54 05N 2 00W
Wharton Cheshire England **42** C1 53 12N 2 31W
Wheathampstead Hertfordshire England **34** C3 51 49N 0 17W
Wheatley Oxfordshire England **32** A2 53 22N 0 52W
Wheaton Minnesota U.S.A. **104** A3 45 49N 96 30W
Wheaton Aston Staffordshire England **35** B3 52 43N 2 12W
Wheeler Lake Alabama U.S.A. **103** I3 34 00N 87 00W
Wheeling West Virginia U.S.A. **105** D2 40 05N 80 43W
Wheldrake North Yorkshire England **43** H3 53 54N 0 57W
Whernside *sum.* North Yorkshire England **44** B1 54 14N

2 23W
Whickham Tyne and Wear England 44 C1 54 57N 1 40W
Whiddy Island Cork Irish Republic 48 B1 51 41N 9 30W
Whipsnade Bedfordshire England 34 B3 51 52N 0 33W
Whiston Merseyside England 42 B2 53 25N 2 50W
Whiston South Yorkshire England 43 G2 53 24N 1 20W
Whitburn Lothian Scotland 45 C1 55 52N 3 42W
Whitburn Tyne and Wear England 44 C1 54 57N 1 21W
Whitby North Yorkshire England 40 D3 54 29N 0 37W
Whitby Ontario Canada 105 E2 43 52N 78 56W
Whitchurch Buckinghamshire England 33 B2 51 53N 0 51W
Whitchurch Hampshire England 32 A2 51 14N 1 20W
Whitchurch Shropshire England 36 B2 52 58N 2 41W
White r. U.S.A. 102 F5 43 00N 103 00W
White r. U.S.A. 103 H4 35 00N 92 00W
White Bay Newfoundland Canada 101 X3 50 30N 55 15W
Whitecourt Alberta Canada 100 L3 54 10N 115 38W
Whitefield Greater Manchester England 42 D2 53 34N 2 18W
Whitehaven Cumbria England 44 A1 54 33N 3 35W
Whitehead Antrim Northern Ireland 48 F4 54 45N 5 43W
Whitehorse Yukon Territory Canada 100 I5 60 41N 135 08W
White Horse, Vale of Berkshire England 32 A2 51 35N 1 30W
Whitehouse Northern Ireland 49 D1 54 39N 5 55W
Whiteland Indiana U.S.A. 104 C1 39 32N 86 05W
White Mountains New Hampshire U.S.A. 105 F2 44 00N 72 00W
White Nile see Bahr el Abiad
White Nile see Bahr el Jebel
White Nile Dam Sudan 78 D2 14 18N 32 30E
Whiteparish Wiltshire England 31 F3 51 01N 1 39W
White River tn. Ontario Canada 104 C3 48 35N 85 16W
Whitesand Bay Cornwall England 31 C2 50 20N 4 25W
White Sea Russia 70 F9 66 00N 37 30E
White Volta r. Ghana 93 E4 9 30N 1 30W
Whitfield Kent England 33 D2 51 09N 1 17E
Whithorn Dumfries & Galloway Scotland 46 D1 54 44N 4 25W
Whitland Dyfed Wales 38 B1 51 50N 4 37W
Whitley Bay tn. Tyne and Wear England 44 C2 55 03N 1 25W
Whitney Ontario Canada 105 E3 45 29N 78 15W
Whitney, Mount California U.S.A. 102 C4 36 35N 118 17W
Whitstable Kent England 33 D2 51 22N 1 02E
Whittier California U.S.A. 107 B2 33 58N 118 02W
Whittington Derbyshire England 43 F1 53 17N 1 25W
Whittington Shropshire England 36 B2 52 52N 3 00W
Whittlesey Cambridgeshire England 33 B3 52 34N 0 08W
Whitton Humberside England 40 D2 53 43N 0 38W
Whitwell Derbyshire England 43 G1 53 18N 1 12W
Whitwell Hertfordshire England 34 C3 51 52N 0 16W
Whitwick Leicestershire England 35 E3 52 44N 1 20W
Whitworth Lancashire England 42 D2 53 40N 2 10W
Whyalla Australia 86 F3 33 04S 137 34E
Wiarton Ontario Canada 105 D2 44 44N 81 10W
Wiay i. Western Isles Scotland 46 A4 57 23N 7 13W
Wichita Kansas U.S.A. 103 G4 37 43N 97 20W
Wichita r. Texas U.S.A. 102 F3 33 00N 100 00W
Wichita Falls tn. Texas U.S.A. 102 G3 33 55N 98 30W
Wick Highland Scotland 46 E5 58 26N 3 06W
Wickersley South Yorkshire England 43 G2 53 26N 1 17W
Wickford Essex England 33 C2 51 38N 0 31E
Wickham Hampshire England 32 A1 50 54N 1 10W
Wickham Market Suffolk England 33 D3 52 09N 1 22E
Wicklow co. Irish Republic 48 E2 52 55N 6 25W
Wicklow Wicklow Irish Republic 48 E2 52 59N 6 03W
Wicklow Head c. Irish Republic 48 E2 52 58N 6 00W
Wicklow Mountains Irish Republic 48 E3 53 00N 6 20W
Widford Hertfordshire England 34 D3 51 50N 0 04E
Widnes Cheshire England 42 B2 53 22N 2 44W
Wien (Vienna) Austria 69 C2 48 13N 16 22E
Wiener Neustadt Austria 69 C2 47 49N 16 15E
Wieprz r. Poland 69 D3 51 00N 23 00E
Wierden Netherlands 64 F4 52 21N 6 35E
Wiesbaden Germany 63 A2 50 05N 8 15E
Wigan Greater Manchester England 42 C2 53 33N 2 38W
Wigginton Staffordshire England 35 C2 52 39N 1 42W
Wigston Leicestershire England 36 C2 52 36N 1 05W
Wigton Cumbria England 44 A1 54 49N 3 09W
Wigtown Dumfries & Galloway Scotland 46 D1 54 52N 4 26W
Wigtown Bay Dumfries & Galloway Scotland 46 D1 54 10N 4 20W
Wijchen Netherlands 64 E3 51 48N 5 44E
Wijde Blik l. Netherlands 65 E2 52 13N 5 04E
Wil Switzerland 61 C2 47 28N 9 03E
Wilberfoss Humberside England 40 D2
Wilhelmshaven Germany 63 A2 53 32N 8 07E
Wilhelm-Pieck-Stadt-Guben Germany 63 B2 51 59N 14 42E
Wilkes Land geog. reg. Antarctica 121 68 00S 105 00E
Wilkes-Barre Pennsylvania U.S.A. 105 E2 41 15N 75 50W
Willaston Cheshire England 42 A1 53 17N 3 02W
Willebroek Belgium 64 D3 51 04N 4 22E
Willemstad Curaçao 109 K2 12 12N 68 56W
Willenhall West Midlands England 35 B2 52 36N 2 02W
Willesden Greater London England 34 C2 51 33N 0 14W
Williamsburg Virginia U.S.A. 105 E1 37 17N 79 43W
Williams Lake tn. British Columbia Canada 100 K3 52 08N 122 09W
Williamson West Virginia U.S.A. 105 D1 37 42N 82 16W
Williamsport Pennsylvania U.S.A. 105 E2 41 16N 77 03W
Williamstown Kentucky U.S.A. 105 D1 38 39N 84 32W
Willington Derbyshire England 35 D3 52 51N 1 34W
Willington Durham England 44 C1 54 43N 1 41W
Williston North Dakota U.S.A. 102 F6 48 09N 103 39W
Williston Lake British Columbia Canada 100 K4 49 27N 80 37W
Williton Somerset England 31 D3 51 10N 3 20W
Willmar Minnesota U.S.A. 104 A3 45 06N 95 03W
Willoughby Warwickshire England 35 E1 52 18N 1 16W
Willow Springs Missouri U.S.A. 104 B1 36 59N 91 59W
Wilmington Delaware U.S.A. 105 E1 39 46N 75 31W
Wilmington Kent England 34 D2 51 25N 0 12E
Wilmington North Carolina U.S.A. 103 K3 34 14N 77 55W
Wilmslow Cheshire England 42 D1 53 20N 2 15W
Wilson North Carolina U.S.A. 103 K4 35 43N 77 56W
Wilton Wiltshire England 31 F3 51 05N 1 52W
Wiltshire co. England 31 E3/F3 51 30N 2 00W
Wiluna Australia 86 C4 26 37S 120 12E
Wimbledon Greater London England 34 C2 51 25N 0 13W
Wimborne Minster Dorset England 31 F2 50 48N 1 59W
Wimereux France 64 A2 50 46N 1 37E
Wincanton Somerset England 31 E3 51 04N 2 25W
Winchburgh Lothian Scotland 45 D1 55 57N 3 26W
Winchelsea East Sussex England 33 C1 50 55N 0 42E
Winchester Hampshire England 32 A2 51 04N 1 19W
Winchester Virginia U.S.A. 103 K4 39 11N 78 12W
Wind River Range mts. Wyoming U.S.A. 102 E5 43 00N 109 00W
Windermere l. Cumbria England 44 B1 54 20N 2 57W
Windermere tn. Cumbria England 44 B1 54 23N 2 54W
Windhoek Namibia 95 C3 22 34S 17 06E
Windlesham Surrey England 34 A2 51 22N 0 39W
Windsor Berkshire England 34 B2 51 29N 0 38W
Windsor Newfoundland Canada 101 X2 48 58N 55 40W
Windsor Ontario Canada 105 D2 42 18N 83 00W
Windward Islands Lesser Antilles 109 L2 12 30N 62 00W
Windward Passage sd. Cuba/Haiti 109 J3/J4 20 00N 73 00W
Windygates Fife Scotland 45 D2 56 12N 3 03W
Wing Buckinghamshire England 34 A3 51 54N 0 44W
Wingate Durham England 44 C1 54 55N 1 23W
Wingerworth Derbyshire England 43 F1 53 13N 1 28W
Wingham Ontario Canada 105 D2 43 54N 81 19W
Winisk Ontario Canada 101 R4 55 20N 85 15W
Winisk Lake Ontario Canada 101 R3 52 30N 87 30W
Winisk River Ontario Canada 101 R4 54 50N 87 00W
Winkleigh Devon England 31 D2 50 51N 3 56W
Winkler Manitoba Canada 104 A3 49 12N 97 55W
Winnebago, Lake Wisconsin U.S.A. 104 C2 44 00N 88 00W
Winnemucca Nevada U.S.A. 102 C5 40 58N 117 45W
Winnipeg Manitoba Canada 104 A3 49 53N 97 10W
Winnipeg, Lake Manitoba Canada 101 P3 52 30N 97 30W
Winnipegosis, Lake Manitoba Canada 101 O3 52 10N 100 00W
Winnipesaukee, Lake New Hampshire U.S.A. 105 F2 43 00N 72 00W
Winona Minnesota U.S.A. 104 B2 44 02N 91 37W
Winschoten Netherlands 64 G5 53 07N 7 02E
Winscombe Avon England 31 E3 51 28N 2 52W
Winsford Cheshire England 42 C1 53 11N 2 31W
Winslow Arizona U.S.A. 102 D4 35 01N 110 43W
Winslow Buckinghamshire England 33 B2 51 57N 0 54W
Winston-Salem North Carolina U.S.A. 103 J4 36 05N 80 18W
Winterbourne Avon England 31 E3 51 30N 2 31W
Winterswijk Netherlands 64 F3 51 58N 6 44E
Winterthur Switzerland 61 C2 47 30N 8 45E
Winterton-on-Sea Norfolk England 33 D3 52 43N 1 42E
Winton Australia 86 G5 22 22S 143 00E
Wirksworth Derbyshire England 36 C3 53 05N 1 34W
Wirral p. Merseyside England 42 A2 53 20N 3 03W
Wisła r. Poland 69 C3 53 00N 19 00E
Wisbech Cambridgeshire England 33 C3 52 40N 0 10E
Wiscasset Maine U.S.A. 105 G2 44 01N 69 41W
Wisconsin state U.S.A. 104 B3 45 00N 90 00W
Wisconsin r. Wisconsin U.S.A. 104 B2 43 00N 90 00W
Wisconsin Rapids tn. Wisconsin U.S.A. 104 C2 44 24N 89 50W
Wishaw Strathclyde Scotland 45 C1 55 47N 3 56W
Wismar Germany 63 B2 53 54N 11 28E
Wisłok r. Poland 69 D3 50 00N 22 00E
Wissembourg France 61 C2 49 02N 7 57E
Wissey r. Norfolk England 33 C3 52 38N 0 50E
Wistow North Yorkshire England 43 G3 53 48N 1 06W
Witham Essex England 33 C2 51 48N 0 38E
Witham r. Lincolnshire England 36 D3 53 05N 0 10W
Witheridge Devon England 31 D2 50 55N 3 42W
Withernsea Humberside England 41 E2 53 44N 0 02E
Witley Surrey England 34 B1 51 08N 0 39W
Witney Oxfordshire England 32 A2 51 48N 1 29W
Witten Germany 62 D2 51 25N 7 19E
Wittenberg Germany 63 B2 51 53N 12 39E
Wittenberge Germany 63 B2 52 59N 11 45E
Wittlich Germany 63 A1 49 59N 6 54E
Wittstock Germany 63 B2 53 10N 12 30E
Wiveliscombe Somerset England 31 D3 51 03N 3 19W
Wivenhoe Essex England 33 C2 51 52N 0 58E
Woburn Bedfordshire England 34 B3 51 59N 0 38W
Woburn Sands tn. Bedfordshire England 34 B4 52 01N 0 39W
Włocławek Poland 69 C3 52 39N 19 01E
Woerden Netherlands 65 D2 52 05N 4 53E
Woking Surrey England 34 B1 51 20N 0 34W
Wokingham Berkshire England 33 B2 51 25N 0 51W
Woldingham Surrey England 34 C1 51 17N 0 02W
Wolf-Bay tn. Québec Canada 101 W3 50 14N 60 40W
Wolfen Germany 63 B2 51 41N 12 17E
Wolfenbüttel Germany 63 B2 52 10N 10 33E
Wolfsberg Austria 69 B2 46 50N 14 50E
Wolfsburg Germany 63 B2 52 27N 10 49E
Wolin Poland 63 B2 53 51N 14 38E
Wollaston Lake Saskatchewan Canada 101 O4 58 20N 103 00W
Wollaston Lake tn. Saskatchewan Canada 101 O4 58 05N 103 38W
Wollaston Northamptonshire England 36 D2 52 16N 0 41W
Wollongong Australia 86 I3 34 25S 150 52E
Wolsingham Durham England 44 C1 54 44N 1 52W
Wolverhampton West Midlands England 35 B2 52 36N 2 08W
Wolverton Buckinghamshire England 33 B3 52 04N 0 50W
Wolvey Warwickshire England 35 D2 52 29N 1 21W
Wombourne Staffordshire England 35 B2 52 32N 2 11W
Wombwell South Yorkshire England 43 F2 53 32N 1 24W
Wompah Australia 86 G4 29 04S 142 05E
Wonersh Surrey England 34 B1 51 12N 0 33W
Wŏnju South Korea 81 K5 37 24N 127 52E
Wŏnsan North Korea 81 K5 39 07N 127 26E
Woodbridge New Jersey U.S.A. 106 A1 40 33N 74 16W
Woodbridge Suffolk England 33 D3 52 06N 1 19E
Wood Buffalo National Park Alberta Canada 100 M4 60 00N 113 00W
Woodburn Northern Ireland 49 D2 54 43N 5 50W
Woodford Greater London England 34 D2 51 37N 0 02E
Woodford Halse Northamptonshire England 36 C2 52 10N 1 13W
Wood Green Greater London England 34 C2 51 38N 0 06W
Woodhall Spa Lincolnshire England 36 D3 53 09N 0 14W
Woodhouse South Yorkshire England 43 F2 53 22N 1 23W
Woodlands tn. Manitoba Canada 104 A4 50 12N 97 40W
Woodlark Island Papua New Guinea 86 I8 9 00S 152 30E
Woods, Lake of the North America 104 B3 49 00N 94 00W
Woodseaves Staffordshire England 35 B3 52 49N 2 19W
Woodstock New Brunswick Canada 101 V2 46 10N 67 36W
Woodstock Ontario Canada 105 D2 43 07N 80 46W
Woodstock Oxfordshire England 32 A2 51 52N 1 21W
Woodstock Vermont U.S.A. 105 F2 43 37N 72 33W
Woodsville New Hampshire U.S.A. 105 F2 44 08N 72 02W
Woodville New Zealand 87 C2 40 20S 175 54E
Woodward Oklahoma U.S.A. 102 G4 36 26N 99 25W
Wool Dorset England 31 E2 50 41N 2 14W
Woolacombe Devon England 31 C3 51 10N 4 13W
Wooler Northumberland England 44 B2 55 33N 2 01W
Woolwich Greater London England 34 D2 51 29N 0 04E
Woore Shropshire England 35 A3 52 59N 2 24W
Wooster Ohio U.S.A. 105 D2 40 46N 81 57W
Wootton Bassett Wiltshire England 31 F3 51 33N 1 54W
Worcester & Birmingham Canal West Midlands England 35 B1 52 15N 2 08W
Worcester Hereford and Worcester England 35 B1 52 11N 2 13W
Worcester Massachusetts U.S.A. 105 F2 42 17N 71 48W
Worcester Republic of South Africa 95 C1 33 39S 19 26E
Workington Cumbria England 44 A1 54 39N 3 33W
Worksop Nottinghamshire England 43 G1 53 18N 1 07W
Worland Wyoming U.S.A. 102 E5 44 01N 107 58W
Wormhoudt France 64 B2 50 53N 2 28E
Worms Germany 63 A1 49 38N 8 23E
Worms Head c. West Glamorgan Wales 38 B1 51 34N 4 20W
Worplesdon Surrey England 34 B1 51 17N 0 37W
Worsbrough South Yorkshire England 43 F2 53 33N 1 29W
Worthing West Sussex England 33 B1 50 48N 0 23W
Worthington Minnesota U.S.A. 104 A2 43 37N 95 36W
Wotton-under-Edge Gloucestershire England 31 E3 51 39N 2 21W
Woverley Hereford & Worcester England 35 B2 52 24N 2 16W
Wragby Lincolnshire England 36 D3 53 39N 1 23W
Wrangell Alaska U.S.A. 100 I4 56 28N 132 23W
Wrangell Mountains Alaska U.S.A. 100 G5 62 00N 143 00W
Wrangle Lincolnshire England 36 E3 53 02N 0 07E
Wrath, Cape Highland Scotland 46 C5 58 37N 5 01W
Wrekin, The mt. Shropshire England 36 B2 52 41N 2 32W
Wrexham Clwyd Wales 38 D3 53 03N 3 00W
Wright Peak Antarctica 121 73 15S 94 00W
Wrigley Northwest Territories Canada 100 K5 63 16N 123 39W
Wrinehill Staffordshire England 35 A4 53 02N 2 23W
Writtle Essex England 33 C2 51 44N 0 26E
Wrocław Poland 69 C3 51 05N 17 00E
Wrotham Kent England 34 D1 51 19N 0 19E
Wroughton Wiltshire England 31 F3 51 31N 1 48W
Wroxham Norfolk England 33 D3 52 42N 1 24E
Wuhai China 81 G5 39 40N 106 40E
Wuhan China 81 H4 30 35N 114 19E
Wuhu China 81 I4 31 23N 118 25E
Wukari Nigeria 93 G4 7 49N 9 49E
Wülfrath Germany 62 C2 51 17N 7 03E
Wunstorf Germany 63 A2 52 26N 9 26E
Wupper r. Germany 62 D1 51 14N 7 17E
Wuppertal Germany 62 C2 51 15N 7 10E
Wurno Nigeria 93 G5 13 18N 5 29E
Würzburg Germany 63 A1 49 48N 9 57E
Wusul Jiang (Ussuri) r. China/Russia 81 L7 47 00N 134 00E
Wutongqiao China 81 F3 29 21N 103 48E
Wuxi China 81 J4 31 35N 120 19E
Wuyi Shan mts. China 81 I3 26 00N 116 30E
Wuzhou China 81 H2 23 30N 111 21E
Wye Kent England 33 C2 51 11N 0 56E
Wye r. Hereford and Worcester England 36 B1 51 58N 2 35W
Wymondham Norfolk England 33 D3 52 34N 1 07E
Wyndham Australia 86 D6 15 30S 128 09E
Wyoming state U.S.A. 102 E5 43 00N 108 00W
Wyre r. Lancashire England 42 B3 53 52N 2 52W

X

Xaafuun Somalia 94 J10 10 27N 51 15E
Xaidulla China 77 D7 36 27N 77 46E
Xam Nua Laos 81 F2 20 25N 103 50W
Xánthi Greece 68 D3 41 07N 24 56E
Xiaguan China 81 F3 25 33N 100 09E
Xiamen China 81 I2 24 28N 118 05E
Xi'an China 81 G4 34 16N 108 54E
Xiangfan China 81 H4 32 05N 112 03E
Xiangtan China 81 H3 27 48N 112 55E
Xianyang China 81 G4 34 22N 108 42E
Xieng Khouang Laos 80 C7 19 21N 103 23E
Xigaze China 81 C3 29 18N 88 50E
Xi Jiang r. China 81 H2 23 30N 111 00E
Xingtai China 81 H5 37 08N 114 29E
Xining China 81 F5 36 35N 101 55E
Xinjiang Uygur Zizhiqu (Sinkiang Uighur Autonomous Region) admin. China 81 B6/C6 41 00N 85 00E
Xinjin China 81 J5 39 25N 121 58E
Xiqing Shan mts. China 81 F4 34 00N 102 30E
Xizang Zizhiqu (Tibet Autonomous Region) admin. China 81 B4/C4 33 30N 85 00E
Xizhuang China 82 G1 39 51N 116 20E
Xochimiko Mexico 108 E3 19 08N 99 09W
Xuanhua China 81 I6 40 36N 115 01E
Xuchang China 81 H4 34 03N 113 48E
Xuwen China 81 H2 20 25N 110 08E
Xuzhou China 81 I4 34 17N 117 18E

Y

Yaba Nigeria 92 C3 6 29N 3 27E
Yablonovy Range mts. Russia 71 M6/N6 51 30N 110 00E
Yabrūd Syria 78 P11 33 58N 36 39E
Yaizu Japan 82 C1 34 54N 138 20E
Yakima r. Washington U.S.A. 102 B6 47 00N 120 00W
Yakima Washington U.S.A. 102 B6 46 37N 120 30W
Yakutat Alaska U.S.A. 100 H4 59 29N 139 49W
Yakutsk Russia 71 O8 62 10N 129 50E
Yalding Kent England 34 E1 51 14N 0 26E
Yalu r. China / North Korea 81 K6 42 00N 127 00E
Yamagata Japan 82 D2 38 16N 140 19E
Yamaguchi Japan 82 B1 34 10N 131 28E
Yamal Peninsula Russia 71 I10/J10 72 00N 70 00E
Yamato Japan 83 A2 35 29N 139 27E
Yambio Sudan 94 E8 4 34N 28 21E
Yambol Bulgaria 68 E3 42 28N 26 30E
Yamburg Russia 71 J9 68 19N 77 09E
Yamoussoukro Côte d'Ivoire 93 D4 6 50N 5 20W
Yamuna r. India 76 L4 28 43N 17 13E
Yamunanagar India 77 D6 30 07N 77 17E
Yana r. Russia 71 P9 69 00N 135 00E
Yanbu'al Baḩr Saudi Arabia 78 E3 24 07N 38 04E
Yancheng China 81 J4 33 23N 120 10E
Yangon see Rangoon
Yangquan China 81 H5 37 52N 113 29E
Yangtze see Jinsha Jiang, Chang Jiang
Yanji China 81 K6 42 52N 129 32E
Yanjing China 81 E3 29 01N 98 38E
Yankton South Dakota U.S.A. 104 A2 42 53N 97 24W
Yantai China 81 J5 37 30N 121 22E
Yao Japan 82 C1 34 36N 135 37E
Yaoundé Cameroon 93 H3 3 51N 11 31E
Yap Islands Pacific Ocean 118 D8 9 30N 138 09E
Yap Trench Pacific Ocean 118 D8 10 00N 139 00E
Yaqui r. Mexico 108 C5 28 00N 109 50W
Yare r. Norfolk England 33 D3 52 37N 1 30E
Yaritagua Venezuela 109 K2 10 05N 69 07W
Yarkant He r. China 71 J3 36 00N 76 00E
Yarlung Zangbo Jiang (Tsangpo) r. China 81 D3 29 00N 92 30E
Yarmouth Isle of Wight England 32 A1 50 42N 1 29W
Yarmouth Nova Scotia Canada 101 V1 43 50N 66 08W
Yarnfield Staffordshire England 35 B3 52 54N 2 12W
Yaroslavl' Russia 70 F7 57 34N 39 52E
Yarrow Water r. Borders Scotland 46 E2 55 35N 3 10W
Yarumal Colombia 114 B14 6 59N 75 25W
Yasawa i. Fiji 118 T16 16 50S 177 30E
Yasawa Group is. Fiji 118 T16 17 00S 177 40E
Yate Avon England 31 E3 51 32N 2 25W
Yateley Hampshire England 33 B2 51 20N 0 51W
Yathkyed Lake Northwest Territories Canada 101 P5 62 30N 97 30W
Yatsushiro Japan 81 B1 32 32N 130 35E
Yatton Avon England 31 E3 51 24N 2 49W
Yauza r. Russia 65 M2 55 46N 37 40E
Yawatahama Japan 82 B1 33 27N 132 24E
Yaxley Cambridgeshire England 33 B3 52 31N 0 16W
Yazd Iran 79 H5 31 54N 54 22E
Yazoo r. Mississippi U.S.A. 103 H3 33 00N 90 00W
Ye Myanmar 80 B7 15 15N 97 50E
Ye Xian China 81 I5 37 10N 119 55E
Yeadon West Yorkshire England 43 E3 53 52N 1 41W
Yealmpton Devon England 31 C2 50 21N 3 59W
Yekaterinburg (Sverdlovsk) Russia 70 I7 56 52N 60 35E
Yell i. Shetland Islands Scotland 47 B2 60 35N 1 10W
Yell Sound Shetland Islands Scotland 47 B2 60 30N 1 15W
Yellowknife Northwest Territories Canada 100 M5 62 30N 114 29W
Yellow Sea (Huang Hai) China 81 J5 35 30N 122 30E
Yellowstone r. U.S.A. 102 E6 46 00N 108 00W
Yellowstone Lake Wyoming U.S.A. 102 D5 44 30N 110 20W
Yelverton Devon England 31 C2 50 30N 4 05W
YEMEN REPUBLIC 78 F2
Yenisey r. Russia 71 K8 64 00N 87 30E
Yenisey, Gulf of Russia 71 J10/K10 72 30N 80 00E
Yeniseysk Russia 71 L7 58 27N 92 13E
Yeo r. Avon England 31 E3 51 20N 2 50W
Yeo r. Dorset/Somerset England 31 E2 51 00N 2 35W
Yeovil Somerset England 31 E2 50 57N 2 39W
Yeppoon Australia 86 I5 23 05S 150 42E
Yerevan Armenia 70 G4 40 10N 44 31E
Yerres r. France 60 C1 48 40N 2 36E
Yesil r. Turkey 78 E7 41 00N 36 25E
Yes Tor sum. Devon England 31 C2 50 42N 4 00W
Yetts O'Muckhart Central Scotland 45 C2 56 12N 3 37W
Yeu Myanmar 77 H4 22 49N 95 26E
Ye Xian China 81 G1 37 10N 119 55E
Yiannitsá Greece 68 D3 40 46N 22 24E
Yibin China 81 F3 28 42N 104 30E
Yichang China 81 H4 30 46N 111 20E
Yinchuan China 81 G5 38 30N 106 19E
Yingkou China 81 J6 40 40N 122 17E
Yining China 81 B6 43 50N 81 28E
Yirga 'Alem Ethiopia 94 G9 6 48N 38 22E
Yiyang China 81 H3 28 39N 112 10E
Yoakum Texas U.S.A. 103 G2 29 18N 97 20W
Yogyakarta Indonesia 80 E2 7 48S 110 24E
Yoichi Japan 82 D3 43 14N 140 47E
Yokadouma Cameroon 93 I3 3 26N 15 06E
Yokkaichi Japan 82 C1 34 58N 136 38E
Yokohama Japan 83 B2 35 27N 139 38E
Yokosuka Japan 83 B2 35 18N 139 38E
Yokote Japan 82 D2 39 20N 140 31E
Yola Nigeria 93 H4 9 14N 12 32E
Yonago Japan 82 B2 35 27N 133 20E
Yonkers New York U.S.A. 106 C2 40 56N 73 52W
Yonne r. France 61 B2 48 00N 3 15E
York North Yorkshire England 43 G3 53 58N 1 05W
York Pennsylvania U.S.A. 105 E1 39 57N 76 44W
York, Cape Australia 86 G7 10 42S 142 32E
York Factory Manitoba Canada 101 Q4 57 08N 92 25W
Yorkshire Dales National Park North Yorkshire
Yorkshire Wolds hills Humberside England 40 D3 54 00N 0 45W
Yorkton Saskatchewan Canada 101 O3 51 12N 102 29W
York, Vale of North Yorkshire England 40 C3 54 10N 1 20W
Yŏsu South Korea 81 K4 34 50N 127 30E
You Jiang r. China 81 G2 23 30N 107 00E
Youghal Cork Irish Republic 48 D1 51 51N 7 50W
Youngstown Ohio U.S.A. 105 D2 41 05N 80 40W
Yoxall Staffordshire England 35 C3 52 46N 1 46W
Yoxford Suffolk England 33 D3 52 16N 1 30E
Yser see Ijzer
Ystalfera West Glamorgan Wales 38 C1 51 47N 3 47W
Ystrad Aeron Dyfed Wales 38 B2 52 10N 4 10W
Ystradgynlais West Glamorgan Wales 38 C1 51 47N 3 45W
Ytterhogdal Sweden 67 C3 62 10N 14 55E
Yu Jiang r. China 81 G2 23 00N 109 00E
Yuan Jiang r. Asia 72 30 00N 112 00E
Yuba City California U.S.A. 102 B4 39 09N 121 36W
Yūbari Japan 82 D3 43 04N 141 59E
Yucatan p. Mexico 108 G3 19 00N 89 00W
Yucatan Basin Caribbean Sea 119 R9 20 00N 85 00W
Yuci China 81 H5 37 40N 112 44E
Yuetot France 61 B2 49 37N 0 45E
YUGOSLAVIA 68 C3
Yukagir Plateau Russia 71 R9 66 30N 156 00E
Yü-kitka l. Finland 67 F4 66 15N 28 30E
Yukon Delta Alaska U.S.A. 100 C5 62 45N 164 00W
Yukon River U.S.A./Canada 100 D5 63 30N 159 40W
Yukon Territory Canada 100 H5 64 15N 135 00W
Yuma Arizona U.S.A. 102 D3 32 40N 114 39W
Yumen China 81 E5 39 54N 97 43E

Abbreviations used in the gazetteer

admin.	administrative area
A.C.T.	Australian Capital Territory
b.	bay or harbour
c.	cape, point or headland
can	canal
C.I.S.	Commonwealth of Independent States
co.	county
d.	desert
dep.	depression
est.	estuary
fj.	fjord
g.	gulf
geog. reg.	geographical region
G.R.A.	Government Residential Area
hist. site	historical site
i.	island
is.	islands
ist.	isthmus
l.	lake, lakes, lagoon
mt.	mountain
mts.	mountains
p.	peninsula
plat.	plateau
pn.	plain
r.	river
rd.	road
r.s.	research station
reg.	region
rep.	republic
res.	reservoir
salt l.	salt lake
sd.	sound, strait or channel
sum.	summit
tn.	town
U.A.E.	United Arab Emirates
U.K.	United Kingdom
U.S.A.	United States of America
v.	valley
vol.	volcano

Abbreviations used on the maps

A.C.T.	Australian Capital Territory
Ákr.	Ákra
App.	Appennino
Arch.	Archipelago
Arg.	Argentina
Arq.	Arquípelago
Austl.	Australia
C.	Cape; Cabo; Cap
Col.	Colombia
D.C.	District of Columbia
Den.	Denmark
E.	East
Ec.	Ecuador
Eq.	Equatorial
Fj.	Fjord
Fr.	France
G.	Gunung; Gebel
I.	Island; Île; Isla; Ilha
Is.	Islands; Îles; Islas; Ilhas
J.	Jezioro
Jez.	Jezero
Kep.	Kepulauan
M.	Muang
Mt.	Mount; Mountain; Mont
Mte.	Monte
Mts.	Mountains; Monts
N.	North
Nat. Pk.	National Park
Neths.	Netherlands
N.P.	National Park
N.Z.	New Zealand
Pa.	Passage
Peg.	Pegunungan
Pen.; Penin.	Peninsula
Pl.	Planina
Port.	Portugal
P.P.	Pulau-pulau
proj.	projected
Pt.	Point
Pta.	Punta
Pte.	Pointe
Pto.	Porto; Puerto
R.	River; Rio
Ra.	Range
Res.	Reservoir
Résr.	Réservoir
S.	South; San
S.A.	South Africa
Sa.	Sierra
Sd.	Sound
Sev.	Severnaya
Sp.	Spain
St.	Saint
Ste.	Sainte
Str.	Strait
Terr.	Territory
U.A.E.	United Arab Emirates
u/c.	under construction
U.K.	United Kingdom
U.N.	United Nations
U.S.A.	United States of America
U.S.S.R.	Union of Soviet Socialist Republics
W.	West

Glossary

Ákra	cape (Greek)		Lago	lake (Italian; Portuguese; Spanish)
Älv	river (Swedish)		Laguna	lagoon (Spanish)
Bahia	bay (Spanish)		Ling	mountain range (Chinese)
Bahr	stream (Arabic)		Llyn	lake (Welsh)
Baie	bay (French)		-misaki	cape (Japanese)
Bugt	bay (Danish)		Mont	mountain (French)
Cabo	cape (Portuguese; Spanish)		Montagne	mountain (French)
Cap	cape (French)		Monts	mountains (French)
Capo	cape (Italian)		Monti	mountains (Italian)
Cerro	hill (Spanish)		More	sea (Russian)
Chaîne	mountain range (French)		Muang	city (Thai)
Chapada	hills (Portuguese)		Mys	cape (Russian)
Chott	salt lake (Arabic)		-nada	gulf; sea (Japanese)
Co	lake (Chinese)		Ostrova	islands (Russian)
Collines	hills (French)		Ozero	lake (Russian)
Cordillera	mountain range (Spanish)		Pegunungan	mountain range (Indonesian)
Costa	coast (Spanish)		Pendi	basin (Chinese)
Côte	coast (French)		Pic	summit (French; Spanish)
-dake	peak (Japanese)		Pico	summit (Spanish)
Danau	lake (Indonesian)		Pik	summit (Russian)
Dao	island (Chinese)		Planalto	plateau (Portuguese)
Dasht	desert (Persian; Urdu)		Planina	mountain range (Bulgarian; Serbo-Croat)
Djebel	mountain (Arabic)		Poluostrov	peninsula (Russian)
Do	island (Korean; Vietnamese)		Puerto	port (Spanish)
Embalse	reservoir (Spanish)		Pulau-pulau	islands (Indonesian)
Erg	dunes (Arabic)		Puncak	mountain (Indonesian)
Estrecho	strait (Spanish)		Punta	cape (Italian; Spanish)
Estreito	strait (Portuguese)		Ras; Râs	cape (Arabic)
Gebel	mountain (Arabic)		Ra's	cape (Persian)
Golfe	gulf, bay (French)		Rio	river (Portuguese)
Golfo	gulf, bay (Italian; Spanish)		Río	river (Spanish)
Gölü	lake (Turkish)		Rivière	river (French)
Gora	mountain (Russian)		Rubha	cape (Gaelic)
Gunto	islands (Japanese)		Salina	salt pan (Spanish)
Gunung	mountain (Indonesian; Malay)		-san	mountain (Japanese)
Hafen	harbour (German)		-sanchi	mountains (Japanese)
Hai	sea (Chinese)		-sanmyaku	mountain range (Japanese)
Ho	river (Chinese)		Sebkra	salt pan (Arabic)
Hu	lake (Chinese)		See	lake (German)
Île; Isle	island (French)		Selat	strait (Indonesian)
Ilha	island (Portuguese)		Seto	strait (Japanese)
Inseln	islands (German)		Shan	mountains (Chinese)
Isla	island (Spanish)		-shima	island (Japanese)
Istmo	isthmus (Spanish)		-shotō	islands (Japanese)
Jabal; Jebel	mountain (Arabic)		Sierra	mountain range (Spanish)
Jezero	lake (Serbo-Croat)		Song	river (Vietnamese)
Jezioro	lake (Polish)		-suidō	strait (Japanese)
Jiang	river (Chinese)		Tassili	plateau (Berber)
-jima	island (Japanese)		Tau	island (Chinese)
-kaikyō	strait (Japanese)		Teluk	bay (Indonesian)
Kamen'	rock (Russian)		-tō	island (Japanese)
Kap	cape (Danish)		Tonle	lake (Cambodian)
Kepulauan	islands (Indonesian)		-wan	bay (Japanese)
-ko	lake (Japanese)		-zaki	cape (Japanese)
Lac	lake (French)		Zaliv	bay (Russian)